012016936

621.3

KU-405-365

WITHDRAWN
FROM STOCK

ΡN
92
N

COMPUTER-AIDED DESIGN OF MICROWAVE CIRCUITS

The Artech House Microwave Library

Introduction to Microwaves by Fred E. Gardiol

Microwaves Made Simple: Principles and Applications by W. Stephen Cheung and Frederic H. Levien

Microwave Tubes by A. S. Gilmour, Jr.

Electric Filters by Martin Hasler and Jacques Neirynck

Nonlinear Circuits by Martin Hasler and Jacques Neirynck

Microwave Technology by Erich Pehl

Receiving Systems Design by Stephen J. Erst

Microwave Mixers by Stephen A. Maas

Feedback Maximization by B.J. Lurie

Applications of GaAs MESFETs by Robert Soares, et al.

GaAs Processing Techniques by Ralph E. Williams

GaAs FET Principles and Technology by James V. DiLorenzo and Deen D. Khandelwal

Dielectric Resonators, Darko Kajfez and Pierre Guillon, eds.

Modern Spectrum Analyzer Theory and Applications by Morris Engelson

Design Tables for Discrete Time Normalized Lowpass Filters by Arild Lacroix and Karl-Heinz Witte

Microwave Materials and Fabrication Techniques by Thomas S. Laverghetta

Handbook of Microwave Testing by Thomas S. Laverghetta

Microwave Measurements and Techniques by Thomas S. Laverghetta

Principles of Electromagnetic Compatibility by Bernhard E. Keiser

Linear Active Circuits: Design and Analysis by William Rynone, Jr.

The Design of Impedance-Matching Networks for Radio-Frequency and Microwave Amplifiers by Pieter L.D. Abrie

Microwave Filters, Impedance Matching Networks, and Coupling Structures by G.L. Matthaei, Leo Young, and E.M.T. Jones

Analysis, Design, and Applications of Fin Lines by Bharathi Bhat and Shiban Koul

Microwave Engineer's Handbook, 2 vol., Theodore Saad, ed.

Handbook of Microwave Integrated Circuits by R.K. Hoffmann

Microwave Integrated Circuits, Jeffrey Frey and Kul Bhasin, eds.

Computer-Aided Design of Microwave Circuits by K.C. Gupta, Ramesh Garg, and Rakesh Chadha

Microstrip Lines and Slotlines by K.C. Gupta, R. Garg, and I.J. Bahl

Advanced Mathematics for Practicing Engineers by Kurt Arbenz and Alfred Wohlhauser

Microstrip Antennas by I.J. Bahl and P. Bhartia

Antenna Design Using Personal Computers by David M. Pozar

Microwave Circuit Design Using Programmable Calculators by J. Lamar Allen and Max Medley, Jr.

Stripline Circuit Design by Harlan Howe, Jr.

Microwave Transmission Line Filters by J.A.G. Malherbe

Electrical Characteristics of Transmission Lines by W. Hilberg

Microwave Diode Control Devices by Robert V. Garver

Tables for Active Filter Design by Mario Biey and Amedeo Premoli

Active Filter Design by Arthur B. Williams

Laser Applications by W.V. Smith

Ferrite Control Components, 2 vol., Lawrence Whicker, ed.

Microwave Remote Sensing, 3 vol., by F.T. Ulaby, R.K. Moore, and A.K. Fung

COMPUTER-AIDED DESIGN OF MICROWAVE CIRCUITS

K.C. Gupta

Department of Electrical Engineering
Indian Institute of Technology, Kanpur

Ramesh Garg

Department of Electrical Engineering
Indian Institute of Technology, Kanpur

Rakesh Chadha

Advanced Centre for Electronic Systems
Indian Institute of Technology, Kanpur

Artech

Copyright © 1981
ARTECH HOUSE, INC.
685 Canton St.
Norwood, MA 02062

Printed and bound in the United States of America
All rights reserved. No parts of this book may be reproduced or utilized in any
form or by any means, electronic or mechanical, including photocopying, record-
ing, or by an information storage and retrieval system, without permission in writing from the publisher.
Library of Congress Catalog card number: 81-69400
Standard Book Number: 0-89006-106-8

87   10   9   8   7   6   5

Preface

With the introduction of hybrid microwave integrated circuits (MICs), computer-aided design (CAD) techniques have become an essential tool for microwave circuit designers. The circuit design process has become increasingly complex because a large variety of active and passive components are now available for use at microwave frequencies and the increased complexity of modern systems demands more precise and accurate design of circuits and subsystems. Also the hybrid MIC approach provides a very limited possibility of trimming or adjusting the circuit after it has been fabricated.

The area of computer-aided circuit design — including computer-aided microwave circuit design — has undergone rapid advances in recent years. Although there are a number of books available on the CAD of electronic circuits at lower frequencies, there is no book dealing with the CAD of microwave circuits. Since the area of CAD of microwave circuits has now matured, a book on this topic is expedient; the present book is an endeavour in this direction. It is designed to provide a detailed exposition of the concepts and techniques used in the computer-aided analysis and design of microwave circuits.

Any CAD process consists of three important segments, namely, i) modelling, ii) analysis, and iii) optimization. This book discusses these three aspects vis-a-vis microwave circuits. We discuss modelling of various constituents of microwave circuits. These include transmission lines, discontinuities, lumped elements, planar components, and semiconductor devices. Network representation suitable for analysis is introduced and matrix techniques for analysis of microwave circuits are discussed. Sensitivity analysis and various optimization techniques are presented.

The book is divided into five parts. In Part I, the first chapter describes the evolution of microwave circuits and introduces the concept of the computer-aided circuit design. Chapter Two is a review of the various representations used for microwave circuits.

Modelling of active and passive components is a crucial part of any circuit design; this is discussed in the eight chapters that make up Part II. At microwave frequencies, there is a need to characterize precisely not only the constituent components, but also the associated parasitic reactances. This book contains seven chapters devoted to characterization of various transmission structures, discontinuities, lumped elements, planar components, and semiconductor devices. Sensitivities of various components are useful in tolerance analysis and optimization of circuits. A chapter is devoted to the characterization of the sensitivities of transmission structures. Accurate characterizations of some of these elements (for instance semiconductor devices) is obtained by measurement of S-parameters over the frequency range of interest. Computer-aided measurement techniques using network analyzers are commonly employed. One chapter is devoted to these techniques including six-port measurement concepts.

Circuit analysis is the most important component of the computer-aided design approach. Part III deals with various methods used for analysis. Microwave circuit analysis is usually carried out in terms of S-matrices. Various chapters deal with the evaluation of the S-matrix of the overall network using the known S-matrices for the individual components, the sensitivity analysis, the tolerance analysis, and the time-domain analysis. All these analyses involve solutions of matrix equations, techniques for which are discussed in a separate chapter.

There are several techniques available for optimization of microwave circuits. Both direct search and gradient methods have been used. Basic concepts in optimization, one-parameter optimization, and multi-parameter optimization techniques are discussed in the three chapters in Part IV. Methods discussed include pattern search, Rosenbrock's method, simplex method, Newton-Raphson method, Davidon-Fletcher-Powell method, and a method for optimizing least square objective functions.

Part V includes two chapters describing CAD programs. A microwave circuit analysis program (MCAP) developed at IIT Kanpur is described. The final chapter, contributed by Mr. Les Besser of Compact Engineering, is a review of some commercially available programs.

Several algorithms have been included in this book in Chapter Thirteen and in later chapters. These have been written in an ALGOL type language and could be skipped over in the first reading when the reader is not familiar with this type of language.

This book evolved from a set of lecture notes first prepared for a graduate course on CAD of microwave circuits offered at IIT Kanpur in the spring semester of 1978. Part of the material has been used subsequently for a course on microwave circuits. Work on CAD of microwave integrated circuits carried out at IIT Kanpur formed a part of a project sponsored by the Department of Electronics (Government of India, New Delhi) and contributed to the contents of this book. Parts of this material were used for a series of seminars delivered at Eidgenossische Technische Hochschule, Zurich in summer 1979 and appeared as an internal publication (Bericht Nr. 79-10) of the Mikrowellen Laboratorium there.

The proposed book will serve microwave circuit designers and graduate students in microwaves. It could be used as a supplementary text for courses on microwave circuits and computer-aided network analysis and design. Part V on CAD programs may be read without going through the rest of the book. Chapter 19 on MCAP could be used directly for analysis of microstrip and stripline circuits.

The authors are grateful to Mr. Les Besser for contributing Chapter 20. Discussions with several colleagues at IIT Kanpur and at Eidgenössische Technische Hochschule Zurich are thankfully acknowledged. Facilities extended by the Department of Electrical Engineering and the Advanced Center for Electronic Systems at IIT Kanpur are acknowledged. The typing of the manuscript has been handled efficiently by Mr. C.M.

Abraham and the art-work has been done by Mr. R.K. Bajpai and Mr. J.C. Verma. The preparation of the manuscript has been supported by the Quality Improvement Programme of IIT Kanpur. This support is thankfully acknowledged.

Thanks are also due to Dr. H.E. Green and Academic Press for their permission to include Table 5.1 from their publication.

K.C. Gupta
Ramesh Garg
Rakesh Chadha

Contents

Chapter 4

SENSITIVITIES OF TRANSMISSION STRUCTURES

Chapter 5

CHARACTERIZATION OF DISCONTINUITIES-I
Coaxial Lines and Waveguides

Chapter 6

**CHARACTERIZATION OF
DISCONTINUITIES – II**
Striplines and Microstrip Lines

Chapter 7

Chapter 8

Chapter 9

Chapter 10

Part III Analysis

Chapter 11

Chapter 12

SENSITIVITY ANALYSIS OF MICROWAVE CIRCUITS   371

Chapter 13

Chapter 14

Chapter 15

Part IV Optimization

Chapter 16

Part V CAD Programs

Chapter 19

Chapter 20

Part I

Introduction

1

Microwave Circuits and Computer-Aided Design

1.1 EVOLUTION OF MICROWAVE CIRCUITS

For a long time the words "microwave circuits" were synonymous with "waveguide circuits." Waveguide was recognized as a useful transmission structure for microwave frequencies in the early thirties. Works by Southworth [1-3] and others at Bell Telephone Laboratories deserve mention in this respect. It was soon realized that a short length of waveguide, with suitable modifications, might function as a radiator and also as a reactive element. Resonant cavities and horn antenna are mentioned in an early article by Southworth [1]. Modern waveguide circuitry had its beginning in the efforts to obtain both a more efficient transfer of microwave power from a source to a waveguide transmission line — thereby providing the elements of a transmitter, and again in the efficient recovery of microwave power at the receiving end — thereby providing the elements of a receiver. This lead to the development of several components like traveling detectors, wavemeters, terminations, etc. Some idea of the techniques used in 1934 can be obtained by recalling that optical benches were commonly used to set up microwave experiments [4]. Several photographs of equipment of those days are available in an article surveying the history of the progress of microwave arts published in the fiftieth anniversary issue of IRE Proceedings [4].

The principle of multiple reflections from discontinuities and the associated principle of cavity resonance played an important part in the development of microwave technology. In some cases, these principles were used to match a source of microwave power to a waveguide. In others, they served to match the waveguide to a receiver, such as a crystal detector. In still others, they served to pass freely a band of frequencies. Together, these principles formed the foundations of microwave circuits.

One of the key features of microwave circuits has been the empirical adjustment or tuning of characteristics by screws and irises (and even by denting!) in waveguides. In the beginning it was an art that was learned by trial and error. This came to be known as "plumbing" and had been for quite a long time a practical tool for microwave engineers.

Perhaps the greatest single contribution to the engineering analysis of microwave circuits was by Phillip H. Smith [5] who provided a graphical tool for solving otherwise complicated transmission line problems. Not only were laborious calculations avoided, but, while solving the problems on a Smith Chart, one could visualize the step-by-step processes under way. Few gadgets of microwave circuitry have been more useful than the Smith Chart.

Rapid developments in microwave circuits took place during the Second World War when special laboratories were set up at the Massachusetts Institute of Technology and at Columbia University to apply microwave techniques to radar problems. Many significant developments in microwave circuits took place during these years, but were published later. A few of those deserve mention. Fox developed [6] devices by which phase could be added progressively to a waveguide. Another product is a hybrid tee (or magic tee) [7] and still another equally significant one was the first directional coupler [8]. All these devices found practical uses immediately. Another direction of wartime evolution was the extension of filter techniques to higher frequencies, leading to transmission line filters. Simultaneously, analytical tools were also developed. The classical description of network performance in terms of voltages, currents, impedance and admittance matrices, was replaced by a description based on the transmitted and the reflected wave variables, leading to the concept of scattering matrix.

The scattering matrix formalism allows simpler representation of multiport microwave networks.

At this stage in the development of microwave circuits, two basic transmission structures were employed frequently. These were the waveguide and the coaxial TEM mode line. Waveguides provided higher power capability and low loss that lead to high Q resonant cavities. Coaxial lines provided inherently wider bandwidth because of the absence of dispersion effects. Also, the concept of impedance could be easily interpreted in the case of coaxial lines. This simplified the design of components. These two transmission structures grew as important components for microwave circuits. Often their roles have been complementary; sometimes they appear in the same module.

It was at this stage that a very useful microwave technique emerged from a special adaptation of two-conductor transmission line theory. Introduced by Barrett and Barnes [9] in 1951, this structure, as used presently, consists of a thin strip of conductor sandwiched between two dielectric plates metalized on outside. This structure is known as a stripline. Early stripline work used razor blades and glue to cut the thin strips and paste them on dielectric sheets. With the availability of copper clad laminates (first introduced for printed circuits) the stripline techniques have developed into a predictable and precise technology. First detailed account of the stripline circuits was made available by the Sanders Tri-plate Manual [10] published in 1956. A comprehensive account of stripline circuits is available in a book by Harlan Howe, Jr. [11]. The most significant feature of a stripline transmission structure is that the characteristic impedance of the line is controlled by the width of the central strip which is fabricated by photo-etching a copperclad dielectric substrate. The two dimensional nature of the stripline circuit configuration permits the interconnection of many components without the need to break the outer conductor shielding. This also allows the placement of the input and output ports with a high degree of flexibility.

Striplines were found very convenient for use in parallel-line couplers because of the natural coupling between two strips placed close to each other. The principles of the coupled line directional coupler were introduced by Wheeler [12] in 1952. Even today a vast majority of directional couplers use a stripline configuration.

Also in the early fifties, another type of transmission structure was conceived [13, 14], consisting of a single dielectric laminate with a conducting strip on one side and a complete conducting coating on the other side. This structure is known as a microstrip line. Microstrip line enjoyed a brief spell of popularity and intensive investigations in the fifties, but was not readily accepted for microwave use due to the high loss per unit length occasioned by radiation. This was largely a result of the low dielectric constant (about 2.5) of the substrate materials then in use. Further developments were prevented by the lack of availability of both the high dielectric constant, low loss materials and the suitable methods for processing and production.

Ever increasing demands for miniaturized microwave circuitry for use in weapons, aerospace and satellite applications lead to renewed intensity of interest in microstrip circuits in 1960s. An elegant analysis of microstrip structure based on conformal mapping transformation was described by Wheeler [15, 16]. The technology of high dielectric constant, low loss dielectric materials and that of deposition of metallic films were perfected [17] and became easily available in the late sixties. This lead to rapid developments in the use of microstrip lines.

The availability of a planar microwave transmission line structure like microstrip line coupled with the rapid developments in microwave semiconductor devices and the techniques of thin film deposition and photolithography eventually resulted in the technology of microwave integrated circuits [18-21]. Microwave integrated circuits (MICs) represent an extension of hybrid integrated circuit technology to microwave frequencies. Today, MICs consist mostly of passive components and circuits in the form of conducting patterns deposited on ceramic or dielectric substrates plus active devices mounted on these circuits in the form of chips or in specially designed packages. In addition to microstrip, other types of lines called slotline and coplanar lines [22, 23] have been used in some MICs. Slotline consists of a slot in the conducting pattern on one side of a dielectric substrate. The other side of the substrate does not contain any metallization. Coplanar lines also involve a metallization pattern, but only on one side of the substrate.

Another recent trend in microwave circuits is the use of lumped elements. Previously, lumped elements could not be used because the size of available lumped elements was comparable to the wavelength at microwave frequencies. With the use of photolithography and thin film techniques, the size of elements (capacitors, inductors, etc.) can be reduced so much that these elements can be used up to J-band frequencies [24, 25]. Use of lumped elements on dielectric substrates, along with the semiconductor devices in chip form mounted thereon, is an attractive option for microwave integrated circuits. Cost reduction of the order of one fiftieth or more has been predicted with the use of these type of circuits [24]. Apart from reduction in size, there is another advantage of lumped elements: circuit design and optimization techniques perfected at lower frequencies can now be directly used in the microwave frequency range.

In addition to lumped elements and one-dimensional transmission line components, two-dimensional planar components have also been proposed for use in microwave circuits [26]. These components are compatible with stripline and microstrip line and provide a useful alternative in microwave circuit design.

The next generation of MICs could be monolithic microwave integrated circuits on semiconductor substrates [27, 28]. Semiconductor substrates used include high resistivity silicon, high resistivity gallium arsenide, and low resistivity silicon with a silicon dioxide layer. Difficulties arise firstly from the need to use a variety of microwave semiconductor devices which cannot be fabricated by a common process, and secondly, because of the requirement of large substrate areas when distributed elements (transmission line sections) are used for passive functions. Recent trends [29] indicate that GaAs technology holds the key to microwave monolithic integrated circuits. GaAs MESFETs [30] are likely to play a dominant role in GHz-bandwidth analog amplifiers and gigabit rate digital integrated circuits.

Microwave integrated circuits (hybrid or monolithic) exhibit almost the same advantages as those available in the case of integrated circuits at lower frequencies [31], namely: (a) improved system reliability, (b) reduced volume and weight, and (c) eventual cost reduction when a large number of standardized items are required.

As in the case of low frequency integrated circuits, the MICs are responsible for both the expansion of present markets and the opening of many new applications, including a host of non-military uses.

There are some difficulties associated with the use of MICs [31]. Before MICs became popular, the microwave circuit designers and users had the flexibility to incorporate tuners and adjustment screws in circuits in order to optimize the performance of the circuit after fabrication. MICs, especially if they have to meet high reliability claims, are devoid of these trimming arrangements. Consequently, devices used therein need to be characterized precisely and the circuits have to be designed more accurately. Computer-aided design, simulation, and optimization [32, 33] techniques have therefore become a necessity.

1.2 COMPUTER-AIDED DESIGN APPROACH

A classical procedure for the design of microwave circuits is outlined in Figure 1.1. One starts with the desired specifications and arrives at an initial circuit configuration. Available design data and previous experience are helpful in selecting this initial configuration. Analysis and synthesis procedures are used for deciding values of various parameters of the circuit. A laboratory model is constructed for the initial design, and measurements are carried out for evaluating its characteristics. Performance achieved is compared with the desired specifications; if the given specifications are not met, the circuit is modified. Adjustment, tuning, and trimming mechanisms incorporated in the circuit are used for carrying out these modifications. Measurements are carried out again and the results compared with the desired specifications. The sequence of modifications, measurements, and comparison is carried out iteratively until the desired specifications are achieved. At times the specifications are compromised in view of the practically feasible performance of the circuit. The final circuit configuration thus arrived at is passed on for prototype fabrication.

The above procedure has been used for the design of microwave circuits for quite some time. However, it has become increasingly difficult to use this iterative and empirical method successfully be-

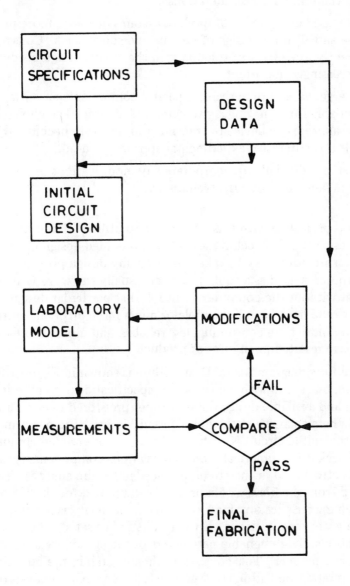

Figure 1.1　Conventional procedure for microwave circuit design.

cause of the following considerations:

i)   Increased complexity of modern systems demands more pre-
      cise and accurate design of circuits and subsystems. Conse-
      quently, the effect of tolerances in the circuit design becomes
      increasingly important.

ii)   A larger variety of active and passive components are now
      available for achieving a given circuit function. The choice of
      the appropriate device or transmission structure becomes diffi-
      cult if the iterative experimental approach is used.

iii) It is very difficult to incorporate any modifications in the cir-
      cuits fabricated by MIC technology.

A method of dealing with this situation is to utilize "Computer-
Aided Design (CAD)" techniques. Computer-aided design in its
strict interpretation may be taken to mean any design process where
the computer is used as a tool. However, usually the word CAD implies that without the computer as a tool, that particular design
process would have been impossible or much more difficult, more
expensive, more time consuming, less reliable, and more than likely
would have resulted in an inferior product.

A typical flow diagram for CAD procedure is shown in Figure 1.2.
As before, one starts with a given set of specifications. Synthesis
methods and available design data (at times pre-stored in computer
memory) help to arrive at the initial circuit design. The performance of this initial circuit is evaluated by a computer-aided circuit
analysis package. Numerical models for various components (passive and active) used in the circuit are needed for the analysis. These
are called from the library of subroutines developed for this purpose.
Circuit characteristics obtained as results of the analysis are compared
with the given specifications. If the results fail to satisfy the desired
specifications, the designable parameters of the circuit are altered in
a systematic manner. This consistutes the key step in the optimization. Several optimization strategies include sensitivity analysis of
the circuit for calculating changes in the circuit parameters. The
sequence of circuit analysis, comparison with the desired performance, and parameter modification is performed iteratively until the
specifications are met or the optimum performance of the circuit

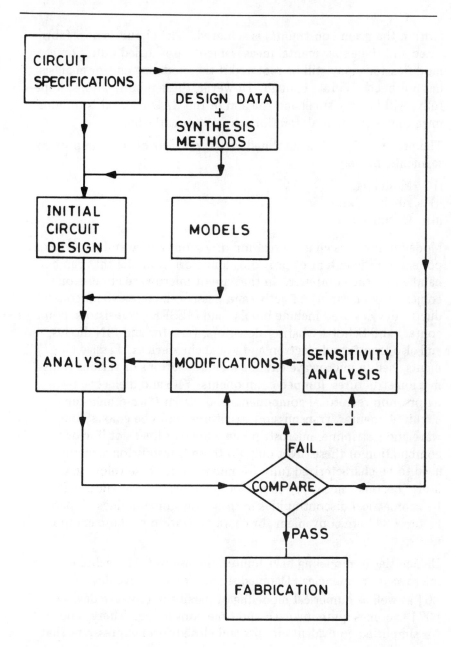

Figure 1.2   CAD procedure for microwave circuit design.

(within the given constraints) is achieved. The circuit is now fabricated and the experimental measurements are carried out. Some modifications may still be required if the modeling and/or analysis has not been accurate enough. However, these modifications, hopefully, will be very small and the aim of the CAD method is to minimize the experimental iterations as far as practicable.

The process of CAD, as outlined above, consists of three important segments, namely:

i)   Modeling,
ii) Analysis, and
iii) Optimization.

Modeling involves characterization of various active and passive components to the extent of providing a numerical model that can be handled by the computer. In the case of microwave circuits one comes across a variety of active and passive elements. Semiconductor devices used include bipolar and MESFET transistors, point contact and Schottky barrier detectors, varactor and PIN diodes, and also transferred electron and avalanche devices. Passive elements used in microwave circuits include sections of various transmission structures, lumped components, YIG and dielectric resonators, non-reciprocal components and planar (two-dimensional) circuit elements. Transmission structures could be coaxial line, waveguide, stripline, microstrip line, coplanar line, slot line or a combination of these. Not only do these transmission structures need to be characterized fully for impedance, phase velocity, etc., it also becomes necessary to model the parasitic reactances caused by geometrical discontinuities in these transmission lines. S-parameters [34] are convenient for characterization of these components.

Difficulties in modeling have limited the use of CAD techniques at microwave frequencies. Detailed simulation of active devices [35, 36] as well as numerical modeling of passive microwave devices [37] becomes quite involved and time consuming. There is need for simplified equivalent circuits and closed-form expressions that possess sufficient accuracy for circuit design. This type of information for microstrip line, slot line, coplanar line, and for microstrip discontinuities is contained in a recent book [23]. At times

it becomes necessary to measure the S-parameters of a particular
device or component and use this empirically derived "model" in
the CAD program. An automatic network analyzer [38, 39] with
system error compensation and calibration procedures is very useful for this purpose. Recently developed six-port network techniques [40, 41] would make the network analyzer systems simpler.

Analysis provides the response of a specified circuit configuration
to a given set of inputs. Computer-aided analysis [42] is perhaps
the most developed and most widely used aspect of CAD. Microwave circuit analysis involves evaluation of S-parameters of the
overall circuit in terms of the given S-parameters of constituent
components of the circuit. Many times microwave circuits can be
expressed as a cascade combination of two-port components. In
such cases, the matrix representing the overall network can be obtained by the multiplication of ABCD matrices (or transfer scattering matrices) [32] of individual two-port components. For more
involved topologies, multiport connection methods [42] are available. Matrix manipulations and inversions involved in these methods
can be efficiently performed by sparse-matrix techniques [43].
Another aspect related to the evaluation of circuit performance is
the computation of circuit sensitivities. This involves calculation
of the effect of variations in designable parameters on the circuit
performance [44]. The results are useful for two purposes: tolerance analysis of the circuit, and optimization using gradient methods.

The process of iterative modifications of circuit parameters in order
to achieve a given objective (i.e., to meet a set of given specifications)
is termed as optimization. Methods of optimization developed for a
variety of other disciplines [45] are useful for the design of microwave circuits also. These methods can be classed in two groups [46]:
gradient methods and direct search methods. In the gradient methods,
information about the derivatives of performance functions (with
respect to designable parameters) is used to arrive at the modified
set of parameters at each step in moving towards the optimum solution. These derivatives (or gradients) are obtained from the sensitivity analysis of the circuit at each step. Direct search methods,
on the other hand, do not use gradient information and the optimization is carried out by searching for the "optimum" solution
in a systematic manner. For microwave circuit design, the direct

search methods have been more popular [32, 47] because of the
additional complexity involved in carrying out the sensitivity
analysis for gradient methods. However, some recently developed
gradient methods [48, 49] are considered superior to other types
of optimization techniques and are finding applications in CAD of
microwave circuits [50].

1.3 OUTLINE OF THE BOOK

The material in the rest of the book is divided into nineteen chapters.

Chapter Two describes three types of representations used for
characterizing components and circuits at microwave frequencies.
The ABCD parameters and the transfer scattering matrix (T-matrix)
representations are applicable to two-port components (or networks)
only. Since two-port components occur very frequently in microwave circuits these representations are discussed in fair detail. Scattering matrix representation is very convenient for the measurement
and characterization of microwave components and is also applicable
to general n-port networks. Properties of S-matrices and their
relationship with other representations are also discussed. An appendix to this chapter contains ABCD, S- and T-matrices for some
two-port components commonly used in microwave circuits.

The next eight chapters, chapters three through ten, describe various
aspects related to the modeling of microwave circuit elements. Chapter Three deals with characterization of various types of transmission
structures. Coaxial line, waveguides, and various transmission lines
used in MICs are discussed. Coupled striplines and coupled microstrip lines are also included. Closed-form expressions for various
characteristics, their accuracies, and the ranges of their validity are
given.

Sensitivity analysis of various transmission structures is discussed in
Chapter Four. Sensitivity values are useful for tolerance analysis
and optimization using gradient methods. The expressions for various
sensitivities are derived from the closed form expression for characteristic parameters presented in Chapter Three. These expressions are
then used to evaluate the worst case change in characteristic impedances and phase velocities due to typical tolerances in fabrication

and material parameters. For coupled lines, change in the coupling coefficient and the input impedance, when used as directional coupler, are described.

Chapters Five and Six present the characterizations of various types of discontinuities (parasitic as well as those incorporated intentionally) in various transmission structures. Chapter Five deals with discontinuities in coaxial lines and rectangular waveguides. Coaxial line discontinuities discussed include capacitive gaps, steps, windows, and stubs. In the case of rectangular waveguides, results are given for posts, strips, diaphragms, steps, right-angled bends, T-junctions, circular apertures, and elliptical apertures. Equivalent circuits for discontinuities and closed form expressions for various circuit elements are given.

Chapter Six describes discontinuities in striplines and microstrip lines. The discontinuities included are: open-end, gap in the strip conductor, step in the strip width, right-angled bend, T-junction, round hole (in striplines), notch (in microstrip lines), and cross junction (in microstrip circuits). Closed form expressions are given for various elements of the equivalent circuits.

Chapter Seven includes design information about lumped elements used in MICs. Resistors, inductors of various types (wire, strip and spirals), and capacitors (sandwich and interdigital) are discussed. Because of the approximate nature of design formulas available, measurements of lumped elements become necessary for modeling them accurately. Measurement techniques specifically suited for this purpose are described.

In addition to lumped elements and transmission lines, MICs use two-dimensional planar components. These components can be viewed as generalizations of microstrip line and stripline components with their transverse dimension comparable to the wavelength. Various methods for analysis and design of these components are discussed in Chapter Eight. These include: Green's function method for some regular shapes, segmentation and desegmentation methods for composite shapes, and numerical techniques for arbitrary shapes. Concepts of frequency and impedance scaling, as applicable to these components, are introduced.

Modeling microwave semiconductor devices forms the subject matter of Chapter Nine. The devices included are: Schottky-barrier and point-contact diodes, varactor diodes, PIN diodes, bipolar transistors and MESFET, and Gunn and impatt diodes. Lumped circuit models for these devices are discussed. The effect of package parasitics is included. Typical values of circuit elements are given. Closed form approximate expressions for the circuit elements of some of the device models are also included. For bipolar transistors and MESFETs, small-signal equivalent circuits are given. Impatt diodes have been characterized for both the small-signal and the large-signal conditions. A non-linear lumped circuit model is presented for the Gunn diode. The model is valid for all the modes of operation.

For several circuits and elements where exact characterization is not available or where parameter values vary from unit to unit (as for semiconductor devices), measurements are needed for their modeling. Chapter Ten deals with measurement techniques used for this purpose. Brief descriptions of the networks analyzer, automatic network analyzer and six-port network analyzer are given. The measurement of S-parameters is discussed. De-embedding and unterminating techniques to extract the component characteristics from measured data are described. Methods for system error measurement and correction are given.

The next five chapters are devoted to circuit analysis techniques. Chapter Eleven describes the evaluation of circuit parameters. The use of symmetry to simplify the circuit analysis is pointed out. Methods for analysis of cascaded two-ports and arbitrarily connected two-ports are discussed. General techniques applicable to arbitrarily connected multiports are treated in detail. Segmentation and desegmentation techniques for two-dimensional planar components are also included.

Chapter Twelve deals with sensitivity analysis of microwave circuits. Two methods of evaluating network sensitivities (namely, the finite difference method and the adjoint network method) are given. The adjoint network method is discussed in detail. For this purpose, Tellegen's theorem in wave variables is introduced and is used to derive the adjoint network. Evaluation of sensitivities in the case when the "subnetwork growth method" is used for analysis is also included. These methods enable one to calculate the sensitivity of circuit performance when the sensitivities of the parameters of individual components are available. Derivatives of S-parameters for components commonly used in microwave circuits are presented for this purpose. When the variation in circuit parameters is large, a slightly different formulation is needed. This is also discussed.

Chapter Thirteen on tolerance analysis includes the worst case and statistical tolerance analyses. The method of analysis for the worst case calculation includes the formulation for vector performance parameters also. An algorithm useful for this purpose is discussed. Statistical analysis includes the commonly used method of moments and Monte-Carlo techniques.

Time domain analysis of microwave circuits is dealt with in Chapter Fourteen. Transient analysis of transmission lines, using the method of characteristics, is discussed. For the networks consisting of both the transmission line sections and lumped components, three methods are discussed. These are the Laplace transform method, the companion network approach, and the state variable approach. In the Laplace transform method, the step response for the total network is evaluated from the step response admittance matrices for the constituent components of the network. The companion network approach is based on approximating the differential equations for the transient analysis by the corresponding difference equations.

Chapter Fifteen deals with matrix solution techniques used in computer-aided network analysis. Gaussian elimination, L-U factorization, and sparse matrix techniques are discussed.

Optimization techniques used in CAD of circuits are discussed in Chapters Sixteen, Seventeen and Eighteen. Chapter Sixteen contains a description of basic concepts, objective function formulation, consideration of constraints present, and one-dimensional search methods.

Chapter Seventeen deals with the direct search methods of optimization. These include pattern search, Rosenbrock's method, Powell's method of conjugate directions, and the simplex method.

Optimization methods using gradient information form the subject matter of Chapter Eighteen. The methods discussed include the steepest descent method, the generalized Newton-Raphson method and the Fletcher-Powell method. Techniques for optimizing least square objective functions are also discussed.

The last two chapters of the book describe some of the CAD programs. A program for the analysis of microstrip and stripline circuits is presented in Chapter Nineteen. Chapter Twenty gives an overview of commercially available CAD programs for microwave circuits.

REFERENCES

[1]   Southworth, G.C., "Hyper-Frequency Waveguides — General Considerations and Experimental Results," *Bell Sys. Tech. J.*, Vol. 15, April 1936, pp. 284-309.

[2]   Carson, J.R., S.P. Meade, and S.A. Schelkunoff, "Hyper-Frequency Waveguides — Mathematical Theory," *Bell Sys. Tech. J.*, April 1936, pp. 310-333.

[3]   Southworth, G.C., "Some Fundamental Experiments with Waveguides," *Proc. IRE*, Vol. 25, July 1937, pp. 807-822.

[4]   Southworth, G.C., "Survey and History of the Progress of Microwave Arts," *Proc. IRE*, Vol. 50, No. 5, May 1962, pp. 1199-1206.

[5]   Smith, P.H., "Transmission Line Calculator," *Electronics*, Vol. 12, Jan. 1939, pp. 29-31. and Smith, P.H., "An Improved Transmission Line Calculator," *Electronics*, Vol. 17, Jan. 1944, pp. 130-133, 318, 320, 322, 324-325.

[6]   Fox, A.G., "An Adjustable Waveguide Phase Changer," *Proc. IRE*, Vol. 35, Dec. 1947, pp. 1489-1498.

[7]   Tyrrell, W.A., "Hybrid Circuits for Microwaves," *Proc. IRE*, Vol. 35, Nov. 1947, pp. 1294-1306.

[8]   Mumford, W.W., "Directional Couplers," *Proc. IRE*, Vol. 35, Feb. 1947, pp. 160-165.

[9]   Barrett, R.M., and M.H. Barnes, "Microwave Printed Circuits," *National Conf. on Airborne Electronics, IRE*, Ohio, May 1951.

[10]   Peters, R.W., *et al.*, *Handbook of Tri-plate Microwave Components*, Sanders Associates, Nashua, New Hampshire, 1956.

[11]   Howe, H., Jr., *Stripline Circuit Design*, Dedham, Mass: Artech House, 1974.

[12]   Wheeler, H.A., "Directional Coupler," U.S. Patent No. 2,606,974 filed 16 May 1946, issued 12 Aug. 1952.

[13]   Greig, D.D., and H.F. Engelmann, "Microstrip — A New Transmission Technique for the Kilomegacycle Range," *Proc. IRE*, Vol. 40, Dec. 1952, pp. 1644-1650.

[14] Assadourian, F., and E. Rimai, "Simplified Theory of Micro-
      strip Transmission Systems," *Proc. IRE*, Vol. 40, Dec. 1952,
      pp. 1651-1657.

[15] Wheeler, H.A., "Transmission Line Properties of Parallel
      Wide Strips by Conformal Mapping Approximation," *IEEE
      Trans. Microwave Theory Tech.*, Vol. MTT-12, 1964, pp.
      280-289.

[16] Wheeler, H.A., "Transmission Line Properties of Parallel
      Strips Separated by a Dielectric Sheet," *IEEE Trans. Mi-
      crowave Theory Tech.*, Vol. MTT-13, 1965, pp. 172-185.

[17] Schilling, S.W., *et al.*, "The Real World of Micromin Sub-
      strates — Part 1 to Part 5," *Microwaves*, Vol. 7, Dec. 1968,
      pp. 52-56; Vol. 8, Jan. 1969, pp. 44-46, 57-60; Sept. 1969,
      pp. 36-38; Dec. 1969, pp. 54-57; Vol. 10, March 1971,
      pp. 54-56.

[18] "Microwave Integrated Circuits," Special Issue, *IEEE Trans.
      on Electron Devices*, Vol. ED-15, July 1968.

[19] "Microwave Integrated Circuits," Special Issue, *IEEE Trans.
      on Microwave Theory and Techniques*, Vol. MTT-19, July
      1971.

[20] Gupta, K.C., and Amarjit Singh (Eds.), *Microwave Integrated
      Circuits*, New Delhi, Wiley Eastern Pvt. Ltd.; and New York,
      Halsted Press (John Wiley and Sons), 1974.

[21] Frey, J., ed., *Microwave Integrated Circuits*, Dedham, Mass:
      Artech House, 1974.

[22] Cohn, S.B., "Slot Line on a Dielectric Substrate," *IEEE
      Trans. Microwave Theory Tech.*, Vol. MTT-17, 1969, pp.
      768-778.

[23] Gupta, K.C., R. Garg, and I.J. Bahl, *Microstrip Lines and
      Slotlines*, Dedham, Mass: Artech House, 1979.

[24] Aitchison, C.S., *et al.*, "Lumped Microwave Circuits — Part
      I to Part V," *Design Electronics*, Sept. 1971, pp. 23-28;
      Oct. 1971, pp. 30-39; Nov. 1971, pp. 42-51. Also *Philips
      Tech. Rev.*, Vol. 32, 1971, pp. 305-314.

[25] Pengelly, R.S., and D.C. Rickard, "Design, Measurements and Application of Lumped Elements up to J-band," *Proc. 7th European Microwave Conf.*, 1977, Copenhagen, pp. 460-464.

[26] Okoshi, T., and T. Miyoshi, "The Planar Circuit — An Approach to Microwave Integrated Circuitry," *IEEE Trans. Microwave Theory Tech*, Vol. MTT-20, 1972, pp. 245-252.

[27] Mehal, E.W., and R.W. Wacker, "GaAs Integrated Microwave Circuits," *IEEE Trans. Electron Devices*, Vol. ED-15, July 1968, pp. 513-516.

[28] Hasan, M.M., and S.K. Mullick, "Monolithic MICs" in *Microwave Integrated Circuits*, K.C. Gupta and Amarjit Singh, Eds., Halsted Press (John Wiley and Sons), 1974.

[29] "Future of Microwaves is Monolithic," Editorial, *Microwave System News*, Vol. 8, No. 11, 1978, p. 60.

[30] "Microwave Field-Effect Transistors," Special Issue, *IEEE Trans. Microwave Theory Tech.*, Vol. MTT-24, June 1976.

[31] Gupta, K.C., *Microwaves*, New Delhi: Wiley Eastern Ltd., 1979 and New York: Halsted Press (John Wiley), 1980, Ch. 10 on "Microwave Integrated Circuits."

[32] Perlman, B.S., and V.G. Gelnovatch, "Computer Aided Design, Simulation and Optimization," in *Advances in Microwaves*, L. Young and H. Sobol, Eds., Vol. 8, New York: Academic Press, 1974.

[33] White, J.F., *Semiconductor Control*, Dedham, Mass: Artech House, 1977, see Ch. 6 on "Mathematical Techniques and Computer Aided Design," pp. 177-243.

[34] "S-Parameters, Circuit Analysis and Design," Hewlett Packard, *Application Note No. 95*, September 1968.

[35] Lee, C.M., *et al.*, "Semiconductor Device Simulation," *IEEE Trans. Microwave Theory Tech.*, Vol. MTT-22, 1974, pp. 160-177.

[36] Hartmann, K., and M.J.O. Strutt, "Computer Simulation of Small Signal and Noise Behaviour of Microwave Bipolar Transistors up to 12 GHz," *IEEE Trans. Microwave Theory Tech.*, Vol. MTT-22, 1974, pp. 178-183.

[37]   Silvester, P., and Z.J. Csendes, "Numerical Modeling of Passive Microwave Devices," *IEEE Trans. Microwave Theory Tech.*, Vol. MTT-22, 1974, pp. 190-201.

[38]   Hackborn, R.A., "An Automatic Network Analyzer System," *Microwave Journal*, Vol. 11, No. 5, 1968.

[39]   Oliver, B.M., and J.M. Cage, *Electronic Measurements and Instrumentation*, New York: McGraw Hill, 1971.

[40]   Hoer, C.A., "A Network Analyzer Incorporating Two Six-Port Reflectometers," *IEEE Trans. Microwave Theory Tech.*, Vol. MTT-25, 1977, pp. 1070-1074.

[41]   Engen, G.F., "The Six-Port Reflectometer: An Alternative Network Analyzer," *IEEE Trans. Microwave Theory Tech.*, Vol. MTT-25, 1977, pp. 1075-1080.

[42]   Monaco, V.A., and P. Tiberio, "Computer-Aided Analysis of Microwave Circuits," *IEEE Trans. Microwave Theory Tech.*, Vol. MTT-22, 1974, pp. 249-263.

[43]   Bonfatti, F., *et al.*, "Microwave Circuit Analysis by Sparse-Matrix Techniques," *IEEE Trans. Microwave Theory Tech.*, Vol. MTT-22, 1974, pp. 264-269.

[44]   Bandler, J.W., and R.T. Seviora, "Wave Sensitivities of Networks," *IEEE Trans. Microwave Theory Tech.*, Vol. MTT-20, 1972, pp. 138-147.

[45]   Rao, S.S., *Optimization — Theory and Applications*, New Delhi, Wiley Eastern Limited, 1978.

[46]   Bandler, J.W., "Optimization Methods for Computer-Aided Design," *IEEE Trans. Microwave Theory Tech.*, Vol. MTT-17, 1969, pp. 533-552.

[47]   Bandler, J.W., "Computer Optimization of Inhomogeneous Waveguide Transformers," *IEEE Trans. Microwave Theory Tech.*, Vol. MTT-17, 1969, pp. 563-571.

[48]   Fletcher, R., and M.J.D. Powell, "A Rapidly Convergent Descent Method of Minimization," *Comput. J.*, Vol. 6, June 1963, pp. 163-168.

[49]   Fletcher, R., "A New Approach to Variable Metric Algorithms," *Comput. J.*, Vol. 13, Aug. 1970, pp. 317-322.

[50]   Sanchez-Sinencio, E., and T.N. Trick, "CADMIC — Computer-Aided Design of Microwave Integrated Circuits," *IEEE Trans. Microwave Theory Tech.*, Vol. MTT-22, 1974, pp. 309-316.

2

Microwave Network Representation

A general microwave circuit is a multiport network, as shown in Figure 2.1, which consists of several components connected by sections of transmission lines (or waveguides). These networks may be characterized in terms of voltages and currents at various ports. This procedure is followed at lower frequencies and an impedance matrix, or an admittance matrix or a hybrid matrix representation is used [1]. At microwave frequencies, voltages and currents are replaced by normalized wave variables, and the resulting scattering matrix formulation [2-5] is commonly used.

A large variety of components used at microwave frequencies are two-port components with a single input port and a single output port. Several microwave circuits may be expressed as a cascaded combination of such two-port components. Analysis of these circuits becomes very convenient if the individual two-ports are characterized in terms of ABCD parameters [3]. The scattering matrix formulation is not very convenient for the analysis of cascaded two-ports. However, there is another representation that uses wave variables and allows cascaded networks to be analyzed easily. This is known as transfer scattering matrix formulation. The three types of representations mentioned above are reviewed in this chapter.

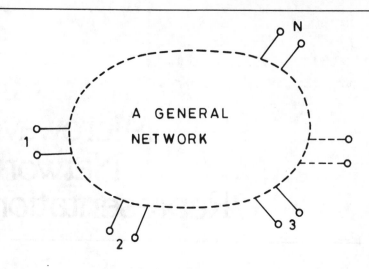

Figure 2.1   A general N-port network.

In addition to these three representations, conventional impedance and admittance matrices also find specific applications in microwave circuit design. In the two-dimensional microwave planar circuits discussed in Chapter 8, the third dimension of the components is assumed to be much smaller than the wavelength, and a voltage could be conveniently defined in terms of the E-field along this direction. An impedance Green's function which defines voltage at any point in terms of the current at some other point is used to find the Z-matrix. The Y-matrix formulation is very convenient when networks or some of their ports are connected in parallel. These matrices have also been used in time domain analysis discussed in Chapter 14. Relationships for transformations from Z- and Y-matrices to scattering matrix and vice-versa are described in Section 2.2.

2.1 ABCD PARAMETERS

ABCD parameters for a two-port network, such as shown in Figure 2.2(a), are defined by

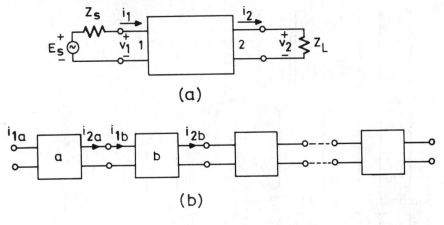

(a)

(b)

Figure 2.2   (a)   A two-port network.
            (b)   A cascaded chain of two-port networks.

$$\begin{bmatrix} v_1 \\ i_1 \end{bmatrix} = \begin{bmatrix} A & B \\ C & D \end{bmatrix}\begin{bmatrix} v_2 \\ i_2 \end{bmatrix} . \tag{2.1}$$

Note that i_2 is shown to flow outward and becomes i_1 of the next two-port network in a cascaded chain as shown in Figure 2.2(b). Thus, if there are two networks "a" and "b" cascaded as shown in Figure 2.3, we have

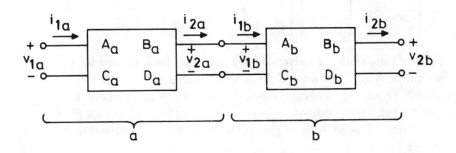

Figure 2.3   Cascade connection of 2 two-port networks.

$$\begin{bmatrix} v_{1a} \\ i_{1a} \end{bmatrix} = \begin{bmatrix} A_a & B_a \\ C_a & D_a \end{bmatrix} \begin{bmatrix} v_{2a} \\ i_{2a} \end{bmatrix} \tag{2.2}$$

and also

$$\begin{bmatrix} v_{2a} \\ i_{2a} \end{bmatrix} = \begin{bmatrix} v_{1b} \\ i_{1b} \end{bmatrix} = \begin{bmatrix} A_b & B_b \\ C_b & D_b \end{bmatrix} \begin{bmatrix} v_{2b} \\ i_{2b} \end{bmatrix} . \tag{2.3}$$

Combining (2.2) and (2.3),

$$\begin{bmatrix} v_{1a} \\ i_{1a} \end{bmatrix} = \begin{bmatrix} A_a & B_a \\ C_a & D_a \end{bmatrix} \begin{bmatrix} A_b & B_b \\ C_b & D_b \end{bmatrix} \begin{bmatrix} v_{2b} \\ i_{2b} \end{bmatrix}$$

$$= \begin{bmatrix} A & B \\ C & D \end{bmatrix} \begin{bmatrix} v_{2b} \\ i_{2b} \end{bmatrix} \tag{2.4}$$

where [ABCD] in (2.4) is the product of two individual ABCD-matrices. Generalizing this analysis for the case of N two-ports cascaded together, we get for the resultant matrix

$$\begin{bmatrix} A & B \\ C & D \end{bmatrix} = \begin{bmatrix} A & B \\ C & D \end{bmatrix}_1 \begin{bmatrix} A & B \\ C & D \end{bmatrix}_2 \cdots \begin{bmatrix} A & B \\ C & D \end{bmatrix}_N . \tag{2.5}$$

Thus, a long chain of network elements may be analyzed simply by multiplying their individual ABCD matrices to obtain the overall ABCD matrix. This representation provides an efficient way for the analysis of networks that can be represented as cascaded two-ports. The analysis of cascaded two-ports is discussed in detail in Chapter 11.

Various performance functions for a network may be obtained from its ABCD matrix. Referring to Figure 2.2(a) we may derive the following relations.

The driving point impedance at the input port is given by

$$Z_{in} = (A Z_L + B) / (C Z_L + D) \qquad (2.6)$$

where the load impedance Z_L is equal to v_2/i_2. The driving point impedance at the output port may be written as

$$Z_{out} = (D Z_s + B) / (C Z_s + A) \qquad (2.7)$$

where the source impedance Z_s is equal to $(E_s - v_1) / i_1$. The voltage transfer coefficient (from the source to the output port) becomes

$$v_2/E_s = Z_L / (A Z_L + B + C Z_s Z_L + D Z_s) . \qquad (2.8)$$

The voltage reflection coefficient at the input port is given by

$$\Gamma_{in} = \{(Z_{in} - Z_s^*) / (Z_{in} + Z_s)\} \qquad (2.9)$$

whereas the voltage reflection coefficient at the output port may be written as

$$\Gamma_{out} = (Z_{out} - Z_L^*) / (Z_{out} + Z_L) . \qquad (2.10)$$

The ABCD matrices for some typical microwave circuit elements are listed in the Appendix 2.1 at the end of this chapter. These parameters have been derived by applying Kirchhoff's laws and/or transmission line equations to the various networks.

ABCD matrices exhibit the following characteristics:

i)   For reciprocal networks,

$$AD - BC = 1 .$$

ii) For symmetrical networks (which remain unaltered when the two ports are interchanged, we have $A = D$.

Normalized ABCD Matrix

ABCD parameters as defined above may be normalized by dividing the parameter B and multiplying the parameter C by a reference impedance Z_o. We may write the normalized ABCD matrix as

$$[ABCD]_n = \begin{bmatrix} A & B/Z_o \\ \\ CZ_o & D \end{bmatrix} . \qquad (2.11)$$

It may be noted that in (2.11) all the four parameters are dimensionless. Quite often, the normalizing impedance Z_o is the characteristic impedance of the transmission lines connected to the two ports of the network. For example, consider a transmission line section of length ℓ and an impedance Z interposed between two lines of impedance Z_o as shown in Figure 1 of Appendix 2.1. The normalized ABCD matrix for this component may be written as

$$[ABCD]_n = \begin{bmatrix} \cos\beta\ell & j\,\dfrac{Z}{Z_o}\,\sin\beta\ell \\[2em] j\,\dfrac{Z_o}{Z}\,\sin\beta\ell & \cos\beta\ell \end{bmatrix} . \qquad (2.12)$$

Normalized ABCD matrices for several elements in cascade can be multiplied together to obtain the overall normalized ABCD matrix, provided the reference impedance Z_o is the same for all the elements.

2.2 SCATTERING PARAMETERS

2.2.1 Definition and General Properties

The use of ABCD parameters at microwave frequencies is not very convenient from the measurements point of view. Also, its main advantage of cascading network components does not hold when the network consists of components with three or more ports and when the topology is different. Scattering matrix formulation is a more general method of representing microwave networks.

A scattering matrix represents the relationship between variables a_n (proportional to the incoming wave at nth port) and variables b_n (proportional to the outgoing wave at nth port) defined in the following manner

$$a_n = v_n^+ / \sqrt{Z_{on}} \qquad (2.13)$$

$$b_n = v_n^- / \sqrt{Z_{on}} \qquad (2.14)$$

where v_n^+ and v_n^- represent voltages corresponding to the incoming and the outgoing waves in the transmission line (or the waveguide) connected to the n*th* port and Z_{on} is the characteristic impedance of the line (or waveguide). Knowledge of v_n^+ and v_n^- is not required to evaluate coefficients of the scattering matrix. Relationships between b_n's and a_n's for a two-port network may be written as

$$b_1 = S_{11} a_1 + S_{12} a_2 , \qquad (2.15)$$

and

$$b_2 = S_{21} a_1 + S_{22} a_2 . \qquad (2.16)$$

In general, for an n-port network, we have

$$b = S a \qquad (2.17)$$

where S is an n x n matrix (2 x 2 for a two-port network). The matrix S is known as the scattering matrix of the network.

The average power flowing into the port n may be evaluated by using (2.13) and (2.14). For this purpose, v_n and i_n may be written as (from transmission line theory)

$$v_n = v_n^+ + v_n^- = \sqrt{Z_{on}} \, (a_n + b_n) , \qquad (2.18)$$

and

$$i_n = \frac{1}{Z_{on}} (v_n^+ - v_n^-) = \frac{1}{\sqrt{Z_{on}}} (a_n - b_n) . \qquad (2.19)$$

Power flowing into the port n is given by

$$W_n = \frac{1}{2} \, \text{Re}(v_n \, i_n^*) = \frac{1}{2} (a_n a_n^* - b_n b_n^*) . \qquad (2.20)$$

This shows that W_n is equal to the power carried into the port n by the incident wave ($\frac{1}{2} a_n a_n^*$) less the power reflected back ($\frac{1}{2} b_n b_n^*$).

Advantages of S-matrix Representation

One of the advantages of S-matrices is the ease of measurement. The ABCD parameters discussed earlier are not a convenient set to measure at microwave frequencies. At lower frequencies the measurements are carried out by using open circuit (or short circuit) terminations at one of the ports and measuring voltage and/or current at the other port. At microwave frequencies an ideal open circuit is extremely difficult to realize, and it is equally difficult to establish the exact location of a short circuit. The S-parameter measurements, on the other hand, are carried out by terminating one or the other port with the normalizing impedance Z_o (usually 50 ohms). Quantities like the reflection coefficient and the transmission coefficient, commonly measured at microwave frequencies, can be expressed directly in terms of the scattering parameters.

Another important advantage of the S-matrix approach emerges from the fact that the S-parameters are defined on the basis of traveling waves and, unlike terminal currents or voltages, the wave variables do not vary in magnitude along a lossless line. This allows the S-parameters for an unknown device to be measured relatively far away from its physical location. The effect of the intermediate length of the low loss line may be eliminated by modifying the phase of the measured data. This is equivalent to the shifting of the reference planes. On the other hand, if the ABCD (or Z- or Y-) parameters were used, they would vary with distance not only in phase but in magnitude also.

Some of the important characteristics of S-matrices are listed below:

i)   For a reciprocal network the S-matrix is symmetrical, i.e.

$$S = S^t \tag{2.21}$$

where the subscript t indicates the transpose of a matrix.

ii)   For a lossless passive network

$$\sum_{n=1}^{N} |S_{ni}|^2 = \sum_{n=1}^{N} S_{ni} S_{ni}^* = 1 \tag{2.22}$$

$$\text{for all } i = 1, 2, \ldots N$$

i.e., the inner product of any column of the scattering matrix with its own conjugate equals unity. Equation (2.22) is a direct consequence of the power conservation property of a lossless passive network.

iii) Again for lossless passive networks, the power conservation condition yields an orthogonality constraint given by

$$\sum_{n=1}^{N} S_{ns} S_{nr}^* = 0 \text{ (for all s, r} = 1, 2, \ldots N, s \neq r) \ . \quad (2.23)$$

This equation states that the inner product of any column of the scattering matrix with the complex conjugate of any other column is zero.

The conditions (2.22) and (2.23) restrict the number of independent elements in an N x N scattering matrix to $N(N + 1)/2$. A matrix that satisfies these two conditions is called a unitary matrix. In terms of matrix operations these conditions imply

$$A^* = [A^t]^{-1} \ . \quad (2.24)$$

The above equation states that in the case of a lossless passive network, the complex conjugate of the scattering matrix is equal to the inverse of its transpose.

Examples of Scattering Matrices

Examples of S-matrices for some of the most commonly used two-port components are listed in Appendix 2.1 along with ABCD and T-parameters for these components. The S-matrix for a lossless transmission line (given in row 1 of Appendix 2.1) may be used to find the modified S-matrix for a network when the reference plane for any of its ports is shifted down the transmission line (or the waveguide) connected to that port. If an additional line length ℓ is connected to the jth port, it can be shown that each of the coefficients S_{ij} or S_{ji} (i.e. the matrix elements involving j) will be multiplied by the factor $e^{-j\beta\ell}$ while the coefficient S_{jj} will be multiplied by $e^{-j2\beta\ell}$.

2.2.2 Relationship with Other Representations

Relationship Between S-matrix and ABCD matrix

As mentioned earlier S-parameters are not suitable for analyzing cascaded networks and therefore, for this application, their conversion to ABCD parameters is desirable. The following equivalences may be used for the conversion:

From S-matrix to ABCD matrix

$$A = (1 + S_{11} - S_{22} - \Delta S)\sqrt{Z_{01}/Z_{02}} \; / \; (2S_{21}) \quad (2.25)$$

$$B = (1 + S_{11} + S_{22} + \Delta S)\sqrt{Z_{01} Z_{02}} \; / \; (2S_{21}) \quad (2.26)$$

$$C = (1 - S_{11} - S_{22} + \Delta S)/(2S_{21} \sqrt{Z_{01} Z_{02}}) \quad (2.27)$$

$$D = (1 - S_{11} + S_{22} - \Delta S)\sqrt{Z_{02}/Z_{01}} \; /(2S_{21}) \quad (2.28)$$

where Z_{01} and Z_{02} are normalizing impedances for S-parameters at ports 1 and 2 respectively, and

$$\Delta S = (S_{11} S_{22} - S_{21} S_{12}). \quad (2.29)$$

It may be noted that for $S_{21} = 0$, ABCD parameters become indeterminate. The parameter S_{21} represents the forward transmission coefficient and is seldom zero in microwave circuits.

From ABCD matrix to S-matrix

$$S_{11} = \frac{A Z_{02} + B - C Z_{01} Z_{02} - D Z_{01}}{A Z_{02} + B + C Z_{01} Z_{02} + D Z_{01}} \quad (2.30)$$

$$S_{12} = \frac{2(AD - BC)\sqrt{Z_{01} Z_{02}}}{A Z_{02} + B + C Z_{01} Z_{02} + D Z_{01}} \quad (2.31)$$

$$S_{21} = \frac{2\sqrt{Z_{01} Z_{02}}}{A Z_{02} + B + C Z_{01} Z_{02} + D Z_{01}} \quad (2.32)$$

and

$$S_{22} = \frac{-A Z_{02} + B - C Z_{01} Z_{02} + D Z_{01}}{A Z_{02} + B + C Z_{01} Z_{02} + D Z_{01}}. \quad (2.33)$$

The factor $(AD - BC)$ in (2.31) is equal to unity for reciprocal networks and therefore S_{12} becomes equal to S_{21}.

Relationships Between S-matrix and Y- and Z-matrices

If the voltages and currents (directed inwards) are denoted by vectors v and i respectively, the admittance and the impedance matrices are defined by

$$i = Y \, v \text{ and } v = Z \, i \tag{2.34}$$

where

$$Z = Y^{-1} . \tag{2.35}$$

Port voltages and port currents are related to the wave variables a_n and b_n by (2.18) and (2.19) respectively. This leads to the following relationships between S-matrix and Y- and Z-matrices [6].

S-matrix from Z-matrix: S-matrix may be evaluated from Z-matrix [6] using the following relation

$$S = \sqrt{Y_o} \, (Z - Z_o)(Z + Z_o)^{-1} \sqrt{Z_o} \tag{2.36}$$

where $Z_o, \sqrt{Z_o}$ and $\sqrt{Y_o}$ are diagonal matrices with diagonal elements given by $Z_{01}, Z_{02}, \ldots Z_{0N}$; $\sqrt{Z_{01}}, \sqrt{Z_{02}}, \ldots \sqrt{Z_{0N}}$; and $1/\sqrt{Z_{01}}, 1/\sqrt{Z_{02}}, \ldots 1/\sqrt{Z_{0N}}$ respectively. $Z_{01}, Z_{02}, \ldots, Z_{0N}$ represent the normalizing impedances at various ports of the network.

S-matrix from Y-matrix: For conversion from Y-matrix to S-matrix, we have [6]

$$S = \sqrt{Z_o} \, (Y_o - Y)(Y_o + Y)^{-1} \sqrt{Y_o} \tag{2.37}$$

where Y_o is a diagonal matrix of normalizing admittances at various ports with diagonal elements given by $1/Z_{01}, 1/Z_{02}, \ldots 1/Z_{0N}$.

One can invert these relations to obtain Z- and Y- matrices in terms of the S-matrix. We obtain

$$Z = \sqrt{Z_o} \, (I + S)(I - S)^{-1} \sqrt{Z_o} \tag{2.38}$$

and

$$Y = \sqrt{Y_o} \, (I - S)(I + S)^{-1} \sqrt{Y_o} \tag{2.39}$$

where I is the identity matrix.

2.3 TRANSFER SCATTERING MATRIX REPRESENTATION

As mentioned earlier, the scattering matrix representation is not
suitable for the analysis of cascaded two-ports. An alternative approach is to convert from S-matrix to ABCD matrix as discussed
above. Another way to analyze the cascaded networks is by defining a new set of scattering parameters (in terms of wave variables)
with properties analogous to ABCD representation regarding matrix
multiplication of cascaded element blocks. The inability to cascade
S-matrices is the result of the fact that part of the variables at a
port are independent, the rest being dependent; i.e., b_1 and b_2 are
dependent on a_1 and a_2, which are independent. By analogy with
the definition of ABCD matrix, if we arrange the scattering parameters in such a manner that all the parameters at the port 1 (i.e.,
a_1 and b_1) are the dependent variables, and the output waves a_2 and
b_2 are the independent variables, we have the basis for a new set
which will have properties similar to those of the ABCD set. Thus,
for two-port networks, we define a new set of parameters known
as transfer scattering or T-parameters [6,7] as

$$\begin{bmatrix} b_1 \\ a_1 \end{bmatrix} = \begin{bmatrix} T_{11} & T_{12} \\ T_{21} & T_{22} \end{bmatrix} \begin{bmatrix} a_2 \\ b_2 \end{bmatrix}. \tag{2.40}$$

The T-parameters defined above are related to the S-parameters as
follows:

$$T_{11} = (-S_{11} S_{22} + S_{12} S_{21})/S_{21} \tag{2.41}$$

$$T_{12} = S_{11}/S_{21} \tag{2.42}$$

$$T_{21} = -S_{22}/S_{21} \tag{2.43}$$

$$T_{22} = 1/S_{21}. \tag{2.44}$$

As in the case of ABCD parameters, the T-parameters also become
indeterminate when the forward transmission coefficient S_{21} is
zero.

T-parameters for various two-port elements can be obtained by
using (2.41) - (2.44). The overall T-parameters of a cascaded

chain are obtained by multiplying individual T-matrices. The scattering matrix for the overall network may be obtained from the overall T-matrix by using the following relations:

$$S_{11} = T_{12} / T_{22} \tag{2.45}$$

$$S_{12} = T_{11} - (T_{12} \ T_{21} / T_{22}) \tag{2.46}$$

$$S_{21} = 1 / T_{22} \tag{2.47}$$

$$S_{22} = -T_{21} / T_{22} \ . \tag{2.48}$$

In order to realize conversion of the T-matrix to the S-matrix, the parameter T_{22} should be non-zero. It may be noted that T_{22} is the reciprocal of the forward transmission coefficient S_{21} and is a non-zero quantity.

For reciprocal networks, the T-parameters satisfy the following relation

$$T_{11} \ T_{22} - T_{12} \ T_{21} = 1 \ , \tag{2.49}$$

which is analogous to the relation $AD - BC = 1$ for ABCD parameters. When the network is identical looking from the ports 1 and 2, we have $S_{11} = S_{22}$ which leads to

$$T_{21} = -T_{12} \ . \tag{2.50}$$

Transfer scattering matrix representation is preferable to ABCD representation because of the following consideration. The calculations required for the transformation from S-matrix to T-matrix are slightly less complex than those required for S-matrix to ABCD matrix transformation. Also, T-parameters are defined in terms of wave variables normalized with respect to impedances at various ports exactly in the same way as for S-parameters. This allows an easier interchange to two representations.

A convenient way of writing T-parameters is to derive them from S-parameters. They could also be written directly using transmission line equations and Kirchhoff's laws. T-matrices for a few simple cases are given in Appendix 2.1.

The three types of representations for microwave networks described in this chapter are useful for computer-aided analysis and design of microwave circuits to be discussed later.

APPENDIX 2.1: ABCD, S- AND T- MATRICES FOR SOME OF THE COMMONLY USED TWO-PORTS

Element	ABCD matrix	S-matrix	T-matrix
1. A transmission line section (Z_o, $Z, \gamma\ell$, Z_o, length ℓ)	$\begin{bmatrix} CH & ZSh \\[2mm] \dfrac{Sh}{Z} & Ch \end{bmatrix}$	$\dfrac{1}{D_s}\begin{bmatrix} (Z^2 - Z_o^2)\,Sh & 2ZZ_o \\[2mm] 2ZZ_o & (Z^2 - Z_o^2)\,Sh \end{bmatrix}$	$\begin{bmatrix} Ch - \dfrac{Z^2 + Z_o^2}{2ZZ_o}Sh & \dfrac{Z^2 - Z_o^2}{2ZZ_o}Sh \\[3mm] -\dfrac{Z^2 - Z_o^2}{2ZZ_o}Sh & Ch + \dfrac{Z^2 + Z_o^2}{2ZZ_o}Sh \end{bmatrix}$
2. A series impedance (Z, Z_1, Z_2)	$\begin{bmatrix} 1 & Z \\ 0 & 1 \end{bmatrix}$	$\dfrac{1}{D_s}\begin{bmatrix} Z + Z_2 - Z_1 & 2\sqrt{Z_1 Z_2} \\[2mm] 2\sqrt{Z_1 Z_2} & Z + Z_1 - Z_2 \end{bmatrix}$	$\dfrac{1}{D_t}\begin{bmatrix} Z_1 + Z_2 - Z & Z_2 - Z_1 + Z \\[2mm] Z_2 - Z_1 - Z & Z_1 + Z_2 - Z \end{bmatrix}$

where $Sh = \sinh\gamma\ell$, $Ch = \cosh\gamma\ell$ and $D_s = 2ZZ_o\,Ch + (Z^2 + Z_o^2)\,Sh$

where $D_s = Z + Z_1 + Z_2$ and $D_t = 2\sqrt{Z_1 Z_2}$

Element	ABCD matrix	S-matrix	T-matrix
3. A shunt admittance	$\begin{bmatrix} 1 & 0 \\ Y & 1 \end{bmatrix}$	$\dfrac{1}{D_s}\begin{bmatrix} Y_1 - Y_2 - Y & 2\sqrt{Y_1 Y_2} \\ 2\sqrt{Y_1 Y_2} & Y_2 - Y_1 - Y \end{bmatrix}$ where $D_s = Y + Y_1 + Y_2$ and $D_t = 2\sqrt{Y_1 Y_2}$	$\dfrac{1}{D_t}\begin{bmatrix} Y_1 + Y_2 - Y & Y_1 - Y_2 - Y \\ Y_1 - Y_2 + Y & Y_1 + Y_2 + Y \end{bmatrix}$
4. A shunt-connected open-ended stub	$\begin{bmatrix} 1 & 0 \\ \dfrac{jT}{Z} & 1 \end{bmatrix}$	$\dfrac{1}{D_s}\begin{bmatrix} 1 & D_s + 1 \\ D_s + 1 & 1 \end{bmatrix}$ where $T = \tan\beta\ell$ and $D_s = -1 + 2jZ/(Z_o T)$	$\begin{bmatrix} 1 - \dfrac{Z_o}{2Z}T & -j\,\dfrac{Z_o}{2Z}T \\ j\,\dfrac{Z_o}{2Z}T & 1 + j\,\dfrac{Z_o}{2Z}T \end{bmatrix}$
5. A shunt-connected short-circuited stub	$\begin{bmatrix} 1 & 0 \\ \dfrac{1}{jZT} & 1 \end{bmatrix}$	$\dfrac{1}{D_s}\begin{bmatrix} -1 & D_s - 1 \\ D_s - 1 & -1 \end{bmatrix}$ where $T = \tan\beta\ell$ and $D_s = 1 + 2jZT/Z_o$	$\begin{bmatrix} 1 + j\,\dfrac{Z_o}{2ZT} & j\,\dfrac{Z_o}{2ZT} \\ -j\,\dfrac{Z_o}{2ZT} & 1 - j\,\dfrac{Z_o}{2ZT} \end{bmatrix}$

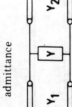

6. An ideal transformer

$Z_o=1$ $n:1$ $Z_o=1$

$$\begin{bmatrix} n & 0 \\ 0 & 1/n \end{bmatrix}$$

$$\frac{1}{n^2+1}\begin{bmatrix} n^2-1 & 2n \\ 2n & 1-n^2 \end{bmatrix}$$

$$\frac{1}{2n}\begin{bmatrix} n^2+1 & n^2-1 \\ n^2-1 & n^2+1 \end{bmatrix}$$

7. π-network

$$\begin{bmatrix} 1+\dfrac{Y_2}{Y_3} & \dfrac{1}{Y_3} \\[2ex] \dfrac{D}{Y_3} & 1+\dfrac{Y_1}{Y_3} \end{bmatrix}$$

$$\frac{1}{D_s}\begin{bmatrix} Y_o^2 - PY_o - D & 2Y_oY_3 \\ 2Y_oY_3 & Y_o^2 + PY_o - D \end{bmatrix}$$

$$\frac{1}{2Y_oY_3}\begin{bmatrix} -Y_o^2 + QY_o - D & Y_o^2 - PY_o - D \\ -Y_o^2 - PY_o + D & Y_o^2 + QY_o + D \end{bmatrix}$$

where $D_s = Y_o^2 + QY_o + D$, $D = Y_1Y_2 + Y_2Y_3 + Y_3Y_1$, $Q = Y_1 + Y_2 + 2Y_3$ and $P = Y_1 - Y_2$

8. T-network

Z_2 Z_o

Z_1 Z_3

Z_o

$$\begin{bmatrix} 1+\dfrac{Z_1}{Z_3} & \dfrac{D}{Z_3} \\[2ex] \dfrac{1}{Z_3} & 1+\dfrac{Z_2}{Z_3} \end{bmatrix}$$

$$\frac{1}{D_s}\begin{bmatrix} -Z_o^2 + PZ_o + D & 2Z_oZ_3 \\ 2Z_oZ_3 & -Z_o^2 - PZ_o + D \end{bmatrix}$$

$$\frac{1}{2Z_oZ_3}\begin{bmatrix} -Z_o^2 + QZ_o - D & -Z_o^2 + PZ_o + D \\ Z_o^2 + PZ_o - D & Z_o^2 + QZ_o + D \end{bmatrix}$$

where $D_s = Z_o^2 + QZ_o + D$, $D = Z_1Z_2 + Z_2Z_3 + Z_3Z_1$, $Q = Z_1 + Z_2 + 2Z_3$ and $P = Z_1 - Z_2$

Element	ABCD matrix	S-matrix	T-matrix
9. A transmission line junction 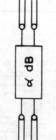 Z_1 Z_2	$\begin{bmatrix} 1 & 0 \\ 0 & 1 \end{bmatrix}$	$\dfrac{1}{D_s}\begin{bmatrix} Z_2 - Z_1 & 2\sqrt{Z_1 Z_2} \\ 2\sqrt{Z_1 Z_2} & Z_1 - Z_2 \end{bmatrix}$	$\dfrac{1}{D_t}\begin{bmatrix} Z_1 + Z_2 & Z_2 - Z_1 \\ Z_2 - Z_1 & Z_1 + Z_2 \end{bmatrix}$

where $D_s = Z_1 + Z_2$ and $D_t = 2\sqrt{Z_1 Z_2}$

Element	ABCD matrix	S-matrix	T-matrix
10. An α-db attenuator — α **dB**	$\begin{bmatrix} \dfrac{A+B}{2} & Z_o\left(\dfrac{A-B}{2}\right) \\[2ex] \dfrac{A-B}{2Z_o} & \dfrac{A+B}{2} \end{bmatrix}$	$\begin{bmatrix} 0 & B \\ B & 0 \end{bmatrix}$	$\begin{bmatrix} -A & 0 \\ 0 & A \end{bmatrix}$

where $A = 10^{\alpha/20}$ and $B = 1/A$.

REFERENCES

[1] Desoer, C.A., and E.S. Kuh, *Basic Circuit Theory*, New York: McGraw-Hill, 1969.

[2] Collin, R.E., *Foundations of Microwave Engineering*, New York: McGraw-Hill, 1966, Chapter 4 on "Circuit Theory for Waveguiding Systems," pp. 170-182.

[3] Perlman, B.S., and V.G. Gelnovatch, "Computer Aided Design, Simulation and Optimization," in *Advances in Microwaves, Vol. 8*, pp. 332-341, Academic Press, 1974.

[4] Gupta, K.C., *Microwaves*, New Delhi: Wiley Eastern, 1979, Chapter 5 on "Microwave Network Representation."

[5] Hewlett Packard, "S-parameters, Circuit Analysis and Design," *Application Note No. 95*, September 1968.

[6] Kuh, E.S. and R.A. Rohrer, *Theory of Linear Active Networks*, San Francisco, CA: Holden-Day, 1967, p. 271.

[7] Carlin, H.J., and A.B. Giordano, *Network Theory*, Englewood Cliffs: Prentice-Hall, 1964; chapter 4 on "The Scattering Matrix."

[8] Weinberg, Louis, "Fundamentals of Scattering Matrices," *Electro-technology*, Vol. 80, No. 1, July 1967, pp. 55-72.

Part II

Modelling of Circuit Elements

3

Characterization
of
Transmission
Structures

An extensive variety of transmission structures are used at microwave frequencies. These include coaxial line [1], waveguide [1],
stripline [2-8], microstrip line [9], coplanar waveguide [9], coplanar strips [9], slot line [9], coupled striplines [2], and coupled
microstrip lines [9]. These transmission structures are the most commonly used, and their cross-sectional views are shown in Figure 3.1.
Half wavelength, quarter wavelength, and one-eighth wavelength
sections of these lines form the basic building-blocks in various types
of microwave circuits. Characterization of these lines requires
evaluation of their characteristic impedances and propagation constants (i.e. phase velocity and attenuation constant) in terms of
physical parameters (like geometrical cross-section) and properties
of the dielectric and the conductor materials used. In this chapter,
the available design information regarding these transmission lines
are approximate. The maximum error may be from 2 to 5 percent.
This modeling uncertainty may be taken into account in the same
way as for the fabrication tolerances. However, for more accurate
design values of the parameters, the analysis may be carried out by
using numerical methods, the references for which are also given.

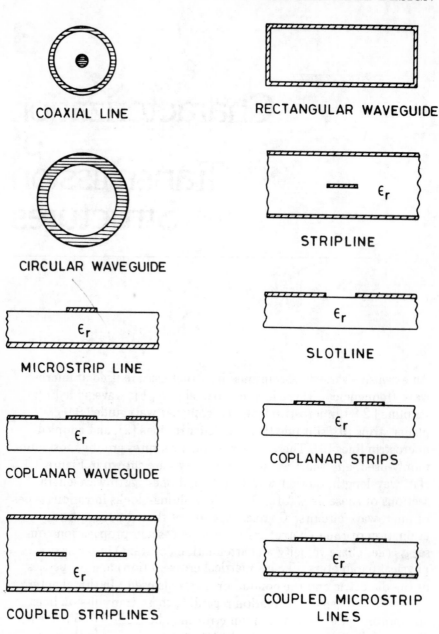

Figure 3.1   Transmission structures commonly used in microwave circuits.

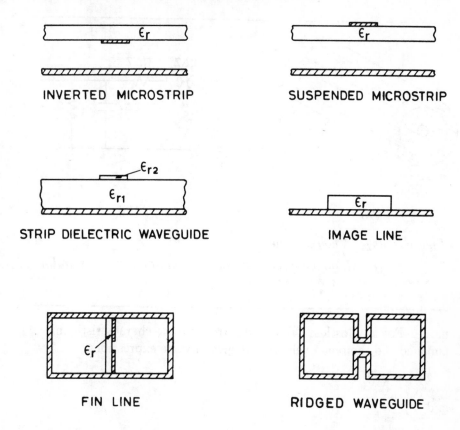

Figure 3.2   Other transmission structures for microwave circuits.

In addition to the various transmission structures discussed in this chapter, there are other transmission lines which are used less often. These include suspended microstrip line [10-11] inverted microstrip line [12], image line [16], fin line [14], ridged waveguide [15] and strip dielectric waveguide [13]. Cross-sectional views of these lines are shown in Figure 3.2, and their characteristics have been discussed in the literature cited.

3.1 COAXIAL LINES

The dominant mode of wave propagation in a coaxial transmission line (shown in Figure 3.3(a)) is the transverse electromagnetic (TEM)

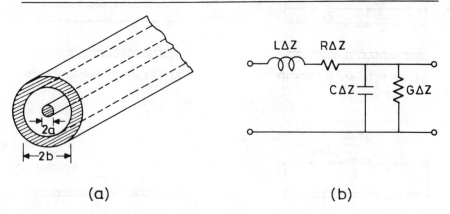

(a)   (b)

Figure 3.3(a)   A coaxial line.

(b)   Lumped circuit representation of a transmission line of length Δz.

mode. For any lossless TEM mode structure the characteristic impedance and the phase velocity are given by the expressions

$$Z_o = \sqrt{L/C} \qquad\qquad (3.1)$$

and

$$v_p = \frac{1}{\sqrt{LC}} \qquad\qquad (3.2)$$

where L and C denote the inductance and the capacitance per unit length of the structure. From (3.1) and (3.2), Z_o may be expressed in terms of v_p and C as

$$Z_o = \frac{1}{v_p C} \cdot \qquad\qquad (3.3)$$

When a structure is homogeneously filled with a dielectric of relative permittivity ϵ_r we have

$$v_p = c / \sqrt{\epsilon_r} \qquad\qquad (3.4)$$

where c is the velocity of electromagnetic waves in free space. In case the dielectric does not fill the structure completely, the relation (3.4) is modified as

$$v_p = c / \sqrt{\epsilon_{re}} \tag{3.5}$$

where ϵ_{re} is called the effective dielectric constant and is related to the capacitance of the structure as

$$\epsilon_{re} = C / C_a \tag{3.6}$$

in which C_a is the capacitance (per unit length) of the structure with the dielectric replaced by air. The concept of effective dielectric constant is applicable to all partially filled TEM mode (or nearly TEM mode) structures and is used for microstrip line and coplanar lines discussed later. For such structures we can write

$$Z_o = \sqrt{C_a / C} \; Z_o^a \tag{3.7}$$

and

$$\beta = \beta_o \sqrt{C/C_a} \tag{3.8}$$

where Z_o^a and β_o are the characteristic impedance and the phase constant, respectively, for the structure with the dielectric replaced by air.

When the losses are also being considered, useful relations for a TEM mode structure are

$$Z_o = \sqrt{(R + j\omega L) / (G + j\omega C)} \tag{3.9}$$

and

$$\gamma = \alpha + j\beta = \sqrt{(R + j\omega L)(G + j\omega C)} \tag{3.10}$$

where R and G denote the series resistance and the shunt conductance per unit length of the structure. The parameters R, L, G and C are the components of the equivalent circuit for a transmission line section as shown in Figure 3.3(b). The propagation constant is denoted by γ (α being the attenuation constant and β the phase constant) and ω is the angular frequency. Equations (3.9) and (3.10) approximate to (3.1) and (3.2) respectively, when the losses are negligible.

Z_o and γ for coaxial lines [1]

For a coaxial line, the values of capacitance and inductance per unit length are obtained from static field analysis. We have

$$C = 2\pi\epsilon \,/\, \ell n(b/a) \qquad\qquad (3.11)$$

and

$$L = \frac{\mu}{2\pi} \, \ell n \,(b/a) \qquad\qquad (3.12)$$

where ϵ and μ are the permittivity and the permeability of the dielectric medium, "b" denotes inner radius of the outer conductor and "a" the radius of the inner conductor. Using (3.11) the characteristic impedance for low loss lines may be written as

$$Z_o = \frac{\eta}{2\pi} \, \ell n \,(b/a) \qquad\qquad (3.13)$$

where η is the intrinsic impedance (= $\sqrt{\mu/\epsilon}$) of the dielectric medium. For air dielectric, we may write

$$Z_o = 60 \, \ell n \,(b/a) \text{ ohm} . \qquad\qquad (3.14)$$

Series resistance R per unit length is given by

$$R = \frac{R_s}{2\pi} \left(\frac{1}{b} + \frac{1}{a} \right) \qquad\qquad (3.15)$$

where R_s is the surface resistivity of the conductors. The conductance G per unit length may be written as

$$G = 2\pi\sigma \,/\, \ell n \,(b/a) = 2\pi\omega\epsilon_o\epsilon_r \, \tan\delta \,/\, \ell n \,(b/a) \qquad (3.16)$$

where σ is the conductivity and $\tan\delta$ is the loss tangent of the dielectric. The attenuation coefficients due to R and G can be calculated as follows:

Attenuation due to conductor,

$$\alpha_c = R/(2 \, Z_o) \text{ nepers/m} . \qquad\qquad (3.17)$$

Attenuation due to dielectric,

$$\alpha_d = G \, Z_o/2 = \sigma\eta/2 = \pi \sqrt{\epsilon_r} \, \tan\delta \,/\, \lambda_o \text{ nepers/m} . \qquad (3.18)$$

Total attenuation, expressed in db/meter, is 8.686 ($\alpha_c + \alpha_d$).

From (3.15) it is seen that R, and hence the attenuation, decreases with an increase in b and a. The upper limit on these dimensions is set by the existence of higher order modes. The lowest order TE wave with circumferential variation (i.e. TE_{01} mode) is significant for this purpose. For this mode the cut-off wavelength is given by

$$\lambda_c \approx 2\pi \left(\frac{b + a}{2} \right) \tag{3.19}$$

i.e., cut-off occurs for wavelength approximately equal to the average circumference.

3.2 WAVEGUIDES [1]

Waveguides of rectangular and circular cross-section find frequent applications. These are discussed in this section.

3.2.1 Rectangular Waveguides

The geometry of a rectangular waveguide and the coordinate system used is shown in Figure 3.4(a). By solving the wave equation subject to the appropriate boundary conditions one obtains [1]

$$\gamma = \sqrt{k_c^2 - k^2} = j \frac{\omega}{v} \sqrt{1 - (f_c/f)^2} \tag{3.20}$$

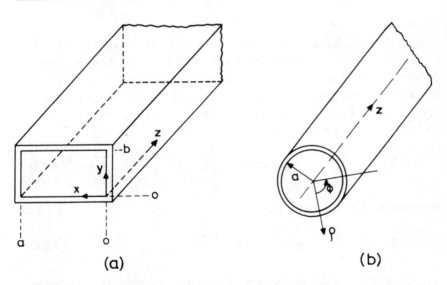

(a)   (b)

Figure 3.4(a)   A rectangular waveguide.

(b)   A circular waveguide.

where γ is the propagation constant, k is the wave number ($= \omega\sqrt{\mu\epsilon}$) in the unbounded dielectric, and v the phase velocity in the dielectric medium. Cut-off wave number k_c and cut-off frequency f_c are related by

$$(k_c)_{m,n} = 2\pi(f_c)_{m,n}\sqrt{\mu\epsilon} = \sqrt{\left(\frac{m\pi}{a}\right)^2 + \left(\frac{n\pi}{b}\right)^2} \quad (3.21)$$

where m and n specify the order of $TE_{m,n}$ or $TM_{m,n}$ modes. From (3.20) one sees that γ is imaginary ($= j\beta$) for $f > f_c$. Phase velocity v and guide wavelength λ_g are calculated from β.

The modes of wave propagation in rectangular waveguide are non-TEM, and the characteristic impedance cannot be defined uniquely. For these structures, Z_0 can be defined either in terms of the voltage-current ratio or in terms of the power transmitted for a given voltage or a given current; i.e.

$$Z_0(v,i) = \frac{v}{i}, \text{ or } Z_0(W,i) = \frac{2W}{i\,i^*}, \text{ or } Z_0(W,v) = \frac{vv^*}{2W}.$$

$$(3.22)$$

For TEM mode lines, these definitions are identical, but for waveguides they lead to three different values of Z_0. All of these three different characteristic impedances may be expressed in terms of the wave impedance Z_z which is defined as the ratio of transverse components of electric and magnetic fields. The wave impedance for TE waves may be expressed as

$$Z_z(TE) = \frac{\omega\mu}{\beta} = \frac{\eta}{\sqrt{1 - (\omega_c^2 / \omega^2)}} \quad (3.23)$$

whereas for TM waves we have

$$Z_z(TM) = \frac{\beta}{\omega\epsilon} = \eta\sqrt{1 - (\omega_c^2 / \omega^2)} . \quad (3.24)$$

For the dominant TE mode in rectangular waveguide, the characteristic impedance is calculated as follows. The voltage v is taken as the maximum voltage from the lower face of the guide to the upper face. The current i is taken as the total longitudinal current in the lower face. The three characteristic impedances defined by (3.22) may then be expressed as

$$Z_o\,(v,i) \;=\; \frac{\pi b}{2a}\;Z_z \tag{3.25}$$

$$Z_o\,(W,i) \;=\; \frac{\pi^2 b}{8a}\;Z_z \tag{3.26}$$

and

$$Z_o\,(W,v) \;=\; \frac{2b}{a}\;Z_z \;. \tag{3.27}$$

Attenuation in waveguides is mainly due to imperfect conductors and may be calculated from the following expressions:

$$(\alpha_c)_{TE_{mo}} \;=\; \frac{8.686\,R_s}{b\eta\sqrt{1-(f_c/f)^2}}\left[1+\frac{2b}{a}\,(f_c/f)^2\right]\;db/m \tag{3.28}$$

$$(\alpha_c)_{TE_{mn}} \;=\; \frac{17.37\,R_s}{b\eta\sqrt{1-(f_c/f)^2}}\left\{(1+b/a)(f_c/f)^2\right.$$
$$\left.+\left[1-(f_c/f)^2\right]\left[\frac{b}{a}\left(\frac{b}{a}\,m^2+n^2\right)\Big/\left(\frac{b^2 m^2}{a^2}+n^2\right)\right]\right\}$$
$$(n\neq0)\;db/m \tag{3.29}$$

and

$$(\alpha_c)_{TM_{mn}} \;=\; \frac{17.37\,R_s}{b\eta\sqrt{1-(f_c/f)^2}}\left\{\left[m^2(b/a)^3+n^2\right]\Big/\right.$$
$$\left.\left[m^2(b/a)^2+n^2\right]\right\}\qquad db/m\;. \tag{3.30}$$

3.2.2 Circular Waveguides

The propagation constant and the wave impedance for waves propagating in the waveguide of circular cross-section (Figure 3.4(b)) are also given by (3.20), (3.23) and (3.24), respectively. The cut-off frequency f_c can be evaluated from the cut-off wave number k_c

which is given for TM modes as

$$(k_c)_{n\ell} = p_{n\ell} / a \tag{3.31}$$

where $p_{n\ell}$ is the ℓth zero of $J_n(x)$ and "a" is the radius of the waveguide. For TE modes we have

$$(k_c)_{n\ell} = p'_{n\ell} / a \tag{3.32}$$

where $p'_{n\ell}$ is the ℓth zero of $J'_n(x)$.

Attenuation caused by imperfect conductivity of walls is given by the following relations. For TM modes

$$\alpha_{n\ell} = 8.686 \frac{R_s}{a\eta} \frac{1}{\sqrt{1-(f_c/f)^2}} \quad \text{db/m} \tag{3.33}$$

whereas for TE modes

$$\alpha_{n\ell} = 8.686 \frac{R_s}{a\eta} \frac{1}{\sqrt{1-(f_c/f)^2}}$$

$$\cdot \left\{ (f_c/f)^2 + \frac{n^2}{p'^2_{n\ell} - n^2} \right\} \quad \text{db/m} . \tag{3.34}$$

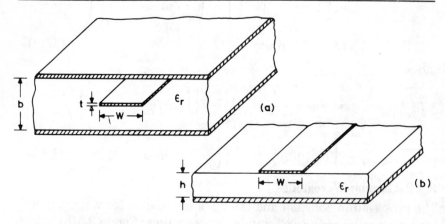

Figure 3.5(a)   A stripline.   (b)   A microstrip line.

3.3 STRIPLINES [4,5,6]

Stripline (shown in Figure 3.5(a)) is one of the most commonly used transmission lines at microwave frequencies. The dominant mode of propagation is TEM, and the design data can be obtained completely by electrostatic analysis.

The analysis of stripline is considerably simplified when the thickness "t" of the central strip is negligible. Cohn [4] has derived, using the conformal mapping technique, an expression for the capacitance of a stripline with $t = 0$. This results in the following equation for the characteristic impedance

$$Z_o \sqrt{\epsilon_r} = 30 \pi \frac{K'(k)}{K(k)} \text{ ohm} \tag{3.35}$$

where $k = \tanh(\pi W/2b)$ and K represents a complete elliptic function of the first kind with K' its complementary function given by

$$K'(k) = K(k') ; \quad k' = \sqrt{1 - k^2} . \tag{3.36}$$

A simple expression for Z_o can be obtained by using an approximation for K/K' (accurate to 8 ppm) as given below:

$$\frac{K(k)}{K'(k)} = \begin{cases} \left[\frac{1}{\pi} \ln\left(2 \, \frac{1 + \sqrt{k'}}{1 - \sqrt{k'}} \right) \right]^{-1} & \text{(for } 0 \le k \le (1/\sqrt{2}) \\ \\ \frac{1}{\pi} \ln\left(2 \, \frac{1 + \sqrt{k}}{1 - \sqrt{k}} \right) & \text{(for } (1/\sqrt{2}) \le k \le 1) \end{cases}$$

$$\tag{3.37}$$
$$\tag{3.38}$$

These formulas yield values for Z_o which are virtually exact.

Analysis for thick striplines has been reported by many authors [2,5,6,7]. The most accurate of these approximate formulas is given by Wheeler [6]. According to this,

$$Z_o \sqrt{\epsilon_r} = 30 \ln \left\{ 1 + \frac{4}{\pi} \frac{b-t}{W'} \left[\frac{8}{\pi} \frac{b-t}{W'} + \sqrt{\left(\frac{8}{\pi} \frac{b-t}{W'} \right)^2 + 6.27} \right] \right\}$$

$$\tag{3.39}$$

where
$$\frac{W'}{b-t} = \frac{W}{b-t} + \frac{\Delta W}{b-t} \tag{3.40}$$

with
$$\frac{\Delta W}{b-t} = \frac{x}{\pi(1-x)}\left\{1 - \frac{1}{2}\ell n\left[\left(\frac{x}{2-x}\right)^2 + \left(\frac{0.0796\,x}{W/b + 1.1x}\right)^m\right]\right\} \tag{3.41a}$$

in which $m = 2\left[1 + \dfrac{2}{3}\dfrac{x}{1-x}\right]^{-1}$ and $x = t/b$.   (3.41b)

For $W'/(b-t) < 10$, (3.39) to (3.41) are stated to yield data which are accurate to within 0.5 percent.

Synthesis Equations for Striplines

For computer-aided design and optimization of stripline circuits, synthesis equations are needed; i.e., strip width W for a given impedance line should be expressed in terms of parameters b, ϵ_r and t. For zero-thickness strips, W/b is obtained as a function of Z_0 and ϵ_r from (3.35) and (3.36) as

$$\frac{W}{b} = \frac{2}{\pi}\tanh^{-1}k \tag{3.42}$$

where

$$k = \begin{cases} \sqrt{1 - \left[\dfrac{e^{\pi x} - 2}{e^{\pi x} + 2}\right]^4} & \text{for } x \geqslant 1 \\[4mm] \left[\dfrac{e^{\pi/x} - 2}{e^{\pi/x} + 2}\right]^2 & \text{for } 0 \leqslant x \leqslant 1 \end{cases}$$

with $x = Z_0\sqrt{\epsilon_r}/(30\pi)$.

The synthesis equation for W/b (with $t \neq 0$) is obtained from (3.39) and is given below [6]

$$\frac{W}{b} = \frac{W_o}{b} - \frac{\Delta W}{b}$$

with $\dfrac{W_o}{b} = \dfrac{8(1-x)}{\pi} \dfrac{\sqrt{e^A + 0.568}}{e^A - 1}$, $A = \dfrac{Z_o \sqrt{\epsilon_r}}{30}$ (3.43)

and $\dfrac{\Delta W}{b} = \dfrac{x}{\pi} \left\{ 1 - \dfrac{1}{2} \ln \left[\left(\dfrac{x}{2-x} \right)^2 + \left(\dfrac{0.0796x}{W_o/b - 0.26x} \right)^m \right] \right\}$

(3.44)

The quantities x and m have been defined earlier in (3.41b).

Stripline Losses

As in the case of other transmission lines, the total loss α_T in stripline can be divided in two parts: the conductor loss and the dielectric loss; i.e.,

$$\alpha_T = \alpha_c + \alpha_d \tag{3.45}$$

where subscripts c and d stand for conductor and dielectric, respectively.

The conductor loss is determined by considering the incremental inductance associated with the penetration of magnetic flux into each of the conducting surfaces [17]. For stripline, it may be evaluated from the following relation [3],

$$\alpha_c = \frac{0.0231 R_s \sqrt{\epsilon_r}}{Z_o} \left\{ \frac{\partial Z_o}{\partial b} - \frac{\partial Z_o}{\partial W} - \frac{\partial Z_o}{\partial t} \right\} \quad \text{db/m} \tag{3.46}$$

where R_s is the sheet resistivity (ohm/square) for the conductor and is given by $\sqrt{\pi f \mu_o \rho}$ with ρ being the resistivity of the conductor. Using relations (3.39) to (3.42) for Z_o, α_c becomes

$$\alpha_c = \frac{-0.0231 R_s \sqrt{\epsilon_r}}{Z_o} \frac{\partial Z_o}{\partial W'} \left\{ 1 + \frac{2W'}{b-t} \right.$$

$$\left. - \frac{1}{\pi} \left[\frac{3x}{2-x} + \ln \frac{x}{2-x} \right] \right\} \quad \text{db/m} \tag{3.47}$$

where $\dfrac{\partial Z_o}{\partial W'} = \dfrac{30\, e^{-A}}{W'\sqrt{\epsilon_r}} \left[\dfrac{3.135}{Q} - \left(\dfrac{8}{\pi}\dfrac{b-t}{W'}\right)^2 (1+Q) \right]$

$$(3.48)$$

with $Q = \sqrt{1 + 6.27\left(\dfrac{\pi}{8}\dfrac{W'}{b-t}\right)^2}.$ (3.49)

It may be observed from (3.47) that for a given value of Z_o, the conductor loss increases with the square root of frequency (because of the frequency dependence of R_s).

The dielectric loss for stripline (or any other TEM mode line) is given by [3]

$$\alpha_d = 27.3\sqrt{\epsilon_r}\,\tan\delta\,/\,\lambda_o \quad \text{db/m} \qquad (3.50)$$

where $\tan\delta$ is the loss tangent of the dielectric. Equation (3.50) shows that the dielectric loss is directly proportional to the frequency and the loss tangent.

The dielectric loss is, in general, very small compared to the conductor loss at microwave frequencies. But at millimeter waves it becomes comparable to the conductor loss because dielectric loss increases linearly with the frequency, whereas conductor loss is proportional to the square root of frequency.

Maximum frequency of operation of a stripline is limited by the excitation of TE modes [8]. For wide lines, the cut-off for the lowest order TE mode is given by

$$f_T(\text{GHz}) = \dfrac{15}{b\sqrt{\epsilon_r}}\,\dfrac{1}{(W/b + \pi/4)} \qquad (3.51)$$

where W and b are in cm. It may be observed that the cut-off frequency, f_T, decreases when either the spacing between the ground planes or the dielectric constant is increased.

3.4 MICROSTRIP LINES [9, 18]

Unlike the stripline, the microstrip line (configuration shown in Figure 3.5(b)) is an inhomogeneous transmission line since the field lines between the strip and the ground plane are not contained entirely in the substrate. Therefore, the mode propagating along the microstrip is not purely TEM but quasi-TEM. For this mode of propagation, the phase velocity in the microstrip is given by (3.5). The effective dielectric constant ϵ_{re} is lower than the dielectric constant of the substrate and takes into account the fields external to the substrate.

The available numerical methods for the characterization of microstrip lines involve extensive computations. Closed form expressions are necessary for optimization and computer-aided design of microstrip circuits. A complete set of design equations for microstrip are presented in this section. These include closed form expressions for the characteristic impedance and effective dielectric constant, and their variation with metal strip thickness and frequency. Expressions for losses are also included.

Characteristic Impedance and Effective Dielectric Constant

The closed form expressions for Z_0 and ϵ_{re} have been reported by Wheeler [19, 20], Schneider [10], and Hammerstad [21]. Wheeler and Hammerstad have also given a synthesis expression for Z_0. The closed form expressions based on [10, 19] are given below:

$$Z_0 = \begin{cases} \dfrac{\eta}{2\pi\sqrt{\epsilon_{re}}} \, \ln\left(\dfrac{8h}{W} + 0.25\dfrac{W}{h}\right) & \text{for } (W/h \leqslant 1) \qquad (3.52\text{a}) \\[3ex] \dfrac{\eta}{\sqrt{\epsilon_{re}}}\left[\dfrac{W}{h} + 1.393 + 0.667\,\ln\left(\dfrac{W}{h} + 1.444\right)\right]^{-1} & \\[2ex] & \text{for } (W/h \geqslant 1) \qquad (3.52\text{b}) \end{cases}$$

where $\eta = 120\,\pi$ ohm, and

$$\epsilon_{re} = \frac{\epsilon_r + 1}{2} + \frac{\epsilon_r - 1}{2}\,(1 + 10\,h/W)^{-1/2} \ . \qquad (3.52\text{c})$$

The maximum relative error in ϵ_{re} and Z_0 is less than two percent. The expressions for W/h in terms of Z_0 and ϵ_r are as follows:

For $A > 1.52$

$$W/h = \frac{8\,\exp(A)}{\exp(2A) - 2} \qquad (3.53\text{a})$$

For A ⩽ 1.52

$$W/h = \frac{2}{\pi} \left\{ B - 1 - \ln(2B-1) + \frac{\epsilon_r - 1}{2\epsilon_r} \left[\ln(B-1) \right. \right.$$

$$\left. \left. + 0.39 - \frac{0.61}{\epsilon_r} \right] \right\} \qquad (3.53b)$$

where

$$A = \frac{Z_o}{60} \left(\frac{\epsilon_r + 1}{2} \right)^{1/2} + \frac{\epsilon_r - 1}{\epsilon_r + 1} \left(0.23 + \frac{0.11}{\epsilon_r} \right)$$

and

$$B = \frac{60 \, \pi^2}{Z_o \sqrt{\epsilon_r}} \quad .$$

These expressions also provide an accuracy better than two percent. The recent closed form expressions by Wheeler [20] provide lower accuracy. However, a single expression holds for the entire range of values of W/h.

The results discussed above assume the strip thickness to be negligible. But, in practice, the strip thickness "t" affects the characteristics. However, when t/h ⩽ 0.005, the agreement between experimental and theoretical results obtained by assuming t/h = 0 is excellent.

Effect of Strip Thickness

A number of expressions have been reported for incorporating the effect of strip thickness in the calculations of Z_o and ϵ_{re} of microstrip. Simple and accurate formulas for Z_o and ϵ_{re} with finite strip thickness are [22],

$$Z_o = \begin{cases} \dfrac{60}{\sqrt{\epsilon_{re}}} \, \ln\left(\dfrac{8h}{W_e} + 0.25 \dfrac{W_e}{h} \right) & (W/h \leqslant 1) \quad (3.54a) \\[6mm] \dfrac{376.7}{\sqrt{\epsilon_{re}}} \left[\dfrac{W_e}{h} + 1.393 + 0.667 \, \ln\left(\dfrac{W_e}{h} + 1.444 \right) \right]^{-1} & (W/h \geqslant 1) \quad (3.54b) \end{cases}$$

where $\dfrac{W_e}{h} = \dfrac{W}{h} + \dfrac{\Delta W}{h}$, with

$$\frac{\Delta W}{h} = \begin{cases} \dfrac{1.25}{\pi}\ \dfrac{t}{h}\left(1 + \ln\dfrac{4\pi W}{t}\right) & (W/h \leqslant 1/2\pi) \quad (3.55a) \\[3em] \dfrac{1.25}{\pi}\ \dfrac{t}{h}\left(1 + \ln\dfrac{2h}{t}\right) & (W/h \geqslant 1/2\pi) \quad (3.55b) \end{cases}$$

$$\epsilon_{re} = \frac{\epsilon_r + 1}{2} + \frac{\epsilon_r - 1}{2}\ F(W/h) - Q \tag{3.56}$$

in which

$$Q = \frac{\epsilon_r - 1}{4.6}\ \frac{t/h}{\sqrt{(W/h)}}\ \text{ and } F(W/h) = (1 + 10\ h/W)^{-1/2}$$
$$\tag{3.57}$$

Effect of Dispersion

The effect of frequency (dispersion) on ϵ_{re} is described accurately through the dispersion model given by Getsinger [23] and modified by Edwards and Owens [24]. The effect of frequency on Z_o has been described by several investigators, and it is found that the results of Bianco *et al.* [25] are closer to numerical values.

The results of Bianco *et al.* for $Z_o(f)$, and Edwards and Owen for $\epsilon_{re}(f)$ may be stated as follows

$$Z_o(f) = Z_{oT} - \frac{Z_{oT} - Z_o}{1 + G(f/f_p)^2} \tag{3.58}$$

and $\epsilon_{re}(f) = \epsilon_r - \dfrac{\epsilon_r - \epsilon_{re}}{1 + G(f/f_p)^2}$ $\tag{3.59}$

where

$$G = \left[\frac{Z_o - 5}{60}\right]^{1/2} + 0.004\ Z_o \tag{3.60}$$

and $f_p(GHz) = 15.66 \, Z_o/h$.   (3.61)

In the above equations h is in mil, Z_o in ohm and Z_{oT} is twice the characteristic impedance of stripline of width W and height 2h. The characteristics Z_o and ϵ_{re} are quasi-static values obtained earlier. Kuester and Chang have reviewed the various numerical methods for dispersion in microstrip [26]. They have also reported [27] an analytical method for dispersion in microstrip which leads to an expression for ϵ_{re} in terms of frequency dependent capacitance and inductance parameters for the line.

Losses

The closed form expressions for the total loss have been reported in the literature [28]. An expression for the conductor loss α_c derived using (3.54) may be written as

$$\alpha_c = \begin{cases} 1.38A \, \dfrac{R_s}{hZ_o} \, \dfrac{32 - (W_e/h)^2}{32 + (W_e/h)^2} & \text{db/m} \quad (W/h \leqslant 1) \;(3.62a) \\[3ex] 6.1 \times 10^{-5} A \, \dfrac{R_s Z_o \epsilon_{re}}{h} \left\{ W_e/h + \dfrac{0.667 \, W_e/h}{W_e/h + 1.444} \right\} \\[2ex] \hspace{4cm} \text{db/m} \quad (W/h \geqslant 1) \;(3.62b) \end{cases}$$

where (W_e/h) is given by (3.55),

$$A = 1 + \frac{h}{W_e} \left(1 + \frac{1}{\pi} \, \ell n \, \frac{2B}{t} \right) \tag{3.63}$$

$$R_s = \sqrt{\pi f \mu_o \rho} \tag{3.64}$$

$$B = \begin{cases} h & \text{for} \left(W/h \geqslant \dfrac{1}{2\pi} \right) \\[3ex] 2\pi W & \text{for} \left(W/h \leqslant \dfrac{1}{2\pi} \right) \end{cases}$$

and ρ is the resistivity of the strip conductor.

Dielectric loss α_d is given by

$$\alpha_d = 27.3 \; \frac{\epsilon_r}{\epsilon_r - 1} \; \frac{\epsilon_{re} - 1}{\sqrt{\epsilon_{re}}} \; \frac{\tan\delta}{\lambda_o} \quad \text{db/m} \tag{3.65}$$

where $\tan\delta$ is the loss tangent of the dielectric. The dielectric loss is normally very small compared with the conductor loss.

3.5 SLOTLINES [9]

The slotline configuration (shown in Figure 3.6) is useful in circuits requiring high impedance lines, series stubs, short circuits, and in hybrid combinations with microstrip circuits in microwave integrated circuits. The mode of propagation is non-TEM and almost transverse electric (TE) in nature. Various methods of analysis discussed in the literature do not lead to closed form expressions for slotline wavelength and impedance. This becomes a serious handicap for circuit analysis and design especially when computer-aided design techniques are used. However, closed form expressions for characteristic impedance and slotline wavelength have been obtained by curve fitting the numerically computed results based on [29].

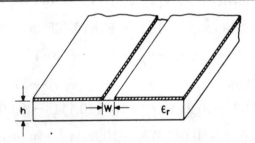

Figure 3.6   A slotline.

Expressions for Characteristic Impedance and Slotline Wavelength

Closed form expressions for characteristic impedance and slotline wavelength have been obtained by curve fitting the results based on Cohn's analysis [30]. These expressions have an accuracy of about

2 percent for the following sets of parameters

$9.7 \leqslant \epsilon_r \leqslant 20$

$0.02 \leqslant W/h \leqslant 1.0$, and

$0.01 \leqslant h/\lambda_o \leqslant (h/\lambda_o)_c$

where $(h/\lambda_o)_c$ is the cut-off value for the TE_{10} surface-wave mode on slotline, and is given by

$$(h/\lambda_o)_c = 0.25 / \sqrt{\epsilon_r - 1} . \tag{3.66}$$

Various parameters for slotline are described in Figure 3.6. The expressions are given below.

a) For 0.02 $\leqslant$ W/h $\leqslant$ 0.2

$$\lambda_s/\lambda_o = 0.923 - 0.195 \ln \epsilon_r + 0.2 \, W/h$$
$$- (0.126 \, W/h + 0.02) \ln (h/\lambda_o \times 10^2) \tag{3.67}$$

$$Z_{os} = 72.62 - 15.283 \ln \epsilon_r + 50 \frac{(W/h - 0.02)(W/h - 0.1)}{W/h}$$
$$+ \ln (W/h \times 10^2) [19.23 - 3.693 \ln \epsilon_r]$$
$$- [0.139 \ln \epsilon_r - 0.11 + W/h (0.465 \ln \epsilon_r + 1.44)]$$
$$\cdot (11.4 - 2.636 \ln \epsilon_r - h/\lambda_o \times 10^2)^2 \tag{3.68}$$

b) For 0.2 $\leqslant$ W/h $\leqslant$ 1.0

$$\lambda_s/\lambda_o = 0.987 - 0.21 \ln \epsilon_r + W/h (0.111 - 0.0022 \, \epsilon_r)$$
$$- (0.053 + 0.041 \, W/h - 0.0014 \, \epsilon_r) \ln (h/\lambda_o \times 10^2) \tag{3.69}$$

$$Z_{os} = 113.19 - 23.257 \ln \epsilon_r + 1.25 \, W/h (114.59 - 22.531$$
$$\ln \epsilon_r) + 20 (W/h - 0.2) (1 - W/h)$$
$$- [0.15 + 0.1 \ln \epsilon_r + W/h (-0.79 + 0.899 \ln \epsilon_r)]$$
$$\cdot \left\{ [10.25 - 2.171 \ln \epsilon_r + W/h (2.1 - 0.617 \ln \epsilon_r) \right.$$
$$\left. - h/\lambda_o \times 10^2]^2 \right\} . \tag{3.70}$$

It is possible to derive more accurate expressions for slotline wavelength when the dielectric constant of the substrate is fixed. Expressions with 1 percent accuracy for the dielectric constant values of 9.7 and 20.0 are given below [31]:

a) ϵ_r = 9.7 and 0.01 $\leqslant$ h/λ_o $\leqslant$ (h/λ_o)$_c$

(i) 0.02 $\leqslant$ W/h $\leqslant$ 0.1

$$\lambda_s/\lambda_o = - (0.126 \text{ W/h} + 0.025) \ell n \,(h/\lambda_o \times 10^2) + 0.283 \text{ W/h}$$
$$+ \ 0.485 \tag{3.71a}$$

(ii) 0.1 $\leqslant$ W/h $\leqslant$ 1.0

$$\lambda_s/\lambda_o = - (0.045 \text{ W/h} + 0.033) \ell n \,(h/\lambda_o \times 10^2) + 0.104 \text{ W/h}$$
$$+ \ 0.507 \tag{3.71b}$$

b) ϵ_r = 20 and 0.01 $\leqslant$ h/λ_o $\leqslant$ (h/λ_o)$_c$

(i) 0.02 $\leqslant$ W/h $\leqslant$ 0.1

$$\lambda_s/\lambda_o = - (0.117 \text{ W/h} + 0.02) \ell n \,(h/\lambda_o \times 10^2) + 0.2 \text{ W/h}$$
$$+ \ 0.345 \tag{3.72a}$$

(ii) 0.1 $\leqslant$ W/h $\leqslant$ 1.0

$$\lambda_s/\lambda_o = - (0.041 \text{ W/h} + 0.031) \ell n \,(h/\lambda_o \times 10^2) + 0.075 \text{ W/h}$$
$$+ \ 0.362 \tag{3.72b}$$

3.6 COPLANAR LINES [9]

Coplanar waveguides are finding extensive applications in microwave integrated circuits. Inclusion of coplanar waveguides in microwave circuits adds to the flexibility of circuit design and improves the performance for some circuit functions. The configuration of a coplanar waveguide (CPW) is shown in Figure 3.7(a). Another promising configuration which is complementary to CPW is known as coplanar strips (CPS) and is shown in Figure 3.7(b). Both of these configurations belong to the category of "coplanar lines" wherein all the conductors are in the same plane (i.e. on the top surface of the dielectric substrate).

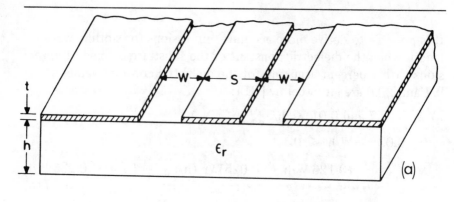

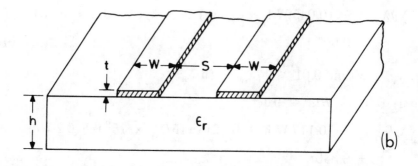

Figure 3.7(a) A coplanar waveguide (CPW).

(b) A "coplanar strips" (CPS) transmission line.

A distinct advantage of these two lines lies in the fact that mounting lumped (active or passive) components in shunt or series configuration is much easier. Drilling holes or slots through the substrate is not needed.

Coplanar waveguides and coplanar strips have been analyzed using quasi-static and full wave methods. Wen [32] has carried out a quasi-static analysis of these transmission lines using conformal mapping and with the assumption that the dielectric substrate is thick enough to be considered infinite. CPW on substrates with finite thickness has also been analyzed using quasi-static approximation [33, 34]. CPS has been analyzed using variational methods [35].

Frequency-dependent behavior of phase velocity and character-istic impedance of CPW and CPS have also been evaluated.

The design equations and data presented in this section are based on the quasi-static analysis. Dispersion effects in coplanar lines have been studied by Yamashita and Atsuki [11] and found to be of the same order as for the microstrip lines. Also, the dispersion for low dielectric constant substrates is almost negligible [11]. These re-sults indicate that the quasi-TEM analysis may be used below X-band frequencies.

Characteristic Impedance and Effective Dielectric Constant

The quasi-static results for CPW given by Wen [32] may be modified for finite dielectric thickness as

$$Z_{ocp} = \frac{30\pi}{\sqrt{\epsilon_{re}}} \frac{K'(k)}{K(k)} \qquad (3.73)$$

where

$$k = \frac{S}{S + 2W} . \qquad (3.74)$$

A closed form expression for ϵ_{re} has been obtained [9] by curve fitting the numerical results of Davis *et al.* [33], and is given below:

$$\epsilon_{re} = \frac{\epsilon_r + 1}{2} \left\{ \tanh \left[0.775 \ln (h/W) + 1.75 \right] + \frac{kW}{h} \left[0.04 \right. \right.$$
$$\left. \left. - 0.7 k + 0.01 (1 - 0.1 \epsilon_r)(0.25 + k) \right] \right\} \qquad (3.75)$$

The accuracy of this expression is better than 1.5 percent for $\epsilon_r \geqslant 9$, $h/W \geqslant 1$ and $0 \leqslant k \leqslant 0.7$, when compared with the results of Davis *et al.* [33].

For CPS, the characteristic impedance can be written as [9]

$$Z_{ocs} = \frac{120 \pi}{\sqrt{\epsilon_{re}}} \frac{K(k)}{K'(k)} \qquad (3.76)$$

where ϵ_{re} is agai l given by (3.75) in which W is now the strip width and S is the spaci..g between the strips. A good agreement is found between the values calculated using the above relations and the avail-able results.

Effect of Strip Thickness

The results discussed above assume infinitesimally thin metallic strip conductor and ground planes. But in practice, metallization has a finite thickness "t" which affects the characteristics. The effect of strip thickness on the impedance of coplanar lines can be taken into account by defining effective values of the strip width and the spacing. This is similar to the concept of increase in microstrip width W due to thickness t as discussed in [22]. For CPW, we can write [9]

$$S_e = S + \Delta \tag{3.77}$$

and

$$W_e = W - \Delta \tag{3.78}$$

where Δ can be evaluated (for all practical values of S/h) from the following relation,

$$\Delta = (1.25\, t/\pi)\,[\,1\, +\, \ln\,(4\,\pi\,S/t)\,]\ . \tag{3.79}$$

The characteristic impedance is found as

$$Z_{ocp} = \frac{30\,\pi}{\sqrt{\epsilon_{re}^t}}\ \frac{K'(k_e)}{K(k_e)} \tag{3.80}$$

where k_e is the effective aspect ratio [9] given by

$$k_e = S_e\,/\,(S_e\, +\, 2W_e) \simeq k\, +\, (1\, -\, k^2)\,\Delta/2W \tag{3.81}$$

and ϵ_{re}^t is the effective dielectric constant for thick CPW. An expression for ϵ_{re}^t is derived by adding a term $A\epsilon_o\epsilon_r\,t/W$, accounting for the increase in capacitance due to the metal thickness, to the expression for capacitance of CPW. The value of A is found empirically such that the results for ϵ_{re}^t agree with the numerically evaluated values given in [36] for ϵ_r = 20 and t/W $\leqslant$ 0.1. It is observed that A = 2.8 gives reasonably accurate (better than 3 percent) results for ϵ_{re}^t . This value of A is quite near to the value of A = 2 obtained by using the simple parallel plate capacitance formulation.

The final expression for ϵ_{re}^t may be written as

$$\epsilon_{re}^t = \epsilon_{re} - \frac{0.7\,(\epsilon_{re} - 1)\,t/W}{[K(k)/K'(k)] + 0.7\,t/W} . \tag{3.82}$$

For coplanar strips, the effect of strip thickness on Z_{ocs} and ϵ_{re} is similar to that in CPW and the closed form expressions are obtained as

$$Z_{ocs} = \frac{120\,\pi}{\sqrt{\epsilon_{re}^t}}\,\frac{K(k_e)}{K'(k_e)} \tag{3.83}$$

where $k_e = S_e/(S_e + 2W_e) \simeq k - (1 - k^2)\,\Delta/2W \tag{3.84}$

with $\Delta = (1.25t/\pi)\,[1 + \ell n\,(4\pi\,W/t)]$. $\tag{3.85}$

The effective dielectric constant for CPS may similarly be written as

$$\epsilon_{re}^t = \epsilon_{re} - \frac{1.4\,(\epsilon_{re} - 1)\,t/S}{[K'(k)/K(k)] + 1.4\,t/S} . \tag{3.86}$$

Losses

When quasi-static approximation is valid, one can use Wheeler's incremental inductance formula [17] for evaluating ohmic losses, and the expression for attenuation in CPW becomes

$$\alpha_c^{cp} = 0.023\,\frac{R_s}{Z_{ocp}}\left[\frac{\partial Z_{ocp}^a}{\partial W} - \frac{\partial Z_{ocp}^a}{\partial S} - \frac{\partial Z_{ocp}^a}{\partial t}\right] \text{ db/m} \tag{3.87}$$

where subscript cp denotes coplanar waveguide. After substituting the expressions for various partial derivatives in (3.87), the final expression for conductor loss becomes

$$\alpha_c^{cp} = 4.88 \times 10^{-4}\,R_s\,\epsilon_{re}\,Z_{ocp}\,\frac{P'}{W\pi}\left(1 + \frac{S}{W}\right)$$

$$\cdot \left\{\frac{\dfrac{1.25}{\pi}\,\ell n\,\dfrac{4\pi S}{t} + 1 + \dfrac{1.25t}{\pi S}}{\left[2 + \dfrac{S}{W} - \dfrac{1.25t}{\pi W}\left(1 + \ell n\,\dfrac{4\pi S}{t}\right)\right]^2}\right\} \text{ db/m} \tag{3.88}$$

where P' is given by

$$P' = \begin{cases} \dfrac{k}{(1-k')(k')^{3/2}} \left[\dfrac{K(k)}{K'(k)} \right]^2 & \text{for } 0 \leqslant k \leqslant 0.707 \\[4mm] \dfrac{1}{(1-k)\sqrt{k}} & \text{for } 0.707 \leqslant k \leqslant 1.0 \end{cases} \qquad (3.89)$$

The expression for the attenuation constant due to dielectric loss in CPW is the same as that for microstrip lines and can be written as

$$\alpha_d = 27.3 \, \frac{\epsilon_r}{\sqrt{\epsilon_{re}}} \cdot \frac{\epsilon_{re} - 1}{\epsilon_r - 1} \cdot \frac{\tan\delta}{\lambda_o} \; db/m \; . \qquad (3.90)$$

In the present case, ϵ_{re} is given by (3.75).

For coplanar strips, the expression for the conductor loss becomes

$$\alpha_c^{cs} = 17.34 \, \frac{R_s}{Z_{ocs}} \, \frac{P'}{\pi S} \left(1 + \frac{W}{S} \right)$$

$$\cdot \left\{ \frac{\dfrac{1.25}{\pi} \ln \dfrac{4\pi W}{t} + 1 + \dfrac{1.25\,t}{\pi W}}{\left[1 + 2\,\dfrac{W}{S} + \dfrac{1.25t}{\pi S} \left(1 + \ln \dfrac{4\pi W}{t} \right) \right]^2} \right\} \; db/m \quad (3.91)$$

where P' is again given by (3.89). The expression for dielectric loss is the same as that given by (3.90).

3.7 COUPLED STRIPLINES

A number of stripline components utilize the coupling between parallel strips in their design. The configuration for the parallel coupled striplines is shown in Figure 3.8. The principal application areas of parallel coupled striplines are directional couplers, delay lines, filters and baluns.

For zero thickness coupled striplines (t = 0) exact formulas for even

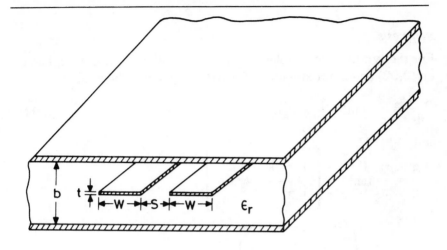

Figure 3.8   A "coupled striplines" configuration.

mode and odd mode impedances have been derived using conformal mapping procedure [37]. These are given as

$$Z_{oe} = \frac{30\pi}{\sqrt{\epsilon_r}} \frac{K(k_e')}{K(k_e)} \tag{3.92a}$$

and

$$Z_{oo} = \frac{30\pi}{\sqrt{\epsilon_r}} \frac{K(k_o')}{K(k_o)} \tag{3.92b}$$

where Z_{oe} and Z_{oo} are the even mode and the odd mode characteristic impedances, respectively. The ratio $K(k') / K(k)$ has been defined in (3.37) and (3.38), and

$$k_e = \tanh\left(\frac{\pi}{2} \frac{W}{b}\right) \tanh\left(\frac{\pi}{2} \frac{W + S}{b}\right) , \quad k_e' = \sqrt{1 - k_e^2} \tag{3.93b}$$

$$k_o = \tanh\left(\frac{\pi}{2} \frac{W}{b}\right) \coth\left(\frac{\pi}{2} \frac{W + S}{b}\right) , \quad k_o' = \sqrt{1 - k_o^2}. \tag{3.93b}$$

Synthesis

For the synthesis of coupled striplines the following formulas, based on (3.92) and approximations for $K(k')/K(k)$, may be used

$$\frac{W}{b} = \frac{2}{\pi} \tanh^{-1} \sqrt{k_e k_o} \tag{3.94}$$

and

$$\frac{S}{b} = \frac{2}{\pi} \tanh^{-1} \left[\frac{1 - k_o}{1 - k_e} \sqrt{\frac{k_e}{k_o}} \right] \tag{3.95}$$

with

$$k_{e,o} = \sqrt{1 - \left(\frac{e^{\pi x} - 2}{e^{\pi x} + 2} \right)^4} \qquad \text{for } 1 \leqslant x \leqslant \infty \tag{3.96a}$$

$$k_{e,o} = \left[\frac{e^{\pi/x} - 2}{e^{\pi/x} + 2} \right]^2 \qquad \text{for } 0 \leqslant x \leqslant 1 \tag{3.96b}$$

and $x = \dfrac{Z_{oe} \sqrt{\epsilon_r}}{30\pi}$ or $\dfrac{Z_{oo} \sqrt{\epsilon_r}}{30\pi}$ for the even and the odd modes, respectively.

Effect of Strip Thickness

Approximate closed form expressions are available which take into account the finite thickness of the strip. These formulas have their best accuracy for $t/b < 0.1$ and $W/b \geqslant 0.35$ [37], and are given below:

$$Z_{oe} = \frac{30\pi (b - t)}{\sqrt{\epsilon_r} \left\{ W + \dfrac{bC_f}{2\pi} A_e \right\}} \tag{3.97a}$$

$$Z_{oo} = \frac{30\pi (b - t)}{\sqrt{\epsilon_r} \left\{ W + \dfrac{bC_f}{2\pi} A_o \right\}} \tag{3.97b}$$

with

$$A_e = 1 + \frac{\ell n \ (1 \ + \ \tanh \ \theta)}{\ell n 2} \qquad (3.98a)$$

$$A_o = 1 + \frac{\ell n \ (1 \ + \ \coth \ \theta)}{\ell n 2} \qquad (3.97b)$$

$$\theta = \pi S/(2b) \qquad (3.98c)$$

and

$$C_f(t/b) = 2 \ \ell n \left(\frac{2b \ - \ t}{b \ - \ t}\right) - \frac{t}{b} \ \ell n \left[\frac{t(2b \ - \ t)}{(b \ - \ t)^2}\right]. \qquad (3.98d)$$

Losses

The total loss in coupled striplines can be divided into dielectric loss α_d and conductor loss α_c. The dielectric loss factor is given by

$$\alpha_d^e = \alpha_d^o = 27.3 \sqrt{\epsilon_r} \tan\delta \ / \ \lambda_o \qquad db/m \ . \qquad (3.99)$$

The conductor loss factor, calculated using the incremental inductance rule of Wheeler [17], is obtained as

$$\alpha_c^e = \frac{0.0231 \ R_s \sqrt{\epsilon_r}}{30\pi \ (b \ - \ t)} \left\{ 60\pi + Z_{oe} \sqrt{\epsilon_r} \left[1 - \frac{A_e}{\pi} \left(\ell n \ \frac{2b - t}{b - t} \right.\right.\right.$$

$$\left.\left.\left. + \frac{1}{2} \ \ell n \ \frac{t(2b \ - \ t)}{(b \ - \ t)^2} \right) + C_f \frac{(1 \ + \ S/b)}{4 \ \ell n 2} \ \frac{sech^2 \theta}{1 \ + \ \tanh\theta} \right] \right\} \qquad db/m$$

$$(3.100a)$$

$$\alpha_c^o = \frac{0.0231 \ R_s \sqrt{\epsilon_r}}{30\pi \ (b \ - \ t)} \left\{ 60\pi + Z_{oo} \sqrt{\epsilon_r} \left[1 - \frac{A_o}{\pi} \left(\ell n \ \frac{2b - t}{b - t} \right.\right.\right.$$

$$\left.\left.\left. + \frac{1}{2} \ \frac{t \ (2b \ - \ t)}{(b \ - \ t)^2} \right) - C_f \frac{(1 \ + \ S/b)}{4 \ \ell n 2} \ \frac{cosech^2 \theta}{1 \ + \ \coth \ \theta} \right] \right\} \qquad db/m.$$

$$(3.100b)$$

3.8 COUPLED MICROSTRIP LINES [38,39]

Coupled microstrip lines are used in a variety of circuit functions, namely directional couplers, filters, impedance matching networks and delay lines. There are numerous papers dealing with the analysis, design and applications of coupled microstrip lines. Both quasi-static and full-wave analyses have been reported.

The properties of coupled lines are determined by the self and mutual inductances and capacitances associated with the two lines. Under the quasi-TEM approximation, the self inductance can be expressed in terms of self capacitance by using a simple relation. It is also found that for most of the practical circuits using symmetric coupled microstrip lines, the mutual inductance and the mutual capacitance are interrelated and it is not necessary to determine the mutual inductance separately. Therefore, only capacitance parameters are evaluated for coupled microstrip lines. These capacitances can be expressed in terms of even and odd mode values for the two modes of propagation.

Even and Odd Mode Capacitances

The geometry of coupled microstrip lines is shown in Figure 3.9. The break-up of total line capacitance into a parallel plate and two fringing capacitances, one for each side of the strip, is also shown. The fringing capacitances for the even mode can be obtained from the fringing capacitance for uncoupled microstrip lines. The odd mode fringing capacitances are determined with the help of an equivalent geometry for coupled striplines and coplanar strips. Using these fringing capacitances the total even and odd mode capacitances may be written as

$$C_e = C_p + C_f + C_f' \qquad\qquad (3.101)$$

$$C_o = C_p + C_f + C_{ga} + C_{gd} \qquad\qquad (3.102)$$

where

$$C_p = \epsilon_o \epsilon_r W/h . \qquad\qquad (3.103)$$

C_f, C_f', C_{ga} and C_{gd} represent various fringing capacitances. C_f is the fringing capacitance of a microstrip line of width W/h, impedance Z_o and effective dielectric constant ϵ_{re} , and is given by

$$2C_f = \sqrt{\epsilon_{re}} \, / \, cZ_o - C_p \, , \qquad c = 3 \times 10^8 \quad \text{m/s.} \qquad (3.104)$$

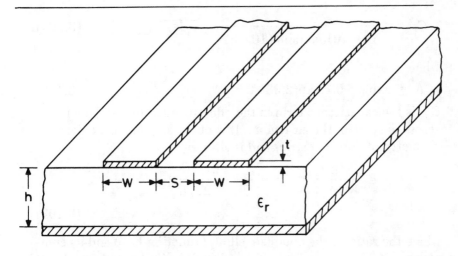

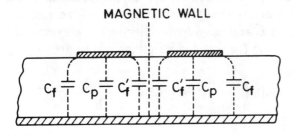

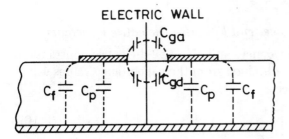

Figure 3.9 A "coupled microstriplines" configuration and break-up of capacitances for the even and odd modes.

The expression for capacitance C_f' is obtained empirically such that the resulting value of even mode capacitance compares with numerical results. The expression for C_f' is found to be

$$C_f' = \frac{C_f}{1 + A(h/s)\tanh(10\,s/h)}\ \sqrt{\epsilon_r/\epsilon_{re}} \qquad (3.105)$$

where

$$A = \exp[\,-0.1\exp(2.33 - 2.53\,W/h)\,]. \qquad (3.106)$$

C_{ga} is the capacitance term in the odd mode for the fringing field across the gap, in the air region. It is obtained from an equivalent geometry of coplanar strips and is given by

$$C_{ga} = \epsilon_o\frac{K(k')}{K(k)}\ ;\quad k = \frac{s/h}{s/h + 2W/h}\ ;\quad k' = \sqrt{1 - k^2}$$

$$(3.107)$$

where the ratio of the complete elliptic function $K(k)$ and its complement $K(k')$ is given by (3.37) and (3.38). C_{gd} represents the capacitance in the odd mode for the fringing field across the gap, in the dielectric region. It is evaluated by modifying the corresponding capacitance expression for coupled striplines and is given by

$$C_{gd} = \frac{\epsilon_o\epsilon_r}{\pi}\ \ell n\left[\coth\left(\frac{\pi s}{4h}\right)\right] + 0.65\,C_f\left[\frac{0.02}{s/h}\sqrt{\epsilon_r}\right.$$

$$\left. + 1 - \epsilon_r^{-2}\right]. \qquad (3.108)$$

Characteristic Impedances and Effective Dielectric Constants

The characteristic impedances and effective dielectric constants for the two modes can be obtained from the capacitance values using the following relations

$$Z_{oi} = \left[c\sqrt{C_i\,C_i^a}\,\right]^{-1} \qquad (3.109)$$

and

$$\epsilon_{re}^i = C_i/C_i^a \qquad (3.110)$$

where i stands for the even or odd mode, and C^a denotes the capacitance with air as dielectric.

Calculations indicate that the even mode capacitance is accurate to within 3% for $\epsilon_r \geqslant 1$. The accuracy for odd-mode capacitance improves for higher values of ϵ_r. However, the characteristic impedances, for both the even and the odd modes, obtained using the above capacitance expressions, yield an accuracy of better than 3% for $0.2 \leqslant W/h \leqslant 2$, $0.05 \leqslant s/h \leqslant 2$, and $\epsilon_r \geqslant 1$.

Effect of Strip Thickness

When the strip conductors are of finite thickness t, capacitances can be evaluated by using the concept of effective width, as enunciated by Wheeler for single microstrip line. An expression for effective width W_t has been obtained by Jansen [40] by modifying the corresponding expression for single microstrip line. These expressions, valid for $s \geqslant 2t$, are reproduced below

$$\frac{W_t^e}{h} = \frac{W}{h} + \frac{\Delta W}{h} \ [1 - 0.5 \ \exp(-0.69 \ \Delta W / \Delta t)] \qquad (3.111)$$

$$\frac{W_t^o}{h} = \frac{W_t^e}{h} + \frac{\Delta t}{h} \qquad (3.112)$$

where

$$\frac{\Delta t}{h} = \frac{1}{\epsilon_r} \ \frac{t/h}{s/h} \qquad (3.113)$$

and ΔW is the increase in strip width of single microstrip line due to strip thickness t given by (3.55). The excess increase Δt in effective width for the odd-mode when compared with the even mode, has been calculated by modeling the excess capacitance, over the $t = 0$ case, by a parallel-plate capacitance.

Due to the increase in even and odd mode capacitances with finite strip thickness, the even and the odd mode impedances decrease. The decrease in odd mode impedance is about 2 percent for $t/h = 0.0047$, and $\epsilon_r = 9.6$. The decrease is negligible for even mode impedance. It is found that the percentage increase in C_o^a (and C_e^a)

with thickness is more than that in C_o (and C_e). Thus effective dielectric constants $\epsilon_{re}^e(t)$ and $\epsilon_{re}^o(t)$ decrease with thickness. The percentage decrease in ϵ_{re}^o is found to be more than that in ϵ_{re}^e because of an additional gap capacitance $2\epsilon_o t/s$, with air as dielectric.

Effect of Dispersion

The dispersive behavior of coupled microstrip lines has been well described using numerical methods [19-22]. Semiempirical expressions by Getsinger [41], and Carlin and Civalleri [42], which describe dispersion in the effective dielectric constant, are very similar. But the results obtained by using Getsinger's formula are closer to experimental values and are widely used. This expression may be written as

$$\epsilon_{re}^i(f) = \epsilon_r - \frac{\epsilon_r - \epsilon_{re}^i}{1 + (f/f_p)^2 G} \tag{3.114}$$

where

$$G = \begin{cases} 0.6 + 0.018\,Z_{oo}, & \text{for odd mode} \\ \\ 0.6 + 0.0045\,Z_{oe}, & \text{for even mode} \end{cases} \tag{3.115}$$

and

$$f_p = \begin{cases} 31.32\,Z_{oo}/h, & \text{for odd mode} \\ \\ 7.83\,Z_{oe}/h, & \text{for even mode.} \end{cases}$$

Here f_p is expressed in GH_z, and h is in mils.

It is seen that an equation similar to (3.114) can be written for the effect of dispersion on impedance also. It is given below:

$$Z_{oi}(f) = Z_{oi}^s - \frac{Z_{oi}^s - Z_{oi}}{1 + (f/f_p)^{1.6} G} \tag{3.117}$$

where G and f_p are given by (3.115) and (3.116), respectively, and Z_{oi} represents the quasi-static value of impedance for coupled microstrip lines. Z_{oi}^s are the corresponding impedances for coupled striplines with the same values of s and W as for the coupled micro-strip lines; but the spacing between the two ground planes is 2h. Values for Z_{oi}^s are twice the values obtained from (3.92).

Losses

Coupled microstrip lines have two types of losses: ohmic and di-electric. The even and odd mode attenuation constants due to ohmic losses in coupled microstrip lines can be determined by using the incremental inductance rule of Wheeler. Its application to the coupled line configuration yields the following expression for the odd mode attenuation constant:

$$\alpha_c^o = \frac{8.686 \, R_s}{240 \, \pi \, Z_{oo}} \cdot \frac{2}{h} \cdot \frac{1}{c \, (C_o^{at})^2}$$

$$\cdot \left[\frac{\partial C_o^{at}}{\partial \, (W/h)} \left(1 + \delta \, \frac{W}{2h} \right) - \frac{\partial C_o^{at}}{\partial \, (s/h)} \left(1 - \delta \, \frac{s}{2h} \right) \right.$$

$$\left. + \frac{\partial C_o^{at}}{\partial (t/h)} \left(1 + \delta \, \frac{t}{2h} \right) \right] \qquad \text{db/m .} \qquad (3.118a)$$

Similarly, for the even mode

$$\alpha_c^e = \frac{8.686 \, R_s}{240 \, \pi \, Z_{oe}} \cdot \frac{2}{h} \cdot \frac{1}{c \, (C_e^{at})^2}$$

$$\cdot \left[\frac{\partial C_e^{at}}{\partial \, (W/h)} \left(1 + \delta \, \frac{W}{2h} \right) - \frac{\partial C_e^{at}}{\partial \, (s/h)} \left(1 - \delta \, \frac{s}{2h} \right) \right.$$

$$\left. + \frac{\partial C_e^{at}}{\partial \, (t/h)} \left(1 + \delta \, \frac{t}{2h} \right) \right] \qquad \text{db/m .} \qquad (3.118b)$$

where

$$\delta = \begin{cases} 1, & \text{for attenuation due to the strips only} \\ \\ 2, & \text{for attenuation due to both the strips and the ground plane} \end{cases}$$

and $c = 1 / \sqrt{\mu_o \epsilon_o}$.

C_o^{at} and C_e^{at} represent odd and even mode line capacitances, respectively, for air as dielectric medium and with finite thickness of strip. R_s is the sheet resistivity of the metallization.

The attenuation due to dielectric loss α_d is given by

$$\alpha_d^e = 27.3 \frac{\epsilon_r}{\sqrt{\epsilon_{re}^e}} \frac{\epsilon_{re}^e - 1}{\epsilon_r - 1} \frac{\tan\delta}{\lambda_o} \qquad db/m \qquad (3.119a)$$

$$\alpha_d^o = 27.3 \frac{\epsilon_r}{\sqrt{\epsilon_{re}^o}} \frac{\epsilon_{re}^o - 1}{\epsilon_r - 1} \frac{\tan\delta}{\lambda_o} \qquad db/m \qquad (3.119b)$$

where $\tan\delta$ is the loss tangent of the dielectric substrate, and λ_o is the free-space wavelength.

The loss calculations are important in the design of filters and couplers. As an approximation, the insertion loss of a coupled-line device with an input impedance of 50 ohm can be taken to be the average of even and odd mode losses.

Synthesis Method

A synthesis method for coupled microstrip lines has been reported by Akhtarzad *et al.* [43]. The procedure involves an intermediate step of computing the strip width for a single line corresponding to impedances $Z_{oe}/2$ and $Z_{oo}/2$. Due to the limitation of single microstrip line formulas used at small W/h values, the results obtained were highly inaccurate for small W/h and s/h combinations. Hinton [44] has shown that the use of better synthesis formulas for single microstrip line reduces the error to less than 3 percent for $\epsilon_r = 9.6, 0.1 \leqslant$ W/h $\leqslant 2$ and $0.05 \leqslant$ s/h $\leqslant 1$ [44].

The value of W/h and s/h for the coupled microstrip lines can be obtained from the simultaneous solution of the following equations

$$\left(\frac{W}{h}\right)_{se} = \frac{2}{\pi} \cosh^{-1}\left(\frac{2H - G + 1}{G + 1}\right) \qquad (3.120)$$

$$\left(\frac{W}{h}\right)_{so} = \frac{2}{\pi} \cosh^{-1}\left(\frac{2H - G - 1}{G - 1}\right)$$

$$+ \frac{8}{\pi(\epsilon_r + 2)} \cosh^{-1}\left(1 + 2\frac{W/h}{s/h}\right)$$

$$\text{for } \epsilon_r \leqslant 6 \quad (3.121a)$$

$$\left(\frac{W}{h}\right)_{so} = \frac{2}{\pi} \cosh^{-1}\left(\frac{2H - G - 1}{G - 1}\right)$$

$$+ \frac{1}{\pi} \cosh^{-1}\left(1 + 2\frac{W/h}{s/h}\right)$$

$$\text{for } \epsilon_r \geqslant 6 \quad (3.121b)$$

$$\text{where } G = \cosh\left[\frac{\pi}{2}\frac{s}{h}\right] \qquad (3.122)$$

$$\text{and } H = \cosh\left[\pi\frac{W}{h} + \frac{\pi}{2}\frac{s}{h}\right]. \qquad (3.123)$$

$\left(\dfrac{W}{h}\right)_{se}$ and $\left(\dfrac{W}{h}\right)_{so}$ are the single-line shape ratios corresponding
to the impedances $Z_{oe}/2$ and $Z_{oo}/2$, respectively. These can be obtained from the synthesis formulas given by (3.53).

An approximate solution of simultaneous equations (3.120) and
(3.121) can be obtained by ignoring the second term in (3.121). A
value of s/h is then given by

$$\frac{s}{h} = \frac{2}{\pi} \cosh^{-1}\left\{\frac{\cosh\left[\frac{\pi}{2}\left(\frac{W}{h}\right)'_{so}\right] + \cosh\left[\frac{\pi}{2}\left(\frac{W}{h}\right)_{se}\right] - 2}{\cosh\left[\frac{\pi}{2}\left(\frac{W}{h}\right)'_{so}\right] - \cosh\left[\frac{\pi}{2}\left(\frac{W}{h}\right)_{se}\right]}\right\}$$

$$(3.124)$$

with $\left(\dfrac{W}{h}\right)'_{so} = 0.78\left(\dfrac{W}{h}\right)_{so} + 0.1\left(\dfrac{W}{h}\right)_{se}.$ (3.125)

The value of s/h, obtained from (3.124), can be used as a starting point for an optimization process for the solution of (3.120) and (3.121).

Characterizations of various transmission structures discussed in this chapter are required for modelling of the sections of these lines used in various microwave circuits.

REFERENCES

[1]   Coaxial lines and waveguides have been discussed in several
        texts. For example see: S. Ramo *et al.*, *Fields and Waves in
        Communication Electronics*, New York: John Wiley, 1965.

[2]   Bahl, I.J., and Ramesh Garg, "Designer's Guide to Stripline
        Circuits," *Microwaves*, Vol. 17, Jan. 1978, pp. 90-96.

[3]   Howe, H., Jr., *Stripline Circuit Design*, Dedham, Mass:
        Artech House, 1974.

[4]   Cohn, S.B., "Characteristic Impedance of Shielded Strip
        Transmission Line," *IRE Trans. Microwave Theory Tech.*,
        Vol. MTT-2, July 1954, pp. 52-55.

[5]   Cohn, S.B., "Problems in Strip Transmission Lines," *IRE
        Trans. Microwave Theory Tech.*, Vol. MTT-3, March 1955,
        pp. 119-126.

[6]   Wheeler, H.A., "Transmission Line Properties of a Stripline
        Between Parallel Planes," *IEEE Trans. Microwave Theory
        Tech.*, Vol. MTT-26, Nov. 1978, pp. 866-876.

[7]   Gunston, M.A.R., *Microwave Transmission-Line Impedance
        Data*, London: Van Nostrand Reinhold, 1972, pp. 38-39.

[8]   Vendelin, G.D., "Limitations on Stripline Q," *Microwave
        J.*, Vol. 13, May 1970, pp. 63-69.

[9]   Gupta, K.C., *et al.*, *Microstrip Lines and Slotlines*, Dedham,
        Mass: Artech House, 1979.

[10]   Schneider, M.V., "Microstrip Lines for Microwave Integrated
        Circuits," *Bell System Tech. J.*, Vol. 48, 1969, pp. 1421-1444.

[11]   Yamashita, E., and K. Atsuki, "Analysis of Microstrip-like
        Transmission Lines by Non-Uniform Discretization of In-
        tegral Equation," *IEEE Trans. Microwave Theory Tech.*,
        Vol. MTT-24, 1976, pp. 195-200.

[12]   Buntschuh, C., "A Study of the Transmission Line Proper-
        ties of Trapped Inverted Microstrip Line," *RADC-TR-74-
        311, AD* No. A-003633, Dec. 1974.

[13]   McLevige, W.V., *et al.*, "New Waveguide Structures for Mil-
        limeter Wave and Optical Integrated Circuits," *IEEE Trans.
        Microwave Theory Tech.*, Vol. MTT-23, 1975, pp. 788-794.

[14]   Davis, R.T., "Millimeter-waves: Controversy Brews Over
       Transmission Media," *Microwaves*, Vol. 15, March 1976,
       pp. 32-42.

[15]   Marcuvitz, N., *Waveguide Handbook*, New York: McGraw
       Hill, 1951, pp. 399-402.

[16]   Knox, R.M., and P.P. Toulios, "Integrated Circuits for the
       Millimeter through Optical Frequency Range," in *Proc.
       Symposium on Submillimeter Waves*, Polytechnic Inst. of
       Brooklyn (N.Y.), March 1970.

[17]   Wheeler, H.A., "Formulas for the Skin Effect," *Proc. IRE*,
       Vol. 30, Sept. 1942, pp. 412-424.

[18]   Bahl, I.J., and D.K. Trivedi, "A Designers Guide to Micro-
       strip," *Microwaves*, Vol. 16, May 1977, pp. 174-182.

[19]   Wheeler, H.A., "Transmission Line Properties of Parallel
       Strips Separated by a Dielectric Sheet," *IEEE Trans. Mi-
       crowave Theory Tech.*, Vol. MTT-13, 1965, pp. 172-185.

[20]   Wheeler, H.A., "Transmission-line Properties of a Strip on
       a Dielectric Sheet on a Plane," *IEEE Trans. Microwave
       Theory Tech.*, Vol. MTT-25, Aug. 1977, pp. 631-647.

[21]   Hammerstad, E.O., "Equations for Microstrip Circuit De-
       sign," in *Proc. European Microwave Conf.*, 1975, pp. 268-
       272.

[22]   Bahl, I.J., and Ramesh Garg, "Simple and Accurate Formu-
       las for Microstrip with Finite Strip Thickness," *Proc. IEEE*,
       Vol. 65, Nov. 1977, pp. 1611-1612.

[23]   Getsinger, W.J., "Microstrip Dispersion Model," *IEEE Trans.
       Microwave Theory Tech.*, Vol. MTT-21, 1973, pp. 34-39.

[24]   Edwards, T.C., and R.P. Owens, "2-18 GHz Dispersion
       Measurements on 10-100 Ohm Microstrip Line on Sap-
       phire," *IEEE Trans. Microwave Theory Tech.*, Vol. MTT-
       24, Aug. 1976, pp. 506-513.

[25]   Bianco, B., *et al.*, "Frequency Dependence of Microstrip
       Parameters," *Alta Frequenza*, Vol. 43, 1974, pp. 413-416.

[26] Kuester, E.F., and D.C. Chang, "An Appraisal of Methods for Computation of the Dispersion Characteristics of Open Microstrip," *IEEE Trans. Microwave Theory Tech.*, Vol. 27, 1979, pp. 691-694.

[27] Kuester, E.F., and D.C. Chang, "Theory of Dispersion in Microstrip of Arbitrary Width," *IEEE Trans. Microwave Theory Tech.*, Vol. MTT-28, March 1980, pp. 259-265.

[28] Pucel, R.A., *et al.*, "Losses in Microstrip," *IEEE Trans. Microwave Theory Tech.*, Vol. MTT-16, 1968, pp. 342-350. Also see correction in *IEEE Trans.*, MTT-16, 1968, p. 1064.

[29] Cohn, S.B., "Slotline on a Dielectric Substrate," *IEEE Trans. Microwave Theory Tech.*, Vol. MTT-17, 1969, pp. 768-778.

[30] Garg, R., and K.C. Gupta, "Expression for Wavelength and Impedance of Slotline," *IEEE Trans. Microwave Theory Tech.*, Vol. MTT-24, 1976, p. 532.

[31] Garg, R., and K.C. Gupta, "Slotline and its Applications in MICs," *ACES (I.I.T. Kanpur) Tech. Report*, TR-34-75, 1975.

[32] Wen, C.P., "Coplanar Waveguide: A Surface Strip Transmission Line Suitable for Non-Reciprocal Gyromagnetic Device Application," *IEEE Trans. Microwave Theory Tech.*, Vol. MTT-17, Dec. 1969, pp. 1087-1090.

[33] Davis, M.E., *et al.*, "Finite-Boundary Correction to the Coplanar Waveguide Analysis," *IEEE Trans. Microwave Theory Tech.*, Vol. MTT-21, Sept. 1973, pp. 594-596.

[34] Hatsuda, T., "Computation of Coplanar-Type Strip Line Characteristics by Relaxation Method and its Applications to Microwave Circuits," *IEEE Trans. Microwave Theory Tech.*," Vol. MTT-23, Oct. 1975, pp. 795-802.

[35] Yamashita, E., and S. Yamazaki, "Parallel-strip Line Embedded in or Printed on a Dielectric Sheet," *IEEE Trans. Microwave Theory Tech.*, Vol. MTT-16, Nov. 1968, pp. 972-973.

[36]   Kitazawa, T., *et al.*, "A Coplanar Waveguide with Thick
        Metal-coating," *IEEE Trans. Microwave Theory Tech.*,
        Vol. MTT-24, Sept. 1976, pp. 604-608.

[37]   Cohn, S.B., "Shielded Coupled-Strip Transmission Line,"
        IRE Trans. Microwave Theory Tech., Vol. MTT-3, October
        1955, pp. 29-38.

[38]   Garg, R., and I.J. Bahl, "Characteristics of Coupled Micro-
        striplines," *IEEE Trans. Microwave Theory Tech.*, Vol.
        MTT-27, July 1979, pp. 700-705. Also see correction in *IEEE
        Trans.*, MTT-28, 1980, p. 272.

[39]   Garg, R., "Design Equations for Coupled Microstrip Lines,"
        Int. J. Electron., Vol. 47, 1979, pp. 587-591.

[40]   Jansen, R.H., "High-speed Computation of Single and Cou-
        pled Microstrip Parameters including Dispersion, High Order
        Modes, Loss and Finite Strip Thickness," *IEEE Trans. Micro-
        wave Theory Tech.*, Vol. MTT-26, Feb. 1978, pp. 75-82.

[41]   Getsinger, W.J., "Dispersion of Parallel-coupled Microstrip,"
        IEEE Trans. Microwave Theory Tech., Vol. MTT-21, 1973,
        pp. 144-145.

[42]   Carlin, H.J., and P.P. Civalleri, "A Coupled-line Model for
        Dispersion in Parallel-coupled Microstrip," *IEEE Trans.
        Microwave Theory Tech.*, Vol. MTT-23, 1975, pp. 444-446.

[43]   Akhtarzad, S., *et al.*, "The Design of Coupled Microstrip
        Lines," *IEEE Trans. Microwave Theory Tech.*, Vol. MTT-
        23, June 1975, pp. 486-492.

[44]   Hinton, J.H., "On Design of Coupled Microstrip Lines,"
        IEEE Trans. Microwave Theory Tech., Vol. MTT-28, March
        1980, p. 272.

4

Sensitivities of Transmission Structures

4.1 INTRODUCTION

In addition to the characterizations of various transmission structures discussed in Chapter 3, there is a need to know the effect of variations in parameters on the characterizations of the transmission structures used in a particular circuit. The analysis leading to this information is called the sensitivity analysis.

4.1.1 Definitions

The sensitivity of a function F with respect to a parameter x is defined as

$$S_x^F = \lim_{\Delta x \to 0} \frac{\Delta F/F}{\Delta x/x} \tag{4.1a}$$

or

$$S_x^F = \frac{x}{F} \frac{\partial F}{\partial x} = \frac{\partial(\ell n F)}{\partial(\ell n x)} . \tag{4.1b}$$

According to (4.1) we may interpret the sensitivity S_x^F as the ratio of the fractional change in the function F to the fractional change in the parameter x, provided that the changes are sufficiently small (approaching zero). S_x^F is sometimes referred to in the literature as the normalized sensitivity, in order to distinguish it from the unnormalized sensitivity, which is simply the partial derivative $\partial F/\partial x$.

When F is a function of several parameters x_1, x_2, x_3, ... x_n, these parameters are represented by a vector and the gradient of F is defined as a column vector consisting of various derivatives $\partial F/\partial x_1$, $\partial F/\partial x_2$, ..., $\partial F/\partial x_n$. We write,

$$\nabla F = \begin{bmatrix} \partial F/\partial x_1 \\ \partial F/\partial x_2 \\ \cdot \\ \cdot \\ \cdot \\ \partial F/\partial x_n \end{bmatrix}. \qquad (4.2)$$

We note that ∇F is equivalent to the unnormalized sensitivity defined above.

4.1.2 Applications of Sensitivity Analysis

There are two major applications of sensitivity (or gradient) evaluation in circuit design: tolerance analysis and optimization. The tolerance analysis can be based on the sensitivity approach and the gradient information is needed in a class of optimization methods.

Tolerance Analysis

The tolerances in the physical and material parameters of a microwave circuit may be due to the limitations of the fabrication technology and/or due to measurement errors. These tolerances in parameters will give rise to deviations from the designed circuit specifications. The problem encountered in the design is to assign tolerances to various parameters in order to yield a circuit that satisfies certain specifications. On the other hand, the requirements of a fabrication technology suitable for achieving a given circuit performance may be specified. A sensitivity analysis is the best way to examine the trade-offs between specifications and tolerances. In addition to parameter tolerances, the models for the components on which the design is based may be approximate. The uncertainties in the value of the model parameters can be of the same order of magnitude as the tolerances in physical parameters. These model uncertainties can be treated in the same manner as the other tolerances [1].

The general problem of determining the deviations in circuit performance because of tolerances in various designable parameters is discussed later in Chapter 13. This chapter deals with the calculation of deviations in the characteristics of transmission structures caused by various fabrication and material tolerances.

Use of Sensitivities in Optimization

Various methods for the optimization of circuit performance are discussed in Chapters 16 to 18. In a typical optimization algorithm the values of the designable parameters are modified iteratively to minimize the "error" or "objective function." The gradient of the performance function is used to arrive at the modified parameter values for the $(j + 1)th$ iteration by adding, to the jth iteration values, increments (or decrements) which depend on the gradient.

Gradients of the characteristics for the transmission structures may be obtained from the sensitivity information presented in this chapter.

4.1.3 Tolerance Analysis of Transmission Lines

Transmission line sections are basic building-blocks in microwave circuits. Therefore, it becomes important to study transmission lines for their sensitivities with respect to the design parameters. Worst case deviations in the characteristics of transmission lines are examined using sensitivity analysis.

Expressions for the change in the characteristics of a transmission line are developed in the following section. The change in characteristic impedance ΔZ is also represented in terms of VSWR performance, which is obtained when the line is connected to a transmission line of exact dimensions. Variation in the phase velocity v is also evaluated.

Change in the Characteristics of a Transmission Line

The change in impedance ΔZ of a transmission line is related to the tolerance ΔB in a parameter B by the relation (using 4.1a))

$$\frac{\Delta Z}{Z_o} = \frac{\Delta B}{B} \; S_B^{Z_o} \tag{4.3}$$

where Z_o is the impedance with ΔB equal to zero. When Z_o is a function of several independent variables B_n, $n = 1, 2, \ldots, N$, the total change in Z_o is given by

$$\frac{\Delta Z}{Z_o} = \sum_{n=1}^{N} \frac{\Delta B_n}{B_n} \, S_{B_n}^{Z_o} . \tag{4.4}$$

The tolerances ΔB_n lead to a spread in the value of ΔZ. The largest possible value of ΔZ determines the worst case behavior, and its value can be obtained from the following relation:

$$\frac{(\Delta Z)_{max}}{Z_o} = \pm \sum_{n=1}^{N} \left| \frac{\Delta B_n}{B_n} \, S_{B_n}^{Z_o} \right| . \tag{4.5a}$$

Similarly, the maximum change $(\Delta v)_{max}$ in the phase velocity v is given by

$$\frac{(\Delta v)_{max}}{v} = \pm \sum_{n=1}^{N} \left| \frac{\Delta B_n}{B_n} \, S_{B_n}^{v} \right| . \tag{4.5b}$$

Equations (4.5) can be used to determine the maximum changes in Z_o and v as a function of tolerances.

The alternative problem of determining the requirements of fabrication technology for the permitted change in transmission line characteristics is considered next.

Determination of Fabrication Accuracy

The fabrication accuracy ΔB_m of a parameter B_m, for a specified value of ΔZ, is obtained from the following relation:

$$\left| S_{B_m}^{Z_o} \right| \cdot \left| \frac{\Delta B_m}{B_m} \right| = \left| \frac{\Delta Z}{Z_o} \right| - \sum_{\substack{n=1 \\ n \neq m}}^{N} \left| \frac{\Delta B_n}{B_n} \, S_{B_n}^{Z_o} \right| . \tag{4.6}$$

Equation (4.6a) holds when the right-hand side is positive. Otherwise, the specified value of ΔZ is not realizable with the given set of ΔB_n values. Similarly, for a specified value of Δv, the value of

ΔB_m may be obtained from

$$\left| S^v_{B_m} \right| \cdot \left| \frac{\Delta B_m}{B_m} \right| = \left| \frac{\Delta v}{v} \right| - \sum_{\substack{n=1 \\ n \neq m}}^{N} \left| \frac{\Delta B_n}{B_n} \; S^v_{B_n} \right|. \quad (4.7)$$

When the criteria of both ΔZ and Δv have to be met, the minimum of two ΔB_m values should be chosen.

The analysis presented above is useful in determining the trade-off between the tolerances and the performance. The requirements of fabrication technology for a specified performance of a transmission line may also be ascertained.

The above formulation is general and can be applied to any type of transmission line. Detailed computations are presented below for coaxial line, rectangular waveguide, stripline, microstrip line, co-planar lines, coupled striplines and coupled microstrip lines.

Evaluation of Sensitivities

Since the definition of sensitivity involves partial derivatives of Z_o and v with respect to one of the parameters, expressions for sensitivities can be obtained if closed form expressions for Z_o and v are available. Closed form expressions for the transmission lines presented in Chapter 3 are used for this purpose. If the fabrication tolerances are smaller than the errors in closed form expressions, numerical methods may be used to determine transmission line parameters for better accuracy.

For planar transmission lines used in MICs, the sensitivity of transmission line characteristics to the metallization thickness is, in general, small. Therefore, it has been neglected in Sections 4.4 to 4.6.

4.2 COAXIAL LINES

Sensitivity expressions for coaxial lines have been obtained by using (3.13) for Z_o and the definition of sensitivity as expressed in (4.1). It is found that

$$S_a^{Z_o} = -S_b^{Z_o} = -\frac{60}{Z_o \sqrt{\epsilon_r}} \qquad (Z_o \text{ in ohms}) \quad (4.8)$$

$$S^{Z_o}_{\epsilon_r} \quad = S^{v \cdot}_{\epsilon_r} \quad = -0.5. \tag{4.9}$$

The above sensitivies are plotted in Figure 4.1. These sensitivity curves have been utilized along with (4.5) to plot the maximum magnitude of the change in impedance, and is shown in Figure 4.2. Also, this figure includes the values of VSWR corresponding to the worst case value of reflection when a line with tolerances is connected to a perfect line (with zero tolerances). This reflection is proportional to ΔZ_o. The tolerance or fabrication accuracy in "a" (or "b") for a specified value of ΔZ and other sets of tolerances can be obtained from (4.6). The fabrication accuracy for a typical case is plotted in Figure 4.3.

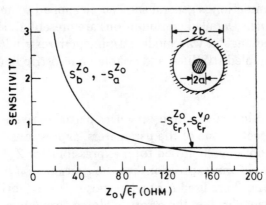

Figure 4.1   *Sensitivities of coaxial line impedance and phase velocity.*

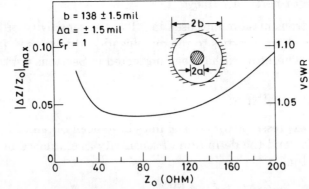

Figure 4.2   *Maximum fractional change in coaxial line impedance because of tolerances.*

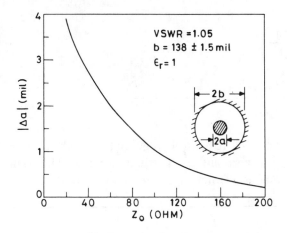

Figure 4.3 *Fabrication accuracy needed for the inner conductor of a coaxial line with the given specifications (VSWR = 1.05, b = 138 ± 1.5 mil, $\epsilon_r = 1$).*

4.3 WAVEGUIDES

Rectangular Waveguides: The characteristics most often used for rectangular waveguides are the phase constant β and the cut-off frequency f_c given by (3.20) and (3.21), respectively. Sensitivities of these characteristics with respect to parameters a, b and ϵ_r are given below:

$$S_a^{f_c} = -\left(\frac{c}{2\pi f_c \sqrt{\epsilon_r}} \cdot \frac{m\pi}{a}\right)^2 = -1 - S_b^{f_c} \qquad (4.10)$$

$$S_b^{f_c} = -\left(\frac{c}{2\pi f_c \sqrt{\epsilon_r}} \cdot \frac{n\pi}{b}\right)^2 = -1 - S_a^{f_c} \qquad (4.11)$$

$$S_{\epsilon_r}^{f_c} = -0.5 \qquad (4.12)$$

$$S_a^{\beta} = \left(\frac{m\pi}{\beta a}\right)^2 = -S_a^v \qquad (4.13)$$

$$S_b^\beta = \left(\frac{n\pi}{\beta b}\right)^2 \tag{4.14}$$

$$S_{\epsilon_r}^\beta = \frac{\omega^2 \mu_o \epsilon_o \epsilon_r}{2\beta^2} = \frac{1 + S_a^\beta + S_b^\beta}{2} . \tag{4.15}$$

For TE_{10} mode in an X-band waveguide (a = 0.9 in., b = 0.4 in.) the value of $S_b^{f_c}$ is zero and $S_a^{f_c}$ is equal to -1.0. The sensitivities with respect to a, as a function of frequency are plotted in Figure 4.4.

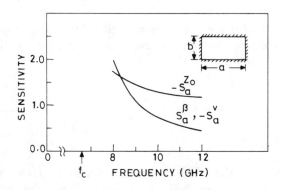

Figure 4.4   *Sensitivities of Z_o, β and v_p for TE_{10} mode in a rectangular waveguide (a = 0.9 inch, b = 0.4 inch and ϵ_r = 1).*

Other characteristics of rectangular waveguide such as wave impedance and characteristic impedance are also needed in circuit analysis, though less frequently. Their sensitivities are given below:

$$S_x^{Z(TE)} = -\frac{1}{x} S_x^\beta \qquad \text{(x is a, b or } \epsilon_r) \tag{4.16}$$

$$S_x^{Z(TM)} = S_x^\beta \qquad \text{(x is a or b)} \tag{4.17}$$

$$S_{\epsilon_r}^{Z(TM)} = S_{\epsilon_r}^\beta - 1 . \tag{4.18}$$

Sensitivities given by (4.16) and (4.17) can be obtained from the curves in Figure 4.4.

The characteristic impedance of a rectangular waveguide cannot be defined uniquely because of the non-TEM nature of the mode of propagation. However, the three definitions for Z_o, for TE_{10} mode (3.25) to (3.27), indicate identical dependence with respect to the parameters a and b. Therefore, Z_o for TE_{10} mode may be written as

$$Z_o = \eta \frac{Kb}{a} \frac{1}{\sqrt{1 - \left[\frac{\lambda_o}{2a} \right]^2}} \tag{4.19}$$

where the constant K depends upon the definition chosen for Z_o. The above equation is used to calculate the sensitivity expressions. These are obtained as

$$S_b^{Z_o} = 1 \tag{4.20a}$$

and

$$S_a^{Z_o} = - \left\{ 1 - \left[\frac{\lambda_o}{2a} \right]^2 \right\}^{-1} . \tag{4.20b}$$

The sensitivity curve defined by (4.20b) is shown in Figure 4.4 for an X-band waveguide.

Circular Waveguides: For the circular waveguide the expressions for the characteristics are given by (3.31) to (3.34); i.e.,

$$f_c = \frac{c}{2\pi a} A , \qquad c = 3 \times 10^8 \text{ m/s} \tag{4.21}$$

$$\beta = \sqrt{\omega^2 \mu_o \epsilon_o \epsilon_r - \left(\frac{A}{a} \right)^2} \tag{4.22}$$

where

$$A = \begin{cases} p_{n\ell} & \text{for TM mode} \\ \\ p'_{n\ell} & \text{for TE mode.} \end{cases}$$

The sensitivities obtained using the above equations are given below
and hold for both the TE and TM modes:

$$S_a^{f_c} = -1 \qquad\qquad\qquad\qquad\qquad (4.23)$$

$$S_a^{\beta} = \left(\frac{A}{\beta a}\right)^2 . \qquad\qquad\qquad\qquad (4.24)$$

Sensitivity expressions for wave impedance are the same as those
for the rectangular waveguide. The sensitivity of β given by (4.24)
has been plotted in Figure 4.5 for TE_{11} mode.

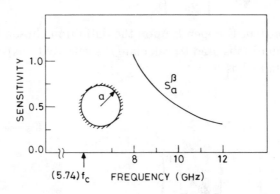

Figure 4.5   Sensitivity of phase constant for TE_{11} mode in a circular waveguide   (a = 1.633 cm, ϵ_r = 1).

4.4 STRIPLINES AND MICROSTRIP LINES

4.4.1 Striplines

For stripline, the characteristics are given by (3.39) to (3.41). The
sensitivity expressions are evaluated as

$$S_W^{Z_o} = \frac{W}{Z_o} \frac{\partial Z_o}{\partial W'} \qquad\qquad\qquad\qquad (4.25)$$

$$S_b^{Z_o} = - \frac{b}{W} \left[\frac{W'}{b-t} - \frac{2}{\pi} \frac{x}{2-x} \right] S_W^{Z_o} \qquad (4.26)$$

$$S_t^{Z_o} = \frac{t}{W} \left\{ \frac{W'}{b-t} - \frac{1}{\pi} \left[\frac{x}{2-x} + \ln \frac{x}{2-x} \right] \right\} S_W^{Z_o} \qquad (4.27)$$

$$S_{\epsilon_r}^{Z_o} = - 0.5 = S_{\epsilon_r}^{v} \qquad (4.28)$$

where $\partial Z_o / \partial W'$ is given by (3.48) and $x = t/b$.

A plot of the above sensitivities is given in Figure 4.6. It may be noted from here that, for high impedance lines ($W < b$), the im-

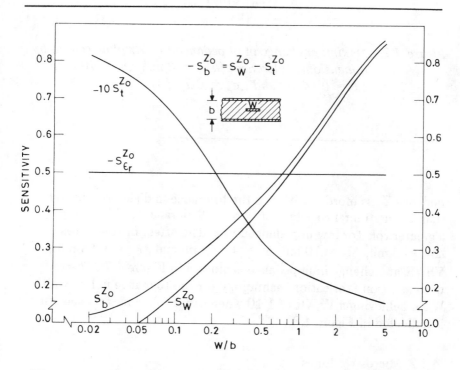

Figure 4.6   Sensitivities of characteristic impedance of a stripline
($\epsilon_r = 2.55$, $b = 125$ mil and $t = 1.4$ mil). [3]

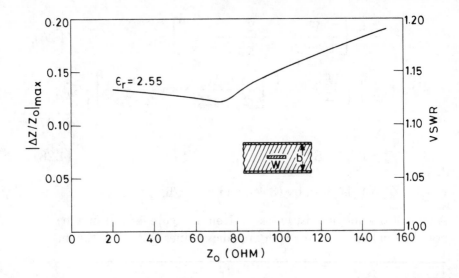

Figure 4.7   *Figure 4.7   Maximum change in impedance of a stripline caused by dimensional tolerances (ΔW = 3 mil, Δb = 10 mil, Δt = 0.14 mil and $\Delta \epsilon_r$ = 0.2). [3]*

pedance Z_o is more sensitive to the tolerance in dielectric constant than to the tolerance values of W or b. Tolerances in W and b play a greater role for low impedance lines. The effect of tolerances ΔW = 3 mil, Δb = 10 mil, Δt = 0.14 mil, and $\Delta \epsilon_r$ = 0.2 on line VSWR and change in impedance is plotted in Figure 4.7. The requirement on fabrication technology for the tolerance in line width W for achieving a VSWR of 1.10 when other tolerances are specified is indicated in Figure 4.8.

4.4.2 Microstrip Lines

For microstrip line, the characteristics Z_o and ϵ_{re} are given by (3.54) to (3.57). The sensitivity expressions evaluated for t = 0 are [3]

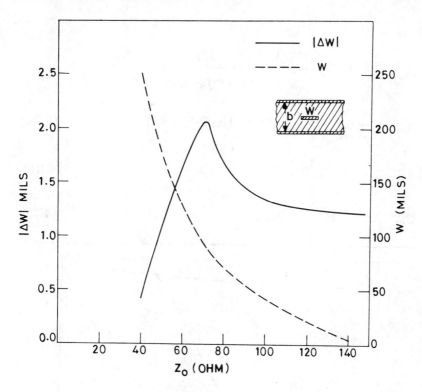

Figure 4.8 *Fabrication accuracy needed for the strip width (ΔW) of a stripline for a given specification (VSWR = 1.10, $\epsilon_r = 2.55 \pm 0.2$, $\Delta b = 10$ mil and $\Delta t = 0.14$ mil). [3]*

$$S_h^{Z_o} = -S_W^{Z_o}$$

$$= \begin{cases} \dfrac{1}{Z_o \sqrt{\epsilon_{re}}} \dfrac{60(8h/W - W/4h)}{(8h/W + W/4h)} + A \quad (\text{for } W/h \leqslant 1) \\ \\ \hspace{4cm} (4.29a) \\ \\ \dfrac{Z_o \sqrt{\epsilon_{re}}}{120\pi}\left[\dfrac{W}{h} + 0.44\dfrac{h}{W} + \dfrac{6h}{W}\left(1 - \dfrac{h}{W}\right)^5\right] + A \\ \\ \hspace{2.5cm} (\text{for } \dfrac{W}{h} \geqslant 1) \quad (4.29b) \end{cases}$$

where

$$A = 1.25 \frac{\epsilon_r - 1}{\epsilon_{re}} \frac{h/W}{(1 + 10h/W)^{3/2}}$$

$$S_{\epsilon_r}^{Z_o} = - \frac{\epsilon_r}{4\epsilon_{re}} \left[1 + (1 + 10h/W)^{-1/2} \right] \qquad (4.30)$$

$$S_{\epsilon_r}^{\epsilon_{re}} = - 2S_{\epsilon_r}^{Z_o} \qquad (4.31)$$

$$S_W^{\epsilon_{re}} = - S_h^{\epsilon_{re}} = 2A \,. \qquad (4.32)$$

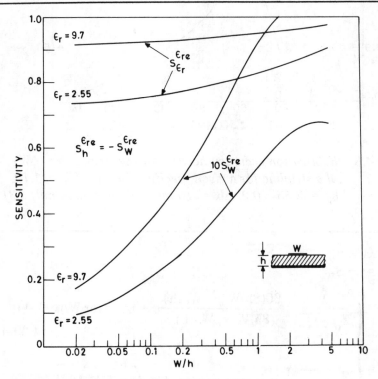

Figure 4.9(a)   Senstivities of effective dielectric constant of a microstrip line (ϵ_r = 9.7 and h = 0.025 inch; ϵ_r = 2.55 and h = 0.0625 inch). [2]

Based on the above equations, sensitivity curves are plotted in Figure 4.9(a) for impedance and in Figure 4.9(b) for effective dielectric constant. It is observed that the behavior of sensitivity curves for the impedance of microstrip lines (Figure 4.9(a)) is similar to that for striplines. Sensitivity curves for effective dielectric constant (Figure 4.9(b)) indicate that ϵ_{re} is most sensitive to tolerance in the dielectric constant. This is expected from physical considerations also. The effect of tolerances on transmission line impedance is shown in Figure 4.10, and the fabrication accuracy, $|\Delta W|$, for a given set of other tolerances and the desired VSWR value is shown in Figure 4.11.

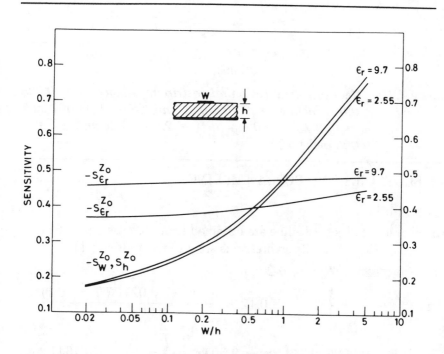

Figure 4.9(b)   *Sensitivities of characteristic impedance of a microstrip line ($\epsilon_r = 9.7$ and $h = 0.025$ inch; $\epsilon_r = 2.55$ and $h = 0.0625$ inch). [2]*

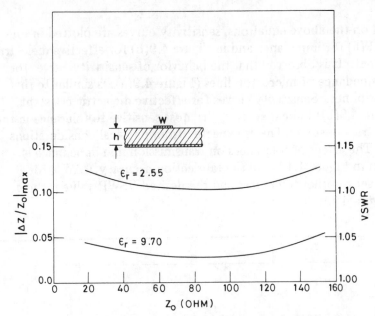

Figure 4.10 Effect of tolerances on microstrip impedance (h = 0.025 ± 0.001 inch, ϵ_r = 9.70 ± 0.20 and $\triangle W$ = ± 0.0001 inch; h = 0.0625 ± 0.005 inch, ϵ_r = 2.55 ± 0.20 and $\triangle W$ = 0.003 inch). [2]

4.5 SLOTLINES AND COPLANAR LINES

4.5.1 Slotlines

The characteristics of slotline are obtained from expressions (3.67) to (3.70). The sensitivity expressions are given as follows [4]:

(i) For 0.02 ⩽ W/h ⩽ 0.2

$$S_W^{Z_{os}} = \frac{50}{Z_{os}} \left\{ 2\frac{W}{h} - 0.12 - \frac{(W/h - 0.02)(W/h - 0.1)}{W/h} \right.$$

$$\left. + 0.0086 \quad (44.28 - 8.50 \ln \epsilon_r) \right\} - \frac{W/h}{Z_{os}} (0.4647 \ln \epsilon_r$$

$$+ 1.44) \quad (11.4 - 2.637 \ln \epsilon_r - h/\lambda_o \times 10^2)^2 \tag{4.33}$$

$$S_h^{Z_{os}} = - S_W^{Z_{os}} + \frac{h}{Z_{os}} \frac{1}{\lambda_o} \frac{\partial Z_{os}}{\partial(h/\lambda_o)} \tag{4.34}$$

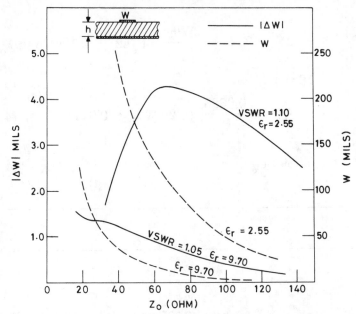

Figure 4.11 Fabrication accuracy of strip width of a microstrip line for given specifications (VSWR = 1.05, ϵ_r = 9.70 ± 0.20 and h = 0.025 ± 0.001 inch; VSWR = 1.10, ϵ_r = 2.55 ± 0.20 and h = 0.0625 ± 0.005 inch). [2]

where

$$\frac{\partial Z_{os}}{\partial (h/\lambda_o)} = -200\,(11.4 - 2.637\,\ln\epsilon_r - h/\lambda_o \times 10^2)$$

$$\cdot\,[\,0.139\,\ln\epsilon_r - 0.11 + 0.4647\,\ln\epsilon_r + 1.44)W/h\,]$$

$$S^{Z_{os}}_{\epsilon_r} = \frac{0.4343\,\epsilon_r}{Z_{os}}\cdot \left\{ 35.19 + 8.50\,\ln\,(W/h \times 10^2) \right.$$

$$+ (0.32 + 1.07\,W/h)\,(11.4 - 2.637\,\ln\epsilon_r - h/\lambda_o \times 10^2)^2$$

$$- 12.14\,(11.4 - 2.637\,\ln\epsilon_r - h/\lambda_o \times 10^2)$$

$$\left. \cdot\,[\,0.139\,\ln\epsilon_r - 0.11 + (0.4647\,\ln\epsilon_r + 1.44)\,W/h\,] \right\}$$

$$(4.35)$$

$$S_W^{\epsilon_{re}} = -2 S_W^{\lambda_s/\lambda_o} = -\frac{2W/h}{\epsilon_{re}} [\ 0.2 - 0.126 \ \ell n \ (h/\lambda_o$$

$$\times 10^2)\ ] \tag{4.36}$$

$$S_h^{\epsilon_{re}} = -S_W^{\epsilon_{re}} + \frac{0.8686}{\epsilon_{re}} (0.29 \ W/h + 0.047) \tag{4.37}$$

$$S_{\epsilon_r}^{\epsilon_{re}} = 0.389 / \epsilon_{re} \ . \tag{4.38}$$

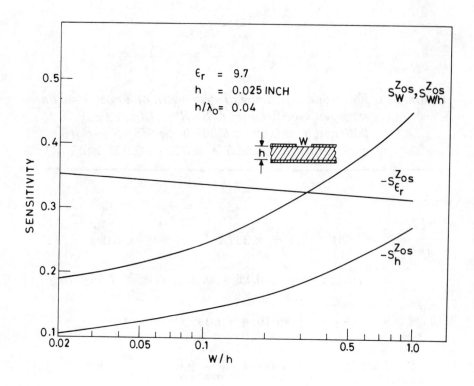

Figure 4.12 Sensitivity curves for the characteristic impedance of slot line. [2]

(ii) For 0.2 ⩽ W/h ⩽ 1.0

$$S_W^{Z_{os}} = \frac{W/h}{Z_{os}} \left\{ 1.25 \, (114.59 - 22.53 \, \ln\epsilon_r) + 24 - 40 \, W/h \right.$$

$$- [\, 10.25 - 2.17 \, \ln\epsilon_r + (2.1 - 0.617 \, \ln\epsilon_r) \, W/h$$

$$- \, h/\lambda_o \times 10^2 \,] \left[(0.9 \, \ln\epsilon_r - 0.79) [\, 10.25 - 2.17 \, \ln\epsilon_r \right.$$

$$+ \, (2.1 - 0.617 \, \ln\epsilon_r) \, W/h - h/\lambda_o \times 10^2 \,] + 2 \, (2.1$$

$$\left. \left. - \, 0.617 \, \ln\epsilon_r) \, [\, 0.15 + 0.1 \, \ln\epsilon_r + (0.9 \, \ln\epsilon_r - 0.79) \, W/h \,] \right] \right\}$$

$$(4.39)$$

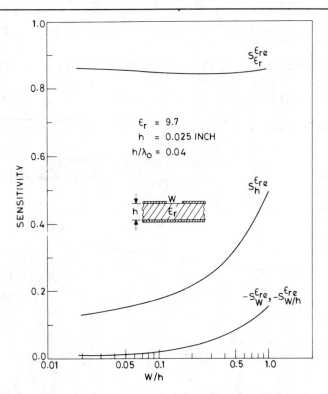

Figure 4.13 Sensitivity curves for the effective dielectric constant of slot line. [2]

$$S_h^{Z_{os}} = - S_W^{Z_{os}} + \frac{h/\lambda_o}{Z_{os}} \frac{\partial Z_{os}}{\partial(h/\lambda_o)} \tag{4.40}$$

where

$$\frac{\partial Z_{os}}{\partial(h/\lambda_o)} = 200 \left[10.25 - 2.17 \, \ell n \epsilon_r + (2.1 - 0.617 \, \ell n \epsilon_r) \, W/h \right.$$

$$\left. - \, h/\lambda_o \times 10^2 \right] \left[0.15 + 0.1 \, \ell n \epsilon_r + (0.9 \, \ell n \epsilon_r - 0.79) \, W/h \right]$$

$$S_{\epsilon_r}^{Z_{os}} = \frac{0.4343 \, \epsilon_r}{Z_{os}} \left\{ 53.55 + 64.85 \, W/h + (0.23 + 2.07 \, W/h) \right.$$

$$\cdot \left[10.25 - 2.17 \, \ell n \epsilon_r + (2.1 - 0.617 \, \ell n \epsilon_r) \, W/h \right.$$

$$\left. - \, h/\lambda_o \times 10^2 \right]^2 - 2(5 + 1.42 \, W/h) \left[0.15 + 0.1 \, \ell n \epsilon_r \right.$$

$$\left. + (0.9 \, \ell n \epsilon_r - 0.79) \, W/h \right] \left[10.25 - 2.17 \, \ell n \epsilon_r + (2.1 \right.$$

$$\left. - 0.617 \, \ell n \epsilon_r) \, W/h - h/\lambda_o \times 10^2 \right] \right\} \tag{4.41}$$

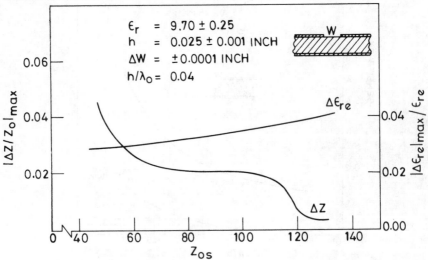

Figure 4.14 Effect of tolerances on the impedance and the effective
dielectric constant of a slot line. [2]

$$S_W^{\epsilon_{re}} = -\frac{2\,W/h}{\epsilon_{re}}\,[\,0.111 - 0.0022\,\epsilon_r - 0.041\,\ln(h/\lambda_o$$

$$\times\ 10^2)\,] \qquad\qquad (4.42)$$

$$S_h^{\epsilon_{re}} = -S_W^{\epsilon_{re}} + \frac{0.8686}{\epsilon_{re}}\,(0.121 + 0.094\,W/h - 0.0032\,\epsilon_r)$$

$$\qquad\qquad (4.43)$$

$$S_{\epsilon_r}^{\epsilon_{re}} = \frac{2}{\epsilon_{re}}\,[\,0.21 + 0.0022\,\epsilon_r\,W/h - 0.0014\,\epsilon_r\,\ln(h/\lambda_o$$

$$\times\ 10^2)\,]\ . \qquad\qquad (4.44)$$

The sensitivity curves, based on (4.33) to (4.44), are plotted in Figures 4.12 and 4.13. The change in impedance and $|\Delta W|$ curves are shown in Figures 4.14 and 4.15, respectively.

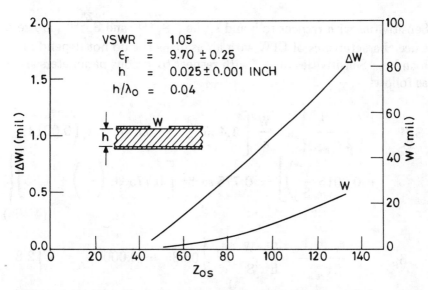

Figure 4.15 Requirement on the fabrication accuracy of slot width as a function of Z_{os} for a slot line. [2]

4.5.2 Coplanar Lines

The sensitivity expressions for coplanar waveguide and coplanar strips are obtained from (3.73) to (3.76). These are given below for the thickness t = 0:

$$S_W^{Z_{ocp}^a} = - S_S^{Z_{ocp}^a} = \frac{60\,P}{Z_{ocp}^a} \cdot \frac{W}{S}\,k^2 \tag{4.45a}$$

where

$$k = S/(S + 2W)$$

$$
P = \begin{cases}
\dfrac{k}{(1 - \sqrt{1 - k^2}\,)(1 - k^2)^{3/4}} & \text{for } 0.0 \leqslant k \leqslant 0.707 \\[4mm]
\dfrac{1}{(1 - k)\sqrt{k}}\left(\dfrac{K'}{K}\right)^2 & \text{for } 0.707 \leqslant k \leqslant 1.0.
\end{cases} \tag{4.45b}
$$

Sensitivities with respect to h and ϵ_r, i.e., $S_h^{Z_{ocp}^a}$ and $S_{\epsilon_r}^{Z_{ocp}^a}$, are zero since characteristics of CPW with air as dielectric do not depend on h and ϵ_r. Sensitivities of ϵ_{re} with respect to various parameters are as follows:

$$
\begin{aligned}
S_W^{\epsilon_{re}} = \frac{\epsilon_r + 1}{2\,\epsilon_{re}} \Bigg\{ & k^3\,\frac{W}{h}\left[1.465\,\frac{W}{S} - 0.647 - \epsilon_r\left(0.0013\right.\right. \\
& \left.\left. + 0.0015\,\frac{W}{S}\right)\right] - 0.775\,\mathrm{sech}^2\left[0.775\,\ell n\left(\frac{h}{W}\right) + 1.75\right]\Bigg\}
\end{aligned} \tag{4.46a}
$$

$$
\begin{aligned}
S_S^{\epsilon_{re}} = \frac{\epsilon_r + 1}{2\,\epsilon_{re}}\,\frac{W}{h}\,\frac{W}{S}\,k^2 \Big\{ & 0.085 - 0.0005\,\epsilon_r - k\,[\,2.8 \\
& - 0.04\,(1 - 0.1\,\epsilon_r)\,]\Big\}
\end{aligned} \tag{4.46b}
$$

$$S_h^{\epsilon_{re}} = - S_W^{\epsilon_{re}} - S_S^{\epsilon_{re}'} \tag{4.46c}$$

$$S_{\epsilon_r}^{\epsilon_{re}} = \frac{\epsilon_r}{2\,\epsilon_{re}} \left\{ \tanh \left[0.775 \,\ell n \left(\frac{h}{W}\right) + 1.75 \right] + \frac{kW}{h} \, [0.04 \right.$$

$$- 0.7k + 0.01 \,(1 - 0.1\,\epsilon_r)\,(0.25 + k)] - 0.001\,\frac{\epsilon_r + 1}{2}$$

$$\left. \frac{kW}{h}\,(0.25 + k) \right\} . \tag{4.46d}$$

The sensitivities of characteristic impedance and effective dielectric constant of coplanar waveguide with respect to various parameters are plotted in Figures 4.16 and 4.17, respectively. The change in impedance is plotted in Figure 4.18 for the set of tolerances mentioned therein. The variation of $(\Delta\epsilon_{re})_{max}/\epsilon_{re}$ is also shown in this figure. It may be noted that ΔZ values are comparable with the corresponding results for microstrip lines (Figure 4.10) and slotlines (Figure 4.14), while results for $\Delta\,\epsilon_{re}/\epsilon_{re}$ are slightly worse.

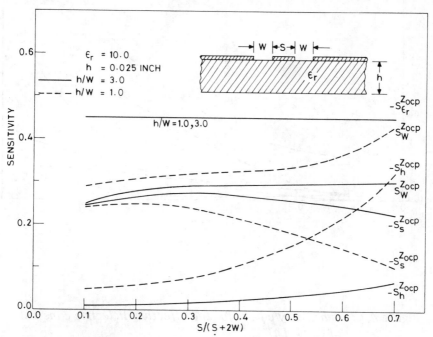

Figure 4.16 Sensitivity curves for the characteristic impedance of CPW. [4]

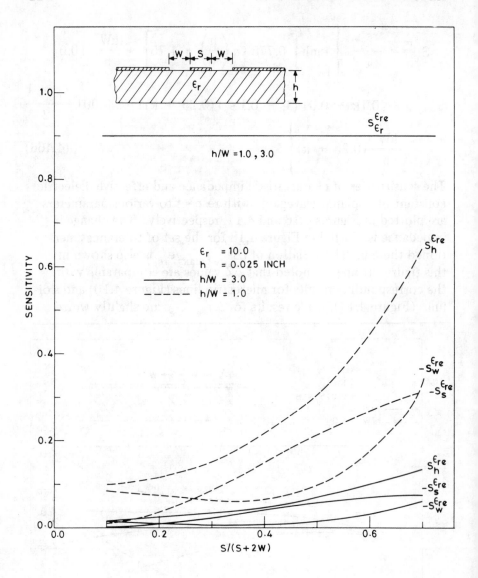

Figure 4.17 *Sensitivity curves for the effective dielectric constant of CPW. [4]*

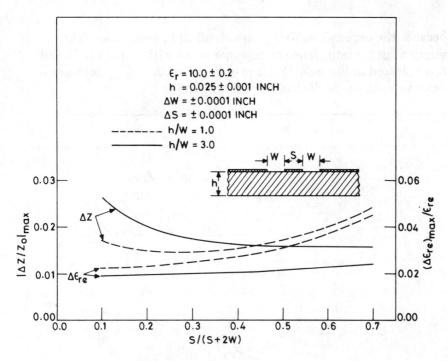

Figure 4.18 Effect of tolerances on the impedance and effective dielectric constant of CPW. [4]

For coplanar strips, the sensitivities of impedance with air as dielectric (Z^a_{ocs}) with respect to parameters S and W are given as follows:

$$S^{Z^a_{ocs}}_W = - S^{Z^a_{ocs}}_S = - \frac{120k\,(1\,-\,k)\,P'}{Z^a_{ocs}} \qquad (4.47a)$$

where

$$P' = P\left[\frac{K}{K'}\right]^2 \qquad (4.47b)$$

and P has been defined earlier in (4.45b).

As for CPW, the sensitivities with respect to h and ϵ_r are zero in this case also. Expressions for sensitivities of ϵ_{re} with respect to various parameters (W,S,h and ϵ_r) are the same as those described for CPW because the expressions for ϵ_{re} are identical in both cases. The sensitivities for impedance of coplanar strips with respect to W and S are plotted in Figure 4.19. It may be noted that Z_{ocs} is less sensitive to variation in W than to variation in S.

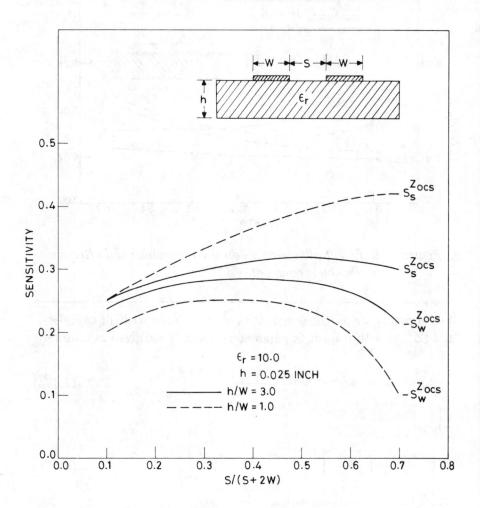

Figure 4.19 Sensitivity curves for the characteristic impedance of CPS. [4]

4.6 COUPLED STRIPLINES AND COUPLED MICROSTRIP LINES

4.6.1 Coupled Striplines

For coupled striplines the characteristics are given by (3.97) and (3.98). The sensitivity expressions are evaluated as:

$$S_W^{Z_{oi}} = -\frac{Z_{oi}\sqrt{\epsilon_r}}{30\,\pi}\;\frac{W}{b-t} \tag{4.48}$$

$$S_b^{Z_{oi}} = \frac{b}{b-t}\left\{1 - \frac{Z_{oi}\sqrt{\epsilon_r}}{30\,\pi}\left[\frac{A_i}{\pi}\;\ell n\left(\frac{2b-t}{b-t}\right)\right.\right.$$
$$\left.\left. + \frac{bC_f}{2\pi}\;\frac{\partial A_i}{\partial b}\right]\right\} \tag{4.49}$$

$$S_s^{Z_{oi}} = -\frac{Z_{oi}\sqrt{\epsilon_r}}{30\,\pi}\;\frac{b}{b-t}\;\frac{sC_f}{2\pi}\;\frac{\partial A_i}{\partial s} \tag{4.50}$$

$$S_t^{Z_{oi}} = \frac{t}{b-t}\left\{-1 + A_i\;\frac{Z_{oi}\sqrt{\epsilon_r}}{60\,\pi^2}\;\ell n\;\frac{2tb-t^2}{(b-t)^2}\right\} \tag{4.51}$$

$$S_{\epsilon_r}^{Z_{oi}} = -0.5 \tag{4.52}$$

where i stands for even mode or odd mode. The quantities A_i and C_f are defined by (3.98), and

$$\frac{\partial A_{e,o}}{\partial b} = -\frac{s}{b}\;\frac{\partial A_{e,o}}{\partial s} \tag{4.53}$$

$$\frac{\partial A_e}{\partial s} = \frac{\pi}{2b\ell n2}\;\frac{\text{sech}^2\dfrac{\pi s}{2b}}{1+\tanh\dfrac{\pi s}{2b}} \tag{4.54a}$$

$$\frac{\partial A_o}{\partial s} = -\frac{\pi}{2b\ell n2}\frac{\cosech^2\frac{\pi s}{2b}}{1 + \coth\frac{\pi s}{2b}} . \tag{4.54b}$$

The even and the odd mode sensitivities can be utilized to determine the change in the coupled line performance due to tolerances. These characteristics may be coupling constant, directivity, insertion loss, input impedance, etc. We shall determine the effect on coupling constant C and impedance Z_o.

Change in Coupling Constant: The maximum change in coupling constant is given by

$$\frac{|\Delta C|_{max}}{C} = \left|\frac{\Delta W}{W} S_W^C\right| + \left|\frac{\Delta b}{b} S_b^C\right| + \left|\frac{\Delta s}{s} S_s^C\right| + \left|\frac{\Delta \epsilon_r}{\epsilon_r} S_{\epsilon_r}^C\right| \tag{4.55}$$

where

$$C = \frac{Z_{oe} - Z_{oo}}{Z_{oe} + Z_{oo}}$$

and

$$S_x^C = \frac{1 - C^2}{2C}\left[S_x^{Z_{oe}} - S_x^{Z_{oo}}\right] .$$

Here, x stands for W, h, s, or ϵ_r.

Change in Impedance: The maximum change in coupled line impedance Z_o, defined as $Z_o = \sqrt{Z_{oe} Z_{oo}}$, can be obtained from

$$\frac{|\Delta Z_o|_{max}}{Z_o} = \frac{1}{2}\left|\frac{\Delta W}{W}\left(S_W^{Z_{oe}} + S_W^{Z_{oo}}\right)\right| + \left|\frac{\Delta b}{b}\left(S_b^{Z_{oe}}\right.\right.$$

$$\left.\left. + S_b^{Z_{oo}}\right)\right| + \left|\frac{\Delta s}{s}\left(S_s^{Z_{oe}} + S_s^{Z_{oo}}\right)\right|$$

$$+ \left|\frac{\Delta \epsilon_r}{\epsilon_r}\left(S_{\epsilon_r}^{Z_{oe}} + S_{\epsilon_r}^{Z_{oo}}\right)\right| . \tag{4.56}$$

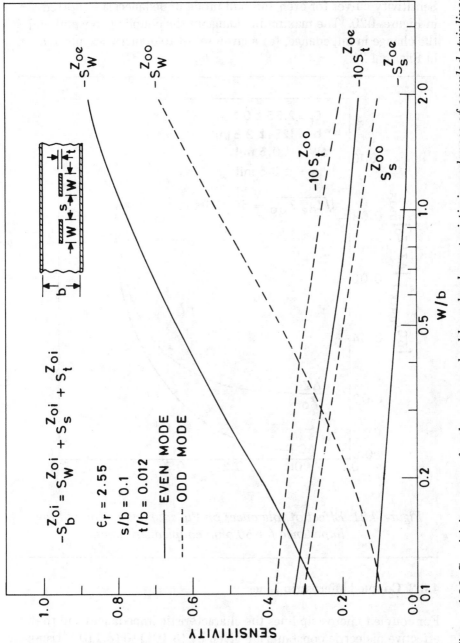

Figure 4.20 Sensitivity curves for the even and odd mode characteristic impedances of coupled striplines.

Sensitivity curves for even and odd mode impedances are plotted
in Figure 4.20. The maximum change in the coupling constant and
the change in impedance, for a given set of tolerances, are plotted
in Figure 4.21.

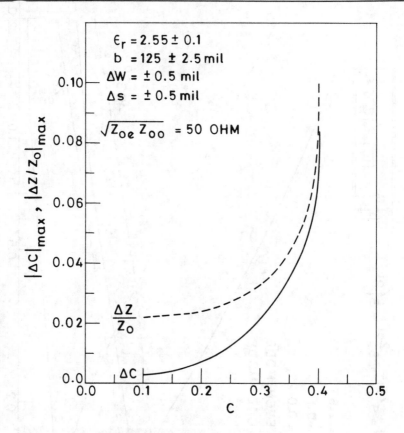

*Figure 4.21 Effect of tolerances on the coupling factor and the
impedance for 50 ohm coupled striplines.*

4.6.2 Coupled Microstrip Lines

For coupled microstrip lines the characteristic impedances and the
effective dielectric constants are given by (3.101) to (3.110). Using
these expressions and the definition of sensitivity, the following

equations for various sensitivities have been obtained

$$S^{Z_{oi}}_{x_j} = -0.5 \left[\frac{x_j}{C_i} \frac{\partial C_i}{\partial x_j} + \frac{x_j}{C_j^a} \frac{\partial C_i^a}{\partial x_j} \right]$$

$$= -0.5 \left[\frac{x_j/h}{C_i} \frac{\partial C_i}{\partial (x_j/h)} + \frac{x_j/h}{C_i^a} \frac{\partial C_i^a}{\partial (x_j/h)} \right] \tag{4.57}$$

$$S^{\epsilon_{re}^i}_{x_j} = \frac{x_j}{C_i} \frac{\partial C_i}{\partial x_j} - \frac{x_j}{C_i^a} \frac{\partial C_i^a}{\partial x_j} \tag{4.58}$$

where i = e or o stands for even or odd mode, respectively; x_j stands for W,h, or s; and C^a represents the capacitance with air as dielectric. We obtain

$$S^{Z_{oi}}_{\epsilon_r} = -0.5 \frac{\epsilon_r}{C_i} \frac{\partial C_i}{\partial \epsilon_r} \tag{4.59}$$

and

$$S^{\epsilon_{re}^i}_{\epsilon_r} = -2 \, S^{Z_{oi}}_{\epsilon_r} . \tag{4.60}$$

For even mode, the various derivatives are obtained as

$$2 \frac{\partial C_e}{\partial (W/h)} = \epsilon_0 \epsilon_r (1 - P) - \frac{1 + P}{cZ_o^a} \left[\frac{\epsilon_{re}}{Z_o^a} \frac{\partial Z_o^a}{\partial (W/h)} \right.$$

$$\left. - \frac{\partial \epsilon_{re}}{\partial (W/h)} \right] - 0.1265 \, A \, P^2 \, Q \, \frac{\tanh(10 \, s/h)}{s/h}$$

$$\cdot \exp(2.33 - 2.53 \, W/h)$$

$$\tag{4.61}$$

$$2 \frac{\partial C_e}{\partial (s/h)} = \frac{A \, P^2 \, Q}{s/h} \left[\frac{\tanh(10 \, s/h)}{s/h} - 10 \, \text{sech}^2 \, (10 \, s/h) \right]$$

$$\tag{4.62}$$

$$\frac{\partial C_e}{\partial \epsilon_r} = \epsilon_o \frac{W}{h} \frac{1-P}{2} \frac{1+P}{2cZ_o^a} \frac{\partial \epsilon_{re}}{\partial \epsilon_r} \qquad (4.63)$$

with

$$P \qquad = [1 + A(h/s)\tanh(10\,s/h)]^{-1}$$

$$Q \qquad = \epsilon_{re}/(cZ_o^a) - \epsilon_o \epsilon_r\, W/h$$

$$A \qquad = \exp[-0.1\exp(2.33 - 2.53\,W/h)]$$

$$\frac{\partial Z_o^a}{\partial (W/h)} =
\begin{cases}
-\dfrac{1}{W/h}\dfrac{60(8h/W - 0.25\,W/h)}{8(h/W + 0.25\,W/h)} & \text{for } (W/h \leqslant 1) \\[4mm]
 & \qquad (4.64a) \\[2mm]
\dfrac{(Z_o^a)^2}{120\pi\,(W/h)}\left[\dfrac{W}{h} + 0.44\dfrac{h}{W} + \dfrac{6h}{W}\left(1 - \dfrac{h}{W}\right)^5\right] & \\[4mm]
 & \text{for } (W/h \geqslant 1)\,(4.64b)
\end{cases}$$

$$\frac{\partial \epsilon_{re}}{\partial (W/h)} = \frac{2.5\,(\epsilon_r - 1)}{\left[\dfrac{W}{h}\right]^2\left[1 + 10\dfrac{h}{W}\right]^{3/2}} \qquad (4.65)$$

$$S_h^{Z_{oi}} = -\left[S_{W/h}^{Z_{oi}} + S_{s/h}^{Z_{oi}}\right]. \qquad (4.66)$$

The derivative expressions for C_e^a are obtained by substituting $\epsilon_r = 1$ in the above equations for derivatives.

For odd mode, the various derivatives are

$$\frac{\partial C_o}{\partial (W/h)} = \frac{\epsilon_o \epsilon_r}{2}\left\{1 - 0.65\left[\frac{0.02}{s/h}\sqrt{\epsilon_r} + 1 - \frac{1}{\epsilon_r^2}\right]\right\}$$

$$+ \frac{\partial C_{ga}}{\partial (W/h)} + \frac{1}{2cZ_o^a}\left\{1 + 0.65\left[\frac{0.02}{s/h}\sqrt{\epsilon_r} + 1\right.\right.$$

$$\left.\left. - \frac{1}{\epsilon_r^2}\right]\right\}\left[\frac{\partial \epsilon_{re}}{\partial (W/h)} - \frac{\epsilon_{re}}{Z_o^a}\frac{\partial Z_o^a}{\partial (W/h)}\right] \qquad (4.67)$$

$$\frac{\partial C_o}{\partial(s/h)} = \frac{\partial C_{ga}}{\partial(s/h)} \left\{ \frac{\epsilon_o \epsilon_r}{4} \ \text{cosech}\left(\frac{\pi}{4} \ \frac{s}{h} \right) + \frac{0.013 \sqrt{\epsilon_r} \ C_f}{(s/h)^2} \right\}$$

$$(4.68)$$

$$\frac{\partial C_o}{\partial \epsilon_r} = \frac{1}{2} \left[\epsilon_o \ \frac{W}{h} + \frac{1}{cZ_o^a} \ \frac{\partial \epsilon_{re}}{\partial \epsilon_r} \right] + \frac{\epsilon_o}{\pi} \ \ell n \left[\coth\left(\frac{\pi}{4} \ \frac{s}{h} \right) \right]$$

$$+ \ 0.325 \left(\frac{1}{cZ_o^a} \ \frac{\partial \epsilon_{re}}{\partial \epsilon_r} - \epsilon_o \ \frac{W}{h} \right) \left[\frac{0.02}{s/h} \ \sqrt{\epsilon_r} + 1 \right.$$

$$\left. - \frac{1}{\epsilon_r^2} \right] + 0.65 \ C_f \left[\frac{0.01}{\sqrt{\epsilon_r}} \ \frac{s}{h} + \frac{2}{\epsilon_r^3} \right] \qquad (4.69)$$

where

$$\frac{\partial C_{ga}}{\partial(W/h)} = \frac{\epsilon_o \ / \ \pi}{k'^{\ 3/2}} \ \frac{2(1 + k')}{s \ / \ h \ + \ 2W/h}$$

$$\frac{\partial C_{ga}}{\partial(s/h)} = - \ \frac{\epsilon_o / \pi}{(1 - k') \ k'^{\ 3/2}} \ \frac{k(1 - k)}{s/h \ + \ 2W/h} \quad \left. \right\} \quad 0 \leqslant k^2 \leqslant 0.5$$

$$(4.70a)$$

$$\frac{\partial C_{ga}}{\partial(W/h)} = \frac{C_{ga}^2}{\pi \ \epsilon_o} \ \frac{\sqrt{k}}{W/h}$$

$$\frac{\partial C_{ga}}{\partial(s/h)} = - \ \frac{C_{ga}^2}{\pi \ \epsilon_o} \ \frac{1}{\sqrt{k} \ (s/h \ + \ 2W/h)} \quad \left. \right\} \quad 0.5 \leqslant k^2 \leqslant 1.$$

$$(4.70b)$$

Sensitivity curves for even and odd mode impedances are plotted in Figure 4.22.

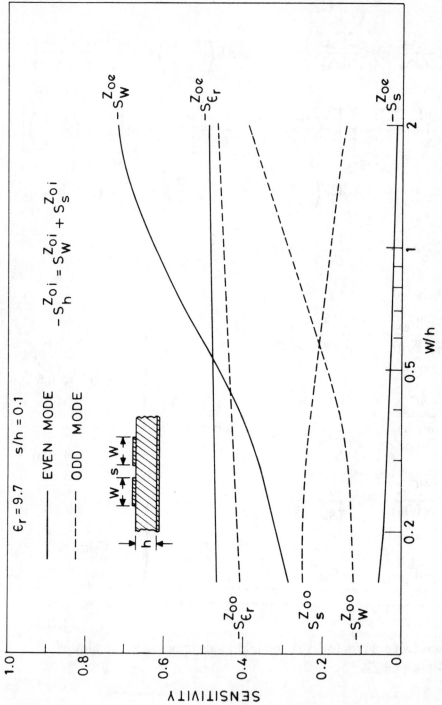

Figure 4.22 Sensivity curves for the even and odd mode characteristic impedances of coupled microstrip lines.

The maximum change in coupling constant and impedance can be determined in the same manner as for coupled striplines, as defined in (4.55) and (4.56). These are plotted in Figure 4.23.

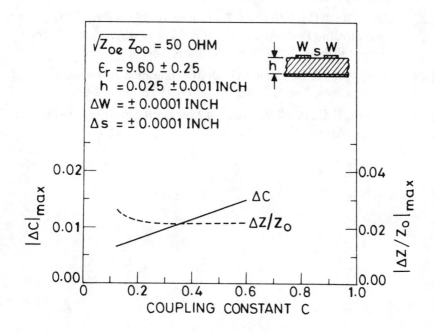

Figure 4.23 *Effect of tolerances on the coupling factor and impedance Z_o of coupled microstrip lines ($Z_o = \sqrt{Z_{oo} Z_{oe}}$ = 50 ohms). [4]*

Expressions for sensitivities of characteristic impedances and phase velocities for various types of transmission structures have been obtained in this chapter. This information, along with the techniques for sensitivity analysis of circuits discussed later in Chapter 12, is useful in the tolerance analysis and optimization of microwave circuits.

REFERENCES

[1]   Bandler, J.W., *et al.*, "Integrated Approach to Microwave
       Design," *IEEE Trans. Microwave Theory Tech.*, Vol. MTT-
       24, Sept. 1976, pp. 584-591.

[2]   Garg, R., "The Effect of Tolerances on Microstrip Line
       and Slotline Performances," *IEEE Trans. Microwave Theory
       Tech.*, Vol. MTT-26, Jan. 1978, pp. 16-19.

[3]   Garg, R., "A Designer's Guide to Tolerance Analysis,"
       Microwaves, Vol. 17, No. 3, March 1978, pp. 54-60.

[4]   Gupta, K.C., *et al.*, *Microstrip Lines and Slotlines*, Dedham,
       Mass: Artech House, 1979.

5

Characterization of Discontinuities I

Coaxial Lines and Waveguides

5.1 INTRODUCTION

Sections of uniform transmission structures, discussed in Chapter 3, constitute the basic building blocks in microwave circuits. However, these sections of lines are invariably accompanied by discontinuities of one type or another. Typical discontinuities are: (i) step change in dimensions (introduced for a change in the impedance level), (ii) bends (right-angled and others), (iii) T-junctions, (iv) short-circuits and open-circuits, etc. The reactances associated with these discontinuities may be called parasitic as they are not introduced intentionally. In a good circuit design, efforts are made to reduce or compensate for these reactances. On the other hand, there are certain discontinuity reactances that are introduced purposefully in order to achieve certain circuit functions. Examples of these are: (i) an iris in a coaxial line, (ii) an inductive or a capacitive post in a waveguide, (iii) a gap in the central conductor of a stripline, etc.

A complete understanding of the design of microwave circuits requires characterizations of the discontinuities present in these circuits. Since the discontinuity dimensions are usually much smaller than the wavelength, the discontinuities are represented by lumped element equivalent circuits. In many cases when the longitudinal dimension of a discontinuity is very short, the equivalent circuit consists of a single shunt or series connected reactance located at the point of the discontinuity. However, when the discontinuity has a larger longitudinal extent, the equivalent circuit is usually a π- or a T- network.

A more complete characterization involves determination of the frequency dependent scattering matrix coefficients associated with the discontinuity. Such analyses are available for several types of discontinuities [1].

Discontinuities are associated with all types of transmission structures. Coaxial line and waveguide discontinuities have been treated in early microwave literature [2]. However, an accurate characterization of discontinuities is considered more essential for microwave integrated circuits. This is because of the fact that the microstrip circuits do not lend themselves to easy adjustments or tuning after the fabrication of the circuit is completed. If a provision is made for adjustments, the main advantages of compactness and reproduceability gained by the use of MIC technology are lost, at least partially. Consequently, microstrip and stripline discontinuities have been studied extensively in recent years [1]. These are discussed in Chapter 6.

For most of the uniform transmission structures used in microwave circuits, the fields are completely described by only a single propagating mode. In contrast, the complete description of the fields at the discontinuity region generally requires an infinite number of nonpropagating modes in addition to the propagating mode. However, the nonpropagating nature of the higher order modes restricts their field distribution to the immediate vicinity of the discontinuity. Hence, the discontinuity fields can be effectively regarded as localized.

The lumped equivalent circuits for various types of discontinuities in coaxial lines and rectangular waveguides are discussed in this chapter. The ranges of validity of the equivalent circuit models are mentioned. Approximate closed form expressions and typical values for the elements of the models are presented. The accuracies of these expressions, as compared with numerical results of rigorous theoretical analyses, are also included.

5.2 COAXIAL LINE DISCONTINUITIES

Various types of coaxial line discontinuities have been discussed in the literature [2]. These include: capacitive gaps, steps, capacitive windows, T-junctions, small elliptical and circular apertures, aperture coupling between two coaxial lines, bifurcation of a coaxial line, etc. The configurations and the equivalent circuits for some of the discontinuities are shown in Figure 5.1. The available results for these are summarized in the following subsection. Scattering matrix representations for these discontinuities can be obtained using the results in Appendix 2.1.

5.2.1 Capacitive Gaps in Coaxial Lines

A gap in the center conductor of a coaxial line, as shown in Figure 5.1(a), introduces mainly a series capacitance in the line. This type of discontinuity finds common use in microwave bandpass filters and DC blocks.

If the gap width is small compared to the wavelength, the problem can be treated electrostatically and the equivalent circuit of the gap discontinuity may be formulated as shown in Figure 5.1(a). For the purpose of analysis, the equivalent circuit may be written as shown in Figure 5.2. The series and shunt capacitances are determined by computing three capacitances: namely, total capacitances of a length of line (i) with a short circuit at plane AA, (ii) with an open circuit at the plane AA, (iii) and with no discontinuity. The section must be sufficiently long to ensure that an undisturbed field distribution is obtained at the end away from the discontinuity. This condition is fulfilled if the line length is equal to or greater than the diameter of the outer conductor. Numerical results for various gap widths and diameter ratios are given in Table 5.1 [3].

The values of capacitances C_1 and C_2, given in Table 5.1, can also be utilized to determine capacitances for the open-end and for the

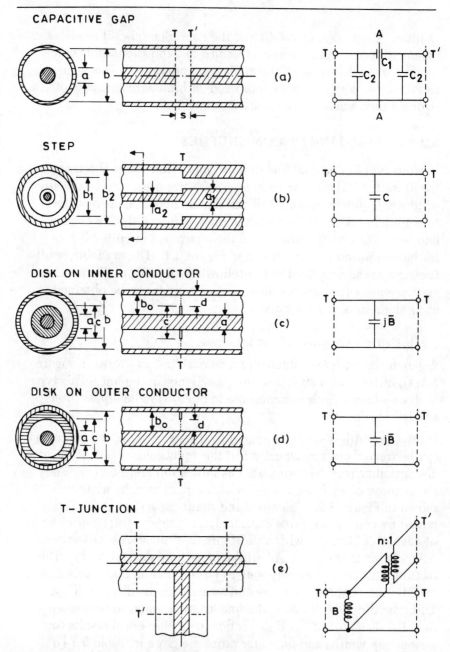

Figure 5.1   Discontinuities in coaxial line and their equivalent circuits.

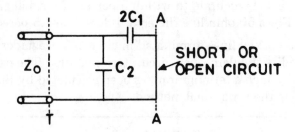

Figure 5.2 *Equivalent circuit for the evaluation of capacitive gap discontinuity.*

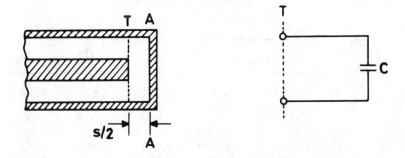

Figure 5.3 *Coaxial line with short circuit at plane AA and its equivalent circuit.*

configuration shown in Figure 5.3. The open-end capacitance is given by C_2, and the capacitance with the shorting plane at a distance s/2 from the inner conductor is C, given by $(2C_1 + C_2)$. A closed form expression for the capacitance C is written as [3]

$$C = \frac{\pi a^2 \epsilon_o \epsilon_r}{2s} + 2a \, \epsilon_o \epsilon_r \, \ell n \left(\frac{b - a}{s} \right)$$

(5.1)

Equation (5.1) is valid under the following restrictions

$$\lambda_o \gg (b - a) \gg s.$$

(5.2)

It is seen that (5.1) is accurate to within 5 percent for small gaps (s/a < 0.1). For a 50 ohm line the error is less than 1.5 percent.

Open-circuited coaxial lines terminated in circular waveguides below cut-off are used as standard open-circuit terminations. The capacitance offered by such a termination has been calculated by Bianco *et al.* [12] using the variational method.

TABLE 5.1

Series (C_1) and Shunt (C_2) Capacitances of Equivalent Circuit for Gaps in Coaxial Lines (pf/$2\pi b$, b in cm) [3].

Gap ratio (s/b)	Diameter ratio (b:a)					
	10:9		4:3		5:3	
	C_1	C_2	C_1	C_2	C_1	C_2
0.05	0.367	0.0354	0.275	0.0143	0.188	0.0082
0.075	0.238	0.0486	0.183	0.0206	0.127	0.0120
0.10	0.173	0.0598	0.136	0.0265	0.0960	0.0156
0.15	0.106	0.0767	0.0858	0.0366	0.0623	0.0221
0.20	0.0718	0.0890	0.0598	0.0450	0.0443	0.0277
0.25	0.0516	0.0985	0.0436	0.0520	0.0328	0.0327
0.30	0.0383	0.106	0.0328	0.0579	0.0249	0.0369

Gap ratio (s/b)	Diameter ratio (b:a)					
	2:1		3:1		5:1	
	C_1	C_2	C_1	C_2	C_1	C_2
0.05	0.138	0.0061	0.0702	0.0039	0.0316	0.0026
0.075	0.0946	0.0089	0.0498	0.0057	0.0231	0.0038
0.10	0.0719	0.0116	0.0384	0.0074	0.0183	0.0050
0.15	0.0474	0.0166	0.0259	0.0105	0.0127	0.0067
0.20	0.0340	0.0210	0.0188	0.0133	0.0093	0.0087
0.25	0.0254	0.0248	0.0143	0.0157	0.0070	0.0102
0.30	0.0194	0.0281	0.0109	0.0178	0.0054	0.0113

5.2.2 Steps in Coaxial Lines

The geometry of the abrupt steps in the inner and the outer conductor diameters occuring simultaneously is shown in Figure 5.1(b). This type of discontinuity is common in coaxial line circuits. The step discontinuity can be represented by a shunt capacitance at the plane of the step as shown in Figure 5.1(b). This capacitance does not vary appreciably with frequency if the cross-sectional dimensions of the line at the plane of discontinuity are small fractions of the wavelength.

Discontinuity capacitance can be computed using the mode matching technique for determining the difference in capacitances between that of the structure with the discontinuity, and that computed by adding the contributions of two single unperturbed lines with cross-sectional dimensions and lengths equal to the actual lines on each side of the step. The lines may be terminated by magnetic walls after a distance equal to one diameter on each side of the step. This technique has been used in [2] and [7].

Gogioso *et al.* [8] have used the variational method to calculate the discontinuity capacitance. The approximate value of shunt capacitance C is obtained by minimizing the following expression with respect to the coefficient e_o and e_1 [8]

$$
C = j \, \frac{2\pi\omega\mu_o\epsilon_o\epsilon_{rl}}{\ln(b_1/a_1)} \left\{ \frac{y_{11}}{\gamma_{11}^2} <E_\rho, \phi_1>^2 + \frac{y_{21}}{\gamma_{21}^2} <E_\rho, \psi_1>^2 \right.
$$

$$
\left. + \sum_{n=2}^{\infty} \frac{y_{1n}}{\gamma_{1n}^2} <E_\rho, \phi_n>^2 + \sum_{n=2}^{\infty} \frac{y_{2n}}{\gamma_{2n}^2} <E_\rho, \psi_n>^2 \right\}
$$

$$
\Big/ <E_\rho, \phi_o>^2 \tag{5.3}
$$

where y_{1n} and y_{2n} are the nth TM mode admittances in regions 1 and 2 respectively, γ_{1n} and γ_{2n} are the TM mode propagation constants, ϕ_n and ψ_n are the corresponding TM mode functions, and ϕ_o is the TEM mode function in region 1. E_ρ is the radial component of the electric field at the discontinuity and is approximated by

$$E_\rho = e_o \phi_o + e_1 \phi_1$$

under the assumption that the first TM mode cut-off frequency is related to the region 2. The coefficients e_o and e_1 have values between zero and unity. The brackets $<\;>$ denote inner products over the region between the inner and the outer conductors.

It has been reported that the results obtained by using the above approach are in very good agreement with the results in [7].

Step discontinuity in a coaxial line due to the change in radius of either conductors has also been analyzed. Closed form expressions for shunt susceptance due to the discontinuity are available in [2].

5.2.3 Capacitive Windows in Coaxial Lines

A capacitive window is formed by a decrease in the gap width between the inner and the outer conductors of a coaxial line. Gap width can be decreased by placing a circular metallic disk on either the inner conductor or the outer conductor.

TABLE 5.2

Values of Parameter p(b/a — 1) used in Modeling of Capacitive
Windows in Coaxial Lines

---

b/a	p(b/a — 1)	b/a	p(b/a — 1)
1.0	3.142	1.6	3.133
1.1	3.141	1.8	3.128
1.2	3.140	2.0	3.123
1.3	3.139	2.5	3.110
1.4	3.137	3.0	3.097
1.5	3.135	4.0	3.073

Disk on the Inner Conductor

The configuration of this discontinuity is shown in Figure 5.1(c). Its equivalent circuit can be represented by a shunt susceptance at the plane of the disk. A closed form expression for the normalized susceptance $\overline{B}$ is given below [2].

$$\overline{B} = \frac{2b_o}{\lambda_o} A_1 \left[4 \ln(\cosec \theta) + \frac{4A \cos^4 \theta}{1 + A \sin^4 \theta} \right.$$

$$\left. + \left(\frac{b_o}{\lambda_o}\right)^2 (1 - 3 \sin^2 \theta)^2 \cos^4 \theta + A_2 \right] \qquad (5.4)$$

where $2b_o = b - a$, $\theta = \pi d/(2b_o)$, $2d = b - c$, and

$$A = \left\{ 1 - \left[\frac{2b_o}{\lambda_o}\right]^2 \right\}^{-1/2} - 1,$$

$$A_1 = \frac{c}{2b_o} \ln\left(\frac{b}{a}\right) \left[\frac{2d}{c \ln(b/c)}\right]^2$$

$$A_2 = \frac{\pi^2}{\gamma_1 \sqrt{1 - \left(\frac{2b_o}{\lambda_{o1}}\right)^2}} \frac{2b_o/c}{\dfrac{J_o^2(p)}{J_o^2(pb/a)} - 1}$$

$$\cdot \left[\frac{J_o(p) N_o(pc/a) - N_o(p) J_o(pc/a)}{(b/c) - 1}\right]^2$$

$$- \left(\frac{\sin 2\theta}{\theta}\right)^2 \bigg/ \sqrt{1 - \left(\frac{2b_o}{\lambda_o}\right)^2} \ .$$

The constant γ_1 for the TM_{01} mode is defined by

$$p = \frac{\pi \gamma_1}{\dfrac{b}{a} - 1} \ .$$

The value of p is obtained from Table 5.2 for various values of b/a.

The expression for B/Y_o in (5.4) has been arrived at by means of a variational method, treating the first higher order TM mode in the exact manner and all other higher modes by parallel plane approximation. Equation (5.4) is valid for $\lambda_o \gamma_1 > (b - a)$ and is estimated to be correct to within a few percent for $b/a < 5$ and for λ_o not too close to the cut-off of the first higher order mode.

Disk on the Outer Conductor

The configuration for this discontinuity and its equivalent circuit are shown in Figure 5.1(d). Equation (5.4) applies to this configuration also, except that now $2d = c - a$ and the constants A_1 and A_2 are rewritten as [2],

$$
A_1 = \frac{a}{c} \, \frac{\ln \dfrac{b}{a}}{\dfrac{b}{a} - 1} \left[\frac{\dfrac{c}{a} - 1}{\ln \dfrac{c}{a}} \right]^2
$$

$$
A_2 = \frac{\pi^2}{\gamma_1 \sqrt{1 - \left(\dfrac{2b_o}{\gamma_1 \lambda_o}\right)^2}} \; \frac{2b_o/c}{1 - \dfrac{J_o^2 (q)}{J_o^2 (qa/b)}}
$$

$$
\cdot \left[\frac{J_o (q) N_o \left(\dfrac{qc}{b}\right) - N_o (q) J_o \left(q \, \dfrac{c}{b}\right)}{1 - (a/c)} \right]^2 - \left(\frac{\sin 2\theta}{\theta}\right)^2
$$

$$
\Bigg/ \sqrt{1 - \left(\frac{2b_o}{\lambda_o}\right)^2}
$$

with $q = \dfrac{\pi \gamma_1}{1 - \dfrac{a}{b}} = \dfrac{b}{a} \, p$.

The validity of the equivalent circuit susceptance is in the same range of parameters as that for the earlier case.

5.2.4 T-junction or Stub in Coaxial Lines

The configuration of a T-junction and its equivalent circuit are shown in Figure 5.1(e). The branch line can be viewed as a shunt circuit in parallel with the main line. Experimental results for a specific set of parameters are available for $\lambda_o = 10$ cm [6].

Other types of discontinuities in coaxial line which occur less frequently; e.g., aperture coupling between two coaxial lines, bifurcation of a coaxial line, small elliptical and circular apertures in the outer conductor, coaxial line radiating into semi-infinite space, coaxial line with infinite central conductor, etc. are discussed in [2].

5.3 RECTANGULAR WAVEGUIDE DISCONTINUITIES

The characterizations of various types of discontinuities in rectangular waveguides have been reported in the literature. These discontinuities include: posts, strips, diaphragms, windows, steps, bends, T-junctions, apertures, etc. The configurations and the equivalent circuits for an inductive post, a capacitive post, a triple inductive post, longitudinal and transverse strips, a thin dielectric post, inductive and capacitive diaphragms, a capacitive strip, apertures, H-plane and E-plane steps, H-plane and E-plane right-angled bends, H-plane and E-plane T-junctions, a thick circular window, and a thin elliptical aperture are shown in Figures 5.4 to 5.10. The equivalent circuit parameters for these discontinuities, given in this section, are quasi-static approximations. Scattering matrix representations corresponding to the equivalent circuits (except that for T-junction) can be obtained from Appendix 2.1.

The discontinuity reactances, given below, have been normalized with respect to the guide impedance, $2\eta b\lambda_g/(a\lambda_o)$. Discontinuity susceptances are also normalized similarly.

5.3.1 Posts in a Waveguide

Inductive Post: An inductive post is realized by using a metallic rod placed across the guide, parallel to the narrow walls and there-

fore parallel to the electric field of the TE_{10} mode. Configuration
for this discontinuity and its equivalent circuit are shown in Figure 5.4(a). Off-centered post, centered post, and resonant post
are discussed below. Closed form equations for the reactances have
been obtained by using the method of field matching and are given
below.

Off-centered Posts [9,2]: The reactances may be written as

$$\overline{X}_b = \frac{a}{\lambda_g}\left(\frac{\pi D}{a}\right)^2\left(1 - \frac{D^2}{16\,x_1^2}\right)^{-1}\sin^2\theta \tag{5.5}$$

$$\overline{X}_a = \overline{X}_o + \frac{\overline{X}_b}{2} - \left(\frac{a\pi^2 D^2}{8\lambda_g}\right)\mathrm{cosec}^2\,\theta$$

$$\cdot\left\{\frac{1}{\lambda_o^2} + \left(\frac{S\cot\theta - S'}{a}\right)^2\left(1 + \frac{D^2}{16\,x_1^2}\right)^{-1}\right\} \tag{5.6}$$

where

$$\overline{X}_o = \frac{aS}{2\lambda_g}\,\mathrm{cosec}^2\,\theta \tag{5.7}$$

$$S = \ln\left[\frac{4a}{\pi D}\sin\theta\right] - 2\sin^2\theta + 2\sum_{m=2}^{\infty}\frac{\sin^2(m\theta)}{m}$$

$$\cdot\left\{\left[1 - \left(\frac{2a}{m\lambda_o}\right)^2\right]^{-1/2} - 1\right\} \tag{5.8}$$

$$S' = \frac{1}{2}\cot\theta - \sin 2\theta + \sum_{2}^{\infty}\sin(2m\theta)\left\{\left[1 - \left(\frac{2a}{m\lambda_o}\right)^2\right]^{-1/2}$$

$$- 1\right\} \tag{5.9}$$

$$\frac{a}{\lambda_g} = \left[\left(\frac{2a}{\lambda_o}\right)^2 - 1\right]^{1/2} \tag{5.10}$$

and

$$\theta = \pi x_1 / a .\tag{5.11}$$

Dimensions x_1, D, and a are shown in Figure 5.4(a). For thin rods, i.e. $D \ll \lambda_o$, the equivalent circuit may be represented by the element X_a alone which may be further approximated by X_o. The equivalent circuit of Figure 5.4(a) is applicable in the wavelength range $a < \lambda_o < 2a$. Expressions (5.5) to (5.7) are accurate to within a few percent for $D/a < 0.10$ and $0.2 < x_1/a < 0.8$.

INDUCTIVE POST

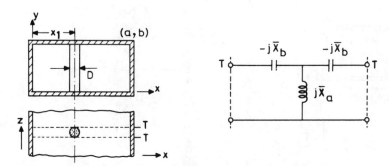

Figure 5.4(a)   *An inductive post in rectangular waveguide and its equivalent circuit.*

RESONANT POST

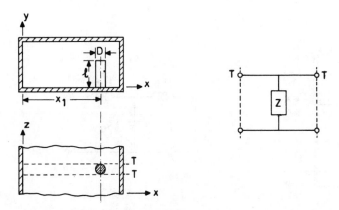

Figure 5.4(b)   *A resonant post in rectangular waveguide and its equivalent circuit.*

CAPACITIVE POST

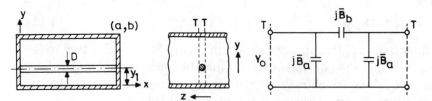

Figure 5.4(c)   A capacitive post in rectangular waveguide and
                 its equivalent circuit.

TRIPLE INDUCTIVE POST

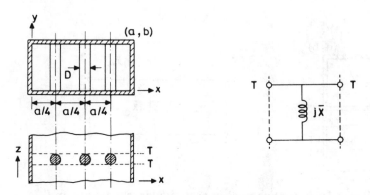

Figure 5.4(d)   A triple inductive post in rectangular waveguide
                 and its equivalent circuit.

DIELECTRIC POST

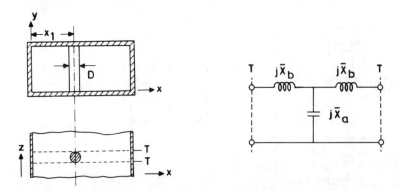

Figure 5.4(e)   A dielectric post in rectangular waveguide and its
                 equivalent circuit.

Numerical values of $\overline{X}_a$ and $\overline{X}_b$ have been plotted in [2] as a function of D/a, with x_1/a as a parameter, for three values of λ_o/a chosen as 1.4, 1.2, and 1.1. It is seen that $\overline{X}_a(\lambda_g/2a)\sin^2(\pi x_1/a)$ decreases with the increase in the value of x_1/a and D/a. For $x_1/a = 0.2$ and $\lambda_o/a = 1.2$, the value of $\overline{X}_o(\lambda_g/2a)\sin^2(\pi x_1/a)$ decreases from 0.96 to 0.38 as D/a is increased from 0.02 to 0.14. The reactance $\overline{X}_b\lambda_g/2a$ increases from 0.0 to 0.06 as D/a increases from 0.0 to 0.25 (for $x_1/a = 0.2$).

In some applications a flat metallic strip is used for an inductive post. An equivalent circuit for this case can be obtained by establishing the equivalence between strip width W and an equivalent rod diameter D. It has been found that this equivalence is given by W = 2D. A more accurate analysis for strips is given in the next section.

Centered Posts $(x_1 = a/2)$ [2]: The reactance expressions in this case are

$$\overline{X}_b = \frac{a}{\lambda g} \frac{(\pi D/a)^2}{1 + 2g^2\left(S' + \dfrac{3}{4}\right)} \tag{5.12}$$

$$\overline{X}_a = \frac{\overline{X}_b}{2} + \frac{a}{2\lambda_g}\left[S - g^2 - \frac{5}{8}g^4 - 2g^4 \left(S' - 2S\lambda_o^2 / \lambda_g^2\right)^2 \right] \tag{5.13}$$

where

$$S = \ln\frac{4a}{\pi D} - 2 + 2\sum_{m=3,5,\ldots}^{\infty} \frac{1}{m}\left\{\left[1 - \left(\frac{2a}{m\lambda_o}\right)^2\right]^{-1/2} - 1\right\} \tag{5.14a}$$

$$S' = \ln\frac{4a}{\pi D} - \frac{5}{2} + \frac{11}{3}\left(\frac{\lambda_o}{2a}\right)^2 - \left(\frac{\lambda_o}{a}\right)^2 \sum_{m=3,5,\ldots}^{\infty}$$

$$m\left\{\sqrt{1-\left(\frac{2a}{m\lambda_o}\right)^2} - 1 + 2\left(\frac{a}{m\lambda_o}\right)^2\right\} \qquad (5.14b)$$

and $g = \dfrac{\pi D}{2\lambda_o}$. $\qquad\qquad\qquad\qquad\qquad (5.15)$

Guide wavelength λ_g has been defined in (5.10). Equations (5.12) to (5.15) are accurate to within a few percent for $D/a < 0.2$. The equivalent circuit for the centered post, shown in Figure 5.4(a), is valid in the range $2a/3 < \lambda_o < 2a$.

Reactance $\overline{X}_b \lambda_g/(2a)$ increases from 0.0 to 0.24 as D/a is increased from 0.0 to 0.25 ($\lambda_o/a = 1.2$). The reactance $\overline{X}_a\lambda_g/(2a)$ decreases from 0.60 to 0.05 as D/a increases from 0.02 to 0.25, for $\lambda_o/a = 1.2$.

Resonant Posts [9]: Configuration for a resonant post in a wave-guide is shown in Figure 5.4(b). The variational method has been used for the analysis. It has been assumed that the current distribution is given by

$$I(y) = I_o \sin[k(\ell - x_1)] \qquad\qquad\qquad (5.16)$$

which is suitable for thin rods ($D \ll \lambda_o$) and when the post is close to the guide wall. In this case, the impedance presented by the post to the waveguide is obtained from

$$Z = \frac{\dfrac{2k\ell - \sin(2k\ell)}{2D\sqrt{\eta\sigma\pi/\lambda_o}} - j\left\{\sin(2k\ell)\ln\left(\dfrac{4x_1}{D}\right) - k(2x_1 - D/2)[2 + \cos(2k\ell)]\right\}}{\dfrac{2\pi x_1^2 \lambda_o\lambda_g}{a^3 b}[1 - \cos(k\ell)]^2}$$

$$(5.17)$$

where η is the wave impedance of the medium and σ is the post conductivity. It can be seen from the impedance expression that the

length required for resonance [Im(z) = 0] is approximately given by
by

$$\ell_t = \frac{\lambda_o}{4} - \frac{x_1 - 0.25\,D}{\ln(4x_1/D)} \quad . \tag{5.18}$$

The above formulas are valid only when the end-capacitance of the post can be neglected; i.e. if $\omega C Z_o$ given by

$$\omega C Z_o = \frac{\pi D^2}{4}\;\frac{\ln(4x_1/D)}{\lambda_o(b-\ell)}$$

is less than about 0.05. However, the end-capacitance can be corrected for by a decrease in the tuning length ℓ_t which may now be written as

$$\ell_t \cong \frac{\lambda_o}{4} - \frac{x_1 - D/4}{\ln(4x_1/D)} - \frac{D^2\,\ln(4x_1/D)}{8(b-\ell)} \tag{5.19}$$

The impedance of the post at resonance, Z_r, reduces to the real term of (5.17). The corresponding insertion loss is given by 20 log [1 + (1/2Z_r)] db.

For a resonant post near the guide center, the reactance expressions are not available in a closed form. However, Marcuvitz [2] has reported experimental results for $\overline{X}_a$ and $\overline{X}_b$ for the following sets of parameters: a = 0.90 in; b = 0.40 in; λ_o = 3.4, 3.2, and 3.0 cm; D = 1/16, 1/8, and 1/4 in; and ℓ/b = 0.25 to 1.0. The reactance values may also be obtained by using the equivalence between the rod and the strip given by D_{eq} = W/2. Expressions for a narrow transverse strip in a waveguide are given in Section 5.3.2. Discontinuity reactances due to the posts having elliptical cross sections have also been analyzed. The results are given in [2].

Capacitive Posts: A capacitive post in a rectangular waveguide can be obtained by placing a metallic rod with its axis perpendicular to the electric field as shown in Figure 5.4(c). We shall assume that the rod is thin (D ≪ b). Expressions for the equivalent circuit elements have been derived by the variational method and are given below [2]

$$\overline{B}_a = \frac{Q\,P^2}{A_2} \tag{5.20}$$

$$\overline{B}_b = \frac{A_1}{Q\,P^2} - \frac{Q\,P^2}{2A_2} \tag{5.21}$$

where $\quad Q = \dfrac{2b}{\lambda_g}\ , \quad P = \dfrac{\pi D}{2b}$

$$A_1 = 1 + \frac{1}{2}\,P^2 Q^2 \left(\ell n\,\frac{\operatorname{cosec}\theta}{2P} + \frac{3}{4} \right)$$

$$+ P^2 Q^2 \sum_{m=1}^{\infty} \cos^2 m\theta \left[\frac{1}{\sqrt{m^2 - Q^2}} - \frac{1}{m} \right] \tag{5.22}$$

$$A_2 = 1 + \frac{1}{2}\,P^2 Q^2 \left[\frac{11}{4} - \ell n\,\frac{\operatorname{cosec}\theta}{2P} \right] + \frac{1}{4}\,P^2 \left(\operatorname{cosec}^2\theta \right.$$

$$\left. - \frac{1}{3} \right) - 2P^2 \sum_{m=1}^{\infty} \cos^2 m\theta \left[m - \frac{Q^2}{2m} - \sqrt{m^2 - Q^2} \right]$$

$$\tag{5.23}$$

with $\theta = \pi y_1 /b.$ \hfill (5.24)

Equations (5.20) and (5.21) are accurate to within a few percent in the range $2b < \lambda_g$, $D/b < 0.1$, and $0.2 < y_1/b < 0.8$. Expressions for the centered post are available in [9] also.

For $2b/\lambda_g = 0.6$, susceptance $\overline{B}_a \lambda_g /2b$ increases from 0.0 to 0.195, and $\overline{B}_b \lambda_g /2b$ increases from 0.0 to 0.22 as D/b is increased from 0.0 to 0.30.

Triple Inductive Posts [9]: The configuration for a triple inductive post is shown in Figure 5.4(d). The presence of two posts on either side of the central one suppresses the higher order even modes generated due to the central post. The expression for the normalized reactance is given as

$$\overline{X} = \frac{a}{2\lambda_g} \sum_{m=3,5,\ldots}^{\infty} \left\{ \left(1 + \sqrt{2} \cos \frac{m\pi}{4} \right) \cos \left(\frac{m\pi D}{2a} \right) \right.$$

$$\left. \left[m^2 - \left(\frac{2a}{\lambda_o} \right)^2 \right]^{-1/2} \right\} . \tag{5.25}$$

The summation over odd values of m indicates that only odd modes contribute to the discontinuity reactance.

Dielectric Posts: The configuration and the equivalent circuit for a dielectric post in a rectangular waveguide are shown in Figure 5.4(e). Expressions for the normalized reactances are given as follows [2]

$$\overline{X}_b = \frac{2a}{\lambda_g} \left(\frac{\pi D}{a} \right)^2 \frac{\sin^2\theta}{P} \tag{5.26}$$

$$-\overline{X}_a = \frac{1}{2} \overline{X}_b + \frac{a}{2\lambda_g} \csc^2\theta \left[Q - S + \frac{\alpha^2}{4} \right] \tag{5.27}$$

where

$$P = \frac{\alpha^2 J_1(\beta)}{J_1(\alpha)} \frac{1}{\alpha J_o(\alpha) J_1(\beta) - \beta J_o(\beta) J_1(\alpha)} - 2 \tag{5.28}$$

$$Q = \frac{J_o(\beta)}{J_o(\alpha)} \frac{1}{\beta J_o(\alpha) J_1(\beta) - \alpha J_o(\beta) J_1(\alpha)} \tag{5.29}$$

$$\alpha = \frac{\pi D}{\lambda_o} , \quad \beta = \frac{\pi D}{\lambda_o} \sqrt{\epsilon_r} , \text{ and } \theta = \pi x_1 /a .$$

The quantity S has been defined in (5.8). The equivalent circuit of Figure 5.4(e) is valid in the wavelength range $a < \lambda_o < 2a$, and for the centered cylinder ($x_1 = a/2$) the range of validity is $2a/3 < \lambda_o < 2a$. Equations (5.26) to (5.29) are accurate to a few percent in the range $D < 0.15a$ and $0.2 < x_1/a < 0.8$ provided that neither $\overline{X}_a$ nor $\overline{X}_b$ are too close to resonance. The resonances imply complete transmission and occur for large values of ϵ_r.

For thin dielectric posts or for low values of ϵ_r such that $\pi D \sqrt{\epsilon_r} \ll \lambda_o$, the equivalent circuit reduces to a simple shunt element and the expression for this shunt reactance is given by

$$-\overline{X} \approx \frac{a}{\lambda_g (\epsilon_r - 1)} \left(\frac{\lambda_o}{\pi D}\right)^2 \operatorname{cosec}^2\theta . \qquad (5.30)$$

The corresponding shunt susceptance is obtained as

$$\overline{B} \approx \frac{\lambda_g (\epsilon_r - 1)}{a} \left(\frac{\pi D}{\lambda_o}\right)^2 \sin^2\theta . \qquad (5.31)$$

The value of reactance $\overline{X}_a$ decreases with the increase in the value of D/a or ϵ_r, and passes through a resonance. Similarly, $\overline{X}_b$ also passes through a resonance. For $D/a = 0.10$ and $\epsilon_r = 4$, the value of $\overline{X}_a$ is 3.12 and $\overline{X}_b = 0.00093$.

LONGITUDINAL STRIP

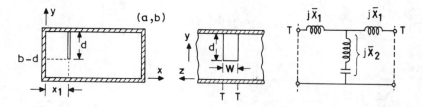

Figure 5.5(a)   A longitudinal reactive strip in rectangular wave-guide and its equivalent circuit.

NARROW TRANSVERSE STRIP

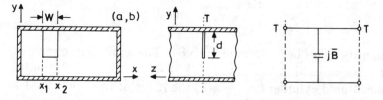

Figure 5.5(b)   A narrow transverse reactive strip in rectangular wave-guide and its equivalent circuit.

5.3.2 Strips in Waveguides

Longitudinal Strips: A thin, perfectly conducting strip in a wave-guide (Figure 5.5(a)) finds applications in E-plane mounted planar circuits, fin-line structures, filters and tuning elements. The expressions for various elements of the equivalent circuit are given below. These have been obtained using the variational method [10].

Normalized reactances $\overline{X}_1$ and $\overline{X}_2$ may be written as [10]

$$\overline{X}_1 = -\overline{X}_2 \pm \frac{Q}{P - 1} \tag{5.32}$$

$$\overline{X}_2 = \pm \left\{ P \left[1 + \left(\frac{Q}{P - 1} \right)^2 \right] \right\}^{1/2} \tag{5.33}$$

where

$$P = \frac{\overline{G}}{\overline{G}^2 + \overline{B}^2} \tag{5.34}$$

$$Q = \frac{-\overline{B}}{\overline{G}^2 + \overline{B}^2} \tag{5.35}$$

where

$$\overline{Y} = \overline{G} + j\overline{B}$$

$$= \frac{1 - \rho}{1 + \rho} = \frac{2 + L(H + A)}{2 + L(H - A)} \tag{5.36}$$

$$A = \frac{1}{\gamma_{10}} \left[1 - e^{-\gamma_{10}W} \right] \tag{5.37}$$

$$H = \frac{2W + \frac{2}{\gamma_{10}} \left[e^{-\gamma_{10}W} - 1 \right]}{1 - e^{-\gamma_{10}W}} \tag{5.38}$$

and ρ is the reflection coefficient. Values of L are different in non-touching strip and touching strip cases. These are given below.

(i) Nontouching Strips (d < b)

In this case the constant L is given by

$$L = \frac{\left(\dfrac{2}{\gamma_{10}}\right)^2 (1 - \cos k_o d)^2 \left[1 - e^{-\gamma_{10}W}\right] \sin^2\theta}{\displaystyle\sum_{n=2}^{\infty} C_n + \sum_{n=1}^{\infty}\sum_{m=1}^{\infty} B_{nm}} \tag{5.39}$$

where

$$C_n = \frac{2(1 - \cos k_o d)^2}{\gamma_{no}^2}\left\{W + \frac{1}{\gamma_{no}}\left[e^{-\gamma_{no}W} - 1\right]\right\}$$
$$\cdot \sin^2(n\theta) \tag{5.40}$$

$$B_{nm} = \frac{4\sin^2(n\theta)}{\gamma_{nm}^2}\left\{W + \frac{1}{\gamma_{nm}}\left[e^{-\gamma_{nm}W} - 1\right]\right\}$$
$$\cdot \left[\frac{k_o^2\left\{\cos\left[\dfrac{m\pi}{b}(b-d)\right] - \cos(m\pi + k_o d)\right\}^2}{k_o^2 - \left(\dfrac{m\pi}{b}\right)^2}\right] \tag{5.41}$$

$$\gamma_{nm} = \left(\frac{m^2\pi^2}{b^2} + \frac{n^2\pi^2}{a^2} - k_o^2\right)^{1/2} \tag{5.42}$$

and $k_o = 2\pi/\lambda_o, \quad \theta = \pi x_1/a.$ (5.43)

(ii) Touching Strips (d = b)

In this case the constant L becomes

$$L = \frac{\dfrac{2}{\gamma_{10}^2}\left[1 - e^{-\gamma_{10}W}\right]\sin^2\theta}{\displaystyle\sum_{n=2}^{\infty} D_n} \tag{5.44}$$

where

$$D_n = \frac{2}{\gamma_{no}^2} \left\{ W + \frac{e^{-\gamma_{no}W} - 1}{\gamma_{no}} \right\} \sin^2(n\theta) . \qquad (5.45)$$

Substitution for P and Q in (5.32) and (5.33) gives four sets of values for $\overline{X}_1$ and $\overline{X}_2$. Two sets are rejected, since they give the conjugate value $\overline{Y}^*$. Another set is rejected on the basis that since the equivalent circuit is lossless its elements should satisfy the Foster reactance theorem which requires $d\overline{X}/d\omega > 0$.

Numerical values of $\overline{X}_1$ and $\overline{X}_2$ as a function of strip width W with λ_o as a parameter are available for d = 0.3 inch [10]. It is seen that $\overline{X}_2$ decreases with the increase in the values of W and λ_o. The behavior of $\overline{X}_1$ is opposite to that of $\overline{X}_2$. For an X-band waveguide with λ_o = 2.5 cm and x_1 = a/2, $\overline{X}_2$ decreases from 1.4 to 0.6 as W is increased from 0.0 to 0.20 inch. For these sets of parameters, $\overline{X}_1$ increases from 0.0 to 0.60. In the case of a centered non-touching strip, the corresponding values for $\overline{X}_2$ and $\overline{X}_1$ vary from 0.70 to 0.05 and from 0.0 to 0.60, respectively. The theoretical results for input susceptance are in very close agreement with the experimental values for a strip of width 0.07 inch mounted in an X-band waveguide. The measurements have been reported in the frequency range 8 GHz to 12 GHz [10].

In the characterization discussed above, the strip is assumed to be infinitesimally thin and narrow (W $\ll \lambda_g$). The current distribution in the strip is taken to be

$$J_y(y) = \sin[k_o(y - b + d)] . \qquad (5.46a)$$

A more accurate assumption should have been

$$J_y(y, z) = \sin[k_o(y - b + d)] \, e^{-\gamma_{10}z} . \qquad (5.46b)$$

However, neglecting the z-variation does not make significant difference at X-band frequencies for W $\leqslant$ 0.20 inch (i.e. W/$\lambda_o \leqslant$ 0.2).

Narrow Transverse Strips: The configuration shown in Figure 5.5(b) has been analyzed using the variational method by Chang and Khan [11]. It has been assumed that the current distribution on the strip is given by

$$J_y(y) = \sin\left(\frac{y - b + d}{2d} \pi\right) . \qquad (5.47)$$

Normalized susceptance is given by

$$
j\overline{B} = \cfrac{\cfrac{2}{\gamma_{10}}\left[\cos\left(\dfrac{\pi x_1}{a}\right) - \cos\left(\dfrac{\pi x_2}{a}\right)\right]^2}{A + \displaystyle\sum_{m=1}^{\infty}\left\{\left[\dfrac{B_m\, b^4}{(4m^2 d^2 - b^2)^2}\right]\cos^2\left[\dfrac{m\pi(b-d)}{b}\right]\right\}}
$$

(5.48)

where

$$
A = \sum_{n=2}^{\infty}\left\{\dfrac{1}{n^2 \gamma_{no}}\left[\cos\left(\dfrac{n\pi x_1}{a}\right) - \cos\left(\dfrac{n\pi x_2}{a}\right)\right]^2\right\}
$$

(5.49)

$$
B_m = \sum_{n=1}^{\infty}\left\{\dfrac{2(k_o^2 - m^2\pi^2/b^2)}{k_o^2\,\gamma_{nm}\,n^2}\left[\cos\left(\dfrac{n\pi x_1}{a}\right) - \cos\left(\dfrac{n\pi x_2}{a}\right)\right]^2\right\}
$$

(5.50)

and γ_{nm} is given by (5.42). Equation (5.48) is applicable at frequencies below cut-off also. It has been found that the theoretical results agree with measurements at X-band frequency for $W < 0.156$ inch and $d < 0.307$ inch [11]. It is seen that the shunt susceptance increases with the strip depth d and the strip width W, and goes through resonance as the frequency or the depth d is increased. For a centered strip in an X-band waveguide with d = 0.02 inch, and at f = 11 GHz the value of $\overline{B}$ increases from 0.50 to 1.50 as W is increased from 0.0 to 0.30 inches.

5.3.3 Diaphragms or Window in Waveguides [9]

Inductive Diaphragms or Window: Figure 5.6(a) shows a rectangular waveguide with diaphragm inserts of lengths d_1 and $(a - d_2)$ so that the window formed is parallel to the electric field and has a width d given by

$$d = d_2 - d_1 \; . \tag{5.51}$$

The location of the window is given by

$$x_o = \frac{d_1 + d_2}{2} \; . \tag{5.52}$$

INDUCTIVE DIAPHRAGM OR WINDOW

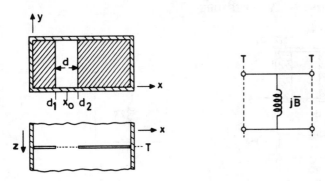

Figure 5.6(a)   An inductive diaphragm or window in rectangular
waveguide and its equivalent circuit.

CAPACITIVE DIAPHRAGM OR WINDOW

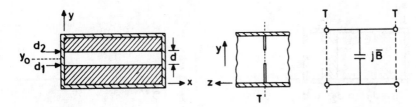

Figure 5.6(b)   A capacitive diaphragm or window in rectangular
waveguide and its equivalent circuit.

CAPACITIVE STRIP

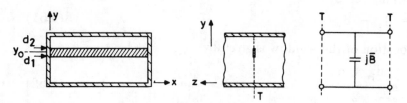

Figure 5.6(c)   A capacitive strip in rectangular waveguide and its equivalent circuit.

DOUBLE SYMMETRICAL APERTURE

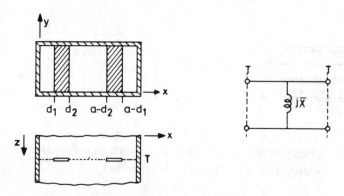

Figure 5.6(d)   A double symmetrical aperture formed by a combination of diaphragms and strips in rectangular waveguide and its equivalent circuit.

SYMMETRICAL DOUBLE INDUCTIVE STRIP

Figure 5.6(e)   A double symmetrical inductive strip in rectangular waveguide and its equivalent circuit.

The field matching technique has been used to determine the equivalent circuit [9]. Normalized susceptance $\overline{B}$ is given by

$$\overline{B} = \frac{-\lambda_g}{a}\left\{\frac{1}{s^2} - 1 - \frac{1}{1 - s^4\delta_2}\left[8c^2\delta_2 + 3\delta_3\right.\right.$$
$$\cdot \left.\left.\frac{\left[4c^2 + s^2 - 1 + s^4\delta_2(4c^2 + 1 - s^2)\right]^2}{(1 - s^4\delta_2)(1 - s^6\delta_3) - 24c^2\delta_3 s^4}\right]\right\} \quad (5.53)$$

with

$$\delta_m = 1 - \left[1 - \left(\frac{2a}{m\lambda_o}\right)^2\right]^{1/2} \quad (5.54)$$

$$c = \cos\left(\frac{\pi x_o}{a}\right)\cos\left(\frac{\pi d}{2a}\right) \quad (5.55)$$

and

$$s = \sin\left(\frac{\pi x_o}{a}\right)\sin\left(\frac{\pi d}{2a}\right). \quad (5.56)$$

In the case of a symmetrical diaphragm ($x_o = a/2$), c approaches zero and $s = \sin(\pi d/2a)$. The resultant equation for $\overline{B}$ becomes

$$\overline{B} = \frac{-\lambda_g}{a}\left\{\frac{1}{s^2} - 1 - \frac{(1 - s^2)^2}{1 - \delta_3 s^6}\left[3\delta_3 + 5\delta_5\right.\right.$$
$$\cdot \left.\left.\frac{\left[2s^2 - 1 + \delta_3 s^6(s^2 - 2)\right]^2}{(1 - \delta_3 s^6)(1 - \delta_5 s^{10}) - 15s^6\delta_5(1 - s^2)^2}\right]\right\} \quad (5.57)$$

An approximate form is obtained by putting $\delta_5 = 0$ in the above equation. Thus, $\overline{B}$ is written as

$$\overline{B} = \frac{-\lambda_g}{a}\left\{\frac{1}{s^2} - 1 - 3\delta_3\frac{(1 - s^2)^2}{1 - \delta_3 s^6}\right\}. \quad (5.58)$$

The quantity $\overline{B}\,a/\lambda_g$ has been plotted in [2] for d/a ranging from
0.5 to 1 and a/λ_o lying between 0.5 and 1.3. For these sets of parameters it varies from 0.96 to 0. The effect of finite thickness of the
window has also been considered in [2].

Capacitive Diaphragms or Window: A capacitive window is obtained by placing diaphragms with edges perpendicular to the electric field. It is shown in Figure 5.6(b) for an asymmetrical diaphragm.
The window parameters are defined in terms of diaphragm parameters as follows

$$d = d_2 - d_1 \tag{5.59}$$

and

$$y_o = \frac{d_1 + d_2}{2}. \tag{5.60}$$

The normalized susceptance $\overline{B}$ for the equivalent circuit can be obtained from the following equations [9]

$$\overline{B} = \frac{4b}{\lambda_g}\left\{ -\ln s + \frac{2c^2\delta_1}{1 + \delta_1 s^2} + \frac{\delta_2\left[\delta_1 s^2(2c^2 + 1 - s^2) + 1 - s^2 - 2c^2\right]^2}{(1 + \delta_1 s^2)^2 (1 + \delta_2 s^4) + 8\delta_2 s^2 c^2(1 + \delta_1 s^2)} \right\} \tag{5.61}$$

with

$$c = \cos\left(\frac{\pi y_o}{b}\right)\cos\left(\frac{\pi d}{2b}\right) \tag{5.62}$$

$$s = \sin\left(\frac{\pi y_o}{b}\right)\sin\left(\frac{\pi d}{2b}\right). \tag{5.63}$$

For the symmetrical window (y_o = b/2), $\overline{B}$ is given by

$$\overline{B} = \frac{2b}{\lambda_g} \left\{ -2 \ln s + \frac{2c^4 \delta_2}{1 + \delta_2 s^4} \right.$$

$$\left. + \frac{\delta_4 \left[\delta_2 s^4 (2c^4 + 1 - s^4) + 1 - s^4 - 2c^4 \right]^2}{(1 + \delta_2 s^4)^2 (1 + \delta_4 s^8) + 8\delta_4 s^4 c^4 (1 + \delta_2 s^4)} \right\}$$

$$(5.64)$$

with s and c now redefined as

$$s = \sin\left(\frac{\pi d}{2b}\right) \qquad (5.65)$$

$$c = \cos\left(\frac{\pi d}{2b}\right) \qquad (5.66)$$

and

$$\delta_n = \frac{1}{\sqrt{1 - \left(\dfrac{b}{n\lambda_g}\right)^2}} - 1 \qquad (5.67)$$

The equivalent circuit shown in Figure 5.6(b) is valid in the range $b < \lambda_g/2$ for the asymmetrical case, and $b < \lambda_g$ for the symmetrical case. The error in (5.61) increases to less than 5 percent at the lower end of the wavelength range. Equation (5.64) has an error less than 5 percent for $b < \lambda_g$ and 1 percent for $b < \lambda_g/2$. The quantity $\overline{B} \lambda_g / b$ can be obtained from graphs in [2] for d/b varying between 0 and 1, and b/λ_g lying between 0 and 1. It varies between 0.6 and 0 for d/b between 0.15 and 1.0.

The effect of finite thickness for the symmetrical window has also been considered in [2]. In this case the equivalent circuit is a π-network.

Capacitive Strips [9]: A capacitive strip is a Babinet's equivalent of a capacitive window. The configuration of a capacitive strip is shown in Figure 5.6(c).

Expression for $\overline{B}$ in the case of a symmetrical capacitive strip is the same as that for a symmetrical diaphragm given in (5.64). It may be noted that 'd' in this formula is still the total aperture and not the width of the strip, i.e., $d = d_1 + (b - d_2)$.

For an unsymmetrical capacitive strip, we have

$$\overline{B} = \frac{4b}{\lambda_g} \ln\left[\frac{\Theta(\beta)}{(1 + s)\Theta(0)}\right] \tag{5.68}$$

where $\Theta(\beta)$ is the Jacobi theta function. The quantity $\Theta(\beta)/\Theta(0)$ can be expressed as

$$\frac{\Theta(\beta)}{\Theta(0)} = \left[\frac{\pi}{2k'K(k)}\right]^{1/2}\left\{1 + 2\sum_{n=1}^{\infty}\left[(-1)^n (q)^{n^2}\right.\right.$$
$$\left.\left. \cdot \cos\frac{n\pi\beta}{K(k)}\right]\right\}.$$

β is obtained from $cn(\beta) = c/(1 + s)$, where $cn(\cdot)$ represents the Jacobi elliptic function. The modulus of the complete elliptic integrals K and K' is,

$$k = \sqrt{\frac{4s}{(1 + s)^2 - c^2}} \quad , \quad k' = \sqrt{1 - k^2}$$

and $q = \exp[-\pi K'(k) / K(k)]$. The parameters c and s have been defined by (5.62) and (5.63), respectively.

Combination of Diaphragms and Strips [9]: Figure 5.6(d) shows a combination of a symmetric inductive diaphragm and a central inductive strip. It can also be called a double symmetrical aperture. The strip reactance $\overline{X}$ is given by

$$\overline{X} = \frac{a}{\lambda_g}\left\{-1 + \frac{K(k)}{2\sin^2\left(\frac{\pi d_2}{a}\right)E(k) + \left[\cos^2\left(\frac{\pi d_2}{a}\right) - \sin^2\left(\frac{\pi d_1}{a}\right)\right]K(k)}\right\}$$

$$\tag{5.69}$$

where E and K are complete elliptic integrals with modulus k given by

$$k = \left[1 - \sin^2\left(\frac{\pi d_1}{a}\right) \text{cosec}^2\left(\frac{\pi d_2}{a}\right) \right]^{1/2} .$$

For $d_1 = 0$, (5.69) reduces to that for a symmetrical inductive diaphragm, and for $d_2 = a/2$, it reduces to that for a single central strip.

Symmetrical Double Inductive Strip: The configuration is shown in Figure 5.6(e) and the reactance expression is obtained as [9]

$$\overline{X} = \frac{a}{\lambda_g} \left\{ -1 + \frac{K(k)}{2\sin^2\left(\frac{\pi d_2}{a}\right) E(k) - \left[\sin^2\left(\frac{\pi d_2}{a}\right) - \sin^2\left(\frac{\pi d_1}{a}\right) \right] K(k)} \right\}$$

(5.70)

with modulus k for E and K given by

$$k = \sin(\pi d_1/a)\,\text{cosec}(\pi d_2/a).$$

For $d_1 = 0$, (5.70) reduces to that for a symmetrical inductive diaphragm, as shown in Figure 5.6(a).

5.3.4 Steps in Waveguides

H-plane Step or Change in the Width of a Waveguide [2]: The geometry of a symmetrical change in the width of a rectangular waveguide is shown in Figure 5.7(a). This discontinuity results from the junction of two rectangular guides and is known as a step in the H-plane. It is assumed in the analysis that each guide propagates only the dominant mode. All higher order modes are cut-off. The expression for the normalized junction reactance for the discontinuity, referred to planes T and T' for the larger guide and the smaller guide, respectively, is obtained as

$$\frac{X}{Z_o} = p\, X_{11} \frac{1 + (q\, X_o)^2}{1 + q^2\, X_o\, X_{22}}$$

(5.71)

H-PLANE STEP (SYMMETRICAL)

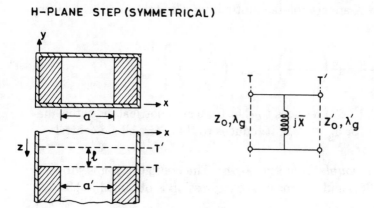

Figure 5.7(a)   A symmetrical H-plane step in rectangular waveguide and its equivalent circuit.

H-PLANE STEP (ASYMMETRICAL)

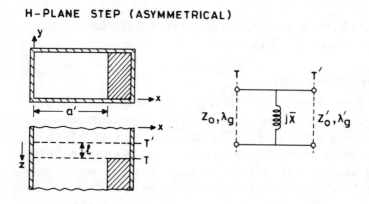

Figure 5.7(b)   An asymmetrical H-plane step in rectangular waveguide and its equivalent circuit.

E-PLANE STEP (SYMMETRICAL)

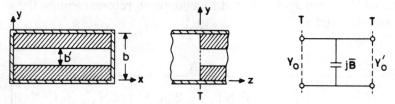

Figure 5.7(c)   A symmetrical E-plane step in rectangular waveguide and its equivalent circuit.

E-PLANE STEP (ASYMMETRICAL)

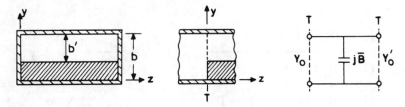

Figure 5.7(d)   An asymmetrical E-plane step in rectangular wave-guide and its equivalent circuit.

$$\frac{Z_o{'}}{Z_o} = \frac{\lambda_g{'}}{\lambda_g} \; \frac{X_{11}}{\alpha \, (X_{22} - X_o)} \; [1 + (q\,X_o)^2] \qquad (5.72)$$

$$\frac{\ell}{a} = \frac{\alpha \, X_o}{\pi} \qquad\qquad (5.73)$$

where $p = 2a/\lambda_g$, $q = 2a'/\lambda_g{'}$, and $\alpha = a'/a$.

The constants X_{11}, X_{22}, and X_{12} are the impedance matrix elements of the T-network referred to a common reference plane T and are obtained as

$$X_{11} = \frac{A}{1 - \dfrac{1}{4A}\left[(A+1)^2 N_{11} + 2(A+1)CN_{12} + C^2 N_{22}\right]}$$

$$X_{22} = \frac{A'}{1 - \dfrac{1}{4A'}\left[(A'+1)^2 N_{22} + 2(A'+1)CN_{12} + C^2 N_{11}\right]}$$

$$X_o = X_{22} - \frac{X_{12}^2}{X_{11}} \approx A' - \frac{C^2}{A} ,$$

where

$$A = \frac{(1-R_1)(1-R_2)+T^2}{(1+R_1)(1-R_2)-T^2} , \qquad R_1 = \left(\frac{1-\alpha}{1+\alpha}\right)^\alpha ,$$

$$A' = \frac{(1+R_1)(1+R_2)+T^2}{(1+R_1)(1-R_2)-T^2} , \qquad R_2 = \left(\frac{1-\alpha}{1+\alpha}\right)^{1/\alpha} ,$$

$$C = \frac{2T}{(1+R_1)(1-R_2)-T^2} , \qquad T = \frac{4\alpha}{\alpha'^2}\sqrt{R_1 R_2}$$

$$N_{11} = 9\theta \left\{ 1 - \frac{16R_1}{\pi\alpha'^2}[E(\alpha)-\alpha'^2 K(\alpha)][E(\alpha')-\alpha^2 K(\alpha')] \right.$$

$$\left. - R_1{}^2 - \alpha^2 T^2 \right\} + \frac{12R_1\alpha^2}{\alpha'^4}[\alpha^2 R_1{}^3 (Q-\theta)$$

$$+ 4R_2{}^3 (Q'-\theta')]$$

$$N_{22} = 9\,\theta\alpha^2 \left\{ 1 + \frac{16R_2}{\pi\alpha'^2} \; E(\alpha)\,[K(\alpha') - E(\alpha')] - R_2{}^2 \right.$$

$$\left. - T^2/\alpha^2 \right\} + \frac{12R_2}{\alpha'^4} \; [4\alpha^2 R_1{}^3\,(Q - \theta) + R_2{}^3(Q' - \theta')]$$

$$N_{12} = 9\,\theta T \left\{ \alpha'^2 - \frac{4E(\alpha)}{\pi} \; [E(\alpha') - \alpha^2 K(\alpha')] + R_1 \right.$$

$$\left. + \alpha^2 R_2 \right\} + \frac{24\alpha}{\alpha'^4} \; \sqrt{R_1 R_2} \; [\alpha^2 R_1{}^3\,(Q - \theta) + R_2{}^3\,(Q' - \theta')]$$

$$Q = 1 - \sqrt{1 - 2\theta}\,, \qquad\qquad Q' = 1 - \sqrt{1 - 2\theta'}$$

$$2\theta = \left(\frac{2a}{3\lambda_o}\right)^2, \qquad\qquad 2\theta' = \left(\frac{2a'}{3\lambda_o}\right)^2$$

and

$$\alpha' = \sqrt{1 - \alpha^2}\,.$$

The functions $K(\alpha)$ and $E(\alpha)$ are complete elliptic integrals of the first and second kinds, respectively.

The equivalent circuit parameter values obtained from the above equations are valid in the range $0.5 < a/\lambda_o < 1.5$ and $2a' > \lambda_o$. The accuracy is better than 1 percent over most of the range and may worsen to within 5 percent at the limit $a/\lambda_o = 1.5$.

Asymmetrical Case: Asymmetrical change in the width of a waveguide is shown in Figure 5.7(b). For this configuration, the expressions for Z_o'/Z_o, X/Z_o, and ℓ/a obtained earlier for the symmetric case hold, but the constants defined below are different. These symbols are redefined as

$$R_1 = \frac{1 + 3\alpha^2}{1 - \alpha^2} \; G^2\,, \qquad R_2 = \frac{3 + \alpha^2}{1 - \alpha^2} \; H^2\,,$$

$$T = \left(\frac{4\alpha}{\alpha'^2}\right)^2 GH$$

$$N_{11} = 4\theta \left[1 - \frac{8\alpha\alpha'^2}{1 + 3\alpha^2} R_1 \ln \frac{1-\alpha}{1+\alpha} - \frac{16\alpha^2}{1+3\alpha^2} R_1 \right.$$

$$\left. - R_1{}^2 - \alpha^2 T^2 \right] + 2 \left(\frac{32}{\alpha'^4} \alpha^2 G \right)^2 [\alpha^4 G^4 (Q - \theta)$$

$$/9 + H^4(Q' - \theta')]$$

$$N_{22} = 4\theta \left[\alpha^2 - \frac{8\alpha\alpha'^2}{3 + \alpha^2} R_2 \ln \frac{1-\alpha}{1+\alpha} + \frac{16\alpha^2}{1+3\alpha^2} R_2 \right.$$

$$\left. - \alpha^2 R_2{}^2 - T^2 \right] + 2 \left(\frac{32}{\alpha'^4} H \right)^2 [\alpha^4 G^4 (Q - \theta)$$

$$+ H^4(Q' - \theta') / 9]$$

$$N_{12} = 4\theta \left[\frac{\alpha'^4}{2\alpha} \ln \frac{1-\alpha}{1+\alpha} + R_1 - \alpha^2 R_2 \right] T$$

$$+ \frac{2}{3} \left(\frac{32\alpha}{\alpha'^4} \right)^2 GH [\alpha^4 G^4 (Q - \theta) + H^4(Q' - \theta')]$$

$$G = \left(\frac{1-\alpha}{1+\alpha} \right)^\alpha , \qquad H = \left(\frac{1-\alpha}{1+\alpha} \right)^{1/\alpha}$$

$$Q = 1 - \sqrt{1 - 2\theta} , \qquad Q' = 1 - \sqrt{1 - 2\theta'}$$

$$2\theta = (a/\lambda_o)^2 , \qquad 2\theta' = (a'/\lambda_o)^2 .$$

The equivalent circuit is valid in the range $0.5 < a/\lambda_o < 1.0$ and has an accuracy of about 1 percent over most of this range. The error may be of the order of 5 percent at the limit $a/\lambda_o = 1.0$.

A plot of the value of normalized reactance $\overline{X} \lambda_g/2a$ is available in [2] for α varying between 0.2 and 1, and $\lambda_o/a = 1.05$ and 2. These results are more accurate than those given by the closed form expressions. It is seen that $\overline{X}\,\lambda_g/2a$ increases from 0 to 6 as α increases from 0.2 to 0.8 ($\lambda_o/a = 1.05$). The value of ℓ/a increases from 0 to 1.04×10^{-2} for α varying between 0 and 0.5. It is symmetric about $\alpha = 0.5$.

E-plane Step or Change in Height of Rectangular Waveguide [2]:
For the E-plane step shown in Figure 5.7(c) the value of normalized junction susceptance can be obtained from the following equations

$$\frac{Y_o}{Y_o{}'} = \frac{b'}{b} = \alpha \tag{5.74}$$

$$
\begin{aligned}
\frac{B}{Y_o} = 2p \Bigg[&\ell n \left(\frac{1 - \alpha^2}{4\alpha} \right) + \frac{\alpha^2 + 1}{2\alpha} \; \ell n(r) \\
&+ 2 \, \frac{A + A' + 2c}{AA' - c^2} + \left(\frac{p}{4} \right)^2 \left(\frac{5\alpha^2 - 1}{1 - \alpha^2} \right. \\
&+ \left. \frac{4}{3} \frac{\alpha^2 c}{A} \right)^2 r^{-4\alpha} \Bigg]
\end{aligned} \tag{5.75}
$$

where

$$A = r^{2\alpha} \frac{1 + \sqrt{1 - p^2}}{1 - \sqrt{1 - p^2}} - \frac{1 + 3\alpha^2}{1 - \alpha^2}$$

$$A' = r^{2/\alpha} \frac{1 + \sqrt{1 - q^2}}{1 - \sqrt{1 - q^2}} + \frac{3 + \alpha^2}{1 - \alpha^2}$$

$$c = \left(\frac{4\alpha}{1 - \alpha^2} \right)^2 , \qquad r = \frac{1 + \alpha}{1 - \alpha}$$

$$p = b/\lambda_g , \qquad q = b' / \lambda_g{}' .$$

The above equivalent circuit is accurate to within 1 percent in the range $b/\lambda_g < 1$. The analysis is based on the assumption of the incidence of the two lowest modes. The value of $\overline{B}\lambda_g/b$ for $b/\lambda_g = 0.8$ is found to decrease from 5.4 to 0.0 as b'/b increases from 0.1 to 1.0.

Asymmetric Case: The configuration for the asymmetric change in waveguide height is shown in Figure 5.7(d). This configuration can be obtained by introducing an electric wall at the plane of symmetry as shown in Figure 5.7(c). Therefore, the same analysis and the same expressions hold for this case also, except that b and b' should be replaced by 2b and 2b', respectively. The value of $\bar{B}$ as a function of b'/b is found to be the same as that for the symmetric case.

5.3.5 Right-Angled Bends or Corners in Waveguides

H-plane Bends [2]: A right-angled bend in the H-plane is shown in Figure 5.8(a). The equivalent circuit parameters for the circuit shown in this figure are given below.

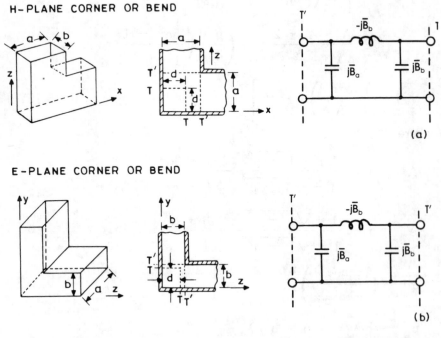

H–PLANE CORNER OR BEND

E–PLANE CORNER OR BEND

Figure 5.8   *Corners or bends in rectangular waveguide and their equivalent circuits: (a) H-plane corner; (b) E-plane corner.*

$$\overline{B}_a = \frac{1}{x}\left[A_1 - x\cot\pi x + \frac{1}{\pi}\left(\frac{1+x^2}{1-x^2}\right) + A_2\right](1+A_3)$$

$$(5.76)$$

$$\overline{B}_a + 2\overline{B}_b = \frac{1}{x}\left[-A_1{}' - x\cot\pi x - \frac{1}{\pi}\left(\frac{1+x^2}{1-x^2}\right)\right.$$

$$\left. + A_2{}'\right](1+A_3{}') \qquad\qquad (5.77)$$

where

$$x = \frac{2a}{\lambda_g} , \qquad A_1 = 0.3366 , \qquad A_1{}' = 0.3071$$

$$A_2 = \frac{\left[0.1801\left(\dfrac{1+x^2}{4-x^2}\right)+0.2021\right]^2}{\dfrac{\sqrt{3-x^2}}{1-\exp\left[-2\pi\sqrt{3-x^2}\,\right]} - 0.1858 - 0.1592\left(\dfrac{1+x^2}{7-x^2}\right)}$$

$$A_2{}' = \frac{\left[0.1801\left(\dfrac{1+x^2}{4-x^2}\right)+0.1669\right]^2}{\dfrac{\sqrt{3-x^2}}{1-\exp(-2\pi\sqrt{3-x^2})} + 0.1432 + 0.1592\left(\dfrac{1+x^2}{7-x^2}\right)}$$

$$A_3 = \begin{cases} 0.01 - 0.0095\,x , & \text{for } 0 \leqslant x \leqslant 1 \\[2mm] -\dfrac{0.00416}{1.5-x} + 0.004 + 0.0019x + 0.002\,x^2 \\[2mm] \qquad\qquad\qquad\qquad \text{for } 1 \leqslant x \leqslant 1.436 \end{cases}$$

$$A_3{}' = -\frac{0.00416}{1.26-x} - 0.0016 + 0.0034x - 0.0026x^2 ,$$

$$\text{for } 0 \leqslant x \leqslant 1.2.$$

The above equations give values which are accurate to within 1 percent for $0 \leqslant 2a/\lambda_g \leqslant 1.2$. An alternative equivalent circuit for the H-plane bend is also shown in Figure 5.8(a). The equivalent circuit parameters, susceptance B and the terminal distance d are given by

$$\overline{B} = \frac{1 + \overline{B}_a{}^2}{\overline{B}_b} + 2\overline{B}_a \tag{5.78}$$

$$\frac{2\pi(a - d)}{\lambda_g} = -\cot^{-1}(\overline{B}_a + 2\overline{B}_b) \tag{5.79}$$

where the susceptances $\overline{B}_a$ and $\overline{B}_b$ are given by (5.76) and (5.77) respectively.

The quantity $2\overline{B}\,a/\lambda_g$ is found to increase from 0.55 to 5.5 as $2a/\lambda_g$ increases from 0.0 to 1.5. For the same set of parameters, d/a decreases from 0.653 to 0.569, $2(\overline{B}_a + 2\overline{B}_b)\,a/\lambda_g$ increases from -0.92 to 0.72, and $(2\overline{B}_b\,a/\lambda_g)^{-1}$ from -1.55 to 2.7.

E-plane Bends [2]: The configuration and the equivalent circuit for an E-plane right-angled bend is shown in Figure 5.8(b). The circuit parameters obtained using the following equations are accurate to within 1 percent in the range $2b/\lambda_g < 1$.

$$\overline{B}_a = -x \left\{ \frac{\cot \pi x}{x} - \frac{1}{\pi x^2} + 0.169 \right.$$
$$\left. + \frac{A_o\, e^{-\pi/2} + (A_1 - A_2)\, e^{-\pi} + A_o{}^2\,(1 + 5\, e^{-\pi})/16}{1 - (1 + 5e^{-\pi})(A_1 - A_2)/4} \right\} \tag{5.80}$$

$$2\overline{B}_b - \overline{B}_a = \frac{1}{\pi x} \left\{ 1 + \pi x \cot \pi x + \pi x^2 \left[0.200 \right. \right.$$
$$\left. + 8 \sum_{n=1}^{\infty} \frac{1}{n(e^{2\pi n} - 1)} \right]$$
$$\left. + \pi x^2 \frac{A_o{}'\, e^{-\pi/2} - (A_1 + A_2)\, e^{-\pi} + A_o{}'^2\,(1 - 3e^{-\pi})/16}{1 + (1 - 3e^{-\pi})(A_1 + A_2)/4} \right\} \tag{5.81}$$

where

$$x = 2b/\lambda_g$$

$$A_o = \frac{4}{\pi} \frac{x^2}{1 - x^2} \quad , \qquad A_o' = A_o - \frac{8}{\sinh(\pi)}$$

$$A_1 = \frac{1}{\pi} \frac{x^2}{1 - 0.5 x^2} \quad ,$$

$$A_2 = \frac{4}{\sqrt{1 - x^2} \left[1 - \exp(-2\pi\sqrt{1 - x^2}) \right]} - \frac{4}{1 - e^{-2\pi}} .$$

An alternative equivalent circuit for the E-plane bend is also shown in Figure 5.8(b). The circuit parameters are given by

$$\overline{B} = \frac{\overline{B}_a^2 + 1}{\overline{B}_b} - 2\overline{B}_a \qquad (5.82)$$

$$\frac{2\pi(b - d)}{\lambda_g} = \cot^{-1} (2\overline{B}_b - \overline{B}_a) \qquad (5.83)$$

where the susceptances $\overline{B}_a$ and $\overline{B}_b$ have been given earlier in (5.80) and (5.81).

The susceptance $\overline{B}\lambda_g/2b$ increases from 1.4 to 6.0 as $2b/\lambda_g$ increases from 0.0 to 0.78. For the same set of parameters, d/b decreases from 0.5 to 0.16, $\overline{B}_b$ $2\pi b/\lambda_g$ from 1.0 to 0.84, and $\overline{B}_a \lambda_g/2b$ increases from 0.88 to 1.54.

5.3.6 T-junctions

H-plane T-junctions [2]: The configuration and the equivalent circuit of a T-junction in the H-plane of a waveguide is shown in Figure 5.9(a). Equivalent circuit parameters are given below. These have been obtained on the assumption that only the dominant mode propagates in each guide. The accuracy of the equations is

H-PLANE   T-JUNCTION

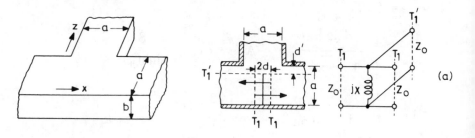

E-PLANE   T-JUNCTION

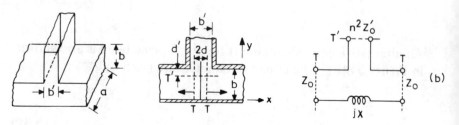

*Figure 5.9   T-junctions in rectangular waveguide and their equi-
valent circuits: (a) H-plane T-junction; (b) E-plane
T-junction.*

better than 15 percent for $0 < 2a/\lambda_g < 1$. For the reference planes
at T_1 and T_1'

$$d \quad = \frac{\lambda_g}{2\pi} \ (\tan^{-1} X_1) - \frac{a}{2} \qquad\qquad (5.84)$$

$$d' \quad = \frac{\lambda_g}{2\pi} \ \tan^{-1} \frac{X_1 X_4 + X_o}{2(X_1 - X_2)} \qquad\qquad (5.85)$$

$$\frac{X}{Z_o} = \frac{1}{2} \ \frac{4(X_2 - X_1)^2 + (X_o + X_1 X_4)^2}{(1 - X_1{}^2)(4X_2 - X_o X_4) - X_1(4 + X_4{}^2 - 4X_2{}^2 - X_o{}^2)}$$

$$(5.86)$$

$$\frac{Z_o{}'}{Z_o} = \frac{4(X_2 - X_1)^2 + (X_c + X_1 X_4)^2}{4(1 + X_1{}^2) X_3{}^2} \tag{5.87}$$

where

$$X_c = X_3{}^2 - X_2 X_4$$

$$X_1 \approx x\left[x \cot\theta - 0.0103 - \frac{\left(\dfrac{4}{5\pi}\dfrac{1 + x^2}{4 - x^2} + 0.2614\right)^2}{\left\{\dfrac{\sqrt{3 - x^2}}{1 - \exp(-2\pi\sqrt{3 - x^2})} - 0.0694\right\}} \right]^{-1}$$

$$X_2 \approx x\left[-\frac{A}{AC + B^2} - 0.057 + \frac{0.085}{1.62 - x^2} \right]$$

$$X_3 \approx x\left[\frac{B}{AC + B^2} \right]$$

$$X_3 + X_4 \approx x\left[\frac{B + C}{AC + B^2} \right]$$

with

$$A = \frac{x}{2}\cot(2\theta) - 0.0322, \quad B = \frac{1}{\pi}\frac{1 + x^2}{1 - x^2} + 0.03246$$

$$C = x\tan\theta + 0.0195, \quad x = 2a/\lambda_g, \text{ and } \theta = \pi a/\lambda_g.$$

The above equations are accurate to within 10 percent for $0 < 2a/\lambda_g < 1.25$. Graphs given in [2] for various circuit parameters are claimed to be accurate to within 1 percent. Alternative equivalent circuits for this discontinuity are also available in [2].

E-plane T-junction [2]: A right-angled T-junction in the E-plane is constituted by two guides of equal width "a" but different heights as shown in Figure 5.9(b). The value of circuit parameters for the equivalent circuit shown in the figure are obtained from the following relations

$$\frac{2\pi}{\lambda_g}\left(\frac{b'}{2} - d\right) = \tan^{-1} A_o \tag{5.88}$$

$$\frac{2\pi d'}{\lambda_g} = \tan^{-1} \frac{A_o A_c + A_b}{A_o - A_a} \tag{5.89}$$

$$n^2 = \frac{2b}{b'} \frac{(1 + A_o^2)(A_b + A_a A_c)}{(A_a - A_o)^2 + (A_b + A_o A_c)^2} \tag{5.90}$$

$$\frac{X}{2Z_o} = \frac{A_o(1 + A_c^2 - A_a^2 - A_b^2) - (1 - A_o^2)(A_a - A_b A_c)}{(A_a - A_o)^2 + (A_b + A_o A_c)^2}$$

$$\tag{5.91}$$

where

$$A_o = \frac{B_a}{Y_o} \quad , \qquad A_a = \frac{B_a - 2B_b - 2B_c}{Y_o}$$

$$A_b = \frac{2b'}{b}\left(\frac{B_c}{Y_o}\right)^2 - A_a A_c \quad , \qquad A_c = \frac{b'}{b} \frac{B_d - B_c}{Y_o}$$

$$\frac{B_a}{Y_o} \approx \frac{\pi b'}{\lambda_g}\left[1 - \frac{\alpha}{\pi} + \frac{8}{\pi^2}\left(\frac{2b'}{\lambda_g}\right)^2 (1 - 0.736\alpha)\right]$$

$$\frac{B_b}{Y_o} \approx \frac{1.1\,b'}{\lambda_g}\left[1 - 0.454\alpha + 0.032\,\alpha^2\right]$$

$$\frac{B_c}{Y_o} \approx \frac{\lambda_g}{2\pi b'}$$

$$\frac{B_d}{Y_o} \approx \frac{b}{\lambda_g}\left[2 - 2\ell n\,(4\alpha) + 2.2\alpha - 0.668\alpha^2 + 0.064\alpha^3\right]$$

where

$$2\alpha = \frac{b'}{b} = \frac{Y_o}{Y_o'} \quad .$$

The above equations are valid in the range $2b < \lambda_g$ or $2b' < \lambda_g$

according as $b > b'$ or $b < b'$, respectively. The accuracy of expressions is within 10 percent. For more accurate numerical values, the reader is referred to [2].

Graphs for d/b, d'/b, n^2, and $X\lambda_g/bZ_o$ have been plotted as functions of b'/b with b/λ_g as a parameter in [2]. It is seen that for b/λ_g = 0.6, and b'/b increasing from 0 to 0.8, the quantity d/b' increases from 0 to 0.05, d'/b increases from 0 to 0.2, n^2 decreases from 1.0 to 0.69, and $X\lambda_g(bZ_o)$ from 0 to -0.3.

5.3.7 Circular and Elliptical Apertures in Waveguides [2]

Thick Circular Apertures: A centered circular aperture in a thick metallic plate transverse to the direction of propagation in a rec-

THICK CIRCULAR APERTURE

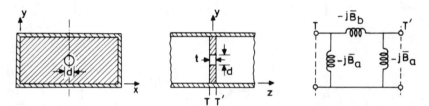

Figure 5.10(a) A thick circular aperture in rectangular waveguide and its equivalent circuit.

THIN ELLIPTICAL APERTURE

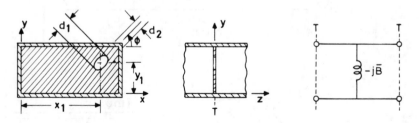

Figure 5.10(b) A thin elliptical aperture in rectangular waveguide and its equivalent circuit.

tangular waveguide is shown in Figure 5.10(a). The equivalent circuit parameters given below are valid in the wavelength range b $<$ λ_g.

$$\overline{B}_a = \frac{\overline{B}}{2} + |\overline{Y}_o'| \tanh \frac{\pi t}{|\lambda_g'|} \tag{5.92}$$

$$\overline{B}_b = |\overline{Y}_o'| \operatorname{cosech} \frac{2\pi t}{|\lambda_g'|} \tag{5.93}$$

where

$$\overline{Y}_o' = -j \frac{0.446 \, ab \, \lambda_g}{d^3} \, p \left[\frac{1 - (0.853 \, d/a)^2}{2J_1'(\pi d/2a)} \right]^2$$

$$\overline{B} = \frac{\lambda_g}{a} \left[\frac{\pi b}{24d \, q^2(x)} - 1 + A_1 - (a/\lambda_o)^2 \, A_2 \right]$$

with

$$A_1 = \frac{b}{4d \, q^2(x)} \sum_{\substack{n,m = -\infty \\ n, m \neq 0}}^{\infty \quad \infty} (-1)^n \left[\frac{3\theta - 6 \tan \frac{\theta}{2} + \tan^3 \frac{\theta}{2}}{9} \right.$$

$$\left. - (\beta/\alpha)^2 \frac{1 - 2 \cos \theta \sin^2 \frac{\theta}{2} - \left(\tan \frac{\theta}{2} - 1 \right)^2}{15 \tan \frac{\theta}{2}} \right]$$

$$A_2 = \frac{4b^3}{a^3 q^2(x)} \sum_{-\infty}^{+\infty} \sum_{-\infty}^{+\infty} \left[n^2 + \frac{(mb/a)^2}{1 + \sqrt{1 - (2b/\lambda_o \alpha)^2}} \right]$$

$$\underset{\substack{n \text{ even} \quad m \text{ odd} \\ (n = 0; m = 1) \\ \text{omitted}}}{}$$

$$\cdot \; \frac{q^2 \left(\dfrac{\alpha x a}{b} \right)}{\alpha^5}$$

$$x \;\; = \frac{\pi d}{2a} \;, \qquad \alpha = \sqrt{n^2 + \left(\frac{mb}{a} \right)^2}$$

$$\sin \theta \;\; = \frac{d}{\alpha a} \;, \qquad \beta = \sqrt{n^2 - \left(\frac{mb}{a} \right)^2}$$

$$q(x) \;\; = \frac{1}{x} \left(\frac{\sin x}{x} - \cos x \right)$$

$$|\lambda_g'| \;\; = 1.706 \; d/p$$

$$p \;\; = \sqrt{1 - \left(\frac{1.706 \; d}{\lambda_o} \right)^2}$$

The values of relative reactances $\overline{X}_a$ and $\overline{X}_b$ are available [2] as a function of thickness t ranging from 0.0 to 0.20 inch, for a 0.375 inch hole in X-band waveguide. Wavelength λ_o is taken to be 3.20 cm. It is seen that for this set of parameters, $\overline{X}_b$ increases from 0.0 to 0.53, and $\overline{X}_a$ decreases from 0.44 to 0.18.

Zero Thickness Apertures: For a centered circular aperture in a zero thickness plate, the equivalent circuit is represented by shunt susceptance given by $\overline{B}$ only.

Small Elliptical Apertures in Zero-thickness Plates; The configuration for this geometry is shown in Figure 5.10(b). Equivalent circuit parameters have been obtained using the integral equation method. It has been assumed that the largest dimension of the aperture is small compared with λ_o/π and $a < \lambda_o < 2a$.

$$\overline{B} = \frac{\lambda_g}{a} \left(\frac{a^2 b}{4\pi M} - 1 \right) \tag{5.94}$$

where

$$M = (M_1 \cos^2 \phi + M_2 \sin^2 \phi) \sin^2 (\pi x_1 /a)$$

with

$$M_1 = \frac{d_1{}^3}{6} \frac{\pi}{4} \frac{\epsilon^2}{K(\epsilon) - E(\epsilon)}$$

and

$$M_2 = \frac{d_1 d_2{}^2}{6} \frac{\pi}{4} \frac{\epsilon^2}{E(\epsilon) - (1 - \epsilon^2) K(\epsilon)} .$$

$K(\epsilon)$ and $E(\epsilon)$ are complete elliptic integrals of the first and second kinds, respectively. The eccentricity ϵ is given by

$$\epsilon = \sqrt{1 - \left(\frac{d_2}{d_1}\right)^2} .$$

For the special case of an off-centered circular aperture $d_1 = d_2 = d$, and

$$M = \frac{d^3}{6} \sin^2 (\pi x_1 /a) . \tag{5.95}$$

REFERENCES

[1] Gupta, K.C., *et al.*, *Microstrip Lines and Slotlines*, Dedham, Mass: Artech House, 1979, Chapters 3 and 4 on "Microstrip discontinuities."

[2] Marcuvitz, N. (Ed.), *Waveguide Handbook*, New York: McGraw-Hill, 1951.

[3] Green, H.E., "The Numerical Solution of Transmission Line Problems," in *Advances in Microwaves*, Vol. 2, New York: Academic Press, 1967, pp. 327-393.

[4] Whinnery, J.R., *et al.*, "Coaxial-line Discontinuities," *Proc. I.R.E.*, Vol. 32, Nov. 1944, pp. 695-709.

[5] Whinnery, J.R., and H.W. Jamieson, "Equivalent Circuits for Discontinuities in Transmission Lines," *Proc. I.R.E.*, Vol. 32, Feb. 1944, pp. 98-115.

[6] Montgomery, C.G., *et al.*, *Principles of Microwave Circuits*, New York: McGraw-Hill, 1948, Sec. 9.6, p. 295.

[7] Somlo, P.I., "The Computation of Coaxial-line Step Capacitance," *IEEE Trans. Microwave Theory Tech.*, Vol. MTT-15, Jan. 1967, pp. 48-53.

[8] Gogioso, L., *et al.*, "A Variational Approach to Compute the Equivalent Capacitance of Coaxial Line Discontinuities," in *Proc. Int. Microwave Symposium*, 1979, pp. 580-583.

[9] Lewin, L., *Theory of Waveguides*, London: Newnes-Butterworths, 1975.

[10] Chang, K., and P.J. Khan, "Equivalent Circuit of a Narrow Axial Strip in Waveguide," *IEEE Trans. Microwave Theory Tech.*, Vol. MTT-24, Sept. 1976, pp. 611-615.

[11] Chang, K., and P.J. Khan, "Analysis of a Narrow Capacitive Strip in Waveguide," *IEEE Trans. Microwave Theory Tech.*, Vol. MTT-22, May 1974, pp. 536-541.

[12] Bianco, B., *et al.*, "Open-circuited Coaxial Lines as Standards for Microwave Measurements," *Electron. Lett.*, Vol. 16, March 8, 1980, pp. 373-374.

6

Characterization
of
Discontinuities II

Striplines and
Microstrip Lines

As in the case of coaxial lines and waveguides, the characterization
of discontinuity reactances is also essential in the case of striplines
and microstrip lines. Various types of discontinuities in striplines
and microstrip lines include open end, gap, step in width, bend, tee-
and cross-junctions, etc. These are shown in Figure 6.1. Examples
of circuits and circuit elements, wherein these discontinuities occur
frequently, are also shown in this figure.

Most of the discontinuities listed in Figure 6.1 contribute to parasitic reactances. These discontinuity reactances (with the exception
of gap, hole, and notch in the strip conductor) are not introduced
intentionally. In this respect, the situation is different from the
waveguide discontinuities described in Section 5.3, wherein most of
the discontinuities are introduced purposely for realizing specific
circuit functions.

Discontinuities in striplines and microstrip lines involve an abrupt
change in the dimensions of the strip conductor, giving rise to a

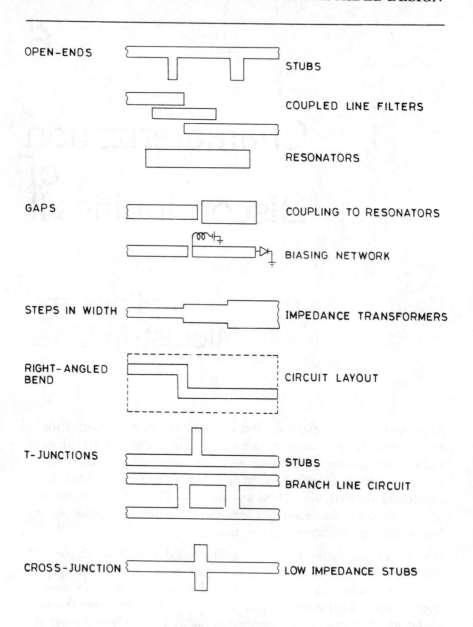

Figure 6.1   Various types of stripline and microstrip discontinuities and their typical circuit applications.

change in the electric and the magnetic field distributions. The altered electric field distribution can be represented by an equivalent capacitance, and the changed magnetic field distribution can be expressed in terms of an equivalent inductance. The discontinuity is characterized by evaluating these capacitances and inductances. Characterizations for various important discontinuities are summarized in this chapter. Lumped element equivalent circuits of various types of discontinuities in striplines and microstrip lines are discussed. Approximate closed form expressions for the circuit elements are given. The accuracy of these expressions is mentioned. Typical ranges of values for the circuit elements are given. The scattering matrix representation for most of the discontinuities can be obtained from Appendix 2.1. For T-junctions, the scattering matrices are given in Sections 6.1.6 and 6.2.6.

In addition to the discontinuities discussed in this chapter, there are discontinuity configurations, which occur in some circuits, for which adequate characterizations are not available. Also, on occasion, one comes across certain ranges of parameters (e.g. ϵ_r of substrates, values of Z_o, etc.) for which the approximate expressions reported in this chapter do not hold. In either case, measurements are needed in order to obtain models for the discontinuities. Measurement techniques discussed in Chapter 10 may be used for this purpose.

6.1 STRIPLINE DISCONTINUITIES

The discontinuities in the center conductor of striplines have been studied comprehensively by Oliner [1], and Altschuler and Oliner [2]. Some of the important discontinuities are treated here. These include an open end, a round hole, a step, a gap, a right-angled bend and a T-junction. These configurations and their equivalent circuits are shown in Figure 6.2. The approximate closed form expressions given in this section are based on [1,2,3]. In these expressions, a bar over the reactances and susceptances means that they are normalized with respect to Z_o and Y_o, respectively. For the analysis of discontinuities, the strip width W of the center conductor is replaced by an equivalent strip width D which is given by

$$
D = \begin{cases}
b\,\dfrac{K(k)}{K(k')} + \dfrac{t}{\pi}\,[1 - \ln(2t/b)] & (\text{for } W/b \leqslant 0.5) \qquad (6.1a) \\[3mm]
W + \dfrac{2b}{\pi}\,\ln 2 + \dfrac{t}{\pi}\,[1 - \ln(2t/b)] & \\[3mm]
& (\text{for } W/b > 0.5) \qquad (6.1b)
\end{cases}
$$

where

$$ k = \tanh(\pi W/2b) . $$

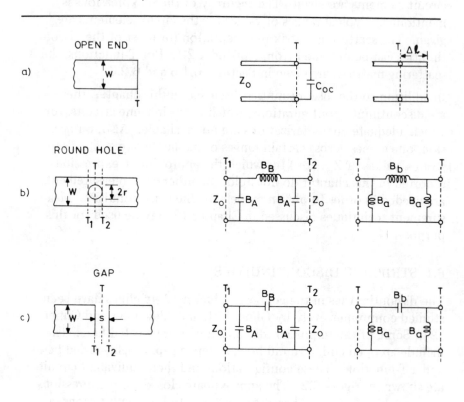

Figure 6.2   *(a) An open end discontinuity in stripline and micro-strip line and its equivalent circuits; (b) A round hole discontinuity in stripline and its equivalent circuits; (c) A gap discontinuity in stripline and microstrip line and its equivalent circuits.*

6.1.1 Open-End

The equivalent circuit of an open-ended stripline is represented by an excess capacitance. It can also be expressed as an equivalent length of a transmission line $\Delta\ell$, as shown in Figure 6.2a. This means that an effective open circuit is located at a distance $\Delta\ell$ from the physical open-end. The extension $\Delta\ell$, is given by

$$\beta\Delta\ell = \tan^{-1}\left[\frac{\delta + 2W}{4\delta + 2W}\ \tan(\beta\delta)\right] \tag{6.2}$$

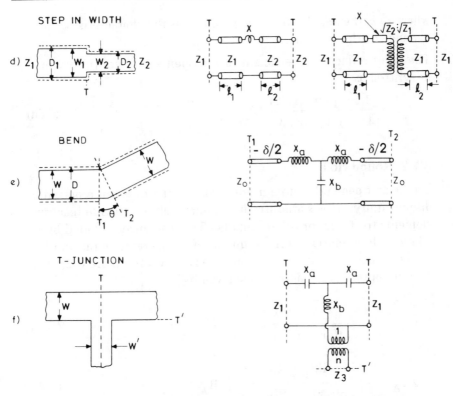

Figure 6.2   *(d) A step (in width) discontinuity in stripline and its equivalent circuits; (e) An arbitrary bend discontinuity in stripline and its equivalent circuit; (f) A T-junction discontinuity in stripline and its equivalent circuit.*

where

$$\delta = \frac{b \ln 2}{\pi} \quad , \quad \beta = \frac{2\pi}{\lambda} \quad \text{and} \quad \lambda = \frac{\lambda_o}{\sqrt{\epsilon_r}} \quad .$$

The value of $\Delta\ell$ increases from 0.095b to 0.19b as W/b increases from 0.15 to 1.95. It increases asymptotically to 0.22b.

The open-circuit capacitance C_{oc} may be obtained from the value of $\beta \Delta\ell$ by using the following relation

$$C_{oc} = \frac{\beta \Delta\ell}{\omega Z_o} \tag{6.3}$$

where ω is the angular frequency and Z_o is the characteristic impedance of the stripline.

The input reflection coefficient of the open-end discontinuity may be written as

$$S_{11} = \frac{1 - j \tan (\beta \Delta\ell)}{1 + j \tan (\beta \Delta\ell)} \tag{6.3a}$$

6.1.2 Round Hole

Unlike an open-end, a hole in the strip conductor is not a parasitic discontinuity. Holes are introduced purposely to provide reactive elements for filters or other circuits. The reactance provided by a hole is dominantly a series inductance. Edge representation of the equivalent circuit for a round hole is shown in Figure 6.2(b). The susceptances B_A and B_B are given by

$$\overline{B}_A = \frac{1 + \overline{B}_a \cot(\beta r)}{\cot(\beta r) - \overline{B}_a} \tag{6.4a}$$

$$2\overline{B}_B = \frac{1 + 2\overline{B}_b \cot(\beta r)}{\cot(\beta r) - 2\overline{B}_b} - \overline{B}_A \tag{6.4b}$$

where

$$\overline{B}_b = -\frac{3}{16\beta} \frac{bD}{r^3} \quad , \quad \overline{B}_a = \frac{1}{4\overline{B}_b} \quad . \tag{6.5}$$

Alternatively, a center-line representation of the equivalent circuit shown in Figure 6.2(b) can be used. In this case, all the three susceptances are inductive and are given by (6.5). It is observed through computations that with the increase in hole diameter $\overline{B}_a$ decreases, whereas $\overline{B}_b$ increases. Also, $\overline{B}_b$ is much larger than $\overline{B}_a$ for the same set of parameters. For example, $\overline{B}_a = -0.025$ and $\overline{B}_b = -10$ for $2r/W = 0.6$ in a 50 ohm line.

6.1.3 Gap

A gap discontinuity is also introduced intentionally to provide a dominantly capacitive series reactance. Its equivalent circuit is a π-network of three capacitances as shown in Figure 6.2(c). The series capacitance C_{12} arises from the electric field between the strip conductors constituting the gap. The shunt capacitance C_1 is a result of the disturbance in the electric field distribution of the stripline at the edge of the gap. As the gap width 's' is increased, C_{12} decreases to zero and C_1 tends to the value of end-capacitance for the open-ended line. The susceptances B_A and B_B are given by

$$\overline{B}_A = \frac{1 + \overline{B}_a \cot(\beta s/2)}{\cot(\beta s/2) - \overline{B}_a} = \frac{\omega C_1}{Y_o} \qquad (6.6a)$$

$$2\overline{B}_B = \frac{1 + (2\overline{B}_b + \overline{B}_a) \cot(\beta s/2)}{\cot(\beta s/2) - (2\overline{B}_b + \overline{B}_a)} - \overline{B}_A = \frac{2\omega C_{12}}{Y_o} \qquad (6.6b)$$

where

$$\lambda \overline{B}_a = - 2b \ln \cosh(\pi s/2b) \qquad (6.7a)$$

$$\lambda \overline{B}_b = b \ln \coth(\pi s/2b) . \qquad (6.7b)$$

It is observed that $\overline{B}_A$ increases and $\overline{B}_B$ decreases with the increase in gap width. $\overline{B}_a$ approaches an asymptotic value for $s/W = 1.5$ in a 50 ohm line. For $s/W = 1$, the value of $\overline{B}_A$ is 0.18 and $\overline{B}_B$ is 0.007.

A center-line representation for the equivalent circuit can be used in this case also. This is shown in Figure 6.2(c). The susceptances B_a and B_b are given by (6.7).

6.1.4 Step in Width

This type of discontinuity is formed by the junction of two lines having different widths, i.e. different impedances. An equivalent circuit, shown in Figure 6.2(d), consists of a series inductive reactance and two line lengths ℓ_1 and ℓ_2. The lengths ℓ_1 and ℓ_2 ($= -\ell_1$) account for the shift of the effective junction plane towards the line of smaller width (i.e. the higher impedance). In the approximate formulation used [2], ℓ_1 and ℓ_2 depend only on the spacing between the strip and the ground plate.

The parameters X, ℓ_1 and ℓ_2 are given by

$$\frac{X}{Z_1} = \frac{2D_1}{\lambda} \, \ell n \, \text{cosec} \, (\pi D_2 / 2D_1) \qquad (6.8)$$

and

$$\ell_1 = -\ell_2 = \frac{b \, \ell n \, 2}{\pi} \, . \qquad (6.9)$$

The scattering matrix, with normalizing impedances at the two ports taken as Z_1 and Z_2 respectively, may be written as

$$[S] = \frac{1}{\Delta} \begin{bmatrix} (Z_2 - Z_1 + jX) \, e^{-j2\beta\ell_1} & 2\sqrt{Z_1 Z_2} \\ \\ 2\sqrt{Z_1 Z_2} & (Z_1 - Z_2 + jX) \, e^{j2\beta\ell_1} \end{bmatrix} \qquad (6.10)$$

where

$$\Delta = Z_1 + Z_2 + jX \, . \qquad (6.11)$$

For equal normalizations at the two ports, the equivalent circuit is written by including an ideal transformer as shown in Figure 6.2(d).

6.1.5 Bend

The equivalent circuit for a bend is shown in Figure 6.2(e). This circuit representation holds for bends at any arbitrary angle. Theoretical formulas for X_a and X_b are derived [1] from the results for an E-plane bend in a parallel plate waveguide by means of the

Babinet equivalence procedure. Reactances for a $90°$ bend are given by

$$\lambda \overline{X}_a = D[1.756 + 4(D/\lambda)^2] \qquad (6.12a)$$

and

$$\lambda \overline{X}_b = D[0.0725 - 0.159(\lambda/D)^2] . \qquad (6.12b)$$

For a bend at an arbitrary angle, the equivalent reactances are given by

$$\lambda \overline{X}_a = 2D \left[\psi(x) + 1.9635 - \frac{1}{x} \right] \qquad (6.13a)$$

$$\overline{X}_b = -\frac{\lambda}{2\pi D} \cot(\theta/2) \qquad (6.13b)$$

where, with θ in degrees,

$$x = \frac{1}{2}[1 + \theta/180] , \quad \frac{1}{2} < x < 1 . \qquad (6.14)$$

$\psi(x)$ is the logarithmic derivative of Γ function and is tabulated in [27]. An approximate closed form expression for $\psi(x)$ may be written as [28]

$$\psi(x) = 0.5223 \ln x + 0.394. \qquad (6.15)$$

Accuracy of the above relation is about 3 percent in the range $\frac{1}{2} < x < 1$.

The scattering matrix for the bend at an arbitrary angle may be obtained from that of a T-network given in (8) of Appendix 2.1 with $Z_1 = Z_2 = jX_a$ and $Z_3 = jX_b$. It may be noted that the planes T_1 and T_2, which are perpendicular to the strips on the two sides of the bend, intersect at the meeting point of the inside edges of the equivalent width strips (width D) rather than that of the physical strips of width W. This leads to an excess line length $\delta/2$ which should be considered on each side of the T-network shown in Figure 6.2(e). When these extra lengths are taken into account, all the four S-parameters get multiplied by $\exp(j\beta\delta)$ where

$$\delta = (D - W) \tan \theta/2 . \qquad (6.16)$$

6.1.6 T-junction

The equivalent circuit for a T-junction is shown in Figure 6.2(f).
In this case, a transformer is used as a circuit element to model
the discontinuity and appears even when the normalizing impedances of lines at the main line ports are taken as Z_1 each and that
in the side branch as Z_3. The three elements X_a, X_b, and n are
given by

$$\frac{X_a}{Z_1} = \overline{X}_a = - \frac{D_3^{\,2}}{D_1 \lambda} \; (0.785 \, n)^2 \tag{6.17}$$

$$\frac{X_b}{Z_1} = \overline{X}_b = - \frac{\overline{X}_a}{2} + \frac{1}{n^2} \left\{ \frac{B_t}{2Y_1} + \frac{2D_1}{\lambda} \left[\ell n2 + \frac{\pi D_3}{6D_1} \right. \right.$$

$$\left. \left. + \frac{3}{2} \left(\frac{D_1}{\lambda} \right)^2 \right] \right\} \qquad (\text{for } D_3/D_1 < 0.5) \tag{6.18a}$$

$$\frac{X_b}{Z_1} = \overline{X}_b = - \frac{\overline{X}_a}{2} + \frac{2D_1}{\lambda n^2} \left[\ell n \frac{1.43 \, D_1}{D_3} + 2 \left(\frac{D_1}{\lambda} \right)^2 \right]$$

$$(\text{for } D_3/D_1 > 0.5) \tag{6.18b}$$

where n $= \sin(\pi D_3/\lambda) \, / \, (\pi D_3/\lambda),$ \hfill (6.19)

and

$$\frac{B_t}{2Y_1} = \frac{2D_1}{\lambda} \left[\ell n \, \text{cosec} \, \frac{\pi D_3}{2D_1} + \frac{1}{2} \left(\frac{D_1}{\lambda} \right)^2 \cos^4 \frac{\pi D_3}{2D_1} \right].$$

$$\tag{6.20}$$

In case the impedances at all the three ports are normalized to unity,
a change in the transformer turns ratio is needed. In this case,

$$X_a{}' = X_a/Z_1 \; , \quad X_b{}' = X_b/Z_1 \; \text{ and } n' = n\sqrt{Z_1/Z_3} \; . \tag{6.21}$$

S-matrix: When the normalizing impedances are Z_1 (at the main line
ports) and Z_3 (at the side branch) the scattering matrix parameters

are given as

$$S_{11} = S_{22} = -\frac{Z_1{}^2 + 2X_a X_b + X_a{}^2 - 2j\dfrac{Z_3}{n^2}X_a}{(Z_1 + jX_a)\,\Delta}$$

$$(6.22)$$

$$S_{12} = S_{21} = \frac{2Z_1\left(\dfrac{Z_3}{n^2} + jX_b\right)}{(Z_1 + jX_a)\,\Delta} \tag{6.23}$$

$$S_{13} = S_{23} = S_{31} = S_{32} = \frac{2\sqrt{Z_1 Z_3/n^2}}{\Delta} \tag{6.24}$$

$$S_{33} = \frac{Z_1 - 2\dfrac{Z_3}{n^2} + j(X_a + 2X_b)}{\Delta} \tag{6.25}$$

with

$$\Delta = Z_1 + 2Z_3/n^2 + j(X_a + 2X_b) \; .$$

6.2 MICROSTRIP DISCONTINUITIES

Various types of discontinuities occurring in microstrip circuits are shown in Figure 6.1. These discontinuities have been studied extensively and a detailed review is given in [4]. A collection of closed form expressions for various important discontinuities is available in [5]. The capacitive components of the discontinuities have been obtained through analyses by Benedek and Silvester [6], Silvester and Benedek [7, 8], Farrar and Adams [9, 10], Maeda [11], Horton [12] and Itoh et al. [13]. The inductive components have been determined by Thomson and Gopinath [14], and Gopinath et al. [15]. Several experimental measurements on the characterization of discontinuities have been reported. Some of the prominent ones are Napoli and Hughes [16], Easter [17], Stephens and Easter [18], and Groll and Weidmann [19]. The dynamic behavior of discontinuities has been studied by Wolff and Menzel [20], and Mehran [21, 22]. An excellent comparison of theoretical and experimental results on discontinuities has been reported by Buontempo and Reggiani [23].

Closed form expressions for various discontinuity reactances [5] are given in this section. Numerical results of Silvester and Benedek have been used for deriving the closed form expressions for the discontinuity capacitances. The results of Gopinath et al. have been used for arriving at the inductance expressions.

The configuration of various discontinuities in microstrip and their equivalent circuits are identical to stripline discontinuities shown in Figure 6.2. Approximate expressions for various reactance elements, their range of validity and the maximum error with respect to numerical results are discussed below. The range of parameters covers the commonly used dielectric constants and aspect ratios. The relations are accurate to about 5 percent in most of the cases.

6.2.1 Open-End

The closed form expression for apparent increase $\Delta\ell$ in line length due to the open-end capacitance has been obtained by modifying the expression derived by Hammerstad [24]. It is given below

$$\frac{\Delta\ell}{h} = 0.412 \left\{ \frac{\epsilon_{re} + 0.3}{\epsilon_{re} - 0.258} \right\} \left(\frac{W/h + 0.264}{W/h + 0.8} \right) \qquad (6.26)$$

where ϵ_{re} is the effective dielectric constant. For $W/h \geqslant 0.2$ and $2 \leqslant \epsilon_r \leqslant 50$, (6.26) yields results which are within 4 percent of the numerical results [7].

The open-circuit capacitance C_{oc} may be obtained from the value of $\Delta\ell/h$ by using the following equation

$$\frac{C_{oc}}{W} = \frac{\Delta\ell}{h} \frac{1}{W/h} \frac{\sqrt{\epsilon_{re}}}{cZ_o} \qquad (6.27)$$

where c is the velocity of light in free space and ϵ_{re} is the effective dielectric constant corresponding to the impedance Z_o. For a 50 ohm line on a substrate with ϵ_r = 9.6, the value of C_{oc}/W is found to be 55 pF/m.

The effect of dispersion on $\Delta\ell$ has been analyzed by Itoh [25]. It is seen that at millimeter wavelengths the value of $\Delta\ell$ is considerably smaller than that computed by using the quasi-static approximation. However, for frequencies up to about 10 GHz, the quasi-static approach gives reasonably good results.

6.2.2 Gap

As in the case of stripline circuits, the study of gap in microstrip is useful in the design of DC blocks, end-coupled filters, coupling element to resonators, etc. Its equivalent circuit is a π-network, as shown in Figure 6.2(c). The edge-line representation, shown in this figure, holds also for microstrip, and the corresponding susceptances can be obtained from the equivalent circuit capacitances C_1 and C_{12}. These are expressed in terms of C_{even} and C_{odd} as follows [6]

$$C_1 = \tfrac{1}{2} C_{even} \tag{6.28}$$

$$C_{12} = \tfrac{1}{2} (C_{odd} - \tfrac{1}{2} C_{even}) \tag{6.29}$$

where C_{even} and C_{odd} are the equivalent circuit parameters for the gap when it is excited symmetrically and anti-symmetrically, respectively. The closed form expressions for C_{even} (C_e) and C_{odd} (C_o) for ϵ_r = 9.6 and $0.5 \leqslant W/h \leqslant 2$ are given below

$$C_o/W \,(pF/m) = (s/W)^{m_o} \exp(K_o) \tag{6.30}$$

$$C_e/W \,(pF/m) = (s/W)^{m_e} \exp(K_e) \tag{6.31}$$

where

$$m_o = \frac{W}{h} (0.267 \ln W/h - 0.3853)$$

$$\left. \right\} \text{for } (0.1 \leqslant s/W \leqslant 1.0)$$

$$K_o = 4.26 - 0.631 \ln W/h$$

$$m_e = 0.8675, \quad K_e = 2.043 \,(W/h)^{0.12} \;(\text{for } 0.1 \leqslant s/W \leqslant 0.3)$$

$$m_e = \frac{1.565}{(W/h)^{0.16}} - 1, \quad K_e = 1.97 - \frac{0.03}{W/h}$$

$$(\text{for } 0.3 \leqslant s/W \leqslant 1.0) \quad (6.32)$$

The values of C_e and C_o for other values of ϵ_r in the range $2.5 \leqslant \epsilon_r \leqslant 15$ can be calculated by using the following scaling relations

$$C_e(\epsilon_r) = C_e(9.6) \ (\epsilon_r/9.6)^{0.9} \tag{6.33a}$$

$$C_o(\epsilon_r) = C_o(9.6) \ (\epsilon_r/9.6)^{0.8} . \tag{6.33b}$$

The above expressions give results which are accurate to within 7 percent for the above mentioned set of parameters. The value of C_{12}, for $\epsilon_r = 8.875$ and $W = h = 0.508$ mm, has been found to decrease from 0.032 to 0.0015 as 's' increases from 0.02 mm to 1.0 mm.

6.2.3 Notch

A notch or a narrow transverse slit in the strip conductor of a microstrip line can be introduced to realize a pure series inductance. The configuration of this discontinuity and its equivalent circuit are shown in Figure 6.3(a). The value of the series inductance L_N can be obtained from the following approximate relation [26]

$$\frac{L_N}{h} \ (\mu H/m) = 2 \left[1 - \frac{Z_o}{Z_o{'}} \sqrt{\frac{\epsilon_{re}}{\epsilon_{re}{'}}} \right]^2 \tag{6.34}$$

where ϵ_{re} and $\epsilon_{re}{'}$ are the effective dielectric constants for microstrip lines with widths W and (W − b), respectively, and Z_o and $Z_o{'}$ are the corresponding impedances. The above expression for L_N is valid for $0 \leqslant b/W \leqslant 0.9$ and $a \leqslant h$.

6.2.4 Step in Width

This type of discontinuity is formed by the junction of two lines having different widths, i.e. different impedances. For discussing microstrip step discontinuity, an equivalent circuit shown in Figure 6.3(b) is used. This is an alternative to the equivalent circuit shown in Figure 6.2(d) and consists of a shunt capacitance C_s in the plane of junction and series inductors L_1 and L_2 on either side of it.

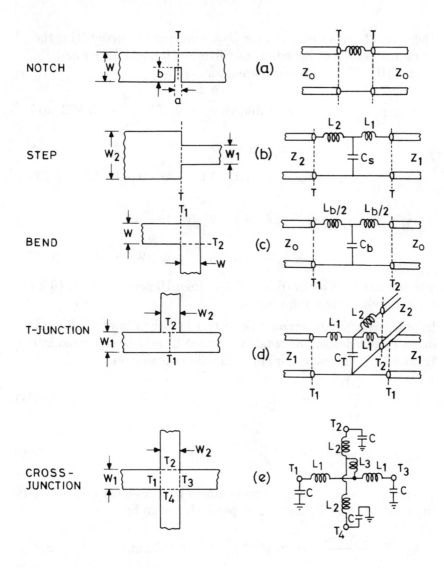

Figure 6.3 *(a)* *A notch discontinuity in microstrip line and its equivalent circuit; (b) A step in microstrip line and its equivalent circuit; (c) A bend in microstrip line and its equivalent circuit; (d) A T-junction in microstrip line and its equivalent circuit; (e) A cross-junction in microstrip line and its equivalent circuit.*

The closed form expressions for C_s are derived by curve fitting the numerical results of Benedek and Silvester [6], and Farrar and Adams [9]. The expressions are given below

$$\frac{C_s}{\sqrt{W_1 W_2}} \; (\text{pF/m}) \; = \; (4.386 \; \ell n \; \epsilon_r \; + \; 2.33) \; \frac{W_2}{W_1} \; - \; 5.472 \; \ell n \, \epsilon_r$$

$$- \; 3.17$$

$$\text{for } \epsilon_r \leqslant 10, \quad 1.5 \leqslant W_2/W_1 \leqslant 3.5 \quad (6.35a)$$

$$\frac{C_s}{\sqrt{W_1 W_2}} \; (\text{pF/m}) \; = \; 56.46 \; \ell n \; (W_2/W_1) \; - \; 44$$

$$\text{for } \epsilon_r \; = \; 9.6, \quad 3.5 \leqslant W_2/W_1 \leqslant 10. \quad (6.35b)$$

The percentage error in (6.35a) is less than 10 percent, while (6.35b) is accurate to within 0.5 percent.

In order to take into account the effect of discontinuity inductances in the circuit design, the total inductance L_s may be separated into L_1 and L_2 (as a first order approximation) as follows

$$L_1 \; = \; \frac{L_{w1}}{L_{w1} \; + \; L_{w2}} \; L_s \qquad\qquad (6.36a)$$

$$L_2 \; = \; \frac{L_{w2}}{L_{w1} \; + \; L_{w2}} \; L_s \qquad\qquad (6.36b)$$

where L_{w1} and L_{w2} are the inductances per unit length of microstrip lines with widths W_1 and W_2 respectively, given by

$$L_w \; = \; \frac{Z_o \sqrt{\epsilon_{re}}}{c} \; (\text{H/m}) \; , \qquad c \; = \; 3 \; \times \; 10^8 \; \text{m/s} \; . \qquad (6.37)$$

The numerical results of Gopinath *et al.* [15] have been used to obtain the expression for L_s. It is given below

$$\frac{L_s}{h} \; (\text{nH/m}) \; = \; 40.5 \left(\frac{W_2}{W_1} \; - \; 1.0 \right) - \; 32.57 \; \ell n \; \frac{W_2}{W_1}$$

$$+ \; 0.2 \left(\frac{W_2}{W_1} \; - \; 1 \right)^2 . \qquad\qquad (6.38)$$

Equation (6.38) has an error of less than 5 percent for $W_2/W_1 \leqslant 5$ and $W_1/h = 1.0$. Computations show that both C_s and L_s increase with an increase in the ratio W_2/W_1. For $\epsilon_r = 9.6$ and $W_2 = 2W_1$, the values of C_s/hC_{w1} and L_s/hL_{w1} are 0.5 each, where C_{w1} is the capacitance per unit length of microstrip line with width W_1.

6.2.5 Right-angled Bend

A right-angled bend is normally used for introducing flexibility in the layout of the circuit design. The equivalent circuit of Figure 6.3(c) is used for a right angled bend (without any change in line impedance at the bend). In this case we denote the shunt capacitance by C_b and the series inductances by $L_b/2$ each. The closed form expressions are given below

$$\frac{C_b}{W} \text{ (pF/m)} = \begin{cases} \dfrac{(14\epsilon_r + 12.5)\, W/h - (1.83\epsilon_r - 2.25)}{\sqrt{W/h}} + \dfrac{0.02\epsilon_r}{W/h} \\ \hspace{4cm} \text{(for } W/h < 1) \quad (6.39a) \\[2mm] (9.5\epsilon_r + 1.25)\, W/h + 5.2\epsilon_r + 7.0 \\ \hspace{4cm} \text{(for } W/h \geqslant 1) \quad (6.39b) \end{cases}$$

$$\frac{L_b}{h} \text{ (nH/m)} = 100\,(4\sqrt{W/h} - 4.21)\ . \tag{6.40}$$

Equations (6.39) are accurate to within 5 percent for $2.5 \leqslant \epsilon_r \leqslant 15$ and $0.1 \leqslant W/h \leqslant 5$. The accuracy of (6.40) is within about 3 percent for $0.5 \leqslant W/h \leqslant 2.0$ when compared with the numerical results of Thomson and Gopinath [14].

For $\epsilon_r = 9.9$ and at $f = 5.0$ GHz, it is seen that C_b/W increases from 15.0 to 200 pF/m as W/h is increased from 0.1 to 2.0. For the same set of parameters, L_b/hL_w increases from -0.37 to $+0.5$.

6.2.6 T-Junction

The circuits used for modelling microstrip T-junctions differ from (but are essentially equivalent to) that discussed for stripline. An equivalent circuit is shown in Figure 6.3(d) and consists of series inductances L_1 in the main line and L_2 in the stub arm, and junction capacitance C_T. In the design of stubs, the inductance L_2 plays a significant role in determining stub length, while for branch-line couplers and SPDT switches both L_1 and L_2 are equally important.

The expressions for the equivalent circuit parameters for a T-junction with a main line impedance of 50 ohms and for $\epsilon_r = 9.9$ are given below

$$C_T/W_1 \text{ (pF/m)} = \frac{100}{\tanh(0.0072 Z_o)} + 0.64 Z_o - 261$$

$$\text{(for } 25 \leqslant Z_o \leqslant 100) \quad (6.41)$$

where Z_o is the characteristic impedance (in ohms) of stub,

$$\frac{L_1}{h} \text{ (nH/m)} = -\frac{W_2}{h} \left[\frac{W_2}{h} \left(-0.016 \frac{W_1}{h} + 0.064 \right) \right.$$

$$\left. + \frac{0.016}{W_1/h} \right] L_{w1} \quad \text{for } 0.5 \leqslant (W_1/h , W_2/h) \leqslant 2.0$$

$$(6.42a)$$

$$\frac{L_2}{h} \text{ (nH/m)} = \left\{ \left(0.12 \frac{W_1}{h} - 0.47 \right) \frac{W_2}{h} + 0.195 \frac{W_1}{h} \right.$$

$$\left. - 0.357 + 0.0283 \sin \left(\pi \frac{W_1}{h} - 0.75 \pi \right) \right\} L_{w2}$$

$$\text{for } 1 \leqslant W_1/h \leqslant 2 , 0.5 \leqslant W_2/h \leqslant 2$$

$$(6.42b)$$

where L_w is the inductance per unit length (nH/m) for a microstrip of width W and is obtained from (6.37).

Equations (6.41) and (6.42) have an estimated error of less than 5 percent. For $\epsilon_r = 9.9$ and $Z_1 = 50$ ohm, the value of C_T/W_1 decreases from 300 to -20 pF/m as Z_2 increases from 25 to 100 ohm. The reactances L_1/hL_{w1} and L_2/hL_{w2} vary from -0.02 to -0.22 and from -0.3 to -0.85, respectively, for $W_1/h = 1.0$ and W_2/h increasing from 0.5 to 2.0.

Scattering matrix representation for the T-junction discontinuity
is obtained as

$$S_{11} = S_{22} = \frac{\overline{Z}_{in} - 1}{\overline{Z}_{in} + 1} \qquad (6.43a)$$

$$S_{12} = S_{21} = \frac{(1 - S_{11})\overline{X}_3 (1 + \overline{X}_2)}{(1 + \overline{X}_2)(1 + \overline{X}_1 + \overline{X}_3) + \overline{X}_3(1 + \overline{X}_1)} \qquad (6.43b)$$

$$S_{13} = S_{31} = S_{23} = S_{32} = \frac{(1 - S_{11})\,\overline{X}_3(1 + \overline{X}_1)}{(1 + \overline{X}_2)(1 + \overline{X}_1 + \overline{X}_3) + \overline{X}_3(1 + \overline{X}_1)} \qquad (6.43c)$$

$$S_{33} = \frac{\overline{Z}'_{in} - 1}{\overline{Z}'_{in} + 1} \qquad (6.43d)$$

where

$$\overline{Z}_{in} = \frac{(1 + \overline{X}_1)(1 + \overline{X}_2)(1 + \overline{X}_3)}{(1 + \overline{X}_1)(1 + \overline{X}_1 + \overline{X}_2 + \overline{X}_3) + (1 + \overline{X}_2)(\overline{X}_1 + \overline{X}_3)}$$

$$\overline{Z}'_{in} = \frac{(1 + \overline{X}_1)(\overline{X}_2 + \overline{X}_3)}{1 + \overline{X}_1 + 2(\overline{X}_2 + \overline{X}_3)}$$

with

$$\overline{X}_1 = \frac{j\omega L_1}{Z_o}, \quad \overline{X}_2 = \frac{j\omega L_2}{Z_o} \quad \text{and} \quad \overline{X}_3 = \frac{1}{j\omega Z_o C_T} .$$

6.2.7 Cross-Junction

One of the most common applications of a cross-junction is in the
realization of low impedance stubs. When a low impedance stub
has a strip width large enough to cause possible excitation of higher
order modes in the microstrip, one of the possible solutions is to
employ two stubs in parallel connected on either side of the main
line. The impedance of each of the two stubs is equal to twice the

impedance of the simulated stub. The equivalent circuit suggested by Gopinath *et al.* [15] and Easter [17] is shown in Figure 6.3(e). The expressions for C, L_1 and L_3 are given as

$$\frac{C}{W_1}\left(\frac{pF}{m}\right) = \frac{1}{4}\left[\left\{37.61\,\frac{W_2}{h} - 13.42\left(\frac{W_2}{h}\right)^{\frac{1}{2}} + 159.38\right\}\right.$$

$$\left.\ell n\,\frac{W_1}{h} + \left(\frac{W_2}{h}\right)^3 + 74\,\frac{W_2}{h} + 130\right]\left(\frac{W_1}{h}\right)^{-1/3}$$

$$- 60 + \frac{0.5}{W_2/h} - 0.375\,\frac{W_1}{h}\left(1 - \frac{W_2}{h}\right)$$

for ϵ_r = 9.9, $0.3 \leqslant W_1/h \leqslant 3$ and $0.1 < W_2/h \leqslant 3$

$$\tag{6.44}$$

$$\frac{L_1}{h}\left(\frac{nH}{m}\right) = \left[\left\{165.6\,\frac{W_2}{h} + 31.2\sqrt{\frac{W_2}{h}} - 11.8\left(\frac{W_2}{h}\right)^2\right\}\frac{W_1}{h}\right.$$

$$\left. - 32\,\frac{W_2}{h} + 3\right]\left(\frac{W_1}{h}\right)^{-3/2}$$

for $0.5 \leqslant (W_1/h,\ W_2/h) \leqslant 2.0$

$$\tag{6.45a}$$

$$-\frac{L_3}{h}\left(\frac{nH}{m}\right) = 337.5 + \left(1 + \frac{7}{W_1/h}\right)\frac{1}{W_2/h} - 5\,\frac{W_2}{h}$$

$$\cdot \cos\left[\frac{\pi}{2}\left(1.5 - \frac{W_1}{h}\right)\right]$$

for $0.5 \leqslant (W_1/h, W_2/h) \leqslant 2.0$.

$$\tag{6.45b}$$

The equation for L_2/h is obtained by replacing W_1 by W_2 and vice versa in (6.45a). The above expressions are accurate to within 5 percent.

Computations show that for $\epsilon_r = 9.9$ and $Z_1 = 50$ ohm the value of C/W_1 decreases from 32.5 to -22.5 pF/m as Z_2 increases from 25 to 100 ohms. Inductances L_1/hL_{w1} and L_3/hL_{w1} increase from 0.2 to 0.6 and from -0.9 to -0.8, respectively, as W_2/h increases from 0.5 to 2.0 ($W_1/h = 1.0$).

REFERENCES

[1]   Oliner, A.A., "Equivalent Circuits for Discontinuities in
        Balanced Strip Transmission Line," *IRE Trans. Microwave
        Theory Tech.*, Vol. MTT-3, March 1955, pp. 134-143.

[2]   Altschuler, H.M., and A.A. Oliner, "Discontinuities in the
        Center Conductor of Symmetric Strip Transmission Line,"
        IRE Trans. Microwave Theory Tech., Vol. MTT-8, May
        1960, pp. 328-339.

[3]   Bahl, I.J., and R. Garg, "A Designer's Guide to Stripline
        Circuits," *Microwaves*, Vol. 17, No. 1, Jan. 1978, pp. 90-96.

[4]   Gupta, K.C., *et al.*, *Microstrip Lines and Slotlines*, Dedham,
        Mass: Artech House, 1979.

[5]   Garg, R., and I.J. Bahl, "Microstrip Discontinuities," *Int. J.
        Electronics*, Vol. 45, No. 1, 1978, pp. 81-87.

[6]   Benedek, P., and P. Silvester, "Equivalent Capacitance for
        Microstrip Gaps and Steps," *IEEE Trans. Microwave Theory
        Tech.*, Vol. MTT-20, Nov. 1972, pp. 729-733.

[7]   Silvester, P., and P. Benedek, "Equivalent Capacitances of
        Microstrip Open Circuits," *ibid.*, Vol. MTT-20, Aug. 1972,
        pp. 511-516.

[8]   Silvester, P., and P. Benedek, "Microstrip Discontinuity Ca-
        pacitances for Right-Angled Bends, T-junctions and Cross-
        ings," *ibid.*, Vol. MTT-21, May 1973, pp. 341-346. (Also
        correction: Vol. MTT-23, May 1975, p. 456).

[9]   Farrar, A., and A.T. Adams, "Matrix Methods for Microstrip
        Three-Dimensional Problems," *ibid.*, Vol. MTT-20, Aug.
        1972, pp. 497-504.

[10]   Farrar, A., and A.T. Adams, "Computation of Lumped Micro-
        strip Capacities by Matrix Methods — Rectangular Sections
        and End Effect," *ibid.*, Vol. MTT-19, May 1971, pp. 495-
        497.

[11]   Maeda, M., "Analysis of Gap in Microstrip Transmission
        Lines," *ibid.*, Vol. MTT-20, June 1972, pp. 390-396.

[12] Horton, R., "The Electrical Characterization of a Right-Angled Bend in Microstrip Line," *ibid.*, Vol. MTT-21, June 1973, pp. 427-429.

[13] Itoh, T., *et al.*, "A Method for Computing Edge Capacitance of Finite and Semi-Finite Microstrip Lines," *ibid.*, Vol. MTT-20, 1972, pp. 847-849.

[14] Thomson, A.F., and A. Gopinath, "Calculation of Microstrip Discontinuity Inductances," *ibid.*, Vol. MTT-23, Aug. 1975, pp. 648-655.

[15] Gopinath, A., *et al.*, "Equivalent Circuit Parameters of Microstrip Change in Width and Cross-Junctions," *ibid.*, Vol. MTT-24, March 1976, pp. 142-144.

[16] Napoli, L.S. and J.J. Hughes, "Foreshortening of Microstrip Open Circuits on Alumina Substrates," *ibid.*, Vol. MTT-19, June 1971, pp. 559-561.

[17] Easter, B., "The Equivalent Circuit of Some Microstrip Discontinuities," *ibid.*, Vol. MTT-23, Aug. 1975, pp. 655-660.

[18] Stephens, I.M., and B. Easter, "Resonant Techniques for Establishing the Equivalent Circuits for Small Discontinuities in Microstrip," *Electronics Lett.*, Vol. 7, Sept. 23, 1971, pp. 582-584.

[19] Groll, H., and W. Weidmann, 'Measurement of Equivalent Circuit Elements of Microstrip Discontinuities by a Resonant Method," *NTZ*, Vol. 28, No. 2, 1975, p. 74.

[20] Wolff, I., and W. Menzel, "A Universal Method to Calculate the Dynamical Properties of Microstrip Discontinuities," in *Proc. 5th Europ. Micro. Conf.*, (Hamburg), 1975, pp. 263-267.

[21] Mehran, R., "The Frequency-Dependent Scattering Matrix of Microstrip Right-Angle Bends, T-Junctions and Crossings," *AEU*, Vol. 29, 1975, pp. 454-460.

[22] Mehran, R., "Frequency Dependent Equivalent Circuits for Microstrip Right-Angle Bends, T-Junctions and Crossings," *AEU*, Vol. 30, 1975, pp. 80-82.

[23]   Buontempo, V. and M. Reggiani, "Determinations of Trans-
        mission Line and Discontinuity Characteristics in Microwave
        Integrated Circuits," *Rev. Tecnica Selenia*, Vol. 2(2), 1975,
        pp. 33-52.

[24]   Hammerstad, E.O., "Equations for Microstrip Circuit Design,"
        in *Proc. 5th Europ. Micro Conf.*, (Hamburg), 1975, pp. 268-
        272.

[25]   Itoh, T., "Analysis of Microstrip Resonators," *IEEE Trans.
        Microwave Theory Tech.*, Vol. MTT-22, Nov. 1974, pp. 946-
        952.

[26]   Hoefer, W.J.R., "Equivalent Series Inductivity of a Narrow
        Transverse Slit in Microstrip," *IEEE Trans. Microwave
        Theory Tech.*, Vol. MTT-25, Oct. 1977, pp. 822-824.

[27]   Jahnke, E., and F. Emde, *Table of Functions*. New York,
        N.Y: Dover Publications, p. 16, 1945.

[28]   Chadha, R., and K.C. Gupta, "A Microwave Circuit Analysis
        Program," *Tech. Report DOE/EE/36-6*, Department of Elec-
        trical Engineering, I.I.T. Kanpur (India), May 1979.

7

Lumped Elements in Microwave Circuits

7.1 BASIC CONSIDERATIONS

Passive elements in conventional microwave circuits are mostly distributed and employ sections of transmission lines and waveguides. This is because the sizes of discrete lumped elements (resistors, inductors, and capacitors) used in electronic circuits at lower frequencies become comparable to the wavelength at microwave frequencies. However, if the sizes of lumped elements can be reduced to much smaller than the wavelength, they should also be acceptable at microwave frequencies. Lumped elements, for use at microwave frequencies, are designed on the basis of this consideration. With the advent of photolithography and thin film techniques, the sizes of elements can be reduced such that these elements may be used up to J-band frequencies [1-4].

Lumped elements are especially suitable for monolithic MICs and for broadband hybrid circuits with minimal size requirements, such as large ratio impedance transformers. Impedance transformations of the order of 20:1 have been reported at 6 GHz [1]. Moreover, the associated loss is small. Therefore, high-power devices which have very low impedance values can be easily tuned with large impedance transformers using lumped elements. Consequently, lumped elements find applications in high power oscillators, amplifiers, and low noise circuits.

The use of lumped elements provides improvement in bandwidth in several circuits. This results from the use of lumped resonant structures. For this reason, lumped elements are recommended for applications in circuits such as varactor tuned Gunn diode oscillators.

Computer-aided design of circuits using lumped elements requires a complete and accurate characterization of thin film lumped elements at microwave frequencies. This necessitates the development of comprehensive mathematical models which take into account the presence of ground planes, proximity effect, fringing fields, parasitics, etc. In this chapter, the available design and characterization details of lumped elements are discussed.

Like MICs using distributed elements, circuits using lumped elements are fabricated on dielectric substrates. However, the purpose of a substrate in lumped element circuits is mainly to provide the physical support and isolation between the various elements, whereas for MICs using distributed elements most of the energy is stored or propagates within the substrate. Therefore, the quality of substrate required for lumped elements is less critical. Nevertheless, for most lumped elements there is a fringing field extending into the substrate, and in order to avoid excessive dielectric loss, the substrate should have a low value of loss tangent. For low value of interturn capacitance in spiral inductors, substrates with low dielectric constant are preferable. Fused quartz has been frequently used for these circuits. When lumped elements are combined with MICs using distributed elements, the usual substrates such as alumina are used.

The three basic building-blocks for circuit design — inductors, resistors, and capacitors — are available in lumped form. Design considerations for these elements are discussed in the following sections. Equivalent circuits, with parasitics included, are given. S-matrix representation for these equivalent circuits can be obtained using Appendix 2.1.

7.2 DESIGN OF LUMPED ELEMENTS

Design of resistors, inductors, and capacitors at microwave frequencies may be arrived at by considering them as very short sections (much smaller than the wavelength) of TEM transmission lines. Consider a transmission line with series inductance per unit length L, resistance per unit length r, shunt capacitance per unit length C, and shunt conductance per unit length g. By using transmission line theory, input impedance of a length ℓ of the transmission line terminated in an impedance Z_L is given by

$$Z_{in} = Z_o \frac{Z_L \cosh \gamma\ell + Z_o \sinh \gamma\ell}{Z_o \cosh \gamma\ell + Z_L \sinh \gamma\ell} \tag{7.1}$$

where Z_o is the characteristic impedance of the transmission line given by

$$Z_o = \left(\frac{r + j\omega L}{g + j\omega C} \right)^{\frac{1}{2}} \tag{7.2}$$

and γ is the propagation constant given by

$$\gamma = \sqrt{(r + j\omega L)(g + j\omega C)} . \tag{7.3}$$

When $\gamma\ell \ll 1$, Z_{in} may be written as

$$Z_{in} = Z_o \frac{Z_L + Z_o \gamma\ell}{Z_o + Z_L \gamma\ell} . \tag{7.4}$$

7.2.1 Resistors and Inductors

When a small section ($\gamma\ell \ll 1$) of a transmission line is terminated in a short circuit, the input impedance as evaluated from (7.4) may be written as:

$$Z_{in} = Z_o \gamma\ell = (r + j\omega L) \ell . \tag{7.5}$$

This section of transmission line will behave like a resistor or like an inductor depending on the value of r as compared with that of ωL. However, in order to realize an inductor or a resistor, it is not necessary to have both the conductors of a transmission line. A single metallic strip on a dielectric substrate may be used for this purpose.

A lumped inductor may be realized using a metallic strip or a wire either in the form of straight section or a circular or square spiral.

Straight sections of ribbons and wires are used for low inductance values typically of the order of 2 to 3 nH. Spiral inductors have higher Q and can provide higher inductance values. The important characteristics to be considered for the design of inductors are the inductance value and the loss. These two determine the Q factor. In addition, one should take into account the effect of the presence of the ground plane while designing inductors. These aspects are considered in the section below.

Strip or Ribbon Inductors

Thin conductor strips of rectangular cross-section deposited on dielectric substrates are often used for low inductance values. In this case, values of r and L in (7.5) correspond to that of the metallic strip. The quantity r is the AC resistance per unit length and L is the self inductance per unit length. Terman [5] has given the formulas for r and L. The total resistance R_{ac} is given by

$$R_{ac} = r \ell = \frac{K R_s \ell}{\text{perimeter}} = \frac{K R_s \ell}{2(W + t)} \qquad (7.6)$$

where R_s is the sheet resistance in ohms per square, W is the width, and t is the thickness of metallic ribbon. K is a correction factor that takes into account the crowding of the current at the corners of the ribbon. Value of K is a function of W/t and varies from about 1.3 to 2 as the ratio W/t varies from 1 to 100. For W/t = 10, the value of K is about 1.55. For other values of W/t, the value of K may be obtained from the graph in [5]. For $5 < W/t < 100$, the following approximation may be used

$$K = 1.4 + 0.217 \ell n \left(\frac{W}{5t} \right) . \qquad (7.7)$$

Inductance of a rectangular strip in free space, far from other conductors or magnetic materials, is given by [5]

$$L \ell = 5.08 \times 10^{-3} \ell \left\{ \ell n \frac{\ell}{W + t} + 1.193 + 0.2235 \frac{W + t}{\ell} \right\} \qquad (7.8)$$

where $L \ell$ is in nanohenries and all dimensions are in mils.

Effect of Frequency and Ground Plane: Inductance values at high frequencies decrease due to the skin effect. The decrease in value is about 4 percent at 1 kHz and remains constant at higher frequencies [6]. The presence of a ground plane also affects the inductance value which decreases as the ground plane is brought nearer [6]. This decrease can be taken into account by means of a correction factor K_g. With this correction, the effective inductance L_E may be written as

$$L_E = K_g L_R \tag{7.9}$$

where L_R is the free-space inductance value. Chaddock [7] has measured the decrease in the value of inductance. His results can be written in closed form as

$$K_g = 0.57 - 0.145 \ln(W/h) \tag{7.10}$$

where W is the ribbon width and h is its spacing from the ground plane.

The unloaded Q of the strip inductor may be written as

$$Q = \omega L/R_{ac} . \tag{7.11}$$

For a copper strip ($R_s = 2.61 \times 10^{-7} f^{1/2}$) and for W/t = 10, one obtains

$$Q = 4.81 \times 10^7 f^{1/2} W \frac{L}{K} . \tag{7.12}$$

Using this expression, values of Q greater than 100 can be obtained with wide strips ($\ell/W < 15$), for an inductance of 1 nanohenry or greater at about 1 GHz. For these equations to hold good, the thickness t must be appreciably greater than twice the skin depth.

The strip inductors are practicable for inductances of 2 nanohenries or less, and are typically about 110 mils long (with $\ell/W = 10$). This length is less than one turn of a 40 mil diameter spiral coil. For larger inductances, many spiral turns are necessary and the above expression does not hold good.

Spiral Inductors

The configuration of a flat spiral strip inductor is shown in Figure 7.1(a). An expression for the inductance of a spiral inductor with n turns may be written as [5, 8, 9]

$$L_s(nH) = 0.01\,\pi n^2 a \left\{ \ln\frac{8a}{c} + \frac{1}{24}\left(\frac{c}{a}\right)^2 \left(\ln\frac{8a}{c} + 3.583\right) - \frac{1}{2}\right\} \tag{7.13}$$

where $a = (d_o + d_i)/4$ (i.e. average radius), $c = (d_o - d_i)/2$ and d_i and d_o are the minimum and the maximum diameters (in mils), respectively. Wheeler [10] has derived the following simple approximation which gives numerical values that are within a few percent of (7.13) over most of the range:

$$L_s(nH) = \frac{n^2 a^2}{8a + 11c} \tag{7.14}$$

where all the dimensions are in mils. Measurements have shown the inductance values to be within 20 percent of theoretical calculations [15].

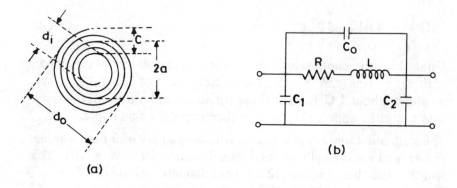

(a)

(b)

Figure 7.1   (a) Configuration of a spiral inductor; (b) Equivalent circuit for a spiral inductor.

The resistance of the spiral inductor may be written as

$$R = K' \pi na\, R_s/W \tag{7.15}$$

where K' is a correction factor, similar to K for straight ribbons, and accounts for the current crowding. From (7.14) and (7.15), Q for the flat spiral coil may be written as

$$Q = \frac{2 \times 10^{-9}\, f\, W\, na}{K'\, R_s\, (8a + 11c)} \tag{7.16}$$

where a, c and W are in mils. The equivalent circuit for the spiral configuration does not consist of an inductance alone. There are associated parasitics in the form of self-capacitance and inter-turn capacitance, C_o, as well as the shunt fringing capacitances C_1 and C_2 due to the effects of ground [4]. The equivalent circuit for a spiral inductor including parasitics is shown in Figure 7.1(b). The series resistance R accounts for the loss. The typical range of values for parasitic elements for a spiral with diameter in the range of 1.0 to 5.0 mm on an alumina substrate are as follows: C_o is nearly 0.15 pF, C_1 ranges from 0.1 to 0.2 pF, C_2 ranges from 0.05 to 0.1 pF, and Q at 4 GHz ranges from 80 to 100. An empirical relation for C_o may be written as [4]

$$C_o(pF) = 0.035\, d_o + 0.06 \tag{7.17}$$

where d_o is the outer diameter of spiral in mm.

Some salient considerations useful in the design of inductors may be summarized as follows:

1. The spiral should have the widest ribbon possible (W large) while keeping the overall diameter (d_o) small. This implies that the separation between the turns should be as small as possible.

2. There should be some space at the center of the spiral inductor to allow the flux lines to pass through, thus increasing the stored energy per unit length. It has been pointed out [9] that d_i/d_o = 1/5 optimizes the value of Q.

3. The surface resistance R_s increases as $f^{1/2}$. Therefore, Q of the inductor increases only as the square root of frequency. However, it has been found experimentally that Q increases only up to a certain frequency and then falls off rapidly [1,17]. This is

probably due to the current crowding and the radiation at higher frequencies. The measured values of Q are found within 2/3 of the theoretical value with $K' = 1$. An assigned value of K' (= 1.5) gives reasonable agreement with the expression (7.16). Q's of about 100 have been achieved.

4. It has been shown that for the same d_o, the Q of a circular spiral will be higher (by about 10 percent) than that of a square spiral, although the inductance is significantly (about 20 percent) less.

5. Multi-turn coils have higher Q (because of higher inductance per unit area) but, because of inter-turn capacitance, they have lower self-resonance frequencies. When the dielectric constant of the substrate is increased, inter-turn capacitance increases and the self-resonance frequency is reduced. This produces an increase in the reactance (and hence in the apparent inductance) of the inductor.

Wire Inductor

This type of inductor is used in MICs as a bonding wire for connections to active devices and to other massive components. The free-space inductance of a wire of diameter d is given by [5]

$$L_w(nH) = 5.08 \times 10^{-3} \, \ell \, [\ell n \, (4\ell/d) - 1] \tag{7.18}$$

where ℓ and d are measured in mils. The resistance R of a wire of length ℓ is obtained from

$$R = R_s \frac{\ell}{\pi d} \tag{7.19}$$

and Q factor may be obtained from

$$Q_w = \frac{2\pi f L_w}{R} . \tag{7.20}$$

Comparing the above equation for Q with that for the strip inductors one finds that, for a value of d equal to ribbon width W, the wire inductor has a higher Q. This is due to the fact that the surface area (for carrying current) is larger for a wire.

The effect of the ground plane on the inductance value of a wire

has also been considered [5]. If the wire is at a distance h above
the ground plane,

$$L_w(nH) = 5.08 \times 10^{-3} \ell \left\{ \ell n \frac{4h}{d} + \ell n \left[\frac{\ell + \sqrt{\ell^2 + d^2/4}}{\ell + \sqrt{\ell^2 + 4h^2}} \right] \right.$$

$$\left. + \sqrt{1 + \frac{4h^2}{\ell^2}} - \sqrt{1 + \frac{d^2}{4\ell^2}} - 2 \frac{h}{\ell} + \frac{d}{2\ell} \right\}$$

$$(7.21)$$

where ℓ, d and h are expressed in mils.

7.2.2 Capacitors

A lumped capacitor may be visualized as a small length of an open-
circuited line (Figure 7.2a) for which the input impedance may be
written as

$$Z_{in} = Z_o \coth \gamma\ell . \tag{7.22}$$

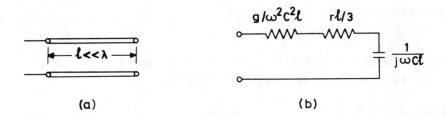

(a)   (b)

Figure 7.2   (a) *An open-circuited line used as a capacitor; (b) Equivalent circuit for the capacitor in (a).*

When $\gamma\ell \ll 1$, (7.22) may be simplified as

$$Z_{in} \cong \frac{Z_o}{\gamma\ell} = \frac{1}{g\ell + j\omega C\ell} = \frac{g}{\omega^2 C^2 \ell} + \frac{1}{j\omega C\ell} . \tag{7.23}$$

The equivalent circuit will thus have a resistance $g/(\omega^2 C^2 \ell)$ in series with the capacitor $C\ell$. A second order approximation (still ignoring L) yields:

$$Z_{in} = \frac{Z_o}{\gamma\ell} + \frac{Z_o \gamma\ell}{3} \approx \frac{g}{\omega^2 C^2 \ell} + \frac{r\ell}{3} + \frac{1}{j\omega C\ell} \quad . \quad (7.24)$$

This represents a series circuit of two resistors and a capacitor as shown in Figure 7.2(b). The second term represents the series resistance responsible for the conductor loss and may be written as

$$\frac{r\ell}{3} = \frac{2R_s\ell}{3W} \quad\quad\quad (7.25)$$

where $r = 2R_s/W$. It may be noted that only inside surfaces of width W contribute to conductor loss and the factor 2 accounts for the loss on the two plates of the capacitor. The other resistive component $g/(\omega^2 C^2 \ell)$ is due to the dielectric loss and may be written as $1/(Q_d \omega C\ell)$ where Q_d is the dielectric Q given by $\omega C/g$. The total Q may thus be written as

$$1/Q = 1/Q_c + 1/Q_d \quad\quad\quad (7.26)$$

where the conductor Q is

$$Q_c = (1/\omega C\ell)(3W/2R_s\ell) \quad . \quad\quad\quad (7.27)$$

Q_c for a square capacitor (W = ℓ) with copper plates and having a total capacitance C_T (in pF) may be written as

$$Q_c = \frac{2.9 \times 10^4}{f^{3/2} \, C_T} \quad\quad\quad (7.28)$$

where f is in GHz.

In order to have a large value of capacitance per unit area, it becomes necessary to decrease the distance between the two conductors (top and bottom) of the transmission line section. Since the normal thickness of alumina substrates used is of the order of 25 mils, for large capacitances a metal-dielectric-metal structure is fabricated on the top surface of the substrate. This configuration is shown in Figure 7.3(a). The dielectric (usually silicon dioxide) used for this sandwich configuration is typically 0.02 to 0.04 mil (0.5 to 1.0 µm) thick. This type of capacitor has been fabricated with dielectric Q of 600 at 1 GHz. Q values at higher frequency are lower in accordance with (7.28).

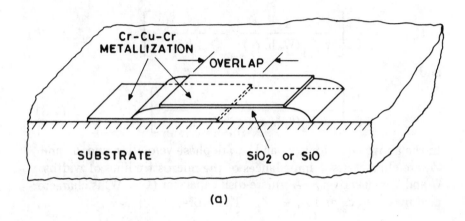

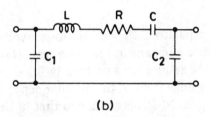

Figure 7.3   (a) Configuration of an overlay capacitor; (b) Equivalent circuit for the capacitor in (a).

An accurate calculation of the capacitance for sandwich capacitors should take into account the effect of fringing field. This calculation has been reported by Wolff and Knoppik [11]. In this analysis, a rectangular capacitor is considered as a microstrip line having a length ℓ and width W. The capacitance may be written as

$$C = \frac{\epsilon_o \epsilon_r W \ell}{h} + 2 C_{e1} + 2 C_{e2} \qquad (7.29)$$

where C_{e1} and C_{e2} are edge capacitances given by

$$C_{e1} = \frac{1}{2} \left[\frac{1}{v_1 Z_1 (W, h, \epsilon_r)} - \frac{\epsilon_o \epsilon_r W}{h} \right] \ell \qquad (7.30)$$

and

$$C_{e2} = \frac{1}{2} \left[\frac{1}{v_2 Z_2 (\ell, h, \epsilon_r)} - \frac{\epsilon_o \epsilon_r \ell}{h} \right] W . \qquad (7.31)$$

In the above equations, v_1 and v_2 are phase velocities, and Z_1 and Z_2 are characteristic impedances of the microstrip lines of widths W and ℓ, respectively. A square disk capacitor ($\ell = W$) is characterized by $v_1 = v_2$ and $Z_1 = Z_2$. Therefore,

$$C_{e1} = C_{e2} = \frac{1}{2} \left\{ \frac{W}{vZ(W, h, \epsilon_r)} - \frac{\epsilon_o \epsilon_r W^2}{h} \right\} . \qquad (7.32)$$

For circular shaped capacitors, the calculations involve evaluating an equivalent dielectric constant in the same way as for the microstrip line and using the results for a uniformly filled configuration. It is assumed that the edge field of the circular capacitor with a large radius r_o (say $r_o/h > 10$) is similar to that of the rectangular disc capacitor. This assumption yields

$$\epsilon_{eq} = \frac{\epsilon_o \epsilon_r \pi r_o^2 + \pi r_o h \left[\dfrac{1}{v Z(2r_o, h, \epsilon_r)} - \dfrac{2 \epsilon_o \epsilon_r r_o}{h} \right]}{\epsilon_o \pi r_o^2 + \pi r_o h \left[\dfrac{1}{v Z(2r_o, h, \epsilon_r = 1)} - (2\epsilon_o r_o/h) \right]} \qquad (7.33)$$

where $Z(2r_o, h, \epsilon_r)$ is the characteristic impedance, and v is the phase velocity for a microstrip line of width $W = 2r_o$. The capacitance of a circular disk may be written as [11]

$$C = \frac{\epsilon_o \, \epsilon_{eq} \, \pi \, r_o^2}{h} \left\{ 1 + \frac{2h}{\pi r_o} \left[\ln \left(\frac{\pi r_o}{2h} \right) + 1.7726 \right] \right\} .(7.34)$$

The equivalent circuit for a sandwich capacitor is shown in Figure 7.3(b). Here, R represents losses in the capacitor. Parasitics are represented by a series inductance L and fringing capacitances C_1 and C_2 due to the ground [4]. Series inductance is typically 0.5 nH for nominal 1 mm by 0.5 mm dimensions (0.25 mm overlap). The fringing capacitances C_1 and C_2 vary between 0.05 and 0.2 pF.

Another configuration for lumped capacitors with low capacitance values is the interdigital geometry shown in Figure 7.4(a). In this geometry, both the conductors of the capacitor are in the same plane, which is the top surface of the dielectric substrate used. This type of capacitor can be fabricated by the technique used for the fabrication of conventional microstrip circuits and does not require any additional processing steps when incorporated in microstrip circuits.

An analysis for interdigital capacitor has been reported by Alley [12]. The capacitance between two sets of digits in interdigital structure is found by using the capacitance formula for the odd mode in coupled microstrip lines, with the ground plane spacing tending to an infinitely large value. When the effect of the ground plane cannot be ignored, it is necessary to consider the contribution of the even mode also. Design formula in this case has been presented by Alley [12]. For Figure 7.4(a), we have [12]

$$C(pF) = \ell (\epsilon_r + 1) [(N - 3) A_1 + A_2] \qquad (7.35)$$

where N is the number of fingers, A_1 = 0.225 pF/in., A_2 = 0.252 pF/in. for infinite thickness of substrate or no ground plane, and ℓ is measured in inches. The Q of the interdigital capacitor is given as

$$Q_c = \frac{1}{\omega C \, R_{series}} \qquad (7.36)$$

where

$$R_{series} = \frac{4}{3} \frac{\ell}{XN} R_s \qquad (7.37)$$

and X is the width of a cell, as shown in Figure 7.4(a).

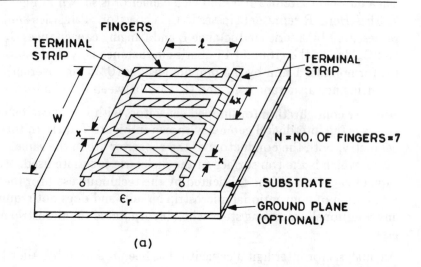

(a)

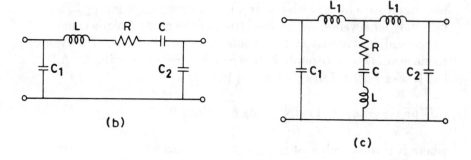

(b)   (c)

Figure 7.4   (a) Configuration of an interdigital capacitor; (b) Equivalent circuit for series mounting; (c) Equivalent circuit for shunt mounting.

As in the case of sandwich geometry, both the dielectric loss and the conductor loss determine the Q factor. The Q of a 2.83 pF capacitor (N = 40, ℓ = 44.8 mils, X = 2 mils) fabricated on a 24 mil thick alumina substrate (99.5 percent purity) has been measured to be 677 at 1.92 GHz [12].

Because of the inductance contributed by the equivalent transmission line, the interdigital capacitors show multiple resonances. Change in the capacitance value with frequency depends on the ratio W/ℓ. The optimum value of W/ℓ may be found numerically so that the capacitance variation with frequency is minimum. As an example, for W/ℓ = 1.66 and N = 24, the capacitance value is constant up to a frequency of 3 GHz.

Interdigital capacitors, with Q's comparable to those for the sandwich type, have been fabricated directly on alumina substrate without using any additional dielectric material. They appear to be lumped up to 3 GHz and values from 0.1 to 10 pF can be achieved. For higher capacitance values, sandwich capacitors should be used. The interdigital approach for capacitors requires a relatively large area (500 by 70 mil for 12 pF value as compared with 22 by 22 mil for 1 μm thick SiO_2 capacitor). However, this type may be preferred for low capacitance values because only a single layer of metallization is required.

Taking into account the parasitics, equivalent circuits for an interdigital capacitor are shown in Figure 7.4 (b and c) [4]. The equivalent circuit for a series mounted configuration is shown in Figure 7.4(b) and that for shunt usage is shown in Figure 7.4(c).

Lumped resonators can be obtained by suitably combining lumped inductors and lumped capacitors. When interdigital capacitors are used the fabrication of the resonator involves only a single process. Both series and parallel resonant circuits are possible and have been used in filter circuits [13, 14]. The resonant circuit configurations are shown in Figure 7.5. It has been demonstrated [14] that lumped element parallel-resonant circuits with single-turn inductors can be fabricated for operation from 5 to 10 GHz, with resistance values of about one ohm or less. This corresponds to Q values between 10 and 90.

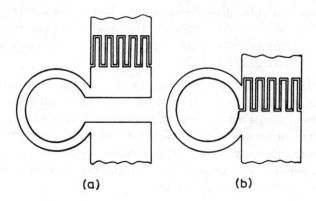

                              (a)   (b)

*Figure 7.5   Lumped element resonators: (a) Series resonator;
              (b) Shunt resonator.*

The measured values of inductance agree with the inductance formulas (7.8), (7.13), and (7.18) to within 20 percent. The discrepancy may be due to the presence of extraneous capacitance and
inductance, due to approximations in the closed form design expressions, and also because of measurement uncertainties. The
measured Q is approximately half that predicted by the ohmic
loss and the inductance formulas. These low values of measured
Q may occur because the conductor is not formed from the bulk
material. For capacitors, also, there is a discrepancy between the
measured and calculated Q values.

Design formulas with about 20 percent error are not very useful
for computer-aided design. These formulas can, at best, serve as
a guideline for initial design. Therefore, it becomes necessary to
model lumped elements on the basis of measured values. Measurement techniques for the accurate characterization of lumped
elements are described in the following section.

7.3 MEASUREMENTS OF LUMPED ELEMENT PARAMETERS

Because of the small size of lumped elements, special techniques
are needed for measurement of their parameters. Basically, there

are three different techniques for measuring the reactance and the Q of lumped elements. These are: (i) direct impedance measurement using reflection technique, (ii) embedding the lumped element in a resonant structure so that the perturbations yield information about the lumped element, and (iii) the study of the susceptance of a combination of a lumped inductor and a lumped capacitor near resonance.

Direct impedance measurement for characterizing the lumped element may be carried out by means of precision coaxial slotted lines, reflectometers and network analyzers. Slotted line techniques yield accurate information only up to 2.5 GHz. The measurement of Q and reactances at higher frequencies becomes difficult because the line losses approach the resistance of the element. Details of the technique of direct impedance measurement are available in [15].

The resonator method for lumped elements can be used up to 12 GHz. This technique is based on measurements of resonance frequency and Q of a resonant transmission line. By connecting a lumped element to the line, the frequency of resonance and Q are perturbed, and from the perturbations, the impedance of the element can be found. Since the transmission line resonates at multiples of the fundamental frequency, the impedance of the lumped element can be found at various frequencies.

Consider a transmission line open at one end and connected to a lumped element at the other end as shown in Figure 7.6. This combination will resonate when

$$jX = jZ_o \cot \theta \tag{7.38}$$

where X is the reactive part of the impedance of the lumped element and θ is the electrical length of the transmission line given by

$$\theta = 2\pi f \ell / v \tag{7.39}$$

where f, ℓ, and v are the frequency of resonance, the length of the line, and the velocity of wave propagation, respectively. Without the lumped element attached, this transmission line resonates when the following condition is satisfied:

$$n\pi = 2\pi f_n \ell / v \tag{7.40}$$

where f_n is the nth order resonance frequency. From (7.39) and
(7.40) we can find θ in terms of the two resonance frequencies as

$$\theta = n\pi f/f_n \ . \tag{7.41}$$

Therefore, (7.38) becomes

$$X = Z_o \cot(n\pi f/f_n) \tag{7.42}$$

where f is the resonance frequency for the circuit shown in Figure
7.6, and f_n is the resonance frequency for the same line length with
both ends open.

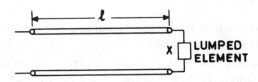

Figure 7.6   Configuration of an open-ended transmission line terminated by a lumped element at one end.

In a practical set-up, the value of f_n is measured first. Then the
lumped element is attached and resonant frequency f measured.
Alternatively, two identical lines may be fabricated on the same
substrate and the lumped element attached to one of them. With
this arrangement, multiple resonance frequencies for the two lines
can be measured and the value of reactance obtained over a range
of discrete frequencies.

The Q factor of a lumped component can be evaluated from the
measurement of Q for the unloaded line and for the line loaded
with the component. Since the total power loss is equal to the
sum of the power losses in the line and the element, we can write

$$\frac{U_{01}}{Q_{01}} = \frac{U_0}{Q_o} + \frac{U_1}{Q_1} \qquad (7.43)$$

where U_{01}, U_0, and U_1 are the energies stored in the combined system, the unloaded line, and the element, respectively, and Q_{01}, Q_0, and Q_1 are the respective Q factors. U_{01} is the sum of U_0 and U_1. Values of Q_{01} and Q_0 are measured experimentally. The energies U_1 and U_0 are calculated as follows. The energy stored in the transmission line, U_0, is given by

$$U_o = \frac{1}{2} \frac{L_o}{\beta} \int_o^\theta [I_o \sin(\beta x)]^2 \ d(\beta x)$$

$$= \frac{1}{8} \frac{Z_o}{\omega} I_o^2 (2\theta - \sin 2\theta) = I_o^2 A \qquad (7.44)$$

where L_o is the inductance per unit length of the line and θ is the electrical length defined in (7.39). The energy stored in the lumped element is calculated in terms of the current flowing through the element. For an inductor, the stored energy is given by

$$U_1 = \frac{1}{2} L (I_o \sin \theta)^2 = I_o^2 B . \qquad (7.45)$$

The value of Q_1, obtained from (7.43) to (7.45), is given as

$$Q_1 = B \left(\frac{A + B}{Q_{o1}} - \frac{A}{Q_o} \right)^{-1} \qquad (7.46)$$

where A and B have been defined in (7.44) and (7.45), respectively.

The accuracy of this measurement technique increases as the difference $(U_1/Q_1 - U_0/Q_o)$ increases. Thus, for greater accuracy, both the unmodified Q of the transmission line Q_o, and the ratio of the energy stored in the lumped element to that of the line, U_1/U_o, should be as large as possible. The ratio U_1/U_o is dependent on the impedance of the line.

Coaxial line resonators, microstrip resonators, and coplanar line resonators have been used for these measurements. For half-wave resonators, the lumped element can be series-mounted in the middle

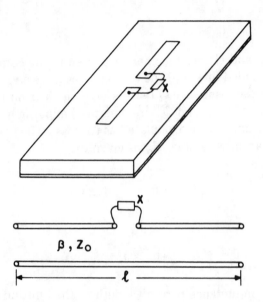

Figure 7.7   Series mounting of a lumped element in the middle of a resonator.

of the resonator as shown in Figure 7.7. Placing the lumped element in this manner modifies the resonant frequency for those modes of the resonator for which the current has a non-zero value at the location of the element. The fundamental mode of resonance and the odd harmonics have this property. For series mounting in the middle of the line, (7.42) holds with f replaced by f/2 and Z_o by $2Z_o$. It is also possible to shunt mount the components in the middle of a transmission line resonator. In this case, only even harmonics of the fundamental mode will be affected, and f should be replaced by f/2 and Z_o by $Z_o/2$ in (7.42).

Aitchison *et al.* [16] point out that lumped elements can be characterized by studying the susceptance of the parallel resonant network of a lumped inductor and a capacitor combination near resonance. Measurement of the complex susceptance and VSWR near resonance enables complete characterization, since: (a) dB/dω at resonance is equal to 2C; (b) the resonant frequency is known and C has been determined, therefore L can be calculated; (c) G is obtained from the VSWR at the resonant frequency, and Q of the circuit can be calculated from

$$Q = \frac{\omega}{2G} \frac{dB}{d\omega} \quad \text{at resonance.} \tag{7.47}$$

The Q values of the individual elements are not easily separated.

For measurements, the parallel-resonant circuit (Figure 7.8) is fabricated on a quartz disk (0.5 mm thick) and connected across a coaxial line, followed by a circular waveguide near cutoff to simulate open-circuit conditions. The coaxial line test fixture is shown in Figure 7.9.

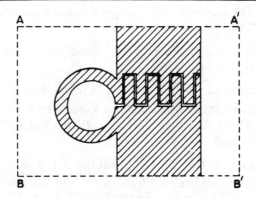

Figure 7.8   Parallel resonant circuit for measurements.

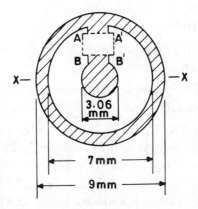

Figure 7.9   Coaxial line test fixture for lumped element character-ization.

REFERENCES

[1]   Caulton, M., "Lumped Elements in Microwave Integrated
       Circuits," in *Advances in Microwaves*, Vol. 8, L. Young
       and H. Sobol, (Eds.), New York: Academic Press, 1974.

[2]   Gupta, K.C., "Lumped Elements for MICs," in *Microwave
       Integrated Circuits*, K.C. Gupta and A. Singh, (Eds.), New
       Delhi, Wiley Eastern, 1974, Ch. 6.

[3]   Gupta, K.C., *Microwaves*, New Delhi: Wiley Eastern, 1979,
       Ch. 11.

[4]   Pengelly, R.S., and D.C. Rickard, "Design, Measurement
       and Application of Lumped Elements up to J-band," in
       Proc. 7th European Microwave Conf., (Copenhagen), 1977,
       pp. 460-464.

[5]   Terman, F.E., *Radio Engineer Handbook*, New York: Mc-
       Graw-Hill, 1943, p. 51.

[6]   Gopinath, A., and P. Silvester, "Calculation of Inductance
       of Finite-Length Strips and its Variations with Frequency,"
       IEEE Trans. Microwave Theory Tech., Vol. MTT-21, 1973,
       pp. 380-386.

[7]   Chaddock, R.E., "The Application of Lumped Element
       Techniques to High Frequency Hybrid Integrated Circuits,"
       Radio and Electronics Engg. (GB), Vol. 44, 1974, pp. 414-420.
       1974.

[8]   Grover, F.W., *Inductance Calculations*, Princeton, NJ: Van
       Nostrand, 1946.

[9]   Dukes, J.M.C., *Printed Circuits: Their Design and Applica-
       tion.* London: Macdonald, 1961.

[10]   Wheeler, H.A., "Simple Inductance Formulas for Radio
       Coils," *Proc. IRE*, Vol. 16, Oct. 1928, pp. 1398-1400.

[11]   Wolff, I., and N. Knoppik, "Rectangular and Circular Micro-
       strip Disk Capacitors and Resonators," *IEEE Trans. Micro-
       wave Theory Tech.*, Vol. MTT-22, Oct. 1974, pp. 857-864.

[12]   Alley, G.D., "Interdigital Capacitors and Their Applications
       to Lumped-element Microwave Integrated Circuits," *IEEE
       Trans. Microwave Theory Tech.*, Vol. MTT-18, Dec. 1970,
       pp. 1028-1033.

[13]   Aitchison, C.S., *et al.*, "Lumped Microwave Circuits: Part
        III: Filters and Tunnel-diode Amplifiers," *Design Electron-
        ics*, Vol. 9, No. 2, Nov. 1971, pp. 42-51.

[14]   Aitchison, C.S., "Lumped Components for Microwave Fre-
        quencies," *Philips Tech. Rev.*, Vol. 32, No. 9/10/11/12, 1971,
        pp. 305-314.

[15]   Daly, D.A., *et al.*, "Lumped Elements in Microwave Inte-
        grated Circuits," *IEEE Trans. Microwave Theory Tech.*,
        Vol. MTT-15, Dec. 1967, pp. 713-721.

[16]   Aitchison, C.S., *et al.*, "Lumped-circuit Elements at Micro-
        wave Frequencies," *IEEE Trans. Microwave Theory Tech.*,
        Vol. MTT-19, Dec. 1971, pp. 928-937.

[17]   Katoh, H., "A Lumped Element Approach to Microwave
        Integrated Circuits," *Trans. of IECE of Japan*, Vol. 56B,
        No. 6, June 1973, pp. 213-220.

8

Two-Dimensional Planar Components

Various types of components for microwave circuits discussed in the earlier chapters may be classified in three categories. Lumped elements discussed in Chapter 7 may be termed *zero-dimensional* since all three dimensions are much smaller than the wavelength, λ corresponding to the frequency of operation. Transmission lines (coaxial lines, striplines, microstrip lines, and coplanar lines) discussed in Chapter 3 may be called *one-dimensional* since their cross-sectional dimensions are much smaller than the wavelength, whereas their lengths are comparable to λ. Waveguides, discussed in Section 3.2, also have cross-sectional dimensions comparable to wavelength and may, on similar considerations, be termed *three-dimensional* components. In addition to these, we have components whose one dimension (i.e., height) is much smaller than λ but the other two dimensions are comparable to (or greater than) λ. These are called *two-dimensional* (2-d) or planar components and are discussed in this chapter.

Three types of configurations for the planar circuits are possible. These are, i) triplate or stripline type, shown in Figure 8.1(a) and (c); ii) open or microstrip type, shown in Figure 8.1(b) and (c); and iii) waveguide type, shown in Figure 8.1(d). The concept of 2-d planar circuits has found several applications in microwave integrated circuits, waveguide circuits, ferrite components, and microstrip antennas. Some of the advantages of the planar circuit approach (PCA) are as follows:

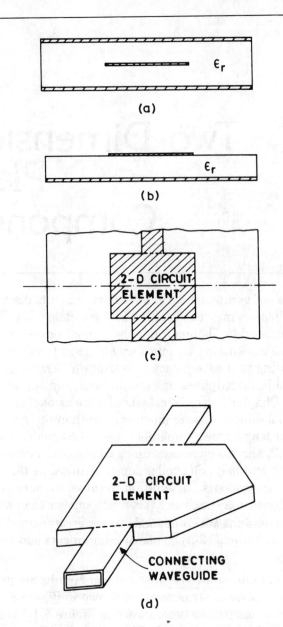

*Figure 8.1   Three types of two-dimensional microwave circuits:
(a) stripline type; (b) microstrip type; (c) plan view
of (a) or (b); and (d) waveguide type.*

a) One-dimensional stripline and microstrip line circuits may be treated as special cases of 2-d circuits. In MICs, actual line lengths become small at high frequencies and line widths become large for low impedance levels (which are normally needed for use with microwave semiconductor devices). In such cases, PCA yields better characterizations of MICs than offered by the transmission line approach.

b) PCA is also applicable to the analysis of discontinuities in striplines and microstrip lines. By optimizing the discontinuity configuration, its effect can be compensated for. This helps to improve performance.

c) Several new designs can be obtained by using the PCA. For example, it has been shown [1] that a circular disc resonator can also be used as a 3-db hybrid.

d) Planar circuits, fabricated on ferrite substrates, may also be analyzed by PCA and extension of techniques used for analyzing circuits on dielectric substrates. This method has been used to obtain the optimum shape of a wideband circulator [2].

e) In microstrip antennas, the aperture field distribution can be evaluated by treating them as planar components with magnetic walls. PCA can be used to evaluate the field along the periphery of these components.

f) With the use of photoetching techniques, planar circuits are easier to fabricate than the three-dimensional waveguide circuits.

8.1 BASIC CONCEPTS [3]

Consider a stripline type planar circuit shown in Figure 8.2. Basic equations for obtaining circuit parameters for the equivalent multiport are discussed in this section.

In the circuit in Figure 8.2, an arbitrarily shaped thin conductor is sandwiched midway between two ground conductors spaced 2d apart. This circuit is excited symmetrically with respect to the upper and the lower ground conductors. There are several ports along the periphery. The widths of these ports are denoted by W_i,

W_j, etc. The rest of the periphery is open-circuited. The coordinate axes are chosen such that the central conducting patch lies in the x-y plane and is perpendicular to the z-axis. Thus, while the dimensions along x and y coordinates are comparable to the wavelength, the thickness along the z-direction is negligible. Therefore, the fields can be assumed to be constant along the z-direction.

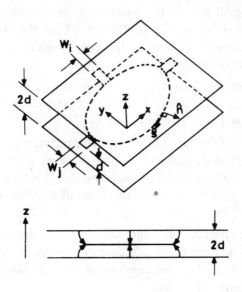

Figure 8.2   Configuration of a stripline type planar circuit.

The general Helmholtz equation, valid for a source free region, is given as

$$(\nabla^2 + k^2) E = 0 , \qquad k^2 = \omega^2 \mu\epsilon \tag{8.1}$$

where μ and ϵ denote the permeability and permittivity of the dielectric material and ω is the angular frequency. The above relation holds good for describing the field within the dielectric. At the

center conductor and at the ground planes the tangential components of the electric field are zero. A magnetic wall is assumed to
exist at the periphery of the 2-d component. Since the fields do
not vary along the z-direction, both E_x and E_y equal zero within
the dielectric region. The fringing field at the periphery is taken
into account by shifting the magnetic wall by a certain distance
from the physical periphery. This shift is shown in Figure 8.3. For
stripline type planar circuits, the shift δ in the magnetic wall is given
by [4],

$$\delta = \frac{2d \ln 2}{\pi} .$$ (8.2)

This value of δ is exact for a semi-infinite patch only, but can be
used in most practical cases. For rectangular patches, the value of
δ can be obtained using (6.2). For microstrip type circuits [5], the
value of δ is obtained from the expression (7.31) for the fringing
capacitance at a microstrip edge.

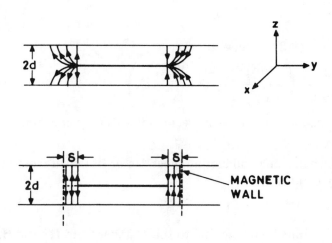

*Figure 8.3   Shift in the magnetic wall to account for the fringing
field.*

It may be noted that the fields above and below the central patch must be oppositely directed. In the discussions below, the E and H can be taken to be the fields on one side of the central patch (the lower side, for instance).

Since E_x and E_y are zero, the E-field in two-dimensional components may be written as

$$E = \hat{a}_z\, E_z(x,y) \tag{8.3}$$

where $\hat{a}_z$ is a unit vector along the z-direction, and E_z is a function of x and y coordinates only. Substituting (8.3) in (8.1) and setting $\partial E_z/\partial z$ equal to zero, we obtain

$$(\nabla_T^2 + k^2)\, E_z = 0 \tag{8.4}$$

where $\nabla_T^2 = \dfrac{\partial^2}{\partial x^2} + \dfrac{\partial^2}{\partial y^2}$. Using Maxwell's equation, the magnetic field can be written as

$$H = -\frac{1}{j\omega\mu}\, \nabla \times E \tag{8.5}$$

which, using (8.3), reduces to

$$H = \frac{1}{j\omega\mu}\left(-\frac{\partial E_z}{\partial y}\, \hat{a}_x + \frac{\partial E_z}{\partial x}\, \hat{a}_y\right) \tag{8.6}$$

where $\hat{a}_x$ and $\hat{a}_y$ are unit vectors along the x and y coordinates respectively.

Surface current on a conducting sheet can be obtained from the boundary condition

$$J_s = \hat{n} \times (H_1 - H_2) \tag{8.7}$$

where $\hat{n}$ is a unit vector normal to the boundary and H_1 and H_2 are magnetic fields on the two sides of a conducting sheet. For the central conductor of a stripline type 2-d circuit, $H_1 = -H_2$ and thus

$$J_s = \frac{2}{j\omega\mu}\left(\frac{\partial E_z}{\partial x}\, \hat{a}_x + \frac{\partial E_z}{\partial y}\, \hat{a}_y\right) \text{ amps/m} . \tag{8.8}$$

For a microstrip type planar circuit (with the periphery extended to take care of the fringing fields), there is no magnetic field above the upper conducting plane and so the factor of 2 in (8.8) will not be used to obtain the surface current on the conducting patch.

The expression for J_s in (8.8) is valid at all points on the central patch including the periphery. For points on the periphery, J_s can be rewritten in terms of components which are normal and tangential to the periphery. We have

$$J_s = \frac{2}{j\omega\mu} \left(\frac{\partial E_z}{\partial s} \, \hat{s} + \frac{\partial E_z}{\partial n} \, \hat{n} \right) \quad \text{amps/m} \qquad (8.9)$$

where $\hat{s}$ and $\hat{n}$ are unit vectors tangential and normal to the periphery as shown in Figure 8.2. For points on the periphery where there are no coupling ports, the normal component of the surface current must be zero, or

$$\frac{\partial E_z}{\partial n} = 0 . \qquad (8.10)$$

The planar circuit can be excited either by microstrip lines (or striplines) connected to the coupling ports or by coaxial lines. When excited by a coaxial line as shown in Figure 8.4, the current flow at the point of excitation is along the z-direction. At a coupling port

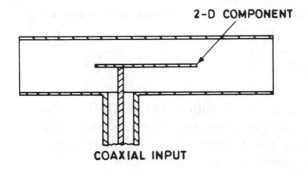

Figure 8.4   Coaxial line excitation of a planar circuit.

on the periphery, the planar circuit can be excited by a stripline (or microstrip) and in this case the current flow (at the coupling port) is normal to the periphery. The current flowing in at a coupling port is obtained using (8.9):

$$i = - \frac{2}{j\omega\mu} \int_W \frac{\partial E_z}{\partial n} \, ds \qquad (8.11)$$

where W is the width of the coupling port and ds is the incremental distance along the periphery. The negative sign in (8.11) implies that the current i flows inwards whereas $\hat{n}$ in (8.9) points outwards.

The characterization of the planar components can be carried out in terms of an RF voltage v on the central conductor. Since $\partial E_z/\partial z = 0$, we have from (8.3),

$$v = - E_z d \ . \qquad (8.12)$$

Equations (8.4), (8.10) and (8.11) can now be written as follows:

$$(\nabla_T^2 + k^2) v = 0 \qquad (8.13)$$

with

$$\frac{\partial v}{\partial n} = 0 \qquad (8.14)$$

for points on the periphery where there are no coupling ports. The current flowing in at a coupling port is expressed as

$$i = \frac{2}{j\omega\mu d} \int_W \frac{\partial v}{\partial n} \, ds \ . \qquad (8.15)$$

The solution of (8.13), with (8.14) and (8.15) as the boundary conditions, leads to the characterization of stripline type of planar components. Governing equations for other types of planar circuits can be obtained using similar procedures.

Various methods for characterizing a planar component using the above approach depend upon the geometry of the central patch. When the planar circuit has a *simple* geometrical shape, the Green's function approach discussed in Sections 8.2 and 8.3 is most convenient. Green's functions are presently available for rectangles, circles, annular rings, some types of triangles, and some circular and annular sectors. Using these Green's functions, the impedance matrix characterization of the circuit can be obtained for the specified ports locations.

When the geometrical shape of the planar circuit is made up of simpler shapes for which the Green's functions are available, the *segmentation* method can be used to find the characteristics of the overall circuit from those of the various segments. In a complementary analysis technique called *desegmentation* method, some *simple* shapes (whose Green's functions are available) are added to the configuration to be analyzed so that the resulting shape is also *simple*. In such a case, the characterization for the circuit as a whole can be obtained from those of the shapes added and that of the resultant shape. Segmentation and desegmentation methods are discussed in Sections 8.4 and 11.3.

Numerical methods are used to analyze an arbitrarily shaped planar circuit. One such technique, contour integral method, is discussed in Section 8.5.

8.2 GREEN'S FUNCTION APPROACH [3]

This method can be employed when the shape of the 2-d patch is relatively simple. The Green's function — which gives voltage at any point for a unit source current excitation elsewhere — is obtained analytically. When the locations of the ports are specified, the impedance matrix of the component can be easily derived using the Green's function.

If a planar component is excited by a current density J_z in the z-direction at any arbitrary point (x_o, y_o) inside the periphery (as shown in Figure 8.5), the wave equation can be written as

$$(\nabla_T^2 + k^2) v = -j\omega\mu \, d \, J_z \; . \tag{8.16}$$

When the circuit is excited by a stripline, J_z denotes a fictitious RF current density injected normally into the circuit. It may be noted that the line current density $J_n \left(= \dfrac{2}{j\omega \, \mu d} \dfrac{\partial v}{\partial n} \right)$, being injected

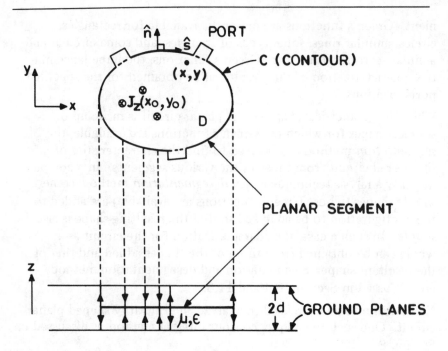

Figure 8.5   *Location of exciting current sources $J_z(x_o, y_o)$ and the field point (x,y) in a planar circuit.*

into the circuit at coupling ports located on the periphery, can equivalently be considered as fed normal to the circuit (along the z-direction) with the magnetic wall condition $\partial v/\partial n = 0$ imposed all along the periphery. This can be explained as follows. When the stripline is connected to a coupling port there is some amount of current in the central strip which flows into the planar component. Half of this current flows in opposite directions in each of the two ground planes. At the boundary where the strip is connected to the planar component, we may consider that the current loops get completed by equivalent currents along the z-direction, as shown in Figure 8.6. These equivalent currents may be evaluated as follows. At the periphery, the magnetic field can be written from (8.6) and (8.12) as

$$H = \frac{1}{j\omega\mu d}\left(\frac{\partial v}{\partial n}\,\hat{s} - \frac{\partial v}{\partial s}\,\hat{n}\right). \tag{8.17}$$

This must equal the magnetic field on the other side of the interface between the planar segment and the feeding line. If the magnetic wall condition is imposed all along the periphery of the planar component, the tangential component of the magnetic field at the periphery is zero. In the present model, there is a change in magnetic field at the periphery (where coupling ports are located). The equivalent fictitious surface current J_s in the z-direction, obtained from the boundary condition (8.7), may be written as

$$J_s = -\frac{1}{j\omega\mu d}\frac{\partial v}{\partial n}\,\hat{a}_z \quad \text{amps/m} . \tag{8.18}$$

J_s is in the negative z-direction in the region below the conducting patch as shown in Figure 8.6. We may now treat the planar component to be excited by line currents along the z-direction at the coupling ports and impose $\partial v/\partial n = 0$ all along the periphery.

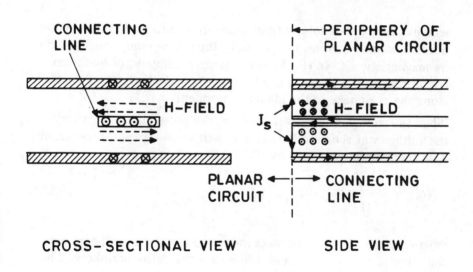

CROSS-SECTIONAL VIEW   SIDE VIEW

Figure 8.6   Representation of H_{tan} at the interface between the planar circuit and the connecting line by an equivalent current density J_s in z-direction, (dotted lines signify H lines; solid lines are current lines).

The Green's function $G(r \mid r_o)$ for (8.16) is obtained by applying a unit line current source $\delta(r - r_o)$ flowing along the z-direction in the region below the central patch and located at $r = r_o$. The Green's function $G(r \mid r_o)$ is a solution of

$$(\nabla_T^2 + k^2)\, G(r \mid r_o) = -j\omega\mu d\, \delta(r - r_o) \tag{8.19}$$

with the boundary condition at the periphery given by

$$\frac{\partial G}{\partial n} = 0 . \tag{8.20}$$

The voltage at any point on the planar element may now be written as

$$v(x, y) = \iint_D G(x,y \mid x_o, y_o)\, J_z(x_o, y_o)\, dx_o\, dy_o \tag{8.21}$$

where $J_z(x_o, y_o)$ denotes a fictitious source current density injected normally and D denotes the region of the planar component enclosed by magnetic walls. In (8.21), other terms arising out of boundary conditions do not appear since both $\partial v/\partial n$ and $\partial G/\partial n$ equal zero all along the periphery of the planar component.

When the source current is fed only at the ports on the periphery, the voltage v at the periphery can be written in terms of line current J_s in the z-direction, given by (8.18), as

$$v(s) = -\int_C G(s \mid s_o)\, J_s(s_o)\, ds_o \tag{8.22}$$

where s and s_o are the distances measured along the periphery and the integral on the right-hand side is over the entire periphery. Since the line current $J_s(s_o)$ is present only at the coupling ports, we may write (8.22) as

$$v(s) = -\sum_j \int_{W_j} G(s \mid s_o)\, J_s(s_o)\, ds_o \tag{8.23}$$

where the summation on the right-hand side is over all the coupling ports and W_j indicates the width of the jth coupling port. From (8.15) and (8.18), the current i_j fed in at the jth port can be written in terms of the equivalent line current in the z-direction as

$$i_j = -2 \int_{W_j} J_s(s_o) \ ds_o \ .$$

(8.24)

If the widths of the coupling ports are assumed to be small so that the line current density J_s is distributed uniformly over the width of the port, we have from (8.24)

$$J_s(s_o) \Big|_{\text{for jth port}} = -\frac{i_j}{2W_j} \ .$$

(8.25)

Substituting (8.25) in (8.23), $v(s)$ is obtained as

$$v(s) = \sum_j \frac{i_j}{2W_j} \int_{W_j} G(s \mid s_o) \ ds_o \ .$$

(8.26)

Equation (8.26) gives voltage at any point on the periphery. To obtain the voltage v_i at the ith coupling port, we take the average voltage over the width of the port. We have

$$v_i = \frac{1}{W_i} \int_{W_i} v(s) \ ds$$

$$= \sum_j \frac{i_j}{2W_i W_j} \int_{W_i} \int_{W_j} G(s \mid s_o) \ ds_o \ ds \ .$$

(8.27)

From (8.27) above, the elements of the impedance matrix of the planar component can be written as

$$z_{ij} = \frac{1}{2W_i \ W_j} \int_{W_i} \int_{W_j} G(s \mid s_o) \ ds_o \ ds \ .$$

(8.28)

We can thus determine the impedance matrix of the component and the scattering matrix can easily be obtained from (2.36).

In the above discussion, it is assumed that the current injected into a port is distributed uniformly over the width of the coupling port. This would imply that the width of the coupling port is small in comparison to the wavelength and the dimensions of the planar component. For cases where this assumption is not valid, each coupling port can be divided into a multiple number of subports over which the current can be assumed to be uniformly distributed. The impedance matrix of the component is obtained for all the subports.

The multiple subports at each coupling port are combined as follows [6]. It is assumed that only the TEM mode is present in the stripline at the location of the coupling port. This is a valid assumption if the coupling ports are at a certain distance from the planar circuit since any higher order modes, excited by the discontinuity at the junction of the stripline and the planar circuit, would decay along the stripline. The intermediate striplines are treated as portions of the planar circuit.

Since only TEM mode is assumed to be present at a coupling port, the voltages at the subports of a coupling port are the same. Thus, one can make use of the parallel connection of subports. This implies that the total current injected in a port is divided into its various subports. This combination requires inversion of the Z-matrix to obtain the admittance matrix. In general, if ports I and J are divided into subports, $I = \{i_1, i_2, \ldots\}$ and $J = \{j_1, j_2, \ldots\}$ then the term Y_{IJ} of the overall admittance matrix is given as

$$Y_{IJ} = \sum_{k \in I} \sum_{\ell \in J} y_{k\ell} \qquad (8.29)$$

where $y_{k\ell}$ are the terms of the admittance matrix with multiple subports. The overall scattering matrix can be obtained from the admittance matrix using (2.37).

8.3 EVALUATION OF GREEN'S FUNCTIONS

The evaluation of Green's function, for a given shape of 2-d component, requires solution of (8.19) with the boundary condition (8.20). There are two methods for obtaining the Green's function:

i) the method of images, and ii) the expansion of Green's function in terms of eigenfunctions.

8.3.1 Method of Images [7]

An analytical solution of the differential equation (8.19) can be obtained if the right-hand side is a periodic function. For this purpose, additional current sources of the type $\delta(r - r_s)$ are placed at points r_s outside the region of the planar component. These additional sources can be obtained by taking multiple images of the line source at r_o with respect to the various magnetic walls of the planar component. The source term in (8.19) is modified and the boundary condition satisfied by the voltage v produced by the source and its images. It should be noted that the additional sources are all outside the region of the planar component and therefore the solution G still represents the Green's function for the geometrical shape of the planar component. For a rectangular planar component the positions of additional line current sources are shown in Figure 8.7.

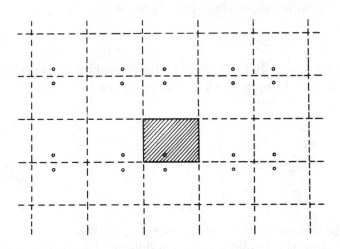

Figure 8.7   *Line current source and its images for calculation of the Green's function for a rectangular component.*

The source pattern used in (8.19) is now periodic and therefore its Fourier series expansion can be obtained. The Green's function can then be expressed as an infinite series summation of the functions obtained in the Fourier series expansion. These are the eigenfunctions. The coefficients, in the series summation for the Green's function, can then be obtained by substituting it in (8.19).

The method of images, discussed above, is restricted to the shapes enclosed by boundaries which are straight lines. This is because the only mirror which gives a point image for a point source is a plane mirror. Even for polygonal shapes, the images can be uniquely specified in the two-dimensional space only if the internal angle at each vertex of the polygon is a submultiple of π. Thus, the method is restricted to rectangular and some types of triangular shapes.

8.3.2 Expansion of Green's Function in Eigenfunctions [7]

In this method, the Green's function is expanded in terms of known eigenfunctions of the corresponding Helmholtz's equation given by (8.13) and (8.14).

Let the eigenfunctions of (8.13), which satisfy (8.14), be ψ_n, and the corresponding eigenvalues be k_n^2, so that

$$\nabla_T^2 \psi_n + k_n^2 \psi_n = 0 \qquad\qquad (8.30)$$

where n represents all the required indices defining a particular ψ_n. Moreover, the eigenfunctions ψ_n can be shown to form an orthonormal set, such that

$$\iint\limits_{D} \psi_n^* \psi_m \, dx \, dy = \begin{cases} 1, \text{ if } n = m \\ \\ 0, \text{ otherwise} \end{cases} \qquad (8.31)$$

where the superscript * denotes a complex conjugate and the region of integration D is bounded by the periphery of the planar component, at which ψ_n satisfies the boundary condition $\partial \psi_n / \partial n = 0$. It should be noted that the Green's function $G(r \mid r_o)$ also satisfies similar boundary conditions as given by (8.20). Assuming that the functions ψ_n form a complete set of orthonormal functions, it is possible to expand $G(r \mid r_o)$ in a series of ψ_n. Let

$$G(r \mid r_o) = \sum_m A_m \psi_m (r) . \tag{8.32}$$

Substituting (8.32) into (8.19) and using (8.30), we get

$$\sum_m A_m (k^2 - k_m^2) \psi_m (r) = - j\omega\mu d\, \delta (r - r_o) . \tag{8.33}$$

Multiplying both sides of the above equation by $\psi_n^* (r)$ and integrating over the region D, we obtain

$$\sum_m A_m (k^2 - k_m^2) \iint_D \psi_m (r)\, \psi_n^* (r)\, dx\, dy = - j\omega\mu d\, \psi_n^* (r_o)$$

$$\tag{8.34}$$

which, by virtue of the orthonormal property (8.31), reduces to

$$A_n (k^2 - k_n^2) = - j\omega\mu\, d\psi_n^* (r_o) . \tag{8.35}$$

We then have

$$A_n = \frac{j\omega\mu d\, \psi_n^* (r_o)}{k_n^2 - k^2} \tag{8.36}$$

so that

$$G(r \mid r_o) = j\omega\mu d \sum_n \frac{\psi_n (r)\, \psi_n^* (r_o)}{k_n^2 - k^2} \tag{8.37}$$

is the required Green's function expansion. For a lossless circuit ψ_n are real and the complex conjugate is not needed in (8.37).

It may be noted that though the Green's functions given by (8.37) contain an intrinsic singularity at $r = r_o$, this does not cause any error in evaluating the impedance matrices using (8.28).

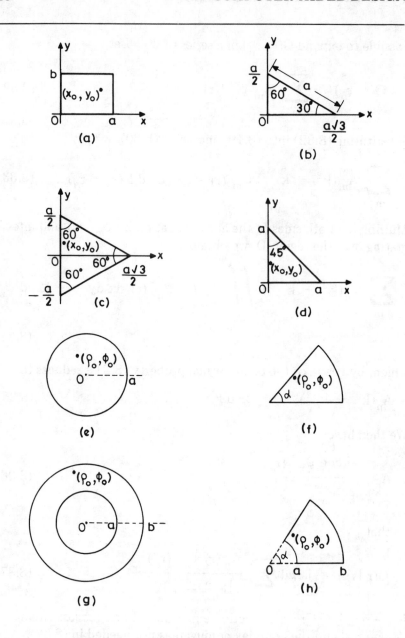

Figure 8.8   *Various planar circuit configurations for which Green's functions are available.*

This method is restricted to the cases where the eigenfunctions are
known. For shapes enclosed by straight edges, eigenfunctions can
be obtained only if the internal angle at each vertex is a submultiple of π. Eigenfunctions can also be obtained for shapes like circles, rings, etc.

8.3.3 Green's Functions for Various Configurations

In this section Green's functions for some planar shapes, shown in
Figure 8.8, are given. In the expressions that follow, σ_i is given by

$$\sigma_i \triangleq \begin{cases} 1, & \text{if } i = 0 \\ \\ 2, & \text{otherwise .} \end{cases} \tag{8.38}$$

a) A rectangle: The Green's function for the rectangle shown in
Figure 8.8(a) is given as [8]

$$G(x,y \mid x_o, y_o) = \frac{j\omega\mu d}{ab} \sum_{n=0}^{\infty} \sum_{m=0}^{\infty}$$

$$\frac{\sigma_m \sigma_n \cos(k_x x_o) \cos(k_y y_o) \cos(k_x x) \cos(k_y y)}{k_x^2 + k_y^2 - k^2} \tag{8.39}$$

where

$$k_x = \frac{m\pi}{a} \quad \text{and} \quad k_y = \frac{n\pi}{b} .$$

b) A $30° - 60°$ right-angled triangle: The Green's function for the
triangle shown in Figure 8.8(b) is given as [9]

$$G(x, y \mid x_o, y_o) = 8j\omega\mu d \sum_{m=-\infty}^{\infty} \sum_{n=-\infty}^{\infty}$$

$$\frac{T_1(x_o, y_o) T_1(x, y)}{16\sqrt{3}\,\pi^2 (m^2 + mn + n^2) - 9\sqrt{3}\,a^2 k^2} \tag{8.40}$$

where

$$
T_1(x, y) = (-1)^\ell \cos\left(\frac{2\pi \ell x}{\sqrt{3}\, a}\right) \cos\left[\frac{2\pi(m - n)y}{3a}\right]
$$
$$
+ (-1)^m \cos\left(\frac{2\pi mx}{\sqrt{3}\, a}\right) \cos\left[\frac{2\pi(n - \ell)y}{3a}\right]
$$
$$
+ (-1)^n \cos\left(\frac{2\pi nx}{\sqrt{3}\, a}\right) \cos\left[\frac{2\pi(\ell - m)y}{3a}\right] \quad (8.41)
$$

with the condition that

$$
\ell = -(m + n) . \quad (8.42)
$$

c) *An equilateral triangle:* The Green's function for the equilateral triangle shown in Figure 8.8(c) is given as [9]

$$
G(x, y \mid x_o, y_o) = 4 j\omega\mu d \sum_{m = -\infty}^{\infty} \sum_{n = -\infty}^{\infty}
$$

$$
\frac{T_1(x_o, y_o) T_1(x, y) + T_2(x_o, y_o) T_2(x, y)}{16\sqrt{3}\, \pi^2 (m^2 + mn + n^2) - 9\sqrt{3}\, a^2 k^2} \quad (8.43)
$$

where $T_1(x, y)$ is given by (8.41) and

$$
T_2(x, y) = (-1)^\ell \cos\left(\frac{2\pi \ell x}{\sqrt{3}\, a}\right) \sin\left[\frac{2\pi(m - n)y}{3a}\right]
$$
$$
+ (-1)^m \cos\left(\frac{2\pi mx}{\sqrt{3}\, a}\right) \sin\left[\frac{2\pi(n - \ell)y}{3a}\right]
$$
$$
+ (-1)^n \cos\left(\frac{2\pi nx}{\sqrt{3}\, a}\right) \sin\left[\frac{2\pi(\ell - m)y}{3a}\right] . \quad (8.44)
$$

As for $T_1(x,y)$, the integer ℓ in $T_2(x,y)$ is given by (8.42).

d) *A right-angled isosceles triangle:* The Green's function for the right-angled isosceles triangle shown in Figure 8.8(d) is given by [9]

$$
G(x, y \mid x_o, y_o) = \frac{j\omega\mu d}{2} \sum_{m = 0}^{\infty} \sum_{n = 0}^{\infty} \frac{\sigma_m \sigma_n T(x_o, y_o) T(x, y)}{(m^2 + n^2)\pi^2 - a^2 k^2}
$$

$$
(8.45)
$$

where

$$T(x, y) = \cos\frac{m\pi x}{a} \cos\frac{n\pi y}{a} + (-1)^{m+n} \cos\frac{n\pi x}{a} \cos\frac{m\pi y}{a} .$$

(8.46)

e) A circle: The Green's function for the circle shown in Figure 8.8(e) is given by [1]

$$G(\rho, \phi \mid \rho_o, \phi_o) = \frac{d}{j\omega\epsilon\pi a^2}$$

$$+ j\omega\mu d \sum_{n=0}^{\infty} \sum_{m=1}^{\infty} \frac{\sigma_n J_n(k_{mn}\rho_o) J_n(k_{mn}\rho) \cos[n(\phi - \phi_o)]}{\pi(a^2 - n^2/k_{mn}^2)(k_{mn}^2 - k^2) J_n^2(k_{mn}a)}$$

(8.47)

where $J_n(\cdot)$ represents Bessel's function of the n*th* order, and k_{mn} satisfy

$$\frac{\partial}{\partial\rho} J_n(k_{mn}\rho) \bigg|_{\rho=a} = 0 .$$

(8.48)

The subscript m in k_{mn} denotes the m*th* root of (8.48). For zeroth order Bessel's function, the first root of (8.48) is taken to be the non-zero root.

f) A circular sector: The Green's functions for circular sectors are available only when the sector angle α is a submultiple of π. For the circular sector shown in Figure 8.8(f) for which $\alpha = \pi/\ell$, the Green's function is given as [10]

$$G(\rho, \phi \mid \rho_o, \phi_o) = \frac{2\ell d}{j\omega\epsilon\pi a^2}$$

$$+ 2j\,\ell\,\omega\,\mu d \sum_{n=0}^{\infty} \sum_{m=1}^{\infty} \frac{\sigma_n J_{n_i}(k_{mn_i}\rho_o) J_{n_i}(k_{mn_i}\rho) \cos(n_i\phi_o) \cos(n_i\phi)}{\pi[a^2 - n_i^2/k_{mn_i}^2](k_{mn_i}^2 - k^2) J_{n_i}^2(k_{mn_i}a)}$$

(8.49)

where $n_i = n\ell$, and k_{mn_i} are given by

$$\left.\frac{\partial}{\partial\rho} J_{n_i}(k_{mn_i}\rho)\right|_{\rho = a} = 0 \qquad\qquad (8.50)$$

g) *An annular ring:* The Green's function for the annular ring shown in Figure 8.8(g) is given as [10]

$$G(\rho, \phi \mid \rho_o, \phi_o) = \frac{d}{j\omega\epsilon\pi(b^2 - a^2)} +$$

$$j\omega\mu d \sum_{n=0}^{\infty} \sum_{m=1}^{\infty} \frac{\sigma_n F_{mn}(\rho_o) F_{mn}(\rho) \cos[n(\phi - \phi_o)]}{\pi[(b^2 - n^2/k_{mn}^2) F_{mn}^2(b) - (a^2 - n^2/k_{mn}^2) F_{mn}^2(a)] (k_{mn}^2 - k^2)}$$

$$(8.51)$$

where

$$F_{mn}(\rho) = N_n'(k_{mn}a) J_n(k_{mn}\rho) - J_n'(k_{mn}a) N_n(k_{mn}\rho)$$

$$(8.52)$$

and k_{mn} are solutions of

$$\frac{J_n'(k_{mn}a)}{N_n'(k_{mn}a)} = \frac{J_n'(k_{mn}b)}{N_n'(k_{mn}b)} . \qquad\qquad (8.53)$$

In the above relations $N_n(\cdot)$ denotes Neumann's function of order n and $J_n'(\cdot)$ and $N_n'(\cdot)$ denote first derivatives with respect to the arguments.

h) *An annular sector:* As in the case of circular sectors, the Green's function for annular sectors are available only if the sector angle α is a submultiple of π. For the annular sector shown in Figure 8.8(h) for which $\alpha = \pi/\ell$, the Green's function is given as [10]

$$G(\rho, \phi \mid \rho_o, \phi_o) = \frac{2\ell d}{i\omega\epsilon\pi(b^2 - a^2)}$$

$$+ 2j\ell\omega\mu d \sum_{n=0}^{\infty} \sum_{m=1}^{\infty} \frac{\sigma_n F_{mn_i}(\rho) F_{mn_i}(\rho_o) \cos(n_i\phi_o) \cos(n_i\phi)}{\pi[(b^2 - n_i^2/k_{mn_i}^2) F_{mn_i}^2(b) - (a^2 - n_i^2/k_{mn_i}^2) F_{mn_i}^2(a)] (k_{mn_i}^2 - k^2)}$$

$$(8.54)$$

where $n_i = n\ell$, and F_{mn_i} ($\cdot$) is defined in (8.52). The values of k_{mn_i} are obtained from (8.53).

8.4 SEGMENTATION AND DESEGMENTATION [11, 6, 12]

As discussed in the previous section, the impedance matrix for a planar circuit of *simple* geometrical shape can be obtained from the Green's function when port locations are specified. The Green's functions have been listed for several geometrical shapes. If the shape of the planar circuit is the one for which the Green's function is not available, an attempt is made to obtain the given shape by addition or removal of the *simple* shapes for which Green's functions are known [11, 12]. Most of the circuits one comes across can be treated in this manner. The characteristics of the given shape are then obtained from those of the *simple* shapes involved. These ideas are illustrated by considering two planar circuit shapes for which Green's functions are not available.

The planar component shown in Figure 8.9(a) can be considered to be made up of two rectangles joined along the common side AB as shown in Figure 8.9(b). To obtain the impedance matrix for this circuit, we consider two rectangular components joined at a discrete number of ports along AB, as shown in Figure 8.9(c). Increasing the numbers of ports along the side AB provides greater accuracy, as in the case of wide external ports discussed in Section 8.2. The overall impedance matrix can be obtained from the impedance matrices of the two components [6]. This is an example of *segmentation* method. A general method of analysis based on segmentation is discussed in Chapter 11.

Consider another planar circuit shape shown in Figure 8.10(a). This shape is obtained by removing a sector of a circle from a rectangle. To obtain the impedance matrix for the circuit shown in Figure 8.10(b), the impedance matrices are obtained for the rectangular and circular sector components shown in Figures 8.10(c) and 8.10(d) respectively. The impedance matrix for the circuit shown in Figure 8.10(e) can be obtained from those of the circuit of Figure 8.10(c) and the component in Figure 8.10(d). This technique is called *desegmentation* and is discussed in Chapter 11.

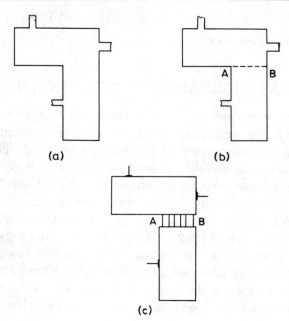

(a)   (b)

(c)

Figure 8.9   An illustration of the segmentation method for analysis of planar components.

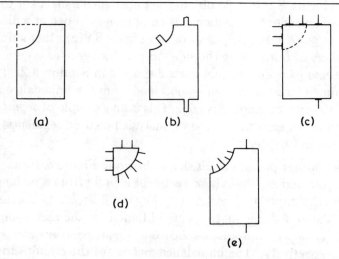

(a)   (b)   (c)

(d)

(e)

Figure 8.10   An illustration of the desegmentation method for analysis of planar components.

8.5 NUMERICAL METHODS FOR ARBITRARY SHAPES

We can use numerical techniques to analyze planar circuits of arbitrary shapes in cases where neither the segmentation nor the desegmentation method can be applied. Two methods which have been discussed in literature for this purpose are the finite element approach [13], and a contour integral approach [3]. The former is an extension of the well known finite element methods [14] and involves the integration of basis functions over the entire conducting patch which is divided into numerous subsections. The contour integral method proposed for analysis of planar circuits involves only a line integral along the periphery. This method is discussed in this section.

The contour integral method is based on the Green's theorem in cylindrical coordinates. The RF voltage at any point $M(s)$ inside the periphery of an arbitrarily shaped planar circuit shown in Figure 8.11(a) is given by

$$4jv(s) = \oint_C \left\{ H_o^{(2)}(kr) \frac{\partial v(s_o)}{\partial n} - v(s_o) \frac{\partial H_o^{(2)}(kr)}{\partial n} \right\} ds_o$$

(8.55)

where $H_o^{(2)}$ is the zeroth-order Hankel function of the second kind and r is the straight line distance between the point $M(s)$ and the source point on the periphery (given by $L(s_o)$). The integral on the right-hand side of (8.55) is carried out over the entire periphery. The RF voltage at any point *just* inside the periphery can be derived from the above relationship. We obtain

$$2jv(s) = \oint_C \left\{ k \cos \theta \, H_1^{(2)}(kr) v(s_o) + j\omega\mu d \frac{J_n(s_o)}{2} H_o^{(2)}(kr) \right\} ds_o$$

(8.56)

where $H_1^{(2)}$ is the first-order Hankel function of the second kind, and J_n denotes line current density flowing into the circuit. The variables s and s_o denote distances along the contour C and r is the straight line distance between the two points M and L (given by s and s_o) as shown in Figure 8.11(a). The angle θ is the angle made by the straight line joining points M and L with the normal to the periphery at L. Line current density J_n, flowing into the circuit at a coupling port, is given by

$$J_n = \frac{2}{j\omega\mu d} \frac{\partial v}{\partial n} . \qquad (8.57)$$

For the numerical calculation of the impedance matrix we divide the periphery into N sections having arbitrary widths W_1, W_2, ... W_N as shown in Figure 8.11(b). The periphery is divided in such a manner that each coupling port contains an integral number of such sections. For greater accuracy, wider coupling ports may be divided into multiple number of sections. We set N sampling points, one at the center of each section, and assume that each section is a straight edge. It is further assumed that the widths of the sections are so small that magnetic and electric fields can be considered constant over each section.

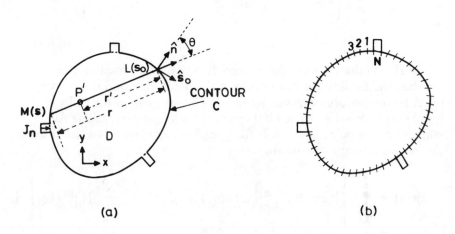

(a)   (b)

Figure 8.11   (a) Configuration of a planar component for analysis
by contour integral method; (b) Division of the peri-
phery in N sections for the analysis.

Under the assumptions outlined above, the line integral in (8.56) can be replaced by summation over the N sections. The resulting expression is given by

$$2jv_\ell = \sum_{m=1}^{N} \left\{ k \, v_m \, G_{\ell m} + \frac{j\omega\mu d}{2} \, i_m \, F_{\ell m} \right\} \tag{8.58}$$

where v_ℓ is the voltage over the ℓth section and i_m ($= J_n \, W_m$) is the total current flowing into the mth section. The matrix elements $G_{\ell m}$ and $F_{\ell m}$ are given as

$$G_{\ell m} = \begin{cases} \displaystyle\int_{W_m} \cos\theta \, H_1^{(2)} \, (kr) \, ds_o \,, & \text{if } \ell \neq m \\[20pt] 0 \,, & \text{otherwise} \end{cases} \tag{8.59}$$

and

$$F_{\ell m} = \begin{cases} \dfrac{1}{W_m} \displaystyle\int_{W_m} H_o^{(2)} \, (kr) \, ds_o \,, & \text{if } \ell \neq m \\[20pt] 1 - \dfrac{2j}{\pi} \left(\ell n \, \dfrac{kW_\ell}{4} - 1 + \gamma \right), & \text{otherwise} \,. \end{cases} \tag{8.60}$$

In (8.60) above, γ ($= 0.5772\ldots$) denotes the Euler's constant.

In the above discussion we assume that the current can be fed into the planar circuit from all the N sections and i_m denotes the current fed from the mth section. This yields the impedance matrix for the N-port circuit — which can be used to obtain the impedance matrix for any specified number and location of ports on the planar circuit being analyzed. Equation (8.58) is written for each section ℓ on the periphery of the planar circuit. All these equations combined together in matrix form become

$$\mathbf{A} \, \mathbf{v} = \mathbf{B} \, \mathbf{i} \tag{8.61}$$

where v and i are the voltage and the current vectors at each section. A and B denote N by N matrices, determined by the shape of the circuit. The elements of these matrices, obtained from (8.58), are

$$a_{\ell m} = -k\, G_{\ell m} \text{ for } \ell \neq m \;,\qquad\qquad\qquad (8.62a)$$

$$a_{\ell\ell} = 2j \qquad\qquad\qquad\qquad (8.62b)$$

and

$$b_{\ell m} = j\, \frac{\omega\mu d}{2}\, F_{\ell m} \;. \qquad\qquad\qquad (8.63)$$

From (8.61), the impedance matrix for the N sections, considered as ports, is obtained as

$$Z_N = A^{-1}\, B \;. \qquad\qquad\qquad\qquad (8.64)$$

In practice, the coupling ports are connected to only a few of the N sections. Rows and columns corresponding to the sections which are open-circuited can be deleted from Z_N. If each coupling port covers only one section, the matrix thus obtained (after deleting rows and columns corresponding to the open sections from Z_N) is the required impedance matrix. If some coupling ports extend to more than one section, the sections in these coupling ports are like subports and the procedure detailed in Section 8.2 can be used to obtain the overall admittance matrix at the coupling ports (and hence impedance matrix, if desired).

8.6 SCALING FOR PLANAR CIRCUITS

Once a planar circuit has been designed for a given set of specifications, the principle of scaling may be used to design a circuit with similar specifications at a different frequency or with different (scaled) impedances at all the ports. Design of a stripline type circuit from a microstrip type circuit (and vice versa) is also possible through scaling. For the purposes of scaling, the dimensions considered include the extension of the periphery to account for the fringing field in open boundary planar circuits.

8.6.1 Frequency Scaling

The concept of frequency scaling applicable to stripline, microstrip, and waveguide circuits [15, 16] can be applied to the 2-d planar circuits also. If all the linear dimensions in the planar patch are reduced by a scaling factor K and the planar patch is deposited on a substrate of height d/K, the response of the modified circuit at frequency f will be the same as that of the original circuit on a substrate of height d at frequency f/K. For example, if a circuit has been designed at 1 GHz on a 5 mm thick substrate, the design can be used at 10 GHz by scaling down all the linear dimensions of the patch by a factor of 10 and fabricating it on a 0.5 mm thick substrate.

It may be noted that for stripline type circuits, extension of the boundary because of the fringing field is proportional to the height of the substrate. Thus, actual physical dimensions may be used for the purposes of frequency scaling.

8.6.2 Impedance Scaling

The concept of impedance scaling can be applied to another planar circuit which has impedance values at all the coupling ports scaled by some factor and has the same frequency response for the scattering parameters. The new circuit is deposited on a substrate of different height and all dimensions of the 2-d patch remain the same. If the planar patch is deposited on a substrate of height Kd, the S-matrix of the new circuit would be the same as that of the original circuit on substrate height d. For the new circuit, the impedances at all the coupling ports are multiplied by the factor K.

The two types of scaling concepts discussed above may be combined together. For example, if the height of the substrate remains unchanged and the linear dimensions are scaled up by a factor K, the S-matrix of the modified circuit at the frequency f/K is the same as that of the original circuit at frequency f, but all the impedance levels in the modified circuit are scaled down by the factor K.

8.6.3 Design of a Stripline Type Circuit from a Microstrip Type Planar Circuit (and Vice Versa)

The concept of scaling can also be applied to obtain an equivalent design in the microstrip type configuration from the design in the stripline type configuration, and vice versa. The scattering matrix response of a stripline type planar circuit with spacing 2d between the ground planes will be the same as that of a microstrip type planar circuit with substrate height d, provided the linear dimensions (between the magnetic walls) are the same in both cases. It may be noted that the characteristic impedance values at the coupling ports for the microstrip type circuit will be twice the corresponding values for the stripline type circuit. Impedance scaling technique can be used in conjunction with the above conversion to get the desired impedance values at the coupling ports.

These scaling techniques provide an additional flexibility in design and are likely to be useful for carrying over the design of microwave circuits to millimeter wave frequencies.

REFERENCES

[1]   Okoshi, T., *et al.*, "Planar 3-db Hybrid Circuit," *Electron. Commun. Japan*, Vol. 58-B, August 1975, pp. 80-90.

[2]   Miyoshi, T., and S. Miyauchi, "The Design of Planar Circulators for Wide-band Operation," *IEEE Trans. Microwave Theory Tech.*, Vol. MTT-28, March 1980, pp. 210-214.

[3]   Okoshi, T., and T. Miyoshi, "The Planar Circuit — An Approach to Microwave Integrated Circuitry," *IEEE Trans. Microwave Theory Tech.*, Vol. MTT-20, April 1972, pp. 245-252.

[4]   Altschuler, H.M., and A.A. Oliner, "Discontinuities in the Center Conductor of Symmetric Strip Transmission Line," *IRE Trans. Microwave Theory Tech.*, Vol. MTT-8, May 1960, pp. 328-339.

[5]   Gupta, K.C., *et al.*, *Microstrip Lines and Slotlines*, Dedham, MA: Artech House, 1979, p. 130.

[6]   Chadha, R., and K.C. Gupta, "Segmentation Method Using Impedance-Matrices for Analysis of Planar Microwave Circuits," *IEEE Trans. Microwave Theory Tech.*, Vol. MTT-29, Jan. 1981, pp. 71-74.

[7]   Morse, P.M., and H. Feshbach, *Methods of Theoretical Physics*, New York: McGraw Hill, 1953, Ch. 7.

[8]   Okoshi, T., and T. Takeuchi, "Analysis of Planar Circuits by Segmentation Method," *Electron. Commun. Japan*, Vol. 58-B, August 1975, pp. 71-79.

[9]   Chadha, R., and K.C. Gupta, "Green's Functions for Triangular Segments in Planar Microwave Circuits," *IEEE Trans. Microwave Theory Tech.*, Vol. MTT-28, Oct. 1980, pp. 1139-1143.

[10]   Chadha, R., and K.C. Gupta, "Green's Functions for Circular Sectors, Annular Rings and Annular Sectors in Planar Microwave Circuits," *IEEE Trans. Microwave Theory Tech.*, Vol. MTT-29, Jan. 1981, pp. 68-71.

[11]   Okoshi, T., *et al.*, "The Segmentation Method — An Approach
       to the Analysis of Microwave Planar Circuits," *IEEE Trans.
       Microwave Theory Tech.*, Vol. MTT-24, October 1976,
       pp. 662-668.

[12]   Sharma, P.C., and K.C. Gupta, "Desegmentation Method for
       Analysis of Two-Dimensional Microwave Circuits," *IEEE
       Trans. Microwave Theory Tech.*, Vol. MTT-29, Oct. 1981
       (to appear).

[13]   Silvester, P., "Finite Element Analysis of Planar Microwave
       Networks," *IEEE Trans. Microwave Theory Tech.*, Vol.
       MTT-21, Feb. 1973, pp. 104-108.

[14]   Zienkiewicz, O.C., *The Finite Elements Method*, London:
       McGraw-Hill, 1977.

[15]   Schneider, M.V., "Millimeter-wave Integrated Circuits,"
       IEEE G-MTT Int. Microwave Symp. Digest, 1973, pp. 16-18.

[16]   Schneider, M.V., and W.W. Snell, Jr., "A Scaled Hybrid Inte-
       grated Multiplier from 10 to 30 GHz," *B.S.T.J.*, Vol. 50,
       July/August 1971, pp. 1933-1942.

9

Models for Microwave Semiconductor Devices

Recent advances in semiconductor device technology have enabled microwave engineers to use solid state devices extensively for various applications. Devices like PIN diodes, varactor diodes, Schottky-barrier diodes, and point-contact diodes are now universally used in circuits such as mixers, harmonic multipliers, parametric amplifiers, phase shifters, and detectors. Gunn diodes, impatts, bipolar transistors, and MESFET's are being used as microwave sources for low-noise and medium power applications. MESFET's and Gunn diodes can be used in ultra-fast logic circuits as well.

The behavior of a semiconductor device for a given geometry and doping profile is governed by the device physics, and can be represented by a set of equations. The solution of these equations yields the device characteristics. For circuit design we are interested only in the terminal characteristics of a device. The terminal behavior can be modelled by an equivalent circuit consisting of lumped components.

Basically, two approaches are used for the modelling of semiconductor devices. The first is based on device physics and translates the physical structure and operating mechanisms of the device into a circuit model. For several devices the operating mechanisms are rather complicated. Simplifying assumptions become necessary and the closed-form solutions are not always available. An alternative approach is based on the measurement of terminal characteristics from which the value of parameters are obtained for a qualitatively derived lumped circuit model. This is called the 'black-box approach' or the 'experimental approach'.

The device model should preferably consist of a minimum number of elements. However, a large number of elements may be required to increase the range of validity and the accuracy of the model. Therefore, the number of elements is a compromise between the complexity of the model, its accuracy, and the range of validity.

Frequency independent equivalent circuits are particularly desirable because they simplify the device characterization data. For devices operating at large signal levels, it becomes convenient if the small-signal parameters of the device can be obtained from the large-signal model.

Equivalent circuits for a number of semiconductor devices used in microwave circuits, are discussed in this chapter. Typical values of circuit elements are given. Closed-form approximate expressions for the circuit elements of some of the device models are also included.

Parameters of most of the semiconductor devices vary from unit to unit. Therefore, experimental measurements often become necessary to find values of various parameters in a model. Experimental measurement techniques used for this purpose are discussed in Chapter 10.

9.1 SCHOTTKY-BARRIER AND POINT-CONTACT DIODES

Schottky-barrier Diodes

A Schottky-barrier diode is a metal-semiconductor junction diode, for which the following conditions are satisfied:

(a)   The work-function for the metal is substantially greater than kT, so that when viewed from the semiconductor side, the barrier height is large compared with kT/e.

(b)   The thickness of the depletion layer is large compared with an electron wavelength h/mc, so that the tunnelling is negligible.

(c) The concentrations of both the electrons and the holes within the depletion layer are much less than those of the ionized impurities.

Schottky-barrier diodes find applications in mixers, detectors, waveform clipping (or clamping) circuits, sampling gates, and fast switches. Compared to point-contact diodes, they also yield a better noise figure in mixer circuits. They are more rugged and reproducible.

The equivalent circuit for the Schottky-barrier diode is shown in Figure 9.1. Nomenclature of the circuit elements, and their typical values are given in Table 9.1. S-parameters for the series mounted diodes can be obtained by representing the equivalent circuit in terms of an equivalent impedance, and using (2) of Appendix 2.1. For shunt mounting, (3) of Appendix 2.1 should be used after finding equivalent admittance for the diode.

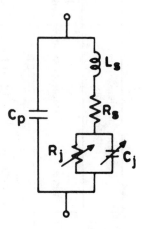

Figure 9.1   Equivalent circuit for Schottky-barrier diodes, varactor diodes and PIN diodes. C_p and L_s are package reactances.

TABLE 9.1

Typical Values for the Elements of Equivalent Circuits for Schottky-barrier Diodes, Varactor Diodes and PIN Diodes (L_s = 0.02 nH, C_p = 0.12 pF)

Symbol	Element	Schottky-barrier diodes at zero bias		Varactor diodes at zero bias		PIN diodes	
		Mixer type	Detector type	Harmonic generator type	Parametric amplifier type	Reverse bias state (0 mA)	Forward bias state (10 mA)
C_j	junction capacitance	0.36 pF	0.12 - 0.15 pF	1-5 pF	0.15 - 0.70 pF	0.1 pF	20 pF
R_j	junction resistance	270 ohm	5 - 170 K ohm	10 M ohm	10 M ohm	20 K ohm	0.8 ohm
R_s	series resistance	4 - 6 ohm	4 - 10 ohm	0.7 ohm	0.4 ohm	0.5 - 2 ohm	0.5 - 2 ohm

Point-contact Diodes

Point-contact diodes are used most extensively in the reception of microwave signals, either as mixers in superhetrodyne receivers or as low-level detectors in video receivers. A point-contact diode consists of a very thin metal-semiconductor barrier in the form of a point-contact. The equivalent circuit for this type of diode is identical to that for the Schottky-barrier diode discussed earlier.

9.2 VARACTOR DIODES

A varactor diode is a variable-reactance, non-linear circuit element. The variable reactance is provided by the junction capacitance, which varies as a function of applied voltage. Varactor diodes find many applications such as modulators, harmonic generators, para-metric amplifiers, upconverters, and tuning elements.

The active element of a varactor diode is the p-n junction (or the metal-semiconductor junction in the case of Schottky-barrier va-ractor diodes). The junction capacitance, C_j, is given by

$$C_j = \frac{C_{jo}}{(1 - V/\phi)^\gamma} \tag{9.1}$$

where C_{jo} is the zero-bias junction capacitance, V is the applied bias (assumed positive when forward biased), ϕ is the contact potential, and the constant γ is the capacitance-voltage slope exponent. The junction resistance, R_j, is defined by

$$R_j = V/I \tag{9.2}$$

with

$$I = I_s \left[\exp \frac{qV}{nkT} - 1 \right] \tag{9.3}$$

where q is the electronic charge, k is the Boltzmann's constant, T is the absolute temperature, and I_s is the reverse saturation current. The ideality factor n is about 2 for point-contact diodes and about 1.06 for Schottky-barrier diodes.

The equivalent circuit for a packaged diode, under reverse bias, is shown in Figure 9.1. The nomenclature and the typical values for the equivalent circuit elements are given in Table 9.1.

9.3 PIN DIODES

PIN diodes can be used for attenuating, levelling, and amplitude
modulating the microwave signals by controlling the bias current
through the device. It can be used as a switch, pulse modulator,
and phase shifter, when the bias current is switched ON and OFF
or varied in discrete steps.

A PIN diode consists of a layer of intrinsic (high resistivity) material
of finite thickness sandwiched between highly doped p and n type
materials. When the diode is forward biased, carriers are injected
into the intrinsic or I-region. These carriers, viz., holes and electrons
have a finite lifetime before recombination. The density of the
charge in the intrinsic region determines the conductance of the
device. The lifetime, τ, determines the approximate low frequency
limit of useful application of the device. This frequency limit may
be approximated by $f_o = 1/(2\pi\tau)$. Lifetimes are in the range 0.01
μsec to well over 3 μsec. At frequencies well below f_o, the PIN diode
behaves as an ordinary p-n junction, so that an RF signal incident
on the diode gets rectified. In the vicinity of f_o, the diode begins
to behave as a linear resistor with a small nonlinear component. At
frequencies well above f_o, the diode behaves essentially as a pure
linear resistor whose value can be controlled by a d.c. or low frequency control signal.

At zero bias or under the reverse bias state, the I layer is partially
depleted of charge carriers. The resistance of the depleted portion
is normally very high, of the order of a few tens of kilo-ohms.

The high frequency ($> f_o$) equivalent circuit for a packaged PIN
diode is shown in Figure 9.1. Some typical values for the equivalent circuit parameters are given in Table 9.1.

For analog applications of PIN diode, the bias current can have any
value between the forward bias ($\sim$ 10 mA) and the reverse bias
($\sim$ 0 mA) states. The resistance, R_j, varies accordingly. An empirical relation for R_j, which is typical of Hewlett-Packard PIN diodes [1], is given below

$$R_j = 26 I_o^{-0.87} \tag{9.4}$$

where I_o is the forward bias current in mA. Equation (9.4) holds
for the range of bias currents between 20 μA and 10 mA.

9.4 BIPOLAR TRANSISTORS AND MESFET'S

9.4.1 Bipolar Transistors

Basic operation of a microwave bipolar transistor is identical to that of transistors at low frequencies. The maximum operating frequency, ω_T, is limited by the transit time between the emitter and the collector, T_{ec}. This consists of emitter-base junction charging time, base transit time, collector depletion layer transit time, and collector depletion layer charging time. The contributions from the first and last terms can be reduced by decreasing the emitter-base and collector-base junction capacitances, respectively. This can be achieved by minimizing the emitter, the base, and the collector areas. However, for maximum emitter current and hence maximum power output, the emitter periphery should be as large as possible. The ratio of emitter periphery to base area is known as the aspect ratio. The interdigitated structure, as shown in Figure 9.2, is commonly used to achieve high values of the aspect ratio. Other geometries used are: overlay, emitter mesh, and diamond configurations [2].

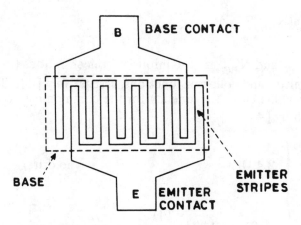

Figure 9.2   Configuration for an interdigitated bipolar transistor.

Transit Time

The expression for the transit time for a microwave bipolar transistor may be written as [3]

$$T_{ec} \overset{\triangle}{=} \frac{1}{\omega_T} = \frac{R_E}{\alpha_o}(C_E + C_c) + \frac{1 + m\alpha_o}{\alpha_o \, \omega_\alpha} + \frac{x}{2 \, v_L}$$

$$+ \frac{C_c}{\alpha_o}(R_E' + R_s) \tag{9.5}$$

where the elements R_E, R_E', R_s, C_c, and C_E are defined in the T-equivalent circuit for the microwave bipolar transistor chip [3] shown in Figure 9.3(a). The factor 'm' is the excess phase shift due to the drift-diffusion mechanism of carrier transport in the base region. It can be approximated by [4]

$$m = 0.22 + 0.098 \, \eta \, . \tag{9.6}$$

Here η is an electric field parameter given by

$$\eta = \ln(N_{BE}/N_{BC}) \tag{9.7}$$

where N_{BE} and N_{BC} are the impurity concentrations (in atoms/cm^3) at the emitter and collector junctions, respectively [4]. The frequency ω_α is the alpha cut-off frequency for the common-base configuration. It is given by [4]

$$\omega_\alpha = \begin{cases} 2.4 \, D/W^2 & \text{(no drift)} \\ \\ (1.21 + 0.09\eta) \, \dfrac{2D}{W^2} \left[\dfrac{\eta^2/2}{\eta - 1 + e^{-\eta}} \right] & \text{(with drift field)} \end{cases} \tag{9.8}$$

where D is the diffusion constant and W is the electrical base width.

The quantities ω_α, m, and α_o are related to the current amplification factor α by the following approximate expression

$$\alpha = \alpha_o \frac{e^{-j\omega\left[\dfrac{m}{\omega_\alpha} + \dfrac{x}{2v_L}\right]}}{1 + j\omega/\omega_\alpha} . \qquad (9.9)$$

The transit time across the collector depletion layer, given by $x/2v_L$, depends on x, the width of the depletion layer, and v_L, the scattering limited saturation velocity of carriers. The value of v_L for silicon is about 8 x 10^6 cm/s and 'x' for silicon is obtained from

$$x(cm) = 3.64 \times 10^3 \left(\frac{V + \phi}{N}\right)^{\frac{1}{2}} \qquad (9.10)$$

where V is the applied reverse bias to the collector, ϕ is the contact potential (~ 0.7 V), and N is the doping concentration (expressed as atoms/cm^3) in the epitaxial layer.

Equivalent Circuit

The small signal T-equivalent circuit for the microwave bipolar transistor chip in the common-emitter configuration is shown in Figure 9.3(a). Approximate closed-form expressions for some of the circuit elements are as follows [4]:

Base spreading resistance, R_b: The base spreading resistance, R_b, can be obtained from the following relation

$$R_b = R_{bb}/W \qquad (9.11)$$

with

$$\frac{1}{R_{bb}} = q \mu \int_o^W N(x) \, dx \qquad (9.12)$$

where μ is the mobility and N(x) is the impurity distribution of carriers in the base region.

Space-charge resistance of the emitter, R_E: The emitter resistance is given by

$$R_E = \frac{kT}{q I_E} . \qquad (9.13)$$

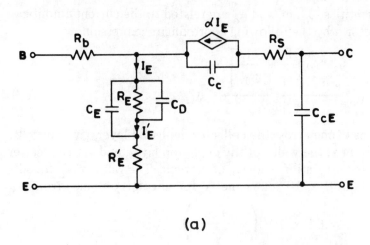

(a)

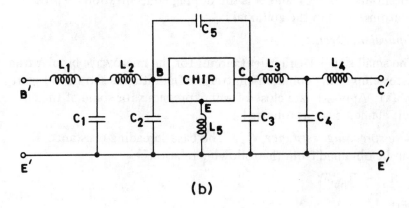

(b)

Figure 9.3   (a) *Equivalent circuit for the bipolar transistor chip;*
              (b) *Equivalent circuit for the packaged transistor.*

Emitter-base junction capacitance, C_E: C_E is given by the following
expression for the junction capacitance

$$C_E \approx A_E \left\{ \frac{\epsilon_o \epsilon_r q N_{BE}}{2(V + \phi)} \right\}^{1/2}$$ (9.14)

where A_E is the emitter area, and N_{BE} is the impurity concentration in the base at the emitter edge. Voltage V is the applied bias and is positive when the emitter-base junction is forward biased.

Diffusion capacitance, C_D: The value of C_D is given by

$$C_D = (R_E \omega_\alpha)^{-1} .$$ (9.15)

Collector-base junction capacitance, C_c: The value of C_c for silicon may be calculated as follows:

$$C_c = A_c \sqrt{\frac{\epsilon_o \epsilon_r}{2 \mu \rho (V + \phi)}}$$ (9.16)

where A_c is the collector area, ρ is the resistivity of the collector epitaxial region and μ is the mobility.

Typical values for the elements of the equivalent circuit are given in Table 9.2.

TABLE 9.2

Typical Values for the Elements of the Equivalent Circuit for the Microwave Bipolar Transistor Chip Designed for Low Noise, High Gain Applications

Symbol	Element	Typical Values
R_E'	emitter spreading resistance	8.6 ohm
R_s	collector spreading resistance	7.0 ohm
R_E	space-charge resistance of the emitter	0.7 ohm
C_E	emitter-base junction capacitance	1.0 pF
C_c	collector-base junction capacitance	0.005 pF
C_{cE}	collector-emitter capacitance	0.05 pF
R_b	base spreading resistance	14.7 ohm
α_o	common-base current amplification factor at zero frequency	0.99

The equivalent circuit for the packaged transistor is shown in Figure 9.3(b) [5] and the typical values for the package parasitics are included in Table 9.3.

TABLE 9.3

Typical Values for the Elements of Package Parasitics of the Bipolar Transistor

Symbol	Element	Typical Values
$C_1, C_2,$ C_3, C_4	capacitances between the different connections of the package	C_1 : 0.06 to 0.1 pF C_2 : 0.01 to 0.012 pF C_3 : 0.001 to 0.003 pF C_4 : 0.01 to 0.013 pF
C_5	capacitance between the input and the output	0.005 pF
L_1, L_4	lead inductances between the reference plane and the package edge	L_1 : 0.2 to 0.3 nH L_4 : 0.4 to 0.6 nH
L_2, L_3	lead inductances between the package edge and the gold wire connection	0.2 to 0.5 nH
L_5	inductance of the gold wire from the chip to the emitter terminal	0.3 to 0.6 nH

S-Matrix

Scattering parameters for the equivalent circuit shown in Figure 9.3(a), with normalizing impedance Z_o on either side, are given below [3].

$$S_{11} = \frac{Z_{in} - Z_o}{Z_{in} + Z_o} \qquad (9.17)$$

where

$$Z_{in} = R + 1 / (j\omega C)$$

with

$$R = R_b + R_E + R_E'$$

$$C = [\omega_T' (R_E + R_E')]^{-1}$$

and

$$\omega_T' = \frac{\omega_T}{1 + \dfrac{\omega_T C_c Z_o}{\alpha_o}}$$

$$S_{22} = \frac{Z_{out} - Z_o}{Z_{out} + Z_o} \tag{9.18}$$

where

$$Z_{out} = \frac{R_o}{1 + j\omega R_o C_o}$$

with

$$R_o = (\omega_T C_c)^{-1}$$

$$C_o = C_{cE} + \frac{C_c}{1 + m\,\alpha_o}$$

$$|S_{12}| = \frac{2Z_o(R_E + R_E')\sqrt{1 + R_E'}}{(R + Z_o)(R_o + Z_o)\sqrt{1 + (\omega T_o)^2}} \tag{9.19a}$$

$$\angle S_{12} = -\tan^{-1}(\omega T_o) \tag{9.19b}$$

where

$$T_o = \frac{1}{\omega_\alpha} + C_E R_E \ .$$

$$|S_{21}| = \frac{2Z_o \omega_T'}{\omega(R + Z_o)} \qquad (9.20a)$$

$$\angle S_{21} = \frac{\pi}{2} - \tan^{-1}\left[\frac{-1}{\omega C(R + Z_o)}\right] - \tan^{-1}(\omega T_d)$$

$$(9.20b)$$

where

$$C = [\ \omega_T'(R_E + R_E')\ ]^{-1}$$

$$T_d = \frac{m}{\omega_\alpha} + \frac{x}{2v_L} + \frac{C_c}{\alpha_o}(R_E + R_E') \ .$$

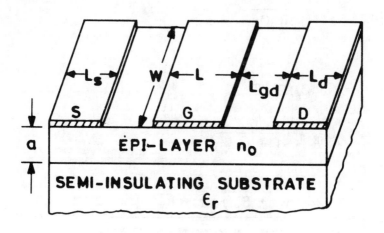

Figure 9.4   Configuration for MESFET.

9.4.2 MESFET'S

The basic configuration for an FET with the Schottky-barrier gate, commonly called MESFET, is shown in Figure 9.4. At times, another 'gate' is added to enhance the functional capability of the device. These devices are called dual gate FET's [6].

As shown, a MESFET consists of a semi-insulating GaAs substrate on which an n-type expitaxial layer (also called a channel) of about 0.2 μm thickness is deposited by epitaxial growth. Sometimes a buffer layer is introduced between the epi-layer and the semi-insulating substrate. The buffer layer restricts the diffusion of impurities from the substrate. The source and the drain electrodes are deposited on the active layer or epi-layer using photolithography technique. Another contact, a metal-semiconductor Schottky junction, is added between the source and the drain. This is called the 'gate'. The gate length is typically 0.5 to 0.7 μm and source-drain spacing is about 2 μm.

Metal-semiconductor FET's (MESFET's) find applications as low-noise amplifiers, power amplifiers, oscillators, mixers, modulators, limiters, and in logic circuits. For all these applications the device should be characterized and the equivalent circuit obtained. The most commonly used small-signal equivalent circuit for an FET in the common-source configuration is shown in Figure 9.5 [7]. This FET model includes the device chip and the external resistances that arise due to the bulk resistance of the semiconductor and the contact resistance at the metalization. The package parasitics are not included. The nomenclature and the typical values for the circuit elements are given in Table 9.4.

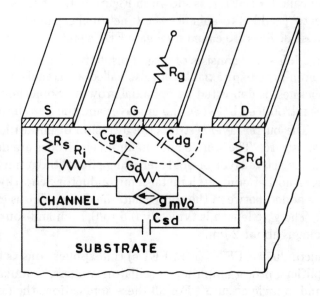

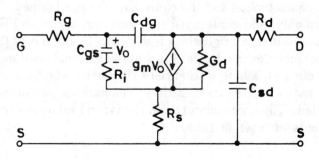

Figure 9.5   Common-source small-signal equivalent circuit for
             MESFET.

TABLE 9.4

Typical Values for the Elements of an Equivalent Circuit for the MESFET Chip at 3 GHz (V_{DD} = 4V and V_{GG} = 0V)

Symbol	Element	Typical Values
g_{mo}	transconductance of the device	40 to 53 m mho
G_d	output conductance	0.66 m mho
C_{gs}	gate-to-source capacitance	0.42 pF
C_{dg}	drain-to-gate feedback capacitance	0.04 pF
R_i	undepleted channel resistance	0.53 ohm
τ_o	phase delay	10 ps
R_g		3 to 4 ohm
R_s	due to the contact resistance at the metallization and bulk resistance	3.3 to 5.5 ohm
R_d	of the semiconductor	4.2 to 7.0 ohm
C_{sd}	source-to-drain capacitance	1.09 pF

Closed-form approximate expressions for the calculation of some of the circuit elements, based on device geometry, are given below [8]:

(i) Transconductance, g_m: Transconductance is the ratio of small change in drain current produced by a small change in gate voltage when the source to drain voltage is fixed. Its value can be obtained from the relation

$$g_m = g_{mo}\, e^{-j\omega\tau_o} \qquad (9.21)$$

where

$$g_{mo} = 4\epsilon_o\, \epsilon_r\, v_s\, f_g(s, p, \xi)\, W/a \qquad (9.22)$$

with

$$f_g(s, p, \xi) = \frac{(1 - s)\cosh(\theta) - (1 - p)}{[2p(1 - p) + \xi(L_1/L)]\cosh(\theta) - 2p(1 - p)}$$

(9.23)

The quantities p, s, ξ, θ, τ_o, etc. are defined at the end of the Section.

(ii) Drain resistance, r_D ($= 1/G_D$): Drain resistance is the ratio of the change in drain voltage to the differential change in drain current when the gate voltage is fixed. It can be expressed in the form

$$r_d = \frac{f_r(s, p, \xi)}{4\,\epsilon_o\,\epsilon_r\,v_s\,W/a}$$

(9.24)

where

$$f_r(s, p, \xi) = \frac{1}{1 - p}\left\{\left[2p(1 - p) + \xi\frac{L_1}{L}\right]\cosh(\theta)\right.$$

$$\left. - 2p(1 - p)\right\}$$

(9.25)

(iii) Gate-to-source capacitance, C_{gs}: Gate-to-source capacitance is approximately equal to the rate of change of the free charge on the gate electrode with respect to the gate bias voltage, when the drain potential is held fixed. An approximate expression for C_{gs} is

$$C_{gs} \approx 2\,\epsilon_o\,\epsilon_r\,W\,f_c(s, p, \xi)$$

(9.26)

where

$$f_c(s, p, \xi) = 1.56 + f_{c_1} + f_{c_2}$$

(9.27)

with

$$f_{c_1} = \frac{2}{f_1}\frac{L_1}{a}\left\{f_g\left[\frac{2p^2(1 - p)^2 + f_2}{1 - p}\right] - s(1 - s)\right\}$$

(9.28)

$$f_{c_2} = 2f_g \frac{L_2}{a} + \left(1 - 2pf_g\right)\left[2 \frac{L}{a} \frac{p}{\xi\cosh(\theta)} + \tanh(\theta)\right]$$
(9.29)

$$f_1 = p^2 - s^2 - \frac{2}{3}(p^3 - s^3)$$
(9.30)

and

$$f_2 = \frac{2}{3}(p^3 - s^3) - \frac{1}{2}(p^4 - s^4) .$$
(9.31)

(iv) Drain-to-gate and source-to-drain capacitances, C_{dg} and C_{sd}:
These are parasitic elements of FET and their values can be obtained
from the following (assuming $L_s \gg L_{sd}$, $L_d \gg L$, $L_s = L_d$):

$$C_{dg} = C_{sd} = \epsilon_o (\epsilon_r + 1) W \frac{K(k')}{K(k)}$$
(9.32)

The ratio $K(k)/K(k')$ is obtained from (3.37) and (3.38) with
k for C_{dg} and C_{sd} being given, respectively, by

$$k_{dg} = \left(\frac{L_{dg}}{L + L_{dg}}\right)^{1/2}$$

and

$$k_{sd} = \frac{\sqrt{L_{sd}(2L_s + L_{sd})}}{L_s + L_{sd}} .$$

Equation (9.32) holds when the substrate is infinitely thick. For
finite thickness h of the substrate, $(\epsilon_r + 1)$ in (9.32) should be replaced by $2 \epsilon_{re}$ with the value of ϵ_{re} obtained from (3.75).

(v) Source series-resistance, R_s [9]: Source series-resistance consists of the resistance R_{ss} of the epitaxial layer between the source
and gate, and the ohmic contact resistance R_{cs}. The value of R_{ss}
is determined by the material resistance, the layer thickness "a"
and the source to gate distance L_{sg}, and is given by

$$R_{ss} = \frac{L_{sg}R_s}{W}$$
(9.33)

where R_s is the surface resistance of epi-layer given by

$$R_s = (e \mu n_o a)^{-1} \qquad (9.34)$$

and μ is the low-field mobility of electrons. The contact resistance R_{cs} is given by

$$R_{cs} = \frac{\sqrt{R_s \rho_c}}{W} \; \coth (L_s \sqrt{R_s / \rho_c}) \qquad (9.35)$$

where ρ_c is the specific contact resistance (ohm-cm^2) [10].

(vi) Drain series-resistance, R_D: This can be estimated in the same way as R_s.

(vii) Gate resistance, R_g [9]: The gate resistance R_g can be obtained from

$$R_g = \frac{1}{4} \frac{\rho W}{3tL} \qquad (9.36)$$

where t is the thickness of the deposited gate metal film, and ρ is the specific resistivity (ohm-cm) of the gate material.

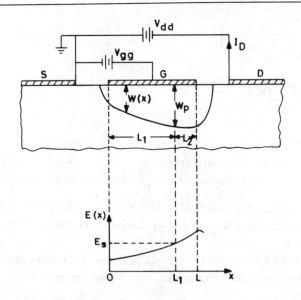

Figure 9.6   Cross-sectional diagram for the idealized FET showing potentials used.

Various symbols which occur in (9.21) to (9.36) are defined below:

τ_o : time required for electrons to traverse the gate length at the scattering-limited velocity. For a 1 μm gate GaAs FET, τ_o $\approx L/v_s = 10^{-4}/(2 \text{ x } 10^7) = 5$ psec.

v_s : scattering-limited velocity (or saturation velocity) of electrons

$$\left.\begin{array}{ll} s & : \sqrt{W_s/W_{oo}} \\[2mm] p & : \sqrt{W_p/W_{oo}} \end{array}\right\} \quad 0 < s < p \leqslant 1$$

W_{oo} : pinch-off voltage or gate to channel potential required to deplete the channel of carriers, and is given by

$$W_{oo} = \frac{e\,n_o}{2\,\epsilon_o\,\epsilon_r}\,a^2\,, \quad \epsilon_o = 8.854 \text{ x } 10^{-14} \text{ F/cm}$$

n_o : doping density in the channel (atoms/cm^3)

ϵ_r : dielectric constant of the substrate (12.5 for GaAs)

a : thickness of epitaxial layer (Figure 9.4)

W_s : channel potential at the source end, and referred to the gate electrode

$$W_s = V_{sg} + \phi$$

W_p : channel potential at the pinch-off point, and referred to the gate electrode (Figure 9.6)

$$W_p = V_{sg} + \phi - V_p$$

V_{sg} : source-to-gate potential (with source at ground)

$$V_{sg} = V_{gg}, \text{ applied potential (Figure 9.6)}$$

ϕ : Schottky-barrier potential (typically 0.8 - 0.9 V for Schottky junctions using gold as metal)

V_p : channel potential at the pinch-off point ($x = L_1$), i.e.

$$V_p = V(L_1)$$

ξ : saturation index, given by $E_s L/W_{oo}$ (of the order of 0.05 to 0.40)

E_s : saturation field, i.e., electric field in the channel at $x = L_1$
(E$_s$ for GaAs $\sim$ 3.9 kV/cm)

L : length of the gate electrode (Figure 9.4)

L_1 : $L \dfrac{f_1(s,p)}{\xi(1-p)}$

L_2 : $L - L_1$ (Figure 9.6)

L_s : length of the source electrode (Figure 9.4)

L_{sd} : inter-electrode spacing between the source and the drain electrodes

L_{gd} : inter-electrode spacing between the gate and the drain electrodes (Figure 9.4)

W : gate width (Figure 9.4)

θ : $\pi L_2/(2a)$.

The value of p is obtained by solving the following transcedental equation

$$V_{dd} = - W_{oo} \left[p^2 - s^2 + \frac{2}{\pi} \frac{a}{L} \xi \sinh(\theta) \right] \qquad (9.37)$$

where V_{dd} is the applied bias potential (Figure 9.6).

Y-Parameters

The equivalent circuit, shown in Figure 9.5, has been analyzed to obtain y-parameters for the device. It has been assumed that $\omega C_{gs} R_i \ll 1$. The y-parameters are given below [7]

$$y_{11} = \omega^2 C_{gs}^2 (R_i + R_s + R_g) \delta^2 + j\omega(\delta C_{gs} + C_{dg}) \qquad (9.38a)$$

$$y_{12} = -j\omega C_{dg} \qquad (9.38b)$$

$$y_{21} = g_{mo}\delta - j\omega[C_{dg} + g_{mo}\delta \{ \tau_o + \delta C_{gs}(R_s + R_g) \}] \qquad (9.38c)$$

$$y_{22} = \delta G_d + j\omega(C_{dg} + C_{sd}) \qquad (9.38d)$$

where

$$\delta = \frac{1}{1 + R_s(g_{mo} + G_d)} \ . \qquad (9.39)$$

The y-parameters can be converted into S-parameters using standard transformations.

9.5 GUNN AND IMPATT DIODES

9.5.1 Gunn Diodes

The Gunn diode is a two-terminal, bulk effect, negative resistance device. It can be fabricated from n-type semiconducting materials like GaAs, InP, $GaAs_x P_{1-x}$, etc. The negative resistance characteristics of these materials arise from negative differential mobility (i.e., a decrease in the carrier velocity with an increase in the electric field) when biased above a threshold value of the electric field. This behavior is called transferred electron effect and the devices exhibiting it are known as transferred electron devices. These devices find several applications as oscillators and amplifiers.

Since the Gunn diode is a two-terminal device, it can be represented by an equivalent impedance for any specified operating conditions (voltage applied and circuit impedance looking from device terminals). Several circuit designs use measured values of this impedance. A model which can be used under various operating conditions has been derived, using general modelling considerations, and is discussed in this section. This nonlinear lumped circuit model for Gunn diodes is reported by Chua and Sing [11]. It is valid for various modes of operation — specifically, the transit-time mode, the delayed-domain mode, the quenched-domain mode, and the LSA mode, provided the Gunn diode satisfies the stable domain requirement of $n_o L > 10^{12}/cm^2$. The model incorporates a timing circuit to simulate the domain nucleation and extinction phenomena automatically.

The equivalent circuit model for the Gunn diode chip is shown in Figure 9.7. It is based on the assumption that a single high-field domain exists and propagates without change of shape, with a domain velocity $v_D(t)$, from the cathode to the anode. Further, the electric field is assumed to be quasi-static.

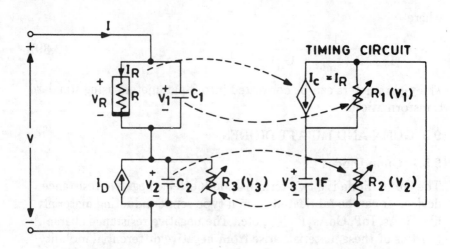

Figure 9.7   Equivalent circuit model for Gunn diode chip.

The equivalent circuit of Figure 9.7 can be divided into two parts: the high field domain part and the bulk sample. The propagating high field domain, characterized by an excess voltage V_2, has the 'static' characteristics defined by the current source I_D. The dynamic effects of the domain are incorporated by shunting the stable-domain current source with a voltage dependent domain capacitance C_2. The entire bulk sample is represented by the ohmic device resistance, R, shunted by the bulk capacitance C_1, and placed in series with the domain elements. These elements are defined below:

$$\text{Cathode to anode capacitance,} \quad C_1 = \frac{\epsilon_o \epsilon_r A}{L} \tag{9.40}$$

$$\text{Domain capacitance,} \quad C_2 = \frac{\epsilon_o \epsilon_r A}{W} \tag{9.41}$$

The nonlinear bulk resistor, R, is obtained from

$$V_R/R = I_R = A \, e \, n_o \, v(E) \Big|_{E \, = \, V_R/L}. \tag{9.42}$$

Nonlinear controlled current source, I_D, for zero diffusion assumption, is given by

$$I_D = C_2 \int_{E_o}^{E_m} [\, v(E_o) - v(E) \,]\, dE - I \qquad (9.43)$$

where E_m, the 'peak' domain field, is given by

$$E_m = \frac{V_1}{L} + \sqrt{\frac{2\, e n_o V_2}{\epsilon_o \epsilon_r}}$$

and the variables are defined as follows:

n_o : uniform donor concentration outside the domain

L : length of the Gunn diode

A : area of cross-section of the Gunn diode

ϵ_r : dielectric constant of the semiconductor

V_2 : excess voltage across the domain given by

$$V_2 = \frac{\epsilon_o \epsilon_r}{e\, n_o} \int_{E_o}^{E_m} (E - E_o)\, dE \ , \quad E : \text{field inside the domain}$$

V_1 : voltage component due to the uniform field E_o, given by
$$V_1 = E_o L$$

V : impressed voltage, $V_1 + V_2$

W : stable-domain width $\approx \dfrac{\epsilon_o \epsilon_r}{e\, n_o} (E_m - E_o)$

I : external device current $= A e n_o v(E_o)$.

The non-linear variation of the electron drift velocity $v(E)$ with electric field can be represented by the following relation

$$v(E) = \frac{\mu E + v_s(E/E_c)^4}{1 + (E/E_c)^4} \tag{9.44}$$

where, for GaAs, $\mu = 8000$ cm^2 / V-sec, $E_c = 4000$ V/cm and $v_s = 8 \times 10^6$ cm/s.

The model described by the elements R, C_1, I_D, and V_2 is valid for the quenched-domain mode and the LSA mode. To describe the transit-time mode and the delayed-domain mode, a 'timing circuit' is added to track the domain motion, and it causes the domain capacitor C_2 to discharge quickly whenever the domain reaches the anode.

The timing circuit for the zero diffusion case is shown in Figure 9.7 along with the rest of the equivalent circuit. The three voltage-controlled nonlinear resistors behave like relays which are activated whenever a prescribed threshold voltage is reached, namely:

$$R_1(V_1) = \begin{cases} 0, & \text{if } V_1 \geq E_t L \\ \infty, & \text{if } V_1 \leq E_t L \end{cases} \tag{9.45}$$

where E_t is the threshold field intensity when the drift velocity curve $v(E)$ attains its maximum,

$$R_2(V_2) = \begin{cases} 0, & \text{if } V_2 = 0 \\ \infty, & \text{if } V_2 \neq 0 \end{cases} \tag{9.46}$$

and

$$R_3(V_3) = \begin{cases} \tau_d/C_2, & \text{if } V_3 \geq A e n_o L \\ \infty, & \text{if } V_3 < A e n_o L \end{cases} \tag{9.47}$$

where τ_d is the time constant for the domain to collapse (usually a few hundred picoseconds) and V_3 is the voltage across the 1F capacitor shown in Figure 9.7.

It may be pointed out that the above mentioned simple equations hold for the zero-diffusion case only. Modes for constant diffusion and non-zero diffusion cases have been discussed in [11].

9.5.2 Impatt Diodes

An impatt or an avalanche diode has an n^+–p–i–p^+ structure. The superscript '+' indicates a heavy doping and i stands for intrinsic, meaning an equal number of available holes and electrons. The structure is sufficiently reverse biased to sweep the entire region between n^+ and p^+ terminals free of carriers. Because of the abrupt n^+–p junction the electric field is highest there. The ionisation starts there and the avalanche breakdown takes place. This leads to the generation of electron-hole pairs. Electrons are collected at the positive terminal, whereas holes drift to the right, cross the remaining depletion layer at an almost constant velocity, and are collected at the p^+–terminal.

A complete analysis of the impatt diode shows that, (i) the diode exhibits a resonance frequency at which the diode susceptance changes from inductive to capacitive, and (ii) the real part of the diode impedance becomes negative at frequencies well below this resonance frequency and remains negative over octaves of the frequency range. The negative resistance of the diode is made use of in impatt oscillators and amplifiers.

(a) Small-signal equivalent circuit: The equivalent circuit of the impatt diode, when the amplitude of the sinusoidal voltage is less than one volt, is shown in Figure 9.8 [12]. It can be used over an octave frequency range centered at the frequency of maximum negative conductance. The equivalent circuit parameters are defined in Table 9.5 and their typical values are also given there.

The values of equivalent circuit elements can be obtained directly by measuring the terminal impedance of the device and then fitting the element values (treated as parameters) in the impedance expression for the modelled equivalent circuit. For the circuit shown in Figure 9.8, the calculated impedance is obtained as

$$Z_{eq}(\omega) = \frac{(R_1 + R_2) + j\omega(L - R_2R_3C + R_1R_2C - R_1R_3C) - \omega^2 LC(R_1 - R_3)}{1 + j\omega C(R_2 - R_3) - \omega^2 LC}$$

$$(9.48)$$

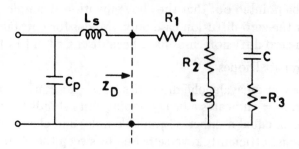

Figure 9.8   Equivalent circuit for a packaged impatt diode.

Alternatively, the diode terminal impedance may be determined from the device structure, material properties, and the operating point. This impedance is then equated to $Z_{eq}(\omega)$ of (9.48). The device impedance, Z_D, may be obtained as follows:

$$Z_D(\omega) = R_s + \frac{\ell_d^{\,2}}{\epsilon_o \epsilon_r A v_s} \left[\frac{1}{1 - (\omega/\omega_a)^2} \right] \frac{1 - \cos\theta}{\theta^2}$$

$$+ \frac{1}{j\omega C_d} \left[1 - \frac{\sin\theta}{\theta} + \frac{\dfrac{\sin\theta}{\theta} + \ell_a/\ell_d}{1 - (\omega_a/\omega)^2} \right] \quad (9.49)$$

where

R_s : series resistance of the diode

ω_a : avalanche frequency

v_s : saturated velocity of carriers in semiconductor

ϵ_r : permittivity of the semiconductor

A : area of cross-section of the diode

ℓ_a : length of the avalanche region

TABLE 9.5

Typical Values for the Elements of the Equivalent Circuit for Impatt Diode Chip

Symbol	Element	Typical Values
C	junction capacitance	0.19 pF
L	avalanche inductance	2.5 nH
R_1	series resistance	58 ohm
R_2	avalanche resistance	32 ohm
R_3	negative resistance	43 ohm

ℓ_d : length of the drift region

C_d : drift region capacitance (= $\epsilon_o \epsilon_r A/\ell_d$)

θ : $\omega \tau_d$

τ_d : transit time of drift region (= ℓ_d/v_s).

Equation (9.49) can be written in terms of four independent diode parameters: τ_d, C_d, ℓ_a/ℓ_d, and ω_a. The first three parameters can be found from the doping profile measurements. The fourth, ω_a, depends upon the operating point (I_{dc}) also and can be measured or estimated.

The equivalent circuit parameters can be determined analytically by comparing (9.48) and (9.49). Making some approximations, we get for the circuit elements,

$$R_1 = R_s + 0.25a(1 + 0.06 a^2)/b \qquad (9.50)$$

$$R_2 = R_1 - 0.03 a^3/b \qquad (9.51)$$

$$R_3 = R_2 \qquad (9.52)$$

$$C = 1/(\omega_a^2 L) \qquad (9.53)$$

and

$$L = \frac{1 - 0.1 a^2 + \ell_a/\ell_d}{2b\omega_a}$$

$$+ \sqrt{\left[\frac{R_2}{\omega_a}\right]^2 + \left[\frac{1 - 0.1a^2 + \ell_a/\ell_d}{2b\,\omega_a}\right]^2}$$

(9.54)

where

$$a = \omega_a \tau_d \text{ and } b = \omega_a C_d .$$

Large-signal equivalent circuit [13]: The small-signal equivalent circuit shown in Figure 9.8 can be also used for the large-signal case, with the assumption that R_2 and L are quadratic functions of peak RF voltage across the diode. One can express R_2 and L as

$$R_2 = R_{2SS} (1 + r_1 V_1 + r_2 V_1^2)$$ (9.55)

$$L = L_{SS} (1 + \ell_1 V_1 + \ell_2 V_1^2)$$ (9.56)

where R_{2SS} and L_{SS} are small-signal values, and $r_1, r_2, \ell_1,$ and ℓ_2 are constants specifying non-linearity. The values of these constants can be obtained to give a good fit between the diode conductance G_D and G_{eq}. Some other criteria may also be used for determining these constants. For a particular diode, values of these constants have been found to be [13]:

$$r_1 = 10^{-2}/V, \qquad r_2 = 8 \times 10^{-4}/V,$$

$$\ell_1 = 3 \times 10^{-3}/V \text{ and } \ell_2 = 7 \times 10^{-5}/V .$$

As in the case of Gunn diode circuits, many impatt diode circuits have been designed based on the simple equivalent impedance representation of the impatt diode. This impedance is measured experimentally for the conditions under which the device is to be used.

REFERENCES

[1] "Selection and Use of Microwave Diode Switches and Limiters," *Hewlett Packard Application Note No. 932*, May 1973.

[2] Gupta, K.C., *Microwaves*, New Delhi: Wiley Eastern, 1979, Ch. 4.

[3] White, M.H., and M.O. Thurston, "Characterization of Microwave Transistors," *Solid-State Electron.*, Vol. 13, 1970, pp. 523-542.

[4] Cooke, H.F., "Microwave Transistors: Theory and Design," *Proc. IEEE*, Vol. 59, Aug. 1971, pp. 1163-1181.

[5] Hartmann, K., *et al.*, "Equivalent Network for Three Different Microwave Bipolar Transistor Packages in the 2-10 GHz Range," *Electron. Lett.*, Vol. 7, Sept. 9, 1971, pp. 510-511.

[6] Liechti, C.A., "Characteristics of Dual-gate GaAs MESFETs," *Proc. 1974 European Microwave Conf.*, pp. 87-91.

[7] Mimura, T., *et al.*, "GaAs Microwave MOSFET," *IEEE Trans. Electron. Devices*, Vol. ED-25, June 1978, pp. 573-579.

[8] Pucel, R.A., *et al.*, "Signal and Noise Properties of Gallium Arsenide Microwave Field-effect Transistors," in *Advances in Electronics and Electron Physics*, L. Marton, Ed., Vol. 38, New York: Academic Press, 1975, pp. 195-265.

[9] Furutsuka, *et al.*, "GaAs Dual-gate MESFET's," *IEEE Trans. Electron Devices*, Vol. ED-25, June 1978, pp. 580-586.

[10] Ogawa, M., *et al.*, "Submicron Single-gate and Dual-gate GaAs MESFET's with Improved Low Noise and High Gain Performance," *IEEE Trans. Microwave Theory Tech.*, Vol. MTT-24, June 1976, pp. 300-305.

[11] Chua, L.O., and Y.W. Sing, "A Nonlinear Lumped Circuit Model for Gunn Diodes," *Int. J. Circuit Theory Applications*, Vol. 6, No. 4, Oct. 1978, pp. 375-408.

[12] Gupta, M.S., "A Small-signal and Noise Equivalent Circuit for IMPATT Diodes," *IEEE Trans. Microwave Theory Tech.*, Vol. MTT-21, Sept. 1973, pp. 591-594.

[13] Gupta, M.S., "Large-signal Equivalent Circuit for IMPATT-diode Characterization and its Application to Amplifiers," *IEEE Trans. Microwave Theory Tech.*, Vol. MTT-21, Nov. 1973, pp. 689-694.

10

Measurement
Techniques
for
Modelling

In earlier chapters, we have discussed modelling of various types of components used in microwave circuits. However, in several instances, the analytical models are not very accurate. Discontinuities in various transmission structures provide examples of this behavior. Discontinuity characterization for several newer transmission structures, like slot lines, coplanar waveguides, coplanar strips, etc., are not yet available. Also, there are several components (like semiconductor devices, lumped resistors, inductors, and capacitors) for which the parameter values vary considerably from unit to unit. This is caused by tolerances in various fabrication processes involved. In these, and similar situations, models required for CAD can be arrived at only through precise experimental measurements.

Measurements of S-parameters for multiport components, and of input impedances (or complex reflection coefficients) for one-port devices, provide the characterization needed for modelling. This chapter describes the techniques used for this purpose.

10.1 MICROWAVE NETWORK ANALYZERS

Instruments used for the measurement of S-parameters of microwave networks are called network analyzers. Three types of network analyzers are discussed in this section. These instruments
provide remarkable improvements in speed, convenience, and accuracy over the previously used slotted line and reflectometer
techniques.

10.1.1 Network Analyzer

As discussed in Chapter 2, scattering parameters for a multiport
network are defined as the ratio of the outgoing to the incoming
wave variables. We have

$$S_{mn} = b_m/a_n \Big|_{a_i = 0 \, (i \neq n)} . \tag{10.1}$$

Thus, the evaluation of S_{mn} involves obtaining the ratio of two
complex quantities b_m and a_n. Network analyzers are designed
for processing the signals proportional to b_m and a_n in order to
determine their complex ratio.

Usually, a_m, b_m, etc., cannot be measured right at the port location,
but are sampled with the help of a linear measurement network, as
shown in Figure 10.1. In general, the sample signals b_3 and b_4 are
related to a_m and b_m by a set of linear relations, given as:

$$b_3 = A \, a_m + B \, b_m \tag{10.2}$$

$$b_4 = C \, a_m + D \, b_m \tag{10.3}$$

where A, B, C, and D are complex constants. The measurement network is designed to make A and D equal to zero so that b_3 and b_4
are proportional to b_m and a_m, respectively. The basic set-up for
such a microwave network analyzer is illustrated in Figure 10.2.
The system is driven by a swept-frequency oscillator. The measurement network for evaluation of S_{mm} (Figure 10.2a) is essentially
a dual-directional coupler connected as a reflectometer. In the case
of measurement of S_{mn} (m ≠ n), it is essentially a power divider
as shown in Figure 10.2(b). There are two outputs from the measurement network: a reference signal and a reflected or transmitted
signal containing information about S_{mm} or S_{mn}. These signals are

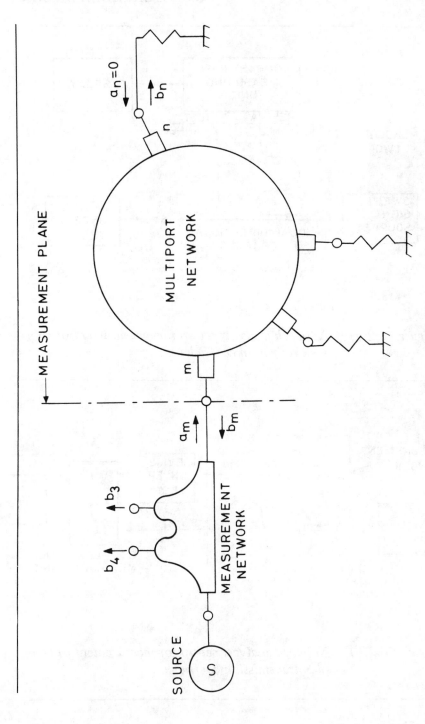

Figure 10.1   Set-up for measurement of S_{mm} of a multiport network.

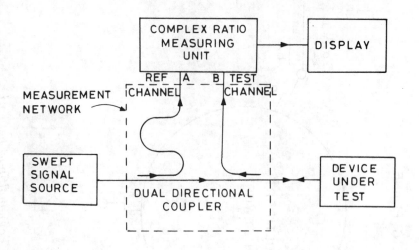

Figure 10.2(a)   *Network analyzer set-up for measurement of com-plex reflection coefficient.*

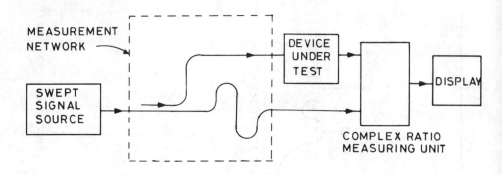

Figure 10.2(b)   *Network analyzer set-up for measurement of com-plex transmission coefficient.*

fed into the complex ratio measuring instrument, where the magnitude and phase of S_{mn} or S_{mm} are measured. The display unit puts the data in a format selected by the user. Data can be organized as either magnitude and phase information on meter readouts or plotted on a polar display.

The most significant part of a network analyzer is the complex ratio measuring unit. Accurate measurement of complex signal ratios at microwave frequencies is both difficult and expensive. Conventional network analyzers convert the test and reference channel signals to a lower frequency by a sampling harmonic converter. Amplitude ratio as well as phase difference is measured at the lower frequency (typically 278 kHz). A detailed block diagram for frequency translation by means of sampling technique is shown in Figure 10.3. In a sampling harmonic converter, the local oscillator of a conventional hetrodyne system is replaced by a pulse generator which generates a train of very narrow pulses. When the pulse width is narrow compared to the period of the applied RF signal, the sampler becomes a harmonic mixer with equal efficiency for each harmonic. Thus, sampling-type mixing has the advantage that a single system can operate over an extremely wide input frequency range. To make the system capable of swept-frequency operation, an internal phase-lock loop keeps the gate generator tuned to the incoming signal. When the loop is unlocked, it automatically tunes back and forth across a portion of the octave-band selected by the user. When any harmonic of the frequency of the tracking gate generator is 20 MHz (first IF) more than the input frequency, the loop stops searching and locks. Search and lock-on are normally completed in about 20 μs.

Since the frequency conversion described above is a linear process, the down-converted signals have the same relative amplitudes and phases as the microwave test and reference signals. Further processing of the test and reference signals is done at the IF frequency. The IF signals are applied to a pair of matched AGC amplifiers which keep the signal level in the reference channel constant and vary the gain in the test channel so that the test signal level does not change when variations common to both the channels occur. This is equivalent to taking a ratio and removing the effects of power variations in the signal source. After a second frequency translation, the amplitude

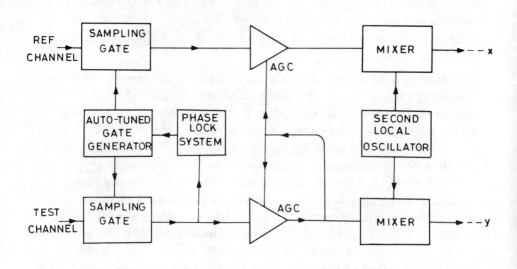

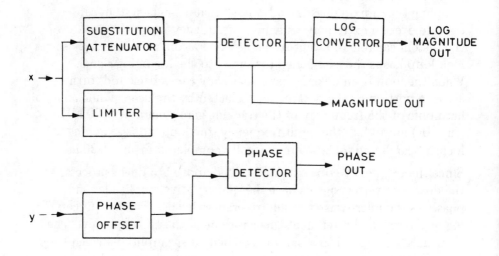

*Figure 10.3   Frequency converter and subsequent processing units
of a network analyzer.*

detection and the phase comparison are done at a lower frequency, typically 278 kHz.

The display unit reads directly the amplitude and the phase of the scattering parameter S_{mm} or S_{mn}.

10.1.2 Automatic Network Analyzer

Automatic network analyzer systems offer vast improvements in speed, convenience and accuracy over the manually operated network analyzer system discussed in Section 10.1.1. Automatic analyzers are able to accurately characterize an unknown device exclusive of system hardware errors, store the results, and represent them in virtually any mathematical form. The measured data may be utilized directly in CAD and simulation studies. In contrast to the previous system, where the key to improved accuracy was usually an improved hardware item, the automatic network analyzer can measure hardware imperfections and correct the measurements accordingly. It is not necessary to assume A and D in (10.2) and (10.3) to be equal to zero (which would be true only if the hardware were perfect). The system evaluates all four constants, A, B, C, and D, as part of the measurement procedure. Departures of A and D from the zero value constitute system errors. In an automatic network analyzer set up, these values are stored in and corrected for by the digital computer.

A block-diagram of an automatic microwave network analyzer system is shown in Figure 10.4. The analyzer measures the S-parameters of the two-port network connected as shown in the figure. The test unit is configured electromechanically, under computer control, to select a transmitted (from port 1 to port 2 or from port 2 to port 1) or reflected (from port 1 or from port 2) signal which is fed to the test channel of the frequency converter. The reference channel of the frequency converter is fed with a known fraction of the input signal. The signal applied to the test unit is derived from a frequency source which is also programmed under computer control.

The network analyzer portion of the system is similar to that of the manually operated system shown in Figure 10.3. In the present case, the signal frequency and various switches are set by sending

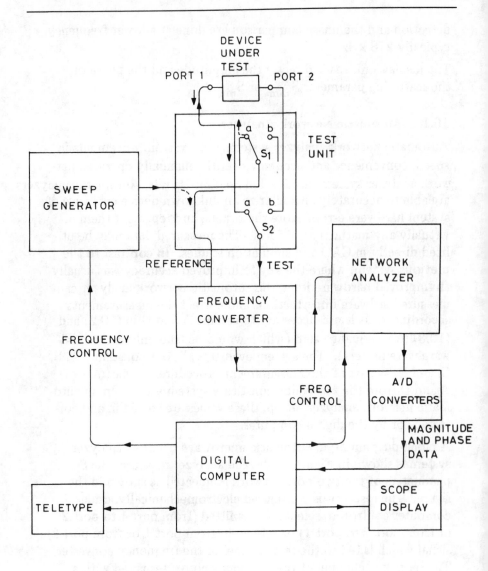

Figure 10.4   Block diagram of an automatic network analyzer set-up.

commands through the digital computer. Two analog-to-digital converters digitize the magnitude and phase information for the computer input. The computer controls all important functions of the microwave instruments. Also, it stores the system's own frequency dependent errors (both amplitude and phase) and performs necessary mathematical calculations.

The automatic network analyzer system operates as follows. First, the computer sets the sweep generator and the network analyzer to the required frequency and routes the microwave signal through the multiplexer to the test unit. Next, the S-parameter to be measured is selected, and the resulting amplitude and phase information is digitized and transferred to the computer. Finally, the raw measurement data are corrected for system errors (previously measured and stored) and displayed in an appropriate form on the scope or the teletype. The operation of error correction is very important and is the unique characteristic of the automatic network analyzer system. System error measurement and correction are discussed in detail in Section 10.3.

10.1.3 Six-port Network Analyzer

In the network analyzers discussed in subsections 10.1.1 and 10.1.2, the key operation is conversion of the test and reference signals to a lower frequency for measurement of the phase difference. This frequency conversion complicates the design of network analyzers and makes their cost prohibitive. However, frequency conversion becomes necessary when we wish to measure *both the magnitudes and the phases* of b_3 and b_4. If only the magnitudes of b_3 and b_4 are sufficient (as for example when one needs only VSWR and not the complex input reflection coefficient), simple power detectors can be used and hetrodyning for the frequency conversion would not be needed. In such a case, (10.2) and (10.3) may be rewritten, with reference to the measurement plane shown in Figure 10.6(a), as

$$P_3 = |b_3|^2 = |A\,a + B\,b|^2 \tag{10.4}$$

$$P_4 = |b_4|^2 = |C\,a + D\,b|^2 \tag{10.5}$$

where P_3 and P_4 are the measured powers, and the proportionality

factors have been absorbed in the constants A, B, C, and D which now
stand redefined. As the phase information is not contained in P_3 and
P_4, two additional detectors are required whose responses P_5 and P_6
are also related linearly to a and b and may be written as

$$P_5 = |E\,a + F\,b|^2 \qquad\qquad\qquad\qquad\qquad (10.6)$$

$$P_6 = |G\,a + H\,b|^2 \qquad\qquad\qquad\qquad\qquad (10.7)$$

where E, F, G, and H are additional complex constants of the measurement network. The measurement objective is to determine b
and a through observations of P_3, P_4, P_5, and P_6 and under the
assumption that A, B, . . ., H are known. For this purpose, the solution of the system of quadratic equations (10.4) through (10.7) is
needed.

Figure 10.5   *Graphical representation of evaluation of complex*
                reflection coefficient in a six-port network analyzer

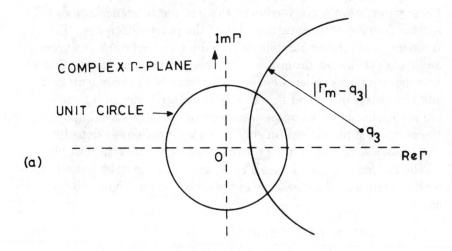

(a)   *Locus of Γ_m when two detectors of measurement*
        network are used

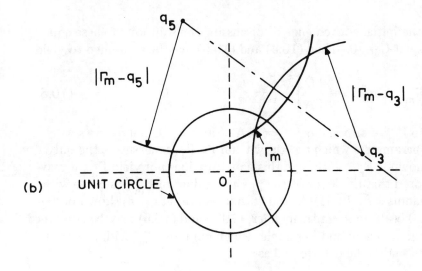

(b)

(b) Evaluation of Γ_m with three detectors of the measurement network

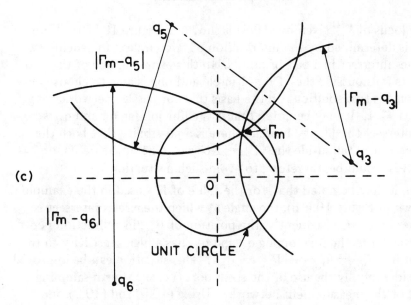

(c)

(c) Evaluation of Γ_m with four detectors of the measurement network

For the initial convenience of discussing the solution of these equations, let $C = 0$. Then (10.4) and (10.5) may be combined to yield

$$| \Gamma_m - q_3 |^2 = \left| \frac{D}{A} \right|^2 \frac{P_3}{P_4} \tag{10.8}$$

where $\Gamma_m = a/b$ and $q_3 = -B/A$. Since A, D, and q_3 are system parameters which are known and P_3/P_4 is measured, the only unknown is Γ_m. Although this equation does not yield Γ_m, it may be noted that the locus of the possible values of Γ_m is a circle with the radius $\sqrt{P_3/P_4}$ $|D/A|$ and with its center at q_3, as shown in Figure 10.5(a). In a similar manner, (10.5) and (10.6) may be combined and the radius of another circle, which contains Γ_m, with center at q_5 ($= -F/E$) be determined as

$$| \Gamma_m - q_5 |^2 = \left| \frac{D}{E} \right|^2 \frac{P_5}{P_4} . \tag{10.9}$$

The locus of Γ_m given by (10.9) is shown in Figure 10.5(b). Here Γ_m is determined by the intersection of two circles. In general, two circles intersect in a pair of points. In this example, one of the two points falls outside the $|\Gamma| = 1$ circle and one is able to choose between the two solutions on the basis that for passive networks $|\Gamma_m| \leqslant 1$. It may be noted that if the line joining q_3 and q_5 were to intersect the $|\Gamma| = 1$ circle, there is a possibility that both the intersections fall inside the $|\Gamma| = 1$ circle. One of the design objectives would be, therefore, to avoid such a situation.

Also, it may be noted that, for the value of Γ_m used in the example shown in Figure 10.5(b), the angle at which the circles intersect is rather small. Consequently, the position of Γ_m, in a direction perpendicular to the line joining q_3 and q_5, has a high sensitivity to the error in $|\Gamma_m - q_3|$ or $|\Gamma_m - q_5|$. This situation can be improved considerably by the use of the sixth port (i.e. the fourth sampling port of the measurement network). Using (10.5) and (10.7), one may write

$$| \Gamma_m - q_6 |^2 = \left| \frac{D}{G} \right|^2 \frac{P_6}{P_4} \tag{10.10}$$

where $q_6 = -H/G$. This provides a third circle upon which Γ_m must lie and which under ideal conditions must pass through the intersection of the other two circles, as shown in Figure 10.5(c). In practice, because of measurement errors, the three circles will not intersect in a point, and some sort of statistical averaging is useful. Thus, the measurement of P_6 enhances the accuracy and at the same time the double root ambiguity is also resolved. Also, it may be recognized that the accuracy with which small values of Γ_m are measured is determined primarily by the precision with which the radii, i.e., the ratios P_3/P_4, etc., are measured. Thus, a large dynamic range for the detectors is not required.

It is not necessary to assume C to be exactly zero. A non-zero value of C alters the above procedure but the basic philosophy remains the same.

A six-port measurement system can be realized practically by using quadrature and $180°$ hybrids [7] as shown in Figure 10.6(a). The values of q_3, q_5, and q_6 in this case are $j\sqrt{2}$, $-\sqrt{2}(1 + j)$, and $\sqrt{2}(1 - j)$, and are shown in Figure 10.6(b) in Γ plane. Let us consider the power outputs at various detectors when a 20 mW source is used. For $\Gamma_m = 0$, a = 0 and $|b|^2 = 5$ mW, and therefore $P_3 = P_4 = P_5 = P_6 = 3.75$ mW. When the load is replaced by a sliding short, $|\Gamma_m| = 1$ and the maximum values of P_3, P_5, and P_6 are about 10.93 mW, 8.44 mW and 8.44 mW, respectively, whereas the minimum values are about 0.32 mW, 0.94 mW, and 0.94 mW, respectively. Thus, the maximum dynamic range required in the case of P_3 is given by $P_{max}/P_{min} = 10.93$ mW/0.32 mW $\cong 15$ dB.

10.2 SYSTEM ERROR MEASUREMENT AND CORRECTION

10.2.1 General Considerations

Accuracy of measurement at microwave frequencies is limited by imperfections in the system hardware used. The measurement networks used in network analyzers have non-zero losses. Directional couplers have finite directivity, coupling errors, and residual VSWR. Switches have finite isolation and a non-zero value for the insertion loss. All these, and other similar imperfections limit the accuracy of measurements performed by the network analyzer. In the past, constant efforts were made to minimize these errors by designing

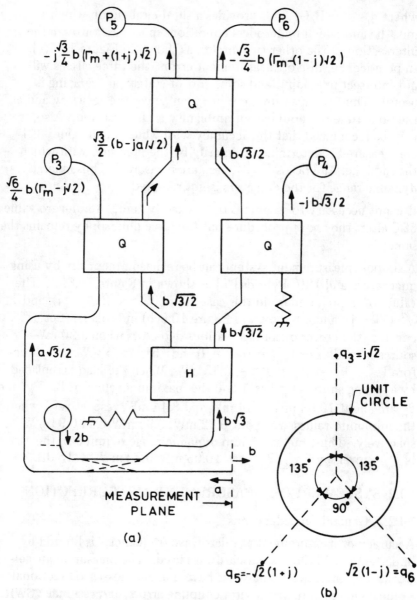

(a)

Figure 10.6(a)   Realization of a six-port network analyzer with
one 180° and three quadrature hybrids.

(b)   Locations of q_3, q_4 and q_5 for the circuit configuration shown in (a).

more and more perfect hardware items. However, it is now recognized and accepted that one can correct for these errors rather than try to eliminate them completely. System error calibration and correction provides not only higher accuracy, but also keeps the system cost at a reasonable level by relaxing the rigid specifications for hardware items.

In order to connect the device or the network under test to the measurement system, one needs connectors, some finite lengths of intervening transmission lines, and, in several cases, transitions (or adapters) from one type of transmission medium to another. Consequently, the actual measurements are usually made at, and refer to, some reference plane physically removed from the device or the network under test. In such cases, the device or the network can be considered as if embedded in the connecting network which is interposed between the device or network to be tested and the measurement system, as shown in Figure 10.7(a). Deduction of the characteristics of the device or the network under test from measurements made at the outputs of the intervening connecting network is termed *de-embedding* [8]. The process of de-embedding requires an accurate characterization of the intervening connecting network. The complexity of the characterization procedure of the connecting network depends upon whether the device or the network under test is a one-port, a two-port or a multiport. In general, the electrical properties of the connecting network can be determined by conducting a series of measurements with known embedded devices. Once the connecting network is characterized, the parameters of the embedded device or the network can be computed from the measured data.

The procedure for eliminating errors introduced by the connecting network is the same as that for the compensation of system errors of the analyzer. An imperfect network analyzer may be viewed as a combination of an 'ideal' network analyzer system and an imperfect connecting network, as shown in Figure 10.7(b).

For the characterization of system imperfection, connectors, etc., one needs certain "standard" components like short-circuits, matched terminations, through-lines, open-circuits, etc., in the same transmission medium as that used for the circuit under test. In some instances, as for microstrip lines, these standards are not easily available. In such cases the calibration is carried out by using standards in a different

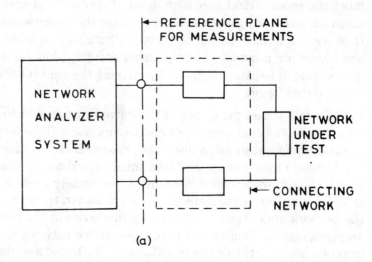

(a)

Figure 10.7(a)   *"Connecting network" used for measurements with a network analyzer system.*

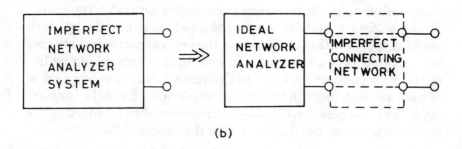

(b)

Figure 10.7(b)   *Imperfect network analyzer viewed as an ideal network analyzer plus an imperfect connecting network.*

medium such as coaxial lines with APC connectors. The circuit characterization thus obtained includes that of the adapters used. A separate characterization of these adapters is needed in order to evaluate the characteristics of the circuit alone. A method for the characterization of adapters is discussed in sub-section 10.2.5.

The procedure for calibration and error correction for one-port, two-port and multi-port networks are discussed separately in this section. Signal-flow graph technique [14] is a very convenient tool for formulating these problems and has been used for this purpose.

10.2.2 One-port Device Measurements

Consider a one-port device to be connected to port 1 of the test unit shown in Figure 10.4. The device presents a complex reflection coefficient ρ_L at the reference plane of this port. The situation can be described by the signal-flow graph shown in Figure 10.8. The parameters r_{00}, r_{10}, r_{01}, and r_{11} are scattering parameters of the equivalent connecting network, corresponding to system errors. The main contributors to the error parameters of the system are the following:

r_{00} : directivity error of the couplers, and the finite isolation between the test and the reference channels

r_{10}, r_{01} : tracking variations of the coupling coefficients, and of the reference and test channels of the frequency converter

r_{11} : mismatch of connectors, and of internal loads.

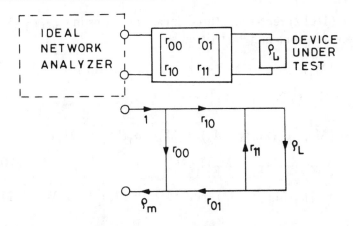

Figure 10.8   *Signal flow graph for measurements on a one-port device.*

From the signal-flow graph in Figure 10.8(a), the measured reflection coefficient ρ_m can be expressed in terms of ρ_L and r-parameters as

$$\rho_m = r_{00} + \frac{r_{10}\, r_{01}\, \rho_L}{1 - r_{11}\, \rho_L}. \tag{10.11}$$

Error parameters r_{00}, r_{11}, and the product $r_{01}\, r_{10}$ can be determined by measuring three different reference standards with accurately known reflection coefficients ρ_L. If M_i (i = 1, 2, 3) are the three values of the measured reflection coefficient ρ_m, corresponding to the three different standard reflections ρ_i(i = 1, 2, 3) connected to the port 1, we have

$$M_i = r_{00} + \frac{r_{10}\, r_{01}\, \rho_i}{1 - r_{11}\, \rho_i}$$

or

$$M_i = r_{00} + M_i \rho_i r_{11} - \rho_i \Delta r \tag{10.12}$$

where

$$\Delta r = r_{00}\, r_{11} - r_{01}\, r_{10}. \tag{10.13}$$

Equation (10.12) represents three linear equations in r_{00}, r_{11} and Δr. Their solutions may be written as

$$\Delta r = [M_1 \rho_1 (M_2 - M_3) + M_2 \rho_2 (M_3 - M_1) + M_3 \rho_3 (M_1 - M_2)] / N \tag{10.14}$$

$$r_{00} = [M_1 \rho_2 \rho_3 (M_2 - M_3) + M_2 \rho_3 \rho_1 (M_3 - M_1) + M_3 \rho_1 \rho_2 (M_1 - M_2)] / N \tag{10.15}$$

$$r_{11} = - [\rho_1 (M_2 - M_3) + \rho_2 (M_3 - M_1) + \rho_3 (M_1 - M_2)] / N \tag{10.16}$$

where

$$N = \rho_2 \rho_3 (M_2 - M_3) + \rho_3 \rho_1 (M_3 - M_1) + \rho_1 \rho_2 (M_1 - M_2). \tag{10.17}$$

The product $r_{10} r_{01}$ can be determined from (10.13), and (10.14) to (10.16).

The choice of the reflection standards ρ_i depends upon the fabrication accuracy, the type of transmission structure used, and the proximity limitations for placing them in the measurement set-up [10]. Preferably, the standards are: a short ($\rho_L = -1$), an open ($\rho_L = 1$), and a perfect match ($\rho_L = 0$). The latter leads to a direct measurement of the parameter r_{00}.

Once r_{00}, r_{11} and $r_{10} r_{01}$ are determined, the reflection coefficient ρ_t can be obtained from the measured value ρ_m by rewriting (10.11) as

$$\rho_t = \frac{\rho_m - r_{00}}{r_{10} r_{01} + r_{11}(\rho_m - r_{00})} . \tag{10.18}$$

At times, as for example in de-embedding problems [8], the characterization of the connecting network is available in terms of its Z-parameters. Relations corresponding to (10.12) and (10.18) may now be written as

$$Z_{mi} = Z_{11} - \frac{Z_{12} Z_{21}}{Z_{22} + Z_{Li}}$$

and

$$Z_t = \frac{Z_{12} Z_{21}}{Z_{11} - Z_m} - Z_{22}$$

where Z_m is the value of the impedance measured at the input of the interconnecting network, Z_{Li} are the standard impedances used for characterization of the interconnecting network, and Z_t is the impedance of the device under test. In this case, also, three values of Z_{Li} are needed for evaluating Z_{11}, Z_{22} and the product $Z_{12} Z_{21}$.

10.2.3 Two-port Measurements

When a two-port network is connected between port 1 and port 2 of the test unit, the signal-flow graph for the system may be drawn as shown in Figure 10.9. Parameters r_{33}, r_{23}, r_{22}, and r_{32} for port 2 are similar to r_{00}, r_{10}, r_{11}, and r_{01} for port 1. Parameters

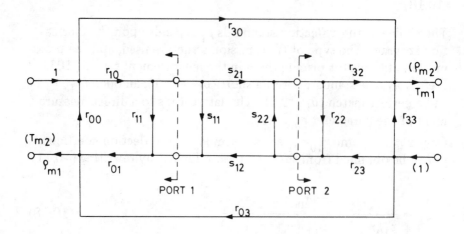

Figure 10.9   Signal flow graph for measurements on a two-port network.

r_{30} and r_{03} are mainly contributed by the finite isolation of the internal switches. S_{11}, S_{21}, S_{12}, and S_{22} are the scattering parameters of the device under test. Signals shown without parentheses apply when the switch S_1 (in Figure 10.4) is in position "a" while the signals indicated in parentheses apply when the switch S_2 is in position "b" which converts port 2 into the input port for the test signal.

Some of the error parameters, viz., r_{00}, r_{11}, and $r_{01} r_{10}$ can be determined by reflection measurements at port 1, as discussed earlier. Parameters r_{33}, r_{22}, and $r_{32} r_{23}$ can be evaluated by similar measurements at port 2. Two-port transmission measurements with the device under test replaced by a through-line are used for evaluating parameters r_{30}, r_{03}, and products $r_{10} r_{32}$ and $r_{01} r_{23}$.

When a through-line of length ℓ, having zero reflections at both ends and a transmission $T = e^{-j\beta\ell}$, is connected between the two ports, the signal-flow graph of Figure 10.9 can be simplified to the one shown in Figure 10.10. The measured transmission T_s can be expressed as

$$T_s = r_{30} + \frac{r_{10}r_{32}\,T}{1 - r_{11}r_{22}\,T^2} \,. \tag{10.19}$$

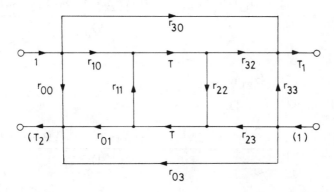

Figure 10.10   Signal flow graph for calibration with a through-line.

When the error parameters r_{11} and r_{22} have been determined by the reflection measurements, two transmission measurements (with different lengths of the through-line) must be performed for the determination of r_{30} and $r_{10}r_{32}$. Alternatively, the value of r_{30} can be found by making a transmission measurement when no connection exists between the ports (i.e. when $T = 0$). Then the parameter $r_{10}r_{32}$ can be determined from the measurement of a through-line using

$$r_{10}r_{32} = \frac{(T_s - r_{30})(1 - r_{11}r_{22}\,e^{-j2\beta\ell})}{e^{-j\beta\ell}} \tag{10.20}$$

since $T = e^{-j\beta\ell}$, $j\beta$ being the propagation constant of the through-line.

The error parameters r_{03} and $r_{01} r_{23}$ can be determined by making a similar measurement with the switch S_1 in "b" position.

Now that the errors of the imperfect 2-port measurement setup have been measured, the scattering parameters ρ_{m1}, ρ_{m2}, T_{m1}, and T_{m2} (shown in Figure 10.9) can be corrected for these errors to obtain S_{11}, S_{21}, S_{12}, and S_{22}. Using the signal-flow graph of Figure 10.9, we have

$$\rho_{m1} = r_{00} + \frac{S_{11}r_{01}r_{10}(1 - S_{22}r_{22}) + S_{21}S_{12}r_{22}r_{01}r_{10}}{D_3}$$

(10.21)

$$T_{m1} = r_{30} + \frac{S_{21}r_{32}r_{10}}{D_3} \tag{10.22}$$

$$\rho_{m2} = r_{33} + \frac{S_{22}r_{32}r_{23}(1 - S_{11}r_{11}) + S_{21}S_{12}r_{11}r_{32}r_{23}}{D_3}$$

(10.23)

$$T_{m2} = r_{03} + \frac{S_{12}r_{23}r_{01}}{D_3} \tag{10.24}$$

where

$$D_3 = 1 - S_{11}r_{11} - S_{22}r_{22} - S_{12}S_{21}r_{11}r_{22}$$
$$+ S_{22}S_{11}r_{11}r_{22} \ . \tag{10.25}$$

An explicit solution to the scattering parameters of the device under test has been presented in [11] and extended to include the leakage paths r_{30} and r_{03} in [9]. The solution is as follows:

$$S_{11} = \{G(1 + r_{22}H) - r_{22}EF\} /N_1 \tag{10.26}$$

$$S_{12} = E/N_1 \tag{10.27}$$

$$S_{21} = F/N_1 \tag{10.28}$$

$$S_{22} = \{H(1 + r_{11}G) - r_{11}EF\} /N_1 \tag{10.29}$$

where

$$N_1 = (1 + r_{11}G)(1 + r_{22}H) - r_{11}r_{22} EF \qquad (10.30)$$

$$E = (T_{m2} - r_{03})/(r_{01}r_{23}) \qquad (10.31)$$

$$F = (T_{m1} - r_{30})/(r_{10}r_{32}) \qquad (10.32)$$

$$G = (\rho_{m1} - r_{00})/(r_{01}r_{10}) \qquad (10.33)$$

$$H = (\rho_{m2} - r_{33})/(r_{23}r_{32}) . \qquad (10.34)$$

Some variations of the above calibration procedure are also available [12, 13].

10.2.4 Three-port and Multiport Measurements

Scattering parameters of three-port and multi-port networks are measured with two of the ports connected to the measuring system at a time and others terminated in matched loads. A typical measurement connection is shown in Figure 10.11. When the ports m and n are connected to a network analyzer system (shown in Figure 10.4), four S-parameters (S_{mn}, S_{nm}, S_{nn}, and S_{mm}) can be obtained by a method similar to the one used for two-port measurements. System errors can be measured and corrected for by following the procedure outlined for two-port measurements. This method will yield accurate results if the matched loads connected to the remaining ports, the connectors or adapters used for connecting them, and the connectors used at ports m and n are perfect. Usually, standard matched loads are used, but the imperfections in the connecting networks at the various ports need to be characterized and corrected for.

The situation is shown in Figure 10.12. It may be pointed out that, while the imperfections of the connectors at the two-ports connected to the measurement system may be combined with the system imperfections, the connectors at the other ports must be characterized separately. This characterization procedure for the connectors is discussed in Section 10.2.5.

Once the characterization of the multiport circuit and the connectors used has been arrived at, the effect of the connectors can be eliminated by using the desegmentation method discussed in Chapter 8 for the case of two-dimensional components. General equations for the desegmentation procedure are developed in Section 11.3.2. They get

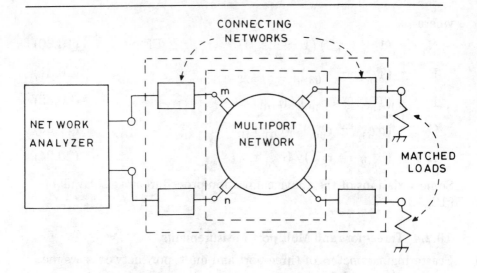

Figure 10.11   Connecting networks in case of multiport network
               measurement.

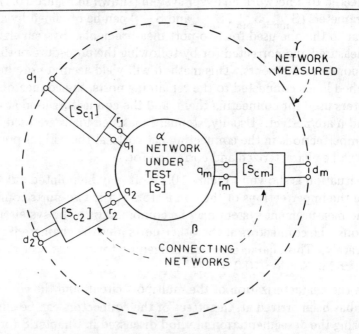

Figure 10.12   Modelling of a multiport network with imperfect
               connectors.

simplified in the present de-embedding problem. An example of a three-port circuit is given in Section 11.3.2.

10.2.5 Characterization of Connectors

As mentioned earlier, characterization of connectors or adapters connected to the various ports of a circuit is needed in two cases: (i) when calibration standards are not available in the same transmission medium as used for the circuit itself, and (ii) when a multiport circuit is being characterized. In this section, we describe a procedure by which the S-parameters of a connector can be obtained. This method can be used when two identical connectors are available for carrying out the measurements. Let A be the transmission medium in which standards are available and let B be the medium used for the circuit. Consider a uniform transmission line of length ℓ in the medium B. Connectors to medium A are added on either side of the line as shown in Figure 10.13(a). Let S_{11}, S_{12}, S_{21}, and S_{22} denote the unknown S-parameters of the connector with the subscript 1 referring to the port of the connector on side A and 2 referring to the port on side B. The reflection coefficient ρ on either side of the circuit in Figure 10.13(a) can be written from the flowgraph shown in Figure 10.13(b) and may be expressed as

$$\rho = S_{11} + \frac{S_{12}\, S_{22}\, S_{21}\, e^{-2j\beta\ell}}{1 - S_{22}^2\, e^{-2j\beta\ell}}. \tag{10.35}$$

The transmission coefficient τ between two ports of the circuit shown in Figure 10.13(a) can be expressed as

$$\tau = \frac{S_{12}\, S_{21}\, e^{-j\beta\ell}}{1 - S_{22}^2\, e^{-2j\beta\ell}}. \tag{10.36}$$

Coefficients ρ and τ are measured using a network analyzer. To a first order approximation $|S_{22}| \ll 1$, (10.35) and (10.36) reduces to

$$\rho = S_{11} + S_{12}\, S_{22}\, S_{21}\, e^{-2j\beta\ell} \tag{10.37}$$

and

$$\tau = S_{12} S_{21}\, e^{-j\beta\ell}. \tag{10.38}$$

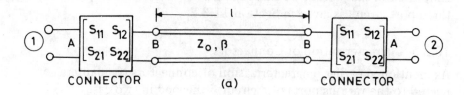

Figure 10.13(a)   Circuit configuration used for characterization
                  of connectors.

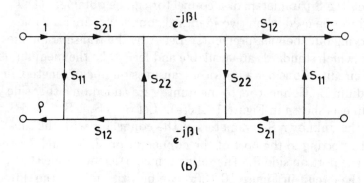

(b)

Figure 10.13(b)   Signal flow diagram for connector characterization.

The product $S_{12} S_{21}$ can be evaluated directly from (10.38) as

$$S_{12} S_{21} = \tau e^{j\beta\ell} \,. \tag{10.39}$$

By measuring ρ and τ for the two different non-commensurate values
of ℓ, unknowns S_{11} and S_{22} can also be evaluated. The mean value
of the product $S_{12}S_{21}$ obtained from the measurements of the two
line lengths may be considered. S_{11} and S_{22} are obtained using
(10.37) as

$$S_{11} = \frac{\rho_1 e^{-2j\beta\ell_2} - \rho_2 e^{-2j\beta\ell_1}}{e^{-2j\beta\ell_2} - e^{-2j\beta\ell_1}} \tag{10.40}$$

$$S_{22} = \frac{\rho_2 - \rho_1}{S_{12} S_{21}(e^{-2j\beta\ell_2} - e^{-2j\beta\ell_1})} \tag{10.41}$$

where ρ_1 and ρ_2 are the reflection coefficients for the line lengths ℓ_1 and ℓ_2, respectively. Equations (10.40) and (10.41) can be used if $\beta(\ell_2 - \ell_1)$ does not equal $n\pi$. For best accuracy, the two lengths should differ by a quarter wavelength.

Even though two line lengths have been considered in the above discussion, a larger number of line lengths may actually be used to characterize the connectors. The data reduction techniques discussed in the next section can be used to obtain the S-parameters of the connector.

Another method for connector characterization is given in [15]. However, this method requires calibration standards like matched loads to be fabricated in the transmission medium used for the circuit.

Once the S-parameters of the connector are determined, they can be used to eliminate the effect of connectors from the measurements using the desegmentation method.

10.3 DATA REDUCTION TECHNIQUES

As discussed in the previous section, calibration of system imperfections and characterization of connecting networks is carried out experimentally by making a number of measurements on standard terminating or through networks. Three reflection standards are needed for calibration of the system for one-port measurements. For two-port networks, two additional transmission standards are needed. Multiport measurements require separate characterization of connectors or adapters, for which two additional through-line measurements are needed.

The computations following these measurements may be formulated in terms of solving a set of linear equations with the number of unknowns equal to the number of independent equations available. For one-port measurements, three linear equations are given by (10.12) with i = 1, 2, 3 and the three unknowns are r_{00}, r_{11}, and Δr. For two-port measurements, two sets of two equations each are involved. From (10.19), we have

$$T_{si} = r_{30} + r_{10}r_{32} \, T_i \, / \, (1 - r_{11} r_{22} T_i^2) \; ; \; i = 1,2 \quad (10.42)$$

and the two unknowns are r_{30} and $r_{10}r_{32}$. We can obtain two similar equations for r_{03} and $r_{01}r_{23}$ by means of measurements with the switch S_i in the b position. For connector measurements discussed in Section 10.2.5, one transmission measurement yields the product $S_{12}S_{21}$ and two linear equations given by (10.37) are available for two unknowns S_{11} and S_{22}.

In all the above cases, the accuracy of measurement can be improved by carrying out a larger number of measurements than the minimum. The resultant set of linear equations may be written as

$$A x = b \qquad\qquad\qquad (10.43)$$

where A is an m x n matrix, m being the number of measurements carried out and n the number of unknown variables to be determined. For the case being considered, $m > n$. The vector x contains n unknowns to be determined and b is the vector of m measured quantities. The m elements of b have perturbations due to random measurement errors and this may result in all the m equations being linearly independent.

Since A is rectangular, the equations will not generally have a unique solution and indeed may not even be consistent. In such cases x can be chosen [16] to yield a least-square solution of (10.43). That is, x should be found so that the sum of squares

$$\|A x - b\|^2 \quad = (A x - b)^*(A x - b)$$
$$= x^* A^* A x - x^* A^* b - b^* A x + b^* b$$
$$(10.44)$$

is minimum. Here, superscript * indicates the complex conjugate of the transpose. Differentiating (10.44) with respect to x and equating to zero gives

$$A^* A x = A^* b. \qquad\qquad\qquad (10.45)$$

Now, if $A^* A$ is non-singular we have a unique solution given by

$$x = (A^* A)^{-1} A^* b. \qquad\qquad\qquad (10.46)$$

This data reduction technique is very general and is used in computer controlled network analyzers to improve measurement accuracy. Measurement and data reduction techniques are useful for modelling several microwave components whose analytical characterizations are not available.

REFERENCES

[1] Oliver, B.M., and J.M. Cage, *Electronic Measurements and Instrumentation*, New York: McGraw-Hill, 1971.

[2] Hackborn, R.A., "An Automatic Network Analyzer System," *Microwave J.*, Vol. 11, Nov. 5, 1968.

[3] Adam, S.F., *Microwave Theory and Applications*, Englewood Cliffs (NJ): Prentice-Hall, 1969, pp. 347-502.

[4] Hoer, C.A., "Using Six-port and Eight-port Junctions to Measure Active and Passive Circuit Parameters," National Bureau of Standards, *Tech. Note 673*, 1975.

[5] Engen, G.F., "The Six-port Reflectometer: An Alternative Network Analyzer," *IEEE Trans. Microwave Theory Tech.*, Vol. MTT-25, 1977, pp. 1075-1083.

[6] Engen, G.F., "Advances in Microwave Measurement Science," *Proc. IEEE*, Vol. 66, 1978, pp. 374-384.

[7] Engen, G.F., "An Improved Circuit for Implementing the Six-port Technique for Microwave Measurements," *IEEE Trans. Microwave Theory Tech.*, Vol. MTT-25, 1977, pp. 1080-1083.

[8] Bauer, R.F., and P. Penfield, Jr., "De-embedding and Un-terminating," *IEEE Trans. Microwave Theory Tech.*, Vol. MTT-22, 1974, pp. 282-288.

[9] Rehnmark, S., "On the Calibration Process of Automatic Network Analyzer Systems," *IEEE Trans. Microwave Theory Tech.*, Vol. MTT-22, 1974, pp. 457-458.

[10] Da Silva, E.F., and M.K. McPhun, "Calibration of Microwave Network Analyzer for Computer Corrected S-parameter Measurements," *Electron. Lett.*, Vol. 9, March 1973, pp. 126-128.

[11] Kruppa, W., and K.F. Sodomsky, "An Explicit Solution for the Scattering Parameters of a Linear Two-port Measured with an Imperfect Test Set," *IEEE Trans. Microwave Theory Tech.*, Vol. MTT-19, Jan. 1971, pp. 122-123.

[12] Hand, B.P., "Developing Accuracy Specifications for Automatic Network Analyzer Systems." *Hewlett-Packard J.*, Vol. 21, Feb. 1970, pp. 16-19.

[13]   Franzen, N.R., and R.A. Speciale, "A New Procedure for System Calibration and Error Removal in Automated S-parameter Measurements," *Proc. 5th European Microwave Conf.*, Hamburg 1975, pp. 69-73.

[14]   Chua, L.O., and P.M. Lin, *Computer-Aided Analysis of Electronic Circuits: Algorithms and Computational Techniques*, Englewood Cliffs, N.J.: Prentice-Hall, 1975, Chapter 14.

[15]   Uhlir, A., Jr., "Correction for Adapters in Microwave Measurements," *IEEE Trans. Microwave Theory Tech.*, Vol. MTT-22, 1974, pp. 330-332.

[16]   Barnett, S., *Matrices in Control Theory with Applications to Linear Programming*, New York: Van Nostrand, 1971, p. 130.

Part III

Analysis

11

Evaluation
of
Circuit
Performance

As pointed out in Chapter 1, computer-aided design of a circuit involves repeated analyses of the circuit. The analysis consists of evaluation of the overall circuit performance parameters from the characterizations of the individual components. This chapter discusses various techniques for analyzing microwave circuits.

As discussed in earlier chapters, microwave circuits may contain lumped components in addition to distributed components. The lumped components can originate from the equivalent circuit models of the active devices or can be present as such in these circuits. A lumped circuit is usually analyzed using the branch-node topology [1] and the overall circuit is characterized in terms of an impedance matrix, an admittance matrix or a hybrid matrix. The distributed components are present as sections of transmission lines, planar elements, directional couplers, circulators, etc. A distributed circuit is analyzed using the multiport representation and the overall circuit is usually characterized in terms of scattering parameters, T-parameters, or the ABCD parameters. Since a circuit, in general, may contain lumped as well as distributed components, it will be convenient for analysis if both types of components are characterized either as lumped equivalents or as multiport equivalents. It has been found that distributed components can be modelled only approximately as lumped equivalents, whereas multi-terminal lumped elements can be transformed exactly into multiport circuits [2]. Therefore, microwave circuits are normally characterized as multiport networks. As discussed in Chapter 2, two-port and multiport networks may be represented in terms of S-parameters, whereas two-port components can be represented in terms of ABCD and T-matrices also.

11.1 CIRCUITS CONSISTING OF TWO-PORTS

A number of circuit elements used at microwave frequencies are two-ports and, therefore; several microwave circuits can be expressed as combinations of two-ports only. Analysis of circuits consisting of two-port components is discussed in this section. The two-ports can be connected in cascade or there can be series, parallel or hybrid connections of the components. The series or parallel connections of two-ports may also result in a multiport network.

11.1.1 Use of Symmetry in the Circuit Analysis

Frequently, multiport networks which exhibit symmetry about a certain plane can be analyzed by carrying out the analysis for the two circuits which are the even and odd mode half-sections of the original network. The even and odd mode half-sections are obtained by considering only half of the circuit on one side of the plane of symmetry and having a magnetic wall at the plane of symmetry in the even mode case and an electric wall in the odd mode case.

For symmetrical two-port networks, the even and odd mode half-sections are usually one-ports. These two one-port circuits are analyzed with electric and magnetic walls at the plane of symmetry. A symmetrical two-port circuit is shown in Figure 11.1(a). The reflection coefficients are evaluated with an open circuit or a short circuit at the plane of symmetry, as shown in Figure 11.1(b). The scattering matrix of the original two-port can then be obtained as

$$S_{11} = S_{22} = \tfrac{1}{2}(S_{11e} + S_{11o}) \qquad\qquad (11.1a)$$

$$S_{12} = S_{21} = \tfrac{1}{2}(S_{11e} - S_{11o}) . \qquad\qquad (11.1b)$$

For symmetrical four-port networks [3], the even and odd mode half-sections are usually two-ports. In many cases these two-ports can be considered as cascades of smaller two-ports. A four-port network having a plane of symmetry is shown in Figure 11.2(a). It can be analyzed by considering the two two-port circuits shown in Figure 11.2(b). The scattering matrix for the overall network can be obtained from the even and odd mode scattering matrices and using the relations given below [3]:

$$S_{44} = S_{11} = \tfrac{1}{2}(S_{11e} + S_{11o})$$

$$S_{33} = S_{22} = \tfrac{1}{2}(S_{22e} + S_{22o})$$

$$S_{34} = S_{21} = \tfrac{1}{2}(S_{21e} + S_{21o})$$

$$S_{43} = S_{12} = \tfrac{1}{2}(S_{12e} + S_{12o})$$

$$S_{13} = S_{42} = \tfrac{1}{2}(S_{12e} - S_{12o})$$

$$S_{31} = S_{24} = \tfrac{1}{2}(S_{21e} - S_{21o})$$

$$S_{14} = S_{41} = \tfrac{1}{2}(S_{11e} - S_{11o})$$

$$S_{23} = S_{32} = \tfrac{1}{2}(S_{22e} - S_{22o}) .$$

$$(11.2)$$

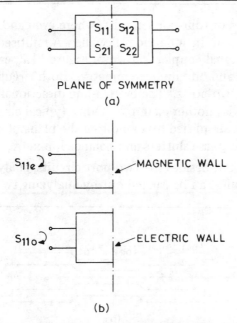

PLANE OF SYMMETRY

(a)

S_{11e} ⟶ MAGNETIC WALL

S_{11o} ⟶ ELECTRIC WALL

(b)

Figure 11.1(a)   A two-port network with a plane of symmetry.

(b)   Even mode and odd mode half-sections of a two-port symmetrical network.

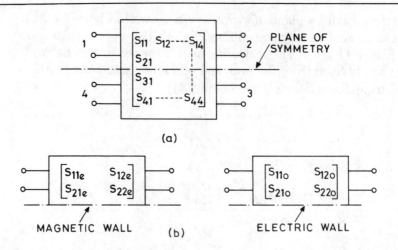

Figure 11.2(a)   A four-port network with a plane of symmetry.

(b)   Even mode and odd mode half-sections of a four-port symmetrical network.

Some examples of four-port circuits, where even and odd mode symmetry can be used, include the following. A multisection parallel-coupled directional coupler, shown in Figure 11.3, can be analyzed using the even and odd mode symmetry. Both circuits can be treated as cascades of two-ports. The branch-line directional coupler shown in Figure 11.4 is another example. Other typical circuits for which analysis can be simplified by exploiting the plane of symmetry are hybrid coupled phase shifters and balanced mixers.

Thus, we see that, besides the two-port circuits, analysis of several multiport circuits can be carried out by analyzing two-port circuits.

$$Z_{oe1} \quad Z_{oo1} \quad Z_{oe2} \quad Z_{oo2} \quad Z_{oe3} \quad Z_{oo3}$$

(a)

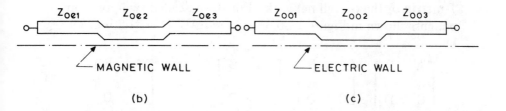

MAGNETIC WALL   ELECTRIC WALL

(b)   (c)

Figure 11.3(a) A three-section parallel coupled directional coupler.

(b) Even mode half section for the three-section coupler.

(c) Odd mode half section for the three-section coupler.

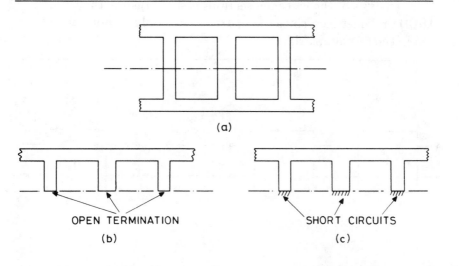

(a)

OPEN TERMINATION   SHORT CIRCUITS

(b)   (c)

Figure 11.4(a) A three-branch directional coupler.

(b) Even mode half section of the coupler in (a).

(c) Odd mode half section of the coupler in (a).

11.1.2 Analysis of Cascaded Two-ports

Cascaded sections of two-ports can be analyzed by multiplying ABCD or T-matrices of individual sections to yield the ABCD or

T-matrix of the overall network. For the cascaded two-port components shown in Figure 11.5, the *overall* ABCD matrix is given by

$$\begin{bmatrix} A & B \\ C & D \end{bmatrix} = \begin{bmatrix} A & B \\ C & D \end{bmatrix}_1 \begin{bmatrix} A & B \\ C & D \end{bmatrix}_2 \cdots \begin{bmatrix} A & B \\ C & D \end{bmatrix}_N \quad (11.3)$$

where the subscripts on the terms on the right-hand side of (11.3) indicate the ABCD matrix for the corresponding component. The T-matrix for the cascade can also be obtained by multiplying the T-matrices of the individual components. We have, for the cascade

$$[T] = [T]_1 \, [T]_2 \cdots [T]_N \, . \qquad (11.4)$$

Thus, analysis of the cascaded sections is simplified by the use of ABCD or T-matrices, since the matrices need only be multiplied to obtain the overall matrix.

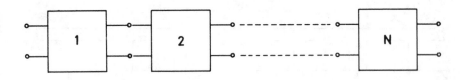

Figure 11.5   A cascade of two-port components.

In general, S-matrices are used for the characterization of microwave circuits. Therefore, for cascaded components, ABCD or T-matrices may have to be obtained from S-matrices and again, for the overall cascade, the S-matrix must be obtained from overall ABCD or T-matrix. As discussed earlier in Chapter 2, T-matrices are preferred over ABCD matrices. The transformations from S- to T-matrices and S- to ABCD matrices, and vice-versa, are discussed in Chapter 2.

It is useful to express the scattering matrix of a cascade of two-port components in terms of component scattering matrices. Let the components A and B, with S-matrices S^A and S^B respectively, be connected in cascade as shown in Figure 11.6. Let a_{1A}, b_{1A}, a_{1B}, etc., represent normalized wave variables at the ports of the two components. We have

$$b_{1A} = S_{11}^A a_{1A} + S_{12}^A a_{2A} \tag{11.5a}$$

$$b_{2A} = S_{21}^A a_{1A} + S_{22}^A a_{2A} \tag{11.5b}$$

and

$$b_{1B} = S_{11}^B a_{1B} + S_{12}^B a_{2B} \tag{11.6a}$$

$$b_{2B} = S_{21}^B a_{1B} + S_{22}^B a_{2B} . \tag{11.6b}$$

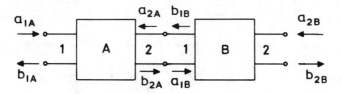

Figure 11.6   Two components, A and B, connected in cascade.

If port 2 of A and port 1 of B have the same normalizing impedances, we have

$$b_{2A} = a_{1B} \tag{11.7a}$$

and

$$b_{1B} = a_{2A} . \tag{11.7b}$$

By eliminating b_{2A}, b_{1B}, a_{1B} and a_{2A} from (11.5) and (11.6) we obtain:

$$
\begin{bmatrix} b_{1A} \\ b_{2B} \end{bmatrix} =
\begin{bmatrix}
S_{11}^A + \dfrac{S_{12}^A S_{11}^B S_{21}^A}{1 - S_{22}^A S_{11}^B} & \dfrac{S_{12}^A S_{12}^B}{1 - S_{22}^A S_{11}^B} \\[4mm]
\dfrac{S_{21}^A S_{21}^B}{1 - S_{22}^A S_{11}^B} & S_{22}^B + \dfrac{S_{21}^B S_{22}^A S_{12}^B}{1 - S_{22}^A S_{11}^B}
\end{bmatrix}
\begin{bmatrix} a_{1A} \\ a_{2B} \end{bmatrix}
$$

$$(11.8)$$

where the matrix on the right-hand side is the S-matrix of the cascade and is denoted by S^{AB}. This relation can be used repeatedly to obtain the overall S-matrix of a cascade with a large number of components.

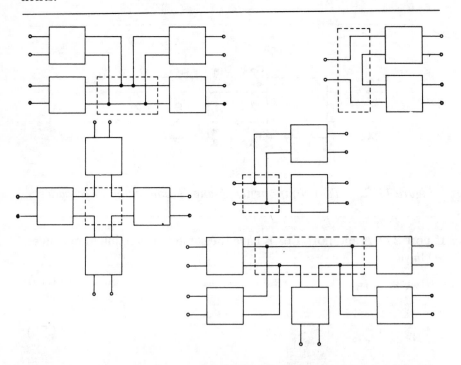

Figure 11.7   Examples of arbitrarily connected two-port components.

11.1.3 Analysis of Arbitrarily Connected Two-ports

Two-port components can be combined arbitrarily to yield a multi-port network. Some examples of these connections are shown in Figure 11.7. These circuits can be analyzed by characterizing such a connection as a "dummy" multi-port component (indicated by dotted lines in Figure 11.7), and then using any of the multiport connection methods described in the next section. To do so, the S-matrix of the multiport connection is required.

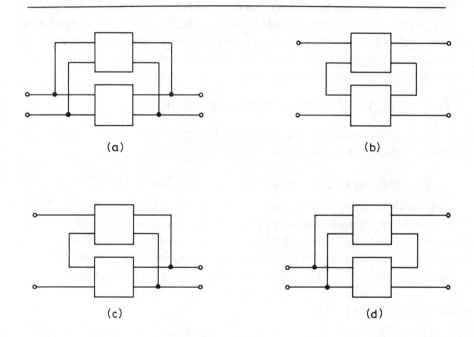

(a)

(b)

(c)

(d)

Figure 11.8(a)   *A parallel-parallel connection of two two-port components.*

      (b)   *A series-series connection of two two-port components.*

      (c)   *A series-parallel connection of two two-port components.*

      (d)   *A parallel-series connection of two two-port components.*

Two-port components can be combined in series or parallel to yield a two-port network. Four different configurations which are possible for such connections are shown in Figure 11.8. These circuits can be analyzed by using Y-, Z-, H- or G-matrices [4] also. The Y-matrix characterization for the parallel-parallel connection (Figure 11.8a) can be obtained by simply adding Y-matrices of the two components. For the series-series connection (Figure 11.8b), the individual Z-matrices are added to yield the overall Z-matrix. For the series-parallel connection (Figure 11.8c), the H-matrices, and for the parallel-series connection (Figure 11.8d), the G-matrices are added to obtain the overall matrix. Even though very little effort is spent in adding these matrices, these representations have the drawback that Y-, Z-, H- or G- matrices are computed from the S-matrices and vice-versa.

11.2 ARBITRARILY CONNECTED NETWORKS

Techniques for evaluating circuit parameters of an arbitrarily interconnected network are discussed in this section.

11.2.1 Analysis Using Connection-Scattering Matrix [5]

This method is applicable when the network contains arbitrarily interconnected multiports and independent generators. Consider a network with m multiport components. It should be pointed out that no unconnected (i.e. external) ports are allowed in this network. For the *ith* component having n_i ports, the incoming and outgoing wave variables (a_i and b_i respectively) at its ports are related by

$$b_i = S_i a_i .$$ (11.9)

This is valid for all the components except the independent generators. An independent generator is described by the relation

$$b_g = S_g a_g + c_g$$ (11.10)

where c_g is the wave impressed by the generator. It may be noted that, for generators which are isolated (or matched), S_g in (11.10) is zero.

The governing relations for all the m components can be put together in the form

$$b = S a + c$$ (11.11)

where

$$a = \begin{bmatrix} a_1 \\ a_2 \\ \cdot \\ \cdot \\ \cdot \\ a_m \end{bmatrix}, \quad b = \begin{bmatrix} b_1 \\ b_2 \\ \cdot \\ \cdot \\ \cdot \\ b_m \end{bmatrix}, \quad c = \begin{bmatrix} c_1 \\ c_2 \\ \cdot \\ \cdot \\ \cdot \\ c_m \end{bmatrix}$$

and

$$S = \begin{bmatrix} S_1 & \cdots & 0 & \cdots & 0 \\ \cdot & \cdots & \cdot & \cdots & \cdot \\ \cdot & \cdots & \cdot & \cdots & \cdot \\ \cdot & \cdots & \cdot & \cdots & \cdot \\ 0 & \cdots & S_i & \cdots & 0 \\ \cdot & \cdots & \cdot & \cdots & \cdot \\ \cdot & \cdots & \cdot & \cdots & \cdot \\ 0 & \cdots & 0 & \cdots & S_m \end{bmatrix}. \tag{11.12}$$

The matrix S in (11.12) is a block diagonal matrix whose submatrices along the diagonal are the scattering matrices of various components and 0's represent null matrices.

Equation (11.11) contains the characterizations of individual components but does not take into account the constraints imposed by interconnections. For a pair of connected ports, the outgoing wave variable at one port must equal the incoming wave variable at the other, assuming that the wave variables at the two connected ports are similarly normalized. For example, if port j of one component is connected to port k of another component as shown in Figure 11.9, the incoming and outgoing waves satisfy

$$a_j = b_k$$

and

$$a_k = b_j,$$

or

$$\begin{bmatrix} b_k \\ b_j \end{bmatrix} = \begin{bmatrix} 0 & 1 \\ 1 & 0 \end{bmatrix} \begin{bmatrix} a_k \\ a_j \end{bmatrix}. \tag{11.13}$$

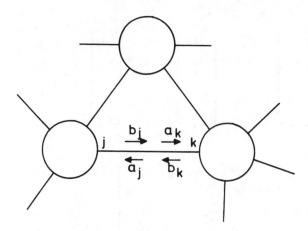

Figure 11.9   *A subnetwork showing port j of a component connected to port k of the other component.*

The matrix on the right-hand side of (11.13) can be recognized as
the inverse of the S-matrix of the interconnection. The elements
of this matrix are 1's and 0's because the normalizing impedances for
the two ports are taken to be equal. In case of unequal normalizations at ports j and k, the elements of the matrix in (11.13) are obtained as the inverse of the corresponding S-matrix of the junction.
If the two normalizing impedances are Z_1 and Z_2, the matrix in
(11.13) is given by the inverse of the S-matrix of a junction of two
lines with unequal impedances given in Appendix 2.1(9).

The relations given by (11.13) are written together for all the interconnected ports in the network and put in the form

$$b = \Gamma a \qquad\qquad (11.14)$$

where Γ is a connection matrix describing the topology. In each row
of Γ all elements are zero except an entry 1 in the column indicating
the interconnection. If the element (j,k) of Γ is 1, it implies that the
port j is connected to the port k. As mentioned above, the entries in
Γ are 1's and 0's only if the two normalizations at each connection
are equal.

Substituting for b from (11.14) into (11.11), we obtain

$$\Gamma a = S a + c$$

or

$$(\Gamma - S) a = c .$$ (11.15)

Setting,

$$W = \Gamma - S$$ (11.16)

we have

$$a = W^{-1} c .$$ (11.17)

In the above equation c is a vector of the impressed wave variables and W is called the connection scattering matrix. The main diagonal elements in W are the negative of the reflection coefficients at the various components ports, the elements corresponding to the ports of the same component are negative of the transmission coefficients and all other elements are zero except those corresponding to the two ports connected together (the Γ matrix elements). The zero nonzero pattern in W depends only on the topology and does not change with component characterizations or frequency. The non-zero entries would change, except the 1's which indicate the connections.

The solution of (11.17) gives the incoming waves a at all the component ports in the network; then the outgoing waves b can be obtained from (11.14).

11.2.2 Multiport Connection Method [5]

In this method also, the scattering matrix for the network is determined using the S-matrices of individual components. This method is applicable when the network contains arbitrarily interconnected multiport components without independent generators. When one or more independent generators are present, these can be treated as existing outside the remaining network N (as shown in Figure 11.10) and the present method yields the S-matrix for the network N.

Consider a network N of multiport components shown in Figure 11.10. This network contains c ports internal to the network (which are connected) and p ports external to it. If there are m components in the network the governing relations for all the components can be written together (as in (11.11)) as

$$b = S a .$$ (11.18)

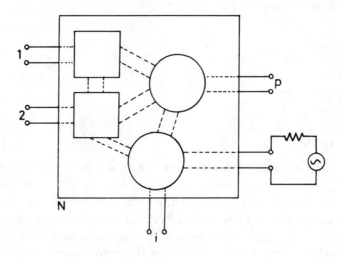

*Figure 11.10   An arbitrarily connected network with p external
ports.*

The rows and columns in (11.18) can be reordered so that the wave
variables are separated into two groups; the first corresponding to
the p external ports, and the second to c internally connected ports.
Equation (11.18) can now be written as

$$\begin{bmatrix} b_p \\ \\ b_c \end{bmatrix} = \begin{bmatrix} S_{pp} & S_{pc} \\ \\ S_{cp} & S_{cc} \end{bmatrix} \begin{bmatrix} a_p \\ \\ a_c \end{bmatrix} \qquad (11.19)$$

where b_p and a_p are the wave variables at the p external ports and
b_c and a_c are the wave variables at the c internal ports. The interconnection constraints for the c internal ports can be written as

$$b_c = \Gamma a_c \qquad (11.20)$$

where Γ is the connection matrix obtained in the same way as in the
previous section. From (11.19) and (11.20), we get

$$\Gamma\, a_c = S_{cp}\, a_p + S_{cc}\, a_c$$

or

$$a_c = (\Gamma - S_{cc})^{-1}\, S_{cp}\, a_p \ . \tag{11.21}$$

Substituting this in (11.19), we get

$$b_p = [\, S_{pp} + S_{pc}\, (\Gamma - S_{cc})^{-1}\, S_{cp}\,]\, a_p \tag{11.22}$$

or, the network scattering matrix S_p is given by

$$S_p = S_{pp} + S_{pc}\, (\Gamma - S_{cc})^{-1}\, S_{cp} \ . \tag{11.23}$$

Equations (11.21) and (11.20) can be used to obtain the wave variables at the internal ports for any arbitrary excitation at the p external ports.

Using this information and the adjoint network approach discussed in the following chapter, one can obtain sensitivities of the network scattering parameters.

The matrix $(\Gamma - S_{cc})$ in (11.21) and (11.23) has characteristics similar to the W matrix in (11.16), namely: (i) it is highly sparse, and (ii) the zero nonzero pattern is independent of the component characterizations and depends only on the topology.

Even though direct connections of two ports have been assumed in the formulations given in this section, it does not in any way restrict the kind of networks that can be analyzed using the above approaches. Any other connection can itself be characterized as a separate component as discussed in Section 11.1.3.

11.2.3 An Example

In the example of a simple circuit shown in Figure 11.11, circuit parameters are obtained by separately using both methods described in Sections 11.2.1 and 11.2.2. The circuit contains a two-port component A, characterized by S^A; a three-port component B, characterized by S^B; and a one-port component C, characterized by S^C. The method described in Section 11.2.2 is directly applicable in this case. The ports are numbered as shown in the figure. Characterizations for the three components are put together as in (11.19):

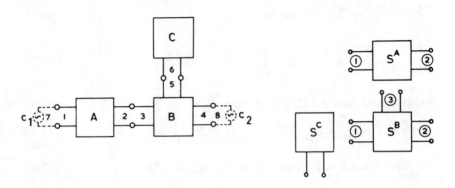

Figure 11.11   The network considered in the example of Sec. 11.2.3.

$$
\begin{bmatrix} b_1 \\ b_4 \\ b_2 \\ b_6 \\ b_5 \\ b_3 \end{bmatrix} = \begin{bmatrix} S_{11}^A & 0 & S_{12}^A & 0 & 0 & 0 \\ 0 & S_{22}^B & 0 & 0 & S_{23}^B & S_{21}^B \\ S_{21}^A & 0 & S_{22}^A & 0 & 0 & 0 \\ 0 & 0 & 0 & S^C & 0 & 0 \\ 0 & S_{32}^B & 0 & 0 & S_{33}^B & S_{31}^B \\ 0 & S_{12}^B & 0 & 0 & S_{13}^B & S_{11}^B \end{bmatrix} \begin{bmatrix} a_1 \\ a_4 \\ a_2 \\ a_6 \\ a_5 \\ a_3 \end{bmatrix} .
$$

$$(11.24)$$

The connection matrix Γ can be written as

$$
\begin{bmatrix} b_2 \\ b_6 \\ b_5 \\ b_3 \end{bmatrix} = \begin{bmatrix} 0 & 0 & 0 & 1 \\ 0 & 0 & 1 & 0 \\ 0 & 1 & 0 & 0 \\ 1 & 0 & 0 & 0 \end{bmatrix} \begin{bmatrix} a_2 \\ a_6 \\ a_5 \\ a_3 \end{bmatrix} .
$$

$$(11.25)$$

Using (11.24) and (11.25) in (11.23), the overall scattering matrix is given by

$$
S_p = \begin{bmatrix} S^A_{11} & 0 \\ 0 & S^B_{22} \end{bmatrix} +
$$

$$
\begin{bmatrix} S^A_{12} & 0 & 0 & 0 \\ 0 & 0 & S^B_{23} & S^B_{21} \end{bmatrix}
\begin{bmatrix} -S^A_{22} & 0 & 0 & 1 \\ 0 & -S^C & 1 & 0 \\ 0 & 1 & -S^B_{33} & -S^B_{31} \\ 1 & 0 & -S^B_{13} & -S^B_{11} \end{bmatrix}^{-1}
\begin{bmatrix} S^A_{21} & 0 \\ 0 & 0 \\ 0 & S^B_{32} \\ 0 & S^B_{12} \end{bmatrix}
$$

$$(11.26)$$

For arbitrary inputs at the two external ports, the incoming wave variables at the internal ports can be found using (11.21), as follows:

$$
\begin{bmatrix} a_2 \\ a_6 \\ a_5 \\ a_3 \end{bmatrix} =
\begin{bmatrix} -S^A_{22} & 0 & 0 & 1 \\ 0 & -S^C & 1 & 0 \\ 0 & 1 & -S^B_{33} & -S^B_{31} \\ 1 & 0 & -S^B_{13} & -S^B_{11} \end{bmatrix}^{-1}
\begin{bmatrix} S^A_{21} & 0 \\ 0 & 0 \\ 0 & S^B_{32} \\ 0 & S^B_{12} \end{bmatrix}
\begin{bmatrix} a_1 \\ a_4 \end{bmatrix} .
$$

$$(11.27)$$

The outgoing wave variables $[\, b_2 \; b_6 \; b_5 \; b_3 \,]^t$ at the internal ports can be obtained by substituting the above relation in (11.25).

To obtain the S-parameters for this circuit using the method given in Section 11.2.1, we put independent generators at the external ports. The generators (shown dotted in Figure 11.11) are single port components and they are characterized by

$$
b_7 = c_1 \tag{11.28a}
$$

and

$$
b_8 = c_2 . \tag{11.28b}
$$

The relation between b's, a's and c's for all the components of the circuit can now be written in the form of (11.11) as

$$
\begin{bmatrix} b_1 \\ b_2 \\ b_3 \\ b_4 \\ b_5 \\ b_6 \\ b_7 \\ b_8 \end{bmatrix}
=
\begin{bmatrix}
S_{11}^{A} & S_{12}^{A} & 0 & 0 & 0 & 0 & 0 & 0 \\
S_{21}^{A} & S_{22}^{A} & 0 & 0 & 0 & 0 & 0 & 0 \\
0 & 0 & S_{11}^{B} & S_{12}^{B} & S_{13}^{B} & 0 & 0 & 0 \\
0 & 0 & S_{21}^{B} & S_{22}^{B} & S_{23}^{B} & 0 & 0 & 0 \\
0 & 0 & S_{31}^{B} & S_{32}^{B} & S_{33}^{B} & 0 & 0 & 0 \\
0 & 0 & 0 & 0 & 0 & S^{C} & 0 & 0 \\
0 & 0 & 0 & 0 & 0 & 0 & 0 & 0 \\
0 & 0 & 0 & 0 & 0 & 0 & 0 & 0
\end{bmatrix}
\begin{bmatrix} a_1 \\ a_2 \\ a_3 \\ a_4 \\ a_5 \\ a_6 \\ a_7 \\ a_8 \end{bmatrix}
+
\begin{bmatrix} 0 \\ 0 \\ 0 \\ 0 \\ 0 \\ 0 \\ c_1 \\ c_2 \end{bmatrix}.
$$

$$(11.29)$$

The interconnection matrix Γ now becomes

$$
\begin{bmatrix} b_1 \\ b_2 \\ b_3 \\ b_4 \\ b_5 \\ b_6 \\ b_7 \\ b_8 \end{bmatrix}
=
\begin{bmatrix}
0 & 0 & 0 & 0 & 0 & 0 & 1 & 0 \\
0 & 0 & 1 & 0 & 0 & 0 & 0 & 0 \\
0 & 1 & 0 & 0 & 0 & 0 & 0 & 0 \\
0 & 0 & 0 & 0 & 0 & 0 & 0 & 1 \\
0 & 0 & 0 & 0 & 0 & 1 & 0 & 0 \\
0 & 0 & 0 & 0 & 1 & 0 & 0 & 0 \\
1 & 0 & 0 & 0 & 0 & 0 & 0 & 0 \\
0 & 0 & 0 & 1 & 0 & 0 & 0 & 0
\end{bmatrix}
\begin{bmatrix} a_1 \\ a_2 \\ a_3 \\ a_4 \\ a_5 \\ a_6 \\ a_7 \\ a_8 \end{bmatrix}
$$

$$(11.30)$$

Using (11.17), the incoming wave variables at the ports are determined as

$$
\begin{bmatrix} a_1 \\ a_2 \\ a_3 \\ a_4 \\ a_5 \\ a_6 \\ a_7 \\ a_8 \end{bmatrix}
=
\begin{bmatrix}
-S^A_{11} & -S^A_{12} & 0 & 0 & 0 & 0 & 1 & 0 \\
-S^A_{21} & -S^A_{22} & 1 & 0 & 0 & 0 & 0 & 0 \\
0 & 1 & -S^B_{11} & -S^B_{12} & -S^B_{13} & 0 & 0 & 0 \\
0 & 0 & -S^B_{21} & -S^B_{22} & -S^B_{23} & 0 & 0 & 1 \\
0 & 0 & -S^B_{31} & -S^B_{32} & -S^B_{33} & 1 & 0 & 0 \\
0 & 0 & 0 & 0 & 1 & -S^C & 0 & 0 \\
1 & 0 & 0 & 0 & 0 & 0 & 0 & 0 \\
0 & 0 & 0 & 1 & 0 & 0 & 0 & 0
\end{bmatrix}^{-1}
\begin{bmatrix} 0 \\ 0 \\ 0 \\ 0 \\ 0 \\ 0 \\ c_1 \\ c_2 \end{bmatrix}
$$

$$(11.31)$$

and the outgoing wave variables at all the ports, b, can be determined using (11.30) and (11.31).

The values of the wave variables at all the ports can thus be obtained for any combination of values of c_1 and c_2. If $c_1 = 1$ and $c_2 = 0$, the values of b_1 and b_4 (at the external ports) correspond to S_{11} and S_{21}, respectively, of the overall scattering matrix. Similarly, for $c_1 = 0$ and $c_2 = 1$, the parameters S_{12} and S_{22} correspond to the values b_1 and b_4, respectively.

11.2.4 Analysis by Subnetwork Growth Method [6]

Using the technique described in Section 11.2.2 to obtain the S-matrix of a network with multiport components, a matrix of order equal to the number of interconnected ports must be inverted. When the network contains many interconnected ports, the order of the matrix to be inverted will become quite large. The computational effort of inverting the matrix can be reduced considerably if the entire network is not taken at once, but is partitioned into a number of subnetworks. The S-matrices of the subnetworks are obtained separately and are then combined to obtain the overall S-matrix of the network. This approach has been discussed in [6] and has been utilized to develop a microwave circuit analysis program [6].

Determination of Computational Effort

For a network with p external ports and c connected ports, the number of long-operations required for the determination of S_p in (11.23) is given as

$$N = p^2c + pc^2 + \alpha c^3 \tag{11.32}$$

where the first two terms arise from the multiplication of matrices and the third term is due to the inversion of the c x c matrix. Depending upon the algorithm used for inversion, the factor α is a constant, almost equal to unity. A long-operation means multiplication or division of two numbers, since the time required for these operations is much larger than that required for addition or subtraction. As shown in (11.32), the computation time required increases rapidly with c.

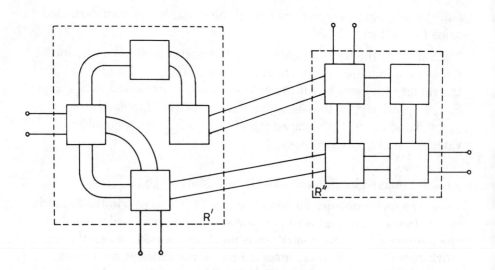

Figure 11.12   A network considered as two subnetworks R' and R" connected together.

Let the network be considered in the form of two subnetworks R' and R'' connected together, as shown in Figure 11.12. The overall scattering matrix can be determined in three steps; the first two steps determining separately the S-matrices of the two subnetworks and the third step connecting together the two subnetworks thus obtained. In such a case, the total number of long-operations required for the evaluation of S-matrix is obtained by using (11.32) for the three steps, and we have

$$N_s = p_1^2 \, c_1 + p_1 c_1^2 + \alpha c_1^3 + p_2^2 \, c_2 + p_2 c_2^2 + \alpha c_2^3$$

$$+ \; p^2 c^* + p c^{*2} + \alpha c^{*3} \tag{11.33}$$

where p_1 and p_2 are the numbers of external ports, and c_1 and c_2 are the numbers of internal ports for the two subnetworks R' and R'', respectively. In the above equation, c^* denotes the number of connected ports between the two subnetworks. If we assume that the two subnetworks have an equal number of external ports and an equal number of internal ports, then

$$p_1 = p_2 = \frac{p + c^*}{2} \tag{11.34a}$$

and

$$c_1 = c_2 = \frac{c - c^*}{2} . \tag{11.34b}$$

It may be recalled that $c = c_1 + c_2 + c^*$. Substituting for p_1, p_2, c_1 and c_2 in (11.33), we get

$$N_s = \frac{1}{4} \, (p^2 c + p c^2 + \alpha c^3) + \frac{3}{4} \, (p^2 c^* + p c^{*2} + \alpha c^{*3})$$

$$- \; \frac{1}{4} \, (3\alpha - 1) \, (c - c^*) \, c c^* . \tag{11.35}$$

The number of long-operations given by (11.35) are less than those given by (11.32). This result can be extended to each subnetwork and it will be seen that a faster computation of the overall S-matrix is achieved by adding only two components in each step. If the network has m components (11.23) is used $(m - 1)$ times.

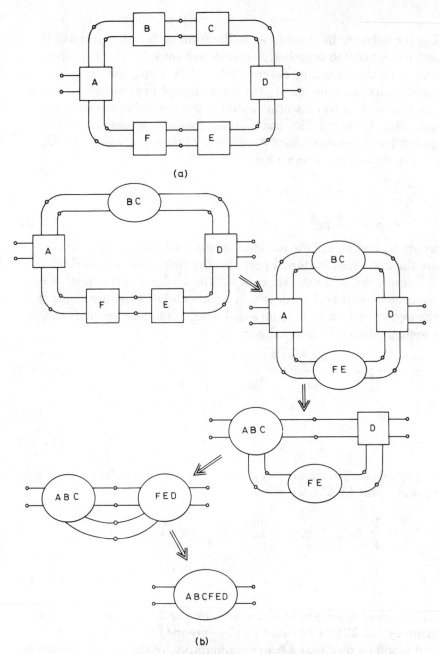

(a)

(b)

Figure 11.13(a)   A network example considered for the subnetwork growth method.

(b)   Changes in topology as different components are connected together in subnetwork growth method for the circuit shown in (a).

It is desirable to obtain an optimal ordering in which the components should be combined so that the total number of long-operations required is minimum. An algorithm for suboptimal ordering has been given by Monaco and Tiberio [6]. It states that, at each stage, those two components should be connected together whose combination would result in the smallest number of external ports. An example of this ordering is shown in Figure 11.13. Components B and C are combined first to give subnetwork BC. F and E are combined next, followed by the combination of A and BC. After these, FE and D are combined and finally ABC and FED are combined to yield the S-matrix of the overall two-port network. The successive alterations in the topology after each step are shown in Figure 11.13(b).

Since (11.23) is used repeatedly to obtain S_p for combining two multiport components, an improved method for evaluating (11.23) is desirable. An improvement is possible for the present case when only two components are being connected together. The 'c' connected ports are divided into two groups 'q' and 'r', so that 'q' contains ports of one component and 'r' contains ports of the other component. Further, the subgroups 'q' and 'r' are numbered so that q_1 is connected to r_1, q_2 is connected to r_2, and so on. The component matrices can now be written together as

$$
\begin{bmatrix} b_p \\ b_q \\ b_r \end{bmatrix} = \begin{bmatrix} S_{pp} & S_{pq} & S_{pr} \\ S_{qp} & S_{qq} & 0 \\ S_{rp} & 0 & S_{rr} \end{bmatrix} \begin{bmatrix} a_p \\ a_q \\ a_r \end{bmatrix} . \tag{11.36}
$$

In the above equation S_{qr} and S_{rq} are null matrices shown as **0** since 'q' and 'r' ports belong to different components. The connection matrix for this case is of the type

$$
\Gamma = \begin{bmatrix} 0 & I \\ I & 0 \end{bmatrix} . \tag{11.37}
$$

The matrix $(\Gamma - S_{cc})$, to be inverted in (11.23), is given as

$$
(\Gamma - S_{cc}) = \begin{bmatrix} -S_{qq} & I \\ I & -S_{rr} \end{bmatrix} . \tag{11.38}
$$

The inverse of $(\Gamma - S_{cc})$ can now be written as

$$(\Gamma - S_{cc})^{-1} = \begin{bmatrix} S_{rr}(I - S_{qq}S_{rr})^{-1} & (I - S_{rr}S_{qq})^{-1} \\ (I - S_{qq}S_{rr})^{-1} & S_{qq}(I - S_{rr}S_{qq})^{-1} \end{bmatrix}$$

$$\triangleq \begin{bmatrix} M_{11} & M_{12} \\ M_{21} & M_{22} \end{bmatrix}, \tag{11.39}$$

and requires the inverse of two matrices of order c/2. Further simplification is possible since, in this case, the p external ports can also be divided into two groups: ports p_1 from component 1 and ports p_2 from component 2. The submatrices S_{pp}, S_{pc} and S_{cp} are of the type

$$S_{pp} = \begin{bmatrix} S_{1p} & 0 \\ 0 & S_{2p} \end{bmatrix}. \tag{11.40}$$

$$S_{pc} = [\, S_{pq} \quad S_{pr} \,] = \begin{bmatrix} S_{1pq} & 0 \\ 0 & S_{2pr} \end{bmatrix} \tag{11.41}$$

and

$$S_{cp} = \begin{bmatrix} S_{qp} \\ S_{rp} \end{bmatrix} = \begin{bmatrix} S_{1qp} & 0 \\ 0 & S_{2rp} \end{bmatrix} \tag{11.42}$$

where subscripts 1 and 2 refer to groups p_1 and p_2, respectively. The overall S-matrix can now be written as

$$S = \begin{bmatrix} S_{1p} + S_{1pq} M_{11} S_{1qp} & S_{1pq} M_{12} S_{2rp} \\ \\ S_{2pr} M_{21} S_{1qp} & S_{2p} + S_{2pr} M_{22} S_{2rp} \end{bmatrix}. \quad (11.43)$$

This requires a smaller number of long-operations than if one uses (11.23) directly since two matrices to be inverted are of order c/2 and matrices to be multiplied are also of smaller orders.

For obtaining the wave variables at the connected ports, (11.21) can be used, which for the present case can be expressed as

$$\begin{bmatrix} a_q \\ \\ a_r \end{bmatrix} = \begin{bmatrix} M_{11} S_{1qp} & M_{12} S_{2rp} \\ \\ M_{21} S_{1qp} & M_{22} S_{2rp} \end{bmatrix} \begin{bmatrix} a_{1p} \\ \\ a_{2p} \end{bmatrix} \quad (11.44)$$

where a_{1p} and a_{2p} are the incoming wave variables at the external ports p_1 and p_2, respectively.

11.3 CIRCUITS CONSISTING OF TWO-DIMENSIONAL PLANAR COMPONENTS

As discussed in Chapter 8, two-dimensional planar components of some *simple* shapes are analyzed using Green's functions. The techniques of segmentation and desegmentation are employed to analyze planar circuits of shapes which are obtained by addition or removal from the regular shapes, as shown in Figure 8.7. The mathematical formulations for these techniques are discussed in this section. These techniques may also be used when a circuit contains other types of components in addition to two-dimensional planar components.

11.3.1 Segmentation Method [7,8]

When the shape of the planar circuit can be considered to be made up of some *simple* shapes, the segmentation method can be used to analyze the circuit. In this method, we replace continuous connections at the boundaries of *simple* shapes (which constitute the planar circuit), by the multiple number of ports covering the entire interconnections. If a large number of ports are considered at the interconnections, the characteristics of the circuit obtained by means of this analysis converge to the actual circuit characteristics. Green's functions can be used to obtain characteristics of each of the *simple* shaped components and the overall characteristics are obtained therefrom.

If the S-matrices of the individual components are obtained, the overall S-matrix can be evaluated using the method described in Section 11.2.2. The c-ports would now refer to the ports at the boundaries between the components of *simple* shapes.

In order to combine S-matrices in the segmentation method, a considerable effort is needed to compute S-matrices for each of the components. Reduction in the computational effort can be achieved if Z-matrices of individual components are combined to give the overall Z-matrix from which the overall S-matrix may be obtained using (2.36). Segmentation methods using Z-matrices are described next [8].

The voltage variables and the current variables for the connected ports and the external ports can be grouped separately as in the multiport connection method discussed in Section 11.2.2, and the Z-matrices of various components can be written as

$$
\begin{bmatrix} v_p \\ v_c \end{bmatrix} = \begin{bmatrix} Z_{pp} & Z_{pc} \\ Z_{cp} & Z_{cc} \end{bmatrix} \begin{bmatrix} i_p \\ i_c \end{bmatrix}
\tag{11.45}
$$

where v_p and i_p are the voltage and the current variables at the p external ports, and v_c and i_c are the corresponding variables at the internal ports. Equation (11.45) does not take into account the constraints imposed by the interconnections. The constraints are: (i) the voltages at the two connected ports are equal and, (ii) the currents are equal and oppositely directed. For all the internal ports, these constraints can be expressed as

$$
\Gamma_1 v_c = 0,
\tag{11.46a}
$$

and

$$
\Gamma_2 i_c = 0
\tag{11.46b}
$$

where $\boldsymbol{\Gamma}_1$ and $\boldsymbol{\Gamma}_2$ matrices with c/2 rows and c columns are given by the circuit topology. In these matrices, each row describes a connection so that all elements in a row are zero except the two elements corresponding to the two connected ports. The two non-zero entries in a row are 1 and -1 for matrix $\boldsymbol{\Gamma}_1$. For matrix $\boldsymbol{\Gamma}_2$, both of these are 1.

Substituting for v_c from (11.45) into (11.46a), we obtain

$$\boldsymbol{\Gamma}_1 Z_{cc} i_c = -\boldsymbol{\Gamma}_1 Z_{cp} i_p . \tag{11.47}$$

Multiplying (11.46b) by j (= $\sqrt{-1}$) and then combining with (11.47), the relation between i_c and i_p can be expressed as

$$\begin{bmatrix} \boldsymbol{\Gamma}_1 Z_{cc} \\ \\ j\boldsymbol{\Gamma}_2 \end{bmatrix} i_c = \begin{bmatrix} -\boldsymbol{\Gamma}_1 Z_{cp} \\ \\ 0 \end{bmatrix} i_p \tag{11.48}$$

where 0 is a null matrix with c/2 rows and p columns. In (11.48), the matrix on the left-hand side is a square matrix of order c x c. The current variables i_c can thus be written as

$$i_c = \begin{bmatrix} \boldsymbol{\Gamma}_1 Z_{cc} \\ \\ j\boldsymbol{\Gamma}_2 \end{bmatrix}^{-1} \begin{bmatrix} -\boldsymbol{\Gamma}_1 Z_{cp} \\ \\ 0 \end{bmatrix} i_p . \tag{11.49}$$

It should be noted that the Z-matrices for lossless circuits are purely imaginary. Equation (11.46b) was multiplied by j so that the matrix, to be inverted in (11.49), is purely imaginary. Multiplication and inversion of purely imaginary matrices can be carried out with the same computational effort as for real matrices.

Substituting the expression for i_c from (11.49) into (11.45), the overall network impedance matrix is obtained as

$$Z_p = Z_{pp} - Z_{pc} \begin{bmatrix} \boldsymbol{\Gamma}_1 Z_{cc} \\ \\ j\boldsymbol{\Gamma}_2 \end{bmatrix}^{-1} \begin{bmatrix} \boldsymbol{\Gamma}_1 Z_{cp} \\ \\ 0 \end{bmatrix} . \tag{11.50}$$

Alternate Formulation for Further Reduction in the Computational Effort

Further savings in computational effort can be achieved if the connected ports are suitably subgrouped and the Z-matrix formulation used as follows. The connected ports are subgrouped in a manner similar to that of Section 11.2.4. The 'c' connected ports are divided into groups 'q' and 'r', each containing $c/2$ ports. This is done in such a way that q_1 and r_1 ports are connected together, q_2 and r_2 ports are connected together, and so on. This involves reordering of rows and/or columns for Z_{cp}, Z_{pc} and Z_{cc} as given in (11.45). The Z-matrices of individual components can now be written together as

$$\begin{bmatrix} v_p \\ v_q \\ v_r \end{bmatrix} = \begin{bmatrix} Z_{pp} & Z_{pq} & Z_{pr} \\ Z_{qp} & Z_{qq} & Z_{qr} \\ Z_{rp} & Z_{rq} & Z_{rr} \end{bmatrix} \begin{bmatrix} i_p \\ i_q \\ i_r \end{bmatrix}. \tag{11.51}$$

In this formulation, the interconnection constraints can be expressed in a much simpler form as

$$v_q = v_r , \tag{11.52a}$$

and

$$i_q + i_r = 0 . \tag{11.52b}$$

Substituting (11.52) into (11.51) and eliminating v_p, v_q and i_r, we obtain

$$(Z_{qq} - Z_{qr} - Z_{rq} + Z_{rr}) i_q = (Z_{rp} - Z_{qp}) i_p$$

or

$$i_q = (Z_{qq} - Z_{qr} - Z_{rq} + Z_{rr})^{-1} (Z_{rp} - Z_{qp}) i_p . \tag{11.53}$$

Substituting (11.53) into the first equation of (11.51) and using $i_r = -i_q$, the Z-matrix of the overall network is obtained as

$$Z_p = Z_{pp} + (Z_{pq} - Z_{pr})(Z_{qq} - Z_{qr} - Z_{rq} + Z_{rr})^{-1}$$

$$(Z_{rp} - Z_{qp}) . \tag{11.54}$$

The relation between v_q and i_p, obtained by substituting (11.53) into the second equation of (11.51), is given as

$$v_q = [\ Z_{qp} + (Z_{qq} - Z_{qr})(Z_{qq} - Z_{qr} - Z_{rq} + Z_{rr})^{-1}$$
$$\cdot (Z_{rp} - Z_{qp})\ ]\ i_p\ . \tag{11.55}$$

In the above formulation, the order of the matrix to be inverted is $c/2$ as compared to the case of (11.50) where a matrix of order 'c' needs to be inverted.

Example

The two methods of segmentation using Z-matrices are illustrated by combining two 3-port resistive subnetworks shown in Figure 11.14. The Z-matrices of the two components are

$$Z_A = \begin{bmatrix} 4 & 3 & 3 \\ 3 & 7 & 3 \\ 3 & 3 & 5 \end{bmatrix} \tag{11.56a}$$

and

$$Z_B = \begin{bmatrix} 7 & 3 & 3 \\ 3 & 5 & 3 \\ 3 & 3 & 5 \end{bmatrix}. \tag{11.56b}$$

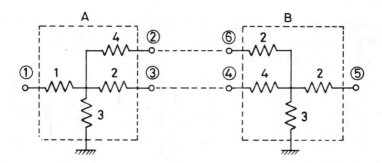

Figure 11.14   Resistive network considered as an example for the segmentation method.

Using the first method, the component characterizations are put in the form

$$
\begin{bmatrix} v_1 \\ v_5 \\ \hline v_2 \\ v_3 \\ v_4 \\ v_6 \end{bmatrix} =
\left[\begin{array}{cc|cccc}
4 & 0 & 3 & 3 & 0 & 0 \\
0 & 5 & 0 & 0 & 3 & 3 \\ \hline
3 & 0 & 7 & 3 & 0 & 0 \\
3 & 0 & 3 & 5 & 0 & 0 \\
0 & 3 & 0 & 0 & 7 & 3 \\
0 & 3 & 0 & 0 & 3 & 5
\end{array} \right]
\begin{bmatrix} i_1 \\ i_5 \\ \hline i_2 \\ i_3 \\ i_4 \\ i_6 \end{bmatrix} .
\tag{11.57}
$$

Matrices $\mathbf{\Gamma}_1$ and $\mathbf{\Gamma}_2$ are obtained as

$$
\begin{bmatrix}
1 & 0 & 0 & -1 \\
0 & 1 & -1 & 0
\end{bmatrix}
\begin{bmatrix} v_2 \\ v_3 \\ v_4 \\ v_6 \end{bmatrix} = \mathbf{0} ,
\tag{11.58}
$$

and

$$
\begin{bmatrix}
1 & 0 & 0 & 1 \\
0 & 1 & 1 & 0
\end{bmatrix}
\begin{bmatrix} i_2 \\ i_3 \\ i_4 \\ i_6 \end{bmatrix} = \mathbf{0} .
\tag{11.59}
$$

The overall Z-matrix, obtained by substituting (11.57) to (11.59) in (11.50), is as follows (note that the matrix $\mathbf{\Gamma}_2$ need not be multiplied by j since Z_{cc} is real).

$$
Z_p =
\begin{bmatrix} 4 & 0 \\ 0 & 5 \end{bmatrix}
-
\begin{bmatrix} 3 & 3 & 0 & 0 \\ 0 & 0 & 3 & 3 \end{bmatrix}
\begin{bmatrix}
7 & 3 & -3 & -5 \\
3 & 5 & -7 & -3 \\
1 & 0 & 0 & 1 \\
0 & 1 & 1 & 0
\end{bmatrix}^{-1}
\begin{bmatrix}
3 & -3 \\
3 & -3 \\
0 & 0 \\
0 & 0
\end{bmatrix}
$$

or

$$
Z_p =
\begin{bmatrix} 4 & 0 \\ 0 & 5 \end{bmatrix}
+ \frac{1}{108}
\begin{bmatrix} -108 & 108 \\ 108 & -108 \end{bmatrix}
=
\begin{bmatrix} 3 & 1 \\ 1 & 4 \end{bmatrix} .
\tag{11.60}
$$

This can be verified to be the Z-matrix of the combination. To obtain the Z-matrix of the combination using the second method, the connected ports are divided into two groups as discussed earlier. For this purpose, the Z-matrices can be written together as

$$
\begin{bmatrix} v_1 \\ v_5 \\ \hline v_2 \\ v_4 \\ \hline v_6 \\ v_3 \end{bmatrix} =
\left[\begin{array}{cc|cc|cc}
4 & 0 & 3 & 0 & 0 & 3 \\
0 & 5 & 0 & 3 & 3 & 0 \\ \hline
3 & 0 & 7 & 0 & 0 & 3 \\
0 & 3 & 0 & 7 & 3 & 0 \\ \hline
0 & 3 & 0 & 3 & 5 & 0 \\
3 & 0 & 3 & 0 & 0 & 5
\end{array}\right]
\begin{bmatrix} i_1 \\ i_5 \\ \hline i_2 \\ i_4 \\ \hline i_6 \\ i_3 \end{bmatrix}
\qquad (11.61)
$$

and the overall Z-matrix is given by substituting (11.61) in (11.54) as

$$
\begin{aligned}
Z_p &= \begin{bmatrix} 4 & 0 \\ 0 & 5 \end{bmatrix} + \begin{bmatrix} 3 & -3 \\ -3 & 3 \end{bmatrix} \begin{bmatrix} 12 & -6 \\ -6 & 12 \end{bmatrix}^{-1} \begin{bmatrix} -3 & 3 \\ 3 & -3 \end{bmatrix} \\
&= \begin{bmatrix} 4 & 0 \\ 0 & 5 \end{bmatrix} + \begin{bmatrix} -1 & 1 \\ 1 & -1 \end{bmatrix} = \begin{bmatrix} 3 & 1 \\ 1 & 4 \end{bmatrix}. \qquad (11.62)
\end{aligned}
$$

11.3.2 Desegmentation Method [9]

This method is applicable in cases where the addition of one or more *simple* shapes to the shape to be analyzed modifies it to another *simple* shape. A few examples of this type are shown in Figure 11.15. As in the case of segmentation method, desegmentation method also involves replacement of continuous connections between various shapes by the multiple number of ports along the interconnection. In order to determine the characteristics of the given circuit using this procedure, it is necessary that the shape to be added has ports other than those along the common boundary.

Let α, as shown in Figure 11.15, denote the shape of the circuit to be analyzed. On the addition of one or more *simple* shapes (denoted by β), a *simple* shape γ is obtained. The characteristics of β and γ can be obtained using Green's function method. Among the ports of the circuit to be analyzed, the ones that are not on the common boundaries between α and β, are denoted as p-ports. If the remaining ports on the circuit α do not cover completely all the boundaries between α and β, additional ports are added to α so that the common boundaries are fully covered. The ports of α on the common boundaries with β are called q-ports. The corresponding ports on β are called r-ports. It should be noted that higher accuracy can be obtained by increasing the number of ports on the common boundary. The ports on β that are not on the common boundary are called d-ports. As explained later, there must be at least as many d-ports on each of the segments in β as the number of r-ports. The d-ports need not be on the periphery of the segment, but can be inside the periphery, as well. The characteristics of the α-shaped circuit can be obtained from the characteristics of components β and γ in terms of either S-matrices, or Z-matrices.

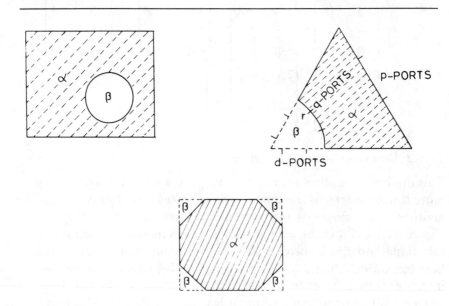

Figure 11.15   Examples of planar circuits suitable for analysis by desegmentation method.

Desegmentation using S-matrices [10]

Governing equations for the components in β and for γ can be written as

$$
\begin{bmatrix} b_r \\ b_d \end{bmatrix} = \begin{bmatrix} S_{rr} & S_{rd} \\ S_{dr} & S_{dd}^{\beta} \end{bmatrix} \begin{bmatrix} a_r \\ a_d \end{bmatrix}
\tag{11.63}
$$

and

$$
\begin{bmatrix} b_p \\ b_d \end{bmatrix} = \begin{bmatrix} S_{pp}^{\gamma} & S_{pd} \\ S_{dp} & S_{dd}^{\gamma} \end{bmatrix} \begin{bmatrix} a_p \\ a_d \end{bmatrix}
\tag{11.64}
$$

where b's and a's denote the outgoing and incoming wave variables, S^{γ} is the scattering matrix of γ, and S^{β} can be directly obtained from scattering matrices of segments in β. To analyze the circuit use

$$
\begin{bmatrix} b_p \\ b_q \end{bmatrix} = \begin{bmatrix} S_{pp}^{\alpha} & S_{pq} \\ S_{qp} & S_{qq} \end{bmatrix} \begin{bmatrix} a_p \\ a_q \end{bmatrix}
\tag{11.65}
$$

where S^{α} is the unknown S-matrix of α. The ports in q and r can be ordered in the same way as in Section 11.3.1. Under these conditions we have

$$
a_q = b_r
\tag{11.66a}
$$

and

$$
b_q = a_r .
\tag{11.66b}
$$

Using segmentation method, the S-matrix of α and those of segments in β can be combined to give the S-matrix of γ. From the discussion in Section 11.2.4, S^{γ} can be expressed as

$$
S^{\gamma} = \begin{bmatrix} S_{pp}^{\alpha} + S_{pq} M_{11} S_{qp} & S_{pq} M_{12} S_{rd} \\ S_{dr} M_{21} S_{qp} & S_{dd}^{\beta} + S_{dr} M_{22} S_{rd} \end{bmatrix}
\tag{11.67}
$$

where

$$M_{12} = (I - S_{rr}S_{qq})^{-1} , \qquad\qquad (11.68a)$$

$$M_{21} = (I - S_{qq} S_{rr})^{-1} , \qquad\qquad (11.68b)$$

$$M_{11} = S_{rr} M_{21} , \qquad\qquad (11.68c)$$

and

$$M_{22} = S_{qq} M_{12} . \qquad\qquad (11.68d)$$

In the desegmentation method, S^{α} is obtained from S^{β} and S^{γ} using the above equations. For this purpose, the number of d-ports must be at least equal to the number of q- or r-ports. The submatrices can be equated from (11.64) and (11.67) to give

$$S_{dd}^{\gamma} = S_{dd}^{\beta} + S_{dr} S_{qq} (I - S_{rr} S_{qq})^{-1} S_{rd} \qquad\qquad (11.69)$$

which results in

$$S_{qq} = (N S_{rr} + I)^{-1} N \qquad\qquad (11.70)$$

where

$$N = (S_{dr}^{t} S_{dr})^{-1} S_{dr}^{t} (S_{dd}^{\gamma} - S_{dd}^{\beta}) S_{rd}^{t} (S_{rd} S_{rd}^{t})^{-1} . \quad (11.71)$$

The other submatrices S^{α} can be obtained as

$$S^{\alpha} = \begin{bmatrix} S_{pp}^{\gamma} - S_{pq} M_{11} S_{qp} & S_{pd} S_{rd}^{t} (S_{rd} S_{rd}^{t})^{-1} (I - S_{rr} S_{qq}) \\ (I - S_{qq} S_{rr}) (S_{dr}^{t} S_{dr})^{-1} S_{dr}^{t} S_{dp} & (N S_{rr} + I)^{-1} N \end{bmatrix} .$$

$$(11.72)$$

To evaluate S^{α} with this procedure, first the submatrix S_{qq} is computed using (11.70), then S_{pq} and S_{qp} are evaluated using (11.72). Submatrix M_{11} is evaluated using (11.68) and finally S_{pp}^{α} is obtained using (11.72).

In the case where d = q, the matrix N in (11.70) reduces to

$$N = S_{dr}^{-1} (S_{dd}^{\gamma} - S_{dd}^{\beta}) S_{rd}^{-1} \qquad\qquad (11.73)$$

and the expressions for S^α reduce to

$$
S^\alpha = \begin{bmatrix} S_{pp}^\gamma - S_{pq} M_{11} S_{qp} & S_{pd} S_{rd}^{-1} (I - S_{rr} S_{qq}) \\ (I - S_{qq} S_{rr}) S_{dr}^{-1} S_{dp} & (N S_{rr} + I)^{-1} N \end{bmatrix}
$$

$$(11.74)$$

where M_{11} is obtained from (11.68), and the submatrices in S^α are evaluated in the same order as for $d > q$.

The scattering matrix S^α corresponds to α, on which additional ports at the boundaries between α and β might have been added. Let the ports of α be divided into o-ports, for which characterization is desired, and e-ports, which were added for desegmentation. The incoming and outgoing wave variables on the segment α are related as

$$
\begin{bmatrix} b_o \\ b_e \end{bmatrix} = \begin{bmatrix} S_{oo}^\alpha & S_{oe}^\alpha \\ S_{eo}^\alpha & S_{ee}^\alpha \end{bmatrix} \begin{bmatrix} a_o \\ a_e \end{bmatrix}
$$

$$(11.75)$$

where S_{oo}^α, S_{oe}^α, S_{eo}^α, S_{ee}^α are obtained by reordering the rows and columns of S^α, and a_o, b_o and a_e, b_e are the wave variables at the o-ports and e-ports, respectively. Characterization is needed only for the o-ports, and thus the open circuit boundary condition can be applied to e-ports giving

$$
a_e = b_e .
$$

$$(11.76)$$

From (11.75) and (11.76), we obtain

$$
b_o = [S_{oo}^\alpha + S_{oe}^\alpha (I - S_{ee}^\alpha)^{-1} S_{eo}^\alpha] a_o
$$

$$(11.77)$$

or the desired scattering matrix S_p can be expressed as

$$
S_p = S_{oo}^\alpha + S_{oe}^\alpha (I - S_{ee}^\alpha)^{-1} S_{eo}^\alpha .
$$

$$(11.78)$$

In the relations above, I denotes an identity matrix of appropriate size.

As pointed out in the previous chapter, desegmentation can be used as a method for de-embedding of multiport networks. The following example illustrates the formulation presented above for desegmentation using S-matrices, applied to de-embedding of a three-port network.

Example [10]

Consider the case of a 3-port circulator with identical connectors at each port as shown in Figure 11.16. The S-parameters for the overall network (including the connectors) are measured and are obtained as

$$
S^{\gamma} = \begin{bmatrix}
0.0148 + j\,0.0493 & -0.134 + j\,0.0624 & -0.897 + j\,0.185 \\
-0.897 + j\,0.187 & 0.0148 + j\,0.0493 & -0.134 + j\,0.0624 \\
-0.134 + j\,0.0624 & -0.897 + j\,0.187 & 0.0148 + j\,0.0493
\end{bmatrix}.
$$

$$(11.79)$$

The S-parameters for the connectors are known from separate calibration and are as follows:

$$
S = \begin{bmatrix}
0.0568 - j\,0.0374 & -j\,0.0966 - j\,0.9544 \\
-0.0966 - j\,0.9544 & 0.0245 + j\,0.0364
\end{bmatrix}
$$

$$(11.80)$$

where the first row in (11.80) refers to the port of the connector external to the overall network with the other port connected to the circulator.

One can obtain the S-matrix of the circulator (excluding the effect of connectors) using desegmentation with γ-network referring to the overall network, and β-network referring to the three connectors only. In this case, we have $p = 0$ and $q = r = d = 3$. $S^{\gamma}_{dd}\,(= S^{\gamma})$ is known from (11.79) and S^{β} can be obtained from (11.80). $S^{\alpha}\,(= S^{\alpha}_{qq})$ is obtained using (11.70) as

$$
S^{\alpha} = \begin{bmatrix}
0 & 0.1 & 0.995 \\
0.995 & 0 & 0.1 \\
0.1 & 0.995 & 0
\end{bmatrix}.
$$

$$(11.81)$$

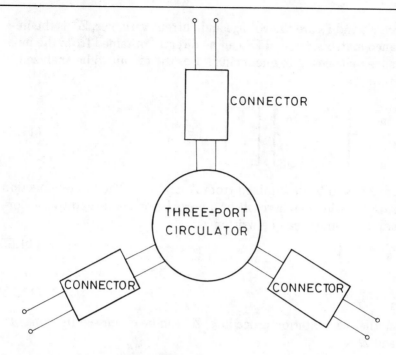

Figure 11.16 *A three-port circulator with connectors considered as an example for de-embedding.*

Desegmentation using Z-matrices

Governing equations in terms of impedance matrix for components in β and γ can be expressed as

$$
\begin{bmatrix} v_r \\ v_d \end{bmatrix} = \begin{bmatrix} Z_{rr} & Z_{rd} \\ Z_{dr} & Z_{dd}^{\beta} \end{bmatrix} \begin{bmatrix} i_r \\ i_d \end{bmatrix}
\tag{11.82}
$$

and

$$
\begin{bmatrix} v_p \\ v_d \end{bmatrix} = \begin{bmatrix} Z_{pp}^{\gamma} & Z_{pd} \\ Z_{dp} & Z_{dd}^{\gamma} \end{bmatrix} \begin{bmatrix} i_p \\ i_d \end{bmatrix}
\tag{11.83}
$$

where v's and i's are the voltage and current variables, Z^γ is the impedance matrix of γ, and Z^β can be directly obtained from the impedance matrices of segments in β. For the circuit to be analyzed, we have

$$\begin{bmatrix} v_p \\ v_q \end{bmatrix} = \begin{bmatrix} Z_{pp}^\alpha & Z_{pq} \\ Z_{qp} & Z_{qq} \end{bmatrix} \begin{bmatrix} i_p \\ i_q \end{bmatrix} \tag{11.84}$$

where Z^α is to be determined from Z^β and Z^γ. The interconnection constraints which are a result of q-ports being connected to the corresponding r-ports can be written as

$$v_q = v_r \tag{11.85a}$$

and

$$i_q + i_r = 0 \ . \tag{11.85b}$$

Using the segmentation procedure, Z^γ can be expressed in terms of Z^α and Z^β as

$$Z^\gamma = \begin{bmatrix} Z_{pp}^\alpha - Z_{pq}(Z_{qq} + Z_{rr})^{-1} Z_{qp} & Z_{pq}(Z_{qq} + Z_{rr})^{-1} Z_{rd} \\ Z_{dr}(Z_{qq} + Z_{rr})^{-1} Z_{qp} & Z_{dd}^\beta - Z_{dr}(Z_{qq} + Z_{rr})^{-1} Z_{rd} \end{bmatrix} .$$

$$\tag{11.86}$$

Carrying out steps similar to those for the S-matrix version of desegmentation, we obtain

$$Z_{qq} = - Z_{rr} - N \tag{11.87}$$

where

$$N = Z_{rd} Z_{rd}^t \left[Z_{dr}^t (Z_{dd}^\gamma - Z_{dd}^\beta) Z_{rd}^t \right]^{-1} Z_{dr}^t Z_{dr} \ . \tag{11.88}$$

Other submatrices in Z^α are

$$Z_{pq} = - Z_{pd} Z_{rd}^t (Z_{rd} Z_{rd}^t)^{-1} N \ , \tag{11.89}$$

$$Z_{qp} = - N (Z_{dr}^t Z_{dr})^{-1} Z_{dr}^t Z_{dp} \ , \tag{11.90}$$

and

$$Z^\alpha_{pp} = Z^\gamma_{pp} - Z_{pq} N^{-1} Z_{qp} . \tag{11.91}$$

For the case in which $d = q$, the expressions for Z^α reduce to

$$N = Z_{rd} (Z^\gamma_{dd} - Z^\beta_{dd})^{-1} Z_{dr} , \tag{11.92}$$

$$Z_{qq} = - Z_{rr} - N , \tag{11.93}$$

$$Z_{pq} = - Z_{pd} (Z^\gamma_{dd} - Z^\beta_{dd})^{-1} Z_{dr} , \tag{11.94}$$

$$Z_{qp} = - Z_{rd} (Z^\gamma_{dd} - Z^\beta_{dd})^{-1} Z_{dp} , \tag{11.95}$$

and

$$Z^\alpha_{pp} = Z^\gamma_{pp} - Z_{pd} (Z^\gamma_{dd} - Z^\beta_{dd})^{-1} Z_{dp} . \tag{11.96}$$

The impedance matrix Z^α corresponds to α on which additional ports at the boundaries between α and β might have been added. One can apply the open circuit condition on these ports, and this amounts to deleting from Z^α the rows and columns corresponding to these ports. The reduced matrix corresponds to impedance matrix for α with the desired ports only.

Example

The desegmentation method using Z-matrices is illustrated by obtaining the Z-matrix of a resistive subnetwork from those of the overall network and another subnetwork shown in Figure 11.17.

The Z-matrices of the γ-network and β subnetwork are given by

$$Z^\gamma = \begin{array}{c} \\ p \\ d \end{array} \begin{array}{c} p \quad\quad d \\ \left[\begin{array}{cc} 3 & 1 \\ 1 & 6 \end{array} \right] \end{array} \tag{11.97}$$

and

$$Z^\beta = \begin{array}{c} \\ r \\ d \end{array} \begin{array}{c} r \quad\quad d \\ \left[\begin{array}{cc} 4 & 3 \\ 3 & 7 \end{array} \right] \end{array} . \tag{11.98}$$

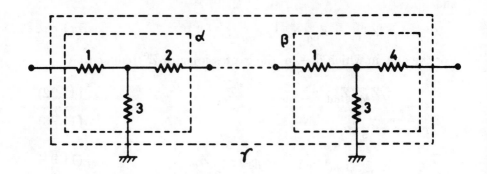

Figure 11.17   A resistive network considered as an example for the
desegmentation method.

The matrix Z^α can be obtained by substituting (11.97) and (11.98)
into (11.92) to (11.96). We have

$$N \quad = 3(6 - 7)^{-1} \ 3 = -9$$
$$Z_{qq} \quad = -4 - (-9) = 5 \ ,$$
$$Z_{pq} \quad = -1(6 - 7)^{-1} \ 3 = 3 \ ,$$
$$Z_{qp} \quad = -3(6 - 7)^{-1} \ 1 = 3 \ ,$$

and

$$Z_{pp} \quad = 3 - 1(6 - 7)^{-1} \ 1 = 4 \ .$$

The matrix Z^α can thus be written as

$$Z_p^\alpha = \begin{bmatrix} 4 & 3 \\ 3 & 5 \end{bmatrix} \tag{11.99}$$

which is seen to be the Z-matrix for the α-subnetwork.

Various methods discussed in this chapter are useful for computer-
aided analysis of microwave circuits.

REFERENCES

[1]   Chua, L.O., and P.M. Lin, *Computer-Aided Analysis of Electronic Circuits: Algorithms and Computational Techniques*, Englewood Cliffs, N.J.: Prentice Hall, 1975.

[2]   Monaco, V.A., and P. Tiberio, "On the Transformation of a Lumped Element Linear Network into a Circuit Composed of Multiports," *Alta Freq.*, Vol. 39, Nov. 1970, pp. 1013-1014.

[3]   Reed, J., and G.J. Wheeler, "A Method of Analysis of Symmetrical Four-port Networks," *IRE Trans. Microwave Theory Tech.*, Vol. MTT-4, Oct. 1956, pp. 246-252.

[4]   Weinberg, L., "Scattering Matrix and Transfer Scattering Matrix," in *Amplifiers*, R.F. Shea, Ed., New York: McGraw-Hill, 1966.

[5]   Monaco, V.A., and P. Tiberio, "Computer-Aided Analysis of Microwave Circuits," *IEEE Trans. Microwave Theory Tech.*, Vol. MTT-22, Mar. 1974, pp. 249-263.

[6]   Monaco, V.A., and P. Tiberio, "Automatic Scattering Matrix Computation of Microwave Circuits," *Alta Freq.*, Vol. 39, Feb. 1970, pp. 59-64.

[7]   Okoshi, T., *et al.*, "The Segmentation Method — An Approach to the Analysis of Microwave Planar Circuits," *IEEE Trans. Microwave Theory Tech.*, Vol. MTT-24, Oct. 1976, pp. 662-668.

[8]   Chadha, R., and K.C. Gupta, "Segmentation Method Using Impedance Matrices for Analysis of Planar Microwave Circuits," *IEEE Trans. Microwave Theory Tech.*, Vol. MTT-29, Jan. 1981, pp. 71-74.

[9]   Sharma, P.C., and K.C. Gupta, "Desegmentation Method for Analysis of Two-dimensional Microwave Circuits," *IEEE Trans. Microwave Theory Tech.*, Vol. MTT-29, Oct. 1981, (to appear)

[10]   Sharma, P.C., and K.C. Gupta, "A Generalized Method for De-embedding of Multiport Networks," (to be published).

12

Sensitivity Analysis of Microwave Circuits

In many network applications, it is desirable to know the effect of changes in the values of various components or parameters on the performance parameters of the network. An analysis of a circuit carried out to obtain this information is called the sensitivity analysis of the circuit [1] - [3]. The sensitivities of transmission structures and other elements yield information as to how changes in the design parameters affect the characterizations of these components. Linking this information with the sensitivity analysis of the circuit, one obtains the sensitivities of performance parameters with respect to the design parameters. Performance parameters of a network may be expressed in terms of S-parameters. Therefore, sensitivities of performance parameters can be obtained from the sensitivities of S-parameters. For example, the voltage gain from a port k to a port i is given by the magnitude of the transfer coefficient, S_{ik} (which equals $|S_{ik}| e^{-j\phi_{ik}}$). Sensitivity of the magnitude $|S_{ik}|$ with respect to a parameter x can be expressed as [4]

$$\frac{\partial |S_{ik}|}{\partial x} = \text{Re} \left[\frac{|S_{ik}|}{S_{ik}} \frac{\partial S_{ik}}{\partial x} \right] \qquad (12.1)$$

where the function Re[·] denotes the real part of the argument.

Similarly, the sensitivity of the phase of S_{ik}, i.e., ϕ_{ik}, with respect to x, can be expressed as [4]

$$\frac{\partial \phi_{ik}}{\partial x} = - \operatorname{Im} \left[\frac{1}{S_{ik}} \frac{\partial S_{ik}}{\partial x} \right] \tag{12.2}$$

where the function $\operatorname{Im} [\cdot]$ denotes the imaginary part of the argument.

Sensitivity analysis can also be used for the exact computation of the group delay. For transmission from a port k to a port i, the group delay is defined as

$$\tau_{ik} = \frac{\partial \phi_{ik}}{\partial \omega} \,. \tag{12.3}$$

Using (12.2), the relation for τ_{ik} can be expressed as

$$\tau_{ik} = - \operatorname{Im} \left[\frac{1}{S_{ik}} \frac{\partial S_{ik}}{\partial \omega} \right] \,. \tag{12.4}$$

Thus, the exact computation of group delay can be carried out by evaluating the sensitivity of the scattering parameter with respect to frequency.

As pointed out in Chapter 4, sensitivity calculations are also used in a class of optimization methods. These optimization techniques are discussed in Chapter 18. There are some optimization methods (like Newton's method discussed in Section 18.2) which also require knowledge of second order sensitivities. According to the definition of group delay given in (12.3), second order sensitivities can also be used to determine the sensitivities of group delay with respect to various design parameters.

There are two methods for carrying out sensitivity analysis of a circuit. One of these is the *finite difference method,* which is applicable to any system in which a particular design parameter is varied and the network is analyzed to get an estimate of the derivatives of performance parameters. The other method is the *adjoint network approach,* which requires the analysis of another network called the adjoint network. Derivatives with respect to all the design parameters can be obtained from the analyses of the original network and a suitably excited adjoint network.

In addition to these two methods, a direct method can be used if the circuit performance parameters are expressed directly in terms of component parameters. In such cases, the sensitivities can be obtained by directly differentiating the expressions for performance parameters.

12.1 FINITE DIFFERENCE METHOD

In order to obtain the sensitivity with respect to a variable, the function is evaluated again after changing the value of the variable. The derivative of the function is obtained from the ratio of the change in the value of the function to the change in the parameter value. Let f be a function of the parameters $x_1, x_2, \ldots, x_n$. The partial derivative of f with respect to x_k can be approximated by

$$\frac{\partial f}{\partial x_k} \approx \frac{f(x_k + \Delta x_k) - f(x_k - \Delta x_k)}{2 \Delta x_k} . \tag{12.5}$$

The accuracy of the derivative is higher for smaller values of Δx_k.

In this method, each of the independent variables in a network is altered one by one and the network is analyzed for each case. Thus, to obtain sensitivities with respect to n variables, 2n analyses are required.[*] Network analysis requires inversion of a matrix and therefore this procedure for evaluating sensitivities is computationally inefficient for large networks. Another disadvantage of the method is that, for small values of Δx_k, the difference of two nearly equal quantities has to be taken in (12.5) and this may lead to numerical errors. For large values of Δx_k, the accuracy of (12.5) is itself limited. Because of these drawbacks, the adjoint network method is preferred.

12.2 ADJOINT NETWORK METHOD [5]

The adjoint network method requires the analyses of the original network and another network called the adjoint network, which is derived from the original network. These two analyses yield the sensitivities with respect to all the variables in the network.

------

[*] (n + 1) analyses would suffice if the derivative is approximated by forward Euler or backward Euler formula in place of (12.5).

To discuss the adjoint network method for obtaining sensitivities of scattering parameters, we first introduce a general theorem. This theorem can be considered a version of Tellegen's Theorem in wave variables.

12.2.1 Tellegen's Theorem in Wave Variables

Consider a general network of multiport components. Let a and b represent normalized incoming and outgoing wave variables at all the ports in the network. Consider another network of multiport components with α and β as normalized incoming and outgoing wave variables at various ports. Now, choose subnetworks of these two networks such that: i) the topologies of the two subnetworks are identical; ii) all the ports for all the junctions in the subnetworks are included; and iii) corresponding ports in the two subnetworks are similarly normalized. Condition (ii) implies that the external ports are excluded from the subnetworks. An example of two subnetworks satisfying these conditions is shown in Figure 12.1. If a_s and b_s represent incoming and outgoing wave variables at all the ports within the subnetwork, these are related as

$$b_s = \Gamma_s a_s \tag{12.6}$$

where Γ_s is the interconnection matrix accounting for the topology and the normalizations of the subnetwork. The method for obtaining the interconnection matrix has been discussed in Section 11.2.1. Corresponding incoming and outgoing wave variables α_s and β_s in the other subnetwork are also related by the same interconnection matrix Γ_s in accordance with the assumptions stated above. We have

$$\beta_s = \Gamma_s \alpha_s . \tag{12.7}$$

For reciprocal junctions where $\Gamma_s = \Gamma_s^t$, it can be shown, using (12.6) and (12.7), that

$$b_s^t \alpha_s - a_s^t \beta_s = a_s^t (\Gamma_s^t - \Gamma_s) \alpha_s = 0 . \tag{12.8}$$

The above result is valid for any two subnetworks of same topology. Therefore, it is also valid for two complete networks with identical topology. For complete networks, the external ports, if any, should be connected to either generators or loads.

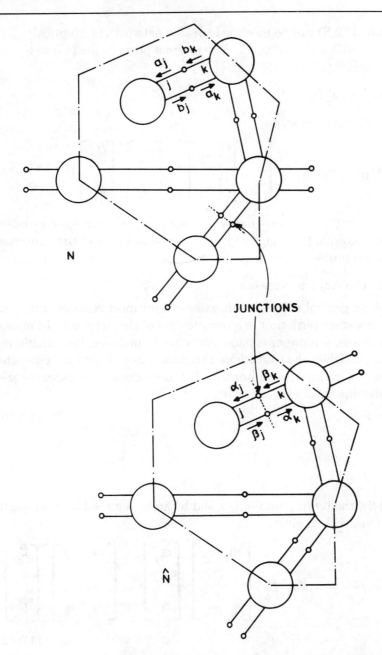

Figure 12.1   *An example of two subnetworks satisfying Tellegen's theorem.*

Equation (12.8) can be modified for two networks of identical
topology with external ports. The internal ports in the two networks satisfy (12.8), that is

$$b_c^t \alpha_c - a_c^t \beta_c = 0 \ .$$

Using this, one can write

$$b_p^t \alpha_p - a_p^t \beta_p = \begin{bmatrix} b_p \\ b_c \end{bmatrix}^t \begin{bmatrix} \alpha_p \\ \alpha_c \end{bmatrix} - \begin{bmatrix} a_p \\ a_c \end{bmatrix}^t \begin{bmatrix} \beta_p \\ \beta_c \end{bmatrix} \qquad (12.9)$$

where, as in the previous chapter, subscript p indicates wave variables
at the p external ports and c indicates wave variables at the c internally
connected ports.

12.2.2 The Adjoint Network

Consider a general network consisting of multiport components. Let
there be a small deviation in a parameter ϕ of the network. In microwave circuits, ϕ represents parameters like impedance, line length, etc.
Further, consider the case where the change in ϕ affects the characterization of a multiport component. If this component is characterized
by scattering matrix S such that

$$b = S \ a \ , \qquad (12.10)$$

then

$$\frac{\partial b}{\partial \phi} = \frac{\partial S}{\partial \phi} a + S \frac{\partial a}{\partial \phi} \ . \qquad (12.11)$$

In (12.9), the terms containing a and b can be replaced by their partial
derivatives with ϕ, giving

$$\frac{\partial b_p^t}{\partial \phi} \alpha_p - \frac{\partial a_p^t}{\partial \phi} \beta_p = \begin{bmatrix} \partial b_p/\partial \phi \\ \partial b_c/\partial \phi \end{bmatrix}^t \begin{bmatrix} \alpha_p \\ \alpha_c \end{bmatrix} - \begin{bmatrix} \partial a_p/\partial \phi \\ \partial a_c/\partial \phi \end{bmatrix}^t \begin{bmatrix} \beta_p \\ \beta_c \end{bmatrix}$$

$$(12.12)$$

where the variables α and β refer to the other network described in
Section 12.2.1. In the right-hand side of (12.12), the term relating

to the component under consideration can be written as

$$\partial b^t / \partial \phi \; \boldsymbol{\alpha} - \partial a^t / \partial \phi \; \boldsymbol{\beta} . \tag{12.13}$$

Using (12.11), the above expression reduces to

$$\left[a^t \frac{\partial S^t}{\partial \phi} + \frac{\partial a^t}{\partial \phi} S^t \right] \boldsymbol{\alpha} - \frac{\partial a^t}{\partial \phi} \boldsymbol{\beta}$$

or

$$a^t \frac{\partial S^t}{\partial \phi} \boldsymbol{\alpha} + \frac{\partial a^t}{\partial \phi} (S^t \boldsymbol{\alpha} - \boldsymbol{\beta}). \tag{12.14}$$

In this expression, $\boldsymbol{\alpha}$ and $\boldsymbol{\beta}$ are incoming and outgoing wave variables corresponding to the ports of component affected by ϕ in the other network, which is topologically identical to the original network. The above discussion is valid for any arbitrary characterizations in the other network. If, for the component under consideration, we define

$$\boldsymbol{\beta} = S^t \boldsymbol{\alpha} \tag{12.15}$$

the expression (12.14) reduces to

$$a^t \frac{\partial S^t}{\partial \phi} \boldsymbol{\alpha} . \tag{12.16}$$

If all the components in the other network are defined as in (12.15), the network described by $\boldsymbol{\alpha}$ and $\boldsymbol{\beta}$ is called the *adjoint* of the original network.

The right-hand side of (12.12) can be rewritten using expressions similar to (12.14) for each component of the network. Equation (12.12) now becomes

$$\frac{\partial b_p^t}{\partial \phi} \boldsymbol{\alpha}_p - \frac{\partial a_p^t}{\partial \phi} \boldsymbol{\beta}_p = \sum_i a_i^t \frac{\partial S_i^t}{\partial \phi} \boldsymbol{\alpha}_i + \sum_i \frac{\partial a_i^t}{\partial \phi} (S_i^t \boldsymbol{\alpha}_i - \boldsymbol{\beta}_i) .$$

$$\tag{12.17}$$

Since all components constituting the adjoint network are defined by

$$\boldsymbol{\beta}_i = S_i^t \boldsymbol{\alpha}_i \tag{12.18}$$

equation (12.17) reduces to

$$\frac{\partial b_p^t}{\partial \phi} \alpha_p - \frac{\partial a_p^t}{\partial \phi} \beta_p = \sum_i a_i^t \frac{\partial S_i^t}{\partial \phi} \alpha_i. \qquad (12.19)$$

Normally, a parameter ϕ affects the characterization of one component only, leaving the characterizations of other components unchanged. For such a case, we have

$$\frac{\partial b_p^t}{\partial \phi} \alpha_p - \frac{\partial a_p^t}{\partial \phi} \beta_p = a^t \frac{\partial S^t}{\partial \phi} \alpha \qquad (12.20)$$

where a, S and α correspond to the affected component, and $\partial S/\partial \phi$ for other components is taken to be zero. It may be pointed out here that if the change in ϕ affects the characterization of more than one component then the right-hand side of (12.20) should be summed over all such components. For example, when sensitivities with respect to frequency are needed in group delay evaluation, the right-hand side of (12.20) has to be summed over all frequency dependent components in the network.

If the network is matched at all the external ports, then $\partial a_p/\partial \phi$ is zero. This condition reduces (12.20) to

$$\frac{\partial b_p^t}{\partial \phi} \alpha_p = a^t \frac{\partial S^t}{\partial \phi} \alpha \qquad (12.21a)$$

or

$$\sum_{k \in E} \alpha_k \frac{\partial b_k}{\partial \phi} = a^t \frac{\partial S^t}{\partial \phi} \alpha \qquad (12.21b)$$

where E represents the set of p external ports. It may be seen that (12.21) relates the changes in responses at external ports to the changes in the characterization of the component affected by a change in ϕ and thus yields sensitivity of port responses with respect to ϕ. Sensitivities with respect to other parameters can be found by deriving the right-hand side of (12.21) for the affected components.

This requires the partial derivatives of the component submatrices (which are discussed in the next subsection). Also, the sensitivities with respect to all the parameters can be determined from two analyses, one of the original network and the other of the adjoint network. For a reciprocal component, $S = S^t$ and the adjoint network contains the original component itself. If all the components are reciprocal, then the adjoint network is the same as the original network.

Evaluation of Gradients

Consider a network for which we wish to evaluate the gradient of the term S_{ij} of the network scattering matrix. For $i \neq j$, the insertion loss from port j to port i is given by

$$S_{ij} = \frac{b_i}{a_j} \tag{12.22}$$

with the condition that all other a_k's ($k \neq j$) are zero; in other words, jth external port is excited by a matched generator and all other external ports are terminated in matched loads. If $a_j = 1$, (12.21b) can be written as

$$\sum_{k \in E} \alpha_k \frac{\partial S_{kj}}{\partial \phi} = a^t \frac{\partial S^t}{\partial \phi} \alpha \ . \tag{12.23}$$

Now, if we make $\alpha_i = 1$, and set all other $\alpha_k = 0$, $k \in E$; we obtain

$$\frac{\partial S_{ij}}{\partial \phi} = a^t \frac{\partial S^t}{\partial \phi} \alpha \tag{12.24}$$

where the ith external port in the adjoint network is excited by a matched generator and all other external ports terminate in matched loads.

The gradients of any S_{ij} are determined by exciting suitably ($a_j = \alpha_i = 1$ as discussed above) the original network and the adjoint network. If the gradient of reflection coefficient at an external port of a network with all reciprocal components is needed, the adjoint network is the same as the original one and is excited also in the same way. Thus, in this case, only one analysis is required to evaluate the gradient.

The analysis of the adjoint network does not require much additional effort. Using the connection scattering matrix method of Section 11.2.1, W^{-1} in (11.17) is the transpose of W^{-1} of the original network and for reciprocal networks it is the same as W^{-1} of original network. W^{-1} for the adjoint network is easily determined and it is multiplied by the source vector c of this network to obtain wave variables inside the network. If the adjoint network is analyzed using the multiport connection method of Section 11.2.2, $(\Gamma - S_{cc})^{-1} S_{cp}$ for the adjoint network is easily determined from the analysis of the original network and, using (11.21), the wave variables inside the network can be determined for any excitation α_p.

The above discussion of obtaining sensitivities for an adjoint network can be extended to obtain second order derivatives of the network scattering matrix with respect to various parameters. For this purpose, we require the derivatives of the incoming wave variables at the ports of the affected component with respect to a parameter in the network. A number of analyses of adjoint network must be performed. More details of the procedure for obtaining second order derivatives are given in [5].

12.2.3 Comparison with the Direct Method

Consider the cascade of two two-port components shown in Figure 11.6. The overall S-matrix for the cascade has been given in (11.8). Consider perturbation in a parameter x which is totally contained in component A, i.e. the change in x does not affect the characterization of component B. Using (11.8), we can directly write the derivative of S_{11}^{AB} with respect to x as

$$\frac{\partial S_{11}^{AB}}{\partial x} = \frac{\partial S_{11}^{A}}{\partial x} + \frac{S_{11}^{B} \left(S_{12}^{A} \dfrac{\partial S_{21}^{A}}{\partial x} + \dfrac{\partial S_{12}^{A}}{\partial x} S_{21}^{A} \right)}{(1 - S_{22}^{A} S_{11}^{B})}$$

$$+ \frac{S_{12}^{A} S_{21}^{A} (S_{11}^{B})^2}{(1 - S_{22}^{A} S_{11}^{B})^2} \frac{\partial S_{22}^{A}}{\partial x} . \tag{12.25}$$

If the component A is reciprocal, $S_{21}^A = S_{12}^A$ and (12.25) can be written as

$$\frac{\partial S_{11}^{AB}}{\partial x} = \frac{\partial S_{11}^A}{\partial x} + 2 \frac{\partial S_{21}^A}{\partial x} \frac{S_{21}^A S_{11}^B}{1 - S_{22}^A S_{11}^B}$$

$$+ \left[\frac{S_{21}^A S_{11}^B}{1 - S_{22}^A S_{11}^B} \right]^2 \frac{\partial S_{22}^A}{\partial x} . \qquad (12.26)$$

The same result is obtained below using the adjoint network method. If both components are assumed to be reciprocal, the adjoint network is the same as the original network. To obtain the derivative of overall S_{11}, both networks are excited by unit excitations at port 1 of the original network. The incoming wave variables at the two ports of component A can be found (using (11.21)) as

$$a = \alpha = \left[1 \quad \frac{S_{21}^A S_{11}^B}{1 - S_{22}^A S_{11}^B} \right]^t . \qquad (12.27)$$

Using (12.24), the derivative of S_{11}^{AB} can be written as

$$\frac{\partial S_{11}^{AB}}{\partial x} = \left[1 \quad \frac{S_{21}^A S_{11}^B}{1 - S_{22}^A S_{11}^B} \right] \begin{bmatrix} \dfrac{\partial S_{11}^A}{\partial x}, & \dfrac{\partial S_{21}^A}{\partial x} \\[2ex] \dfrac{\partial S_{12}^A}{\partial x}, & \dfrac{\partial S_{22}^A}{\partial x} \end{bmatrix} \begin{bmatrix} 1 \\[2ex] \dfrac{S_{21}^A S_{11}^B}{1 - S_{22}^A S_{11}^B} \end{bmatrix}$$

$$\qquad (12.28)$$

which on multiplication yields (12.26).

It should be pointed out that even when component B is non-reciprocal, (12.27) is still valid and the adjoint network method gives the same result as in (12.26).

12.2.4 Evaluation of Gradients for Subnetwork Growth Method [4, 6]

In the adjoint network method for obtaining sensitivities, we need to know the values of the wave variables at all the ports of the affected components. When the networks are analyzed using the subnetwork growth method described in Section 11.2.4, where only one component is connected at a time, the wave variables at all the component ports are not directly available. In this section we discuss one of the approaches [6] for obtaining the wave variables at all the component ports when the analysis is carried out by connecting one component at a time. For this purpose, the analysis procedure is slightly modified so that one component is added *to the subnetwork already formed.* The network is thus recomposed by growth by connecting one multiport component to the subnetwork formed. When there is more than one component to be connected to the same subnetwork, there is a rule to follow in selecting the component to be connected first. The multiport to be connected first should be the one which after connection gives rise to the subnetwork with the least number of ports.

Consider a network with m multiport components. The network is analyzed by connecting components one by one to the subnetwork formed, as discussed above. Let E_k denote the *kth* component in the sequence and Σ_k be the subnetwork formed after connecting k components. Also, Σ_k is formed by interconnecting the subnetwork Σ_{k-1} and component E_k. The wave variables at the connected ports between Σ_{k-1} and E_k (denoted by $a_c(E_k, \Sigma_{k-1})$) can be obtained in terms of the wave variables incident on ports of Σ_k (denoted by $a_p(\Sigma_k)$). Since only two subnetworks are being connected at a time, the procedure detailed in (11.36) to (11.44) is used for analysis. Let $a_c(E_k, \Sigma_{k-1})$ be subgrouped into $a_c(E_k)$ and $a_c(\Sigma_{k-1})$, indicating wave variables incident on ports of E_k and Σ_{k-1}, respectively. Similarly, $a_p(\Sigma_k)$ is subgrouped into $a_p(E_k, \Sigma_k)$ and $a_p(\Sigma_{k-1}, \Sigma_k)$ indicating wave variables incident on ports of E_k and Σ_{k-1}, respectively. We can write

$$
\begin{bmatrix}
a_p(E_k, \Sigma_k) \\
\\
a_p(\Sigma_{k-1}, \Sigma_k)
\end{bmatrix}
= P_k \, a_p(\Sigma_k)
\tag{12.29}
$$

where P_k is a square matrix containing 1's and 0's needed to reorder the variables in $a_p(\Sigma_k)$ for this partitioning.

From (11.44), we can obtain $a_c(E_k, \Sigma_{k-1})$ in terms of $a_p(\Sigma_k)$ as

$$a_c(E_k, \Sigma_{k-1}) = \begin{bmatrix} a_c(E_k) \\ a_c(\Sigma_{k-1}) \end{bmatrix} = R_k \begin{bmatrix} a_p(E_k, \Sigma_k) \\ a_p(\Sigma_{k-1}, \Sigma_k) \end{bmatrix} = R_k P_k a_p(\Sigma_k)$$

$$(12.30)$$

where R_k is obtained in terms of submatrices of (11.44), while analyzing the network for the overall scattering matrix. The objective here is to obtain the values of wave variables inside the network N, in terms of the wave variables incident on external ports. To achieve this, we proceed backwards, using (12.30) to obtain wave variables between E_m and Σ_{m-1}, then use these to obtain wave variables between E_{m-1} and Σ_{m-2}, and so on. The wave variables at the connected ports between E_m and Σ_{m-1} are obtained using (12.30) (with $k = m$) as

$$\begin{bmatrix} a_c(E_m) \\ a_c(\Sigma_{m-1}) \end{bmatrix} = R_m \begin{bmatrix} a_p(E_m, \Sigma_m) \\ a_p(\Sigma_{m-1}, \Sigma_m) \end{bmatrix} = R_m P_m a_p(\Sigma_m) \ .$$

$$(12.31)$$

The external ports of Σ_{m-1} consist of: i) external ports of Σ_m which are from Σ_{m-1}, and ii) connected ports between Σ_{m-1} and E_m, which are from Σ_{m-1}. This is shown in Figure 12.2. Thus, $a_p(\Sigma_{m-1})$ consists of $a_p(\Sigma_{m-1}, \Sigma_m)$ and $a_c(\Sigma_{m-1})$ as

$$a_p(\Sigma_{m-1}) = \begin{bmatrix} a_p(\Sigma_{m-1}, \Sigma_m) \\ a_c(\Sigma_{m-1}) \end{bmatrix} .$$

$$(12.32)$$

We can obtain $a_p(\Sigma_{m-1}, \Sigma_m)$ from $a_p(\Sigma_m)$ by omitting the rows corresponding to waves not incident on Σ_{m-1}. Similarly, $a_c(\Sigma_{m-1})$ can be obtained from the right-hand side of (12.31) by omitting rows of $(R_m P_m)$ corresponding to waves not incident on Σ_{m-1}. Let the

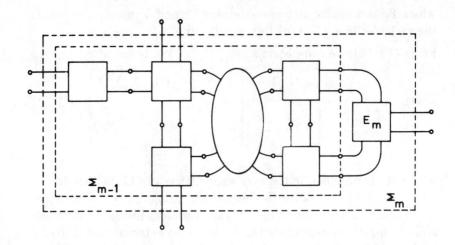

Figure 12.2   Interconnection of a subnetwork Σ_{m-1} and an element E_m.

operation of omitting rows be denoted by $|_{m-1}$. We thus have from (12.31) and (12.32)

$$a_p(\Sigma_{m-1}) = \begin{bmatrix} I(n) \mid_{m-1} \\ \\ (R_m P_m) \mid_{m-1} \end{bmatrix} a_p(\Sigma_m) \qquad (12.33a)$$

where $I(n)$ is an identity matrix of order n, the number of external ports of the network. Equation (12.33a) may be rewritten as

$$a_p(\Sigma_{m-1}) = T_{m-1} a_p(\Sigma_m) \qquad (12.33b)$$

where

$$T_{m-1} = \begin{bmatrix} I(n) \mid_{m-1} \\ \\ (R_m P_m) \mid_{m-1} \end{bmatrix}. \qquad (12.34)$$

To continue the pattern of back substitution, we must reorder the variables in $a_p(\Sigma_{m-1})$ into subgroups $a_p(E_{m-1}, \Sigma_{m-1})$ and

$a_p(\Sigma_{m-2}, \Sigma_{m-1})$. Proceeding as before, we get

$$a_c(E_{m-1}, \Sigma_{m-2}) = R_{m-1} P_{m-1} T_{m-1} a_p(\Sigma_m) \quad (12.35)$$

which gives

$$a_p(\Sigma_{m-2}) = \begin{bmatrix} T_{m-1} \Big|_{m-2} \\ \\ \left(R_{m-1} P_{m-1} T_{m-1} \right) \Big|_{m-2} \end{bmatrix} a_p(\Sigma_m)$$

$$= T_{m-2} a_p(\Sigma_m) . \quad (12.36)$$

Therefore, for an arbitrary k

$$a_p(\Sigma_k) = T_k a_p(\Sigma_m) \quad (12.37a)$$

with

$$T_k = \begin{bmatrix} T_{k+1} \Big|_k \\ \\ \\ \left(R_{k+1} P_{k+1} T_{k+1} \right) \Big|_k \end{bmatrix} = \begin{bmatrix} I(n) \Big|_k \\ \left(R_m P_m \right) \Big|_k \\ \left(R_{m-1} P_{m-1} T_{m-1} \right) \Big|_k \\ \vdots \\ \left(R_{k+1} P_{k+1} T_{k+1} \right) \Big|_k \end{bmatrix}$$

$$(12.37b)$$

and

$$a_c(E_k, \Sigma_{k-1}) = R_k P_k T_k a_p(\Sigma_k) . \quad (12.38)$$

It should be pointed out here that to set up T_k the matrix elements have already been obtained for evaluating $a_c(E_{k+1}, \Sigma_k)$. At the end of this back substitution process (i.e. when k = 1), we can put together the waves incident on all the components as

$$\begin{bmatrix} a_c(E_m, \Sigma_{m-1}) \\ a_c(E_{m-1}, \Sigma_{m-2}) \\ \vdots \\ a_c(E_2, E_1) \end{bmatrix} = \begin{bmatrix} R_m P_m \\ R_{m-1} P_{m-1} T_{m-1} \\ \vdots \\ R_2 P_2 T_2 \end{bmatrix} a_p(\Sigma_m) .$$

$$(12.39)$$

With some additional computations, the wave variables at all the internal ports are thus known in terms of incoming wave variables at the external ports of the network.

Example

The circuit shown in Figure 11.13a is an example of the procedure just described. This circuit is redrawn in Figure 12.3 and E_1 ..., E_6 indicates the order in which components are added to the subnetwork. The number of components m equals 6, and the number of external ports n equals 2.

When Σ_5 and E_6 are connected, we have

$$[a_7 \; a_{11} \; a_{12} \; a_{13}]^t = R_6 \, P_6 \, [a_1 \; a_{14}]^t$$

$$\text{or} \quad \begin{bmatrix} a_7 \\ a_{11} \\ a_{12} \\ a_{13} \end{bmatrix} = R_6 \begin{bmatrix} 1 & 0 \\ 0 & 1 \end{bmatrix} \begin{bmatrix} a_1 \\ a_{14} \end{bmatrix} \tag{12.40}$$

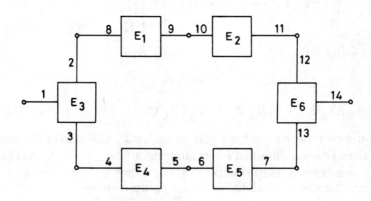

Figure 12.3   An example of a network analyzed by subnetwork growth method as modified for gradient evaluation.

where P_6 for the network is an identity matrix. R_6 in (12.40) is a 4×2 matrix obtained from submatrices as given in (11.44). From (12.40), we can obtain $(a_7 \; a_{11})^t$ by deleting the last two rows from $R_6 \times P_6$, which corresponds to the $|_5$ operation. We thus have

$$
a_p(\Sigma_5) = \begin{bmatrix} a_1 \\ a_7 \\ a_{11} \end{bmatrix} = \begin{bmatrix} 1 & 0 \\ (R_6 \; P_6) \big|_5 \end{bmatrix} \begin{bmatrix} a_1 \\ a_{14} \end{bmatrix} \tag{12.41}
$$

where the first row in the matrix of the right-hand side of (12.41) is obtained by the $|_5$ operation on an identity matrix. We thus have

$$
T_5 = \begin{bmatrix} 1 & 0 \\ (R_6 P_6) \big|_5 \end{bmatrix}. \tag{12.42}
$$

The submatrices for R_5 are obtained after subgrouping $a_p(\Sigma_5)$. We have $[a_7 a_1 a_{11}]^t = P_5 [a_1 a_7 a_{11}]^t$, or

$$
\begin{bmatrix} a_7 \\ a_1 \\ a_{11} \end{bmatrix} = \begin{bmatrix} 0 & 1 & 0 \\ 1 & 0 & 0 \\ 0 & 0 & 1 \end{bmatrix} \begin{bmatrix} a_1 \\ a_7 \\ a_{11} \end{bmatrix}. \tag{12.43}
$$

From (12.43), one can write

$$
a_c(E_5, \Sigma_4) = \begin{bmatrix} a_5 \\ a_6 \end{bmatrix} = R_5 P_5 T_5 \begin{bmatrix} a_1 \\ a_{14} \end{bmatrix} \tag{12.44}
$$

and

$$
a_p(\Sigma_4) = \begin{bmatrix} a_1 \\ a_5 \\ a_{11} \end{bmatrix} = T_4 \begin{bmatrix} a_1 \\ a_{14} \end{bmatrix} \tag{12.45a}
$$

where

$$T_4 = \begin{bmatrix} T_5 \big|_4 \\ \\ R_5\, P_5\, T_5 \big|_4 \end{bmatrix}.$$

(12.45b)

Proceeding in the manner described above, wave variables at all the internal ports can be obtained.

12.3 EVALUATION OF DIFFERENTIAL SCATTERING MATRICES

In this section, we obtain partial derivatives of S-matrices ($\partial S/\partial \phi$) for some typical elements. Sensitivity invariants for S-matrices are useful for obtaining these derivatives, and these are discussed in the following section.

12.3.1 Sensitivity Invariants for Scattering Matrices [7]

Some sensitivity invariants of S-matrices exist for networks composed of lumped resistors, inductors, capacitors, uniform transmission lines, and controlled sources. These sensitivity invariants for S-matrices are obtained by first considering the sensitivity invariants for Z-matrices. Considering the adjoint network N we can write the Tellegen's theorem as

$$\sum_c v_c \,\hat{i}_c = \sum_p v_p \,\hat{i}_p$$

(12.46)

where v_c and v_p are the voltages across the internal ports and external ports, respectively, for the original network; and $\hat{i}_c$ and $\hat{i}_p$ are the currents into the corresponding ports for the adjoint network. The unnormalized sensitivity of the element (i,j) of the overall impedance matrix with respect to a parameter p_k contained in an element with impedance matrix Z_e is given as

$$\frac{\partial Z_{ij}}{\partial p_k} = \hat{i}_B^t \, \frac{\partial Z_e}{\partial p_k} \, i_B$$

(12.47)

where $\hat{i}_B$ and i_B carry currents into the component ports for the adjoint and original networks, respectively. Here, we assume that the original network is excited by a unit current source at port j and the adjoint network is excited by a unit current source at port i, with all other ports in both the networks kept open.

For individual components, the variables are defined as: R_i for lumped resistors, L_i for lumped inductors, D_i (= $1/C_i$) for lumped capacitors, Z_i for characteristic impedances of uniform transmission lines, and r_{mi} for transfer resistances of current controlled voltage sources. Thus, the set of parameters considered are

$$\{z\} = \{R_i, L_i, D_i, Z_i, r_{mi}\} .$$
(12.48)

If p_k is one of the parameters listed in (12.48), then the component in which it is contained has an impedance matrix which is homogeneous of degree one. In other words, if p_k is contained in Z_e, then

$$p_k \frac{\partial Z_e}{\partial p_k} = Z_e$$
(12.49a)

and if p_k is not contained in Z_e

$$p_k \frac{\partial Z_e}{\partial p_k} = 0 .$$
(12.49b)

From (12.49a) and (12.47), it follows that if p_k is contained in Z_e,

$$p_k \frac{\partial Z_{ij}}{\partial p_k} = \hat{i}_B^t Z_e i_B$$
$$= \hat{i}_B^t v_B .$$
(12.50)

From (12.50), the sum over all the parameters p_k in (12.48) is given by

$$\sum_{p_k} p_k \frac{\partial Z_{ij}}{\partial p_k} = \sum_c v_c \hat{i}_c$$
(12.51)

which, using (12.46), reduces to

$$\sum_{p_k} p_k \frac{\partial Z_{ij}}{\partial p_k} = \sum_p v_p \hat{i}_p .$$
(12.52)

Since the adjoint network is excited by a unit current source at the external port i and all other external ports are open-circuited, the right-hand side of (12.52) is equal to v_i. Further, since the original network is excited by a unit current source at the external port j and all other ports are open-circuited, we have

$$\sum_p v_p\, i_p = v_i = Z_{ij}\, i_j = Z_{ij} \; . \tag{12.53}$$

It follows from (12.52) and (12.53) that

$$\sum_{p_k} p_k\, \frac{\partial Z_{ij}}{\partial p_k} = Z_{ij} \; . \tag{12.54}$$

Since the choice of indices (i,j) in the above discussion was arbitrary, we can conclude that

$$\sum_{p_k} p_k\, \frac{\partial Z}{\partial p_k} = Z \; . \tag{12.55}$$

From (12.54), it follows that

$$\sum_{p_k} \frac{p_k}{Z_{ij}}\, \frac{\partial Z_{ij}}{\partial p_k} = 1 \; . \tag{12.56}$$

The sum of normalized sensitivities of Z_{ij} is unity, independent of Z_{ij}. As the above discussion implies, if the component impedance matrices are homogeneous of degree one in the impedance parameters of (12.48), (as seen by (12.49)), the overall Z-matrix exhibits the same property.

To obtain sensitivity invariants in terms of the S-matrix of the network, we write S in terms of Z, as given by (2.36), and differentiate[*] to obtain

$$\frac{\partial S}{\partial p_k} = 2\,[\sqrt{Z_o}\,]\,(Z + Z_o)^{-1}\, \frac{\partial Z}{\partial p_k}\,(Z + Z_o)^{-1}\,[\sqrt{Z_o}\,] \; . \tag{12.57}$$

---

[*]Using the general formula
$$\frac{\partial}{\partial x}\, A^{-1} = -A^{-1}\, \frac{\partial A}{\partial x}\, A^{-1}$$

Taking the sum $p_k(\partial S/\partial p_k)$ over all p_k's in $\{z\}$ of (12.48) (excluding Z_{oi}'s, the normalizing impedances at various ports), we get

$$\sum_{p_k} p_k \frac{\partial S}{\partial p_k} = 2\,[\sqrt{Z_o}]\,(Z + Z_o)^{-1}$$

$$\cdot \sum_{p_k} p_k \frac{\partial Z}{\partial p_k}\,(Z + Z_o)^{-1}\,[\sqrt{Z_o}] \qquad (12.58)$$

which upon using (12.55) reduces to

$$\sum_{p_k} p_k \frac{\partial S}{\partial p_k} = 2\,[\sqrt{Z_o}]\,(Z + Z_o)^{-1}\,Z(Z + Z_o)^{-1}\,[\sqrt{Z_o}]$$

$$= \frac{1}{2}\,(I - S^2)\ . \qquad (12.59)$$

where S^2 indicates the product of S with itself and I is the identity matrix. It may be noted that p_k in (12.58) does not include normalizing impedances. If the summation is carried out over all normalizing impedances we get

$$\sum_{Z_{oi}} Z_{oi} \frac{\partial S}{\partial Z_{oi}} = -2\,[\sqrt{Z_o}]\,(Z + Z_o)^{-1}\,[\sqrt{Z_o}]$$

$$+ 2\,[\sqrt{Z_o}]\,(Z + Z_o)^{-1}\,Z_o(Z + Z_o)^{-1}\,[\sqrt{Z_o}]$$

$$= -2\,[\sqrt{Z_o}]\,(Z + Z_o)^{-1}\,Z(Z + Z_o)^{-1}\,[\sqrt{Z_o}]$$

$$= \frac{1}{2}\,(S^2 - I)\ . \qquad (12.60)$$

We see from (12.59) and (12.60) that, if the summation is carried out over all parameters in $\{z\}$ as well as all Z_{oi}'s, one gets

$$\sum_{p_k'} p_k' \frac{\partial S}{\partial p_k'} = 0\ , \qquad (12.61)$$

where p_k' indicates the parameters in $\{z\}$ as well as the normalizing impedances. It may be pointed out that p_k could be the corresponding admittance parameters also, in which case the expression on the right-hand side in (12.59) is negative. Hence, the sum of sensitivities with respect to all $\{z\}$ or $\{y\}$ parameters of the network, normalizing impedances or admittances included, is zero for all networks.

12.3.2 Differential S-matrices for Typical Components

The invariants derived above can be used for individual components also. In general, a component contains only one parameter of $\{z\}$, or its dual $\{y\}$. In such a case, we obtain from (12.59)

$$\frac{\partial S}{\partial \phi} = \frac{1}{2\phi} \; (I - S^2) \tag{12.62a}$$

when ϕ is a parameter from $\{z\}$, and

$$\frac{\partial S}{\partial \phi} = \frac{1}{2\phi} \; (S^2 - I) \tag{12.62b}$$

when ϕ is a parameter from $\{y\}$. For example, consider a series impedance Z interposed between two transmission lines of impedance Z_o. The S-matrix for this combination is given in Appendix 2.1, as

$$S = \frac{1}{(Z + 2Z_o)} \begin{bmatrix} Z & 2Z_o \\ \\ 2Z_o & Z \end{bmatrix}. \tag{12.63}$$

Its sensitivity can be obtained as

$$\frac{\partial S}{\partial Z} = \frac{1}{2Z} \; (I - S^2) = \frac{2Z_o}{(Z + 2Z_o)^2} \begin{bmatrix} 1 & -1 \\ -1 & 1 \end{bmatrix} \tag{12.64}$$

which is the same as obtained through direct differentiation. Since Z_o is the normalizing impedance on both ports of this component, $\partial S/\partial Z_o$ can be obtained from (12.60) as

$$\frac{\partial S}{\partial Z_o} = \frac{1}{2Z_o} \; (S^2 - I) = - \frac{2Z}{(Z + 2Z_o)^2} \begin{bmatrix} 1 & -1 \\ -1 & 1 \end{bmatrix} \tag{12.65}$$

which can be obtained by means of direct differentiation also. Hence, if the component contains only one parameter of $\{z\}$ or $\{y\}$, (12.62a) or (12.62b) can be used to obtain the derivative of the scattering matrix. Also, if the normalizing impedance is Z_{oi} on all the ports of a component, then

$$\frac{\partial S}{\partial Z_{oi}} = \frac{1}{2Z_{oi}} (S^2 - I) \tag{12.66a}$$

and

$$\frac{\partial S}{\partial Y_{oi}} = \frac{1}{2Y_{oi}} (I - S^2) \tag{12.66b}$$

where Y_{oi} is the characteristic admittance on all ports of the component. In cases where the normalizing impedances are different for the different ports of a component, direct differentiation has to be performed to obtain derivatives of S-matrix with respect to the normalizing impedances. Differential S-matrices for some typical components are listed in Appendix 12.1. For several other components given in Appendix 2.1, differential S-matrices can be obtained by using (12.62) and (12.66).

12.4 AN EXAMPLE ON EVALUATION OF SENSITIVITIES

A two-section maximally flat impedance transformer shown in Figure 12.4a is considered for evaluating sensitivities of the reflection coefficient. The effect of discontinuity reactance is ignored in order to keep the example simple. For finding the gradient using adjoint network method, the circuit is treated as a cascade of two-ports as shown in Figure 12.4(b). The performance parameter of interest is the reflection coefficient at the input port. All the components in this circuit are reciprocal and so the adjoint network is the same as the original network. The derivatives of S_{11} are to be obtained with respect to the line impedances Z_1 and Z_2.

In order to obtain the derivatives of S_{11}, both the original and the adjoint networks are excited by a matched source with output wave amplitude equal to unity at port 1, and port 2 is terminated in matched load. The analysis of the circuit at the center frequency gives normalized wave variables as shown in Figure 12.5(a). A change in Z_1

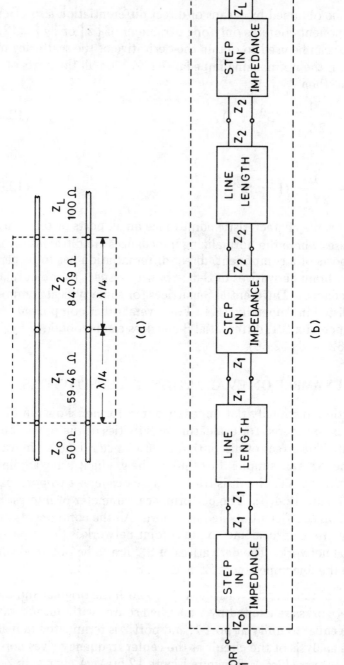

*Figure 12.4(a)   A two-section quarter wave transformer circuit.
(b)   The quarter wave transformer of (a) represented as a cascade of two-port components.*

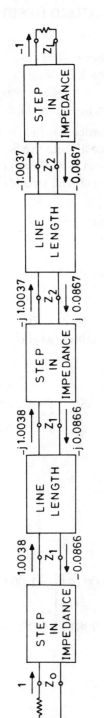
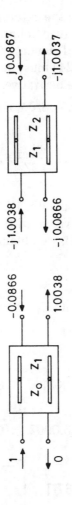
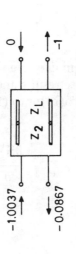

Figure 12.5 (a)   Values of wave variables inside the network of Figure 12.4(b).
(b)   Values of wave variables at three impedance steps in the transformer.

or Z_2 affects the S-matrices of the two steps at either end of the line section Z_1 or Z_2. S-matrices of components marked "line length" are unaffected by the change in Z_1 or Z_2. Normalized wave variables at the three affected steps are shown again in Figure 12.5(b).

The circuit is matched at both the external ports, hence $\partial a_p/\partial \phi = 0$ and (12.21) holds. Since a change in line impedance affects the S-matrices of two components of the network, the term $a^t (\partial S^t/\partial \phi) \, \alpha$ on the right-hand side of (12.24) must be summed over the two affected components to find the derivative.

Four matrices corresponding to $\partial S/\partial \phi$, namely

$$\frac{\partial S_{\text{step 1}}}{\partial Z_1}, \quad \frac{\partial S_{\text{step 2}}}{\partial Z_1}, \quad \frac{\partial S_{\text{step 2}}}{\partial Z_2} \quad \text{and} \quad \frac{\partial S_{\text{step 2}}}{\partial Z_3}, \text{ are obtained}$$

from the formulae given in Appendix 12.1 (item 2 with $Z = 0$). Substituting these results and the values of the wave variables (as shown in Figure 12.5(b)) into (12.24), we obtain

$$\frac{\partial S_{11}}{\partial Z_1} = a^t_{\text{step 1}} \frac{\partial S^t_{\text{step 1}}}{\partial Z_1} \alpha_{\text{step 1}} + a^t_{\text{step 2}} \frac{\partial S^t_{\text{step 2}}}{\partial Z_1} \alpha_{\text{step 2}}$$

or

$$\frac{\partial S_{11}}{\partial Z_1} = [1 \quad -0.0866] \begin{bmatrix} 0.0083 & -0.0007 \\ -0.0007 & -0.0083 \end{bmatrix} \begin{bmatrix} 1 \\ -0.0866 \end{bmatrix}$$

$$+ [-1.0038j \quad 0.0867j] \begin{bmatrix} -0.0081 & 0.0014 \\ 0.0014 & 0.0081 \end{bmatrix} \begin{bmatrix} -1.0038j \\ 0.0867j \end{bmatrix}$$

$$= 0.016642 . \tag{12.67}$$

Similarly,

$$\frac{\partial S_{11}}{\partial Z_2} = [-1.0038j \quad 0.0867j] \begin{bmatrix} 0.0057 & -0.001 \\ -0.001 & -0.0057 \end{bmatrix} \begin{bmatrix} -1.0038j \\ 0.0867j \end{bmatrix}$$

$$+ [-1.0037 \quad 0] \begin{bmatrix} 0.0059 & 0.0005 \\ 0.0005 & -0.0059 \end{bmatrix} \begin{bmatrix} -1.0037 \\ 0 \end{bmatrix}$$

$$= -0.011823 . \tag{12.68}$$

These values of $\partial S_{11}/\partial Z_1$ and $\partial S_{11}/\partial Z_2$ can be used for circuit optimization or tolerance analysis. When the above circuit is realized using striplines, the sensitivity of S_{11} with respect to ϵ_r may be calculated from

$$\frac{\partial S_{11}}{\partial \epsilon_r} = \left(\frac{\partial S_{11}}{\partial Z_1} \frac{\partial Z_1}{\partial \epsilon_r} + \frac{\partial S_{11}}{\partial Z_2} \frac{\partial Z_2}{\partial \epsilon_r} \right)$$

$$+ \left(\frac{\partial S_{11}}{\partial \theta_1} \frac{\partial \theta_1}{\partial \epsilon_r} + \frac{\partial S_{11}}{\partial \theta_2} \frac{\partial \theta_2}{\partial \epsilon_r} \right) \tag{12.69}$$

where θ_1 and θ_2 are electrical lengths of two sections, respectively, and ϵ_r is the relative dielectric constant of the substrate, assumed to be uniform over the circuit area. However, we assume that Z_0 and Z_L are not influenced by substrate parameters.

12.5 LARGE CHANGE SENSITIVITIES [8]

Evaluation of sensitivities of network performance parameters can be used to calculate changes in performance caused by a small perturbation in circuit parameters. This information is of use in circuit optimization as well as in tolerance analysis. However, in the case of tolerance analysis, if parameter tolerances are not very small, the change in performance obtained using sensitivities would not be exact since the higher order terms are neglected in this method. Hence, if the deviation is large, it is also desirable to obtain the characterization of the perturbed network. This section describes an approach to analyzing a perturbed network using a method which requires less computational effort than that required to analyze the network again.

Consider a network with m components, including independent generators. The network is analyzed using connection scattering matrix approach described earlier in Section 11.2.1. The wave variables are obtained using

$$b = S a + c \qquad\qquad (12.70)$$

$$b = \mathbf{\Gamma} a , \qquad\qquad (12.71)$$

and

$$a = (\mathbf{\Gamma} - S)^{-1} c . \qquad\qquad (12.72)$$

Now, let us suppose that a parameter ϕ is perturbed in the network, causing changes in the characterization of the S-matrix for the kth component from S_k to S_k^*. If the changed parameter is not one of the components of c, Equation (12.70) for the perturbed network can be modified to

$$b^* = S^* a^* + c \qquad\qquad (12.73)$$

where the asterisk indicates that the variable corresponds to the perturbed network, For the kth component, (12.70) gives

$$b_k^* = S_k^* a_k^* + c_k . \qquad\qquad (12.74)$$

Let

$$S_k^* = S_k + \Delta S_k . \qquad\qquad (12.75)$$

Therefore, (12.74) can be written as

$$b_k^* = S_k a_k^* + \Delta S_k a_k^* + c_k$$

$$= S_k a_k^* + (c_k + \Delta c_k) \qquad\qquad (12.76)$$

where

$$\Delta c_k = \Delta S_k a_k^* . \qquad\qquad (12.77)$$

The perturbed component can thus be replaced by the unperturbed component with a set of supplementary impressed waves at its ports. The wave variables a^*, at all the component ports, can now be written as

$$a^* = (\mathbf{\Gamma} - S)^{-1} c^* \qquad\qquad (12.78)$$

where

$$c^* = c + \Delta c .$$ (12.79)

From (12.78) and (12.79), we have

$$a^* = (\Gamma - S)^{-1} c + (\Gamma - S)^{-1} \Delta c$$ (12.80)

which, using (12.72), reduces to

$$a^* = a + (\Gamma - S)^{-1} \Delta c .$$ (12.81)

Since the perturbed parameter affects only the characterization of the kth component, Δc is nonzero only for rows corresponding to the ports of the kth component. If the n ports of the kth component are numbered as $k_1, k_2, \ldots, k_n$, (12.81) can be written as

$$a^* = a + (\Gamma - S)^{-1} \left| \begin{pmatrix} 1, & \ldots, & N \\ k_1, & \ldots, & k_n \end{pmatrix} \right. \Delta c_k$$ (12.82)

where the marker of the type

$$\left| \begin{pmatrix} m, & \ldots, & n \\ p, & \ldots, & q \end{pmatrix} \right.$$

is used to denote a matrix reduced to the elements of the rows m, ..., n and the columns p, ..., q. For the present case, in (12.82) for $(\Gamma - S)^{-1}$, only the columns corresponding to ports of the kth component have been retained. In (12.82), a^* contains incoming wave variables at ports of all the components. Incoming wave variables at ports of the kth component are contained in a^* in its rows $k_1, \ldots, k_n$. Hence, we can write

$$a_k^* = a_k + (\Gamma - S)^{-1} \left| \begin{pmatrix} k_1, & \ldots, & k_n \\ k_1, & \ldots, & k_n \end{pmatrix} \right. \Delta c_k$$ (12.83)

which, on multiplying both sides by ΔS_k, reduces to

$$\Delta c_k = \Delta S_k a_k + \Delta S_k (\Gamma - S)^{-1} \left| \begin{pmatrix} k_1, & \ldots, & k_n \\ k_1, & \ldots, & k_n \end{pmatrix} \right. \Delta c_k .$$ (12.84)

We can obtain Δc_k from (12.84) as

$$\Delta c_k = \left[I - \Delta S_k (\Gamma - S)^{-1} \Big|_{\left(\begin{array}{c} k_1, \ldots, k_n \\ k_1, \ldots, k_n \end{array}\right)} \right]^{-1} \Delta S_k \, a_k \quad (12.85)$$

where I is an identity matrix of order n. The value of c_k as obtained above can be substituted in (12.82) to obtain incoming wave variables at all the component ports in the network.

The matrix inversion required in (12.85) involves a matrix of size n only, and hence the additional computational effort for large change sensitivity evaluation is small. It should be noted here that, if the perturbation in a parameter affects more than one component, then Δc would be nonzero in the rows corresponding to the ports of all the affected components. The above discussion is still valid except that the size of matrix to be inverted would now be larger. It would be equal to the sum of the numbers of ports of all affected components.

Various aspects of sensitivity analysis discussed in this chapter are useful for the tolerance analysis discussed in Chapter 13 and optimization techniques discussed in Chapter 18.

APPENDIX 12.1: DIFFERENTIAL SCATTERING MATRICES FOR SOME TYPICAL COMPONENTS

Component	Variable Parameter	Differential S-matrices
1. A transmission line section	a) ℓ	$-j\beta \begin{bmatrix} 0 & e^{-j\beta\ell} \\ e^{-j\beta\ell} & 0 \end{bmatrix}$
2. A series impedance	a)* Z	$\dfrac{2}{D_s^2}\begin{bmatrix} Z_1 & -\sqrt{Z_1 Z_2} \\ -\sqrt{Z_1 Z_2} & Z_2 \end{bmatrix}$
	b) Z_1	$\dfrac{1}{D_s^2}\begin{bmatrix} -2(Z+Z_2) & (Z-Z_1+Z_2)\sqrt{\dfrac{Z_2}{Z_1}} \\ (Z-Z_1+Z_2)\sqrt{\dfrac{Z_2}{Z_1}} & 2Z_2 \end{bmatrix}$

Component	Variable Parameter	Differential S-matrices

c) Z_2

$$\frac{1}{D_s^2}\begin{bmatrix} 2Z_1 & (Z+Z_1-Z_2)\sqrt{\dfrac{Z_1}{Z_2}} \\[2ex] (Z+Z_1-Z_2)\sqrt{\dfrac{Z_1}{Z_2}} & -2(Z+Z_1) \end{bmatrix}$$

where $D_s = Z + Z_1 + Z_2$

a)* Y

$$-\frac{2}{D_s^2}\begin{bmatrix} Y_1 & \sqrt{Y_1 Y_2} \\[1ex] \sqrt{Y_1 Y_2} & Y_2 \end{bmatrix}$$

b) Y_1

$$\frac{1}{D_s^2}\begin{bmatrix} 2(Y+Y_2) & (Y-Y_1+Y_2)\sqrt{\dfrac{Y_2}{Y_1}} \\[2ex] (Y-Y_1+Y_2)\sqrt{\dfrac{Y_2}{Y_1}} & -2Y_2 \end{bmatrix}$$

3. A shunt admittance

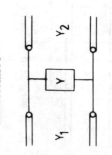

c) Y_2

$$\frac{1}{D_s^2}\begin{bmatrix} -2Y_1 & (Y+Y_1-Y_2)\sqrt{\dfrac{Y_1}{Y_2}} \\[2ex] (Y+Y_1-Y_2)\sqrt{\dfrac{Y_1}{Y_2}} & 2(Y+Y_1) \end{bmatrix}$$

where $D_s = Y + Y_1 + Y_2$

4. An ideal transformer

$Z_0=1$ $Z_0=1$

$n:1$

a) n

$$\frac{2}{(n^2+1)^2}\begin{bmatrix} 2n & 1-n^2 \\[1ex] 1-n^2 & -2n \end{bmatrix}$$

5. A junction of three transmission lines

Y_1, Y_2, Y_3

a) Y_1

$$\frac{1}{D_s^2}\begin{bmatrix} 2(Y_2+Y_3) & (Y_2+Y_3-Y_1)\sqrt{\dfrac{Y_2}{Y_1}} & (Y_2+Y_3-Y_1)\sqrt{\dfrac{Y_3}{Y_1}} \\[2ex] (Y_2+Y_3-Y_1)\sqrt{\dfrac{Y_2}{Y_1}} & -2Y_2 & -2\sqrt{Y_2 Y_3} \\[2ex] (Y_2+Y_3-Y_1)\sqrt{\dfrac{Y_3}{Y_1}} & -2\sqrt{Y_2 Y_3} & -2Y_3 \end{bmatrix}$$

where $D_s = Y_1 + Y_2 + Y_3$

Component	Variable Parameter	Differential S-matrices

6. A transmission line section of impedance Z interposed in a transmission line of impedance Z_o

Z_o $Z, \beta l$ Z_o $\longleftrightarrow l \longleftrightarrow$

a) ℓ

$$R\begin{bmatrix} 2Q\, e^{-j\beta\ell} & 1 + Q^2\, e^{-2j\beta\ell} \\[4pt] 1 + Q^2\, e^{-2j\beta\ell} & 2Q\, e^{-j\beta\ell} \end{bmatrix}$$

where $Q = (Z_o - Z)/(Z_o + Z)$, $R = -j\beta P\, e^{-j\beta\ell}/[1 - Q^2\, e^{-2j\beta\ell}]^2$

with $P = 4ZZ_o/(Z + Z_o)^2$

b)* Z

$$-\frac{1}{2Z}\begin{bmatrix} S^2 + T^2 - 1 & 2\,ST \\[4pt] 2\,ST & S^2 + T^2 - 1 \end{bmatrix}$$

c)* Z_o

$$\frac{1}{2Z_o}\begin{bmatrix} S^2 + T^2 - 1 & 2\,ST \\[4pt] 2\,ST & S^2 + T^2 - 1 \end{bmatrix}$$

where $S = j(Z^2 - Z_o^2)\sin\beta\ell / D_s$; $T = 2ZZ_o/D_s$

with $D_s = 2ZZ_o\cos\beta\ell + j(Z^2 + Z_o^2)\sin\beta\ell$

*These differential scattering matrices are obtained using relations (12.62) and (12.66).

REFERENCES

[1] Calahan, D.A., *Computer-Aided Network Design*, New York: McGraw-Hill, 1972, Ch. 5, "Sensitivity Calculations."

[2] Chua, L.O., and P.M. Lin, *Computer-Aided Analysis of Electronic Circuits: Algorithms and Computational Techniques*, Englewood Cliffs, New Jersey: Prentice-Hall Inc., 1975, Ch. 15, "Frequency-Domain and Time-Domain Sensitivity Calculations."

[3] Fidler, J.K., and C. Nightingale, *Computer Aided Circuit Design*, Middlesex U.K.: Thomas Nelson and Sons Ltd., 1978, Ch. 6 on "Sensitivity."

[4] Iuculano, G., *et al.*, "A Computer Program for Sensitivity and Group Delay Evaluation of Linear Networks," *Alta Freq.*, Vol. 40, Nov. 1971, pp. 873-880.

[5] Bandler, J.W., and R.E. Seviora, "Wave Sensitivities of Networks," *IEEE Trans. Microwave Theory Tech.*, Vol. MTT-20, Feb. 1972, pp. 138-147.

[6] Rauscher, C., "A Fast Evaluation of S-parameter Sensitivities," *A.E.U.*, Band 28, Heft 3, 1974, pp. 113-114.

[7] Sablatash, M., and R. Seviora, "Sensitivity Invariants for Scattering Matrices," *IEEE Trans. Circuit Theory*, Vol. CT-18, Mar. 1971, pp. 282-284.

[8] Rauscher, C., and G. Epprecht, "Large-change Sensitivity Analysis of a Microwave Network by Means of Scattering Parameters," *A.E.U.*, Band 28, Heft 2, 1974, pp. 95-96.

13

Tolerance
Analysis

An important step in the computer-aided design of circuits is the
tolerance analysis [1] - [3]. Once the circuit has been designed to
achieve certain performance criteria, it is desirable to study the
effect of uncertainties in component behavior on the circuit performance. The parameter uncertainties are caused by fabrication
tolerances, modelling approximations, and measurement errors.
The effect of parameter uncertainties on the circuit performance
can be evaluated using the techniques of tolerance analysis discussed in this chapter. To do so, we need to know the possible
uncertainties in the designable parameters of the circuit under
consideration.

There are two broad approaches to tolerance analysis: the worst-
case tolerance analysis and the statistical tolerance analysis. In
the worst-case analysis, one obtains the effect of the worst combination of parameter tolerances on the performance. For this purpose, the deviations in parameter values which have maximum cumulative impact on the performance must be obtained. Circuits
may be designed so that even in the worst-case the performance
criteria are met. This stringent requirement is necessary for the
design of highly reliable systems so that a circuit contained in
the system must perform flawlessly even in the worst-case conditions. Such a circuit would obviously be uneconomical for mass
production.

Statistical tolerance analysis requires not only the tolerances in parameter values but also the information about their statistical distributions within the tolerance limits. This information is used to find the probability that the circuit will meet its specifications. The analysis is useful for circuits which will be produced in large numbers, so that an estimate of yield (percentage of circuits meeting the performance criteria) can be obtained. Tolerance analysis can also be used for design centering and tolerance assignment [4] - [6].

13.1 WORST-CASE ANALYSIS

Given the range of values for each designable parameter, worst-case analysis allows one to obtain the range of values that are taken by various performance parameters. The range of values taken by the designable parameters are governed by their tolerances and the extreme values taken by the performance parameters correspond to the worst-case.

Method of Analysis

Let a set of network performance parameters u_i be controlled by designable parameters p_j. This dependence can be expressed in functional form as

$$u = f(p) \tag{13.1}$$

where the vector u is expressed as

$$u = [u_1, u_2, \ldots, u_m]^t \tag{13.2}$$

and

$$p = [p_1, p_2, \ldots, p_n]^t \tag{13.3}$$

with t representing the transpose. We define tolerances on p_j and u_i as the range of values these variables can take i.e.,

$$p_j^- \leqslant p_j \leqslant p_j^+, \quad \forall j \in \{1, 2, \ldots, n\} \tag{13.4}$$

and

$$u_i^- \leqslant u_i \leqslant u_i^+, \quad \forall i \in \{1, 2, \ldots, m\}. \tag{13.5}$$

The worst-case tolerance analysis problem can now be stated as follows. Given p_j^- and p_j^+ for all j, use the functional relationship (13.1) to obtain u_i^- and u_i^+ for all i. The nominal values of the parameters p_j are denoted by p_j^o, around which the perturbations are considered. The deviation in a performance parameter u_i can be written in terms of perturbations in parameters p_j as

$$\delta u_i = \sum_{j=1}^{n} \left(\frac{\partial u_i}{\partial p_j} \right) \Bigg|_{p_j = p_j^o} \circ \ \delta p_j \qquad (13.6)$$

where the perturbations δp_j are expressed as

$$\delta p_j = p_j - p_j^o , \quad \forall j \in \left\{ 1, 2, \ldots, n \right\} . \qquad (13.7)$$

In (13.6), $\partial u_i / \partial p_j$ are obtained by carrying out the sensitivity analysis of the circuit. To obtain the worst-case deviations in u_i, the worst-case maximum values for the right-hand side of (13.6) are evaluated. The largest change in u_i can be obtained from (13.6) by making p_j in (13.7) take either the value p_j^- or p_j^+ , depending on the sign of $\partial u_i / \partial p_j$. The largest positive value of δu_i is obtained when the signs of δp_j and $\partial u_i / \partial p_j$ are the same for each j, and the largest negative value of δu_i is obtained when the sign of δp_j is chosen to be opposite to the sign of $\partial u_i / \partial p_j$.

If the tolerance in a parameter p_j is large, its contribution to δu_i is obtained differently from that for small changes discussed above. To evaluate this contribution, first the sign of δp_j is decided by the sign of $\partial u_i / \partial p_j$, as in the case of small tolerances. Values of u_i are then calculated for the two values of p_j given by p_j^o and $p_j^o + \delta p_j$, as discussed in the previous chapter (section 12.5). The difference between these two values of u_i is the contribution of large change in parameter p_j to u_i. An alternative to this procedure is to reanalyze the network for parameter values p_j^+ or p_j^- , depending upon the sign of $\partial u_i / \partial p_j$. This is desirable when many of the parameters have large tolerances.

In most cases, the method discussed above can be used to obtain worst-case values. However, if a performance parameter u_i is defined in terms of a vector quantity (e.g. VSWR in terms of reflection coefficient, which is complex) the above procedure may yield pessimistic results. Considering the example of the input VSWR, we can write its derivative with respect to a parameter p_j, using (12.1), as

$$\frac{\partial(\text{VSWR})}{\partial p_j} = \frac{2\,|S_{11}|}{(1 - |S_{11}|)^2}\,\text{Re}\left[\frac{1}{S_{11}}\,\frac{\partial S_{11}}{\partial p_j}\right] \qquad (13.8)$$

and use (13.6) to obtain worst-case VSWR. But this procedure leads to pessimistic results. More accurate results can be obtained if the maximum and the minimum magnitudes of S_{11} are obtained using the general procedure discussed below. These magnitudes can then be used to obtain the worst-case values of VSWR. An algorithm for obtaining the minimum and maximum magnitudes of a vector performance parameter u, is described below.

Worst Case Values for Vector Performance Parameters

We assume that, for each designable parameter p_j, the tolerances in positive and negative directions are equal. In other words, we have

$$p_j^+ + p_j^- = 2p_j^o \text{ , for each j.} \qquad (13.9)$$

The upper and lower limits on a parameter p_j differ equally from its nominal value. The algorithm to be described uses the deviations (in performance) δu_j caused by the deviation in a parameter p_j. The incremental deviations δu_j can be obtained as

$$\delta u_j = \left.\frac{\partial u}{\partial p_j}\right|_{p_j^o} (p_j^+ - p_j^o) \text{ , } \quad j = 1, 2, \ldots, n \text{ .} \qquad (13.10)$$

In general, the modified parameter u can be written as

$$u = u^o + \sum_{j=1}^{n} \mu_j\,\delta u_j \qquad (13.11)$$

where μ_1, μ_2..... μ_n are parameters describing the particular model under consideration and u^o is the nominal value of u. The parameters μ_j take values between -1 and 1, or

$$-1 \leqslant \mu_j \leqslant 1 \text{ , } \quad j = 1, 2, \ldots, n \text{ .} \qquad (13.12)$$

We need to obtain maximum and minimum magnitudes of u from the range of possible values obtained in (13.11) and (13.12).

Evaluation of Worst Case Maximum

The problem of finding the values of u with maximum magnitudes is relatively simple, since in this case the values of μ_j in (13.11) are +1 and −1 only. The problem can be reformulated as follows: given the nominal value u^o and the incremental values δu_j, we are going to determine for each δu_j whether it must be added to or subtracted from u^o to get u_{max} (i.e. μ_j is +1 or −1).

The algorithm for this purpose was obtained empirically [7]. The δu_j's are added to u or subtracted from u , one by one, in a fixed order. (At any stage during the process of obtaining u_{max} , u indicates the sum of u^o and $\mu_j \, \delta u_j$, already added). Whether a particular δu_j is added to or subtracted from u can be decided by checking whether $(u + \delta u_j)$ or $(u - \delta u_j)$ has the higher magnitude, depending upon the sign of the inner product of u and δu_j. If the sign is positive, δu_j is added to u, otherwise it is subtracted. This is illustrated in Figure 13.1. The order in which $\mu_j \, \delta u_j$'s are added to u is decided as follows. At every stage, we select a δu_j out of the remaining δu_j's, so that the magnitude of $(u \pm \delta u_j)$ is highest. This can be done by choosing the j which leads to the highest value of ($\| \delta u_j \|^2 + 2 | u \cdot \delta u_j |$), where $\| x \|$ indicates the norm $\sqrt{(x \circ x)}$ of a multidimensional vector x. The process is re-

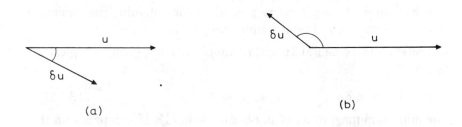

(a)   (b)

Figure 13.1(a) Addition of δu to u for obtaining the worst-case maximum.

(b) Subtraction of δu from u for obtaining the worst-case maximum.

peated till all δu_j's are added or subtracted. This procedure can now be stated as follows.

u $\quad$ = u^o // u^o is the nominal value //

U $\quad$ = $\{1, 2, \ldots, n\}$ // U is the set of available indices of δu_j's //

For all j $= 1$ *to* n *do* $b_j = \delta u_j \cdot \delta u_j$

Repeat

$\quad$ *For all* j $\in$ U *do* $c_j = u \cdot \delta u_j$

$\quad$ Select k $\in$ U such that $(b_k + 2 \, \text{Abs}(c_k))$ has the highest value // Abs( ) takes absolute value //

$\quad$ u = u + $\text{sign}(c_k) \, \delta u_k$ // sign( ) is +1 if the argument is positive

$\qquad\qquad\qquad\qquad\qquad$ otherwise it is -1 //

$\quad$ U = U $- \{k\}$

until U is empty

In the above procedure the sign (c_k) gives the value of μ_k(1 or -1) as described earlier.

Evaluation of Worst Case Minimum

The procedure for finding the worst-case minimum magnitude of u is more intricate, since μ_j in (13.11) can take all possible values between -1 and +1. An iterative procedure for obtaining the minimum magnitude has been obtained empirically [7].

Consider an incremental δu and nominal value u^o, giving a typical u as

$$u = u^o + \mu \, \delta u , \qquad -1 \leqslant \mu \leqslant 1 . \qquad (13.13)$$

The minimum magnitude of u, obtainable in (13.13), depends on the relative orientation of u^o and δu. Consider the three orientations shown in Figure 13.2. For the case shown in Figure 13.2(a), $\mu = -1$ would yield the minimum magnitude value u_{min} . On the other hand, for the case shown in Figure 13.2(b) a negative value of μ, less than 1, will yield u_{min}; whereas for the case shown in Figure 13.2(c), μ will be positive and less than unity. The value of u_{min} can be obtained

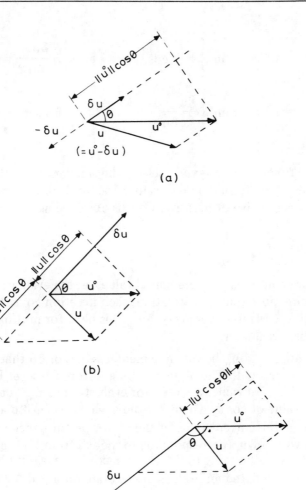

Figure 13.2(a) The case where μ = −1 yields the minimum.

(b) The case where a negative value of μ(less than 1) yields the minimum.

(c) The case where a positive value of μ (less than 1) yields the minimum.

from

$$u_{min} = u^o - \min \left\{ \| u^o \cos \theta \| , \| \delta u \| \right\} \frac{\delta u}{\| \delta u \|} \, sign(\cos \theta)$$

$$= u^o - \min \left\{ \frac{\| u^o \cos \theta \|}{\| \delta u \|} , 1 \right\} \delta u \, sign(\cos \theta)$$

$$(13.14)$$

where the function min $\{x,y\}$ selects the smaller of the two quantities x and y, and sign (x) takes values 1 and -1, depending upon whether x is positive or negative. Cos θ is obtained as

$$\cos \theta = \frac{u^o \circ \delta u}{\| u^o \| \, \| \delta u \|} . \qquad (13.15)$$

If there are a number of incremental values u, the evaluation of u_{min} may require more than one iteration, each iteration consisting of operation (13.14) used for every δu. This need for multiple iterations is discussed later.

Let $\delta u_1, \delta u_2, \ldots \delta u_n$ be the incremental values of δu that can be added or subtracted. The indices of δu are stored as a set U. The order in which δu values are used for evaluation of u_{min} depends upon the value of $\cos \theta$, where θ is the angle between δu and u, with u being the current value of the vector performance parameter. To begin with, a δu_i (corresponding to index i from U) is chosen so that $\cos \theta_i$ corresponding to it has the maximum magnitude. After this step, u is updated and values of $\cos \theta$ are obtained for remaining δu values. Again, a δu_i which gives the maximum magnitude of $\cos \theta$ is chosen and the process repeated until all the indices in the set U have been considered.

The procedure for the first iteration can now be stated as follows:

U = $\{1, 2, \ldots, n\}$

Repeat

   For all j $\in$ U *do*

     begin

       Obtain $\cos \theta_j$ (between u and δu_j) using (13.15)

     end (for j)

Select $k \in U$, such that
$$|\cos \theta_k| \geqslant |\cos \theta_j| \text{ for all } j \in U$$
$$U = U - \{k\}$$
Update u using (13.14)

until U is empty.

The procedure is illustrated in the following example.

Example

Consider the case where the performance parameter u is a complex quantity (i.e. two-dimensional vector) and there are two δu values. Let

$$u^o \doteq 10 + j0$$
$$\delta u_1 = -6 + j\,2\sqrt{3}$$
$$\delta u_2 = 6 + j\,2\sqrt{3} \quad .$$

We know that the worst case minimum for this particular example is zero, since

$$u_{min} = u^o + \frac{5}{6}\,(\delta u_1 - \delta u_2) = 0 \ .$$

However, if the above procedure is used, we have

$$U = \{1, 2\}$$
$$\cos \theta_1 = \frac{10(-6)}{10(4\sqrt{3})} = -\frac{\sqrt{3}}{2}$$
$$\cos \theta_2 = \frac{10(6)}{10(4\sqrt{3})} = \frac{\sqrt{3}}{2} \quad .$$

Let $k = 1$ be chosen initially.

$$u = u^o - \min\left\{\frac{\|u^o \cos \theta\|}{\|\delta u\|}, 1\right\} \delta u \, \text{sign}(\cos \theta)$$
$$= 10 - \min\{1.25, 1\}\,\delta u_1\,(-1)$$
$$= 10 + \delta u_1 = 4 + j\,2\sqrt{3} \quad .$$

Now $U = \{2\}$

$$\therefore \; \cos\theta_2 \;=\; \frac{24 + 12}{2\sqrt{7}\cdot 4\sqrt{3}} \;=\; \frac{9}{2\sqrt{21}}$$

$$u \;=\; u \;-\; \min\left\{ \frac{\|u\cos\theta\|}{\|\,\delta u\,\|}\,,\; 1 \right\}\, \delta u \;\text{sign}(\cos\theta)$$

$$=\; (4 + j\,2\sqrt{3}) \;-\; \min\left\{ \frac{3}{4}\,,\; 1 \right\}\, \delta u_2$$

$$=\; (4 + j\,2\sqrt{3}) \;-\; \frac{3}{4}\,(6 + j\,2\sqrt{3})$$

$$=\; -\frac{1}{2} \;-\; j\,\frac{\sqrt{3}}{2}$$

which is the value of u obtained after the first iteration. Thus, more than one iteration is required to obtain u_{min}.

Procedure Using Multiple Iterations

It should be noted that, if $\mu_j\,\delta u_j$ is added in one iteration, $(1 - \mu_j)\,\delta u_j$ is available for addition and $(1 + \mu_j)\,\delta u_j$ is available for subtraction from u in the next iteration. That is, in the next iteration, the magnitudes of incremental deviations available for addition and subtraction are unequal. Therefore, we store unit vectors along δu_j's as s_j's, and also the magnitudes of δu_j's for movement in the positive s_j direction are stored as g_{1j}, and as g_{2j} for movement in the negative s_j direction.

The value of $\cos\theta_j$ for any s_j is now determined as

$$\cos\theta_j \;=\; \frac{u \circ s_j}{\|u\|} \qquad\qquad\qquad (13.16)$$

To add the deviations along $\pm s_j$ to u the following criterion is adopted:

$$\textit{If } \cos\theta_j > 0, \quad \textit{then } \;\Delta = \min\left\{ \|u\cos\theta_j\|\,,\; g_{2j} \right\}$$
$$\textit{else } \;\Delta = \min\left\{ \|u\cos\theta_j\|\,,\; g_{1j} \right\}$$

$$u \;=\; u \;-\; s_j\,\Delta\,\text{sign}(\cos\theta_j)$$

$$g_{1j} \;=\; g_{1j} \;+\; \Delta\,\text{sign}(\cos\theta_j)$$

$$g_{2j} \;=\; g_{2j} \;-\; \Delta\,\text{sign}(\cos\theta_j)$$

The overall procedure for obtaining u_{min} can now be described as follows:

For all j = 1 *to* n *do*

   begin

      $g_{1j} = \| \boldsymbol{\delta} u_j \|$

      $g_{2j} = g_{1j}$

      $s_j = \boldsymbol{\delta} u_j / g_{1j}$

   end (for j)

$W = \{1, 2, \ldots, n\}$

$u = u^o$

Repeat

   U = W

   Repeat

      For all j $\in$ U *do*

         begin

            Obtain $\cos \theta_j$ (between u and s_j) using (13.16)

         end (for j)

      Select k $\in$ U such that

         $|\cos \theta_k| > |\cos \theta_j|$ for all j $\in$ U

      Add deviation along $\pm s_k$ using the procedure described above

      $U = U - \{k\}$

   until U is empty

 until no further change in u is seen in the previous iteration

$u_{min} = u$

These iterations are continued until the values of u converge. This would happen if, for each i $\in$ W, either s_i is orthogonal to u (i.e., $\cos \theta_i = 0$), or $g_{2i} = 0$ for $\cos \theta_i$ positive, or $g_{1i} = 0$ for $\cos \theta_i$ negative.

A Modified Procedure for Worst-case Minimum

The procedure described above leads to the minimum magnitude value of u (i.e., u_{min}). In some cases, however, the convergence towards u_{min} can be slow. For example, in the case shown in Figure 13.3(a), δu_1 and δu_2 are very nearly orthogonal to u^o. The angles between u^o and δu_1, and u^o and δu_2 are both $(\pi/2 + \alpha)$. If both δu_1 and δu_2 are added to u^o ($\mu = 1$), u_{min} is obtained. However, if the procedure described earlier is used for this case, the convergence to u_{min} is very slow. This is because the magnitude of $\cos \theta_k$ chosen in the first iteration is $|\cos(\pi/2 + \alpha)| = \sin \alpha$, and in all subsequent iterations till convergence its magnitude is $\sin 2\alpha$. This is illustrated in Figure 13.3(b). It is assumed here that deviation along δu_2 is added first. Further, we assume that the magnitudes of incremental deviations δu_1 and δu_2 are large, so that initially the amount of deviations added to u are restricted by their angular position and not by their magnitudes. The convergence can be speeded up if, in subsequent iterations, we take the unit vector along total change in u in the previous iteration, in addition to unit vectors along δu_1, δu_2, ... Besides δu_j values, combinations of δu_j are also considered for incremental deviations to u. For the case shown in Figure 13.3(b), total change in u in the first iteration is AC. If, in the second iteration, we also choose a unit vector along AC, then the $\cos \theta_j$ for the angle θ_j (between the unit vector along AC and u) has higher magnitude than $\cos \theta_j$ for any s_j and u. The angle β, as shown in Figure 13.3(b), is given by

$$\beta = \alpha + \tan^{-1} \left[\frac{\sin 4\alpha}{4(1 - \cos^2\alpha \ \cos 2\alpha)} \right] \qquad (13.17)$$

and tends toward 2α for α approaching zero. Hence, by including the combination of u's in the previous iteration, the magnitude of $\cos \theta_k$ for the unit vector chosen increases from $\sin 2\alpha$ to about $\cos 2\alpha$ (for small values of α). This leads to faster convergence to u_{min}.

We now describe the modified algorithm for obtaining u_{min} so that combinations of δu are included for adding incremental deviations to u.

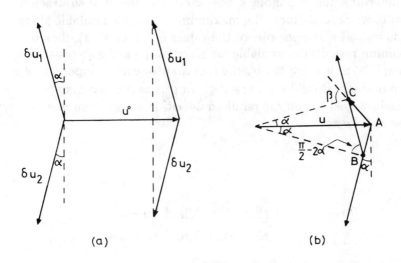

Figure 13.3(a)   *The case where δu_1 and δu_2 are very nearly ortho-*
                   gonal to u_o.

        (b)   *Changes in u in the first iteration for the case*
               shown in (a).

Let us denote unit vectors along combinations of δu_j by $s_{n+1}, \ldots,$
s_k. These unit vectors are linear combinations of $s_1, \ldots, s_n$ and may
be written as

$$s_i = \sum_{j=1}^{n} h_{ij} s_j , \quad \forall i \in \{n+1, n+2, \ldots, k\} . \quad (13.18)$$

To obtain the values of h_{ij} in (13.18), we use a set of variables r_1,
$r_2, \ldots, r_n$ to add up moves along $s_1, s_2, \ldots, s_n$. In every iteration,
the moves along $s_1, s_2, \ldots, s_n$ are added up in variables $r_1, r_2, \ldots,$
r_n. These r's are used to generate a unit vector s_i with $i \in$ $n+1$,
$n+2, \ldots, k$. The unit vector along total change in u in an
iteration is the new s_j. The values of r_j are used to express $s_i (i > n)$
in terms of $s_i (i \leq n)$ in a particular iteration.

To determine the step along s_i that should be added or subtracted from u, we need to know the maximum magnitude available along s_i and $-s_i$. If s_i is along one of the values of u_j ($i \leqslant n$), then the maximum magnitudes available are given by g_{1i} and g_{2i}; otherwise, (when $i > n$) it is limited by the fact that for each component of s_i the movement should not exceed g_{1j} or g_{2j}, as the case may be. The procedure used to add the required deviation along s_i can now be given as follows.

If $i \leqslant n$

   then

      begin

         If $\cos \theta_i > 0$ *then* $\triangle = \text{Min} \left\{ \| u \cos \theta_i \| \, , \, g_{2i} \right\}$

                       else $\triangle = \text{Min} \left\{ \| u \cos \theta_i \|, \, g_{1i} \right\}$

         $u = u - s_i \triangle \text{sign}(\cos \theta_i)$

         $r_i = r_i - \triangle \text{sign}(\cos \theta_i)$

         $g_{1i} = g_{1i} + \triangle \text{sign}(\cos \theta_j)$

         $g_{2i} = g_{2i} - \triangle \text{sign}(\cos \theta_j)$

      end

   else

      begin

         For all $j = 1$ *to* n *do*

            begin

               If $h_{ij} \cos \theta_i > 0$ *then* $b_j = \left| \dfrac{g_{2j}}{h_{ij}} \right|$

                           else $b_j = \left| \dfrac{g_{1j}}{h_{ij}} \right|$

        end (for j)

        $\delta = \text{Min}(b_j)$ over all $j = \left\{ 1, 2, \ldots, n \right\}$ such that $h_{ij} \neq 0$

        $\triangle = \text{Min} \left\{ \| u \cos \theta_i \| \, , \, \delta \right\}$

        $u = u - s_i \triangle \text{sign}(\cos \theta_i)$

For all $j = 1$ *to* n *do*

    begin

        $r_j = r_j - h_{ij} \ \triangle \ \text{sign}(\cos \theta_i)$

        $g_{1i} = g_{1i} + h_{ij} \ \triangle \ \text{sign}(\cos \theta_i)$

        $g_{2i} = g_{2i} - h_{ij} \ \triangle \ \text{sign}(\cos \theta_i)$

    end (for j)

    end

The procedure for one iteration — adding required deviations along unit vectors $s_1, s_2, \ldots, s_k$ whose indices are stored in a set W — can now be described as follows:

For all $j = 1$ *to* n *do* $r_j = 0$

$U = W$

Repeat

  For all $i \in U$ *do*

    begin

      Obtain $\cos \theta_i$ between u and s_i using (13.16)

    end (for i)

  Select k such that $|\cos \theta_k| \geqslant |\cos \theta_i|$ for all $i \in U$

  Add required deviation along s_k to u, using the procedure described above

  $U = U - \{k\}$

until U is empty

Choice of Directions s_i

At the outset, the set W contains indices 1 to n, corresponding to unit vectors along δu_j's. After the first iteration, $n + 1$, the index of s_{n+1} (a unit vector along total change in u accomplished in the first iteration), is added to the set W. After the second iteration $n + 2$, corresponding to s_{n+2} (a unit vector along total change in u accomplished in the second iteration), is also added to W. This is repeated for the first n iterations. After that, the set W remains unaltered in size, but the unit vector along total change in u in an iteration replaces the least recently updated unit vector, in other words, the unit vector replaced n iterations earlier is deleted and replaced by

the present unit vector. The process is continued until no further
change in u is possible. For each $j \leqslant n$, either $\cos \theta_j$ is zero; if
$\cos \theta_j$ is positive, g_{2j} is zero; or if $\cos \theta_j$ is negative, g_{1j} is zero.
The main algorithm can now be stated as follows:

it = 0

For all j = 1 *to* n *do*

    begin

        $g_{1j} = \| \boldsymbol{\delta} u_j \|$

        $g_{2j} = g_{1j}$

        $s_j = \boldsymbol{\delta} u_j / g_{1j}$

    end (for j)

W = $\{ 1, 2, \ldots, n \}$

u = u^o

Repeat

    Do one iteration using the procedure described above

$$\boldsymbol{\delta} u = \sum_{j=1}^{n} r_j s_j$$

    i = n + 1 + it mod n

    it = it + 1

    $s_j = \boldsymbol{\delta} u / \| \boldsymbol{\delta} u \|$

    If it $<$ n *then* W = W + $\{ i \}$

    For all j = 1 *to* n *do* $h_{ij} = r_j / \| \boldsymbol{\delta} u \|$

until $\| \boldsymbol{\delta} u \| < \epsilon$

In the above procedure ϵ is a predetermined criterion used to check
for convergence.

The algorithm described in this section can be used to obtain minimum and maximum magnitudes of any multidimensional parameter
in terms of possible incremental deviations. This is particularly useful
in cases when the deviations are comparable to (or even greater than)

the nominal values of the performance parameters. This situation occurs quite often in microwave circuits since the performance parameters may involve reflection coefficients whose nominal values are usually zero or close to zero. For large tolerances, the incremental deviations are obtained using large change sensitivities. The worst-case analysis problem can also be formulated as a constrained optimization problem.

13.2 STATISTICAL TOLERANCE ANALYSIS [2]

Any worst-case analysis, by its very nature, tends to be pessimistic. On the other hand, the statistical tolerance analysis takes into account the nature of random variations in various circuit parameters to determine the statistics of performance parameters. However, this analysis requires more input information — like probability distributions corresponding to parameter variations — and, thus, gives a more realistic picture. Two approaches commonly used for this purpose are outlined in this section.

13.2.1 Method of Moments

Equation (13.10) can be written in the form

$$\delta u_i = \sum_{j=1}^{n} \delta p_j \frac{\partial u_i}{\partial p_j} . \tag{13.19}$$

Let σ_j^2 be the variance of distribution associated with the parameter p_j. We want to obtain the variance of distribution of parameter u_i. The derivative terms appearing in (13.19) could be treated as scaling factors for the δp_j's, whose variances are σ_j^2 so that the variances of

$$\frac{\partial u_i}{\partial p_j} \delta p_j \text{ become } \left(\frac{\partial u_i}{\partial p_j} \right)^2 \sigma_j^2 . \text{ Now, using the results for variance}$$

of sum of random variables (Appendix 13.1), we may write the variance in u_i as

$$\sigma_{u_i}^2 = \left[\frac{\partial u_i}{\partial p_n} \sigma_1 , \dots, \frac{\partial u_i}{\partial p_n} \sigma_n \right] R \left[\begin{array}{c} \frac{\partial u_i}{\partial p_1} \sigma_1 \\ - - - - \\ \frac{\partial u_i}{\partial p_n} \sigma_n \end{array} \right] \tag{13.20}$$

where R is a correlation matrix for the parameters p_j's. We may thus obtain the variance in the performance parameter from the variances in design parameters p_j's and the sensitivities. This procedure is illustrated by an example given below.

Example

Consider a mismatch between the impedances Z_1 and Z_2 in terms of the reflection coefficient ρ. Ten pairs of sample values of Z_1 and Z_2 are given. Their correlation is calculated using the data shown in Table 13.1.

TABLE 13.1

Sample Values and Deviations for Z_1 and Z_2

Z_1	Z_2	$(Z_1 - \overline{Z}_1)^2$	$(Z_2 - \overline{Z}_2)^2$	$(Z_1 - \overline{Z}_1)(Z_2 - \overline{Z}_2)$
50	50	4.00	0.25	-1.00
55	47.5	9.00	4.00	-6.00
55	45	9.00	20.25	-13.50
47.5	50	20.25	0.25	-2.25
55	50	9.00	0.25	1.50
57.5	45	30.25	20.25	-24.75
52.5	45	0.25	20.25	-2.25
47.5	55	20.25	30.25	-24.75
50	52.5	4.00	9.00	-6.00
50	55	4.00	30.25	-11.00
520	495	110.00	135.00	-90.00

Various statistical calculations are carried out as follows:

Averages: $\overline{Z}_1 = 52.0$ and $\overline{Z}_2 = 49.5$

Standard deviations:
$$\sigma_{z_1} = \sqrt{\frac{1}{10} \times 110} = 3.32$$

$$\text{and } \sigma_{z_2} = \sqrt{\frac{1}{10} \times 135} = 3.67$$

Correlation coefficient:

$$r = \frac{-90.00}{10(3.32)(3.67)} = -0.738 \quad .$$

Reflection coefficient is defined as

$$\rho = \frac{Z_2 - Z_1}{Z_2 + Z_1} \quad .$$

Therefore, average value of reflection coefficient may be defined as

$$\overline{\rho} = \frac{\overline{Z}_2 - \overline{Z}_1}{\overline{Z}_2 + \overline{Z}_1} = -0.0246 \quad .$$

The definition of ρ gives

$$\frac{\partial \rho}{\partial Z_1} = -\frac{2Z_2}{(Z_2 + Z_1)^2} = -0.00961$$

and

$$\frac{\partial \rho}{\partial Z_2} = \frac{2Z_1}{(Z_2 + Z_1)^2} = 0.0101 \quad .$$

Variance in reflection coefficient can now be calculated as

$$\sigma_\rho^2 = \begin{bmatrix} \sigma_{z1} \dfrac{\partial \rho}{\partial Z_1} & \sigma_{z2} \dfrac{\partial \rho}{\partial Z_2} \end{bmatrix} \begin{bmatrix} 1 & r \\ r & 1 \end{bmatrix} \begin{bmatrix} \sigma_{z1} \dfrac{\partial \rho}{\partial Z_1} \\ \sigma_{z2} \dfrac{\partial \rho}{\partial Z_2} \end{bmatrix}$$

$$= \begin{bmatrix} -0.0319 & 0.0371 \end{bmatrix} \begin{bmatrix} 1 & -0.738 \\ -0.738 & 1 \end{bmatrix} \begin{bmatrix} -0.0319 \\ 0.0371 \end{bmatrix}$$

$$= 0.00414 \quad ,$$

and

$$\sigma_\rho = 0.0643 \quad .$$

This value of σ_ρ can be verified by evaluating ρ for each of the pair of values of Z_1 and Z_2 and then calculating the variance.

13.2.2 Monte Carlo Analysis

This method can be used when the sensitivity values are not available, or when large statistical variations are to be considered.

In this method, sets of parameter values are generated from the given statistical distributions of parameters. Circuits corresponding to these sets of parameter values are analyzed for the performance parameters. The statistics of these performance parameters yield information about tolerances.

The procedure simulates sets of parameter values according to the prescribed distributions. For this purpose, generation of random numbers according to the prescribed distributions is required. Most computers have standard subprograms to generate uniformly distributed random numbers in the range [0, 1]. Using these uniformly distributed random numbers, one can generate random numbers for the desired distribution. This requires integration of the probability density function to obtain the cumulative probability function. Parameter values for the prescribed distribution in a given range can be obtained by scaling from the random numbers for that distribution in the range [0, 1].

The parameter values generated above are combined with other parameter values (generated in a similar fashion) in a random way and formed into sets. Each set of parameter values simulates the circuit being analyzed. By analyzing a large number of these simulated circuits, the *statistical* distributions of performance parameters can be easily determined.

The standard deviations calculated from the statistical distributions give more realistic tolerance values. The values of percentage yield (percentage of circuits meeting the specifications) can also be determined from these distributions.

The techniques for worst-case and statistical tolerance analyses discussed in this chapter are useful for evaluating the tolerances and for tolerance assignments.

APPENDIX 13.1 SOME RESULTS FROM PROBABILITY THEORY AND STATISTICS [2, 8]

In this Appendix, we briefly review some of the results from the probability theory and statistics for continuously variable parameters.

Consider a random variable x which takes continuous values from a lower limit x_1 to an upper limit x_2. We define a probability density function h(x) in the range (x_1, x_2) such that h(x) dx gives the probability of occurrence of the random variable in the range (x, x + dx). The function h(x) must then be non-negative in the range (x_1, x_2) and its integral from a to b gives the probability of occurrence of the random variable between these limits, i.e.

$$\int_a^b h(x)\, dx = \text{Prob.}\left\{a \leqslant x \leqslant b\right\} \tag{A13.1}$$

where $x_1 \leqslant a < b \leqslant x_2$. We can now obtain the mean value of x and its variance σ^2 as

$$\overline{x} = \int_{x_1}^{x_2} x\, h(x)\, dx, \tag{A13.2}$$

and

$$\sigma^2 = \int_{x_1}^{x_2} (x - \overline{x})^2\, h(x)\, dx. \tag{A13.3}$$

If the variable x is uniformly distributed in the range $[x_1, x_2]$, the distribution function h(x) is given as

$$h(x) = \frac{1}{x_2 - x_1}. \tag{A13.4}$$

Another example of continuous variation is the Gaussian (normal) distribution given as

$$h(x) = \frac{1}{\sqrt{2\pi}\,\sigma} \quad \exp\left[-\frac{(x - \bar{x})^2}{2\sigma^2}\right]. \tag{A13.5}$$

Discrete Case

In some cases the random variable takes discrete values $x_1, x_2, \ldots,$ x_n. The mean and the variance for this case are obtained as

$$\bar{x} = \frac{1}{n} \sum_{i=1}^{n} x_i, \tag{A13.6}$$

and

$$\sigma^2 = \frac{1}{n} \sum_{i=1}^{n} (x_i - \bar{x})^2. \tag{A13.7}$$

If all values of x are scaled by a factor A, the variance σ^2 gets scaled by A^2 and the mean by A.

Independent Variables

Two random variables x and y are said to be independent if and only if the occurrence of variable x in a range is independent of the occurrence of variable y. Mathematically, it can be stated as:

Prob. $\{a \leqslant x \leqslant b \text{ and } c \leqslant y \leqslant d\} =$

Prob. $\{a \leqslant x \leqslant b\} \cdot$ Prob. $\{c \leqslant y \leqslant d\}$ \tag{A13.8}

for all valid ranges (a,b) and (c,d).

Correlated Variables

The correlation coefficient associated with two random variables x and y is given for the discrete case as

$$r = \frac{1}{n\sigma_x \sigma_y} \sum_{i=1}^{n} (x_i - \bar{x})(y_i - \bar{y}) \tag{A13.9}$$

where σ_x^2 and σ_y^2 are variances associated with random variables x and y, respectively. If the variables x and y are independent, their correlation coefficient r equals zero and indicates that these are uncorrelated. However, the reverse is not true, that is r = 0 (uncorrelated variables) does not imply independence between variables. The correlation coefficient of a random variable with itself is 1.

For random variables $x_1, x_2, \ldots, x_n$, we can define a n × n correlation matrix R such that $r_{ij} = r_{ji}$ gives the correlation coefficient between variables x_i and x_j.

The variance σ_X^2 of a random variable X defined by

$$X = \sum_{i=1}^{n} x_i \qquad\qquad\qquad (A13.10)$$

is given by

$$\sigma_X^2 = \boldsymbol{\sigma} \, \mathbf{R} \, \boldsymbol{\sigma}^t \qquad\qquad\qquad (A13.11)$$

with $\boldsymbol{\sigma} = [\sigma_1, \sigma_2, \ldots, \sigma_n]^t$. The standard deviations $\sigma_1, \sigma_2, \ldots$, correspond to $x_1, x_2, \ldots$ If the random variables $x_1, x_2, \ldots, x_n$ are uncorrelated so that R = I, the above equation reduces to

$$\sigma_X^2 = \sum_{i=1}^{n} \sigma_i^{\,2} \, . \qquad\qquad\qquad (A13.12)$$

REFERENCES

[1]   Geher, K., *Theory of Network Tolerances*, Budapest: Akademiai Kiodo, 1971.

[2]   Calahan, D.A., *Computer-Aided Network Design*, New York: McGraw-Hill, 1972, Ch. 7 on "Tolerance Analysis."

[3]   Fidler, J.K., and C. Nightingale, *Computer Aided Circuit Design*, Middlesex U.K.: Thomson Nelson and Sons Ltd., 1978, Sec. 6.3 on "Tolerance Analysis."

[4]   Director, S.W., and G.D. Hachtel, "The Simplicial Approximation Approach to Design Centering," *IEEE Trans. Circuits and Systems*, Vol. CAS-24, July 1977, pp. 363-372.

[5]   Bandler, J.W., *et al.*, "Integrated Approach to Microwave Design," *IEEE Trans. Microwave Theory Tech.*, Vol. MTT-24, Sept. 1976, pp. 584-591.

[6]   Karafin, B.J., "Optimum Assignment of Component Tolerances for Electrical Networks," *B.S.T.J.*, Vol. 50, No. 4, April 1971, pp. 1225-1242.

[7]   Gupta, K.C., and R. Chadha, "Design Real-World Stripline Circuits," *Microwaves*, Vol. 17, No. 12, Dec. 1978, pp. 70-80.

[8]   Monroe, M.E., *Theory of Probability*, New York: McGraw-Hill, 1951.

[9]   Chambers, R.P., "Random Number Generation on Digital Computers," *IEEE Spectrum*, Vol. 4, Feb. 1967, pp. 48-56.

14

Time Domain Analysis of Microwave Circuits

Methods for frequency domain analysis of microwave circuits have been discussed in Chapter 11. As pointed out there, microwave circuit analysis techniques have become specialized for two reasons. Firstly, microwave circuits use both distributed and lumped elements. Secondly, for several microwave components, a convenient method of characterization is in terms of S-parameters. For time domain analysis also, the techniques used at lower frequencies are modified to incorporate the above mentioned considerations.

There are several applications in which time domain analysis of microwave circuits becomes necessary. These include design of fast switching digital integrated circuits, broadband radar and communication systems, and the study of lightning and EMP (electromagnetic pulse) effects on systems containing transmission lines.

There are three basic approaches used for the transient analysis of electronic circuits. These are: (i) Laplace transform method, (ii) companion network approach, and (iii) state variable approach. The Laplace transform method is applicable to a linear network or the linear part of a general nonlinear network. The other two approaches are applicable to nonlinear networks also. All three methods can be used at microwave frequencies. Before presenting a brief discussion of these methods, a method for the time domain analysis of transmission lines is presented in the following section.

14.1 TRANSIENT ANALYSIS OF TRANSMISSION LINES

One of the simple approaches for the transient analysis of transmission lines is based on the method of characteristics, used for the solution of hyperbolic partial differential equations. This method has been used for uniform transmission lines [1] and can also be extended [2] to non-uniform transmission lines with characteristic impedance Z_o varying along the length.

The set of partial differential equations describing TEM mode transmission lines is written as

$$-\frac{\partial v}{\partial z} = L\frac{\partial i}{\partial t} + R\,i \tag{14.1}$$

$$-\frac{\partial i}{\partial z} = C\frac{\partial v}{\partial t} + G\,v \tag{14.2}$$

where L, R, C, and G are series inductance, series resistance, shunt capacitance, and shunt conductance per unit length of the line. For low loss lines, R and G may be considered negligible. The method of characteristics [3] is used to transform (14.1) and (14.2) into two ordinary differential equations. Each of the resulting equations holds for a different characteristic direction in z-t plane. Along these directions, variables z and t are related and thus a change in t is associated with a change in z. For a uniform line, it can be shown that by substituting

$$\frac{dz}{dt} = 1/\sqrt{LC} \tag{14.3}$$

equations (14.1) and (14.2) may be combined to yield

$$\frac{d}{dt}(v + \sqrt{L/C}\,i) = -\left(\frac{G}{C}\,v + \frac{R}{\sqrt{LC}}\,i\right). \tag{14.4}$$

For a lossless line, (14.4) becomes

$$\frac{d}{dt}(v + \sqrt{L/C}\,i) = 0 \text{ or } \frac{dV_i}{dt} = 0 \tag{14.5}$$

where V_i is defined as $v + \sqrt{L/C}\,i$.

The relations (14.4) and (14.5) are used for time domain analysis of uniform transmission lines. Equation (14.3), which is a prerequisite for (14.4) and (14.5), describes a family of characteristic curves in z-t plane. These are known as *forward characteristics* (f-curves). For uniform transmission lines, L and C are independent of z and therefore, f-curves are straight lines as shown in Figure 14.1. The total length of the transmission line section is divided in N equal parts. The spacing between the adjacent f-curves is Δt along the time axis and Δz along the z-axis. Increments Δt and Δz are related by (14.3).

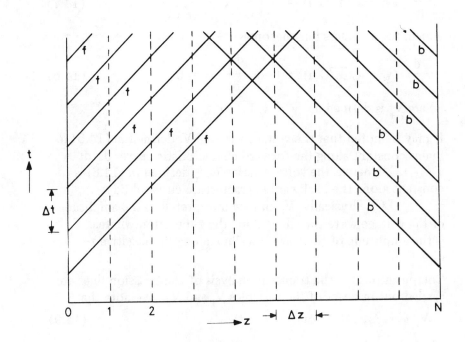

Figure 14.1   *Families of f and b characteristics in the z-t plane for a uniform transmission line.*

The second set of characteristic curves for (14.1) and (14.2) is given by

$$\frac{dz}{dt} = -1/\sqrt{LC} .$$ (14.6)

Along the curves specified by (14.6), z decreases with t and these are termed *backward characteristic* curves or b-curves. These b-curves for a uniform transmission line are also shown in Figure 14.1. Spacing between adjacent b-curves is also Δt and Δz along t and z-axes respectively. Along the b-curves, (14.1) and (14.2) yield

$$\frac{d}{dt} (v - \sqrt{L/C}\ i) = -\left(\frac{G}{C}\ v - \frac{R}{\sqrt{LC}}\ i\right)$$ (14.7)

which, for a lossless line, becomes

$$\frac{d}{dt} (v - \sqrt{L/C}\ i) = 0 \text{ or } \frac{dV_r}{dt} = 0$$ (14.8)

where V_r is defined as $v - \sqrt{L/C}\ i$.

It may be noted that the voltage variable V_i defined in (14.5) remains constant along the forward characteristic curves $dz/dt = 1/\sqrt{LC}$, whereas the voltage variable V_r defined in (14.8) is constant along the backward characteristic curves $dz/dt = -1/\sqrt{LC}$. Physically, V_i may be interpreted as the amplitude of the voltage wave travelling along the z-direction whereas V_r is the amplitude of the wave travelling along the negative z-direction.

Computations for the transient analysis of transmission lines are carried out in terms of the variables V_i and V_r. We note that

$$V_i(z + \Delta z , t + \Delta t) = V_i(z,t)$$ (14.9)

where Δz and Δt are related by (14.3). Similarly, from (14.8) and (14.6), we get

$$V_r(z - \Delta z , t + \Delta t) = V_r(z, t) .$$ (14.10)

Using (14.9) and (14.10), one can calculate V_i and V_r along the line at a time instant $t + \Delta t$ if the values of these variables at the time instant t are known for all points along the line length. If the transmission line extends from z = 0 to z = L, it may be noted that $V_i(0,t)$

and $V_r(L,t)$ cannot be obtained from the application of (14.9) and (14.10), respectively. These two values are obtained from the excitations at the two ends of the transmission line section.

Voltage and current at any point along the line can be evaluated from the values of V_i and V_r as

$$v(z,t) = [V_i(z,t) + V_r(z,t)] / 2 \qquad (14.11)$$

and

$$i(z,t) = [V_i(z,t) - V_r(z,t)] / (2Z_o) \qquad (14.12)$$

where Z_o is the characteristic impedance of the uniform line and is given by $\sqrt{L/C}$.

For numerical evaluation of the time domain behavior, the length of the transmission line is divided into N sections of equal length Δz and corresponding delays equal to the time step Δt, as shown in Figure 14.2. The time interval Δt is the time increment step used for the transient analysis of the circuit. The analysis is now carried out by writing 2N difference equations in the time domain. We have, from (14.9)

$$V_i(n,t) = V_i(n - 1, t - \Delta t), \quad n = 1, 2, \ldots, N \qquad (14.13)$$

and from (14.10)

$$V_r(n,t) = V_r(n + 1, t - \Delta t), \quad n = (N - 1), (N - 2),$$

$$\ldots, 2, 1, 0 \qquad (14.14)$$

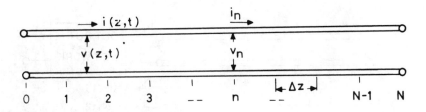

Figure 14.2   *A transmission line length divided into N sections for transient analysis.*

where $V_i(n,t)$ and $V_r(n,t)$ denote the values of the voltage variables V_i and V_r at various points along the transmission line at the time instant t. $V_i(0,t)$ and $V_r(N,t)$ are determined by the transient behavior of the networks connected at the input and output ends, respectively. From the definitions of V_i and V_r, and referring to Figure 14.3(a), V_i at the input end may be written as

$$V_i(0, t) = \frac{[v_o(t)/i_o(t)] + Z_o}{[v_o(t)/i_o(t)] - Z_o} \, V_r(0,t) \qquad (14.15)$$

where $v_o(t)$ is the output voltage and $i_o(t)$ is the output current of the network connected at the input terminals of the transmission line. For linear networks, the ratio $v_o(t) / i_o(t)$ may be obtained from the transient analysis of the input network even without knowing the value of $v_o(t)$. Similarly, V_r at the output end may be written as

$$V_r(N,t) = \frac{[v_N(t)/i_N(t)] - Z_o}{[v_N(t)/i_N(t)] + Z_o} \, V_i(N,t) \, . \qquad (14.16)$$

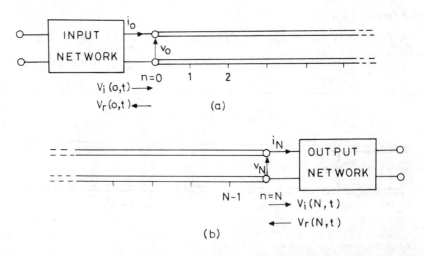

Figure 14.3   Voltages and currents at (a) the input end and (b) the output end of a transmission line section.

As shown in Figure 14.3(b), $v_N(t)$ and $i_N(t)$ represent the input voltage and the input current to the network connected at the output terminals of the transmission line. As in the case of the ratio $v_o(t)/i_o(t)$ in (14.15), the value of $v_N(t)/i_N(t)$ in (14.16) is obtained from the time domain analysis of the output network.

One may often require the transient analysis of a two-port network with transmission lines connected at both the input and the output ports. This configuration is shown in Figure 14.4. A time domain analysis of the network is carried out and the ratios $v_{in}(t)/i_{in}(t)$ and $v_{out}(t)/i_{out}(t)$ are evaluated as a function of time t. $V_i(N,t)$ at port 1 and $V_r(0,t)$ at port 2 are known from the analysis of the lines connected at the respective ports. Equations (14.16) and (14.15) are used for evaluating $V_r(N,t)$ at port 1 and $V_i(0,t)$ at port 2, respectively. These values are utilized to continue the transmission line analysis for the next time step and the response obtained for the time instant $t + \Delta t$.

Figure 14.4   *A two-port network with transmission lines connected at both the ports.*

Example

Consider a length of transmission line with a matched triangular shaped pulse source at one end and a resistive load of value $R = Z_o/2$ at the other end, as shown in Figure 14.5. Let the total delay along the line length be 6 ns. For the time domain analysis, we divide the length in 6 sections (N = 6) and assume that at t = 0 there is no voltage or current along the line length:

$$V_i(n,0) = V_r(n,0) = 0 \qquad n = 1, 2, \ldots, 6 .$$

V_i and V_r at subsequent time instants are calculated by using (14.13) and (14.14), respectively. For t = 6 Δt, $V_r(n,t)$ remains zero. For t = 7 Δt

$$V_i(n, 7\,\Delta t) = [0, 15, 12, 9, 6, 3]^t$$

$V_r(N, 7\,\Delta t)$ is calculated using (14.16). We have

$$V_r(N, 7\,\Delta t) = \frac{0.5\,Z_o - Z_o}{0.5\,Z_o + Z_o} \quad 3 = -1 .$$

For t = 8 Δt, we get

$$V_i(n, 8\,\Delta t) = [0, 0, 15, 12, 9, 6]^t$$

$$V_r(n, 8\,\Delta t) = [0, 0, 0, 0, -1, -2]^t .$$

Voltage distribution along the line at this time instant may be written using (14.11) as

$$v(n, 8\,\Delta t) = [0, 0, 7.5, 6, 4, 2]^t .$$

Equations (14.13), (14.14) and (14.16) are used to continue the analysis further in time domain.

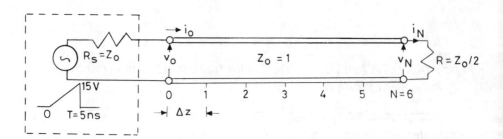

Figure 14.5   *A transmission line with a triangular pulse source at the input and a resistive load at the output.*

14.2 LAPLACE TRANSFORM METHOD [4, 5]

If the frequency domain description of the terminal behavior of a linear network is available, its time domain response can be determined by carrying out the inverse Laplace transform. This also holds for the linear part of a network containing nonlinear elements. Let

$$v(t) = [v_1(t), v_2(t), \ldots, v_n(t)]^t \qquad (14.17)$$

be the vector describing terminal voltages and

$$i(t) = [i_1(t), i_2(t), \ldots, i_n(t)]^t \qquad (14.18)$$

the vector describing terminal currents. Let $V(s)$ and $I(s)$ denote the Laplace transforms of $v(t)$ and $i(t)$, respectively. If the frequency domain behavior of the network is described by its short circuit admittance matrix $Y(s)$ with

$$I(s) = Y(s) \ V(s) \ , \qquad (14.19)$$

the time domain behavior of the network can be expressed as

$$i(t) = y(t) \ast v(t) \qquad (14.20)$$

where $\ast$ denotes convolution. $y(t)$, the inverse Laplace transform of $Y(s)$, is a matrix whose elements are impulse responses. There exist a number of numerical methods for finding inverse transform, but all of these methods require that the function to be inverted decrease at least as fast as $1/s$ for large values of s. For this reason, we rewrite (14.19) as

$$I(s) = A(s) \ s \ V(s) \qquad (14.21)$$

where $A(s) = Y(s)/s$. $\qquad (14.22)$

In the time domain, we have

$$i(t) = a(t) \ast \dot{v}(t) \ U(t) + a(t) \ v(0) \qquad (14.23)$$

where $\dot{v}(t)$ is the time derivative of the port voltage vector, $v(0)$ is its initial value, and $U(t)$ is the unit step function. $a(t)$, the inverse transform of $A(s)$, is a matrix of step responses. Let Δt be the interval between the discrete time points at which the response is being calculated. Then, (14.23) may be written as

$$i(k) = \frac{1}{2} \sum_{j=1}^{k} \left\{ [a(k - j + 1) + a(k - j)] \right.$$

$$\left. \cdot \, [v(j) - v(j - 1)] \right\} + a(k) \; v(0) \quad (14.24)$$

where (k), (j), etc. imply time instants (t = k Δt), (t = j Δt), etc. For each value of j we have approximated the step response by the average of its end-point values and the derivative by the difference of its end-point values. The duration of the time increments is normalized to unity, (Δt = 1). Note that i(k) in (14.24) can be separated into two parts, one relating to the past history and the other depending upon the current value of v(k), as:

$$i(k) = i_o(k) + g_o \; v(k) \qquad k = 1, 2, \ldots \qquad (14.25)$$

where

$$g_o = [a(1) + a(0)] \, / \, 2 \qquad (14.26)$$

$$i_o(k) = \frac{1}{2} \sum_{j=1}^{k-1} \left\{ [a(k - j + 1) + a(k - j)] \right.$$

$$\left. \cdot \, [v(j) - v(j - 1)] \right\} - g_o \; v(k - 1) + a(k) \; v(0) . \quad (14.27)$$

In the above equation, g_o is a matrix with constant elements equal to the step response of the network in the first interval. The current $i_o(k)$ can be regarded as a vector of current sources whose values are determined by the past history of v(k). Thus, $i_o(k)$ is known for a given k.

The transient response can thus be calculated using (14.25) to (14.27). The basic requirement here is the evaluation of the step response matrix a(t). The step response of each element or component in the network is available from its characterization. The key step in the analysis is to combine the individual step responses of the various components to evaluate the step response matrix a(t) for the overall network. A convenient method for this purpose [5] is discussed in the following section.

Combining Subnetworks

For frequency domain analysis (discussed in Chapter 11) there exist various methods of combining the characterization of subnetworks or components to obtain the overall characteristics of the network. When the combination of the subnetworks is to be carried out for time domain analysis, it is desirable to choose the network descriptions so that the resulting network matrix can be obtained conveniently from those of its constituents. If the two component matrices are to be multiplied in frequency domain (as in the case with ABCD matrices for cascaded network), the corresponding operation in the time domain will be the convolution of the two constituent time domain response matrices. Since the convolution operation involves relatively complicated computations, efforts are made to avoid such formulations. On the other hand, if we consider, for example, a circuit with two components described by admittance matrices and connected in parallel, the overall response is given by an admittance matrix which is the sum of the two individual matrices. Since the Laplace transform of a sum is equal to the sum of the two individual Laplace transforms, parallel connections are very conveniently handled in time domain by using admittance matrix descriptions. Basically, this implies that the overall system matrix should contain only sums or differences of individual component responses and products or quotients should not be involved. This is achieved by treating every kind of connection as though it were a parallel connection, so that Y-matrices may be directly added or superimposed.

Let us first consider a parallel connection as shown in Figure 14.6. Here, one port of a three-port network is connected in parallel with one port of a two-port network to form a new four-port network. Let the matrices Y^A and Y^B of the two subnetworks be put together as

$$
\mathbf{Y}_{\text{sub}} =
\begin{bmatrix}
Y^A_{11} & Y^A_{12} & Y^A_{13} & 0 & 0 \\
Y^A_{21} & Y^A_{22} & Y^A_{23} & 0 & 0 \\
Y^A_{31} & Y^A_{32} & Y^A_{33} & 0 & 0 \\
0 & 0 & 0 & Y^B_{44} & Y^B_{45} \\
0 & 0 & 0 & Y^B_{54} & Y^B_{55}
\end{bmatrix}
\tag{14.28}
$$

where superscripts A and B on the elements of the matrix denote the elements of step response admittance matrices of subnetworks A and B respectively. The admittance matrix of the combination, with ports renumbered as $1'$, $2'$, $3'$, $5'$, can be simply written as

$$
\mathbf{Y}' =
\begin{array}{c}
 \\
1' \\
2' \\
3' \\
5'
\end{array}
\begin{array}{ccccc}
1' & \quad 2' & \quad 3' & \quad 5' \\
\begin{bmatrix}
Y^A_{11} + Y^B_{44} & Y^A_{12} & Y^A_{13} & Y^B_{45} \\
Y^A_{21} & Y^A_{22} & Y^A_{23} & 0 \\
Y^A_{31} & Y^A_{32} & Y^A_{33} & 0 \\
Y^B_{54} & 0 & 0 & Y^B_{55}
\end{bmatrix}
\end{array}
\tag{14.29}
$$

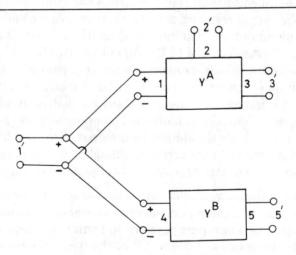

Figure 14.6   *Port 1 of the network A connected in parallel to port 4 of the network B.*

The step response matrix of the network in Figure 14.6 may be written in a similar manner as

$$
a'(t) = \begin{bmatrix}
a_{11}^A + a_{44}^B & a_{12}^A & a_{13}^A & a_{45}^B \\
a_{21}^A & a_{22}^A & a_{23}^A & 0 \\
a_{31}^A & a_{32}^A & a_{33}^A & 0 \\
a_{54}^B & 0 & 0 & a_{55}^B
\end{bmatrix}
\qquad (14.30)
$$

where the various elements of the matrix in (14.30) are elements of step response matrices of subnetworks A and B.

The application of the above procedure to the cascade and series connections requires addition of extra open-circuited ports to the network. Consider the cascade combination of two two-ports as shown in Figure 14.7(a). Since we are interested in simple additive operations on Y^A and Y^B to yield the overall response, the cascade connection of Figure 14.7(a) can be treated as a parallel combination of ports 2 and 3 to form a new three-port network with ports $1'$, $3'$ and $4'$ as shown in Figure 14.7(b). If port $3'$ is open-circuited then the networks of Figures 14.7(a) and (b) are physically identical. The step response matrix of network in Figure 14.7(b) may be written as

$$
a'(t) = \begin{matrix} 1' \\ 3' \\ 4' \end{matrix}
\begin{matrix} \quad 1' \qquad\qquad 3' \qquad\quad 4' \end{matrix}
\begin{bmatrix}
a_{11}^A & a_{12}^A & 0 \\
a_{21}^A & a_{22}^A + a_{33}^B & a_{34}^B \\
0 & a_{43}^B & a_{44}^B
\end{bmatrix}.
\qquad (14.31)
$$

The response of the cascaded network may now be obtained by writing

$$
\begin{bmatrix} i_{1'}(k) \\ 0 \\ i_{4'}(k) \end{bmatrix}
= \begin{bmatrix} i_{01'}(k) \\ i_{03'}(k) \\ i_{04'}(k) \end{bmatrix}
+ \begin{bmatrix} \dfrac{a'(1) + a'(0)}{2} \end{bmatrix}
\begin{bmatrix} v_{1'}(k) \\ v_{3'}(k) \\ v_{4'}(k) \end{bmatrix}.
$$

$$
\qquad (14.32)
$$

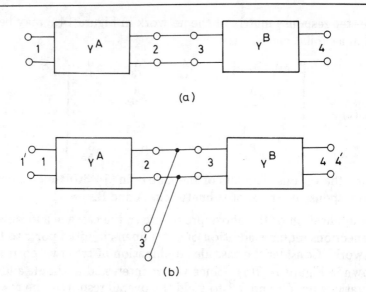

Figure 14.7(a) Cascade connection of two networks.

(b) An open-circuited port 3' connected to the cascade connection for applying Laplace transform method of transient analysis.

$v_{1'}(k)$ and $v_{4'}(k)$ are the known excitations to the network. The initial value of $v_{3'}(0)$ is also known. For $k = 1$, $i_{01'}(k)$, $i_{03'}(k)$ and $i_{04'}(k)$ are found from the previous history (using 14.27) as

$$i_o(1) = - g_o v(0) + a'(1) v(0) = \frac{a'(1) - a'(0)}{2} v(0) .$$

(14.33)

Substituting $i_o(1)$ in (14.32), $i_{1'}(1)$, $i_{4'}(1)$ and $v_{3'}(1)$ can be evaluated in terms of the known excitations $v_{1'}(1)$ and $v_{4'}(1)$. Similarly $i_{1'}(k)$ and $i_{4'}(k)$ may be computed for successive time steps.

Series connection of two ports in terms of additive operations on admittance matrices becomes slightly more complicated. Let us consider the situation where port 1 of subnetwork A is to be series connected to port 4 of subnetwork B, as shown in Figure 14.8. The first

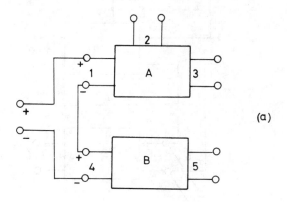

(a)

Figure 14.8(a) Two networks A and B with ports 1 and 4 connected in series.

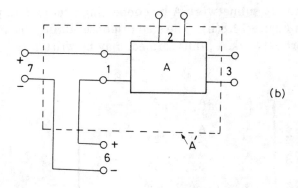

(b)

Figure 14.8(b) Network A modified into A' by incorporating a dummy series T-junction.

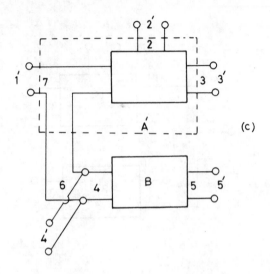

*Figure 14.8(c) Parallel connection of the port 6 of A' and the
                 port 4 of B by creating a dummy open-circuited
                 port 4'.*

step is to modify subnetwork A by connecting a series T to port 1
as shown in Figure 14.8(b). The step response admittance matrix of
the four-port network A', thus formed, may be written as

$$
a^{A'}(t) = \begin{array}{c} \\ 7 \\ 2 \\ 3 \\ 6 \end{array}
\begin{array}{cccc} 7 & 2 & 3 & 6 \\ \end{array}
\begin{bmatrix}
a_{11}^{A} & a_{12}^{A} & a_{13}^{A} & -a_{11}^{A} \\
a_{21}^{A} & a_{22}^{A} & a_{23}^{A} & -a_{21}^{A} \\
a_{31}^{A} & a_{32}^{A} & a_{33}^{A} & -a_{31}^{A} \\
-a_{11}^{A} & -a_{12}^{A} & -a_{13}^{A} & a_{11}^{A}
\end{bmatrix}. \qquad (14.34)
$$

Port 6 of the network A' and port 4 of subnetwork B are now cascaded by introducing an additional port 4' as in the case of the previous example. The overall step response matrix of the resulting
five-port network shown in Figure 14.8(c) may be written as

$$
a'(t) = \begin{array}{c} \\ 1' \\ 2' \\ 3' \\ 4' \\ 5' \end{array}
\begin{array}{ccccc}
1' & 2' & 3' & 4' & 5' \\
\end{array}
\left[
\begin{array}{ccccc}
a_{11}^{A} & a_{12}^{A} & a_{13}^{A} & -a_{11}^{A} & 0 \\
a_{21}^{A} & a_{22}^{A} & a_{23}^{A} & -a_{21}^{A} & 0 \\
a_{31}^{A} & a_{32}^{A} & a_{33}^{A} & -a_{31}^{A} & 0 \\
-a_{11}^{A} & -a_{21}^{A} & -a_{31}^{A} & a_{11}^{A} + a_{44}^{B} & a_{45}^{B} \\
0 & 0 & 0 & a_{54}^{B} & a_{55}^{B}
\end{array}
\right] . \quad (14.35)
$$

As in the previous case, $i(t)$ is evaluated by putting $i_{4'}(t) = 0$ and using (14.25) to (14.27).

These examples demonstrate that any general combination of elements can be analyzed by an extension of these techniques. Implementation of this procedure, however, requires knowledge of step response matrices. These matrices for the two frequently occurring lossless transmission line sections are as follows [5]. For a transmission line section with matched resistance at one end (Figure 14.9a), the step response admittance matrix may be written as

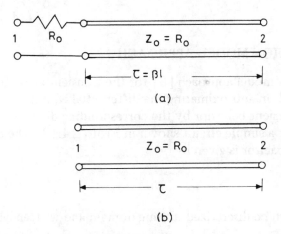

Figure 14.9(a) A transmission line section with a matched series resistor at the input end.

(b) A transmission line section with the electrical length τ.

$$a(t) = \begin{bmatrix} \dfrac{1}{2R_o}\{U(t)+U(t-2\tau)\} & -\dfrac{1}{R_o}U(t-\tau) \\[2em] -\dfrac{1}{R_o}U(t-\tau) & \dfrac{1}{R_o}U(t) \end{bmatrix} \qquad (14.36)$$

where $U(t)$ is the unit step function. For a transmission line section open-circuited at both ends (Figure 14.9(b)), the step response admittance matrix is given by

$$a(t) = \begin{bmatrix} \dfrac{1}{2R_o}[U(t)+U(t-2\tau) \\ \quad +U(t-4\tau)+\ldots] & -\dfrac{2}{R_o}[U(t-\tau) \\ \quad +U(t-3\tau)+\ldots] \\[2em] \dfrac{-2}{R_o}[U(t-\tau)+ \\ \quad U(t-3\tau)+\ldots] & \dfrac{1}{2R_o}[U(t)+2U(t-2\tau) \\ \quad +2U(t-4\tau)\ldots] \end{bmatrix} .$$

$$(14.37)$$

14.3 COMPANION MODEL APPROACH

The companion model approach [6] for the transient analysis of circuits is based on approximating the differential equations representing the transient behavior by the corresponding difference equations. Consider a simple circuit shown in Figure 14.10. The current through the capacitor is given by

$$i = C\frac{dv}{dt} . \qquad (14.38)$$

This relation can be discretized in time domain and written as

$$i^{n+1} = C\frac{(v^{n+1}-v^n)}{\Delta t} \qquad (14.39)$$

where i^{n+1} is an approximation to the capacitor current with superscript $(n+1)$ referring to the particular time instant. Δt is the interval between successive points in time domain. Equation (14.39) can be modelled by the circuit shown in Figure 14.10(b). The conductance G(= C/Δt) and the current source (C/Δt)v^n combination shown in this figure is called the *companion network model* for the capacitor. The approximation for the derivative used in this model is given as

$$\left. \frac{dv}{dt} \right|_{t = t^{n+1}} = \frac{v^{n+1} - v^n}{t^{n+1} - t^n} = \frac{v^{n+1} - v^n}{\Delta t} \qquad (14.40)$$

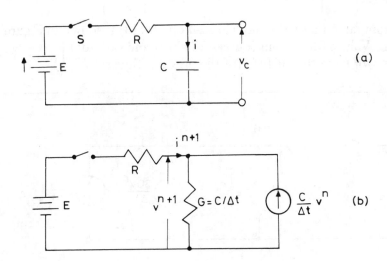

Figure 14.10   (a) A series R-C circuit; and (b) its companion model.

This is known as the *backward Euler formula*. There are other alternative approximations that may be used. The *forward Euler formula* is given by

$$\left. \frac{dv}{dt} \right|_{t = t^n} = \frac{v^{n+1} - v^n}{t^{n+1} - t^n} = \frac{v^{n+1} - v^n}{\Delta t} \qquad (14.41)$$

and the trapezoidal integration rule is given by

$$\left.\frac{dv}{dt}\right|_{t = t^{n+1}} + \left.\frac{dv}{dt}\right|_{t = t^n} = 2\,\frac{v^{n+1} - v^n}{\Delta t} \quad . \qquad (14.42)$$

The trapezoidal rule results in an improvement in accuracy over the Euler formulas for numerical integration [7]. Using (14.42), i^{n+1} in the circuit of Figure 14.10 may be written as

$$i^{n+1} = C\left\{\frac{2v^{n+1}}{\Delta t} - \frac{2v^n}{\Delta t} - \left.\frac{dv}{dt}\right|_{t = t^n}\right\} \quad . \qquad (14.43)$$

The companion network model based on (14.43) is shown in Figure 14.11. Values for current sources $2C\,v^n/\Delta t$ and $C(dv/dt)\big|_{t = t^n}$ are known from the analysis for the previous time step.

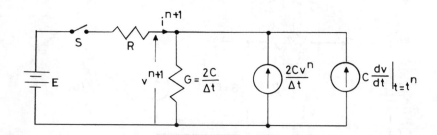

Figure 14.11   A companion model based on trapezoidal rule for series R-C circuit of Figure 14.10(a).

The companion network model for inductors may be written in a similar fashion. When the backward Euler formula is used, the voltage across an inductor (Figure 14.12(a)) becomes

$$v^{n+1} = \frac{L}{\Delta t}\,(i^{n+1} - i^n) \qquad (14.44)$$

and the corresponding companion network is shown in Figure 14.12(b). For the convenience of using nodal admittance matrix method for

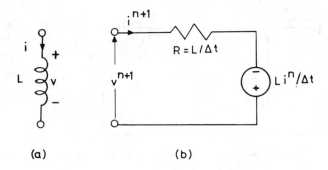

$$\text{(a)} \qquad\qquad\qquad \text{(b)}$$

*Figure 14.12   (a) An inductor; and (b) its companion network
model based on Equation (14.44).*

analysis at discrete time steps, the companion network model of
Figure 14.12(b) is frequently rewritten by replacing the inductance
by a capacitatively loaded gyrator. An ideal gyrator is a two-port
network (shown in Figure 14.13(a)) with

$$
\begin{bmatrix} v_1 \\ i_1 \end{bmatrix}
=
\begin{bmatrix} 0 & 1 \\ 1 & 0 \end{bmatrix}
\begin{bmatrix} v_2 \\ i_2 \end{bmatrix}.
\tag{14.45}
$$

For the capacitor shown in Figure 14.13(a)

$$
i_2 = C \frac{dv_2}{dt}.
$$

At port 1 of the gyrator, (14.45) yields

$$
v_1 = C \frac{di_1}{dt}
\tag{14.46}
$$

or

$$
v_1^{n+1} = \frac{C}{\Delta t} \left\{ i_1^{n+1} - i_1^n \right\}
\tag{14.47}
$$

which is identical to (14.44) with L replaced by C. Thus the companion model of an inductor (Figure 14.12a) can be written as
shown in Figure 14.13(b).

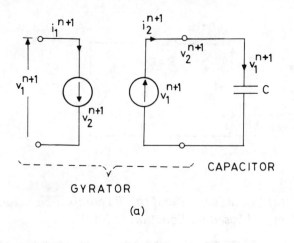

GYRATOR   CAPACITOR

(a)

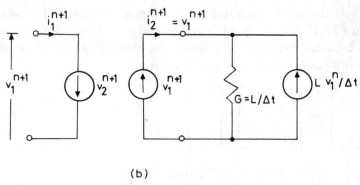

(b)

Figure 14.13   (a) A capacitor loaded gyrator and (b) its application
for writing a companion model for an inductor.

The main advantage of companion network approach is the ease
with which it can be extended to incorporate nonlinear elements.
Companion models for nonlinear elements are obtained by the
linearization of the corresponding equations by Taylor series expansion about the nominal operating point. For a nonlinear conductance shown in Figure 14.14(a), we write

$$i = g(v) \, v \; . \tag{14.48}$$

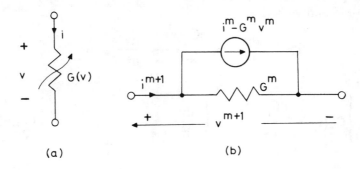

Figure 14.14   *(a) A nonlinear conductance; and (b) its companion
model.*

The form of the right-hand side of (14.48) is decided by the fact
that, in a passive two terminal nonlinear element, setting v to zero
must result in zero current. Expanding i in a truncated Taylor
series about i^o, we have

$$i = i^o + \left.\frac{\partial i}{\partial v}\right|_{v = v^o} (v - v^o) = i^o + G^o v - G^o v^o .$$

$$(14.49)$$

The approximation in (14.49) can be improved by successive iterations. For the m*th* iteration it becomes

$$i^{m+1} = i^m + G^m v^{m+1} - G^m v^m . \qquad (14.50)$$

A companion model based on this approximation is shown in Figure 14.14(b). Such a linearized model may be included in the models
for transient analysis discussed earlier. It may be noted that iterations for various values of m are needed at each time step in the discretized time domain analysis.

A nonlinear capacitance is defined by a nonlinear relationship between charge and voltage, namely

$$q = C_q(v) \, v . \qquad (14.51)$$

For the present analysis, a relationship between current and voltage is required and we write

$$\frac{dq}{dt} = i = C_q(v) \frac{dv}{dt} + \frac{dC_q(v)}{dv} \frac{dv}{dt} v$$

so that

$$i = \left\{ C_q(v) + \frac{dC_q(v)}{dv} v \right\} \frac{dv}{dt} \qquad (14.52)$$

or

$$i = C(v) \frac{dv}{dt} \qquad (14.53)$$

where

$$C(v) = C_q(v) + \frac{dC_q(v)}{dv} v . \qquad (14.54)$$

Similarly, for a nonlinear inductor, we can write

$$v = L(i) \frac{di}{dt} . \qquad (14.55)$$

Equations (14.53) and (14.55) are linearized in a manner similar to that for g(v).

14.4 STATE VARIABLE APPROACH

The state variable approach is a very general method [7, 8, 9] for the time domain analysis of linear and nonlinear networks and systems.

In the state variable approach, a linear time-invariant network is characterized by two equations of the following form

$$\dot{x} = A x + B u \qquad (14.56)$$

and

$$y = C x + D u + (D_1 \dot{u}_1 + \dots) \qquad (14.57)$$

where

u = m component column vector representing the m inputs (independent sources),

y = p component column vector representing the p outputs (voltages and/or currents of interest),

x = n component column vector comprising a set of n independent auxiliary variables, and

A,B,C,D,D_1 = constant, real matrices of appropriate dimensions.

Note that A is always a square matrix of order n.

Equation (14.56) represents a set of n first order differential equations (coupled in general) called *state equations*. The set of auxiliary variables x_1, x_2, . . ., x_n are called the *state variables*, and $x = (x_1, x_2, . . ., x_n)^t$ is called the *state vector*. Equation (14.57) is known as the *output equation*.

For the general nonlinear case, the state equation may be written as

$$\dot{x} = f(x, u, t) . \qquad (14.58)$$

Once the network equations can be manipulated in the form (14.56) or (14.58) it is possible to apply some numerical techniques based on (14.40), (14.41) or (14.42) to provide an approximate solution to the system of equations. The main difficulty lies in the formulation of state equations and, more particularly, the determination of matrix A when equations are in the form (14.56).

The number of equations, n, in (14.56) or (14.58) depends upon the complexity of the network. For a set of n linearly independent equations, the most general solution must contain n arbitrary constants to be determined by n initial conditions. Usually, but not always, these n initial conditions are the values of $x_1, . . ., x_n$ at t = 0. Thus, the order of complexity n of a network is equal to the number of independent initial conditions that can be, and must be, specified in terms of the electrical variables in order to obtain the complete solution of x(t).

It can be shown [8] that, for linear, lumped, and time invariant networks, the order of complexity is equal to the number of independent capacitor voltages and inductor currents. For RLC networks, some of the capacitor voltages and/or inductor currents may not be independent. This happens when: (i) the network has one or more loops consisting of only capacitors and possibly, independent voltage sources, called C-E_i loops; or when (ii) the network has one or more cutsets consisting of only inductors and, possibly, independent current sources, called L-J_i cutsets.

Thus the order of complexity of any RLC network is given by

$$n = b_{LC} - n_C - n_L \tag{14.59}$$

where

b_{LC} = total number of capacitors and inductors

n_C = total number of independent C-E_i loops.

n_L = total number of independent L-J_i cutsets.

For linear, active networks, the number of variables in x could be less than that given by (14.59). A general method for computer formulation of state equations for linear active networks may be divided into two stages. The first stage consists of the formulation of "initial state" equations of the form

$$M^{(o)} \; \dot{x}^{(o)} = A^{(o)} \; x^{(o)} + B^{(o)} \; u \tag{14.60}$$

where the vector $x^{(o)}$ consists of all capacitor voltages and inductor currents, and u comprises all independent sources. $M^{(o)}$ is a constant matrix consisting of the coefficients of the elements of $\dot{x}^{(o)}$. The variables in $x^{(o)}$ may or may not be linearly independent. The dependent variables in $x^{(o)}$ are uncovered and eliminated in the second stage. Equation (14.60) is first reduced to the form

$$\dot{x} = A x + B u + (B_1 \dot{x} + \dots) \tag{14.61}$$

where the elements of x are, in general, a subset of $x^{(o)}$. Now, (14.61) can be put into the normal form (14.56). Details of the computer formulation of state equations and their solutions are given in [9].

As mentioned earlier, the state variable technique can be extended to nonlinear networks, and the normal form of equations in this case is expressed by (14.58). However, the formulation of state equations in this case becomes more complicated since the presence of non-linear elements, characterized by non-monotonic characteristic curves in a network, may lead to the non-existence of the normal-form equation. The non-monotonic characteristics may also arise due to the combination of negative resistors or controlled sources with other components.

A detailed discussion of the topological formulation of state equations for dynamic, nonlinear networks, based on hybrid matrix formulation, is available in [9].

Various approaches for time domain analysis, discussed in this chapter, can be used to analyze microwave circuits.

REFERENCES

[1] Branin, F.H., "Transient Analysis of Lossless Transmission Lines," *Proc. IEEE*, Vol. 55, 1967, pp. 2012-2013.

[2] Dvorak, V., "Transient Analysis of Non-uniform Transmission Lines," *Proc. IEEE*, Vol. 58, 1970, pp. 844-845.

[3] Ames, W.F., *Nonlinear Partial Differential Equations in Engineering*, New York: Academic Press, 1965, Chap. 7.

[4] Silverberg, M., and O. Wing, "Time Domain Computer Solutions for Networks Containing Lumped Nonlinear Elements," *IEEE Trans. Circuit Theory*, Vol. CT-15, 1968, pp. 292-294.

[5] Allen, J.L., "Time-domain Analysis of Lumped-Distributed Networks," *IEEE Trans. Microwave Theory Tech.*, Vol. MTT-27, 1979, pp. 890-896.

[6] Calahan, D.A., *Computer-Aided Network Design*, New York: McGraw-Hill, 1972, Chapter 4, "Transient Analysis of Dynamic Networks," pp. 80-105.

[7] Fidler, J.K., and C. Nightingale, *Computer Aided Circuit Analysis*, Middlesex (U.K.): Thomas Nelson and Sons Ltd., 1978, Chap. 5, "Transient Analysis," pp. 127-169.

[8] Rohrer, R.A., *Circuit Theory — An Introduction to the State Variable Approach*, New York: McGraw-Hill, 1970.

[9] Chua, L.O., and P.M. Lin, *Computer-Aided Analysis of Electronic Circuits: Algorithms and Computational Techniques*, Englewood Cliffs, New Jersey: Prentice-Hall, 1975, Chapters 8 to 11.

15

Matrix Solution Techniques

Various methods of circuit analysis discussed in the preceding chapters have one feature in common. They all require solution of a set of simultaneous linear equations. These equations are put in a matrix form, and several matrix operations (multiplication, inversion, etc.) have to be carried out to obtain the results of the circuit analysis. When a circuit design is optimized (as discussed later in Chapters 16 to 18), it becomes necessary to carry out the circuit analysis repeatedly, once in every iteration of the optimization algorithm. Thus, it becomes very important to have efficient circuit analysis programs. This requires efficient methods to carry out various matrix operations.

Two efficient approaches for the solution of matrix equations are discussed in this chapter. These are: (i) Gaussian elimination, and (ii) L-U decomposition and Forward elimination - Back substitution. Some of the sparse matrix techniques used to reduce storage requirements and improve computational efficiency are also discussed.

15.1 GAUSSIAN ELIMINATION [1,2]

Let us consider the following set of linear, simultaneous equations

$$
\begin{aligned}
a_{11}x_1 + a_{12}x_2 + \ldots + a_{1n}x_n &= b_1 \\
a_{21}x_1 + a_{22}x_2 + \ldots + a_{2n}x_n &= b_2 \\
\vdots \qquad \vdots \qquad\qquad \vdots & \\
a_{n1}x_1 + a_{n2}x_2 + \ldots + a_{nn}x_n &= b_n \;.
\end{aligned}
\tag{15.1}
$$

The above equation can be written in the matrix form

$$
A\,x = b \tag{15.2}
$$

where

$$
x = (x_1, x_2, \ldots, x_n)^t, \quad b = (b_1, b_2, \ldots, b_n)^t, \text{ and}
$$

$$
A = \begin{bmatrix}
a_{11} & a_{12} & \cdots & a_{1n} \\
a_{21} & a_{22} & \cdots & a_{2n} \\
\vdots & \vdots & & \vdots \\
a_{n1} & a_{n2} & \cdots & a_{nn}
\end{bmatrix}.
$$

There are various well known methods for obtaining the solution of (15.2). One of the simplest methods is the use of Cramer's rule, but it is highly inefficient. To solve a set of n equations using Cramer's rule, $N = 2(n + 1)!$ long-operations are required. In this section, we shall discuss Gaussian elimination algorithm wherein the number of long-operations required is of the order of n^3. We first illustrate the procedure by means of a simple example given below.

Example: Consider the solution of the following set of equations

$$
2x_1 + 2x_2 + 3x_3 = 3 \tag{15.3a}
$$

$$
4x_1 + 7x_2 + 7x_3 = 1 \tag{15.3b}
$$

$$
-2x_1 + 4x_2 + 5x_3 = -7. \tag{15.3c}
$$

Using (15.3a) to eliminate x_1 from the other two equations, we get

$$2x_1 + 2x_2 + 3x_3 = 3 \qquad\qquad (15.4a)$$

$$3x_2 + x_3 = -5 \qquad\qquad (15.4b)$$

$$6x_2 + 8x_3 = -4 \ . \qquad\qquad (15.4c)$$

We now eliminate x_2 from (15.4c), to obtain

$$2x_1 + 2x_2 + 3x_3 = 3 \qquad\qquad (15.5a)$$

$$3x_2 + x_3 = -5 \qquad\qquad (15.5b)$$

$$6x_3 = 6 \ . \qquad\qquad (15.5c)$$

The solutions for x_1, x_2 and x_3 can now be obtained in the reverse order by back substitution. Equation (15.4c) gives $x_3 = 1$, which on substitution in (15.4b) gives $x_2 = -2$. Finally, from (15.4a), we have $x_1 = 2$. Equations (15.5) are called *triangular equations* and the process of obtaining solution in the reverse order is called *Back Substitution*.

The basic operations used for triangularization in the above example are:

(i) Multiplication of an equation by a nonzero constant.

(ii) Replacement of j*th* equation by the sum of j*th* equation and α times k*th* equation, where α is any constant and $k \neq j$.

The method used in the example given above is known as *Gaussian elimination* and can be extended to obtain the solution of n simultaneous equations.

For its implementation on a computer, the operations described above can be performed on the augmented matrix $[A|b]$. If M denotes the n $\times$ (n + 1) augmented matrix, the operations for triangularization of A are as listed below:

For all k = 1 *to* n − 1 *do*

    begin

        For all i = k + 1 *to* n *do*

            begin

                $\alpha = -\ m_{ik}/m_{kk}$

For all j = k *to* n + 1 *do* m$_{ij}$ = m$_{ij}$ + α m$_{kj}$

    end (for i)

  end (for k) .

In this algorithm, only the operation (ii) described above is being used. Since each row of M corresponds to an equation, in the innermost loop, the i*th* row is being replaced by the sum of the i*th* row and $(-m_{ik} / m_{kk})$ times the k*th* row. This is being done for columns k to (n + 1) only, since the entries in columns 1 to (k − 1) for rows k to n have already been made zero.

The updating of m$_{ij}$ is carried out $(n - k)(n - k + 2)$ times for each k, from 1 to (n − 1). Therefore, the total number of times the updating is carried out is

$$\sum_{k=1}^{n-1} (n - k)(n - k + 2) = \frac{n(n - 1)(2n + 5)}{6} .$$

$$(15.6a)$$

The number of times α is evaluated is obtained from

$$\sum_{k=1}^{n-1} (n - k) = \frac{n(n - 1)}{2} . \qquad (15.6b)$$

Each updating in the innermost loop requires single multiplication, and evaluation of α requires single division. Therefore, the total number of long-operations needed for triangularization is

$$N_t = \frac{n(n - 1)(2n + 5)}{6} + \frac{n(n - 1)}{2} = \frac{n(n - 1)(n + 4)}{3} .$$

$$(15.7)$$

The above algorithm assumes that the diagonal elements m$_{kk}$ are nonzero. These elements are called *pivots*. To ensure that the pivots are nonzero, the following operations (in addition to the two operations described earlier) may be performed on the augmented matrix:

(iii)   Rows of M may be interchanged. This merely changes the order in which the equations are written. This step may be used to change the value of the pivot element from a very small to a larger value.

(iv)   The columns of A can be interchanged. This implies that the unknowns in x are written in a different order. Information about all column interchanges should be stored so that when x is obtained, values to various variables can be assigned in the correct manner.

Of the above four operations, operations (i) to (iii) are called *elementary row operations*, since these operate on the rows of a matrix. Performing an elementary row operation on a matrix is identical to pre-multiplying the matrix with another matrix that is obtained by performing the identical row operation on an identity matrix.

Once the matrix M is triangularized, we solve the resultant equations in the reverse order obtaining unknowns one at a time. The various steps can be given as

For all j $=$ n *step* $-$ 1 *until* 2 *do*

   begin

   $b_j = b_j / a_{jj}$

   For all i $=$ j $-$ 1 *step* $-$ 1 *until* 1 *do* $b_i = b_i - a_{ij} b_j$

   end (for j)

$b_1 = b_1 / a_{11}$

The terms a_{ij} and b_j above are parts [A|b] of the triangularized matrix M and the solution to x is now given by b. The number of times innermost updating of b_i is carried out is given by

$$(n - 1) + (n - 2) + \ldots + 1 = \frac{n(n - 1)}{2} .$$

This involves one multiplication for each updating of b_i in the innermost loop. There are additional n divisions. Therefore, the number of long-operations in back substitution is given by

$$N_s = n + \frac{n(n - 1)}{2} = \frac{n(n + 1)}{2} . \tag{15.8}$$

Addition of (15.7) and (15.8) gives us the total number of long-operations needed for Gaussian elimination, i.e.,

$$N = \frac{n(n - 1)(n + 4)}{3} + \frac{n(n + 1)}{2}$$

$$= \frac{n^3}{3} + \frac{3n^2}{2} - \frac{5n}{6} . \tag{15.9}$$

In the Gaussian elimination procedure the inverse of matrix A is not explicitly determined. The inverse of A can be obtained using a matrix which is given by augmenting A with an identity matrix of the same dimensions. In this case, M is written as

$$M = [A\,|\,I] \tag{15.10}$$

The matrix A is triangularized by performing row operations, as described earlier, on the augmented matrix M. Now, similar row operations are performed further on M so as to reduce the triangularization and subsequent operations) would now contain the inverse of A. We discuss below the procedure needed after the matrix A is triangularized.

Only the steps on the second portion of M (originally I, now labelled B) are described.

For all j = n *step* − 1 *until* 2 *do*
   begin
      For all k = 1 *to* n *do* b_{jk} = b_{jk} / a_{jj}
      For all i = j − 1 *step* − 1 *until* 1 *do*
         begin
            For all k = 1 *to* n *do* b_{ik} = b_{ik} − $a_{ij}\,b_{jk}$
      end (for i)
   end (for j)

In this procedure the inverse of A gets stored in B. The number of long-operations are now larger since the augmented matrix is of bigger size. The total number of long-operations required to obtain the inverse is about n^3.

15.2 PIVOTING [1, 2]

In this section, we discuss various criteria which can be used for the selection of pivots at a particular stage. Though, in the previous section, the only restriction mentioned was that the pivots should be nonzero, it has been found that even the pivots with small magnitudes may lead to numerical errors. This is because of the finite word length used in the computer on which the computations are carried out. The errors caused by pivots of small magnitude can be illustrated by means of the following example.

Example: Consider the following system of equations

$$\begin{bmatrix} 0.0001 & 1 \\ 10 & 10 \end{bmatrix} \begin{bmatrix} x_1 \\ x_2 \end{bmatrix} = \begin{bmatrix} 5 \\ 60 \end{bmatrix}. \qquad (15.11)$$

The solution of (15.11), correct to five digits, is $x_1 = 1.0001$ and $x_2 = 4.9999$. For Gaussian elimination, the first equation is multiplied by 10^5 and subtracted from the second equation which now becomes

$$- 99990\, x_2 = - 499940 . \qquad (15.12)$$

If the computer uses three digit arithmetic, (15.12) would become

$$- 1.00 \times 10^5\, x_2 = - 5.00 \times 10^5 \qquad (15.13)$$

giving $x_2 = 5.00$. When substituted in the first equation of (15.11), this gives $x_1 = 0.0$, which is grossly incorrect.

Let us also obtain the solution after interchanging the rows in (15.11). Equation (15.11) now becomes

$$\begin{bmatrix} 10 & 10 \\ 0.0001 & 1 \end{bmatrix} \begin{bmatrix} x_1 \\ x_2 \end{bmatrix} = \begin{bmatrix} 60 \\ 5 \end{bmatrix}. \qquad (15.14)$$

Applying Gaussian elimination, the second equation of (15.14) becomes

$$0.9999\, x_2 = 4.9994 \qquad (15.15)$$

which, for a computer using three digit arithmetic, would reduce to

$$1.00\, x_2 = 5.00. \tag{15.16}$$

Hence $x_2 = 5.00$ and on back substitution one gets $x_1 = 1.00$, which is the correct solution for the three digit arithmetic.

The example above illustrates that, if the absolute value of a pivot is too small, a severe numerical error may result. To avoid these errors, a good strategy is to choose the pivot at the kth stage to be the element with the largest absolute value in column k of all rows from k to n. This takes some extra computer time but the improvement in the accuracy of the solution is significant. Further improvement in accuracy is possible by interchanging not only the rows but the columns as well. This method is called *complete pivoting* as compared to *partial pivoting* where only rows are interchanged. Additional time is required for complete pivoting since the unknowns also have to be reordered when the columns are interchanged.

As discussed in Chapter 11, a matrix of the type ($\Gamma - S$) is required to be inverted for analysis. The diagonal elements in this matrix are the reflection coefficients at various component ports. The magnitudes of these reflection coefficients could be very small at certain frequencies. However, in every row of ($\Gamma - S$) there is a unity element corresponding to the interconnection matrix Γ which is independent of frequency. Other elements in ($\Gamma - S$) are elements of the component matrices which are less than unity for passive circuits. The unity elements could serve as ideal pivots since the time required to search for the element of highest magnitude is saved. Also, in the initial stages until the unity elements corresponding to Γ matrix are updated; the division by pivot need not be performed. It may be pointed out that in very rare cases the unity element, corresponding to Γ, may on modification drop to zero. This happens only in some anomalous situations and is not considered here [3].

15.3 L-U FACTORIZATION AND F-B SUBSTITUTION [1,2]

To obtain the solution to (15.2), for more than one set of vector **b**, L-U factorization method [1] is preferred. In this method, matrix A is decomposed into a lower triangular matrix L and an upper triangular matrix U such that

$$A = L U \qquad (15.17)$$

where

$$L = \begin{bmatrix} \ell_{11} & 0 & . & . & 0 \\ \ell_{21} & \ell_{22} & 0 & . & 0 \\ \vdots & \vdots & \vdots & \vdots & \vdots \\ \ell_{n1} & \ell_{n2} & . & . & \ell_{nn} \end{bmatrix} \qquad (15.18)$$

and

$$U = \begin{bmatrix} 1 & u_{12} & . & . & u_{1n} \\ 0 & 1 & . & . & u_{2n} \\ \vdots & \vdots & \vdots & \vdots & \vdots \\ 0 & 0 & . & . & 1 \end{bmatrix} \cdot \qquad (15.19)$$

Equation (15.2) now becomes

$$L U x = b . \qquad (15.20)$$

Solution to (15.20) is obtained in two steps. First, using forward elimination technique, one obtains the solution for y satisfying

$$L y = b . \qquad (15.21)$$

The second step requires the solution for x from

$$U x = y . \qquad (15.22)$$

using the process of back substitution. The elements of U are unity all along the main diagonal and therefore, for the purpose of storage, L and U can be overlapped and stored as T such that

$$T = L + U - I \qquad (15.23)$$

where I is an identity matrix.

15.3.1 L-U Decomposition

In this section, we discuss the procedure for decomposing a non-singular matrix A into L and U matrices. First, we discuss situations when such a decomposition is not directly possible.

In Section 15.1, we saw that a non-singular matrix can be triangularized using elementary row operations. Further, each row can be divided by the diagonal element to make it of the type U. As pointed out in the previous section, the effect of a row operation on a matrix can be obtained by pre-multiplying it with another matrix, say E. The matrix E is obtained by performing the same row operation on an identity matrix (I) of suitable order. For any non-singular matrix A, we can thus write

$$E_m \ E_{m-1} \ \cdots \ E_2 \ E_1 \ A \ = \ U \qquad (15.24)$$

where E_k may be any of the three types of matrices obtained by performing an elementary row operation on an identity matrix. If a_{kk} at every stage is nonzero, we would not need row interchanges and only the row operations (i) and (ii) need be used. Matrices E obtained after row operations (i) and (ii) are lower triangular type since operation (i) is multiplication of a row by a scalar and for operation (ii) we always add α times one row to a latter row. The product of any two lower triangular matrices is also a lower triangular matrix. Therefore, the product $(E_m \ E_{m-1} \ \cdots \ E_2 E_1)$ in (15.24) is lower triangular. The inverse of a lower triangular matrix is also lower triangular. Hence, from (15.24), we have

$$A \ = \ L \ U \qquad (15.25)$$

where

$$L \ = \ (E_m E_{m-1} \ \cdots \ E_1)^{-1}$$
$$= \ E_1^{-1} \ E_2^{-1} \ \cdots \ E_m^{-1} \ . \qquad (15.26)$$

If at some stage the pivot element a_{kk} is zero, then a row interchange operation is needed for the Gaussian elimination to continue. In such a case it can be shown that we can find L and U which satisfy

$$L \ U \ = \ P \ A \qquad (15.27)$$

where P is a *permutation matrix* which is obtained by making all row interchanges needed on an identity matrix. If no row interchanges are required, then obviously P = I.

Various procedures like Crout's algorithm and Dolittle algorithm are available for L-U decomposition [2]. The following describes Dolittle algorithm for L-U decomposition of a matrix. In this algorithm, the diagonal elements at each stage are chosen as pivots and it is assumed that they do not become zero.

For all k = 1 *to* n − 1 *do*
    begin
        For all j = k + 1 *to* n *do* $a_{kj} = a_{kj}/a_{kk}$
        For all i = k + 1 *to* n *do*
            begin
                For all j = k + 1 *to* n *do* $a_{ij} = a_{ij} - a_{ik} a_{kj}$
        end (for i)
    end (for k) .

This procedure transforms **A** into **T**, as given by (15.23). The terms of **L** and **U** both are contained in **A** as

$$\ell_{ij} = a_{ij}, \quad \text{for } j \leqslant i \tag{15.28}$$

and

$$u_{ij} = a_{ij}, \quad \text{for } j > i \tag{15.29a}$$

with

$$u_{ii} = 1. \tag{15.29b}$$

In the above algorithm, the number of times the step involving division is executed is given by

$$(n - 1) + (n - 2) + \ldots + 2 + 1 = \frac{n(n - 1)}{2} .$$

The number of times the step for updating a_{ij} is executed is given by

$$(n - 1)^2 + (n - 2)^2 + \ldots + 4 + 1 = \frac{n(n - 1)(2n - 1)}{6} .$$

The updating of a_{ij} requires single multiplication and so the total number of long-operations needed is given by

$$N_{LU} = \frac{n(n - 1)}{2} + \frac{n(n - 1)(2n - 1)}{6} = \frac{n^3}{3} - \frac{n}{3} .$$

$$\tag{15.30}$$

As discussed in the previous section, the selection of pivot for matrices of the type ($\Gamma - S$) can be done a priori by choosing, in each row, the unity element corresponding to the interconnection matrix Γ as the pivot. This implies that the unknowns must be reordered so that the 1's corresponding to Γ fall on the main diagonal. If an array $g(i)$ gives (for the ith row) the position of the unity element corresponding to Γ, then the algorithm described above for L-U decomposition gets modified as

For all k = 1 *to* n − 1 *do*
  begin
      p = g(k)
      For all j = k + 1 *to* n *do*
        begin
          q = g(j)
          $a_{kq} = a_{kq}/a_{kp}$
        end (for j)
      For all i = k + 1 *to* n *do*
        begin
          For all j = k + 1 *to* n *do*
            begin
              q = g(j)
              $a_{iq} = a_{iq} - a_{ip}a_{kq}$
            end (for j)
        end (for i)
    end (for k)

In the above algorithm, the columns of A are not reordered but the element in column p = g(k) is chosen as the pivot at the kth stage. Since the previous pivots have been chosen from columns g(1), g(2), ..., g(k − 1), the elements in these columns in the kth row and the pivot at the kth stage are parts of L and so are not divided by the pivots. Only the elements in columns g(k + 1), ..., g(n) are divided by the pivot. Similarly, for updating, only the elements in columns g(k + 1), ..., g(n) for rows (k + 1) ... n are updated.

While obtaining the solution using the forward elimination and back substitution, this reordering should be used to assign results to the variables.

It should be pointed out that, for the adjoint network also, L-U factors can be used to obtain the solution. This is because if

$$A x = b \tag{15.31}$$

is used to obtain the solution for the original network, the solution to adjoint network is obtained by solving

$$A^t x' = b' \tag{15.32}$$

where b' is the excitation vector for the adjoint network. If we express

$$A = L U \tag{15.33}$$

we have

$$A^t = U^t L^t . \tag{15.34}$$

15.3.2 Forward Elimination and Back Substitution

In order to solve a set of simultaneous equations using L-U factors, solutions to (15.21) and (15.22) are obtained. Equation (15.21) can be rewritten as

$$
\begin{bmatrix}
\ell_{11} & 0 & \cdots & 0 \\
\ell_{21} & \ell_{22} & \cdots & \cdot \\
\vdots & \vdots & \vdots & \vdots \\
\ell_{n1} & \ell_{n2} & \cdots & \ell_{nn}
\end{bmatrix}
\begin{bmatrix}
y_1 \\
y_2 \\
\vdots \\
y_n
\end{bmatrix}
=
\begin{bmatrix}
b_1 \\
b_2 \\
\vdots \\
b_n
\end{bmatrix} . \tag{15.35}
$$

The unknown y_1 can be obtained directly from the first equation of (15.35). This can then be substituted in the second equation to obtain y_2 and so on, until all the y_i values are obtained.

The solution to (15.22) is obtained as follows. Equation (15.22) can be rewritten as

$$\begin{bmatrix} 1 & u_{12} & \cdots & u_{1n} \\ 0 & 1 & \cdots & u_{2n} \\ \vdots & \vdots & \vdots\vdots\vdots & \vdots \\ 0 & 0 & \cdots & 1 \end{bmatrix} \begin{bmatrix} x_1 \\ x_2 \\ \vdots \\ x_n \end{bmatrix} = \begin{bmatrix} y_1 \\ y_2 \\ \vdots \\ y_n \end{bmatrix}. \qquad (15.36)$$

From (15.36), all the x_i values can be obtained in the reverse order.
The algorithm for forward elimination and back substitution can be
given as follows:

// Forward Elimination //
For all j = 1 *to* n − 1 *do*
   begin
      $b_j = b_j/a_{jj}$
      For all i = j + 1 *to* n *do* $b_i = b_i − a_{ij}\,b_j$
   end (for j)
$b_n = b_n/a_{nn}$
// The values of y_i are now contained in b_i's. //
// Back Substitution //
For all i = n − 1 *step* − 1 *until* 1 *do*
   begin
      For all j = n *step* − 1 *until* i + 1 *do* $b_i = b_i − a_{ij}b_j$
   end (for i)
// The values of x_i are now contained in b_i's. //

In this algorithm, for forward elimination there are n divisions and
$n(n − 1)/2$ multiplications. For the back substitution there are
$n(n − 1)/2$ multiplication operations. Thus, the total number of
long-operations for this algorithm are

$$N_{FB} = n + n(n − 1) = n^2 . \qquad (15.37)$$

We can now write the total number of long-operations needed to obtain the solution of (15.2), using L-U factorization and F-B substitution, from (15.30) and (15.37):

$$N = N_{LU} + N_{FB}$$

$$= \frac{n^3}{3} + n^2 - \frac{n}{3} \ . \tag{15.38}$$

If solutions to (15.2) for different sets of right-hand side vectors are needed then only the Forward-Backward substitution needs to be carried out repeatedly. The L-U decomposition is required only once for the original matrix.

For microwave circuits, where the matrix solution for matrices of the type ($\Gamma - S$) is needed, the previous section covers L-U factorization using the unity elements corresponding to Γ as the pivots. It should be noted that since the pivot at kth stage is chosen from column g(k), the unknowns obtained directly will have to be reordered. Thus, the unknowns are stored in a different array x and the reordering is done while storing them. F-B substitution for such cases is described below.

```
// Forward Elimination //
For all j = 1 to n − 1 do
   begin
      q = g(j)
      x_q = b_j/a_jq
      For all i = j + 1 to n do b_i = b_i − a_iq x_q
   end (for j)
q = g(n)
x_q = b_n/a_nq
```

// Back Substitution //

For all i = n − 1 *step* − 1 *until* 1 *do*
  begin
    p = g(i)
    For all j = n *step* − 1 *until* i + 1 *do*
      begin
        q = g(j)
        x_p = x_p − a_{iq} x_q
      end (for j)
  end (for i)

Applications

The solution to (15.32) is required for sensitivity calculations using adjoint network. In this connection, we note that U^t is a lower triangular matrix with unity diagonal elements, and L^t is an upper triangular matrix with elements of arbitrary values on the diagonal. The solution to (15.32) can be obtained by modifying slightly the procedure for Forward-Backward Substitution as described later for sparse matrices in Section 15.4.3.

Further, in cases where the inverse of a matrix will be post-multiplied by another matrix, the L-U factors of the matrix may be obtained and a set of F-B substitutions is carried out for each column of the matrix to be post-multiplied. For example, to evaluate A^{-1} C, the L-U factors of A are obtained and these factors are used to obtain solution of each column of C using Forward-Backward substitution.

15.4 SPARSE MATRIX TECHNIQUES [4-14]

As discussed in Chapters 11 and 12, the matrices needed to be inverted for network analysis are highly sparse. A *sparse matrix* is one which has a large number of zero elements. For matrices of the type (Γ − S), nonzero elements correspond only to the ports of the same component and to the interconnections of ports. For a typical network, only 5 to 10 percent of entries in (Γ − S) are nonzero.

Further, when the same circuit is analyzed for different values of the parameters for various components, the positions of zeros do not change, i.e., the zero - nonzero pattern in ($\Gamma - S$) depends only on the network topology and not on the component characterizations.

Since the matrices are highly sparse, most of the long-operations to be performed for L-U factorization and F-B substitution will be of the type $0 \times a_{ij}$ and $0/a_{ii}$ which could actually be omitted. Thus, the computational efficiency of the analysis can be improved if we use techniques that omit operations of these types and perform only nonzero operations.

Further, considerable reduction in the storage requirement for the matrix can be achieved if only the nonzero elements are stored and the zero elements are not stored. Suitable data structures are designed so that the position of an element in the matrix and its value can be easily retrieved.

15.4.1 Reordering of Equations

In L-U decomposition, the L-U factors given by T of (15.23) are stored in the same memory locations as the original matrix A. It is possible that a location which is zero in A (and so not stored) may become non-zero on decomposition. In L-U decomposition, an element a_{ij} is updated as

$$a_{ij} \leftarrow a_{ij} - a_{ik} a_{kj} \ .$$

If a_{ij} is zero and a_{ik} and a_{kj} are both nonzero, the element (i,j) which was zero in A becomes nonzero in T. The new nonzero elements thus created are called *fill-ins*. Storage locations should be kept for the fill-ins also.

The number of fill-ins generated is dependent on the ordering of rows and/or columns. If the pivots to be chosen in each row are fixed, then the number of fill-ins generated depends upon the ordering of rows. It is desirable to minimize the fill-ins thus generated. To illustrate the dependence of the number of fill-ins generated on the ordering, we consider the solution of the following equations by L-U factorization.

$$\begin{bmatrix} 2 & 4 & -2 & -6 \\ 3 & 9 & 0 & 0 \\ -2 & 0 & 8 & 0 \\ 2 & 0 & 0 & -12 \end{bmatrix} \begin{bmatrix} x_1 \\ x_2 \\ x_3 \\ x_4 \end{bmatrix} = \begin{bmatrix} 6 \\ -6 \\ 14 \\ 26 \end{bmatrix} \qquad (15.39)$$

To determine the number of fill-ins generated, we need not know the actual values of nonzeros, but only their positions. For instance, the matrix of (15.39) for which L-U factors are needed is of the following type:

$$\begin{array}{cccc} & 1 & 2 & 3 & 4 \\ \begin{array}{c} 1 \\ 2 \\ 3 \\ 4 \end{array} & \begin{bmatrix} X & X & X & X \\ X & X & 0 & 0 \\ X & 0 & X & 0 \\ X & 0 & 0 & X \end{bmatrix} \end{array}$$

where X indicates a nonzero element. On L-U factorization, the matrix gets completely filled and so six fill-ins are generated. The number of long-operations needed for this decomposition is 20.

If the equations in (15.39) are ordered as:

$$\begin{bmatrix} 9 & 0 & 0 & 3 \\ 0 & -12 & 0 & 2 \\ 0 & 0 & 8 & -2 \\ 4 & -6 & -2 & 2 \end{bmatrix} \begin{bmatrix} x_2 \\ x_4 \\ x_3 \\ x_1 \end{bmatrix} = \begin{bmatrix} -6 \\ 26 \\ 14 \\ 6 \end{bmatrix} \qquad (15.40)$$

with pivot elements being kept the same, the matrix for which L-U factors are needed is of the type

$$\begin{array}{cccc} & 2 & 4 & 3 & 1 \\ \begin{array}{c} 2 \\ 4 \\ 3 \\ 1 \end{array} & \begin{bmatrix} X & 0 & 0 & X \\ 0 & X & 0 & X \\ 0 & 0 & X & X \\ X & X & X & X \end{bmatrix} \end{array}$$

where, as before, X indicates a nonzero element. On L-U factorization, the matrix is again of the same type and no fill-ins are generated. The number of nonzero long-operations required for factorization is now six. Thus, the rows and columns of A should be reordered, not only to minimize the generation of fill-ins, but also to reduce the number of long-operations required for L-U decomposition. This can be accomplished by means of the reordering algorithm described next.

Reordering algorithm [8-10]

The objective of this algorithm is to reorder the rows and columns of a matrix A, so that the total number of fill-ins generated is minimum.

To find the order of rows and columns, which gives the overall minimum, requires the evaluation of fill-ins generated for each case. The number of possible cases is n! and it would be highly uneconomical in terms of computer effort required to obtain the global minimum. Hence a sub-optimal or a local minimum is accepted.

The Markowitz reordering algorithm [8] attempts to minimize the number of long-operations needed. As pointed out earlier, the pivot to be chosen in each row is fixed and the algorithm decides at each stage which of the remaining pivot candidates should be chosen as the next pivot. The algorithm is described as follows:

Starting with k = 1 until k = n — 1, at the k*th* step, the number of long-operations required for each pivot candidate are found. The pivot that requires the fewest number of long-operations is chosen to be the next pivot. If there are ties, any one amongst the tied pivot candidates is chosen. The number of nonzero long-operations for updating is the product of nonzeros in the pivoting row (in the columns to be updated) and in the pivoting column (in the rows to be updated). This number added to the number of nonzeros in the pivoting row gives the total number of long-operations needed vis-a-vis a pivot candidate.

The algorithm is used here to reorder the rows and columns of the 6×6 matrix structure shown below.

$$
\begin{array}{c}
\\ 1\\ 2\\ 3\\ 4\\ 5\\ 6
\end{array}
\begin{array}{cccccc}
1 & 2 & 3 & 4 & 5 & 6 \\
\left[\begin{array}{c}X\end{array}\right. & & & X & X & \\
& X & X & X & & \\
X & X & X & & X & \\
X & & & X & & X \\
& X & & X & & \\
& X & X & & & X
\end{array}\left.\right]
$$

The pivot candidates are taken to be the elements on the main diagonal. The number of nonzero long-operations required for updating by each pivot candidate are given in Table 15.1.

TABLE 15.1

Number of long operations required in the example considered

Pivot candidate in row	No. of long-operations Division + Updating Total		
1	2 + 4	=	6
2	2 + 2	=	4
3	3 + 9	=	12
4	2 + 6	=	8
5	1 + 2	=	3
6	2 + 2	=	4

The diagonal element in row 5 is chosen as the pivot and, after performing the operations required for this stage, the matrix becomes of the type shown below.

$$
\begin{array}{c}
\begin{array}{cccccc}
\;5 & 1 & 2 & 3 & 4 & 6
\end{array} \\
\begin{array}{c}
5 \\ 1 \\ 2 \\ 3 \\ 4 \\ 6
\end{array}
\left[
\begin{array}{cccccc}
X & & & X & & \\
X & X & & \boxed{X} & X & \\
 & & X & X & X & \\
X & X & X & X & & \\
 & X & & & X & X \\
 & & & X & X & X
\end{array}
\right]
\end{array}
$$

There is one fill-in generated, and indicated by $\boxed{X}$.

The number of long-operations, for division and updating, required for the next stage, for each of the remaining pivot candidates in the row sequence 1, 2, 3, 4, 6 is: $6(= 2 + 4)$, $4(= 2 + 2)$, $8(= 2 + 6)$, $8(= 2 + 6)$ and $4(= 2 + 2)$, respectively.

As shown, there is a tie between pivot elements in rows 2 and 6. Let us choose the diagonal element in row 2 as the next pivot. After performing the operations required for this stage the matrix becomes of the type shown below.

$$
\begin{array}{c}
\begin{array}{cccccc}
\;5 & 2 & 1 & 3 & 4 & 6
\end{array} \\
\begin{array}{c}
5 \\ 2 \\ 1 \\ 3 \\ 4 \\ 6
\end{array}
\left[
\begin{array}{cccccc}
X & & & X & & \\
 & X & & X & X & \\
X & & X & \boxed{X} & X & \\
X & X & X & X & & \boxed{X} \\
 & X & & & X & X \\
 & & & X & X & X
\end{array}
\right]
\end{array}
$$

Following the above procedure, the matrix, after decomposition, is of the following type

	5	2	6	1	3	4
5	X				X	
2		X			X	X
6			X		X	X
1	X			X	(X)	X
3	X	X		X	X	(X)
4			X	X	(X)	X

The number of fill-ins generated is three and a total of 19 long-operations are required for L-U decomposition. It may be noted that, in the absence of the above reordering, the number of fill-ins would be 5 and the total number of long-operations will be 24. In most practical cases, the improvement by reordering is more significant than seen here.

This procedure for reordering is summarized below. RMA denotes the remainder matrix which initially is set equal to the original matrix A. It is assumed that the pivoting elements in each row are placed at the diagonal. The set RMI stores the indices for the remaining pivot candidates. The operations NZR(i) and NZC(i) give the number of nonzero entries in row i and column i (of RMA) respectively. NOP(i) indicates the number of long-operations needed at the step involving the pivot candidate i.

Let RMA = matrix A; RMI = $\{1, 2, \ldots, n\}$

For all k = 1 *to* n − 1 *do*

   begin

      For each i ∈ RMI *do*

         begin

            Determine NZR(i) and NZC(i)

            $NOP(i) = \{NZR(i) - 1\} + \{NZR(i) - 1\}\{NZC(i) - 1\}$

         end (for i)

      Find i_{min} such that $NOP(i_{min}) = \underset{i}{Min}\,(NOP(i))$

      $p(k) = i_{min}$ // p(k) is the next pivoting row. //

For each r such that $a_{rp(k)} \neq 0$ *do*
    begin
        For each j such that $a_{p(k)j} \neq 0$ *do*
            begin
                If $a_{rj} = 0$ *then*
                    begin
                        // Updating the data structure //
                        Add a_{rj} to RMA
                        NZR(r) = NZR(r) + 1
                        NZC(j) = NZC(j) + 1
                  end
            end (for j)
    end (for r)
    Delete row p(k) and column p(k) from RMA
    RMI = RMI $- \left\{ p(k) \right\}$
  end (for k)
p(n) = RMI

The above procedure puts certain requirements on the data structure to be used for handling the matrix. The operations involved are the following:

i)   Counting of nonzeros in each row and column;

ii)   Searching a column for a nonzero element;

iii) Searching a row for a nonzero element;

iv) Comparing a row with another for finding a nonzero element in a column of one row, which is zero in the corresponding column of the other row;

v)   Inserting a nonzero element in A; and

vi) Deleting a row and column from A.

The data structure to be used should facilitate the implementation of these oprations on the matrix.

15.4.2 Data Structure for Reordering

Use of doubly-linked orthogonal lists [11] is a convenient method
for storing a sparse matrix. These lists record the positions of nonzero elements in the matrix. Since the pivot elements have already
been brought to the diagonal positions, the diagonal elements are
necessarily nonzero and this does not need to be explicitly recorded
in the linked list. Thus, only the positions of the off-diagonal nonzero elements need to be stored. The off-diagonal nonzero elements
are numbered arbitrarily for this purpose. A record is created corresponding to each off-diagonal nonzero element in the matrix. For
the ith element, the record contains six entries and is of the type

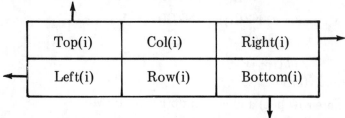

Top(i)	Col(i)	Right(i)
Left(i)	Row(i)	Bottom(i)

where *Col* and *Row* store, for this element, the column number and
row number, respectively. *Left* gives the index number of the element
which is the left-hand side neighbour in the same row, *Right* gives the
index number of the element which is the right-hand side neighbour
in the same row, *Top* gives the index number of the element which
is the upper neighbour in the same column, and *Bottom* gives the
number of the element which is the lower neighbour in the same
column. If an element does not have a neighbour in a particular direction, i.e., if it is the first or the last nonzero element in a row or
column, the corresponding entry in the record is zero.

The above data structure is illustrated by using it on a matrix structure shown below. The number of the off-diagonal nonzero elements
is included as subscripts.

$$
\begin{array}{c c c c c c}
 & 1 & 2 & 3 & 4 & 5 \\
1 & X & & X_1 & X_6 & \\
2 & & X & & X_3 & X_7 \\
3 & X_2 & X_4 & X & & \\
4 & X_{10} & X_5 & & X & \\
5 & & & X_8 & X_9 & X
\end{array}
$$

The records created are shown in Figure 15.1. Two more arrays, *Rowst* and *Colst* are also created so that *Rowst*(j) stores the number of the first off-diagonal nonzero element in row j, and *Colst*(k) stores the value of the first off-diagonal nonzero element in column k. For the matrix structure discussed above and the nonzero elements numbered as in Figure 15.1, the various array entries are given in Table 15.2.

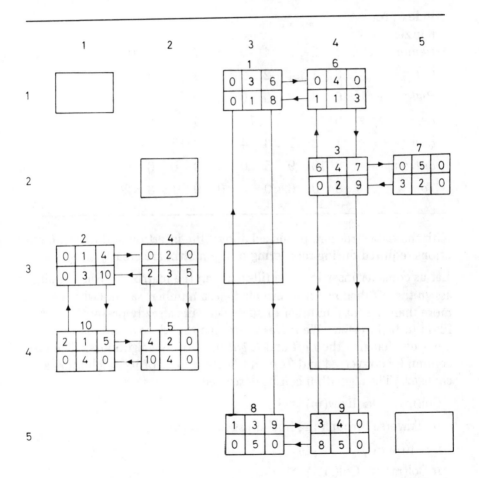

Figure 15.1   Doubly linked orthogonal lists for the matrix example in Section 15.4.2.

TABLE 15.2

Various array entries in the example of doubly-linked orthogonal lists

Rowst	1	3	2	10	8					
Colst	2	4	1	6	7					
Index i for nonzero element	1	2	3	4	5	6	7	8	9	10
Col	3	1	4	2	2	4	5	3	4	1
Right	6	4	7	0	0	0	0	9	0	5
Left	0	0	0	2	10	1	3	0	8	0
Row	1	3	2	3	4	1	2	5	5	4
Bottom	8	10	9	5	0	3	0	0	0	0
Top	0	0	6	0	4	0	0	1	3	2

With the data structure proposed above, the insertion and deletion operations required during reordering of the matrix are greatly simplified.

Let us consider insertion of a fill-in a_{jk} in the matrix A. First of all, we assign the off-diagonal nonzero element a number, say m (which is one more than the total number of such elements already present), to the fill-in to be inserted. We traverse through the jth row and insert the element by changing the *Left* and *Right* links of its neighbours. Then the column k is traversed and *Top* and *Bottom* links of its neighbours are changed. The algorithm can be described as

Col(m) = k; Row(m) = j

// Traverse through the linked list for jth row //

i = Rowst(j)

If Col(m) $<$ Col(i)

    then // Fill-in is the first off-diagonal nonzero element of row j //

       begin

          Left(m) = 0
          Left(i) = m
          Right(m) = i

```
         end
     else
         begin
             ifd = Right(i)
             While ifd ≠ 0 and Col(m) > Col(ifd) do
                 begin
                 i = Right(i)
                 ifd = Right(i)
                 end (while)
         Right(i) = m
         Left(m) = i
         Right(m) = ifd
         If ifd ≠ 0
             then // Fill-in is not the last off-diagonal nonzero
                      element in row j //
                 Left(ifd) = m
     end
NZR(Row(m)) = NZR(Row(m)) + 1 // Add 1 to the number of
                                            nonzeros in jth row //

i = Colst(k)
If Row(m) < Row(i)
    then // Fill-in is the first off-diagonal nonzero element in column k //
        begin
            Top(m) = 0
            Top(i) = m
            Bottom(m) = i
        end
    else
        begin
            ifd = Bottom(i)
            While ifd ≠ 0 and Row(m) > Row(ifd) do
```

> *begin*
>> i = Bottom(i)
>> ifd = Bottom(i)
>
> *end* (while)
>
> Bottom(i) = m
> Top(m) = i
> Bottom(m) = ifd
>
> *If* ifd $\neq$ 0 *then* Top(ifd) = m
>
> *end*

NZC (Col(m)) = NZC(Col(m)) + 1

In the above procedure NZR (j) and NZC (k) store the number of nonzero elements in row j and column k, respectively and so are updated when a fill-in is generated in position (j,k) of A.

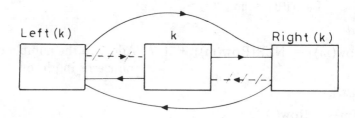

Figure 15.2   *Changes in the left and right pointers of the nearest two elements when a column k is deleted.*

The deletion of a row and a column from the data structure is also simplified. To delete a column from the matrix for each element k in the column, left and right pointers of the adjacent elements in the same row have to be altered as shown in Figure 15.2. The procedure for deleting a column j and a row j from the matrix can be described as follows:

// Deletion of column j //

k = Colst(j)

While k ≠ 0 *do*

   begin

      If Left(k) ≠ 0 *then* Right (Left(k)) = Right(k)

      If Right(k) ≠ 0 *then* Left(Right(k)) = Left(k)

      NZR (Row(k)) = NZR (Row(k)) − 1

      k = Bottom(k)

   end (while)

Colst(j) = 0 // Indicates that the jth column has been deleted //

Deletion of row j is accomplished in the same manner.

In the above procedure, NZR is updated for each row which contains an element in the jth column, as the number of nonzeros reduces by one upon deletion of the column.

15.4.3 L-U Factorization and F-B Substitution [12-14]

A method of L-U factorization and Forward-Backward substitution using sparse matrix techniques is discussed in this section. These operations are greatly simplified by using triangular indexing for the matrix. It is assumed that the matrix is reordered to minimize fill-ins, positions of which have already been determined, and the necessary insertions have been made in the data structure. It should be noted that, at this stage, only the positions of fill-ins have been determined and zeros are stored in these places. The values to be inserted in these positions will be determined during L-U factorization.

All the elements to be stored for matrix A (i.e. nonzeros and fill-ins) are numbered. The pivot elements at the main diagonal are numbered first. The remaining elements are divided into two parts — the elements in L and the elements in U. For each column and row k, from 1 to n − 1, the remaining elements are numbered in the following alternate order: i) the elements in the kth column of L from top to bottom; and ii) the elements in the kth row of U from left to right. For the matrix structure shown below, the element number is shown along with each element that has to be stored.

$$\begin{array}{c} \\ 1 \\ 2 \\ 3 \\ 4 \\ 5 \end{array}
\begin{bmatrix}
X_1 & & X_8 & X_9 & \\
& X_2 & & X_{12} & X_{13} \\
X_6 & X_{10} & X_3 & X_{16} & X_{17} \\
X_7 & X_{11} & X_{14} & X_4 & X_{19} \\
& & X_{15} & X_{18} & X_5
\end{bmatrix}
\begin{array}{c} \\ \end{array}$$

$$\begin{array}{ccccc} 1 & 2 & 3 & 4 & 5 \end{array}$$

Further, an array *Rowcol* can be created such that *Rowcol*(i) stores, for the ith off-diagonal element, its column number if it is from U and its row number if it is from L. For the elements on the main diagonal, *Rowcol*(i) stores the index i itself which is the row as well as the column number. For the matrix structure shown above, *Rowcol* is given as:

Index	1	2	3	4	5	6	7	8	9	10
Rowcol	1	2	3	4	5	3	4	3	4	3

Index	11	12	13	14	15	16	17	18	19
Rowcol	4	4	5	4	5	4	5	5	5

Two arrays *Lcolst* and *Urowst* are also created such that *Lcolst*(k) gives the index number of the top-most off-diagonal element in column k of L and *Urowst*(j) gives the index number of the left-most off-diagonal element in row j of U. For the matrix structure shown above, these arrays are as given below.

Lcolst   6 10 14 18
Urowst   8 12 16 19

The values of the elements are stored in the array A. A(i) gives the values of the element with index number i.

Various nonzero operations required during L-U decomposition for the matrix structure taken above are as follows:

		Index i of the element to be updated	Operation in terms of A(i)
Pivot 1			
Divide:	$a_{13} \leftarrow a_{13}/a_{11}$		$A(8) \leftarrow A(8)/A(1)$
	$a_{14} \leftarrow a_{14}/a_{11}$		$A(9) \leftarrow A(9)/A(1)$
Update:	$a_{33} \leftarrow a_{33} - a_{31}a_{13}$	3	$A(3) \leftarrow A(3) - A(6) \times A(8)$
	$a_{34} \leftarrow a_{34} - a_{31}a_{14}$	16	$A(16) \leftarrow A(16) - A(6) \times A(9)$
	$a_{43} \leftarrow a_{43} - a_{41}a_{13}$	14	$A(14) \leftarrow A(14) - A(7) \times A(8)$
	$a_{44} \leftarrow a_{44} - a_{41}a_{14}$	4	$A(4) \leftarrow A(4) - A(7) \times A(9)$
Pivot 2			
Divide:	$a_{24} \leftarrow a_{24}/a_{22}$		$A(12) \leftarrow A(12)/A(2)$
	$a_{25} \leftarrow a_{25}/a_{22}$		$A(13) \leftarrow A(13)/A(2)$
Update:	$a_{34} \leftarrow a_{34} - a_{32}a_{24}$	16	$A(16) \leftarrow A(16) - A(10) \times A(12)$
	$a_{35} \leftarrow a_{35} - a_{32}a_{25}$	17	$A(17) \leftarrow A(17) - A(10) \times A(13)$
	$a_{44} \leftarrow a_{44} - a_{42}a_{24}$	4	$A(4) \leftarrow A(4) - A(11) \times A(12)$
	$a_{45} \leftarrow a_{45} - a_{42}a_{25}$	19	$A(19) \leftarrow A(19) - A(11) \times A(13)$
Pivot 3			
Divide:	$a_{34} \leftarrow a_{34}/a_{33}$		$A(16) \leftarrow A(16)/A(3)$
	$a_{35} \leftarrow a_{35}/a_{33}$		$A(17) \leftarrow A(17)/A(3)$
Update:	$a_{44} \leftarrow a_{44} - a_{43}a_{34}$	4	$A(4) \leftarrow A(4) - A(14) \times A(16)$
	$a_{45} \leftarrow a_{45} - a_{43}a_{35}$	19	$A(19) \leftarrow A(19) - A(14) \times A(17)$
	$a_{54} \leftarrow a_{54} - a_{53}a_{34}$	18	$A(18) \leftarrow A(18) - A(15) \times A(16)$
	$a_{55} \leftarrow a_{55} - a_{53}a_{35}$	5	$A(5) \leftarrow A(5) - A(15) \times A(17)$
Pivot 4			
Divide:	$a_{45} \leftarrow a_{45}/a_{44}$		$A(19) \leftarrow A(19)/A(4)$
Update:	$a_{55} \leftarrow a_{55} - a_{54}a_{45}$	5	$A(5) \leftarrow A(5) - A(18) \times A(19)$

The order in which the elements are to be updated during L-U decomposition is also stored in array. The elements are updated for each pivot and the order for updating the elements is stored in *Order*. *Order* is a pointer array: each element of it points to the element of A to be updated, in the same order as used in L-U decomposition.

For the matrix structure shown earlier, *Order* would contain the following entries:

Order 3 16 14 4 16 17 4 19 4 19 18 5 5

The array *Pivotst* is used to indicate the beginning of updating operations in *Order* for a pivot. *Pivotst*(k) = r implies that for the k*th* pivot, the elements to be updated are given from *Order*(r) onwards. Thus for the present case *Pivotst* is as follows:

Pivotst 1 5 9 13

We can now write a general algorithm for L-U decomposition in terms of the arrays defined above.

$\ell = 0$

For all i = 1 *to* n − 1 *do*

   begin

     For all k = Urowst(i) *to* Lcolst(i + 1) − 1 *do* A(k) = A(k)/A(i)

     For all j = Lcolst(i) *to* Urowst(i) − 1 *do*

       begin

         For all k = Urowst(i) *to* Lcolst(i + 1) − 1 *do*

           begin

             $\ell = \ell + 1$

             A(Order(ℓ)) = A(Order(ℓ)) − A(j) × A(k)

          end (for k)

       end (for j)

   end (for i)

Only nonzero operations are performed in the above procedure and no searching through the list is required.

We now discuss forward elimination and back substitution using the above data structure so that nonzero operations are avoided. For solution of L y = b, the following nonzero operations are required

	Operations in terms of A(i) and B(i)
$b_1 \leftarrow b_1/a_{11}$	$B(1) \leftarrow B(1)/A(1)$
$b_3 \leftarrow b_3 - a_{31}\, b_1$	$B(3) \leftarrow B(3) - A(6) \times B(1)$
$b_4 \leftarrow b_4 - a_{41}\, b_1$	$B(4) \leftarrow B(4) - A(7) \times B(1)$
$b_2 \leftarrow b_2/a_{22}$	$B(2) \leftarrow B(2)/A(2)$
$b_3 \leftarrow b_3 - a_{32}\, b_2$	$B(3) \leftarrow B(3) - A(10) \times B(2)$
$b_4 \leftarrow b_4 - a_{42}\, b_2$	$B(4) \leftarrow B(4) - A(11) \times B(2)$
$b_3 \leftarrow b_3/a_{33}$	$B(3) \leftarrow B(3)/A(3)$
$b_4 \leftarrow b_4 - a_{43}\, b_3$	$B(4) \leftarrow B(4) - A(14) \times B(3)$
$b_5 \leftarrow b_5 - a_{53}\, b_3$	$B(5) \leftarrow B(5) - A(15) \times B(3)$
$b_4 \leftarrow b_4/a_{44}$	$B(4) \leftarrow B(4)/A(4)$
$b_5 \leftarrow b_5 - a_{54}\, b_4$	$B(5) \leftarrow B(5) - A(18) \times A(4)$
$b_5 \leftarrow b_5/a_{55}$	$B(5) \leftarrow B(5)/A(5)$

The solution y is written over b. For back substitution, to obtain the solution of U x = y (with y stored in b), the nonzero operations are as given below.

$b_4 \leftarrow b_4 - a_{45}\, b_5$	$B(4) \leftarrow B(4) - A(19) \times B(5)$
$b_3 \leftarrow b_3 - a_{34}\, b_4$	$B(3) \leftarrow B(3) - A(16) \times B(4)$
$b_3 \leftarrow b_3 - a_{35}\, b_5$	$B(4) \leftarrow B(4) - A(17) \times B(4)$
$b_2 \leftarrow b_2 - a_{24}\, b_4$	$B(2) \leftarrow B(2) - A(12) \times B(4)$
$b_2 \leftarrow b_2 - a_{25}\, b_5$	$B(2) \leftarrow B(2) - A(13) \times B(2)$
$b_1 \leftarrow b_1 - a_{13}\, b_3$	$B(1) \leftarrow B(1) - A(8) \times B(3)$
$b_1 \leftarrow b_1 - a_{14}\, b_4$	$B(1) \leftarrow B(1) - A(9) \times B(4)$

In back substitution also, the solution x is written over b only. The algorithm for forward elimination and back substitution in terms of the data structure described earlier can be given as follows.

// Forward Elimination //

For all i = 1 *to* n − 1 *do*

   begin

      B(i) = B(i)/A(i)

      For all j = Lcolst(i) *to* Urowst(i) − 1 *do*

         B(Rowcol(j)) = B(Rowcol(j)) − A(j) × B(i)

   end (for i)

B(n) = B(n)/A(n)

// Back Substitution //

For all i = n − 1 *step* − 1 *until* 1 *do*

   begin

      For all j = Urowst(i) *to* Lcolst(i + 1) − 1 *do*

         B(i) = B(i) − A(j) × B(Rowcol(j))

   end (for i)

In the procedure described above, no nonzero operations are performed and searching or sorting is avoided.

F-B Substitution for Sensitivity Calculations

As described in Section 15.3.1, the transpose set of equations must be solved to obtain the sensitivities using the adjoint network. Equation (15.32) must be solved for this purpose. We have

$$A^t x' = (L U)^t x' = U^t L^t x' = b' \qquad (15.41)$$

and therefore we solve

$$U^t y' = b' \qquad (15.42)$$

for y' and then

$$L^t x' = y' \qquad (15.43)$$

to obtain x'. Equations (15.42) and (15.43) can be rewritten as

$$
\begin{bmatrix}
1 & 0 & 0 & \cdots & 0 \\
u_{12} & 1 & 0 & \cdots & 0 \\
u_{13} & u_{23} & 1 & \cdots & 0 \\
\vdots & \vdots & \vdots & \vdots\vdots\vdots & \vdots \\
u_{1n} & u_{2n} & u_{3n} & \cdots & 1
\end{bmatrix}
\begin{bmatrix}
y'_1 \\ y'_2 \\ y'_3 \\ \vdots \\ y'_n
\end{bmatrix}
=
\begin{bmatrix}
b'_1 \\ b'_2 \\ b'_3 \\ \vdots \\ b'_n
\end{bmatrix}
\qquad (15.44)
$$

and

$$
\begin{bmatrix}
\ell_{11} & \ell_{21} & \ell_{31} & \cdots & \ell_{n1} \\
0 & \ell_{22} & \ell_{32} & \cdots & \ell_{n2} \\
0 & 0 & \ell_{33} & \cdots & \ell_{n3} \\
\vdots & \vdots & \vdots & \vdots\vdots\vdots & \vdots \\
0 & 0 & 0 & \cdots & \ell_{nn}
\end{bmatrix}
\begin{bmatrix}
x'_1 \\ x'_2 \\ x'_3 \\ \vdots \\ x'_n
\end{bmatrix}
=
\begin{bmatrix}
y'_1 \\ y'_2 \\ y'_3 \\ \vdots \\ y'_n
\end{bmatrix}.
\qquad (15.45)
$$

The procedure for sparse F-B substitution can easily be modified for the present case. The algorithm for the present case can now be written as

// Forward Elimination //

For all i = 1 *to* n − 1 *do*

    begin

        For all j = Urowst(i) *to* Lcolst(i + 1) − 1 *do*

            B'(Rowcol(j)) = B'(Rowcol(j)) − A(j) × B'(i)

    end (for i)

// Back Substitution //

B'(n) = B'(n)/A(n)

For all i = n − 1 *step* − 1 *until* 1 *do*
> *begin*
> > *For all* j = Lcolst(i) *to* Urowst(i) − 1 *do*
> > > B′(i) = B′(i) − A(j) × B′(Rowcol(j))
> > B′(i) = B′(i)/A(i)
> *end* (for i)

This procedure avoids both nonzero operations and searching through the list.

15.4.4 Remarks on Sparse Matrix Techniques

The discussions on sparse matrix techniques show that only nonzero long-operations need to be performed and storage for zero elements can be saved if proper data structures are used. Doubly-linked orthogonal list structures have been suggested for reordering of rows and columns in order to minimize the fill-ins. Use of triangular indexes minimizes searching time for L-U factorization and F-B substitution.

It should be noted here that though creation of these data structures and then reordering may require some effort, this has to be done only once. Optimization of a typical circuit may require that the circuit be analyzed hundreds of times. If the network is large, the time and storage required for these may be unmanageably large. Using sparse matrix techniques, the reordering of rows and columns is done only once and arrays for triangular indexing are created only once. For a large number of analyses, the time required is drastically reduced in spite of the initial overhead in reordering and creation of arrays.

REFERENCES

[1] Chua, L.O., and P.M. Lin, *Computer-Aided Analysis of Electronic Circuits: Algorithms and Computational Techniques.* Englewood Cliffs, New Jersey: Prentice-Hall, Inc., 1975, Chapter 16, "Introduction to Sparse-Matrix Techniques for Circuit Analysis."

[2] Fox, L., *An Introduction to Numerical Linear Algebra.* New York: Oxford University Press, Inc., 1965.

[3] Bonfatti, F., *et al.*, "Microwave Circuit Analysis by Sparse-matrix Techniques," *IEEE Trans. Microwave Theory Tech.*, Vol. MTT-22, March 1974, pp. 264-269.

[4] Rose, D.J., and R.A. Willoughby, eds., *Sparse Matrices and Their Applications*, New York: Plenum Press, 1972.

[5] Tewarson, R.P., *Sparse Matrices.* New York: Academic Press, 1973.

[6] Bunch, J.R., and D.J. Rose, *Sparse Matrix Computations.* New York: Academic Press, 1976.

[7] Duff, I.S., "A Survey of Sparse Matrix Research,"*Proc. IEEE*, Vol. 65, 1977, pp. 500-535.

[8] Markowitz, H.M., "The Elimination Form of the Inverse and its Application to Linear Programming," *Management Sci.*, Vol. 3, 1957, pp. 255-269.

[9] Duff, L.S., "On the Number of Non-Zeros Added when Gaussian Elimination is Performed on Sparse Random Matrices," *Math. Comput.*, Vol. 28, 1974, pp. 219-230.

[10] Hsieh, H.Y., and M.S. Ghousi, "On Optimal Pivoting Algorithms in Sparse Matrices," *IEEE Trans. Circuit Theory*, Vol. CT-19, 1972, pp. 93-96.

[11] Knuth, D.E., *The Art of Computer Programming.* Vol. 1, Fundamental Algorithms, Reading, MA: Addison-Wesley, 1968.

[12] Gustavson, F.G., *et al.*, "Symbolic Generation of an Optimal Crout Algorithm for Sparse Systems of Linear Equations," *J. Assoc. Comput. Math.*, Vol. 17, 1970, pp. 87-109.

[13]   Curtis, A.R., and J.K. Reid, "The Solution of Large Sparse Unsymmetric Systems of Linear Equations," *J. Inst. Math. Appl.*, Vol. 8, 1971, pp. 344-353.

[14]   Ogbuobiri, E.C., *et al.*, "Sparsity-Directed Decomposition for Gaussian Elimination of Matrices," *IEEE Trans. Power App. Syst.*, Vol. PAS-89, 1970, pp. 141-150.

Part IV

Optimization

16

Introduction to
Optimization

The philosophy of computer-aided design approach has been outlined in Chapter 1. As shown in the flow diagram of Figure 1.2, one starts with a given set of circuit specifications and an initial circuit design. A network model is formulated for analyzing the circuit. Modelling techniques discussed in Chapter 3 through Chapter 10 are used for writing the circuit model. The methods of analysis described in Chapter 11 through Chapter 15 are used for evaluation of circuit performance. Circuit characteristics obtained from the analysis are compared with the given specifications. If the results fail to satisfy the desired specifications, the designable parameters of the circuit are altered in a systematic manner. The sequence of circuit analysis, comparison with the desired performance, and parameter modification, is performed iteratively till the optimum performance of the circuit is achieved. This process is known as optimization and is depicted in the flow-chart shown in Figure 16.1. There are two different ways of carrying out the modification of designable parameters. These are known as gradient methods and direct search methods. Gradient methods use information about the derivatives of the performance functions (with respect to designable parameters) for arriving at the modified set of parameters. This information is obtained from the sensitivity analysis carried out using methods described in Chapter 12. Therefore, in this case, the optimization process gets modified as shown in Figure 16.2. On the other hand, the direct search methods do not use gradient information and parameter modification is carried out by searching for the optimum in a systematic manner.

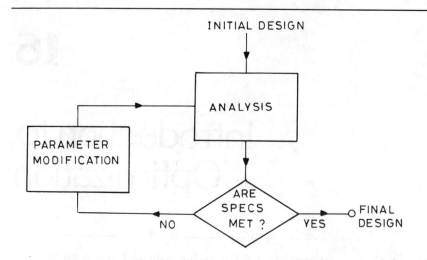

Figure 16.1 Flow-chart of the optimization process.

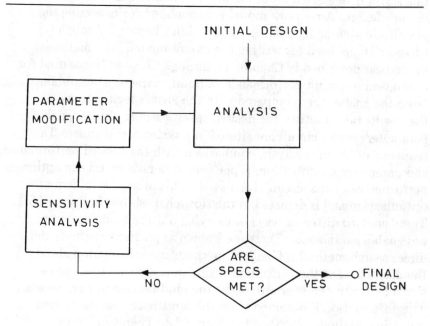

Figure 16.2 Flow-chart of the optimization process using sensitivity analysis for gradient evaluation.

Various aspects of optimization are well documented in the literature [1-10]. This chapter and the two following chapters summarize the important features. This chapter deals with basic concepts, objective function formulation, consideration of constraints, and one-dimensional search methods. The next two chapters describe multi-dimensional optimization techniques using search methods and gradient methods, respectively.

16.1 BASIC CONCEPTS AND DEFINITIONS

Objective function and constraints

The problem of optimization may be formulated as minimization of a scalar *objective function* $U(\phi)$, where $U(\phi)$ is an error function which represents the difference between the performance achieved at any stage and the desired specifications. For example, in the case of a microwave transistor amplifier, the formulation of $U(\phi)$ will involve the specified and achieved values of the gain, the bandwidth, and perhaps the input impedance, noise figure, and dynamic range, also. The objective function $U(\phi)$ is also called the cost function, index or error criterion. Optimization problems are usually formulated as minimization of $U(\phi)$. This does not cause any loss of generality since the minima of a function $U(\phi)$ correspond to the maxima of the function $-U(\phi)$. Thus, by a proper choice of $U(\phi)$, any maximization problem may be reformulated as a minimization problem. ϕ is the set of *designable parameters* whose values may be modified during the optimization process. Usually, for the solution to be feasible, the elements of ϕ are subject to certain *inequality constraints* given by $g(\phi) \geqslant 0$ and certain *equality constraints* $h(\phi) = 0$. For microstrip circuits, elements of ϕ would be the lengths and characteristic impedances of various microstrip sections, values of lumped elements, and parameters of the active devices used. Various constraints arise from the minimum value of the line width that can be etched, the maximum value of line width permissible without exciting higher order modes, available or achievable values of lumped elements, and the limits on parameter values of available active devices. It may be noted that in addition to the elements of ϕ, the value of $U(\phi)$ may depend on several other parameters like frequency, temperature, etc., whose values are not decided by the designer. Hence, these elements are not listed in the set of designable parameters.

The elements of ϕ define a space. A portion of this space where all the constraints are satisfied is called the *feasible region* R or the *design space* R, which may be expressed as

$$R \stackrel{\triangle}{=} \left\{ \phi \mid g(\phi) \geqslant 0, \ h(\phi) = 0 \right\}. \tag{16.1}$$

R is said to be *closed* if equalities are allowed and is said to be *open* if no equalities are allowed. Equation (16.1) defines a closed space. In the optimization process, we look for optimum value of ϕ inside R.

A global minimum of $U(\phi)$, located by a vector ϕ_{min} on the response hypersurface generated by $U(\phi)$, is such that

$$U_{min} \stackrel{\triangle}{=} U(\phi_{min}) < U(\phi) \tag{16.2}$$

for any feasible ϕ not equal to ϕ_{min}. Commonly known methods do not generally guarantee to find a global minimum but yield a local minimum which may be defined as follows:

$$U(\phi_{min}) = \min_{\phi \in R_{\varrho}} U(\phi) \tag{16.3}$$

where R_{ϱ} is a part of R in the local vicinity of ϕ_{min}.

Some features commonly encountered in optimization problems are depicted in Figure 16.3 which is a plot of constant U hypersurfaces for the case of a two-dimensional ϕ vector. This figure shows feasible region, non-feasible region, constant-U contours, a local minimum, global minimum, a saddle point, and a narrow valley. At a saddle point, the function is maximum with respect to variations in some directions and minimum with respect to variations in some other directions.

Some additional features of the objective function $U(\phi)$ may be illustrated by plotting U function for one-dimensional U functions as shown in Figure 16.4(a to d). Figure 16.4(a) shows a *unimodal function* which may be defined as a function having a unique optimum in the feasible region R. It may or may not be continuous. Figure 16.4(b) shows a *strictly convex* function which may be defined as one that can only be overestimated by a linear interpolation between two points on its surface. In such a case we have for $\phi_1 \neq \phi_2$,

$$U(\phi_1 + \lambda[\phi_2 - \phi_1]) < U(\phi_1) + \lambda[U(\phi_2) - U(\phi_1)] \tag{16.4}$$

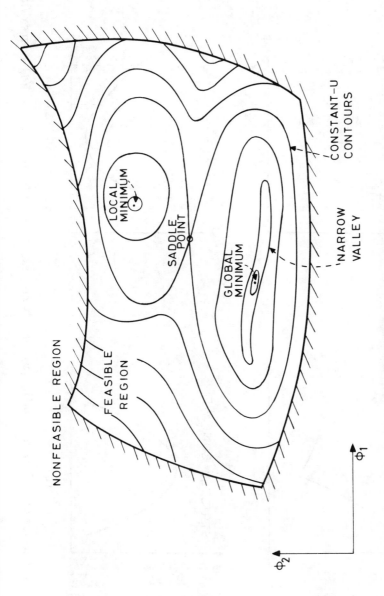

Figure 16.3 Topological representation of a two-dimensional optimization problem.

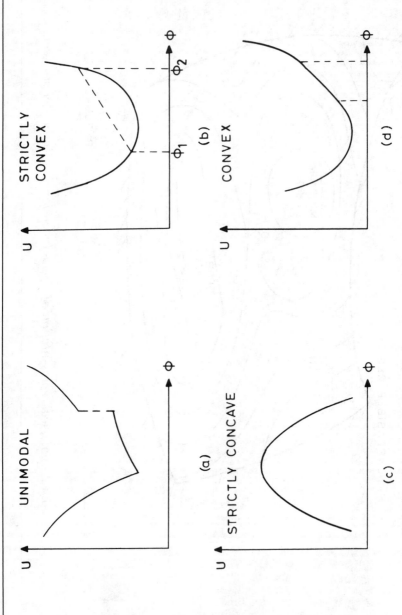

Figure 16.4 Illustrations of (a) unimodal, (b) strictly convex, (c) strictly concave, and (d) convex functions.

where $0 < \lambda < 1$. The negative of a strictly convex function is called a *strictly concave* function, such as the one depicted in Figure 16.4(c). If the two sides in (16.4) become equal, and hence a linear interpolation can occur, we have a *convex function* and the word *strictly* is omitted. Such a function is shown in Figure 16.4(d). The terminology convex and non-convex is also used for the region R in space. A region R is said to be a *convex region* if, for all $(\phi_a, \phi_b) \in$ R, all points given by

$$\phi = \phi_a + \lambda(\phi_b - \phi_a) \qquad 0 \leqslant \lambda \leqslant 1 \qquad (16.5)$$

lie in R. Otherwise, it is a *non-convex region*. Convex and non-convex regions are illustrated in Figures 16.5(a) and (b), respectively.

Taylor Series Expansion

Another general concept used in many optimization methods is that of multi-dimensional Taylor series expansion. The expansion of $U(\phi + \Delta \phi)$ may be written as

$$U(\phi + \Delta\phi) = U(\phi) + \nabla U^t \Delta\phi + \tfrac{1}{2}\Delta\phi^t H\Delta\phi + \ldots \qquad (16.6)$$

where

$$\Delta\phi \overset{\Delta}{=} [\Delta\phi_1, \Delta\phi_2, \ldots, \Delta\phi_k]^t \qquad (16.7)$$

and

$$\nabla U \overset{\Delta}{=} \left[\frac{\partial U}{\partial \phi_1}, \frac{\partial U}{\partial \phi_2}, \ldots, \frac{\partial U}{\partial \phi_k} \right]^t. \qquad (16.8)$$

$\Delta\phi$ defined in (16.7) is called the *increment vector* and ∇U of (16.8) is known as the *gradient vector*. *Hessian matrix* H in (16.6) is a k by k matrix containing second order partial derivatives and is written

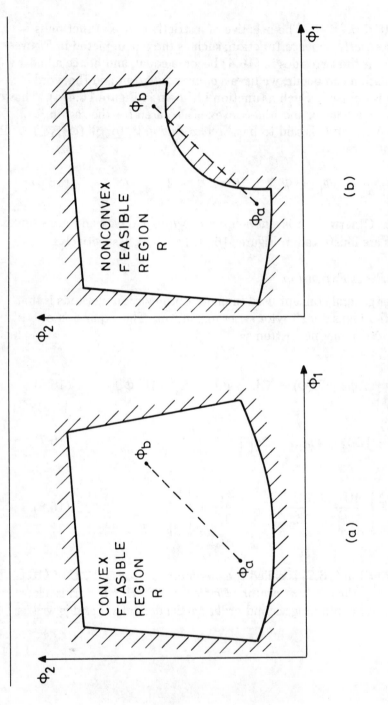

Figure 16.5 (a) Convex and (b) non-convex feasible regions.

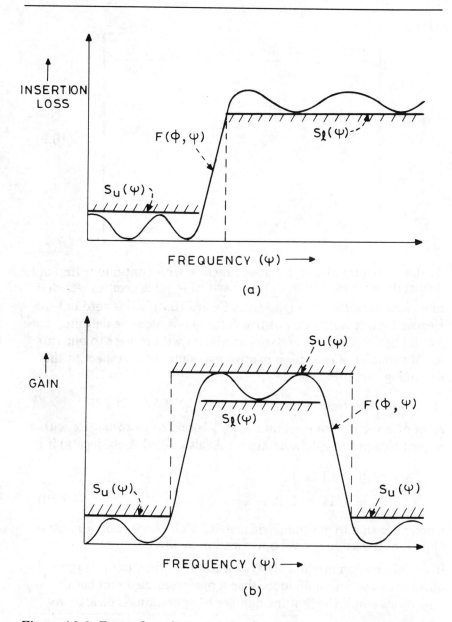

Figure 16.6 Examples of upper response and lower response specifications for (a) a low-pass filter and (b) a band-pass amplifier.

as follows:

$$H \triangleq \begin{bmatrix} \dfrac{\partial^2 U}{\partial \phi_1^2}, & \dfrac{\partial^2 U}{\partial \phi_1 \partial \phi_2} & \cdots & \dfrac{\partial^2 U}{\partial \phi_1 \partial \phi_k} \\[2em] \dfrac{\partial^2 U}{\partial \phi_2 \partial \phi_1}, & \dfrac{\partial^2 U}{\partial \phi_2^2} & \cdots & \dfrac{\partial^2 U}{\partial \phi_2 \partial \phi_k} \\[1em] \vdots & & & \\[1em] \dfrac{\partial^2 U}{\partial \phi_k \partial \phi_1}, & \dfrac{\partial^2 U}{\partial \phi_k \partial \phi_2} & \cdots & \dfrac{\partial^2 U}{\partial \phi_k^2} \end{bmatrix} . \quad (16.9)$$

At the minimum of a continuous function with continuous first order partial derivatives, $\nabla U(\phi_{min}) = 0$ and $H(\phi_{min})$ is positive semidefinite.[*] At a *saddle point* (shown in Figure 16.3), ∇U is zero but the Hessian matrix is neither positive definite nor negative definite. Such a point corresponds to a relative minimum with respect to one subset of variables of ϕ and is a relative maximum with respect to the remaining variables in ϕ.

Conjugate Directions

A set of n vectors (or directions) $\{ s_i \}$ is said to be *conjugate* with respect to a positive definite matrix A (also called A-conjugate) if

$$s_i^t A s_j = 0 \qquad i \neq j$$
$$i,j = 1, 2, \ldots, n \qquad\qquad\qquad (16.10)$$

where A is an n by n symmetric matrix. This concept of conjugate directions is used in several optimization methods.

If a minimization method always locates the minimum of a general quadratic function in no more than a predetermined number of operations and if the limiting number of operations is directly re-

---

[*]A matrix is called positive definite when all its eigenvalues are positive, it is called semidefinite when eigenvalues take only positive and zero values, it is negative definite when all eigenvalues are negative, and negative semidefinite when some eigenvalues are negative and some zero.

lated to the number of variables n, then the method is said to be *quadratically convergent.* If a quadratic function

$$U(\phi) = \phi^t A \phi + b^t \phi + C \qquad (16.11)$$

is minimized sequentially, once along each direction of a set of n linearly independent, A-conjugate directions, the global minimum of U will be located at or before the n*th* step regardless of the starting point.

16.2 OBJECTIVE FUNCTIONS FOR CIRCUIT OPTIMIZATION

16.2.1 General Considerations

The aim of the optimization process is to reduce the differences between the performance realized from a designed circuit and the original specifications. The function which quantifies these differences is called the *objective function.* In order to formulate objective functions for the optimization of circuit designs, the concept of weighted error is useful. Let $S(\psi)$ represent the specified response function (real or complex) of the circuit where ψ is the independent variable, frequency, or time. Also, let $F(\phi, \psi)$ represent the network response at any stage during the design optimization process. $F(\phi, \psi)$ is also called the *approximating function.* A *weighted error function* may be defined as

$$e(\phi, \psi) \overset{\triangle}{=} w(\psi) [F(\phi, \psi) - S(\psi)] . \qquad (16.12)$$

The function $w(\psi)$ is a *weighting function.* The role of the weighting function $w(\psi)$ is to emphasize or deemphasize the difference between $F(\phi, \psi)$ and $S(\psi)$ at selected values of the variable ψ. For example, in the case of a band-pass filter, it may be considered desirable to reduce the transmission loss at two spot frequencies in the pass band. Weighting functions corresponding to these two values of ψ should be kept large.

In order to express the error (or the deviation to be minimized) as a single quantity, we use the norm of the weighted error function $e(\phi, \psi)$. The *pth norm,* when ψ is a continuous variable, is defined as

$$\| e \|_p \overset{\triangle}{=} \left\{ \int_{\psi_1}^{\psi_2} | e(\phi, \psi) |^p \, d\psi \right\}^{1/p} , \quad 1 \leqslant p \leqslant \infty. \quad (16.13)$$

When ψ takes discrete values only

$$\| e \|_p \overset{\triangle}{=} \left\{ \sum_i | e_i(\phi) |^p \right\}^{1/p} , \quad \begin{array}{l} i \in I \\ 1 \leqslant p \leqslant \infty \end{array} \qquad (16.14)$$

where $e_i(\phi) = e(\phi, \psi_i)$ is a component of the *error vector* defined as

$$e(\phi) = [e_1(\phi), e_2(\phi), \ldots, e_n(\phi)]^t . \qquad (16.15)$$

I is an index set relating to the discrete values of ψ in an interval (ψ_ℓ, ψ_u). When there are n discrete values of ψ

$$I \overset{\triangle}{=} (1, 2, \ldots, n) .$$

Two important types of objective functions are obtained using (16.13) and (16.14). These are known as the least p*th* approximation and the minimax approximation.

16.2.2 Least p*th* Approximation
In this case, the objective function is written as

$$U(\phi) = \int_{\psi_1}^{\psi_2} | e(\phi, \psi) |^p \, d\psi \qquad (16.16)$$

or in the discrete case as

$$U(\phi) = \sum_{i \in I} | e_i(\phi) |^p . \qquad (16.17)$$

The minimization of $U(\phi)$ given by (16.16) or (16.17) is known as the *least* p*th approximation*. The minimum thus obtained is the best approximation for the p*th* norm of the error function. A value of $p = 2$ leads to the commonly used least square objective function. In this case, the objective function is the sum of the squares of the errors. The sum of the errors themselves does not lead to an acceptable objective function because of the mutual cancellation of positive and negative errors. When $p = 2$, the norm defined by (16.13) or (16.14) is called a *Euclidean norm* as it basically measures the distance from the origin in the multi-dimensional error space to the tip of the error vector $e(\phi)$ given by (16.15). For the least square case the objective function becomes

$$U(\phi) = \sum_{i=1}^{n} [e_i(\phi)]^2 \tag{16.18}$$

where n is the number of sample points in ψ. In terms of the error vector $e(\phi)$, $U(\phi)$ may be written as

$$U(\phi) = [e(\phi)]^t [e(\phi)] \tag{16.19}$$

and the gradient of $U(\phi)$ becomes

$$\nabla U = 2J^t e(\Phi) \tag{16.20}$$

where J is the n by k Jacobian matrix given by

$$J = \begin{bmatrix} \dfrac{\partial e_1}{\partial \phi_1} & \dfrac{\partial e_1}{\partial \phi_2} & \cdots & \dfrac{\partial e_1}{\partial \phi_k} \\[2ex] \dfrac{\partial e_2}{\partial \phi_1} & \dfrac{\partial e_2}{\partial \phi_2} & \cdots & \dfrac{\partial e_2}{\partial \phi_k} \\[2ex] \vdots & \vdots & & \\[2ex] \dfrac{\partial e_n}{\partial \phi_1} & \dfrac{\partial e_n}{\partial \phi_2} & \cdots & \dfrac{\partial e_n}{\partial \phi_k} \end{bmatrix} . \tag{16.21}$$

The Jacobian matrix may be used to expand the error function $e(\phi)$ in terms of Taylor series as

$$e(\phi + \triangle \phi) \approx e(\phi) + J\triangle\phi. \tag{16.22}$$

When the value of p is greater than 2, the objective function gets adjusted automatically to give even more weight to larger errors. For example, consider an objective function with two error components e_1 (= 1) and e_2 (= 2). For p = 6 and equal weights, U becomes

$$U = (1^6 + 2^6)^{1/6} = (65)^{1/6} \approx 2 . \tag{16.23}$$

Now if we reduce e_1 by 1 (i.e., $e_1 = 0$) we find that U is still 2. On the other hand, if we reduce e_2 by 1 (i.e. e_2 is made unity) the objective function drops immediately from 2 to $2^{1/6} \approx 1$. A further increase in the value of p will enhance this preferential treatment of larger errors.

16.2.3 Minimax Approximation

When p is made infinitely large in (16.13) or (16.14) the following relationship governs the behaviour of the objective function. For well-behaved functions, we have

$$
\max_{[\psi_\varrho, \psi_u]} |e(\phi, \psi)| = \lim_{p \to \infty} \left\{ \frac{1}{\psi_u - \psi_\varrho} \int_{\psi_\varrho}^{\psi_u} |e(\phi, \psi)|^p \, d\psi \right\}^{1/p}
$$

(16.24)

and for the discrete case

$$
\max_i e_i(\phi) = \lim_{p \to \infty} \left\{ \sum_i |e_i(\phi)|^p \right\}^{1/p}, \quad i \in I .
$$
(16.25)

This limiting behaviour for large p leads to direct minimax formulation for the objective function. We write

$$
U(\phi) = \max_{[\psi_\varrho, \psi_u]} [w_u(\psi) \{ F(\phi, \psi) - S_u(\psi) \} ,
$$

$$
-w_\varrho(\psi) \{ F(\phi, \psi) - S_\varrho(\psi) \}]
$$
(16.26)

where $S_u(\psi)$ is the desired upper response specification, $S_\varrho(\psi)$ is the desired lower response specification, $w_u(\psi)$ is the weighting function for $S_u(\psi)$, and $w_\varrho(\psi)$ is the weighting function for $S_\varrho(\psi)$. These quantities satisfy the following restrictions:

$$
S_u(\psi) \geqslant S_\varrho(\psi), w_u(\psi) > 0, \text{ and } w_\varrho(\psi) > 0 .
$$
(16.27)

Under these conditions, $w_u(\psi) \{ F(\phi, \psi) - S_u(\psi) \}$ and $- w_l(\psi) \{ F(\phi, \psi) - S_l(\psi) \}$ are positive when the specifications are not met; they are zero when the specifications are met; and are negative when the specifications are exceeded. The objective is, therefore, to minimize the weighted maximum amount by which the network response fails to meet the specifications, or to maximize the minimum amount by which the network response exceeds the specifications. When there are no upper and lower response specifications but only one desired response specification, we have

$$S_u(\psi) = S_\ell(\psi) = S(\psi) \qquad (16.28)$$

and

$$w_u(\psi) = w_\ell(\psi) = w(\psi) \qquad (16.29)$$

Therefore, (16.26) reduces to

$$U = \max_{[\psi_\ell,\ \psi_u]} \ [\ |\, w(\psi)\, \{\, F(\phi,\, \psi) - S(\psi)\, \}\ |\ ] \qquad (16.30)$$

which is also known as the *Chebyshev* type of objective function.

Examples of upper and lower response specifications for a low-pass filter and a band-pass amplifier are shown in Figure 16.6(a) and (b), respectively. Typical $F(\phi,\, \psi)$ which meet the specifications are also shown in these figures.

One of the difficulties in the minimax formulation described above is the fact that the discontinuous derivatives are generated in ϕ-space when the maximum deviation jumps abruptly from one point on the ψ-axis to another. An alternative to the above formulation which circumvents the difficulty of discontinuous derivatives is to treat U as an additional independent variable subject to two additional constraints [2]. The problem may now be reformulated as: to minimize U subject to

$$U \geqslant w_{ui} \ \{\, F_i(\phi) - S_{ui}\, \} \ , \qquad i \in I_u \qquad (16.31)$$

and

$$U \geqslant - w_{\ell i} \ \{\, F_i(\phi) - S_{\ell i}\, \} \ , \qquad i \in I_\ell \qquad (16.32)$$

and other constraints explicitly stated in the specifications. The index sets I_u and I_ℓ, which are not necessarily disjoint, contain those values of i which refer to the upper and lower specifications, respectively. At a minimum, at least one of the constraints in (16.31) and (16.32) must be an equality, otherwise U could be reduced further without any violation of the constraints. If $U_{min} < 0$, then the minimum amount by which the network response exceeds the specifications has been maximized. If $U_{min} > 0$, then the maximum amount by which the network response fails to meet the specifications has been minimized. When I_u and I_ℓ are infinite, this formulation becomes identical to (16.26). Again, a special case arises when

$$S_{ui} = S_{\ell i} = S_i$$

$$w_{ui} = w_{\ell i} = w_i \qquad\qquad (16.33)$$

$$I_u = I_\ell = I .$$

Equations (16.29) and (16.30) may now be written as

$$U \geqslant w_i[F_i(\phi) - S_i] \qquad\qquad (16.34)$$

and

$$U \geqslant - w_i[F_i(\phi) - S_i] \text{ where } i \in I. \qquad\qquad (16.35)$$

16.3 CONSTRAINTS

Constraints on the values of designable parameters ϕ influence the optimization process considerably. It is rare to find a microwave circuit design problem which is without constraints. For example, there is a lower limit (because of higher order modes) and a practical upper limit (because of the minimum line width that can be etched) on the characteristic impedances of striplines and microstrip lines. Other designable parameters like β of a transistor, Q of a resonator, etc., are all constrained to a small range of easily achievable values. It is necessary to consider the various design constraints before starting and embarking on the optimization process. Two different strategies for handling constraints are: i) transformation of parameters while leaving the objective function unaltered [11], and ii) modification of the objective function by introducing some kind of penalty.

16.3.1 Transformation of Constraints [11]

In most of the cases the constraints may be expressed in terms of upper and lower bounds on the elements of ϕ. We can write

$$\phi_{\ell i} \leqslant \phi_i \leqslant \phi_{ui} , \quad i = 1, 2, \ldots, k .$$ (16.36)

These constraints can be handled by defining ϕ_i' such that

$$\phi_i = \phi_{\ell i} + (\phi_{ui} - \phi_{\ell i}) \sin^2 \phi_i'$$ (16.37a)

or alternatively

$$\phi_i = \tfrac{1}{2} (\phi_{\ell i} + \phi_{ui}) + \tfrac{1}{2}(\phi_{ui} - \phi_{\ell i}) \sin \phi_i' .$$ (16.37b)

If the feasible region is open, i.e., $\phi_{\ell i} < \phi_i < \phi_{ui}$, the following transformations may be used.

$$\phi_i = \phi_{\ell i} + (\phi_{ui} - \phi_{\ell i}) \exp(\phi_i') / [1 + \exp(\phi_i')]$$ (16.38)

or alternatively

$$\phi_i = \phi_{\ell i} + \frac{1}{\pi} (\phi_{ui} - \phi_{\ell i}) \cot^{-1} (\phi_i') .$$ (16.39)

In (16.39), $-\infty < \phi_i' < \infty$ but only solutions within the range $0 < \cot^{-1} \phi_i' < \pi$ are allowed. This transformation has a penalizing effect upon the parameters in the vicinity of the upper and lower bounds. So if the optimum values are expected to lie away from the bounds, this transformation may also introduce a favourable scaling of parameters.

Another type of constraint in microwave circuit design is on the ratio of two parameters. For example, bounds on the ratio of impedances are encountered when dealing with the discontinuity reactances. This may be expressed as

$$\ell \leqslant \phi_2 / \phi_1 \leqslant u, \quad \phi_1 > 0 , \quad \phi_2 > 0 .$$ (16.40)

Transformations

$$\phi_1 = e^{\phi_1'} \cos [\theta_\ell + (\theta_u - \theta_\ell) \sin^2 \phi_2']$$ (16.41)

and

$$\phi_2 = e^{\phi_1'} \sin [\theta_\ell + (\theta_u - \theta_\ell) \sin^2 \phi_2']$$ (16.42)

where

$$0 < \theta_\ell = (\tan^{-1} \ell) < \theta_u = (\tan^{-1} u) < \pi/2$$ (16.43)

ensure that for any ϕ_1' and ϕ_2', the constraints (16.40) are always satisfied.

16.3.2 Penalty for Constraint Violation

A simple way of disallowing a constraint violation is by rejecting any set of parameter values which produces a nonfeasible solution. This may be achieved by freezing the violating parameter or parameters temporarily, and can be easily implemented in direct search methods discussed later in Chapter 17. However, it has been pointed out that a method which simply rejects nonfeasible points can easily terminate at a false minimum [3]. An alternative is to impose a sufficiently large penalty on the objective function when any violation occurs. For this purpose, we add a term

$$\sum_{i=1}^{m} w_i \, g_i^2 \, (\phi) \,, \qquad w_i \begin{cases} = 0 \text{ for } g_i(\phi) \geqslant 0 \\ \\ \\ > 0 \text{ for } g_i(\phi) < 0 \end{cases} \qquad (16.44)$$

to the objective function. It may be noted that all constraints have been put in the form of $g_i(\phi) \geqslant 0$. As long as the constraints are satisfied, the objective functions is not penalized. However, nonfeasible points may be obtained with this formulation. There are other disadvantages also with this approach. Depending upon the type of penalty used, the objective function may be discontinuous or may have steep valleys at the boundaries of the feasible region, and its first or second derivatives may be discontinuous.

16.3.3 Sequential Unconstrained Minimization Technique

This technique [12, 13] for dealing with constraints in optimization problems involves the transformation of the constrained objective into a penalized unconstrained objective of the form

$$P(\phi, r) = U(\phi) + r \, G(\phi) \qquad (16.45)$$

where $G(\phi)$ is continuous in the interior of the feasible region $(g_i(\phi) > 0)$, and $G(\phi) \to \infty$ for any $g_i(\phi) \to 0$ and $r > 0$. Two commonly used forms for $G(\phi)$ are

$$G(\phi) = \sum_{i=1}^{m} \frac{1}{g_i(\phi)} \qquad (16.46)$$

and

$$G(\phi) = - \sum_{i=1}^{m} \log g_i(\phi) . \qquad (16.47)$$

The minimization process starts with selecting a value of ϕ in the interior of R (denoted by R^o and defined as $R^o = \{\phi \,|\, g_i(\phi) > 0\}$ and selecting an initial positive value of $r = r_1$. The function $P(\phi, r)$ of (16.45) is minimized for these chosen values of ϕ and r. Because of the form of (16.46) or (16.47), the minimum $P_{min}(\phi, r_1)$ is expected to lie in R^o. This procedure is repeated for a strictly monotonic decreasing sequence of r values, i.e., $r_1 > r_2 > r_3 \ldots$ $r_j > 0$, with each minimization being started at the previous minimum. For example, the minimization of $P(\phi, r_2)$ is started at $\phi_{min}(r_1)$. Every time r is reduced, the effect of the penalty is reduced and so one would expect that as $j \to \infty$ and $r_j \to o$, $\phi_{min}(r_j) \to \phi_{min}$ and consequently $U_{min}(\phi, r_j)$ tends to the constrained minimum $U_{min}(\phi)$.

Conditions for convergence of the above procedure [12] require that $U(\phi)$ be convex and $g_i(\phi)$ be concave so that the function $P(\phi, r)$ is convex. Nevertheless, the method works successfully for a wide variety of practical problems for which convergence is not readily proved. Bad initial choices of r and ϕ will slow down the convergence. Too large a value of r_1 may render the first few minima of P relatively independent of U, whereas too small a value may render the penalty ineffective except near the boundary where elongated valleys with steep sides are produced. Once the process is started, however, a constant reduction factor of 10 can be used for successive r values. Usually, efficient gradient methods of optimization (discussed later in Chapter 18) are needed to apply this method of sequential unconstrained minimization.

16.4 ONE-DIMENSIONAL OPTIMIZATION TECHNIQUES

It is instructive to look at the methods for minimizing an objective function of a single variable before discussing multi-dimensional optimization. In some cases, the problem itself may be one-dimensional e.g. finding the optimum length of a single transmission line section in a particular transmission line network. Moreover, the one-dimensional minimization techniques are significant because many multi-dimensional optimization techniques (discussed in the next two chapters) call for a one-dimensional search for a minimum in some feasible direction. Since the one-dimensional search is carried out repeatedly, it is desirable to develop efficient algorithms for this purpose.

When the one-dimensional search is used in the optimization procedure for multi-dimensional problems, one starts from a given point in the feasible region in a selected direction. This point and the direction are obtained from the previous iteration of the multi-dimensional search. The derivative of the objective function in the selected direction is negative. The variable in the one-dimensional search is the distance from the starting point. The one-dimensional search is used to find the minimum in this direction.

We can recognize two broad classes of methods available for one-dimensional optimization. The first group consists of elimination methods which chop away sub-intervals not containing the optimum in an efficient manner with no assumptions except that of unimodality. These may also be called *minimax methods* because they minimize the maximum interval which could contain the minimum. The second group consists of approximation or interpolation methods which assume that the function is smooth and well represented by a low order polynomial near the optimum.

16.4.1 Elimination Methods

These methods start with the assumption that the objective function is unimodal in an interval which, for the *jth* iteration, may be termed I^j so that

$$I^j \stackrel{\Delta}{=} u - \ell \tag{16.48}$$

where u and ℓ are the upper and lower limits, respectively. We write

$$\phi_u^j = u \text{ and } \phi_\ell^j = \ell . \tag{16.49}$$

Consider two interior points $\phi_a^j = a$ and $\phi_b^j = b$ in the interval I^j such that $\ell < a < b < u$. Let the values of the objective function evaluated at these points be $U(a) = U_a$ and $U(b) = U_b$. There are two possibilities:

i) $U_a > U_b$, in which case the minimum lies in $[a, u]$ and
     $I^{j+1} = u - a$.

ii) $U_a < U_b$, in which case the minimum lies in $[\ell, b]$ and
     $I^{j+1} = b - \ell$.

Of course, there is the third, but statistically unlikely, possibility
where $U_a = U_b$, in which case the minimum lies in the interval
$[a, b]$ and $I^{j+1} = b - a$.

Whatever the outcome of comparing u_a and u_b, we want

$$I^{j+1} = u - a = b - \ell \tag{16.50}$$

which is achieved by placing a and b symmetrically in the interval
$[\ell, u]$. We want to minimize I^{j+1} and use one of the points again
in our new interval. This leads to

$$I^{j+2} = u - b = a - \ell. \tag{16.51}$$

From (16.50) and (16.51), we note that

$$I^j = I^{j+1} + I^{j+2} . \tag{16.52}$$

The two well known methods of one-dimensional minimization
differ in how the two interior points a and b are selected.

Fibonacci Search

The most effective direct elimination method is the Fibonacci search
method [8, 14]. This method derives its name because of the usage
of the *Fibonacci sequence of numbers* defined by

$$F_o = F_1 = 1$$

$$F_i = F_{i-1} + F_{i-2} \quad i = 2, 3, \ldots, . \tag{16.53}$$

The first few terms of this sequence are 1, 1, 2, 3, 5, 8, 13, 21, . . .
In the Fibonacci search method, the total number of function evalu-
ations $n(n \geq 2)$ is decided first. The interior points ϕ_a^j and ϕ_b^j at the
jth iteration are given by

$$\phi_a^j = \frac{F_{n-j-1}}{F_{n-j+1}} I^j + \phi_\ell^j \qquad (16.54)$$

$$\phi_b^j = \frac{F_{n-j}}{F_{n-j+1}} I^j + \phi_\ell^j \qquad (16.55)$$

where $j = 1, 2, \ldots, n-1$. From (16.55) and (16.54), we have

$$\phi_b^j - \phi_a^j = \frac{F_{n-j} - F_{n-j-1}}{F_{n-j+1}} I^j = \frac{F_{n-j-2}}{F_{n-j+1}} I^j . \qquad (16.56)$$

Thus the symmetry is maintained and each iteration (except the first) actually requires only one function evaluation. Various operations in the jth iteration may be summarized as follows:

If $U_a^j > U_b^j$, then

$$\phi_\ell^{j+1} = \phi_a^j, \phi_a^{j+1} = \phi_b^j, \phi_u^{j+1} = \phi_u^j, U_a^{j+1} = U_b^j \qquad (16.57)$$

and if $U_a^j < U_b^j$, then

$$\phi_\ell^{j+1} = \phi_\ell^j, \phi_b^{j+1} = \phi_a^j, \phi_u^{j+1} = \phi_b^j, U_b^{j+1} = U_a^j. \qquad (16.58)$$

The interval of uncertainty after j iterations is

$$I^{j+1} = \phi_u^j - \phi_a^j = \phi_b^j - \phi_\ell^j \qquad (16.59)$$

reducing the interval I^j by a factor

$$\frac{I^j}{I^{j+1}} = \frac{F_{n-j+1}}{F_{n-j}} . \qquad (16.60)$$

After $n-1$ iterations, the total reduction ratio becomes

$$\frac{I^1}{I^n} = \frac{F_n}{F_{n-1}} \frac{F_{n-1}}{F_{n-2}} \cdots \frac{F_2}{F_1} = F_n. \qquad (16.61)$$

For example, after four function evaluations the initial interval is reduced by a factor of 5, whereas eleven evaluations will reduce the interval by a factor of 144.

In the last (i.e. $(n - 1)th$) iteration both ϕ_a^{n-1} and ϕ_b^{n-1} are given by $\frac{1}{2} I^{n-1} + \phi_\ell^{n-1}$. In this case it becomes necessary to carry out one of the function evaluations at $\frac{1}{2} I^{n-1} + \phi_\ell^{n-1} \pm \delta$ where δ is a small deviation. The final interval of uncertainty is $\frac{1}{2} I^{n-1}$ or $\frac{1}{2} I^{n-1} + \delta$.

In order to achieve an accuracy of σ, the value of n must be such that

$$F_{n-1} < \frac{\phi_u^1 - \phi_\ell^1}{\sigma} \leqslant F_n \qquad (16.62)$$

The above mentioned procedure for the Fibonacci search may be summarized as follows

// Fibonacci Search //

$I^o \quad = u - \ell$

$d \quad = \dfrac{F_{n-2}}{F_n} \; I^o$

$a \quad = \ell + d$

$b \quad = u - d$

$U_a \quad = U(a)$

$U_b \quad = U(b)$

$j \quad = 1$

Loop

   If $U_a > U_b$

      then

         begin

           $\ell = a$

           If $j = n - 1$ *then* EXIT

           $a = b$

           $U_a = U_b$

           $d = \dfrac{F_{n-j-2}}{F_{n-j}} \; (u - \ell)$

```
        b = u − d
    If a = b then b = b + δ
        U_b = U(‛)
    end
else
    begin
        If U_a < U_b
            then
                begin
                    u = b
                    If j = n − 1 then EXIT
                    b = a
                    U_b = U_a
```

$$d = \frac{F_{n-j-2}}{F_{n-j}} (u - \ell)$$

```
                    a = ℓ + d
                    If a = b then a = a − δ
                    U_a = U(a)
                end
            else // Now U_a = U_b //
                begin
                    ℓ = a
                    u = b
                    j = j + 1
                    If j = n − 1 then EXIT
```

$$d = \frac{F_{n-j-2}}{F_{n-j}} (u - \ell)$$

```
                    a = ℓ + d
                    b = u − d
```

$$U_a = U(a)$$
$$U_b = U(b)$$
    end

   end

 $j = j + 1$

forever

Search by Golden Section

The other method of locating interior points in one-dimensional minimization is known as the search by golden section [8, 14]. It has the advantage that the total number of function evaluations n need not be fixed in advance and the method is almost as effective as Fibonacci search.

In this case also, the intervals of uncertainty in successive iterations are related by (16.52). In addition, this method reduces the interval of uncertainty by a constant factor τ at each iteration. Therefore, τ is given by

$$\frac{I^j}{I^{j+1}} = \frac{I^{j+1}}{I^{j+2}} = \tau. \tag{16.63}$$

Relations (16.52) and (16.63) lead to

$$\tau^2 = \tau + 1 \tag{16.64}$$

for which the solution of relevance is

$$\tau = (1 + \sqrt{5})/2 = 1.618034 . \tag{16.65}$$

The division of a line according to (16.52) and (16.63) yields two unequal parts such that the ratio of the whole to the larger part is equal to the ratio of the larger to the smaller. This type of division of a linear segment is called the *golden section of a line*.

The algorithm given for the Fibonacci search can be used for search by golden section also when d is given by $(\tau - 1)^2 (u - \ell)$.

When search by golden section is used for one-dimensional minimization, the reduction ratio after n function evaluations is

$$\frac{I^1}{I^n} = \tau^{n-1} . \tag{16.66}$$

It can be shown that for the Fibonacci search (as $n \rightarrow \infty$)

$$\frac{I^1}{I^n} = F_n \approx \frac{\tau^{n+1}}{\sqrt{5}} . \tag{16.67}$$

The ratio of effectiveness of the Fibonacci search as compared with the golden section is, therefore,

$$\frac{F_n}{\tau^{n-1}} \approx \frac{\tau^2}{\sqrt{5}} = 1.1708 . \tag{16.68}$$

Comparing (16.60) and (16.63) for $j = 1$ and a large value of n, we note that the Fibonacci search and the golden section search start practically at the same rate, the later method ultimately providing an interval of uncertainty only some 17 percent greater than the former. Golden section search is frequently preferred because the number of function evaluations need not be fixed in advance.

16.4.2 Interpolation Methods

These methods approximate the variation of the objective function near the minimum by a low order polynomial which is fitted repetitively through a number of points until the minimum is obtained with the desired accuracy. Methods using quadratic and cubic polynomials are used frequently. In these methods, it is assumed that the function is unimodal and continuous with continuous derivatives in the region of the search. The slope of the objective function at the starting point (generally taken at $\phi = 0$) is assumed to be negative.

Quadratic Interpolation Methods [15, 8]

A quadratic is the lowest order polynomial for which a minimum can exist. Let

$$h(\phi) = a + b\phi + c\phi^2 \tag{16.69}$$

be the quadratic function used for approximating the objective function $U(\phi)$. The necessary condition for the minimum of $h(\phi)$

is that

$$\frac{dh}{d\phi} = b + 2c\phi = 0$$

i.e.,

$$\phi^* = -b/2c \tag{16.70}$$

where ϕ^* locates the minimum of $h(\phi)$. The sufficiency condition for the minimum of $h(\phi)$ is that

$$\left. \frac{d^2h}{d\phi^2} \right|_{\phi^*} > 0, \quad \text{i.e. } c > 0. \tag{16.71}$$

In order to determine the constants a, b, and c in (16.69), we must evaluate $U(\phi)$ at three points. Let A, B, and C be the three values of ϕ where the function $U(\phi)$ is evaluated and let U_A, U_B, and U_C be the corresponding function values, i.e.,

$$U_A = a + bA + cA^2$$

$$U_B = a + bB + cB^2$$

$$U_C = a + bC + cC^2 \ . \tag{16.72}$$

Solution of (16.72) yields

$$a = \left\{ U_A \, BC \, (B - C) + U_B \, CA \, (C - A) + U_C \, AB \, (B - A) \right\} / P \tag{16.73}$$

$$b = \left\{ U_A (B^2 - C^2) + U_B (C^2 - A^2) + U_C (A^2 - B^2) \right\} / P \tag{16.74}$$

and

$$c = -\left\{ U_A (B - C) + U_B (C - A) + U_C (A - B) \right\} / P \tag{16.75}$$

where

$$P = (A - B)(B - C)(C - A) \ . \tag{16.76}$$

From (16.70), (16.74), and (16.75), the minimum of $h(\phi)$ is obtained at

$$\phi^* = -\frac{b}{2c} = \frac{U_A(B^2 - C^2) + U_B(C^2 - A^2) + U_C(A^2 - B^2)}{2\left\{U_A(B-C) + U_B(C-A) + U_C(A-B)\right\}}.$$

$$(16.77)$$

The following procedure can be used to ensure $c > 0$ in the first iteration of curve fitting:

i)   With U_A at $\phi = 0$ and the initial step size t_o known, evaluate U at $\phi = t_o$ and denote this value of U by U_1.

ii) If $U_1 > U_A$, set $U_C = U_1$ and evaluate the function U at $\phi = t_o/2$ to get U_2 and set $t_o = t_o/2$.

iii) If $U_2 \leqslant U_A$, set $U_B = U_2$ and use (16.77) to obtain ϕ^*.
     If $U_2 > U_A$, set $U_C = U_2$ and evaluate the function U at $\phi = t_o/2$ to get the new U_2 and set $t_o = t_o/2$. Repeat step (iii).

iv) If $U_1 \leqslant U_A$, set $U_B = U_1$ and evaluate U at $\phi = 2t_o$ to get U_2.

v)   If $U_2 > U_B$, set $U_C = U_2$ and use (16.77) to obtain ϕ^*. If $U_2 \leqslant U_B$, set $U_A = U_B$, $U_B = U_2$, and $t_o = 2t_o$ and evaluate U at $\phi = 2t_o$ and repeat step (v).

The ϕ^* found by the procedure described above is the location of the minimum of the approximating function $h(\phi)$. It is necessary to ensure that ϕ^* is sufficiently close to the true minimum ϕ_{min} of $U(\phi)$. This can be carried out by comparing $U(\phi^*)$ with $h(\phi^*)$ and considering ϕ^* to be a sufficiently good approximation if they differ by not more than a small amount ϵ. This criterion can be stated as

$$\left| \frac{h(\phi^*) - U(\phi^*)}{U(\phi^*)} \right| \leqslant \epsilon .$$

$$(16.78)$$

If (16.78) is not satisfied, a new quadratic function

$$h'(\phi) = a' + b'\phi + c'\phi^2$$

is used to approximate the function $U(\phi)$. To determine the constants a', b', and c', the best three function values out of the current

U_A, U_B, U_C, and $U(\phi^*)$ can be used. These are selected as follows:

i)   If $\phi^* > B$ and $U(\phi^*) < U_B$, assign $A \leftarrow B, B \leftarrow \phi^*, C \leftarrow C$;

$$(16.79)$$

ii) If $\phi^* > B$ and $U(\phi^*) > U_B$, assign $A \leftarrow A, B \leftarrow B, C \leftarrow \phi^*$;

$$(16.80)$$

iii) If $\phi^* < B$ and $U(\phi^*) < U_B$, assign $A \leftarrow A, B \leftarrow \phi^*, C \leftarrow B$;

$$(16.81)$$

iv) If $\phi^* < B$ and $U(\phi^*) > U_B$, assign $A \leftarrow \phi^*, B \leftarrow B, C \leftarrow C$.

$$(16.82)$$

This process of trying to fit another polynomial to get a better approximation to ϕ^* is known as *refitting* the polynomial. New values of A, B, and C are assigned as in (16.79) through (16.82). A new value ϕ^* can be obtained by carrying out one additional function evaluation. If this ϕ^* also does not satisfy the convergence criteria of (16.78), a new quadratic should be fitted again.

The above procedure for quadratic interpolation is summarized below in the form of an algorithm.

```
// Quadratic Interpolation //
i = 0
A = 0
U_A = U(0)
U_1 = U(t_o)
If U_1 < U_A
    then
        begin
            B = t_o
            U_B = U_1
            U_2 = U(2t_o)
            While U_2 ≤ U_B do
```

begin

$\quad$ A = B

$\quad$ U_A = U_B

$\quad$ B = $2t_o$

$\quad$ U_B = U_2

$\quad$ t_o = $2t_o$

$\quad$ U_2 = $U(2t_o)$

end (while)

$\quad$ C = $2t_o$

$\quad$ U_C = U_2

end

else

$\quad$ *begin*

$\quad$ *Repeat*

$\quad\quad$ C = t_o

$\quad\quad$ U_C = U_1

$\quad\quad$ t_o = $t_o/2$

$\quad\quad$ U_1 = $U(t_o)$

$\quad$ *until* $U_1 < U_A$

$\quad$ B = t_o

$\quad$ U_B = U_1

$\quad$ *end*

Obtain ϕ^* using (16.77)

Repeat

$\quad$ U_ϕ = $U(\phi^*)$

$\quad$ *If* B < ϕ^*

$\quad$ *then*

$\quad\quad$ *begin*

$\quad\quad\quad$ *If* $U_B > U_\phi$

$\quad\quad\quad$ *then*

```
            begin
                A  =  B
                U  = U
                 A    B
                B  = φ*
                U   = U
                 B     φ
            end
        else
            begin
                C  =  φ*
                U   = U
                 C    φ
            end

    end
else
    begin
        If  U  > U
             B    φ
            then
                begin
                    C  =  B
                    U   = U
                     C    B
                    B  = φ*
                    U   = U
                     B    φ
                end
            else
                begin
                    A  =  φ*
                    U   = U
                     A    φ
                end

    end
Obtain φ* using (16.77)
until convergence of φ*
```

Cubic Interpolation Method [16, 8]

This method employs a cubic function

$$h(\phi) = a + b\phi + c\phi^2 + d\phi^3 \tag{16.83}$$

to approximate the objective function $U(\phi)$ between the points A and B. Values of $U(\phi)$ and its first derivative at A and B are used to evaluate the constants a, b, c, and d. We have

$$U_A = a + bA + cA^2 + dA^3 \tag{16.84}$$

$$U_B = a + bB + cB^2 + dB^3 \tag{16.85}$$

$$U_A' = b + 2cA + 3dA^2 \tag{16.86}$$

$$U_B' = b + 2cB + 3dB^2 \ . \tag{16.87}$$

Values of the constants are found as

$$a = U_A - bA - cA^2 - dA^3 \tag{16.88}$$

$$b = \frac{1}{(A - B)^2} \left[B^2 U_A' + A^2 U_B' + 2ABZ \right] \tag{16.89}$$

$$c = \frac{-1}{(A - B)^2} \left\{ (A + B)Z + BU_A' + AU_B' \right\} \tag{16.90}$$

and

$$d = \frac{1}{3(A - B)^2} \left\{ 2Z + U_A' + U_B' \right\} \tag{16.91}$$

where

$$Z = \frac{3(U_A - U_B)}{(B - A)} + U_A' + U_B' \ . \tag{16.92}$$

The minimum of $h(\phi)$ is located by equating $dh/d\phi = 0$, and is given by

$$\phi^* = \frac{-c \pm (c^2 - 3\,bd)^{1/2}}{3d} \ . \tag{16.93}$$

Application of the sufficiency condition for the minimum of $h(\phi)$ leads to

$$\frac{d^2h}{d\phi^2} = 2c + 6d\phi^* > 0. \qquad (16.94)$$

After substituting for the values of b, c, and d, the location of the minimum, ϕ^*, may be expressed as

$$\phi^* = A + \frac{(U_A' + Z \pm Q)}{(U_A' + U_B' + 2Z)} (B - A) \qquad (16.95)$$

where

$$Q = (Z^2 - U_A' U_B')^{1/2}. \qquad (16.96)$$

The two values of ϕ^*, corresponding to the two roots of $h'(\phi)$, indicate the position of a maximum and a minimum of $h(\phi)$. The value of ϕ^* lying in the range A to B is chosen. In order to avoid imaginary values for Q, we should ensure that

$$(Z^2 - U_A' U_B') \geqslant 0. \qquad (16.97)$$

This inequality is automatically satisfied if we choose A and B such that $U_A' < 0$ and $U_B' \geqslant 0$. The value of ϕ^* thus obtained is checked according to (16.78). If this acceptance criteria is not satisfied a new cubic equation

$$h'(\phi) = a' + b'\phi + c'\phi^2 + d'\phi^3 \qquad (16.98)$$

is used to approximate $U(\phi)$. The constants a', b', c', and d' can be evaluated by using the values of the function and its derivative at the best two points out of the three points A, B, and ϕ^* currently available. If $U'(\phi^*) < 0$, ϕ^* and B are taken as the new A and B; otherwise (i.e., if $U'(\phi^*) > 0$) A and ϕ^* are taken as the new A and B. The new ϕ^* is evaluated and convergence checked again. If (16.78) is satisfied, the procedure is stopped and ϕ^* is taken as ϕ_{min}.

The procedure for cubic interpolation is summarized below in the form of an algorithm.

// Cubic Interpolation //

$A = 0$

$U_A = U(0)$

$U_A' = U'(0)$

$U_B = U(t_o)$ // t_o is the starting step length //

$U_B' = U'(t_o)$

While $U_B' < 0$ *do*

  begin

    $A = B$

    $U_A = U_B$

    $U_A' = U_B'$

    $t_o = 2t_o$

    $U_B = U(t_o)$

    $U_B' = U'(t_o)$

  end (while)

$B = t_o$

Obtain ϕ^* using (16.95) and (16.96)

Repeat

  $U_\phi' = U'(\phi^*)$

  If $U_\phi' < 0$

    then

      begin

        $A = \phi^*$

        $U_A = U(\phi^*)$

        $U_A' = U_\phi'$

      end

    else

begin

$B = \phi^*$

$U_B = U(\phi^*)$

$U_B{}' = U_\phi{}'$

end

Obtain ϕ^* using (16.95) and (16.96)

until convergence

Various concepts of optimization introduced in this chapter and the one-dimensional minimization techniques discussed here are employed in the next two chapters where we discuss methods for multi-dimensional optimization.

REFERENCES

[1]   Temes, G.C., and D.A. Calahan, "Computer-Aided Network
        Optimization, the State-of-Art," *Proc. IEEE*, Vol. 55, Nov.
        1967, pp. 1832-1863.

[2]   Waren, A.D., L.S. Lasdon, and D.F. Suchman, "Optimiza-
        tion in Engineering Design," *Proc. IEEE*, Vol. 55, Nov. 1967,
        pp. 1885-1897.

[3]   Bandler, J.W., "Optimization Methods for Computer-Aided
        Design," *IEEE Trans. Microwave Theory and Techniques*,
        Vol. MTT-17, Aug. 1969, pp. 533-552.

[4]   Temes, G.C., "Optimization Methods in Circuit Design,"
        in *Computer Oriented Circuit Design*, F.F. Kuo and W.G.
        Magnuson, Jr., Eds., Englewood Cliffs, N.J.: Prentice-Hall,
        1969.

[5]   Director, S.W., "Survey of Circuit-Oriented Optimization
        Techniques," *IEEE Trans. Circuit Theory*, Vol. CT-18,
        Jan. 1971, pp. 3-10.

[6]   Charalambous, C., "A Unified Review of Optimization,"
        IEEE Trans. Microwave Theory and Techniques, Vol.
        MTT-22, March 1974, pp. 289-300.

[7]   Fidler, J.K., and C. Nightingale, *Computer Aided Circuit
        Design*, Middlesex: Thomas Nelson and Sons Ltd., 1978
        Chapter 7 on "Circuit Optimization."

[8]   Rao, S.S., *Optimization — Theory and Applications*,
        New Delhi: Wiley Eastern Limited, 1978.

[9]   Lavi, A.,and T.P. Vogel, Eds. *Recent Advances in Optimi-
        zation Techniques*, New York: Wiley, 1966.

[10]   Box, M.J., D. Davies, and W.H. Swann, *Non-linear Optimi-
        zation Techniques*, Edinburgh, Scotland: Oliver and Boyd,
        1969.

[11]   Box, M.J., "A Comparison of Several Current Optimiza-
        tion Methods and the Use of Transformation in Constrained
        Problems," *Computer J.*, Vol. 9, May 1966, pp. 67-77.

[12]   Fiacco, A.V., and G.P. McCormick, "The Sequential Un-
        constrained Minimization Technique for Nonlinear Pro-
        gramming, a Primal-Dual Method," *Management Sci.*,
        Vol. 10, Jan. 1964, pp. 360-366.

[13]   Fiacco, A.V., and G.P. McCormick, "Computational
        Algorithm for the Sequential Unconstrained Minimization
        Technique for Non-linear Programming," *Management Sci.*,
        Vol. 10, July 1964, pp. 601-617.

[14]   Wilde, D.J., *Optimum Seeking Methods*, Englewood Cliffs,
        N.J.: Prentice Hall, 1964.

[15]   Powell, M.J.D., "An Efficient Method for Finding the
        Minimum of a Function of Several Variables without
        Calculating Derivatives," *Computer J.*, Vol. 7, July 1964,
        pp. 155-162.

[16]   Fletcher, R., and C.M. Reeves, "Function Minimization
        by Conjugate Gradients," *Computer J.*, Vol. 7, July 1964,
        pp. 149-154.

Direct Search
Optimization
Methods

As pointed out in Chapter 16, various optimization methods may be classified in two groups. Methods that do not make use of the values of the gradient of the objective function are known as *direct search* methods, and are discussed in this chapter. Broadly speaking, these methods rely on the sequential examination of trial solutions in which each solution is compared with the best available up to that time, using a strategy generally based on past experience to decide where the next trial solution should be located. A few commonly used methods are discussed in this chapter.

17.1 PATTERN SEARCH METHODS

One of the simple strategies for direct search optimization is what may be called *one-at-a-time search*. In this method, one parameter is allowed to vary until no further improvement is obtained, then the next parameter is varied and so on. Progress is fairly slow when valleys are not oriented in the direction of any coordinate axis.

The pattern search technique [1] is an improvement over one-at-a-time search and allows one to search along fairly narrow valleys because it attempts to align a search direction along the valley. This technique involves two types of moves in the multi-dimensional ϕ–space. Starting from an initial position, *exploratory moves* are made along the various ϕ-axes in a one-at-a-time manner. The best point resulting from this set of moves defines a *pattern direction* with respect to the initial starting position. A *pattern move* is made in order to find a minimum in the pattern direction. This can be done by using one-dimensional optimization techniques discussed in the previous chapter. The sequence of the exploratory moves and the pattern moves is repeated till the desired optimum is reached.

The two well known pattern search methods, Hooke and Jeeves method [1], and Powell's method [2] differ only in the selection of the axes along which pattern moves are made. In the Hooke and Jeeves method, the pattern directions are decided by exploring along the natural ϕ-parameter axes, whereas in the Powell's method, the set of axes for each sequence of pattern moves is modified with the aim that the resulting selection is a set of conjugate directions. Bandler and MacDonald [3] have modified the Hooke and Jeeves method for minimax objective functions. The response hypersurfaces for minimax objective functions often have a narrow curved valley along which the path of discontinuous derivatives lies. The modified method is called *Razor search* and proceeds in the same way as the pattern search until it terminates. A random point is then selected automatically in the neighbourhood and a second pattern search is initiated until this one also terminates. End points of the two searches (if different) define a new pattern direction, which is explored to find the minimum.

The three methods of pattern search mentioned are presented in this section.

17.1.1 Hooke and Jeeves Method [1]

As indicated earlier, the pattern search method of Hooke and Jeeves is a sequential technique, each step of which consists of two types of moves. The first kind of move (called the exploratory move) is used to explore the local behaviour of the objective function and the second one (called the pattern move) takes advantage of the pattern direction identified in the first step.

One starts with an arbitrarily selected point $\phi_1 = [\phi_{1,1}, \phi_{1,2}, \ldots, \phi_{1,n}]^t$ called the *starting base point* and the prescribed step length $\Delta\phi_i$ along each of the coordinate directions u_i, (i = 1, 2, ..., n).

To start an exploratory move, $U(\phi_1)$ is evaluated. Each of the variables $\phi_{1,i}$ is perturbed about the current base point, to obtain a new temporary base point as

$$\phi_{2,i} = \begin{cases} \phi_{1,i} + \Delta\phi_i, & \text{if } U(\phi_1 + \Delta\phi_i u_i) < U(\phi_1) \\ \phi_{1,i} - \Delta\phi_i, & \text{if } U(\phi_1 - \Delta\phi_i u_i) < U(\phi_1) \\ \phi_{1,i}, \text{ if } U(\phi_1) < \min\left\{ U(\phi_1 + \Delta\phi_i u_i), U(\phi_1 - \Delta\phi_i u_i)\right\}. \end{cases} \tag{17.1}$$

The process in (17.1) is repeated around the temporary base point for i = 1, 2, 3, ..., n. The point ϕ_2 is the *new base point* and, unless $\phi_2 = \phi_1$, a pattern direction s_1 is established as

$$s_1 = \phi_2 - \phi_1. \tag{17.2}$$

A one-dimensional search is carried out along the direction s_1 and the position of the minimum along s_1 may be written as

$$\phi_3 = \phi_2 + \lambda s_1. \tag{17.3}$$

Exploratory moves are carried out with ϕ_3 as the base point and the process continues. If there is no progress in a particular direction u_i, the step length $\Delta\phi_i$ is reduced (say by a factor of two) and the exploratory moves continue. The process is assumed to have converged whenever no progress is made in a particular set of exploratory moves and the step lengths fall below a small quantity ϵ, i.e. when

$$\max_i \left\{ \Delta\phi_i \right\} < \epsilon \quad \text{and} \quad s_j = 0. \tag{17.4}$$

This procedure is summarized below in the form of an algorithm.

// Hooke and Jeeves Method //

$U_\phi = U(\phi)$ // ϕ is the starting point //

Repeat

    $\phi_b = \phi$

    $U_b = U_\phi$

    For all i = 1 *to* n *do*

        begin

            $U_a = U(\phi_b + \Delta\phi_i u_i)$

            If $U_a < U_b$

                then

                    begin

$$\phi_b = \phi_b + \Delta\phi_i \, u_i$$
$$U_b = U_a$$

      end

    else

      begin

$$U_a = U(\phi_b - \Delta\phi_i \, u_i)$$
$$\textit{If } U_a < U_b$$

        then

          begin

$$\phi_b = \phi_b - \Delta\phi_i \, u_i$$
$$U_b = U_a$$

          end

        else $\Delta\phi_i = \Delta\phi_i/2$

      end

    end (for i)

$$s = \phi_b - \phi$$
$$\textit{If } s \neq 0$$

    then

      begin

        Obtain λ such that $U(\phi_b + \lambda s)$ is minimum

$$\phi = \phi_b + \lambda s$$
$$U_\phi = U(\phi)$$

      end

until $\text{Max}_i \left\{ \Delta\phi_i \right\} < \epsilon$ *and* $s = 0$

17.1.2 Powell's Method [2]

Powell's method is an improvement over the basic pattern search method discussed above. It is a widely accepted direct search method and it can be proved to be a method of conjugate directions.

The following theorem [7] helps us to identify conjugate directions in Powell's method. Consider a quadratic function of dimension n and two parallel hyperplanes 1 and 2 of dimension k $<$ n. Suppose that the constrained stationary points of the quadratic in the hyperplanes are ϕ_1 and ϕ_2, respectively. Then, the line joining ϕ_1 and ϕ_2 is conjugate to any line parallel to the hyperplanes. Accordingly, if ϕ_1 and ϕ_2 are two different minima obtained by searches along a direction s starting from two different points, then the vector $(\phi_1 - \phi_2)$ is conjugate to the direction s. Thus, if s_i is chosen along the line joining two minima obtained by searching along s_{i-1}, the directions (s_{i-1}, s_i) are conjugate.

Powell's method for pattern search consists of minization along a set of directions in ϕ-space. To start with, this set coincides with the coordinate directions u_i. The direction of the total increment in one cycle is the pattern direction and is used as the next direction of search. In the second cycle, the pattern direction is included in the set and the first direction u_1 is discarded. In this manner the directions searched in the n*th* cycle are $\{u_n, s_1, s_2, \ldots, s_{n-1}\}$.

To have the first pattern direction s_1 as conjugate to u_n, a search is carried out along u_n before the first cycle. Thus, the directions in the n*th* cycle are conjugate.

Powell's method is a very efficient direct search method because of the quadratic convergence property associated with conjugate directions. This is not because we often get quadratic functions for optimization, but because most of the functions can be approximated very closely by a quadratic function near their minima. In the Taylor's series expansion of an n-dimensional function around its minimum, the terms involving higher derivatives are dominated by the quadratic term and hence $U(\phi)$ approaches a quadratic in the vicinity of the minimum.

The algorithm for the Hooke and Jeeves method given earlier may be modified to suit Powell's method as follows:

// Powell's method //

// ϕ_0 is the starting point //

For all i $= 1$ *to* n *do* $s_i = u_i$

Obtain λ^* to minimize $U(\phi_0 + \lambda s_n)$

$\phi = \phi_0 + \lambda^* s_n$

Repeat

$\phi_a = \phi$

For all i $= 1$ *to* n *do*

    begin

        Obtain λ^* to minimize $U(\phi + \lambda s_i)$

        $\phi = \phi + \lambda^* s_i$

    end

For all i $= 1$ *to* n $- 1$ *do* $s_i = s_{i+1}$

$s_n = \phi - \phi_a$

Obtain λ^* to minimize $U(\phi + \lambda s_n)$

$\phi = \phi + \lambda^* s_n$

until convergence of ϕ

17.1.3 Razor Search Method

It has been pointed out [3] that the minimum for many minimax types of objective functions lies along a path of discontinuous derivative of the $U(\phi)$ function. An example of the objective function of this type is

$$U(\phi) = \min_{\phi} \left\{ \max_{[f_\ell, f_u]} \left[|\rho(\phi, f)| \right] \right\} \tag{17.5}$$

where, in this example, ρ represents the complex reflection coefficient of a multi-sectional inhomogeneous impedance matching transformer. The frequencies f_ℓ and f_u represent the lower and the upper limits of the operating frequency range. ϕ is the set of designable parameters consisting of lengths and impedances (or dimensions) of various sections. Objective functions of this type are found to have a path of the discontinuous derivative situated along a narrow curved valley. The discontinuity in the derivative arises when $U(\phi)$ jumps from one response ripple extremum to another.

The pattern search method of Sec. 17.1.1 is likely to terminate at a false minimum on the path of the discontinuous derivative. The modification suggested by Bandler and MacDonald [3] involves making a random move after one such termination. A new initial point is selected according to the following:

$$\phi_{i,2} = \phi_{i,m1} + k R(i) \qquad i = 1, 2, \ldots, n \tag{17.6}$$

where ϕ_{i,m_1} specify the location of the minimum (possibly a false one) located in one cycle of the pattern search procedure of Hooke and Jeeves, R(i) is a random number between -1 and $+1$, and k is a scaling factor. Another pattern search is started from

$$\boldsymbol{\phi}_2 = \{\phi_{i,2}\} \quad i = 1, 2, \ldots, n \tag{17.7}$$

and, let us say, terminates at $\boldsymbol{\phi}_{m2}$. If $\boldsymbol{\phi}_{m2}$ is almost the same as the terminating point of the first search, one can conclude that the minimum found is a true one and not false. On the other hand, if $\boldsymbol{\phi}_{m2}$ is different from $\boldsymbol{\phi}_{m1}$, a pattern direction is defined by

$$s = \boldsymbol{\phi}_{m2} - \boldsymbol{\phi}_{m1} \tag{17.8}$$

and the pattern search is continued along this direction. Quite often this leads to the true minimum which can be checked by making another random move as in (17.6).

Random moves may also help accelerate the minimization procedure when the ordinary pattern search becomes slow. This has been shown [3] by testing the razor search strategy on the Rosenbrock's function

$$U(\boldsymbol{\phi}) = 100\,(\phi_2 - \phi_1^2) - (1 - \phi_1)^2 . \tag{17.9}$$

This function does not involve discontinuous derivatives. When the razor search method is used without random moves (i.e. the pattern search method), $U(\boldsymbol{\phi})$ becomes 7.4×10^{-3} after 200 function evaluations. In razor search with three random moves, the value of the minimum of $U(\boldsymbol{\phi})$ obtained is 1.6×10^{-6} after 172 function evaluations. Theoretically, the minimum value of $U(\boldsymbol{\phi})$ is zero.

A modification of the pattern search algorithm to incorporate random moves is given below.

// Algorithm Razor //

Obtain $\boldsymbol{\phi}_a$ to minimize $U(\boldsymbol{\phi})$ by the Hooke and Jeeves method with starting point ϕ_1

Repeat

    $\boldsymbol{\phi}_1 = \boldsymbol{\phi}_a$

    For all i = 1 *to* n *do* $\boldsymbol{\phi}_1 = \boldsymbol{\phi}_1 + k\,R(i)\,u_i$

    Obtain $\boldsymbol{\phi}_b$ to minimize $U(\boldsymbol{\phi})$ by Hooke and Jeeves method with starting point ϕ_1.

$$s = \phi_b - \phi_a$$

Obtain λ^* to minimize $U(\phi_b + \lambda s)$

$$\phi_a = \phi_b + \lambda^* s$$

until $\| s \| < \epsilon$

17.2 ROTATING COORDINATES METHOD

In the method of rotating coordinates suggested by Rosenbrock [4], the coordinate system is rotated at each stage of minimization in such a manner that the first axis is oriented towards the locally estimated direction of the valley and all the other axes are made mutually orthogonal and normal to the first one.

Before starting the minimization process, we select a set of initial step lengths $\lambda_1, \lambda_2, \ldots, \lambda_n$ to be taken along the search directions $s_1, s_2, \ldots, s_n$ respectively. At the j*th* stage of minimization (to start with j = 1) we proceed as given below. The set of directions $s_1^{(j)}, s_2^{(j)}, \ldots, s_n^{(j)}$ and the base point are known. For j = 1, these directions are the coordinate directions and the base point is an arbitrary feasible point.

A step of length λ_1 is taken in the direction $s_1^{(j)}$ from the known base point. If the step is successful, λ_1 is multiplied by a constant α, the new point is retained and a success is recorded. If the step is a failure, λ_1 is multiplied by another constant $-\beta$, the new point is discarded and a failure is recorded. A step is said to be successful if the new value of the objective function is less than or equal to the old one. Otherwise it is called a failure. The values of α and β recommended by Rosenbrock are 3.0 and 0.5 respectively.

The search continues sequentially along the directions $s_1^{(j)}, s_2^{(j)}, \ldots,$ $s_{n-1}^{(j)}, s_n^{(j)}, s_1^{(j)}, s_2^{(j)}, \ldots$ until at least one step has been successful and one step has failed in each of the n directions $s_1^{(j)}, s_2^{(j)}, \ldots s_n^{(j)}$. The new set of directions $s_1^{(j+1)}, s_2^{(j+1)}, \ldots, s_n^{(j+1)}$ for use in the next or (j + 1)*th* stage of minimization is obtained by using the Gram-Schmidt orthogonalization procedure [8]. For this purpose, a set of independent directions $p_1, p_2, \ldots, p_n$ is computed as

$$p = [p_1, p_2, \ldots, p_n] =$$

$$[s_1^{(j)}, s_2^{(j)}, \ldots s_n^{(j)}] \begin{bmatrix} L_1 & 0 & 0 & \cdots & 0 \\ L_2 & L_2 & 0 & \cdots & 0 \\ L_3 & L_3 & L_3 & \cdots & 0 \\ \vdots & \vdots & \vdots & & \vdots \\ L_n & L_n & L_n & \cdots & L_n \end{bmatrix} \qquad (17.10)$$

where L_k is the algebraic sum of all the successful step lengths in the corresponding direction, $s_k^{(j)}$, $k = 1, 2, \ldots, n$. The matrix on the right-hand side of (17.10) is lower triangular. It can be seen that p_1 represents the vector joining the starting point and the final point, obtained after the sequence of searches at the jth stage. The vector p_2 denotes the algebraic sum of the successful step lengths in all directions except the first one, and so on. Thus the vectors p_1, p_2, $\ldots$, p_n are linearly independent.

The direction $s_1^{(j+1)}$ is given by

$$s_1^{(j+1)} = p_1 / \| p_1 \| \qquad (17.11)$$

and the other $s_i^{(j+1)}$ are computed as follows:

$$s_i^{(j+1)} = q_i / \| q_i \| \qquad i = 2, 3, \ldots, n \qquad (17.12)$$

where

$$q_i = p_i - \sum_{m=1}^{i-1} [p_i^t s_m^{(j+1)}] s_m^{(j+1)} . \qquad (17.13)$$

The final point obtained at the jth stage is used as the base point for the next stage and the process continues.

The algorithm is terminated either after completing a specified number of stages or when the condition

$$| L_i | \leq \epsilon , \quad \text{for all i} \qquad (17.14)$$

is satisfied, where ϵ is a small number.

The Rosenbrock's method, discussed in this section, can follow curved and steep valleys since the coordinate system in the n-dimensional space can be rotated according to need. The basic Rosenbrock method has been modified [9] so that, in any given cycle, the search is continued in each of the directions until the optimum is found. In other words, a one-dimensional minimization procedure is adopted in each of the search directions. The modified method is expected to be superior to both the Hooke and Jeeves, and the Rosenbrock methods.

The procedure for the Rosenbrock rotating coordinates method is summarized below in the form of an algorithm.

// Algorithm Rotating Coordinates //

$U_\phi = U(\phi)$

For all $i = 1$ *to* n *do* $s_i = u_i$

Repeat

   For all $i = 1$ *to* n *do*

     begin

       $L_i = 0$

       suc(i) = 0

       fail(i) = 0 // *suc* and *fail* are logical arrays //

     end (for i)

   Repeat

     For all $i = 1$ *to* n *do*

     begin

       $U_t = U(\phi + \lambda_i s_i)$

       If $U_t \leqslant U_\phi$

         then

           begin

            $\phi = \phi + \lambda_i s_i$

            $U_\phi = U_t$

            $L_i = L_i + \lambda_i$

            $\lambda_i = \alpha \lambda_i$

$$\text{suc(i)} = 1$$
end
   else
     begin
$$\lambda_i = -\beta \lambda_i$$
$$\text{fail(i)} = 1$$
     end
 end (for i)

ex = 1 // *ex* is a logical variable //

For all i = 1 *to* n *do* ex = ex *and* suc(i) *and* fail(i)

  until ex

Obtain $p_1, p_2, \ldots, p_n$ using (17.10)

$s_1 = p_1 / \| p_1 \|$

For all i = 2 *to* n *do*

  begin

$$q_i = q_i - \sum_{m=1}^{i-1} [p_i^t s_m] \, s_m$$

$$s_i = q_i / \| q_i \|$$

  end (for i)

until $\underset{i}{\text{Max}} \; |L_i| < \epsilon$

17.3 THE SIMPLEX METHOD [5, 6]

The geometrical figure formed by a set of n + 1 points in an n-dimensional space is called a *simplex*. The (n + 1) points are called *vertices* of the simplex. Thus, it is a topological generalization of a triangle which may be called a simplex in two-dimensional space. A tetrahedron is a three-dimensional simplex. When the vertices are equidistant, the simplex is said to be a regular simplex.

The simplex method [5, 6] for minimization of a multi-dimensional objective function starts with an arbitrary shaped simplex in the n-dimensional ϕ-space. The function is evaluated at the n + 1 vertices of the simplex. The simplex modifies and gradually moves towards and shrinks around the optimum point during the iterative process. The manipulation of the simplex is achieved using various operations known as reflection, expansion, contraction and shrinking. In discussing these operations we will use the following notations:

ϕ_h: vertex corresponding to the highest value of U(ϕ) among the vertices of the simplex, i.e.

$$U(\phi_h) = \max_{i = 1 \text{ to } n + 1} \left\{ U(\phi_i) \right\} \tag{17.15}$$

ϕ_s: vertex corresponding to the second highest value of U(ϕ), i.e.

$$U(\phi_s) = \max_{\substack{i = 1 \text{ to } n + 1 \\ i \neq h}} \left\{ U(\phi_i) \right\} \tag{17.16}$$

ϕ_ℓ: vertex corresponding to the lowest value of U(ϕ)

$$U(\phi_\ell) = \min_{i = 1 \text{ to } n + 1} \left\{ U(\phi_i) \right\} \tag{17.17}$$

ϕ_o: centroid of the simplex constituted by all points ϕ_i, other than ϕ_h. It is obtained as

$$\phi_o = \frac{1}{n} \sum_{\substack{i = 1 \\ i \neq h}}^{n + 1} \phi_i . \tag{17.18}$$

The manipulation of the simplex starts with the reflection operation.

Reflection

Since ϕ_h is the vertex corresponding to the highest value of the objective function, it is worthwhile to explore whether the point ϕ_r obtained by reflecting ϕ_h in the opposite face (hyperplane) has a lower value. If this is the case, then we can construct a new simplex by rejecting the point ϕ_h and including the new point ϕ_r. The process of reflection is illustrated in Figure 17.1 for a two-dimensional case. The reflected point is obtained as

$$\phi_r = \phi_o - \alpha (\phi_h - \phi_o) \tag{17.19}$$

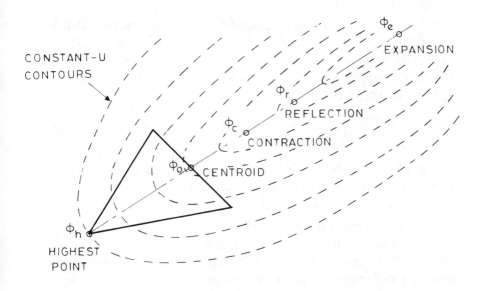

*Figure 17.1 Reflection, expansion and contraction operations in the
simplex method of optimization.*

where $\alpha > 0$ is the reflection coefficient defined as the ratio of the
distance between ϕ_r and ϕ_o, to the distance between ϕ_h and ϕ_o. The
point ϕ_r lies on the line joining ϕ_h to ϕ_o, on the far side of ϕ_o from
ϕ_h with $|\phi_r - \phi_o| = \alpha|\phi_h - \phi_o|$.

The objective function is evaluated at ϕ_r and compared with values
at ϕ_ℓ, ϕ_s and ϕ_h. There are several possibilities: i) $U(\phi_\ell) < U(\phi_r)$
$\leqslant U(\phi_s)$; ii) $U(\phi_r) < U(\phi_\ell)$; iii) $U(\phi_s) < U(\phi_r) < U(\phi_h)$; and
iv) $U(\phi_r) > U(\phi_h)$.

The subsequent operations corresponding to these cases are: i) reflection in new simplex, ii) expansion, iii) contraction, and iv)
shrinking, respectively.

In the first case, the new simplex includes ϕ_r, and ϕ_h is discarded.
ϕ_s now becomes ϕ_h, and ϕ_o is computed again and reflection operation is repeated.

Expansion

If the reflection process gives a point ϕ_r for which $U(\phi_r) < U(\phi_\ell)$, i.e., if the reflection produces a new minimum, one can generally expect the value of the function to decrease further by moving along the direction joining ϕ_o to ϕ_r. This is achieved by the expansion of ϕ_r to ϕ_e by the relation

$$\phi_e = \phi_o - \gamma(\phi_o - \phi_r) \tag{17.20}$$

where $\gamma\,(>1)$ is called the expansion coefficient, defined as the ratio of the distance between ϕ_e and ϕ_o to the distance between ϕ_r and ϕ_o. This operation is also illustrated in Figure 17.1.

The objective function is now evaluated at ϕ_e. If $U(\phi_e) < U(\phi_r)$, we replace the point ϕ_h by ϕ_e and restart the process of reflection. On the other hand, if $U(\phi_e) > U(\phi_r)$, it means that the expansion process is not successful and hence we replace the point ϕ_h by ϕ_r, and restart the process of reflection.

Contraction

If the reflection process yields a point ϕ_r such that $U(\phi_s) < U(\phi_r) < U(\phi_h)$, only a mild improvement has been gained. In this circumstance, we perform a contraction in the direction joining ϕ_o with ϕ_r to check if a better point has been overshot. For contraction we assign

$$\phi_c = \phi_o - \beta(\phi_o - \phi_r) \tag{17.21}$$

where β is called the contraction coefficient $(0 \leq \beta < 1)$ and is defined as the ratio of the distance between ϕ_c and ϕ_o, to the distance between ϕ_r and ϕ_o. This operation is also illustrated in Figure 17.1. The objective function is now evaluated at ϕ_c. If $U(\phi_c)$ is less than $U(\phi_r)$, ϕ_c is retained and replaces ϕ_h. On the other hand, if $U(\phi_r)$ is less than $U(\phi_c)$, ϕ_r is retained and replaces ϕ_h. The next iteration starts with the reflection process again.

Shrinking

The operation of shrinking is resorted to if the reflection process yields a totally unfavourable result, i.e. when $U(\phi_r) > U(\phi_h)$ and no improvement has been gained in computing the reflected point. The implication is that the minimum probably lies within the simplex. The simplex is therefore shrunk about the point of lowest value ϕ_ℓ, by modifying all the other points in the simplex according to

$$\phi_i = \tfrac{1}{2}(\phi_i + \phi_\ell) \ . \tag{17.22}$$

This process is illustrated for a two-dimensional case in Figure 17.2. The reflection process is started again with the new simplex.

The simplex method is assumed to have converged whenever the standard deviation Q of the function at the n + 1 vertices of the current simplex is smaller than some prescribed small quantity ϵ, i.e.

$$Q = \left\{ \sum_{i=1}^{n+1} \frac{[\,U(\phi_i) - U(\phi_o)\,]^2}{n+1} \right\}^{1/2} < \epsilon \ . \tag{17.23}$$

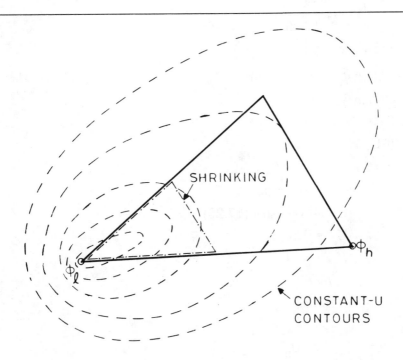

Figure 17.2 Shrinking operation in the simplex method of optimization.

One advantage of the simplex method is that one can start with a larger simplex so that widely separated points are tested at the beginning. This may discourage the simplex from shrinking to a local minimum. The extreme flexibility of size and shape of the simplex gives an intuitive feeling to the correctness of the simplex method.

The simplex procedure is summarized below in an algorithm form.

// Simplex method //

// $\phi_1, \phi_2, \ldots, \phi_{n+1}$ are initialized for the starting simplex //

For all i = 1 *to* n + 1 *do* $U_i = U(\phi_i)$

Repeat

    Obtain h, ℓ and $s \in \{1, 2, \ldots, n+1\}$ such that

$$U_h = \text{Max}\{U_i\}$$
$$U_\ell = \text{Min}\{U_i\}$$
$$U_s = \underset{i \neq h}{\text{Max}}\{U_i\}$$

    Obtain ϕ_o using (17.18)

    Obtain ϕ_r using (17.19)

    $U_r = U(\phi_r)$

    If $U_r < U_\ell$

        then

            begin // Expansion //

                Obtain ϕ_e using (17.20)

                $U_e = U(\phi_e)$

                If $U_e < U_r$

                    then

                        begin

$$\phi_h = \phi_e$$
$$U_h = U_e$$

                    end

                else

```
                begin
                    Φ  = Φ
                     h     r
                    U  = U
                     h     r
                end
        end
    else
        begin
            If U  > U
                r     h
                then
                    begin  // Shrinking //
                        For all i = 1 to n + 1 do
                            begin
                                If i ≠ ℓ
                                    then
                                        begin
                                            Φ  = ½(Φ  + Φ )
                                             i      i     ℓ
                                            U  = U(Φ )
                                             i       i
                                        end
                            end (for i)
                    end
                else
                    begin
                        If U  > U
                            r     s
                            then
                                begin // Contraction //
                                Obtain Φ  using (17.21)
                                        c
                                U  = U(Φ )
                                 c      c
                                If U  < U
                                    c     r
                                    then
```

$$begin$$
$$\phi_h = \phi_c$$
$$U_h = U_c$$
$$end$$
$$else$$
$$begin$$
$$\phi_h = \phi_r$$
$$U_h = U_r$$
$$end$$
$$end$$
$$else$$
$$begin$$
$$\phi_h = \phi_r$$
$$U_h = U_r$$
$$end$$
$$end$$
$$end$$

until convergence

Various methods of optimization discussed in this chapter are based on direct search and do not require the evaluation of gradients. The methods based on gradient evaluation are described in the next chapter.

REFERENCES

[1] Hooke, R., and T.A. Jeeves, "Direct Search Solution of Numerical and Statistical Problems." *Jour. ACM*, Vol. 8, 1961, pp. 212-229.

[2] Powell, M.J.D., "An Efficient Method for Finding the Minimum of a Function of Several Variables without Calculating Derivatives," *Computer J.*, Vol. 7, No. 4, 1964, pp. 303-307.

[3] Bandler, J.W., and P.A. MacDonald, "Optimization of Microwave Networks by Razor Search," *IEEE Trans. Microwave Theory Tech.*, Vol. MTT-17, 1969, pp. 552-562.

[4] Rosenbrock, H.H., "An Automatic Method for Finding the Greatest or Least Value of a Function," *Computer J.*, Vol. 3, Oct. 1960, pp. 175-184.

[5] Spendley, W., G.R. Hext, and F.R. Himsworth, "Sequential Application of Simplex Designs in Optimization and Evolutionary Operation," *Technometrics*, Vol. 4, 1962, p. 441.

[6] Nelder, J.A., and R. Mead, "A Simplex Method for Function Minimization," *Computer J.*, Vol. 7, 1965, p. 308.

[7] Rao, S.S., *Optimization: Theory and Applications*, New Delhi: Wiley Eastern Limited, 1978, p. 270.

[8] Ralston, A., *A First Course in Numerical Analysis*, New York: McGraw-Hill, 1965.

[9] Swann, W.H., "Report on the Development of a New Direct Search Method of Optimization," Central Instrument Laboratory, Imperial Chemical Industries Ltd., England, Research Note 64/3, June 1964.

18

Gradient Methods
for
Optimization

The direct search methods of optimization, discussed in the previous chapter, make repeated use of evaluation of the objective function. However, the derivatives of the objective function are not required. The methods to be discussed in this chapter, on the other hand, make use of the derivatives of the objective function, $U(\phi)$. The primary reason for the use of derivatives or gradient techniques in circuit optimization is that at any point in the design space, the negative gradient direction indicates the direction of the greatest rate of decrease of the objective function at that point. The gradient needed for these methods can be obtained from the sensitivity analysis as discussed in Chapter 12.

Some gradient techniques suitable for circuit optimization are discussed here.

18.1 STEEPEST DESCENT METHOD [1-3]

The steepest descent method is perhaps the simplest gradient technique available for function minimization. It exploits the property noted above by determining a minimum of the objective function along a line in the direction of the gradient. In this method, we start from an initial trial point ϕ_1 and iteratively move towards the optimum point according to the rule

$$\phi_{i+1} = \phi_i + \lambda_i s_i \tag{18.1}$$

where

$$s_i = -\nabla U(\phi) \mid_{\phi_i} / \|\nabla U(\phi)\mid_{\phi_i}\| \tag{18.2}$$

i.e., s_i is given by the negative of the normalized gradient vector at the current value of ϕ in the ith iteration. The function ∇U is defined in (16.8). The step length λ_i is obtained from the one-dimensional search along the s_i direction.

The following convergence criteria can be used to terminate the iterative process:

i) $$\left| \frac{U(\phi_{i+1}) - U(\phi_i)}{U(\phi_i)} \right| \leqslant \epsilon_1 \tag{18.3}$$

ii) $$\left| \frac{\partial U(\phi)}{\partial \phi_k} \right| \leqslant \epsilon_2 , \quad k = 1, 2, \ldots, n. \tag{18.4}$$

iii) $$|\phi_{i+1} - \phi_i| \leqslant \epsilon_3 . \tag{18.5}$$

At the first look, the method of steepest descent may appear to be an efficient technique since each one-dimensional search starts in the "best" direction. However, owing to the fact that the steepest descent direction is a local property, the method is really not effective in most of the problems. Perhaps, it is best to regard its ineffectiveness as a demonstration of the fact that a good local strategy is not necessarily a good global one. An illustration of this is seen in Figure 18.1, where it is seen that the gradient direction at ϕ_0 does not point towards the minimum.

Numerous modifications have been suggested over the years to speed up the convergence of the steepest descent method. One of these is based on the idea of using one-dimensional search in a direction given by

$$s_i = \phi_i - \phi_{i-2} , \quad i \geqslant 2 \tag{18.6}$$

alternately, instead of always using the negative gradient direction. Directions given by (18.6) generally lie in the direction of the mini-

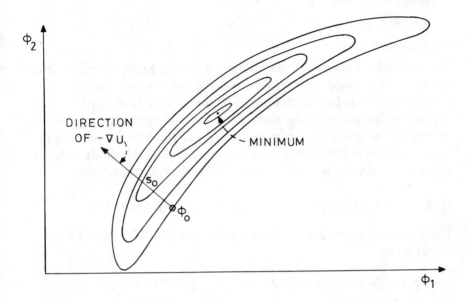

Figure 18.1 An example where steepest descent direction does not point towards the minimum.

mum and their use accelerates the convergence. This method is called a *gradient based partan* (parallel tangent) method [1-3]. The procedure is summarized below in the form of an algorightm.

// Gradient Parallel Tangent //

$\phi_a = \phi$ // ϕ is the starting point //

Obtain s using (18.2)

Obtain λ^* to minimize $U(\phi + \lambda s)$

$\phi = \phi + \lambda^* s$

Repeat

    Obtain s using (18.2)

    Obtain λ^* to minimize $U(\phi + \lambda s)$

    $\phi = \phi + \lambda^* s$

    $s = \phi - \phi_a$

    $\phi_a = \phi$

Obtain λ^* to minimize $U(\phi + \lambda s)$

$\quad = \phi + \lambda^* s$

until convergence.

The methods of steepest descent and parallel tangents are called first order methods since only the first order derivatives are used in their execution. Second order methods include two kinds of approaches: (a) where the second order derivatives are used explicitly, and (b) where, by the use of information from previous steps, knowledge of the second order derivatives is obtained implicitly. Methods of these two kinds are discussed in Sections 18.2 and 18.3, respectively.

18.2 GENERALIZED NEWTON-RAPHSON METHOD [4]

The Taylor series expansion for a multidimensional function $U(\phi)$ is written as

$$U(\phi + \triangle \phi) = U(\phi) + \nabla U^t . \triangle \phi + \frac{1}{2} \triangle \phi^t H(\phi) \triangle \phi + \dots$$

$$(18.7)$$

where $H(\phi)$ is the Hessian matrix defined in (16.9). Consider a point ϕ in the vicinity of the optimum point ϕ_{min} such that

$$\phi_{min} = \phi + \triangle \phi. \qquad (18.8)$$

Differentiating (18.7) and using the fact that

$$\nabla U(\phi_{min}) = 0 \qquad (18.9)$$

we have (neglecting higher order terms)

$$0 \approx \nabla U(\phi) + H(\phi) \triangle \phi. \qquad (18.10)$$

When $H(\phi)$ is non-singular, the set of linear equations given by (18.10) can be easily solved for $\triangle \phi$ as

$$\triangle \phi \approx - H^{-1}(\phi) \nabla U(\phi) \qquad (18.11)$$

where $H^{-1}(\phi)$ is the inverse of the Hessian matrix at ϕ. For a quadratic function $U(\phi)$, the vector $\triangle \phi$ given by (18.11) provides the increments in parameters for the minimum to be reached in exactly one step. When $U(\phi)$ is not quadratic the higher order terms in (18.7) and (18.10) are not negligible and an iterative procedure is required to find the better approximation. The iteration scheme is given by

$$\phi_{i+1} = \phi_i - \lambda_i \, H^{-1}(\phi_i) \nabla U(\phi_i) \tag{18.12}$$

where λ_i is the step length evaluated by using one-dimensional optimization in the direction s_i given by

$$s_i = \left\{ -H^{-1}(\phi_i) \, \nabla U(\phi_i) \right\} . \tag{18.13}$$

Iterations given in (18.12) could also be carried out by using a fixed step length λ. However, the incorporation of a one-dimensional search has several advantages. First, the minimum is approached in less steps than for the fixed λ method. Second, it finds the point of minimum in all cases, whereas the fixed λ method may not converge in some cases. Third, it usually avoids convergence to a saddle point or a maximum. In spite of these many advantages, the Newton-Raphson method discussed above has not become popular because it has the following difficulties, as well.

i)   It requires storage of the n x n $H(\phi_i)$ matrix.

ii)   It becomes difficult (and sometimes impossible) to compute the elements of $H(\phi_i)$ which are second order partial derivatives.

iii)   The method requires the inversion of the matrix $H(\phi_i)$ and the evaluation of the product $H^{-1}(\phi_i) \, \nabla U(\phi_i)$ at each step of the iteration procedure.

These features make the method impractical for problems involving a complicated objective function with a large number of variables.

18.3 DAVIDON-FLETCHER-POWELL METHOD [5, 6]

The main difficulty in the generalized Newton-Raphson method, discussed in Section 18.2, is the evaluation of H and its inverse at each stage of iteration. The Davidon-Fletcher-Powell method overcomes this difficulty by using an approximation to the inverse of Hessian in place of $H^{-1}(\phi_i)$ in equations (18.11) to (18.13). This approximation is gradually improved in the successive stages of iteration. Thus, at the $(i + 1)th$ iteration, an approximation to the inverse of H (say G_i) is used to define the direction of search by

$$s_i = -G_{i-1} \, \nabla U(\phi_i) \tag{18.14}$$

and the results of the search are then used to improve the approximation. Also, this method aims to arrange the successive approximations to the inverse so that the directions generated are conjugate. In each iteration

$$\phi_{i+1} = \phi_i + \lambda_i s_i \tag{18.15}$$

and

$$G_i = G_{i-1} + \frac{s_i s_i^t}{s_i^t H s_i} + B_i . \tag{18.16}$$

Equation (18.16) is formulated as follows. Consider a specially constructed matrix

$$\sum_{j=1}^{p} \alpha_j s_j s_j^t \tag{18.17}$$

which is arranged so that we may find an approximation to H^{-1}. The set of directions $s_i, \ldots, s_p$ are mutually conjugate with respect to the matrix H. If we post-multiply the matrix in (18.17) by $H s_r$ for $r = 1, 2, \ldots, p$, we have, by the conjugacy of s_i,

$$\left(\sum_{j=1}^{p} \alpha_j s_j s_j^t \right) H s_r = \alpha_r s_r s_r^t H s_r . \tag{18.18}$$

If we now set

$$\alpha_r = \frac{1}{s_r^t H s_r} \tag{18.19}$$

we have

$$\left(\sum_{j=1}^{p} \alpha_j s_j s_j^t \right) H s_r = s_r . \tag{18.20}$$

Since s_r is not an eigenvector, (18.20) may be written, for $p = n$,

$$\left(\sum_{j=1}^{n} \alpha_j s_j s_j^t \right) H = I \tag{18.21}$$

where I is an identity matrix. Combining (18.19) and (18.21) we have

$$H^{-1} = \sum_{j=1}^{n} \frac{s_j \, s_j^t}{s_j^t \, H \, s_j} . \tag{18.22}$$

Relation (18.22) suggests that, as each new conjugate direction is generated, the partial sums of (18.22) could be used as approximations to H^{-1}. Although the property of conjugacy has been used to derive (18.22), the use of (18.22) itself does not ensure that s_i will be mutually conjugate. B_i in (18.16) has been added to allow for additional flexibility to ensure conjugacy.

If s_r $(r = 1, 2, \ldots, i-1)$ are mutually conjugate with respect to the Hessian matrix H, then

$$s_r^t \, H \, s_i = 0 \tag{18.23}$$

or

$$s_r^t \, H \, G_{i-1} \, \nabla U(\phi_i) = 0 . \tag{18.24}$$

If

$$s_r^t = s_r^t \, H \, G_{i-1} \tag{18.25}$$

it follows that,

$$s_r^t \, \nabla U(\phi_i) \approx 0 \quad \text{for } r = 1, 2, \ldots, i-1 . \tag{18.26}$$

Equation (18.26) is a general theorem for conjugate directions. The above derivation shows by induction that if the relation (18.25) can be arranged to hold true, then the s_i are mutually conjugate. To arrange that

$$s_r^t \, H \, G_i = s_r^t \quad r = 1, 2, \ldots, i \tag{18.27}$$

holds, we write it for $r = i$ and substitute for G_i from (18.16), so that

$$s_i^t \, H \left(G_{i-1} + \frac{s_i \, s_i^t}{s_i^t \, H \, s_i} + B_i \right) = s_i^t \tag{18.28}$$

or

$$s_i^t \, H \, G_{i-1} + s_i^t + s_i^t \, H \, B_i = s_i^t \tag{18.29}$$

or

$$s_i^t \, H \, (G_{i-1} + B_i) = 0. \tag{18.30}$$

From the definition of Hessian, we may write

$$H \, (\phi_{i+1} - \phi_i) = \nabla U(\phi_{i+1}) - \nabla U(\phi_i) \tag{18.31}$$

which, combined with (18.15), may be written as

$$H \, s_i = \frac{1}{\lambda_i} \left\{ \nabla U(\phi_{i+1}) - \nabla U(\phi_i) \right\}. \tag{18.32}$$

Combining (18.30) and (18.32) and using $H = H^t$, we get

$$\left\{ \nabla U(\phi_{i+1}) - \nabla U(\phi_i) \right\}^t (G_{i-1} + B_i) = 0. \tag{18.33}$$

One of the solutions of (18.33), $B_i = -G_{i-1}$, is trivial in the sense that it reduces (18.16) to

$$G_i = \frac{s_i \, s_i^t}{s_i^t \, H \, s_i} \tag{18.34}$$

which would make G_i a function of only the *ith* conjugate direction. If we set

$$y_i = \nabla U(\phi_{i+1}) - \nabla U(\phi_i) \tag{18.35}$$

and try the solution

$$B_i = \frac{-G_{i-1} \, y_i \, y_i^t \, G_{i-1}}{y_i^t \, G_{i-1} \, y_i} \tag{18.36}$$

we have, by substituting in (18.33),

$$y_i^t \, G_{i-1} - \frac{y_i^t \, G_{i-1} \, y_i \, y_i^t \, G_{i-1}}{y_i^t \, G_{i-1} \, y_i}$$

$$= y_i^t \, G_{i-1} - y_i^t \, G_{i-1} = 0. \tag{18.37}$$

This verifies (18.36) as a solution for B_i. Now B_i, as given by (18.36), may be substituted in (18.16) to use the minimization procedure postulated in (18.14) through (18.16). However, (18.16) assumes that H itself is known and could be used explicitly in approximating H^{-1}. This is possible for only some special cases. In general, we should avoid the explicit use of H and approximate the term $s_i^t H s_i$ in (18.16) by using the value of G_{i-1} obtained in the previous iteration. For this purpose, we write

$$s_i^t H s_i = \frac{(\phi_{i+1} - \phi_i)^t}{\lambda_i} H s_i$$

$$= \frac{\{\nabla U(\phi_{i+1}) - \nabla U(\phi_i)\}^t}{\lambda_i} s_i . \qquad (18.38)$$

Using (18.14), the above relation reduces to

$$s_i^t H s_i = (1/\lambda_i)\{\nabla U(\phi_{i+1}) s_i + [\nabla U(\phi_i)]^t G_{i-1} [\nabla U(\phi_i)]\} . \qquad (18.39)$$

Since the gradient at ϕ_{i+1} is orthogonal to s_i, the first term on the right-hand side of (18.39) becomes zero and we have

$$s_i^t H s_i = (1/\lambda_i) [\nabla U(\phi_i)]^t G_{i-1} [\nabla U(\phi_i)] . \qquad (18.40)$$

The method may now be summarized. For the *ith* stage of iteration we have as follows:

i)   Compute $s_i = -G_{i-1} \nabla U(\phi_i)$ (18.41)

ii)   Calculate λ_i by one-dimensional minimization of $U(\phi_i + \lambda_i s_i)$

iii) Set $\phi_{i+1} = \phi_i + \lambda_i s_i$ (18.42)

      and $y_i = \nabla U(\phi_{i+1}) - \nabla U(\phi_i)$ (18.43)

iv) Compute

$$G_i = G_{i-1} + \frac{\lambda_i s_i s_i^t}{[\nabla U(\phi_i)]^t G_{i-1} [\nabla U(\phi_i)]}$$

$$- \frac{G_{i-1} y_i y_i^t G_{i-1}}{y_i^t G_{i-1} y_i} . \qquad (18.44)$$

To start with, G_o may be taken as an identity matrix. In this case, we have an initial minimization along a steepest descent direction which is usually quite efficient for the first few steps. Choosing $G_o = I$ ensures positive definiteness of G_o. One can show that if G_i is positive definite, G_{i+1} will also be positive definite provided λ_i's are computed accurately. However, with the likelihood of numerical error in computation of λ_i's, it is advisable to check for positive definiteness of G as the iterations proceed and, if necessary, to reset G to an identity matrix.

18.4 OPTIMIZATION OF LEAST SQUARE OBJECTIVE FUNCTIONS

The optimization methods discussed earlier are useful for minimizing any scalar objective function. A least square optimization requires that the sum of the squares of deviations be minimized. The methods discussed thus far can be used by designating U as the sum of the squares of the deviations. In this section, a technique for optimizing least square objectives is presented. This technique is based on Gaussian least squares solution. The algorithm uses the gradients of each of the terms and avoids a one-dimensional search in the design space.

Let the objective function to be minimized be

$$U = f_1^2 + f_2^2 + \ldots + f_m^2 \tag{18.45}$$

where $f_1, f_2, \ldots, f_m$ are the functions of the designable parameters $\phi = \{ \phi_1, \phi_2, \ldots, \phi_n \}$, with $m \geqslant n$. The minimization of U in (18.45) is equivalent to minimizing the norm of an m-dimensional objective function vector

$$f(\phi) = \{ f_1(\phi), f_2(\phi), \ldots, f_m(\phi) \} . \tag{18.46}$$

with $f_1(\phi), f_2(\phi), \ldots, f_m(\phi)$ being its components. The norm of $f(\phi)$ is taken to be $[f(\phi)]^t f(\phi)$ and is equal to U given by (18.45). The value of the vector objective function f at $\phi + \Delta\phi$ can be estimated using Taylor's series expansion as

$$f(\phi + \Delta\phi) \approx f(\phi) + J(\phi)\Delta\phi . \tag{18.47}$$

where the increment $\Delta\phi$ is assumed to be small so that the higher order terms can be neglected and $J(\phi)$ is the Jacobian matrix defined by (16.21).

In this method, $\Delta\phi$ is chosen such that the norm of $f(\phi + \Delta\phi)$, given by the right-hand side of (18.47), is minimum. Using (10.46), the value of $\Delta\phi$ giving minimum value of the norm of $f(\phi) + J(\phi)\Delta\phi$ is given by

$$\Delta\phi = -\left\{ [J(\phi)]^t\, J(\phi) \right\}^{-1} [J(\phi)]^t\, f(\phi) . \tag{18.48}$$

For quadratic functions f, the minimum of (18.45) is achieved in a single step. For higher order objective functions, this process must be repeated, i.e., $f(\phi)$ and $J(\phi)$ are computed at $\phi + \Delta\phi$ and a new $\Delta\phi$ is obtained. This process is repeated until convergence. However, a common problem using this method is that $\Delta\phi$, as computed from (18.48) may become too large. In such cases, and if the Jacobian J is changing rapidly with ϕ, it is desirable to restrict each component of $\Delta\phi$ to a pre-specified value.

The technique can be used for many optimization problems in micro-wave circuits. The scattering parameters are complex and can be considered as the two components of the vector objective function. For example, in the case of minimizing input VSWR, f can be expressed as

$$f = \left\{ \mathrm{Re}(S_{11}),\ \mathrm{Im}(S_{11}) \right\}^t \tag{18.49}$$

which is a two-dimensional vector objective function. As another example, in the design of a branch-line hybrid, the objectives for optimization are to minimize the input VSWR and to equalize the power division. Normally, the scalar objective function would be expressed as

$$U = A|S_{11}|^2 + B|S_{21} - jS_{41}|^2 \tag{18.50}$$

where S_{21} and S_{41} are coupling coefficients which have a phase difference of $90°$, and A and B are weighting constants. The problem can be reformulated in terms of a vector objective function as

$$f = \left\{ a\,\mathrm{Re}(S_{11}),\ a\,\mathrm{Im}(S_{11}),\ b\,\mathrm{Re}(S_{21} - jS_{41}),\ \right.$$
$$\left. b\,\mathrm{Im}(S_{21} - jS_{41}) \right\}^t \tag{18.51}$$

where $a^2 = A$ and $b^2 = B$. The method proposed in this section can now be used to minimize the norm of f. For optimization over a range of frequencies, the objectives at different frequencies can be treated as components of a vector objective function.

The gradient methods of optimization discussed in this chapter are, in general, more efficient than the direct search methods described in the previous chapter.

REFERENCES

[1] Shah, R.V., R.J. Buehler, and O. Kempthorne, "Some Algorithms for Minimizing a Function of Several Variables," *J. SIAM*, Vol. 12, March 1964, pp. 74-92.

[2] Wilde, D.J., *Optimum Seeking Methods.* Englewood Cliffs, N.J.: Prentice Hall, 1964.

[3] Rao, S.S., *Optimization: Theory and Applications.* New Delhi: Wiley Eastern Limited, 1978.

[4] Powell, M.J.D., "Minimization of Functions of Several Variables," in *Numerical Analysis: An Introduction*, J. Walsh, Ed., Washington, DC: Thompson, 1967.

[5] Davidon, W.C., "Variable Metric Method of Minimization," *Argonne National Laboratory Report No. ANL-5990*, 1959.

[6] Fletcher, R., and M.J.D. Powell, "A Rapidly Convergent Descent Method for Minimization," *Computer J.*, Vol. 6, No. 2, 1963, pp. 163-168.

Part V

CAD Programs

19

A Microwave Circuit Analysis Program (MCAP)

This chapter describes a general purpose microwave circuit analysis program called MCAP [1,2,3]. This program evaluates the overall scattering matrix of a multiport circuit from the known S-matrices of the constituent components of the circuit. The subroutines incorporated into the program can handle various stripline and microstrip components. However, the program may be extended for circuits using any other transmission structure by including the relevant subroutines (which characterize various elements).

The characterization of striplines and microstrip lines discussed in Chapter 3 and the modelling of stripline and microstrip discontinuities given in Chapter 6 are used in MCAP. The circuit analysis uses the connection-scattering matrix approach discussed in Section 11.2.1. Since equation (11.17) yields the values of wave variables a at all external as well as connected ports of the circuit, MCAP can be extended to perform the sensitivity analysis using the adjoint network method, as discussed in Chapter 12.

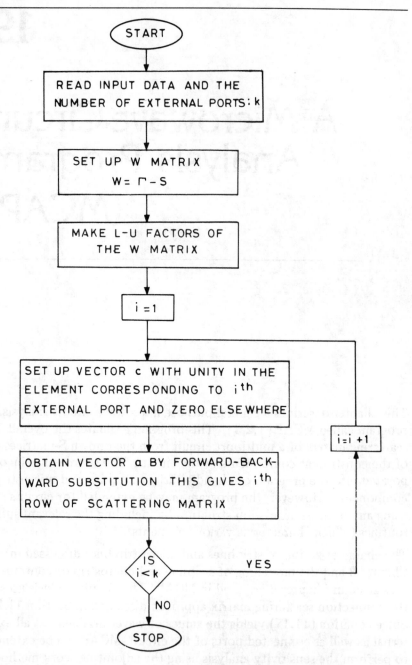

Figure 19.1 Flow-chart for the analysis program MCAP.

19.1 PROGRAM DESCRIPTION

19.1.1 Flow Chart

A flow chart for the analysis program is shown in Figure 19.1. The circuit is divided into basic components whose characterizations are stored in the library of subroutines. The data read in includes description of components, interconnections between ports, and frequency of operation. The program stores the expressions for the evaluation of scattering matrix for all the basic components which constitute the circuit to be analyzed. The interconnection scattering matrix is computed from the interconnection pattern and component scattering matrices. It is factorized into a lower triangular matrix and an upper triangular matrix.

Source vector c is set up with c(i) = 1 for an external port i. The solution for W a = c is obtained by forward backward substitution and the process is repeated for every external port.

19.1.2 Description of Subroutines

i) REDATA: This subroutine reads in the input data. The first line read indicates whether a stripline or a microstrip circuit is being analyzed. The other data consist of description of elements, the interconnections of various ports, and the frequencies at which the scattering matrix is to be computed. It also reads information about whether the discontinuity effects are to be taken into consideration for analysis. It is called by the main program.

ii) ELCODE: Converts the mnemonic code describing the type of element into a numeric code. It is called by the subroutine REDATA.

iii) SETWNC: Sets up the W matrix (= Γ − S) by putting unity elements corresponding to interconnections and inserting the scattering matrices of the components in the network in their proper place. It is called by the main program.

iv) SETUPS: Called repeatedly by the subroutine SETWNC and inserts the scattering matrix of one of the components (at a time) into the W matrix.

v) IMPFWD: Computes the characteristic impedance of a stripline or microstrip line from the width of the strip, other parameters being kept constant. It is called by subroutine REDATA.

TABLE 19.1

Subroutines for Various Elements

Z_0	Transmission line section	LINESC
Z	Shunt admittance across a line	SHNTSC
Z	Series impedance	SERISC
Z_1 Z_2	Change in impedance	STEPSC
	T-junction	TEEJSC
	Open-end	OPNESC
	Bend in strip	BENDSC
	Gap in the strip conductor	GAPSC
	Hole in strip conductor	HOLESC
	Coupled lines	COUPLD
1 2 $N \leq 4$	Externally specified S-parameters	SPARA

vi) WIDTH: This subroutine computes the width of the conducting strip required to get a particular characteristic impedance.

vii) FACTLU: Factorizes the W matrix into a lower triangular matrix and an upper triangular matrix. It is called by the main program.

viii) FORBAK: This subroutine computes the solution by a pair of forward and backward substitutions using the L-U factors obtained by FACTLU. It is called by the main program.

Scattering matrices for the various components are computed by corresponding subroutines, as listed in Table 19.1. These subroutines are called by the subroutine SETWNC.

19.1.3 Example

As an example, a 3 db rat-race hybrid in microstrip configuration is analyzed using MCAP. The circuit configuration is shown in Figure 19.2. This circuit consists of eight components: four T-junctions

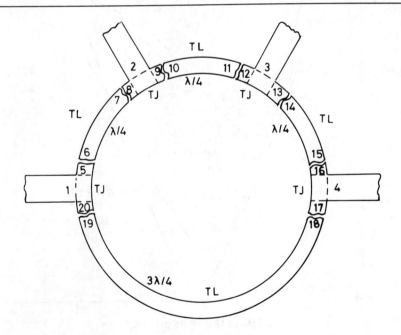

Figure 19.2 Numbering of ports of a rat-race hybrid for analysis using MCAP.

and four microstrip transmission line sections. The circuit has been analyzed twice, first ignoring the parasitic reactances associated with T-junctions and then taking into account the parasitic reactances. The frequency responses for the two cases are shown in Figures 19.3 and 19.4. Substrate height is 0.125 inch, ϵ_r = 2.55, and center frequency is 3 GHz. In Figure 19.3, VSWR variations for ϵ_r = 9.8 are also plotted. It demonstrates that the discontinuity reactance effects are reduced when high dielectric constant substrates are used. This example points out the need to incorporate the effect of discontinuity reactances into microstrip circuit analysis.

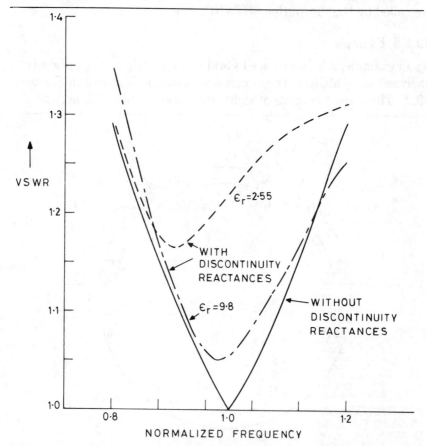

Figure 19.3 VSWR of the rat-race hybrid with and without consider-ing discontinuity reactances.

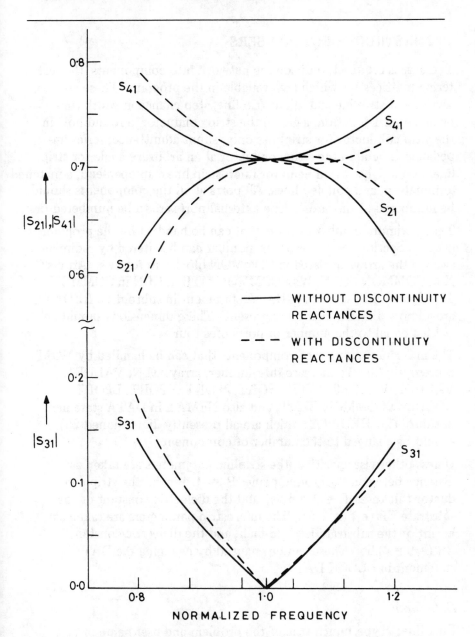

Figure 19.4 Coupling coefficients and the isolation of the rat-race hybrid with and without considering discontinuity reactances.

19.2 INSTRUCTIONS FOR USERS

The user is required to divide the network into components, the scattering matrices for which are available in the program. These are: sections of stripline and microstrip line, step change in width (impedance), a T-junction, a gap in the strip conductor, a round hole in the strip conductor for striplines only, shunt admittance, series impedance, a bend in the strip conductor at an arbitrary angle for striplines and a right-angled bend for microstrip lines, an open-end, a matched termination, and coupled lines. All ports at all the components should be numbered (1 onwards). The external ports are to be numbered first.

The maximum number of ports that can be handled by the program given in Section 19.3 is 56. This number can be altered by redimensioning the arrays declared in COMMON blocks, as follows. Arrays C, X in COMMON SOLN, W in COMMON MTRX, NCN in COMMON TOPO, and also NPMAX in DATA statement in subroutine REDATA are all now dimensioned 60 at present. These dimensions should be at least equal to the number of ports plus four.

The maximum number of components that can be handled by MCAP is presently 25. To increase this number, arrays ELN, VALUE1, VALUE2, VALUE3, TYPE, IPORT, JPORT, KPORT, LPORT, NCODE in COMMON ELMT, and also NEMAX in DATA statement in subroutine REDATA (which are all presently dimensioned 25) should be changed to the number of components.

Unless otherwise specified, the stripline parameters are taken as: distance between the ground planes B = 1/4 inch; the strip conductor thickness T = 1.4 mils; and the dielectric constant of the substrate ER (ϵ_r) = 2.55. The microstrip parameters are taken as: height of the substrate H = 1/8 inch; and the dielectric constant ER (ϵ_r) = 2.55. These can be changed by changing the DATA statement in BLOCK DATA.

Data Input

First line: Type/punch title of the problem and user name or any other information.

Second line: Type/punch M if microstrip circuit is being analyzed, otherwise (i.e. for stripline circuits) it is to be left blank.

The next set of lines gives a description of the components. The description is entered component by component, and requires one line per component.

Col. 2-5, ELN in A4. ELN is the element name which should be a four character name (e.g. TEE7, OP21, 1BND) assigned to each element.

Col. 6-10, IPROT in I5. IPORT is the port number of one of the two ports of two-port components, or port number of one of the two through ports if the component is a T-junction, or any of the four ports in case of coupled line sections.

Col. 11-15, JPORT in I5. JPORT is the port number of the second port in case of two-port components, and port number of the other through port for T-junctions. For coupled lines, it is the number of the port coupled to IPORT.

Col. 16-20, KPORT in I5. KPORT is the port number of the branch line in the case of a T-junction and it is the number of the isolated port for coupled line sections. This field should be left blank for two-port components.

Col. 21-25, LPORT in I5. LPORT is the port number of a directly coupled port for coupled line sections, and it is to be left blank for components having less than four ports. Port numbers for a coupled line section are illustrated in Figure 19.5.

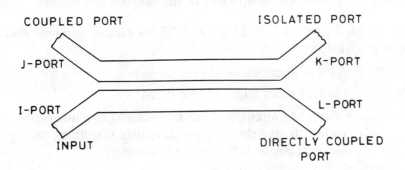

Figure 19.5 Port numbers for a coupled line section.

Col. 26, blank.

Col. 27-28, TYP in A2. TYP describes the type of component as per the following notation:

SA: Shunt admittance
SI: Series impedance
TL: Transmission line section
SW: Step in width
GS: Gap in strip
BS: Bend in strip at arbitrary angle
RH: Round hole in strip
TJ: T-junction
OE: Open end
MT: Matched termination
SP: Externally specified S-parameters
CL: Coupled lines section

Col. 29-30, blank.

Col. 31-42, VALUE 1 in E12.5. For SA, SI, TL, GS, BS, RH, OE or MT type of elements, VALUE1 would be the impedance of the line in ohms or the width of the conducting strip in meters. For SW and TJ type of elements this would be the impedance or the width of the line connected to the port numbered as IPORT. For the SP type of element, this would be left blank and for the CL type of element this would be the even mode impedance (in ohms) or the width (in meters) or the coupling coefficient of the coupled line section.

Col. 43-54, VALUE2 in E12.5. VALUE2 for various elements would be as given below:

For SA: Value of shunt impedance in ohms

For SI: Value of series impedance in ohms

For TL: Length of transmission line in meters. For a microstrip, the length may also be given in radians specifying the electrical length at the center frequency.

For GS: Length of the gap in meters

For SW: Impedance or width of line at port JPORT

For BS: Angle of bend in degrees

For TJ: Impedance or width of line connected at the port KPORT.

For CL: Odd mode impedance in ohms, or the gap between the
           coupled lines in meters or the characteristic impedance of
           the coupled lines, depending upon the corresponding data
           given in VALUE1

For RH: Diameter of the hole in meters

For OE, SP and MT types of elements, this field is to be left blank.

Col. 55-66, VALUE 3 in E12.5. For CL type of element, this would
be the center frequency in Hz if the coupling coefficient is specified
in VALUE1; otherwise it is the length of the coupled line section in
meters. For microstrip transmission line, this would be the center frequency in Hz, otherwise it is left blank.

Col. 67, blank.

Col. 68 — Type/punch W to indicate whether the width of the
conducting strip has been specified in this line (wherever the option
is provided between widths and impedances), otherwise the corresponding values are assumed to be impedances. (The user may specify impedance of a line in ohms or the width of a conductiong strip in metres.
For a component, either impedances only or widths only may be
specified). For coupled line, type/punch C to indicate whether the
coupling coefficient has been specified in this line. For microstrip
transmission line, type/punch R to indicate if length has been specified
in radians.

A blank line is inserted to indicate the end of the circuit component
list.

The next line specifies the number of external ports (IOP) in I1 in
Column 1. The external (unconnected) ports should be numbered
first starting from 1.

The next set of lines specify the interconnections between various
components. Each line gives one interconnection between two connected ports. Columns 6-10 and 16-20 contain the number of two
connected ports in I5 each. The number of these lines thus equals
the number of interconnections.

The next line specifies the starting frequency, WST, the end frequency, WND, the frequency increment or factor, DW, the scale,
NSCALE, (linear or logarithmic) and also the information as to
whether or not the discontinuity reactances are to be taken into
account for analysis.

Type/punch F in Column 1 if the frequencies specified in this line are in Hz, otherwise these are assumed to be in rad./sec.

Type/punch D in Column 3 if the discontinuity effects are to be considered.

Col. 6-20, WST in E15.6

Col. 21-35, WND in E15.6

Col. 36-50, DW in E15.6

Col. 51-53, Type/punch LIN if a linear frequency scale is desired, or LOG, if a logarithmic scale is desired. If the scale is linear, DW is the frequency increment by which the frequency variable is increased at each step. If it is logarithmic, DW is the factor by which the frequency variable is multiplied at each step.

Additional lines are inserted only if SP type of elements are present. These lines give the externally specified S-matrix, in which S-parameters are read in 8E10.3 format in one row per line. If there is more than one SP type of element, then S-parameters for the next SP type of element will follow the S-parameters of the previous SP type of element. S-parameters will have to be given at each frequency at which response is desired.

The output of the program is the scattering matrix of the network, the input VSWR, and the magnitudes of scattering parameters at all the frequency points desired. The circuit description fed in is also printed out for verification by the user. The frequency is printed in 1PE15.6 and in the subsequent lines the scattering matrix and externally specified S-parameters (if any) are printed in 4 (E12.5, 2X, E12.5, 5X) format.

An example which illustrates the use of the program is given. The circuit considered is the 3 db rat-race hybrid described in Section 19.1.3. The circuit is divided into basic components and the port numberings are as shown in Figure 19.2.

The input file is shown in Figure 19.6. The computer printout obtained by running MCAP in this case is shown in Figure 19.7.

```
M    TO SOLVE A HYBRID RING
TEE1  20   5   1   TJ   70.7107   50.000    0.30E10 R
TEE2   8   9   2   TJ   70.7107   50.000    0.30E10 R
TEE3  12  13   3   TJ   70.7107   50.000    0.30E10 R
TEE4  16  17   4   TJ   70.7107   50.000    0.30E10 R
TRL1   6  11       TL   70.7107    1.5708
TRL2  10  15       TL   70.7107    1.5708
TRL3  14  17       TL   70.7107    1.5708
TRL4  18  19       TL   70.7107    4.7124
4
       5    6
       7    8
       9   10
      11   12
      13   14
      15   16
      17   18
      19   20
F   0.240E10      0.360E10      0.0200E10 LIN
```

Figure 19.6 Input file for analysis of the rat-race hybrid.

Figure 19.7 *Output file (initial portion only) obtained by analyzing*
*the rat-race hybrid.**

```
            TO SOLVE A HYBRID RING

     MICROSTRIP LINE CIRCUIT COMPONENTS ARE CONSIDERED
 NE ELN        IP           JP           KP        LP      TYP
   1TEE1       20            5            1                 TJ
   2TEE2        8            9            2                 TJ
   3TEE3       12           13            3                 TJ
   4TEE4       16           17            4                 TJ
   5TRL1        6            7                              TL
   6TRL2       10           11                              TL
   7TRL3       14           15                              TL
   8TRL4       18           19                              TL


      FIRST 4 PORTS ARE TREATED AS   EXTERNAL PORTS
  INTERCONNECTION OF VARIOUS PORTS
                    5                   6
                    7                   8
                    9                  10
                   11                  12
                   13                  14
                   15                  16
                   17                  18
                   19                  20

STARTING FREQ =    2.400000E+09HZ,END FREQ =     3.600000E+09HZ
     BY   2.000000E+08  ON A  LIN  SCALE

     DISCONTINUITY EFFECTS ARE NOT CONSIDERED


                    2.400000E+09 HZ
 S-MATRIX FOR THE OVERALL CIRCUIT IS FOUND AS
-0.50578E-01    0.11777E+00      0.39784E+00   -0.47417E+00
 0.39784E+00   -0.47417E+00      0.17501E+00   -0.31049E-01
-0.65791E-01    0.12427E+00      0.37011E+00   -0.65463E+00
-0.60564E+00    0.46248E+00     -0.65791E-01    0.12427E+00

    VSWR        ----------MAGNITUDE OF S-PARAMETERS----
    1.29403     0.12817E+00                  0.61896E+00

    1.43233     0.61896E+00                  0.17774E+00

    1.43233     0.14061E+00                  0.75201E+00

    1.29403     0.76203E+00                  0.14061E+00



                    2.600000E+09 HZ
 S-MATRIX FOR THE OVERALL CIRCUIT IS FOUND AS
-0.16490E-01    0.78812E-01      0.29504E+00   -0.60458E+00
 0.29504E+00   -0.60458E+00      0.77697E-01   -0.53006E-01
-0.24509E-01    0.77920E-01      0.22641E+00   -0.69329E+00
-0.41302E+00    0.60308E+00     -0.24509E-01    0.77920E-01

    VSWR        ----------MAGNITUDE OF S-PARAMETERS----
    1.17514     0.80519E-01                  0.67273E+00

    1.20764     0.67273E+00                  0.94055E-01
```

*Output shown is continued linewise on the opposite page.

VALUE1	VALUE2	VALUE3	X
0.707107E+02	0.500000E+02		
0.707107E+02	0.500000E+02		
0.707107E+02	0.500000E+02		
0.707107E+02	0.500000E+02		
0.707107E+02	0.175047E-01		R
0.707107E+02	0.175047E-01		R
0.707107E+02	0.175047E-01		R
0.707107E+02	0.625141E-01		R

-0.65791E-01	0.12427E+00	-0.60564E+00	0.46248E+00
0.37011E+00	-0.65463E+00	-0.65791E-01	0.12427E+00
0.17501E+00	-0.31049E-01	0.39784E+00	-0.47417E+00
0.39784E+00	-0.47417E+00	-0.50578E-01	0.11777E+00
	0.14061E+00		0.76203E+00
	0.75201E+00		0.14061E+00
	0.17774E+00		0.61896E+00
	0.61896E+00		0.12817E+00

-0.24509E-01	0.77920E-01	-0.41302E+00	0.60308E+00
0.22641E+00	-0.69329E+00	-0.24509E-01	0.77920E-01
0.77697E-01	-0.53006E-01	0.29504E+00	-0.60458E+00
0.29504E+00	-0.60458E+00	-0.16490E-01	0.78812E-01
	0.81684E-01		0.73095E+00
	0.72933E+00		0.81684E-01

19.3 PROGRAM LISTING

```
00100  C
00200  C          M A I N   P R O G R A M
00300        COMPLEX ST,CX,S(4,4)
00400        DIMENSION SMAG(4,4),VSWR(4)
00500        COMMON /PARA/ B,T,ER,H
00600        COMMON //FREQ// WST,WND,DW,NSCALE
00700        COMMON //FREK// BETA,WP
00800        COMMON //TOPO// NCN(60),C(60),NP,NE,NPT
00900        COMMON //SOLN/ X(60)
01000        COMMON /DAT/ STPI
01100        DATA LIN,LOG /3HLIN,3HLOG/  ← CHAR CONST TOO LONG
01200        ST=(0.0,1.0)
01300        PI=4.0*ATAN(1.0)
01400        CALL REDATA
01500        IOP=NPT=NP
01600        DO 5 J=1,IOP
01700        JP=NP+J
01800        NCN(JP)=JP
01900  5
02000        IF(NSCALE.EQ.LIN)GO TO 10
02100        NW=ALOG10(WND/WST)/ALOG10(DW)+1.5
02200        GO TO 20
02300  10    NW=(WND-WST)/DW+1.5
02400  20    WP=WST
02500        DO 23 J=1,NPT
02600  23
02700        DO 100 I=1,NW
02800        BETA=WP*SQRT(ER)/(0.3E 09)
02900        WW=WP/(2.0*PI)
03000        PRINT 30,WW
03100        CALL SETWNC
03200        CALL FACTLU
03300        DO 25J=1,IOP
03400        JP=NP+J
03500        C(JP)=1.0
03600        CALL FORBAK
03700        C(JP)=0.0
03800        DO 25 JL=1,IOP
03900        JP=NP+JL
04000  25    S(JL,J)=X(JP)
04100  30    FORMAT(//,15X,1PE15.6,' HZ')
```

```fortran
      PRINT 32
32    FORMAT(2X,'S-MATRIX FOR THE OVERALL CIRCUIT IS FOUND AS:')
      DO 35 IP=1,IOP
35    PRINT 40,(S(IP,J),J=1,IOP)
40    FORMAT(1X,4(E12.5,2X,E12.5,5X))
      PRINT 45
45    FORMAT(/4X,'VSWR',6X,'--------MAGNITUDE OF S-PARAMETERS----')
      DO 50 J=1,IOP
50    SMAG(IP,J)=CABS(S(IP,J))
53    VSWR(IP)=(1.+SMAG(IP,IP))/(1.-SMAG(IP,IP))
      DO 55 IP=1,IOP
55    PRINT 57,VSWR(IP),(SMAG(IP,J),J=1,IOP)
57    FORMAT(1X,F10.5,2X,4(E12.5,19X))
      IF(NSCALE.EQ.LIN) GO TO 60
      WP=WP*DW
      GO TO 100
600   WP=WP+DW
100   CONTINUE
      STOP
      END
      BLOCK DATA
      INTEGER SA,SI,TL,SW,GS,BS,TJ,OE,RH,MT,SP,CL
      COMMON /PARA/ B,T,ER,H,SW,GS,BS,TJ,OE,RH,MT,SP,CL
      COMMON /CODE/ SA,SI,TL,SW,GS,BS,TJ,OE,RH,MT,SP,CL
      DATA B,T,ER,H /0.635E-2,0.3556E-4,2.55,0.3175E-2/
      DATA SA,SI,TL,SW,GS,BS,TJ,OE,RH,MT,SP,CL /2HSA,2HSI,2HTL,2HSW,2H
     1GS,2HBS,2HTJ,2HOE,2HRH,2HMT,2HSP,2HCL/
      END
C     SUBROUTINE TO SET MATRIX W
C
      SUBROUTINE SETWNC
      INTEGER ELN,TYPE
      COMPLEX S,W,W(60,60)
      COMMON /MTRX/ W(60,60)
      COMMON /ELM/ ELN(25),VALUE1(25),VALUE2(25),VALUE3(25),TYPE(25),
     1IPORT(25),JPORT(25),KPORT(25),LPORT(25),NCODE(25)
      COMMON /TOPO/ NCN(60),NP,NE,NPT
      COMMON /EMTX/ S(4,4),VAL1,VAL2,VAL3
      COMMON /SETT/ IP,JP,KP,LP
      COMMON /FREK/ BETA,WP
      DO 10 I=1,NPT
```

```
08500          DO 10 J=1,NPT
08600   10     W(I,J)=0.0
08700          DO 20 I=1,NPT
08800          J=NC(I)
08900   20     W(I,J)=1.0
09000          DO 150 I=1,NE
09100          NC=NCODE(I)
09200          IP=IPORT(I)
09300          VAL1=VALUE1(I)
09400          VAL2=VALUE2(I)
09500          VAL3=VALUE3(I)
09600          IF(NC.LE.9.OR.NC.EQ.12)JP=JPORT(I)
09700          GO TO (40,50,60,70,80,90,100,110,120,150,140),NC
09800   40     CALL SHNTSC
09900          CALL SETUPS
10000          GO TO 150
10100   50     CALL SERISC
10200          CALL SETUPS
10300          GO TO 150
10400   60     CALL LINESC
10500          CALL SETUPS
10600          GO TO 150
10700   70     CALL STEPSC
10800          CALL SETUPS
10900          GO TO 150
11000   80     CALL GAPSC
11100          CALL SETUPS
11200          GO TO 150
11300   90     CALL BENDSC
11400          CALL SETUPS
11500          GO TO 150
11600   100    CALL HOLESC
11700          CALL SETUPS
11800          GO TO 150
11900   110    KP=KPORT(I)
12000          CALL TEEJSC
12100          CALL SETUPS
12200          W(JP,KP)=-S(1,3)
12300          W(JP,KP)==S(2,3)
12400          W(KP,IP)==S(3,1)
12500          W(KP,JP)=-S(3,2)
12600
```

```
12700          GO TO 150
12800  120     CALL OPNESC
12900          W(IP,IP)=-S(1,1)
13000  130     GO TO 150
13100          KP=KPORT(I)
13200          LP=I
13300          I=II
13400          CALL SPARA(II)
13500          IF(JP.EQ.0)GO TO 132
13600          CALL SETUPS
13700          IF(LP.NE.0)GO TO 135
13800          IF(KP.EQ.0)GO TO 150
13900          W(IP,KP)=-S(1,3)
14000          W(KP,IP)=-S(2,3)
14100          W(KP,KP)=-S(3,3)
14200          W(KP,IP)=-S(3,2)
14300          GO TO 150
14400  132     GO TO 150
14500  135     W(IP,KP)=-S(1,3);W(IP,LP)=-S(1,4)
14600          W(JP,KP)=-S(2,3);W(JP,LP)=-S(2,4)
14700          W(KP,KP)=-S(3,3);W(KP,JP)=-S(3,2)
14800          W(LP,KP)=-S(4,3);W(LP,JP)=-S(4,2)
14900          W(LP,LP)=-S(4,4)
15000          GO TO 150
15100          GO TO 150
15200          KP=KPORT(I)
15300  140     GO TO 150
15400          KP=KPORT(I)
15500          LP=LPORT(I)
15600          CALL COUPLD
15700          CALL SETUPS
15800          W(IP,KP)=-S(1,3);W(IP,LP)=-S(1,4)
15900          W(JP,KP)=-S(2,3);W(JP,LP)=-S(2,4)
16000          W(KP,KP)=-S(3,3);W(KP,JP)=-S(3,2)
16100          W(LP,KP)=-S(4,3);W(LP,JP)=-S(4,2)
16200          W(LP,LP)=-S(4,4)
16300          CONTINUE
16400  150     CONTINUE
16500          RETURN
16600          END
16700          SUBROUTINE ELCODE(TYP,NC)
16800          INTEGER TYP&SA,SI,TL,SW,GS,BS,TJ,OE,RH,MT,SP,CL
16900          COMMON /CODE/ SA,SI,TL,SW,GS,BS,TJ,OE,RH,MT,SP,CL
```

```
17000       NC=0
17100       IF(ITYP.EQ.SA)NC=1
17200       IF(ITYP.EQ.SI)NC=2
17300       IF(ITYP.EQ.TL)NC=3
17400       IF(ITYP.EQ.SW)NC=4
17500       IF(ITYP.EQ.GS)NC=5
17600       IF(ITYP.EQ.BS)NC=6
17700       IF(ITYP.EQ.RH)NC=7
17800       IF(ITYP.EQ.TJ)NC=8
17900       IF(ITYP.EQ.SP)NC=9
18000       IF(ITYP.EQ.OE)NC=10
18100       IF(ITYP.EQ.MT)NC=11
18200       IF(ITYP.EQ.CL)NC=12
18300       IF(NC.NE.0)RETURN
18400       PRINT 10
18500    10 FORMAT(' INCORRECT CODE FOR ELEMENT TYPE'/'PLEASE CHECK DATA CA
18600      1KDS.STOP.')
18700       STOP
18800       END
18900 C     SUBROUTINE TO READ INPUT DATA
19000 C     -------------------------------
19100       SUBROUTINE REDATA
19200       LOGICAL DISC,MSP
19300       INTEGER TYPE,TYP,APORT,BPORT,D,C,M,R
19400       COMPLEX SI
19500       INTEGER ELN,SA,SI,TL,SW,GS,BS,TJ,OE,RH,X,F,W,BBBB,SP,CL,TITLE(20
19600       COMMON /DAT/ ST,PI
19700       COMMON /DISK/ DISC
19800       COMMON /TOPO/ NCN(60),NP,NE,NPT
19900       COMMON /MSTP/ MSP
20000       COMMON /PARA/ BLT,ER,H
20100       COMMON /ELMT/ ELN(25),VALUE1(25),VALUE2(25),VALUE3(25),TYPE(25),
20200      1IPORT(25),JPORT(25),APORT(25),LPORT(25),NCODE(25)
20300       COMMON /CODE/ SA,SI,TL,SW,GS,BS,TJ,OE,RH,MT,SP,CL
20400       COMMON /FREQ/ WST,WND,DW,NSCALE
20500       DATA BBBB/4H    /
20600       DATA NEMAX,NPMAX /25,56/
20700       DATA LIN,LOG,W,F,C,M,R /3HLIN,3HLOG,1HW,1HF,1HC,1HM,1HR/
20800 C     READ TITLE OF THE PROBLEM IN 20A4 FORMAT
20900       READ 10(TITLE(IT),IT=1,20)
21000    10 FORMAT(20A4)
```

Handwritten margin notes:
- CHAR CONST TOO LONG
- NAM IS A FUNCTION NAM
- SUFFIXES NOT MIXED

```
           PRINT 15,(TITLE(IT),IT=1,20)
15         FORMAT(5X,20A4)
16         READ 16,K
           FORMAT(A1)                         INVALID FORMAT
           IF(K.EQ.M)GO TO 18
           MSP=.FALSE.
17         PRINT 17
           FORMAT(//5X,'STRIPLINE CIRCUIT COMPONENTS ARE CONSIDERED.')
           GO TO 21
18         MSP=.TRUE.
19         PRINT 19
21         FORMAT(//5X,'MICROSTRIP LINE CIRCUIT COMPONENTS ARE CONSIDERED')
           NP=2
           NE=2
C          NOW READ IN THE DESCRIPTION OF ELEMENTS
22         PRINT 22
           FORMAT(2X,'NE','ELN',8X,'IP',8X,'JP',8X,'KP',8X,'LP',4X,'TYP   -MCAP  4/1/OP
          1',11X,'VALUE1',14X,'VALUE2',14X,'VALUE3',4X,'X',/)
           DO 110 NE=1,NEMAX
23         READ 23(ELN(NE),IPORT(NE),JPORT(NE),KPORT(NE),LPORT(NE),TYPE,X
          1(NE),VALUE1(NE),VALUE2(NE),VALUE3(NE),X
           FORMAT(1X,A4,I5,I5,I5,1X,A2,2X,E12.5,E12.5,E12.5,1X,A1)
           IF(ELN(NE).EQ.BBBB)GO TO 126
           TYP=TYPE(NE)
           CALL ELCODE(TYP,NC)
           NCODE(NE)=NC
           IF(NP.LIT.IPORT(NE))NP=IPORT(NE)
           IF(NC.EQ.12.AND.X.EQ.C)GO TO 24
           IF(NC.EQ.12.AND.X.EQ.W)GO TO 25
           IF(NC.EQ.3.AND.X.EQ.R)GO TO 26
           IF(NC.EQ.11.OR.X.NE.W)GO TO 30
           VAL=VALUE1(NE)
           CALL IMPFWD(VAL,Z)
           VALUE1(NE)=Z
           IF(NC.NE.4.AND.NC.NE.8)GO TO 30
           VAL=VALUE2(NE)
           CALL IMPFWD(VAL,Z)
           VALUE2(NE)=Z
           GO TO 30
24         VAL1=VALUE1(NE);VAL2=VALUE2(NE);VAL3=VALUE3(NE)
           CALL IMPFCP(VAL1,VAL2,ZOE;VAL3,ZOO,CPLNTH)
           VALUE1(NE)=ZOE;VALUE2(NE)=ZOO;VALUE3(NE)=CPLNTH
           GO TO 30
```

```
25    VAL1=VALUE1(NE);VAL2=VALUE2(NE)
      CALL IMPED(VAL1,VAL2,ZOE,ZOO)
      VALUE1(NE)=ZOE;VALUE2(NE)=ZOO
      GO TO 30
26    VAL1=VALUE1(NE)
      VAL2=VALUE2(NE)
      VAL3=VALUE3(NE)
      CALL WIDTH(VAL1,WD)
      CALL EREFF(WD,ERE)
      BETA1=2.*PI*VAL3*SQRT(ERE)/(0.3E09)
      TRL=VAL2/BETA1
      VALUE2(NE)=TRL
30    GO TO (40,40,40,40,40,60,91,80,90,96) ,NC
40    IF(NP.LT.JPORT(NE))NP=JPORT(NE)
      PRINT 45, NE,ELN(NE),IPORT(NE),JPORT(NE),TYP,VALUE1(NE),VALUE2(NE
     1)X
45    FORMAT(1X,I3,A4,5X,I5,5X,I5,25X,A2,5X,E15.6,5X,E15.6,21X,A1)
      GO TO 100
60    PRINT 70, NE,ELN(NE),IPORT(NE),JPORT(NE),KPORT(NE),TYP,VALUE1(NE)
     1,VALUE2(NE)
70    FORMAT(1X,I3,A4,5X,I5,5X,I5,5X,I5,15X,A2,5X,E15.6,5X,E15.6)
      IF(NP.LT.JPORT(NE))NP=JPORT(NE)
      IF(NP.LT.KPORT(NE))NP=KPORT(NE)
      GO TO 100
80    PRINT 85, NE,ELN(NE),IPORT(NE),TYP,VALUE1(NE)
85    FORMAT(1X,I3,A4,5X,I5,35X,A2,5X,E15.6)
      GO TO 100
91    IF(LPORT(NE).NE.0) GO TO 97
      IF(KPORT(NE).EQ.0)GOTO 93
92    PRINT 92, NE,ELN(NE),IPORT(NE),JPORT(NE),KPORT(NE),TYP
92    FORMAT(1X,I3,A4,5X,I5,5X,I5,5X,I5,15X,A2)
      IF(NP.LT.JPORT(NE))NP=JPORT(NE)
      IF(NP.LT.KPORT(NE))NP=KPORT(NE)
      GO TO 100
93    IF(JPORT(NE).EQ.0)GOTO 101
94    PRINT 94, NE,ELN(NE),IPORT(NE),JPORT(NE),TYP
      FORMAT(1X,I3,A4,5X,I5,5X,I5,25X,A2)
      IF(NP.LT.JPORT(NE))NP=JPORT(NE)
      GO TO 100
101   PRINT 102, NE,ELN(NE),IPORT(NE),TYP
102   FORMAT(1X,I3,A4,5X,I5,35X,A2)
      GO TO 10
```

```
29800   97   PRINT 99,NE,ELN(NE),IPORT(NE),JPORT(NE),KPORT(NE),LPORT(NE),TYP
29900   99   FORMAT(1X,I3,A4,5X,I5,5X,I5,5X,I5,5X,I5,5X,A2)
30000        IF(NP.LT.JPORT(NE))NP=JPORT(NE)
30100        IF(NP.LT.KPORT(NE))NP=KPORT(NE)
30200        IF(NP.LT.LPORT(NE))NP=LPORT(NE)
30300        GO TO 100
30400   90   PRINT 95,NE,ELN(NE),IPORT(NE),TYP,VALUE1(NE)
30500   95   FORMAT(1X,I3,A4,5X,I5,35X,A2,5X,E15.6)
30600        GO TO 100
30700   96   PRINT 98,NE,ELN(NE),IPORT(NE),JPORT(NE),KPORT(NE),LPORT(NE),TYP,
30800       1VALUE1(NE),VALUE2(NE),VALUE3(NE),X
30900   98   FORMAT(1X,I3,A4,5X,I5,5X,I5,5X,I5,5X,A2,5X,E15.6,5X,E15.6,5X,E15.6)
31000        IF(NP.LT.JPORT(NE))NP=JPORT(NE)
31100        IF(NP.LT.KPORT(NE))NP=KPORT(NE)
31200        IF(NP.LT.LPORT(NE))NP=LPORT(NE)
31300  100   IF(NP.LE.NPMAX)GO TO 110
31400        PRINT 105
31500  105   FORMAT(5X,'NUMBER OF PORTS EXCEEDS NPMAX.STOP.')
31600        STOP
31700  110   CONTINUE
31800        IF(NE.LE.NEMAX)GO TO 120
31900        PRINT 115
32000  115   FORMAT(5X,'NUMBER OF ELEMENTS EXCEEDS NEMAX.STOP.')
32100        STOP
32200  120   NE=NE-1
32300        READ 125,IOP
32400        PRINT 127,IOP
32500  125   FORMAT(I1)
32600  127   FORMAT(//,5X,'FIRST',I2,' PORTS ARE TREATED AS EXTERNAL PORTS')
32700        NPT=NP+IOP
32800  C     NOW READ IN INTERCONNECTIONS OF VARIOUS PORTS
32900        PRINT 128
33000  128   FORMAT(/2X,'INTERCONNECTION OF VARIOUS PORTS')
33100        NJ=(NP-IOP)/2
33200        DO 140 II=1,NJ
33300        READ 130,APORT,BPORT
33400  130   FORMAT(5X,I5,5X,I5)
33500        NCN(APORT)=BPORT
33600        NCN(BPORT)=APORT
33700  140   PRINT 145,APORT,BPORT
33800  145   FORMAT(15X,I5,5X,I5)
33900        READ 150,J,WST,WND,DW,NSCALE
34000  150   FORMAT(A1,1X,A1,2X,E15.6,E15.6,E15.6,A3)
```

```
34100        IF(X.EQ.F) GO TO 170
34200        PRINT 160, WST,WND,DW,NSCALE
34300 160    FORMAT(1X,'STARTING FREQ =',1PE15.6,'RAD/SEC,END FREQ =',1PE15.
34400       16,'RAD/SEC',//5X,'BY',1PE15.6,' ON A ',A3,' SCALE')
34500        GO TO 190
34600 170    PRINT 180, WST,WND,DW,NSCALE
34700 180    FORMAT(/1X,'STARTING FREQ =',1PE15.6,'HZ,END FREQ =',1PE15.6,'HZ
34800       1',/5X,'BY',1PE15.6,' ON A ',A3,' SCALE')
34900        WND=WND*PI*2.0
35000        WST=WST*PI*2.0
35100        IF(NSCALE.EQ.LOG) GO TO 190
35200        DW=DW*PI*2.0
35300 190    IF(J.EQ.D)GO TO 210
35400        DISC=.FALSE.
35500        PRINT 200
35600 200    FORMAT(//,5X,'DISCONTINUITY EFFECTS ARE NOT CONSIDERED')
35700        RETURN
35800 210    DISC=.TRUE.
35900        PRINT 220
36000 220    FORMAT(//,5X,'DISCONTINUITY EFFECTS ARE CONSIDERED')
36100        RETURN
36200        END
36300 C      SUBROUTINE TO CALCULATE S-MATRIX FOR TRANSMISSION LINE
36400 C      =======================================================
36500        SUBROUTINE LINESC
36600        LOGICAL MSP
36700        COMPLEX S,ST
36800        COMMON /EMTX/ S(4,4),VAL1,VAL2,VAL3
36900        COMMON /MSTP/ MSP
37000        COMMON /DAT/ ST,PI
37100        COMMON /FREK/ BETA,WP
37200        IF(MSP)GO TO 10
37300        VAL2=VAL2*BETA
37400        GO TO 20
37500 10     CALL WIDTH(VAL1,WD)
37600        BETA1=WP*SQRT(ERE)/(0.3E09)
37700        VAL2=VAL2*BETA1
37800 20     S(1,1)=0.0
37900        S(1,2)=COS(VAL2)-ST*SIN(VAL2)
38000        S(2,2)=0.0
38100        RETURN
38200        END
```

```
C-------SUBROUTINE TO CALCULATE S-MATRIX FOR STEP IN WIDTH    38500
C-------                                                      38600
        SUBROUTINE STEPSC                                     38700
        LOGICAL DISC,MSP                                      38800
        COMPLEX S,ST,TEMP,C1,C2                               38900
        COMMON /EMTX/ SS(4,4),VAL1,VAL2,VAL3                  39000
        COMMON /DISK/ DISC                                    39100
        COMMON /DAT/ ST,PI                                    39200
        COMMON /PARA/ B,T,ER,H                                39300
        COMMON /FREK/ BETA,WP                                 39400
        COMMON /MSTP/ MSP                                     39500
        REAL LS,LW1,LW2,L1,L2                                 39600
        IF(DISC) GO TO 2                                      39700
        S(1,1)=(VAL2-VAL1)/(VAL2+VAL1)                        39800
        S(1,2)=2.0*SQRT(VAL2*VAL1)/(VAL2+VAL1)                39900
        S(2,1)=S(1,2)                                         40000
        S(2,2)=-S(1,1)                                        40100
        RETURN                                                40200
2       IF(MSP)GO TO 5                                        40300
        TBLD=B*ALOG(2.0)/PI*BETA*2.0                          40400
        RATIO=VAL2/VAL1                                       40500
        IF(VAL1.GT.VAL2)RATIO=VAL2/VAL1                       40600
        X=30.0*(B-T)/SQRT(ER)*BETA*ALOG(1.0/SIN(PI/2.0*RATIO))  40700
        TEMP=VAL2+VAL1+X*ST                                   40800
        S(1,1)=(2*VAL2-VAL1+X*ST)/TEMP                        40900
        S(2,2)=(2*VAL1-VAL2+X*ST)/TEMP                        41000
        S(1,2)=2*(COS(TBLD)+ST*SIN(TBLD))                     41100
        S(2,1)=2*(COS(TBLD)-ST*SIN(TBLD))                     41200
        IF(VAL1.GT.VAL2) GO TO 3                              41300
        S(1,2)=S(1,2)*C2                                      41400
        S(2,1)=S(2,1)*C1                                      41500
        RETURN                                                41600
3       S(1,2)=S(1,2)*C1                                      41700
        S(2,1)=S(2,1)*C2                                      41800
        RETURN                                                41900
5       CALL WIDTH(VAL1,W1)                                   42000
        CALL WIDTH(VAL2,W2)                                   42100
        RETURN                                                42200
        CS=SQRT(W1*W2)*((10.1*ALOG10(ER)+2.33)*W1/W2-12.6*ALOG10  42300
       1(ER)-3.17)*(0.1E-11)                                  42400
        LS=H*(40.5*(W1/W2-1.0)-75.*ALOG10(W1/W2)+0.2*(W1/W2-1.)**2)*  42500
       1(0.1E-08)                                             42600
```

```
42800      CALL EREFF(W1,ERE1)
42900      CALL EREFF(W2,ERE2)
43000      LW1=VAL1*W1*SQRT(ERE1)/(0.3E09)
43100      LW2=VAL2*W2*SQRT(ERE2)/(0.3E09)
43200      L1=(LW1*LS)/(LW1+LW2)
43300      L2=(LW2*LS)/(LW1+LW2)
43400      X1=WP*L1;X2=WP*L2;XB=-1./(WP*CS)
43500      TEMP=VAL1*VAL2+ST*(X2+XS)*VAL2-(X1*X2+X1*XS+X2*X
43600     1S)/TEMP
43700      S11=-(VAL1*VAL2-ST*(X1+XS)*VAL2+ST*(X2+XS)*VAL1+X1*X2+X1*XS+X2*X
43800     1S)/TEMP
43900      S22=-(VAL1*VAL2-ST*(X2+XS)*VAL1+ST*(X1+XS)*VAL2+X1*X2+X1*XS+X2*X
44000     1S)/TEMP
44100      S21=SQRT(VAL2/VAL1)*2./(VAL2+ST*X2)*(ST*(X2+XS)*VAL1*VAL1-VAL1*(
44200     1X1*X2+X1*XS+X2*XS)-ST*X1*VAL1*VAL2+X1*(X1+XS)*VAL2)/TEMP
44300      S12=S21
44400      DL=LS/(LW1+LW2)
44500      TH1=WP*SQRT(ERE1)*DL/(0.3E09)
44600      TH2=WP*SQRT(ERE2)*DL/(0.3E09)
44700      IF(VAL1.GT.VAL2)GO TO 10
44800      S(1,1)=S(1,1)*(COS(2.*TH1)-ST*SIN(2.*TH1))
44900      S(2,2)=S(2,2)*(COS(2.*TH2)+ST*SIN(2.*TH2))
45000      RETURN
45100   10 S(1,1)=S(1,1)*(COS(2.*TH1)+ST*SIN(2.*TH1))
45200      S(2,2)=S(2,2)*(COS(2.*TH2)-ST*SIN(2.*TH2))
45300      RETURN
45400      END
45500 C    SUBROUTINE FOR L-U FACTORIZATION OF W-MATRIX
45600 C    -------------------------------------------
45700      SUBROUTINE FACTLU
45800      COMPLEX W
45900      COMMON /TOPO/ NCN(60),NP,NE,NPT
46000      COMMON /MTRX/ W(60,60)
46100      NP1=NPT-1
46200      DO 20 L=1,NP1
46300      LPR=L+1
46400      LPR=NCN(L)
46500      DO 10I=LPR,NPT
46600      IPR=NCN(I)
46700      W(L,IPR)=W(L,IPR)/W(L,LPR)
46800   10 DO 20J=L1,NPT
46900      DO 20J=L1,NPT
47000      JPR=NCN(J)
```

```
47100  20      W(I,JPR)=W(I,JPR)-W(I,LPR)*W(L,JPR)
47200          RETURN
47300          END
47400  C       SUBROUTINE TO CALCULATE S-MATRIX FOR GAP IN CONDUCTING LINE
47500  C       --------------------------------------------------
47600          SUBROUTINE GAPSC
47700          LOGICAL MSP
47800          COMPLEX S,ST,DEL
47900          COMMON /EMTX/ S(4,4),VAL1,VAL2,VAL3
48000          COMMON /DAT/ ST,PI
48100          COMMON /PARA/ B,T,ER,H
48200          COMMON /FREK/ BETA,WP
48300          COMMON /MSTP/ MSP
48400          REAL MO,ME,KO,KE
48500          IF(MSP)GO TO 4
48600          TEMP=PI/2.0*VAL2/B
48700          BAP=B*BETA/PI*ALOG(COSH(TEMP))
48800          BBP=B*BETA/(2.0*PI)*ALOG(COSH(TEMP)/SINH(TEMP))
48900          BS=BETA*VAL2/2.0
49000          BA=(SIN(BS)+COS(BS)*BAP)/(COS(BS)-BAP*SIN(BS))
49100          BB=0.5*(SIN(BS)+COS(BS)*(2.0*BBP+BAP))/(COS(BS)-(2.0*BBP+BAP)*S
49200         1IN(BS))
49300          DEL=((1.0-2.0*BA*BB-BA**2)+2.0*(BA+BB)*ST)*(COS(BS)-SIN(BS)*ST)
49400          S(1,1)=(1.0+2.0*BB*BA**2)/DEL
49500          S(1,2)=2.0*BB*ST/DEL
49600          S(2,1)=S(1,2)
49700          S(2,2)=S(1,1)
49800          RETURN
49900  4       CALL WIDTH(VAL1,WD)
50000          CALL EREF(WD,ERE)
50100          SW=VAL2/WD;WH=WD/H
50200          MO=WH*(0.619*ALOG10(WH)-0.3853)
50300          KO=4.26-1.453*ALOG10(WH)
50400          IF(SW.LE.0.3.AND.SW.GE.0.1)GO TO 20
50500          IF(SW.GT.1.0.OR.SW.LT.0.1)GO TO 5
50600          ME=1.565/WH**0.16-1.
50700          KE=1.97-0.03/WH
50800          GO TO 25
50900  5       PRINT 10
51000  10      FORMAT(5X,'CONSTRAINTS FOR GAP IN MICROSTRIP VIOLATED'/,5X,
51100         1'CHECK THE VALUES OF S/W,STOP.')
51200          STOP
51300  20      ME=0.8675
```

```
51400  25  KE=2.043*WH**0.12
51500      COD=WD*(0.1E-11)*SW**MO*EXP(KO)
51600      CCEV=COD*(0.1E-11)*SW**ME*EXP(KE)
51700      COD=COD*(ER/9.6)**0.8
51800      CEV=CEV*(ER/9.6)**0.9
51900      CP=0.5*CEV;CG=0.5*(COD-0.5*CEV)
52000      DL=CP*(0.3E09)*VAL1/SQRT(ERE)
52100      BB=WP*CG;BA=WP*CP
52200      DEL=(1./VAL1**2-2.*BA*BB-BA**2)+2.*(BA+BB)*ST/VAL1)*(COS(BL)
52300      1-SIN(BL)*ST)
52400      DEL=(1./VAL1**2-2.*BB*ST/(DEL*VAL1)+BA*BB+BA**2)/DEL
52500      S(1,1)=(1./VAL1**2+2.*BA*BB+BA**2)
52600      S(1,2)=2.*BB*ST/(DEL*VAL1)
52700      S(1,2)=S(1,2);S(2,2)=S(1,1)
52800      RETURN
52900      END
53000      SUBROUTINE TO CALCULATE S-MATRIX FOR ARBITRARY BEND IN STRIPLINE
53100 CCCC AND RIGHT ANGLE BEND IN MICROSTRIP LINE
53200
53300      SUBROUTINE BENDSC
53400      LOGICAL DISC,MSP
53500      COMPLEX S,ST,DEL
53600      COMMON /EMTX/ S(4,4),VAL1,VAL2,VAL3
53700      COMMON /DAT/ ST,PI
53800      COMMON /DISK/ DISC
53900      COMMON /PARA/ BETA,ER,H
54000      COMMON /FREK/ BETA,WP
54100      COMMON /MSTP/ MSP
54200      REAL LB
54300      IF(DISC)GOTO 3
54400      S(1,1)=0.000
54500      S(1,2)=1.000
54600      S(2,1)=1.000
54700      S(2,2)=0.
54800      RETURN
54900  3   IF(MSP)GOTO 5
55000      CALL WIDTH(VAL1,WD)
55100      D=30.0*PI*(B-T)/VAL1
55200      ANRB2=VAL2*PI/360.00
55300      TBL=(D-WD)*SIN(ANRB2)/COS(ANRB2)*BETA
55400      XBM=-1.0/(BETA*D*SIN(ANRB2)/COS(ANRB2))
55500      XSML=0.5+VAL2/360.0
55600  C   SI IS OBTAINED BY CURVE FITTING SZI(X)
```

```
55800        SI=0.5223*ALOG(XSML)+0.394
55900        XA=BETA*D/PI*(SI+1.9635-1.0/XSML)
56000        DEL=(1.0-2.0*XA*XB-XA**2+2.0*ST*(XA+XB))*(COS(TBL)-ST*SIN(TBL))
56100        S(1,2)=2.0*XB*ST/DEL
56200        S(1,1)=S(1,2)
56300        S(2,1)=S(1,2)
56400        S(2,2)=S(1,1)
56500        RETURN
56600        IF(VAL2.NE.90) GO TO 25
56700    5   CALL WIDTH(VAL1,WD)
56800        WH=WD/H
56900        LB=H*100.*(4.*SQRT(WH)-4.21)*(0.1E-08)
57000        IF(WH.GE.1.)GO TO 10
57100        CB=H*(14.*ER+12.5)*WH-(1.83*ER-2.25))/SQRT(WH)+0.02*ER/
57200       1WH)*(0.1E-11)
57300        GO TO 20
57400   10   CB=W*(9.5*ER+1.25)*WH+5.2*ER+7.)*(0.1E-11)
57500   20   XA=WP*LB/2.;XB=-1./(WP*CB)
57600        DEL=VAL1*VAL1-XA*XA-2.*XA*XB+ST*ST*2.*VAL1*(XA+XB)
57700        S(1,2)=ST*2*XB*VAL1/DEL
57800        S(1,1)=(VAL1*VAL1+XA*XB)*VAL1/DEL
57900        S(1,2)=S(1,2);S(2,2)=S(1,1)
58000        S(2,1)=S(1,2)
58100        RETURN
58200   25   PRINT 30
58300   30   FORMAT(/5X,'SUBROUTINE FOR BEND HAVING ANGLE OTHER THAN 90 DEGR
58400       1EE IS NOT INCLUDED,STOP.')
58500        STOP
58600        END
58700 C---------SUBROUTINE TO CALCULATE S-MATRIX FOR HOLE IN STRIPLINE ONLY
58800 C-------------------------------------------------
58900 C        FOR HOLE IN MICROSTRIP EXECUTION WILL STOP
59000 C-------------------------------------------------
59100        SUBROUTINE HOLESC
59200        LOGICAL MSP
59300        COMPLEX S,ST,DEL
59400        COMMON /EMTX/S(4,4),VAL1,VAL2,VAL3
59500        COMMON /DAT/ST,PI,ER
59600        COMMON /PARA/B,T,ER,H
59700        COMMON /FREK/BETA,WP
59800        COMMON /MSTP/MSP
59900        IF(MSP)GO TO 5
60000        D=30.0*PI*(B-T)/VAL1
60100        BBP=1.5*B*D/(BETA*VAL2**3)
             BAP=0.25/BBP
```

```
      BR=BETA*VAL2/2.0
      BA=(SIN(BR)+BAP*COS(BR))/(COS(BR)-BAP*SIN(BR))
      BB=0.5*(-(SIN(BR)+2.0*BBP*COS(BR))/(COS(BR)-2.0*BBP*SIN(BR))-BA)
      DEL=(1.0-2.0*BA-BB-BA**2+2.0*ST*(BA+BB))*(COS(2.0*BR)-ST*SIN(2.0
     1*BR))
      S(1,1)=(1.0+2.0*BA+BB+BA**2)/DEL
      S(1,2)=-2.0*BB*ST/DEL
      S(2,1)=S(1,2)
      S(2,2)=S(1,1)
      RETURN
    5 PRINT 10
   10 FORMAT(/5X,'SUBROUTINE FOR HOLE IN MICROSTRIP IS NOT INCLUDED,
     1STOP.')
      STOP
      END
      SUBROUTINE FORBAK
      COMPLEX X,W,C,R
      COMMON /TOPO/ NCN(60),NP,NE,NPT
      COMMON /MTRX/ W(60,60)
      COMMON /SOLN/ C(60),X(60)
C     FORWARD ELIMINATION
      I=NCN(1)
      X(I)=C(I)/W(1,I)
      DO 20 I=2,NPT
      R=0.0
      IPR=NCN(I)
      I1=I-1
      DO 10 L=1,I1
      LPR=NCN(L)
      R=R+W(I,LPR)*X(LPR)
   10 X(IPR)=(C(I)-R)/W(I,IPR)
C     BACK SUBSTITUTION
      NP1=NPT-1
      DO 40K=1,NP1
      I=NPT-K
      R=0.0
      IPR=NCN(I)
      I1=I+1
      DO 30L=I1,NPT
      LPR=NCN(L)
   30 R=R+W(I,LPR)*X(LPR)
   40 X(IPR)=X(IPR)-R
      RETURN
      END
```

```
C
C     SUBROUTINE TO CALCULATE S-MATRIX FOR SHUNT ADMITTANCE
C
      SUBROUTINE SHNTSC
      COMPLEX S /EMTX/ S(4,4),VAL1,VAL2,VAL3
      YC=1.0/VAL1
      S(1,1)=-VAL2/(VAL2+2.0*YC)
      S(1,2)=2.0*YC/(VAL2+2.0*YC)
      S(2,1)=S(1,2)
      S(2,2)=S(1,1)
      RETURN
      END
C
C     SUBROUTINE TO CALCULATE S-MATRIX FOR SERIES IMPEDANCE
C
      SUBROUTINE SERISC
      COMPLEX S /EMTX/ S(4,4),VAL1,VAL2,VAL3
      S(1,1)=VAL2/(VAL2+2.0*VAL1)
      S(1,2)=2.0*VAL1/(VAL2+2.0*VAL1)
      S(2,1)=S(1,2)
      S(2,2)=S(1,1)
      RETURN
      END
      SUBROUTINE SETUPS
      COMPLEX S,W /EMTX/ S(4,4),VAL1,VAL2,VAL3
      COMMON /MTRX/ W(60,60)
      COMMON /SETT/ IP,JP,KP,LP
      W(IP,JP)=S(1,1)
      W(IP,JP)=S(1,2)
      W(JP,JP)=S(2,1)
      W(JP,JP)=S(2,2)
      RETURN
      END
C
C     SUBROUTINE TO CALCULATE S-MATRIX FOR OPEN END SECTION
C
      SUBROUTINE OPNESC
      LOGICAL DISC,MSP
      COMPLEX S,ST /DISK/ DISC
      COMMON /EMTX/ S(4,4),VAL1,VAL2,VAL3
      COMMON /DATA/ ST,PI,T,EK,H
      COMMON /PARA/ B,T,EK,H
      COMMON /FREK/ BETA,WP
```

```
      COMMON /MSTP/ MSP
      IF(DISC) GO TO 3
      S(1,1)=1.0
      RETURN
    3 IF(MSP)GO TO 5
      CALL WIDTH(VAL1,WD)
      CA=B*ALOG(2.0)/(PI)
      TANBL=(CA+2.0*WD)/(4.0*CA+2.0*WD)*SIN(BETA*CA)/COS(BETA*CA)
      S(1,1)=(1.0-TANBL*ST)/(1.0+TANBL*ST)
      RETURN
    5 CALL WIDTH(VAL1,WD)
      CALL EREFF(WD,ERE)
      WH=WD/H
      DL=0.412*H*(ERE+0.3)*(WH+0.264)/((ERE-0.258)*(WH+0.8))
      RL=DL*WP*SQRT(ERE)/(0.3E09)
      TANBL=SIN(BL)/COS(RL)
      S(1,1)=(1.-ST*TANBL)/(1.+ST*TANBL)
      RETURN
      END
      SUBROUTINE TEEJSC
C------------------------------------------------------
C     SUBROUTINE TO CALCULATE S-MATRIX FOR TEE JUNCTION
C------------------------------------------------------
      LOGICAL DISC,MSP
      REAL NP
      COMPLEX S,ST,DT,ZT
      COMMON /PARA/ B,T,PI,ER,H
      COMMON /DAT/ ST,PI
      COMMON /DISK/ DISC
      COMMON /EMTX/ S(4,4),VAL1,VAL2,VAL3
      COMMON /FREK/ BETA,WP
      COMMON /MSTP/ MSP
      IF(DISC) GO TO 1
      C=VAL1+2.0*VAL2
      S(1,1)=-VAL1/C
      S(1,2)=2.0*VAL2/C
      S(1,3)=2.0*SQRT(VAL1*VAL2)/C
      S(3,3)=(VAL1-2.0*VAL2)/C
      GO TO 30
    1 IF(MSP)GO TO 5
      TH=15.0*PI*(B-T)*BETA/(VAL2*SQRT(ER))
      NP=SIN(TH)/TH
      ZP=VAL2/NP**2
      DUM=0.785*NP*VAL1
      XA=-TH*DUM**2/(PI*VAL2)
```

```
73400        TEMP=15.0*(B-T)*BETA/(VAL1*SQRT(FR))
73500        IF(VAL1/VAL2.LT.0.5)GO TO 2
73600        XB=2.0*VAL1*TEMP/NP**2*(ALOG(1.43*VAL2/VAL1)+2.0*TEMP**2)-XA/2.0
73700        GO TO 4
73800   2    RTY=2.0*TEMP*(ALOG(1.0/SIN(PT/2.0*VAL1/VAL2))+0.5*TEMP**2*COS(PI
73900       1/2.0*VAL1/VAL2)**4)
74000        XB=VAL1/NP**2*(RTY+2.0*TEMP*(ALOG(2.0)+PI/6.0*VAL1/VAL2+1.5*TEMP
74100       1**2))-XA/2.0
74200   4    ZT=VAL1+2.0*ZP+(XA+2.0*XB)*ST
74300        DT=ZT*(VAL1+2.0*ZP+XA*XB+XA**2-2.0*ZP*XA*ST)/DT
74400        S(1,2)=2.0*VAL1*(ZP+XB*ST2)/LT
74500        S(1,3)=2.0*SQRT(VAL1*ZP)/ZT
74600        S(3,3)=(VAL1-2.0*ZP+(XA+2.0*XB)*ST)/ZT
74700        GO TO 30
74800   5    CALL WIDTH(VAL1,W1)
74900        CALL WIDTH(VAL2,W2)
75000        CALL EREFF(W1,ERE1)
75100        CALL EREFF(W2,ERE2)
75200        D1=120.*PI*H/(VAL1*SQRT(ERE1))
75300        D2=120.*PI*H/(VAL2*SQRT(ERE2))
75400        RETA1=WP*SQRT(ERE1)/(0.3E09)
75500        RETA2=WP*SQRT(ERE2)/(0.3E09)
75600        ALEMDA=(0.3E+09)**2/ALEMDA
75700        RZ=VAL1/VAL2;RD=D1/ALEMDA
75800        TEMP=D1*RZ*PI/ALEMDA
75900        AN=SIN(.05*D2*RZ*AN*AN
76000        IF(RZ.GT.2.)GO TO 10
76100        DS1=D1*(2.-0.16*D1*(1.+(2.*RD)**2-2.*ALOG(RZ))*RZ
76200        GO TO 15
76300  10    DS2=D1/2.-0.16*D1*(1.+(2.*RD)**2-2.*ALOG(1./RZ))/RZ
76400  15    IF(RZ.GT.0.5)GO TO 20
76500        RI=RD/VAL1*(-1.-2.*RD)*RZ)
76600        GO TO 25
76700  20    BT=RD/VAL1*(1.-2.*RD)*(3.-RZ-2.)
76800  25    ZN=VAL1*(2.*AN)/DEN
76900        DEN=VAL1*(2.*ZN+ST*RT*VAL1*ZN)/DEN
77000        S(1,1)=2.*SQRT(VAL1*ZN)/DEN
77100        S(1,2)=2.*ZN-ST*RT*VAL1*ZN)/DEN
77200        S(3,3)=(VAL1-2.*ZN-ST*BT*VAL1*ZN)/DS2
77300        TH1=BETA1*DS1;TH2=BETA2*DS2
77400        S(1,1)=S(1,1)*(COS(2.*TH1)+ST*SIN(2.*TH1))
```

```
      SC(1,2)=SC(1,2)*(COS(2.*TH1)+ST*SIN(2.*TH1))
      SC(3,3)=SC(3,3)*(COS(TH1+TH2)+ST*SIN(TH1+TH2))
      SC(3,1)=SC(1,2)
      SC(2,2)=SC(1,3)
      SC(2,1)=SC(1,3)
      SC(3,2)=SC(2,3)
      RETURN
      END
C     SUBROUTINE TO FIND CH. IMPEDANCE FROM WIDTH OF CONDUCTING LINE
C
      SUBROUTINE IMPFWD(WD,Z)
      LOGICAL MSP
      COMPLEX ST
      COMMON /PARA/ B,T,ER,H
      COMMON /MSTP/ MSP
      COMMON /DAT/ ST,PI
      IF(MSP)GO TO 5
      CF=2.0*ALOG((2.0*B-T)/(B-T))-T/B*ALOG(T*(2.0*B-T)/(B-T)**2)
      IF(WD/(B-T).LT.0.35)GO TO 3
      WE=WD
      GO TO 4
3     WE=WD-(0.35*B-WD)**2/(B+12.0*T)
4     Z=30.0*PI*(B-T)/(SQRT(ER)*(WF+B*CF/PI))
      RETURN
5     WH=WD/H
      CALL EREFF(WD,ERE)
      IF(WH.GE.1.)GO TO 10
      Z=60./SQRT(ERE)*ALOG(8./WH+0.25*WH)
      RETURN
10    Z=120.*PI/(SQRT(ERE)*(WH+1.393+0.667*ALOG(WH+1.444)))
      RETURN
      END
C     SUBROUTINE TO FIND WIDTH OF CONDUCTING LINE FROM CH. IMPEDANCE
C
      SUBROUTINE WIDTH (Z,WD)
      LOGICAL MSP
      COMPLEX ST,PI
      COMMON /DAT/ ST,PI
      COMMON /PARA/ B,T,ER,H
      COMMON /MSTP/ MSP
      IF(MSP)GO TO 5
      P=1.0-T/B
```

```
82200          CF=2.0*ALOG(1.0+1.0/P)-T/B*ALOG(1.0/P**2-1.0)
82300          X=30.0*PI*P/(SQRT(ER)*Z)-CF/PI
82400          IF(Z*SQRT(ER)*(1.0+2.3*T/B).GT.120.0) GO TO 3
82500          WD=B**X
82600          RETURN
82700    3     S=6.0*T/B+0.85
82800          WD=B**(S-SQRT(S*S-X*(12.0*T/B+1.0)-0.1225))
82900          RETURN
83000    5     B=60.*PI/(SQRT(ER)*Z)
83100          **.61/ER))
83200          -**H/PI*(B-1.-ALOG(2.*B-1.)+(ER-1.)/(2.*ER)*(ALOG(B-1.)+0.3
83300    19)    20=H/ER))
83400          IF(WD/H.GE.2.)RETURN
83500          A=SQRT((ER+1.)/2.)+Z/60.+(ER-1.)*(0.23+0.11/ER)/(ER+1.)
83600          WD=B**H*EXP(2.*A)/(EXP(2.*A)-2.)
83700          RETURN
83800          END
83900    C     SUBROUTINE TO READ EXTERNAL SUPPLIED S-PARAMETERS
84000    C
84100          SUBROUTINE SPARA(II)
84200          COMPLEX S
84300          COMMON/EMTX/S(4,4),VAL1,VAL2,VAL3
84400          COMMON/SEIT/IP,JP,KP,LP
84500    2     PRINT 2,II
84600          FORMAT(/5X,'EXTERNAL S-MATRIX FOR ELEMENT NUMBER',I4,' IS.')
84700    5     DO 10 I=1,4
84800          READ(8,10)(S(I,J),J=1,4)
84900    10    FORMAT(8E10.3)
85000          IF(LP.NE.0)GO TO 40
85100          IF(KP.NE.0)GO TO 30
85200          IF(JP.NE.0)GO TO 20
85300          PRINT 50,S(1,1)
85400          RETURN
85500    20    DO 25 I=1,2
85600    25    PRINT 50,(S(I,J),J=1,2)
85700          RETURN
85800    30    DO 35 I=1,3
85900    35    PRINT 50,(S(I,J),J=1,3)
86000          RETURN
86100    40    DO 45 I=1,4
86200    45    PRINT 50,(S(I,J),J=1,4)
86300    50    FORMAT(1X,4(E12.5,2X,E12.5,5X))
86400          RETURN
86500          END
86600    C     SUBROUTINE TO FIND ZOE AND ZOO FOR COUPLED LINE FROM WIDTH
```

```
C     AND GAP OF THE COUPLED LINE
      SUBROUTINE IMPED(VAL1,VAL2,ZOE,ZOO)
      LOGICAL MSP
      REAL KKE,KE,KEP,KO,KOP,KKO,K,KP,KK
      COMPLEX ST,PI
      COMMON/DAT/ST,PI
      COMMON/PARA/B,T,ER,H
      COMMON /MSTP/ MSP
      IF(MSP)GO TO 35
      KE=TANH(0.5*PI*VAL1/B)*TANH(0.5*PI*(VAL1+VAL2)/B)
      KEP=SQRT(1.-KE*KE)
      KO=TANH(0.5*PI*VAL1/B)/TANH(0.5*PI*(VAL1+VAL2)/B)
      KOP=SQRT(1.-KO*KO)
      IF(KE*KE.LE.0.5) GO TO 5
      KKE=PI/ALOG(2.0*(1.+SQRT(KEP))/(1.-SQRT(KEP)))
      GO TO 10
    5 KKE=PI/ALOG(2.0*(1.+SQRT(KF))/(1.-SQRT(KE)))
   10 ZOE=30.*PI*KKE/SQRT(ER)
      IF(KO*KO.LE.0.5) GO TO 25
      KKO=PI/ALOG(2.0*(1.+SQRT(KO))/(1.-SQRT(KO)))
      GO TO 30
   15 PRINT 20
   20 FORMAT(/10X,'INCORRECT VALUES FOR WIDTH OR/AND GAP'/10X,
     1'PLEASE CHECK DATA CARDS.STOP.')
      STOP
   25 KKO=ALOG(2.*(1.+SQRT(KOP))/(1.-SQRT(KOP)))/PI
   30 ZOO=30.*PI*KKO/SQRT(ER)
      RETURN
   35 CP=8.85*(0.1E-11)*ER*VAL1/H
      CALL EREFF(VAL1,ERE)
      CALL IMPFWD(VAL1,Z)
      CF=0.5*(SQRT(ERE)/(Z*(0.3E09))-CP)
      A=EXP(-0.1*EXP(2.33-2.53*VAL1/H))
      CFP=CF/(1.+A*H/VAL2*TANH(8.*VAL2/H))*SQRT(ER/ERE)
      KP=VAL2/(H+VAL2/H+2.*VAL1/H))
      K=VAL2/(H+K*K)
      IF(K*K.GE.0.5)GO TO 40
      KK=1.0/PI*ALOG(2.*(1.+SQRT(KP))/(1.-SQRT(KP)))
      GO TO 45
   40 KK=PI/(CALOG(2.*(1.+SQRT(K))/(1.-SQRT(K))))
```

```
45    CGA=8.85*(00.1E-11)*KK
      CGD=8.85*(00.1E-11)*ER/PI*ALOG(1./TANH(PI*VAL2/(4.*H)))+
     110.65*CEA*(00.02*SQRT(ER)*H/VAL2+1.-1./(ER*ER))
      CEA=CEP+CF+CGA+CGD
      COD=CEP+CF+CGA+CGD
      IF(ER-1.)ZERE=1.)GO TO 50
      ER=1.*ZERE
      CED=CEP+CF+CGA+CGD
      GO TO 35
50    ZOE=1./((0.3E09)*SQRT(CEA*CED))
      ZOD=1./((0.3E09)*SQRT(CDA*CUD))
      RETURN;END
C     SUBROUTINE TO CALCULATE S-MATRIX FOR COUPLED LINES
      SUBROUTINE COUPLD
      LOGICAL MSP
      COMPLEX ST,RHO,TRC,DEN
      COMMON/EMTX/S(4,4),VAL1,VAL2,VAL3
      COMMON/DAT/ST,PI
      COMMON/FREK/BETA,WP
      COMMON/PARA/B,F,ER,H
      COMMON/MSTP/MSP
      RZ=SQRT(VAL1/VAL2)
      IF(MSP)GO TO 2
      TH=BETA*VAL3
      GO TO 3
2     ZMILT=SQRT(VAL1*VAL2)
      CALL WIDTH(ZMULT,WD)
      CALL EREFF(WD,ERE)
      BETA1=WP*SQRT(ERE)/(0.3E09)
3     TH=BETA1*VAL3
      DEN=2.0*COS(TH)+ST*SIN(TH)*(PZ+1./RZ)
      RHO=ST*SIN(TH)*(RZ-1./RZ)/DEN
      TRC=2./DEN
      DO 5 J=1,4
      DO 5 J=1,4
5     S(1,2)=RHO;S(1,4)=TRC
      S(2,1)=S(1,2);S(2,3)=S(1,4)
      S(3,2)=S(1,2);S(3,4)=S(1,2)
      S(4,1)=S(1,4);S(4,3)=S(1,2)
      RETURN
      END
```

```
C
C
C
C     SUBROUTINE TO FIND ZOE AND ZOO FROM COUPLING AND CH. IMPEDANCE
C     OF THE COUPLED LINES
C
      SUBROUTINE IMPFCP(VAL1,VAL2,VAL3,ZOE,ZOO,CPLNTH)
      LOGICAL /MSTP/ MSP
      COMMON /FREK/ BETA,WP
      COMMON/PARA/B,T,ER,H
      IF(MSP)GO TO 5
      CPLNTH=(O.3E09)/(VAL3*4.*SQRT(ER))
      GO TO 10
5     CALL WIDTH(VAL2,WD)
      CALL EREFF(WD,ERE)
      CPLNTH=(O.3E09)/(VAL3*4.*SQRT(ERE))
10    ZOE=SQRT((1.+VAL1)/(1.-VAL1))*VAL2
      ZOO=SQRT((1.-VAL1)/(1.+VAL1))*VAL2
      RETURN;END
C     SUBROUTINE TO CALCULATE EFFECTIVE DIELECTRIC CONSTANT ERE
C
      SUBROUTINE EREFF(W,ERE)
      COMMON/PARA/B,T,ER,H
      WH=W/H
      FWH=1./SQRT(1.+12./WH)
      IF(WH.GT.1.)GO TO 5
      FWH=FWH+0.04*(1.-WH)**2
5     ERE=(ER+1.)/2.+(ER-1.)*FWH/2.
      RETURN
      END
```

95400
95500
95600
95700
95800
95900
96000
96100
96200
96300
96400
96500
96600
96700
96800
96900
97000
97100
97200
97300
97400
97500
97600
97700
97800
97900
98000
98100
98200

REFERENCES

[1]   Chadha, R., and K.C. Gupta, "A Microwave Circuit Analysis
       Program," *Tech. Report*, No. DOE/EE/36-6, Dept. of Elec-
       trical Eng., IIT Kanpur, May 1979.

[2]   Chadha, R., and K.C. Gupta, "Computer-Aided Analysis of
       Stripline Circuits Including Discontinuity Reactance Effects,"
       Jour. Instn. Electronics Telecomm. Engrs. (India), Vol. 26,
       1980, pp. 290-292.

[3]   Kumar, G., and K.C. Gupta, "Extension of MCAP for Micro-
       strip Circuit Analysis," *Tech. Report*, No. DOE/EE/36-7,
       Dept. of Electrical Eng., IIT Kanpur, 1980.

20

An Overview of Available CAD Programs*

INTRODUCTION

Preceding chapters have described the modelling, analysis and optimization of microwave circuit design. The microwave industry has been extremely conservative and cautious in applying these modern design aids. According to some sources, a "typical" microwave engineer spends only 10-20% of his working time with design — the rest is taken up by other tasks, often menial, such as searching for component sources, equipment and data, or generating paperwork. Too many circuits are still "designed" by painfully slow workbench experimentation and physical layout. This is in sharp contrast with the semiconductor industry where computer-aided simulation and layout has been widely accepted and practiced since the mid-sixties.

The situation is even worse when production is considered. Production levels too often depend on a machinist's mood, an assembler's attitude, or a technician's time. What is needed is a combination of modern mass production techniques and clever circuit design which should lead to greater standardization.

---

*This chapter has been contributed by Mr. Les Besser, Compact Engineering, Palo Alto, California, USA.

The combination of inefficient design, production, and the lack of new designers has forced management to look for ways to improve the efficiency of their manpower. One answer is the integration of computer aids for design, manufacture, and project management to cut time and costs and increase quality and productivity [1].

Effective, specialized systems for Computer-Aided Design (CAD), Computer-Aided Manufacturing (CAM), Computer-Aided Testing (CAT), and Computer-Aided Project Management (PM) are available from a number of computer system vendors. Some of them are now used by engineering, manufacturing, quality assurance, and project management, yet little has been done to coordinate and integrate computer use in design, manufacture, and management. Although much of the information about a product or a project is common to several of the functions, few of the specialized systems now available are able to communicate directly with each other. Many of them run on different brands of computers. Languages, file formats, and communication protocols vary widely. System integration is therefore an area where much work is still needed.

There are many libraries listing data components, materials, tooling, standards, and test procedures in any factory. Keeping these in machine form for direct use by specialized computer programs will ultimately yield better designs and more reliable products with shorter design cycles.

Human interaction with the systems are now being enhanced through extensive use of computer graphics. Those parts needed for a particular plant or product line can be assembled to fit requirements. Parts of systems in different locations can be linked together via data communication networks.

20.2 INTEGRATED DESIGN AND MANUFACTURING SYSTEM CONCEPT

An ideal design/manufacturing cycle of a microwave amplifier is illustrated in this section. Most of the routine decisions and tedious computations are performed by computers; the human interaction is provided in the form of interactive graphics. Such a concept is called an Integrated Design and Manufacturing System (IDMS) as shown in Figure 20.1, and explained through a microwave amplifier design procedure below.

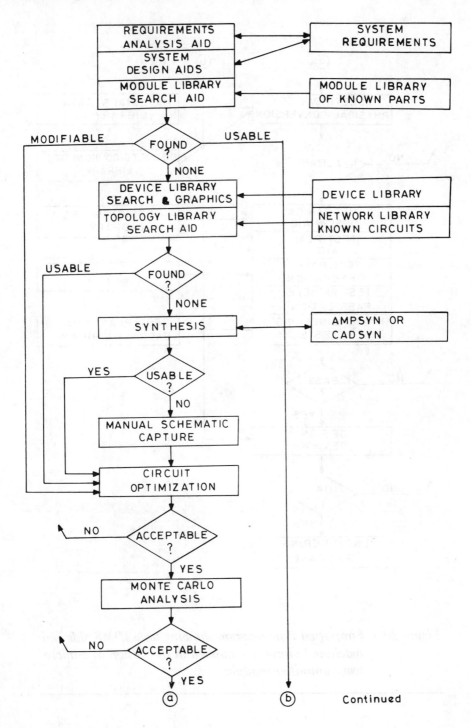

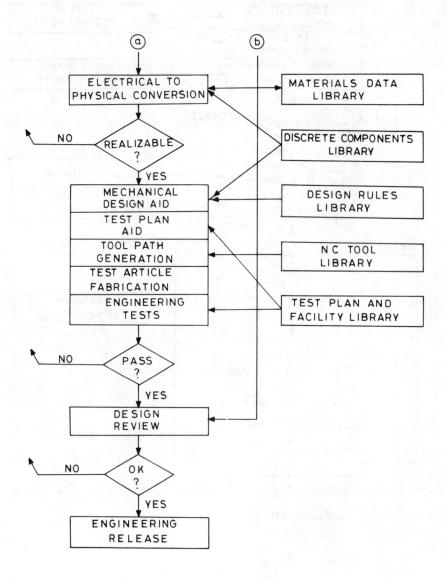

Figure 20.1 Simplified flow diagram showing how IDMS aids and machine libraries are applied in the design of a microwave amplifier module.

Amplifier performance requirements are specified by system engineers. These people use graphic and text-processing features of IDMS to prepare and record amplifier specifications in a segment of the IDMS database. As they do their work, these engineers can search the IDMS library of currently producible modules. In case such a module meets the requirements of the new system, it can be included immediately in the system design.

If the system engineer concludes that a new amplifier is needed, the task is turned over to the component designers. The microwave engineer assigned to amplifier design retrieves the specifications from the IDMS database. In many cases, an existing amplifier can be modified to perform as specified, and the engineer can select one of the existing modules as a starting point for module optimization. The work of describing a totally new module is not needed.

If it is decided to start from scratch rather than to use or modify a known amplifier, the engineer consults the IDMS library of transistor characteristics to select devices that show the best promise of meeting design requirements. This is done by specifying the gain and bandwidth requirements, and the databank provides a list of alternative devices that are able to meet specifications.

When transistors are selected, the program generates equivalent circuits to model the devices [2]. Next, the engineer consults the IDMS library of matching network schematics to select the input, output, and interstage network topologies that appear appropriate to the design. If a set of promising networks is located in the library, they are used as the initial point in the synthesis to follow. If a new topology is needed, the engineer invokes the IDMS network design aids to create and verify the needed schematics. If the network design aid fails to produce a usable topology, the engineer uses the IDMS graphic design aids to create and capture a schematic by manual methods.

With the schematics complete, the engineer uses optimization to refine the electrical characteristics of the amplifier design by adjusting the electrical parameters of the components in the matching networks under the engineer's guidance. All critical circuit parameters, such as gain flatness, impedance match, noise figure, stability, etc., are carefully monitored to assure acceptable performance.

Sometimes the optimization does not converge, indicating that the chosen circuit cannot meet specifications. If this is true, the engineer must seek a change in the specifications or start over with different choices of transistors, number of stages, and/or networks. On the other hand, if one of the electrical designs resulting from the optimization is acceptable, the tolerance effects are examined by using Monte Carlo analysis, permitting the placing of limits on active and passive component values. Finally, the program converts the electrical parameters of transmission lines to physical dimensions on a selected substrate using the material databank. If the optimal electrical design cannot be realized physically within the constraints of real materials, the engineer must repeat portions of this procedure.

If the design can be built, the engineer uses a mechanical layout program contained in the IDMS to do the topological design. This program takes the physical dimensions for the network components from the amplifier design file. If any discrete components, such as chip capacitors, are included in the design, their dimensions are retrieved from a discrete components library. The engineer works with an interactive graphics display to create the mechanical layout of the amplifier, subject to constraints that are drawn from the design rules library. The result of this step is a "drawing" of the amplifier in the design file.

The microwave engineer works with this design and with the library of test facilities and procedures to specify a test plan for the amplifier. The test plan may call for the addition of test point couplers or connections to the mechanical design of the amplifier. It may also call for fabrication of new test fixtures and possibly the acquisition of new test equipment.

When the design has been completed with the addition of any needed test points, the design data are used with library information describing the numerically controlled tools in the plant to generate tool paths for milling the enclosure and preparing the photomasks needed to etch the circuits.

A prototype circuit is then fabricated, assembled, and tested. If the test results show a need for adjustments in the design, selected steps can be carried out to produce another prototype until all specifications are met. Then design test data are submitted for design review. If they fail the design review, more work is needed. This may be as simple as adding a mounting bracket, or as complex as changing the specifications or some fundamental aspect of the design.

Amplifiers that pass design review can be released immediately for production. The documentation that normally accompanies such a release is complete in the IDMS database, having been generated in parallel using the IDMS utilities and libraries. Included are the unit material requirements, tool control information, assembly instructions, and the test plan and performance data for the production item. The released design can also be added to the library of known module designs for possible uses in other equipment. If a new network topology has been created, it can be added to the library of known networks.

This example shows that productivity in microwave design work can be increased considerably through elimination of unnecessary work, through instant availability of relevant data, through computer analysis to complement engineering creativity, and through automatic documentation of results that are directly usable in the manufacturing, quality assurance, and project management of the organization.

Although (as of this writing) the ultimate integrated CAD/CAM system only exists in its conceptual form, the complete solution is not far away; and, in the opinion of the author, it should be available in the early part of this decade.

The remaining section of this chapter describes several commercially available design programs to analyze, synthesize and optimize microwave circuits. The programs are offered through Hewlett-Packard software suppliers and international timesharing services.

20.3 SUMMARY OF MICROWAVE CAD PROGRAMS

Three catagories of programs are discussed here, depending on their hardware requirements, ranging from handheld and desktop calculators to large scale computers. Functionally, the COMPACT series offers analysis and optimization of active and passive circuits, AMPSYN and CADSYN provide matching network synthesis, while FILSYN is a general purpose filter design program.

20.3.1 HANDY-COMPACT®, Circuit Analysis on the HP-41C Handheld Calculator

HANDY-COMPACT® [3], available in the form of a plug-in ROM, provides the user with the capability to examine complex circuit structures using two-port or ladder analysis. This program supplements the larger CAD programs and can be used for preliminary design in a time and cost-effective manner. Students and others with limited access to large CAD programs will find that HANDY-COMPACT® has many of the features of the larger programs at a reduced execution speed.

In two-port mode, analysis is based on S-parameters and requires 10 to 15 seconds to compute the S-matrix for a lumped or distributed element. In ladder mode, analysis requires from 4 to 6 seconds to compute the impedance at each node of a ladder network. The node may be changed at any time. Ladder analysis is useful for matching networks, lossless filters, and other networks where the input impedance is desired or can be used to compute the insertion loss. Ladder analysis can also be used with two-port analysis for series or shunt one-port branches (such as amplifier bias networks) to increase the execution speed.

Each HANDY-COMPACT® function is assigned a name used to execute the desired function. For example, the series Resistor-Capacitor combination is "SRC". The user enters the value for the resistor and capacitor, specifies whether the combination is connected in series or shunt, then enters "XEQ" and "SRC" to compute the S-matrix for the element. The next step would be "XEQ" and "CAS" (execute cascade connection) to connect the element with a previous two-port. No key assignments are made, allowing the designers the freedom to choose their own combinations. All functions may be executed directly from the keyboard or placed in a circuit file for automatic execution. A start, stop, and step frequency register is provided for this purpose, as well as an index register used to recall one- or two-port data at the corresponding frequency.

As an example of the use of the program, a three-element matching network is analyzed. The circuit schematics, frequency response, and a plot of the 3-dB bandwidth response are shown in Figure 20.2.

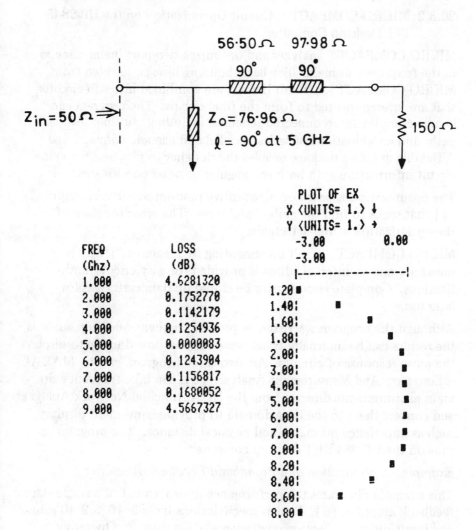

Figure 20.2 Circuit schematic and frequency response of the 2-8 GHz matching network. Printouts were provided by the HP-41C Auxiliary Printer.

20.3.2 MICRO-COMPACT® , Circuit Optimization on the HP-9845 B/T Desktop Computer

MICRO-COMPACT® analyzes and optimizes two-port linear circuits in the frequency domain. The basic building blocks, selected from MICRO-COMPACT® 's circuit library, are combined into sub-circuits that are interconnected to form the final circuit. The program can handle complex interconnected schemes, including multiple feedback paths and combinations of series, parallel and cascade connections. A flexible graphics package enables the designer to plot and map vital circuit information with both rectangular or polar coordinates.

The optimization is based on an adaptive random search technique [4] that seeks to find the global minimum. The error function of the optimization is user-selectable.

MICRO-COMPACT® is self-documenting by means of "HELP" messages, and an internal editor is provided for easy circuit modifications. Complete circuits may be stored on data cartridges for later use.

Although the program is written to provide frequency-domain analysis, the results can be internally transformed to the time domain to display the pulse response of circuits. An associated program, called "MAMA" (Microwave And Measurement Analysis) [5], can take frequency domain measurements directly from the HP Automated Network Analyzer and convert them to the time domain to provide convenient displays, such as impedance mismatch and physical distance. The program runs on the HP-9845B/T desktop computer.

Example: Optimization of a Broadband Feedback Amplifier

This example illustrates the performance improvement of a single-stage feedback amplifier [6]. Design specifications include 10 ± .2 dB gain, and input/output reflection coefficients of les than .2. Operating frequency range is 10 - 2,000 MHz.

The circuit schematic of the amplifier stage is shown in Figure 20.3. At the lower frequencies the resistor of the parallel feedback controls the gain and the input/output impedances. The RL combination rolls off the effect of parallel feedback at 1000 MHz. For frequencies above 1,000 MHz, the gain flatness is maintained by the input/output matching networks. The circuit is now optimized with the error function EF given by

$$EF = \frac{1}{10} \sum_{f = 10}^{f = 2000} \left(|S_{11}|^2 + |S_{22}|^2 + |G_{Desired} - G_{Actual}|^2 \right).$$

(20.1)

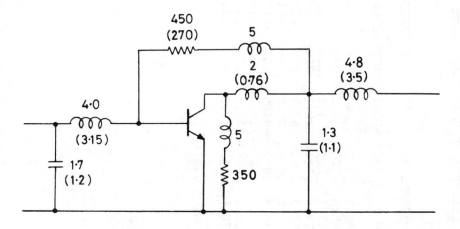

Figure 20.3 Circuit diagram of the 10-2,000 MHz feedback amplifier. Numbers in parentheses are optimized values.

The optimization reduces the error function from 2.92 to 0.59 in 215 function evaluations. The final component values are shown in parentheses on the circuit diagram. The actual computer run is shown in Figure 20.4.

Although the above circuit is relatively simple, optimization can be quite difficult due to potential instability and the presence of several "local minima" that may lead to a false solution. Past experience shows that purely gradient-seeking search techniques are not always capable of locating the optimum design in such cases.

CIRCUIT OPTIMIZATION WITH 6 VARIABLES

INITIAL CIRCUIT ANALYSIS

POLAR S-PARAMETERS IN   50.0 OHM SYSTEM

FREQ.	S11 (MAGN<ANGL)		S21 (MAGN<ANGL)		S21 (MAGN<ANGL)		S22 (MAGN<ANGL)		S21 DB	K FACT.
10.00	.37<	1	3.99<	175.3	.122<	.4	.25<	4	12.03	1.16
100.00	.36<	-15	3.93<	165.5	.120<	-7.2	.25<	2	11.90	1.19
250.00	.35<	-41	3.88<	147.1	.117<	-19.8	.25<	-1	11.78	1.21
500.00	.35<	-80	3.88<	117.8	.111<	-39.1	.25<	-9	11.78	1.26
750.00	.32<	-117	3.89<	92.9	.102<	-57.9	.20<	-27	11.80	1.34
1000.00	.27<	-149	3.89<	67.0	.096<	-75.8	.13<	-56	11.79	1.44
1250.00	.19<	-175	3.88<	35.3	.092<	-94.5	.10<	-118	11.78	1.53
1500.00	.11<	150	3.82<	.1	.087<	-115.0	.16<	179	11.65	1.61
1750.00	.11<	40	3.61<	-35.5	.078<	-137.1	.29<	143	11.15	1.71
2000.00	.28<	-11	3.13<	-70.6	.067<	-158.9	.43<	122	9.90	1.77

OPTIMIZATION BEGINS WITH FOLLOWING VARIABLES

VARIABLES
(1): 1.7000
(2): 4.0000
(3): 450.00
(4): 2.0000
(5): 1.3000
(6): 4.8000

ERR. F.= 2.989
---****----

```
ERR. F. =    .201
ERR. F. =    .171
ERR. F. =    .139
ERR. F. =    .089
ERR. F. =    .087
( 1):..   1.2049
( 2):..   3.1513
( 3):..   270.30
( 4):..   .76444
( 5):..   1.1320
( 6):..   3.4805
ERR. F. =    .087
----*****----
FINAL ANALYSIS FOLLOWS
```

POLAR S-PARAMETERS IN 50.0 OHM SYSTEM

FREQ.	S11 (MAGN<ANGL)	S21 (MAGN<ANGL)	S12 (MAGN<ANGL)	S22 (MAGN<ANGL)	S21 DB	K FACT.
10.00	.17< 5	3.16< 175.8	.164< .7	.08< 18	9.99	1.20
100.00	.16< -11	3.12< 168.0	.162< -5.7	.08< 25	9.88	1.22
250.00	.16< -40	3.10< 153.2	.159< -16.3	.11< 33	9.83	1.24
500.00	.17< -82	3.14< 129.4	.151< -32.7	.15< 32	9.94	1.26
750.00	.19< -127	3.17< 109.6	.138< -49.2	.15< 22	10.01	1.32
1000.00	.20< -161	3.17< 89.4	.127< 64.2	.13< 10	10.01	1.40
1250.00	.18< 174	3.19< 64.3	.121< -78.6	.13< -16	10.07	1.45
1500.00	.16< 151	3.22< 36.8	.116< -94.2	.12< -54	10.16	1.48
1750.00	.16< 110	3.22< 9.9	.107<-110.5	.13< -117	10.17	1.56
2000.00	.20< 61	3.11< -17.0	.098<-126.3	.21< -167	9.84	1.63

Figure 20.4 *Optimization of the 10-2000 MHz amplifier using MICRO-COMPACT. Six components are varied simultaneously by the computer to find the optimum solution.*

20.3.3 SUPER-COMPACT®

This new program replaces the general purpose circuit optimization program, COMPACT, that served the worldwide needs of the microwave industry during the past decade. SUPER-COMPACT® offers unrestricted, simple data input and flexible interactive optimization of one-, two-, three-, or four-port circuits. Users may specify a tailored optimization error function which may include combinations of S-, Y-, and Z-parameters as well as nodal impedances or admittances with arbitrary terminations. Specifications may be different for various input-output pairs allowing simultaneous optimization for desired characteristics (such as coupling and isolation). Circuits may be optimized in different states. For example, the equivalent circuit of a switch can be optimized simultaneously in the "on" and "off" modes. A unique interactive optimization segment allows the user to combine gradient and adaptive random search techniques for maximum efficiency with a high degree of probability to find the global optimum. Interactive graphics plot polar or rectangular charts with the frequency response of any of the available two-, three-, or four-port parameters. In addition, constant-noise, constant-gain, and stability circles may also be plotted on the Smith chart for any given two-port. Displays can be "zoomed-in" to provide close-up views of critical performance areas.

The program includes several databanks to provide information and measured characteristics of transistors and dielectric materials. Local databanks can be created and stored on the user's disk. The databanks can be called at the command level, and can be searched for components meeting specified performance requirements such as maximum gain or minimum noise figures. Direct plotting of device parameters is available.

Microwave designers may describe transmission lines in microstrip, stripline, coplanar waveguide and suspended substrate modes. Component values may be expressed in electrical or physical dimensions. Analysis includes the effects of dispersion, radiation, discontinuities, multi-layer metallization, surface roughness, dielectric, and conductor losses. Closed-form microstrip and stripline approximations offer less than 1% error for most practical dielectric materials. Transmission line synthesis is carried out automatically by computing physical dimensions from electrical parameters.

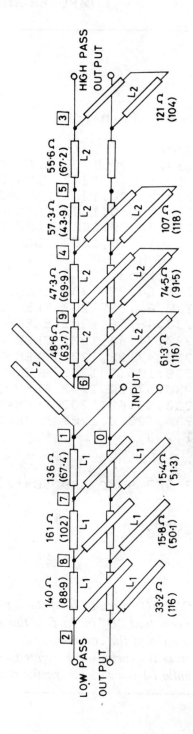

Figure 20.5 Circuit schematic of the microwave diplexer filter. Impedance values shown in parentheses are the optimized values.

```
D: 90
L1: 10GHZ
L2: 10GHZ
* Create three-port block
BLK
* Low-Pass Section
OST 2 0 Z0=?30,33.20,120? ELEN=D F=L1
TRL 2 8 Z0=?30,120.0,120? ELEN=D F=L1
OST 8 0 Z0=?30,30.00,120? ELEN=D F=L1
TRL 8 7 Z0=?30,120.0,120? ELEN=D F=L1
OST 7 0 Z0=?30,30.00,120? ELEN=D F=L1
TRL 7 1 Z0=?30,120.0,120? ELEN=D
+ F=?5GHZ,L1,10GHZ?
* High-Pass Section
OST 1 6 Z0=?30,64.29,120? ELEN=D F=L2
SST 6 0 Z0=?30,61.33,120? ELEN=D F=L2
TRL 6 9 Z0=?30,48.56,120? ELEN=D F=L2
SST 9 0 Z0=?30,74.54,120? ELEN=D F=L2
TRL 9 4 Z0=?30,47.28,120? ELEN=D F=L2
SST 4 0 Z0=?30,106.9,120? ELEN=D F=L2
TRL 4 5 Z0=?30,57.34,120? ELEN=D F=L2
TRL 5 3 Z0=?30,55.60,120? ELEN=D F=L2
SST 3 0 Z0=?30,120.0,120? ELEN=D F=L2
BLK1: 3POR 1 2 3
END
FREQ
STEP 2E9 4E9 5E7 STEP 4E9 5E9 2.5E7
END
OUT
PRI BLK1 S R1=50
END
```

Figure 20.6 SUPER-COMPACT circuit file of the 3-port diplexer filter. The constant "D" in the first line defines the electrical lengths of the commensurate sections. L1 and L2 represent quarter-wave frequencies. L2 is kept constant while L1 is a variable for the optimization.

A typical SUPER-COMPACT® circuit optimization is illustrated by the design of a microwave diplexer filter with passbands of 2-3.3 and 4-5 GHz in a 50-ohm system. The filter is to be realized in coaxial structure.

The initial network, shown in Figure 20.5, was obtained by independent synthesis of two singly-terminated filters (high-pass and low-pass types) assuming ideal (lossless) transmission lines. The quarter-wavelength frequencies of both sections were 10 GHz. The two filters were combined at their unterminated ends to form a three-port diplexer network. Component values in parentheses refer to optimized results.

The SUPER-COMPACT® circuit file description is illustrated in Figure 20.6. Data lines beginning with asterisks (*) are comments — they are used for reference only. A plus sign (+) in the first column indicates continuation. In the left file, the circuit is defined as a three-port through nodal interconnections. The electrical lengths of the transmission lines and their quarter-wave frequencies are specified first, followed by the circuit description. Each element is defined and interconnected in a single input line. Numerical values shown between question marks (?) are the lower and upper limits and initial values for optimization. Note that some of the line impedance values in data file do not correspond to those shown in the schematic. Specifically, impedances above 120 ohms are reduced to 120 ohms, and impedances below 30 ohms are increased to 30 ohms. This was done to investigate the effect of changes necessary to keep physical dimensions in a realistic range.

For physical realization, the transmission line impedances should be held within a 30-120 ohm range. In our filter schematic, the actual impedance range is from 15.45 ohms to 161.5 ohms; therefore, it cannot be constructed in its current form. If the impedances are arbitrarily changed to be within the realizable range, the filter performance becomes unacceptable, as shown in Figure 20.7a. We submitted the filter to a constrained optimization with the allowed 30-120 ohm impedance range. In addition to the fifteen line impedances, the quarter-wave frequency of the commensurate-length lowpass section is also declared to be variable. Even though the low-pass section has six transmission lines, their variable quarter-wave frequencies are kept the same. The error function to be minimized is:

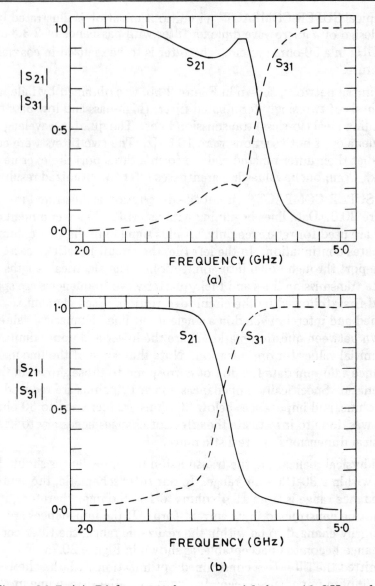

Figure 20.7 (a) Diplexer performance with f_o = 10 GHz and
transmission line impedances set arbitrarily to 30 <
Z < 120.

(b) Results of constrained optimization. Note the
improvement in both passband and stopband per-
formances.

$$
\text{ERRF} = \sum_{f=2,000}^{f=3,300} W_{11}\,|S_{11}|^2 + W_{21}\,|S_{21}-0|^2
$$

$$
+ W_{31}\,|S_{31}-(-20)|^2 + W_{22}\,|S_{22}|^2
$$

$$
+ \sum_{f=4,000}^{f=5,000} W'_{11}\,|S_{11}|^2 + W'_{21}\,|S_{21}-(-20)|^2
$$

$$
+ W'_{31}\,|S_{31}-0|^2 + W'_{33}\,|S_{33}|^2 \tag{20.2}
$$

where S_{21} and S_{31} are given in dB. The W and W' factors represent "weights" associated with the various S-parameters in two different frequency bands. Two of them, W_{31} and W'_{21}, are specified so that their values go to zero if S_{31} and/or S_{21} reach the minimum specified 20 dB stopband attenuation. Also note that $|S_{11}|$ is minimized in both frequency bands, while $|S_{22}|$ and $|S_{33}|$ are only minimized in their respective passbands.

Optimization improved their performance significantly, as shown in Figure 20.7b. The optimized component values are given in parentheses in Figure 20.5.

20.3.4 Lumped Element Matching Synthesis with AMPSYN

The AMPSYN program [8] synthesizes lumped element matching networks and provides for transformation of the lumped design to approximate transmission line equivalents. AMPSYN allows the user to select the necessary topology to absorb the parasitic elements. Impedance transformations are implemented by the program to provide the proper networks for the specified terminating impedance levels. Because the networks are the result of exact calculations, they provide excellent initial values for multistage amplifier circuit. If necessary, these values may be even further refined by optimization.

AMPSYN enables the designer to compare various solutions with different combinations of reflection-zero locations. Such networks have the same frequency response, but different sets of component values allow convenient selection for suitable physical realization or parasitic absorption.

Example: Matching Synthesis with Complex Impedance Terminations

To illustrate the synthesis procedure, we asked AMPSYN to design a fourth-order band-pass matching network between two complex terminations, as shown in Figure 20.8. The desired bandwidth is 100-300 MHz; 0.2 dB equal-ripple response and 0.1 dB minimum insertion loss are specified.

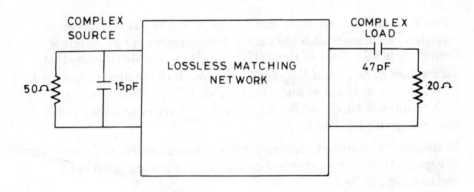

Figure 20.8 Impedance matching synthesis with complex termina-
tions. The first element of the matching network must
be a parallel capacitor and the last one must be a series
capacitor to be consistent with the source and load
parasitics.

The AMPSYN response is shown in Figure 20.9. First, the circuit topology is specified ("TY" command) in terms of series and parallel capacitors and inductors. Next, the circuit is synthesized ("SY" command), and scaled to the specified source impedance and upper cutoff frequency.

The initial synthesis shows that the input capacitor is not enough to absorb the 15 pf source parasitic and the load resistance is lower than the specified 20 ohms. A Norton impedance transformation will most likely take care of the improper load, and the input capacitance could be increased by shifting the reflection zeros to a different combination.

The "PA" command evaluates the input and output capacitance values corresponding to the four possible reflection zero pair positions (OO, IO, OI and II) where "O" stands for right-hand plane and "I" stands for left-hand plane position. Note that the "OI" position yields an output capacitor of 46.19 pf, within 2% of the parasitic of the load, while the input capacitor is 18.27 pf, sufficiently high to absorb the 15 pf source parasitic. We shall use this combination and accept the 46.19 pf value as our load parasitic. At the input, the 18.27 pf capacitor is split into two parallel parts.

The final synthesis is followed by an impedance transformation ("IT" command. The resultant final network is shown in Figure 20.10.

20.3.5 Transmission Line Matching Network Synthesis with CADSYN

CADSYN is a distributed matching network synthesis computer program that offers commensurate (equal) length transmission line network design. Bandwidth, gain slope, transmission line length, insertion loss, ripple, and circuit topology are all selectable and may be modified as desired. Theoretical gain-bandwidth limitations are calculated to predict device performance prior to synthesis [9]. Interactive use of Kuroda's identity, Norton's transformation, duality, and impedance scaling provide the capability to design matching networks with arbitrary impedance transformation and realizable element values. All synthesis and transformation steps are transparent to the user, so even those who are inexperienced in modern synthesis techniques can easily learn to design matching networks with the program.

```
COMMAND: GA
NO. OF ELEMENTS, NO. OF HIGH PASS ELEMENTS =4,2
DESIRED SLOPE (DB/OCTAVE/) = Ø
BANDWIDTH (F UPPER/F LOWER) = 3
MIN BANDPASS INSERTION LOSS (DB) = .1
INBAND RIPPLE (DB) = .2
ENTER RE TO RESTART
       ER FOR EQUIRIPPLE
       MF FOR MAXIMALLY FLAT
       CH FOR LP CHEBYSHEV ? ER

COMMAND: TY
ELEMENT  1 IS CP
ELEMENT  2 IS LS
ELEMENT  3 IS LP
ELEMENT  4 IS CS
COMMAND: SY
RS = 5Ø
NEW FH(GHZ) = .3
R(SOURCE) =    5Ø.ØØØØ OHMS
CP=   13.2975 PF
LS=   21.328Ø NH
LP=   42.1685 NH
CS=   59.6117 PF
R(LOAD)=   12.997Ø OHMS
F UPPER =     Ø.3ØØØ GHZ
  COMMAND: PA
DESIRED LOAD IMPEDANCE = 2Ø
```

```
--------------------------------------------------------
                       INPUT              OUTPUT
ZERO POSITIONS     MAX  CAP (PF)       MIN  CAP (PF)
--------------------------------------------------------
O  O                  13.2975             38.7387
I  O                  15.Ø672             56.Ø384
O  I                  18.2772             46.1966
I  I                  21.7959             63.4964
CHANGE MIL, SLOPE, ALL, OR NOTHING (C/S/A/N):N
COMMAND: MZ
TYPE O TO IMPROVE PARASITIC ABSORPTION ON THE OUTPUT
       I TO IMPROVE ABSORPTION ON THE INPUT


COMPLEX ZERO PAIRS
ZERO 1 REAL PART = Ø.Ø469 IMAG PART =+- Ø.3762 . : O
ZERO 2 REAL PART = Ø.1Ø87 IMAG PART =+- Ø.8726 . : I
```

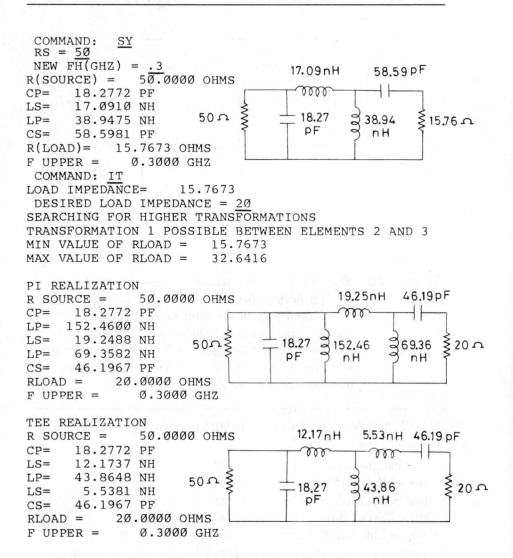

```
COMMAND:   SY
RS = 50
NEW FH(GHZ) = .3
R(SOURCE) =     50.0000 OHMS
CP=     18.2772 PF
LS=     17.0910 NH
LP=     38.9475 NH
CS=     58.5981 PF
R(LOAD)=    15.7673 OHMS
F UPPER =      0.3000 GHZ
  COMMAND: IT
LOAD IMPEDANCE=     15.7673
 DESIRED LOAD IMPEDANCE = 20
SEARCHING FOR HIGHER TRANSFORMATIONS
TRANSFORMATION 1 POSSIBLE BETWEEN ELEMENTS 2 AND 3
MIN VALUE OF RLOAD =    15.7673
MAX VALUE OF RLOAD =    32.6416

PI REALIZATION
R SOURCE =     50.0000 OHMS
CP=     18.2772 PF
LP=    152.4600 NH
LS=     19.2488 NH
LP=     69.3582 NH
CS=     46.1967 PF
RLOAD =     20.0000 OHMS
F UPPER =      0.3000 GHZ

TEE REALIZATION
R SOURCE =     50.0000 OHMS
CP=     18.2772 PF
LS=     12.1737 NH
LP=     43.8648 NH
LS=      5.5381 NH
CS=     46.1967 PF
RLOAD =     20.0000 OHMS
F UPPER =      0.3000 GHZ
```

Figure 20.9 Response of the AMPSYN program. Since the initial synthesis did not provide sufficient input capacitance, the reflection zero combinations are changed to increase the value of C1.

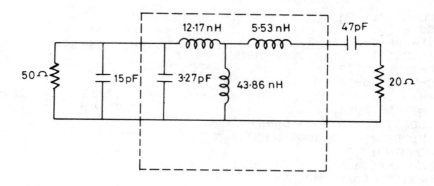

Figure 20.10   *The final matching network shows the splitting of*
the synthesized input capacitor into two parts.
15 pF is already in the source and 3.27 pF is
realized in the circuit. The output capacitor was
so close to 47 pF that for practical purposes it can
be called a "full absorption," leaving no extra ca-
pacitance in the circuit.

CADSYN handles five types of distributed network elements as
follows:

Open Parallel Stub   — OP
Shorted Parallel Stub   — SP
Open Series Stub   — OS
Shorted Series Stub   — SS
Cascade Line (Unit Element) — CL (or UE)

The topology is specified by the user in a simple form. It must be
consistent with the basic network specifications. A convenient list
of valid topologies is available from the program.

The impedance behavior of most practical complex source and load
terminations can be approximated by a resistor and a reactive element, such as a series or parallel transmission line stub, or a cascade
line. The length of the reactive part determines the commensurate

lengths of all transmission lines of the network to be synthesized. The type of element (OP, UE, etc.) places a constraint on the topology selection. Under ideal conditions, the synthesis may be directed to provide "exact parasitic absorption" by setting one of the network elements equal to the reactive part of the termination.

The operation of CADSYN is very similar to that of AMPSYN and is not described here.

20.3.6 FILSYN

FILSYN is a general purpose filter design program that offers exact synthesis of commensurate (equal length) transmission line networks, as well as lumped (LC) elements [10]. The filter types include lowpass, linear-phase low-pass, high-pass bandstop, and band-pass (both conventional and parametric). The passband response may be maximally flat or equal-ripple with monotonic, equal-minima, arbitrary or pica-wise stopband specifications. For more general cases, functional input is also available. Both single and double terminated networks are offered; the former type is particularly useful for diplexer filter design. Users may specify their own topology or the program can provide a suitable one. Predistorted design is available for lossy filter structures.

At the command level, FILSYN offers network manipulations and transformations (both Norton and Kuroda types) for convenient circuit realization. Analysis is given both at the transfer function and at the final circuit levels.

Group delay equalization is offered in two ways: all-pass equalizer sections may be incorporated in the filter or they can be cascaded to the network through the "DEELAY" subprogram. Equalizers may also be designed with lumped or distributed elements.

In addition to passive network realization, FILSYN also provides digital and active filter synthesis. To illustrate a typical filter design, we asked FILSYN for a synthesis of a fifth-order 5 GHz low-pass filter consisting of two unit elements and three parallel open-circuited stubs. The FILSYN response is shown in Figure 20.11 and the corresponding filter and its response are shown in Figure 20.12.

```
PLACER: P, FILSYN: F, LADDER: L, DIGITAL: D OR END: E
> F
ENTER TITLE
> MICROWAVE LOWPASS FILTER
FILTER KIND - LUMPED: 0, BILINEAR DIGITAL: 1 OR MICROWAVE: 2
> 2
ENTER QUARTER WAVE FREQUENCY IN HZ
> 10E9
FILTER TYPE - LOWPASS: 1, HIGHPASS: 2, LIN.-PHASE LOWPASS: 3, BANDPASS: 4
> 1
UPPER EDGE OF THE PASSBAND IN HZ
> 5E9
PASSBAND - MAX.-FLAT: 0, EQUAL-RIPPLE: 1, FUNCTIONAL INPUT: 2
> 1
WHAT IS THE BAND EDGE LOSS IN DB
> .2
STOPBAND - MONOTONIC: 0, EQUAL-MINIMA: 1 OR SPECIFIED: 2
> 0
ENTER NUMBER OF UNIT ELEMENTS
> 2
ENTER FREQUENCY-LOSS PAIR IN UPPER STOPBAND
> 8E9 40
ENTER INPUT TERMINATION IN OHMS
> 50
ENTER OUTPUT TERMINATION (0. INDICATES OPEN OR SHORT)
> 50
```

```
ENTER THE NUMBER OF INCREMENTS (UP TO 5). NO ANALYSIS, ENTER: 0
> 1
ENTER 1 FREQUENCY INCREMENTS IN HZ
> 1E9
ENTER 2 CORNER FREQUENCIES IN HZ
> 0 10E9

GENERAL FILTER SYNTHESIS PROGRAM

MICROWAVE LOWPASS FILTER
  LOW-PASS FILTER
    EQUAL RIPPLE PASS BAND
      BANDEDGE LOSS                              =  0.2000 DB.
      MAX. PASSBAND VSWR                         =  1.5386
      UPPER PASSBAND EDGE FREQUENCY              =  5.0000000D+09 HZ.
      QUARTER-WAVE FREQUENCY                     =  1.0000000D+10 HZ.
  MONOTONIC STOPBAND
    MULTIPLICITY OF ZERO AT QUARTER-WAVE FR.     =  3
    NUMBER OF UNIT ELEMENTS                      =  2
    NUMBER OF FINITE TRANSMISSION ZERO PAIRS     =  0
    OVERALL FILTER DEGREE                        =  5
    INPUT TERMINATION                            =  5.0000000D+01 OHMS
    OUTPUT TERMINATION                           =  5.0000000D+01 OHMS
    REQUESTED TERMINATION RATIO                  =  1.0000000D+00
    NEAREST AVAILABLE TERMINATION RATIO          =  1.0000000D+00
```

Figure 20.11   Interactive response of the FILSYN program. User inputs are underlined.

```
******** COMPUTED PERFORMANCE ********

FREQUENCY      LOSS          PHASE          DELAY
IN HZ          IN DB         IN DEGREES     IN SECONDS

0.00000D+00    0.000000      0.000000       1.15640D-10
1.00000D+09    0.128297      41.294844      1.13411D-10
2.00000D+09    0.179841      82.554002      1.18594D-10
3.00000D+09    0.004177      128.948990     1.41173D-10
4.00000D+09    0.181790      184.052278     1.66182D-10
5.00000D+09    0.200000      263.946581     3.27664D-10
6.00000D+09    12.162432     3.919582       1.53813D-10
7.00000D+09    26.740836     40.051456      6.93280D-11
8.00000D+09    41.395514     60.478958      4.79224D-11
9.00000D+09    61.631075     76.089167      4.00747D-11
1.00000D+10    901.585931    90.000000      3.79446D-11
```

LATTICE: L, COMPUTER CONFIG.: C, INPUT SIDE: IN, OUTPUT SIDE: OUT
> C
WISH TO SEE INTERMEDIATE RESULTS: Y/N
> N
** EVEN NUMBERED BRANCHES ARE SERIES, ODD ONES SHUNT **

MICROWAVE LOWPASS FILTER

```
**** ALL VALUES ARE IMPEDANCES ****

  1    ...R....    5.0000000D+01
  5    ...C....    3.7944610D+01
  7      UE        8.4007706D+01
 13    ...C....    2.4211666D+01
 15      UE        8.4007706D+01
 19    ...C....    3.7944610D+01
 21    ...R....    5.0000000D+01
```

Figure 20.12   A fifth-order microwave lowpass filter realization and its frequency response. The symbols "C" stand for parallel open stubs and "UE" for unit elements (cascade transmission lines).

648 COMPUTER-AIDED DESIGN

REFERENCES[*]

[1] Besser, L., W. Brown, and R. Wales, "System Merges Total Computer Control," *Microwave Systems News*, April 1980.

[2] Medley, M., Jr., and J.L. Allen, "Broadband GaAs FET Amplifier Design Using Negative Image Device Models," *Microwave Theory and Transactions*, Sept. 1979.

Medley, M., Jr., and J.L. Allen, "Improved Device Modelling for Matching Network Synthesis," *MTT Microwave Symposium Digest*, 1979.

[3] Allen, J.L., Ph.D., and M.W. Medley, Jr., *Microwave Circuit Design Using Programmable Calculators.* Dedham: Artech House, Inc., 1980.

[4] Gucker, G.R., "Stochastic Gradient Algorithms for Searching Multidimensional Multinodal Surfaces," Stanford University Center for Systems Research, Information Systems Lab, *Technical Report No. 6778-7*, October 1969.

[5] Stinehelfer, H.E., Jr., and H.E. Stinehelfer, Sr., "Microwave Analysis Using Time Domain Plots Created from Frequency Domain Reflections," *IEEE MTT Symposium Technical Digest*, June 1981.

[6] Besser, L., "Microwave Circuit Design," *Electronic Engineering*, October, 1980.

[7] Besser, L., C. Holmes, M. Ball, M. Medley, and S. March, "Computer-Aided Design for the 1980s," *IEEE MTT Symposium Technical Digest*, June 1981.

[8] Mellor, D.J., "Calculator-Based Synthesis Routine Speeds Microwave Amplifier Design," *IEEE MTT-S International Microwave Symposium Digest*, 1977.

[9] Ku, W.H., and W.C. Petersen, "Optimum Gain-Bandwidth Limitations of Transistor Amplifiers as Reactively Constrained Active Two-Port Networks," *IEEE Transactions on Circuits and Systems*, June 1975.

[10] Szentirmai, G., "Interactive Filter Design by Computer," *IEEE Circuits and Systems*, October and December 1978.

[*]Technical manuals for the described computer programs can be obtained from Compact Engineering (Div. of CGIS), Palo Alto, CA.

Index